CORMAC
GALLAGHER

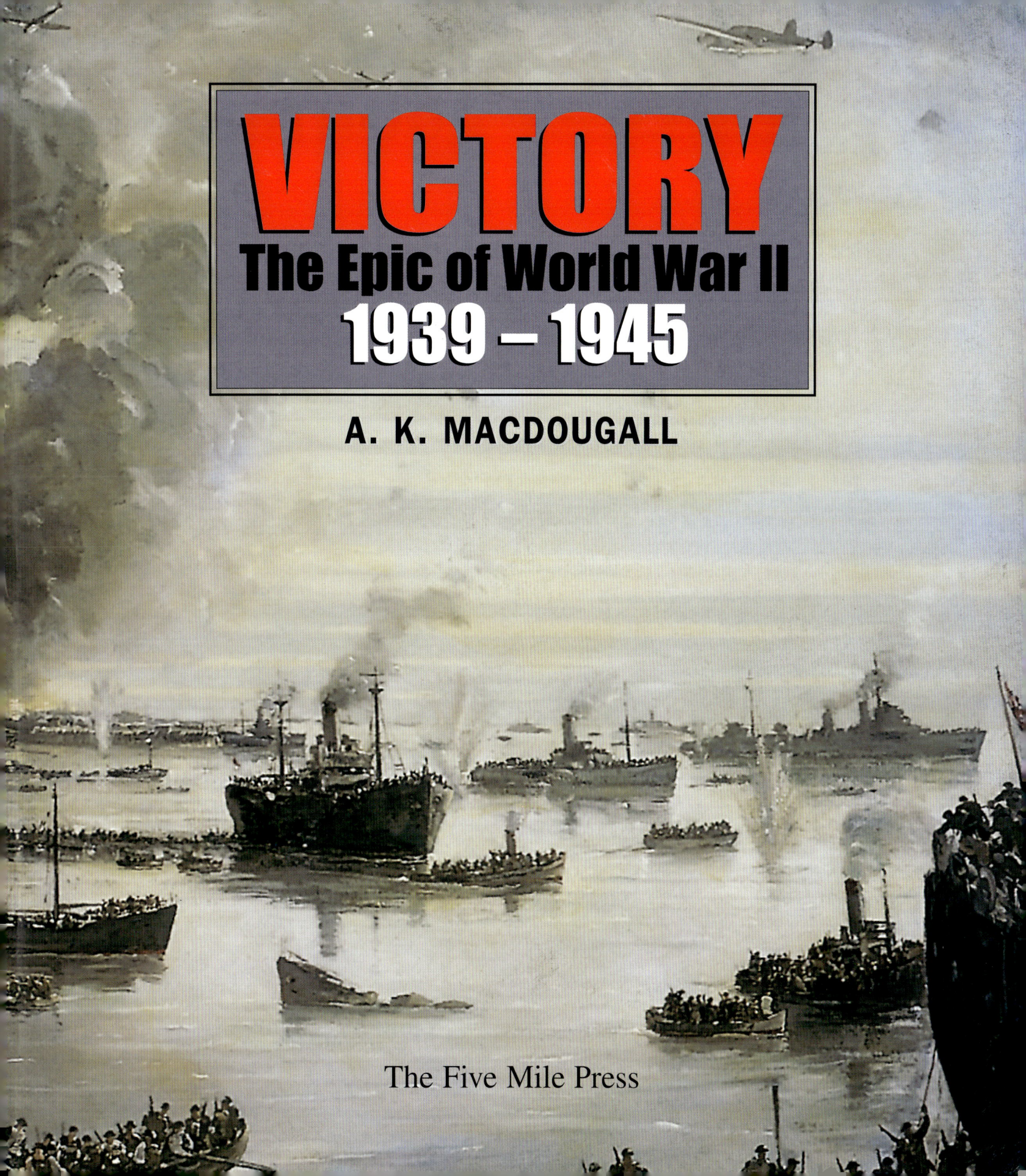

Previous pages: Retreating to the Channel port of Dunkirk, nearly a third of a million British and French troops were saved by the Royal Navy and an armada of small craft over nine days in May–June, 1940, to live and fight another day. From the painting by Charles Cundall in the Imperial War Museum, London (detail).

The Five Mile Press

The Five Mile Press Pty Ltd
950 Stud Road
Rowville Victoria 3178
Australia
Email: publishing@fivemile.com.au
Website: www.fivemile.com.au

First published 2005

Printed in China

Text copyright © A.K. Macdougall/Clarion Editions and The Five Mile Press

Page layouts: A.K. Macdougall
Type design and page make-up: Zoë Murphy
Cover design: Aimee Forde
Edited by Richard McGregor

National Library of Australia Cataloguing-in-Publication data
Macdougall, A.K. (Anthony Keith)
Victory: the epic of World War II, 1939–1945

Includes index.
ISBN 1 74124 605 9 (pbk).
ISBN 1 74124 580 X (hbk).

940.53

PREFACE

In any history of the World War of 1939–45 photographs speak more strongly than words. Their power, horror and ability to haunt the memory are so overwhelming that words are almost superfluous. Yet the most comprehensive narratives of the conflict often lack adequate illustrations, while many pictorial histories contain only a token text, little longer than extended captions. In this book — and in its design — I have attempted to balance a narrative text with an abundance of photographs, while concentrating on the dramatic and desperate first three years of war when the Allied nations reeled in defeat yet evolved the means of achieving victory. The text covers some aspects of the War often neglected in similar books (Italy's role and the Burma campaign, for example). I have drawn extensively from some of my previous writings such as *Anzacs: Australians at War* to sketch the campaigns fought in 1941 and 1942 by British Commonwealth forces, particularly by the Australians and New Zealanders. My gratitude is extended to the great picture archives that I have visited over the years in Canberra, London and Washington (these are listed in the Acknowledgements); to the works too numerous to mention that have provided the information from which the text was woven; and — as always — to my cherished wife Veronica.

A. K. M, 2005

CONTENTS

INTRODUCTION ... 6

PART I
UNCERTAIN PEACE, 1919–39 ... 7

CHAPTER 1
DARK VICTORY, 1918–19 ... 8
From Armistice to Peace Treaty 10   Hitler in Munich 12

CHAPTER 2
THE RISE OF THE DICTATORS, 1919–35 ... 14
The Weimar Republic 17   Italy: The Fascist Path to Power 18
The Birth of the Nazi Party 20   Days of Hope: The mid-1920s 22
Hitler Achieves Power 24   Roosevelt and the New Deal 27

CHAPTER 3
THE MARCH TO WAR, 1935–39 ... 28
1935: Italy Marches 30   Spanish Civil War 31
1937: Japan: Rising Sun, Dark Clouds 33
Special Section: Arming for a New War 36   1938: The Anschluss 43
1938: Czechoslovakia Ceases to Exist 44   1939: The End of
Appeasement 46   The Nazi-Soviet Non-Aggression Pact 47

PART II
THE EDGE OF DEFEAT: 1939–42 ... 49

CHAPTER 4
1939: BLITZKRIEG! ... 50
Germany Invades Poland 50   The British Empire Goes to War 52
Powerful Neutrals 53   The End of Poland 54
British Commonwealth 59   The 'Phoney War' 63   War in the Air 65
The War at Sea 66   Secret Weapons 68   Finland 69

CHAPTER 5
1940: DEFEAT IN THE WEST ... 70
Plans for a German Offensive 70   The End in Finland 72
Denmark Invaded 74   Norway 74   The Fall of Chamberlain 77
Churchill at the Helm 78   Eve of Blitzkrieg 78   Bliztkrieg in the West 80
The Dutch Collapse 80   Belgium Invaded 82   Retreat in Belgium 83
Retreat to Dunkirk 84   Last Days at Dunkirk 87
Italy Enters the War 89   France: The Last Act 90   Britain at Bay 92
The Battle of Britain 93   De Gaulle and Free France 98   The Sea Lanes 100
The USA: From Neutral to Unofficial Ally 102   The Blitz 103
War Against Italy 105   1940: Greece and the Balkans 108

CHAPTER 6
1941: THE WIDENING WAR ... 112
The Australian Victories 115   Rommel: The Desert Fox 118
To Greece 119   The Battle of Matapan 120   The Fall of Yugoslavia 122
The Fall of Greece 124   Tobruk: The Defence 126   The Battle for Crete 129
Sink the *Bismarck*! 134   1941: Ethiopia 135   Iraq 136   Invading Syria 136
Iran 139   Britain at War 140   1941: War in the Air 142
The Origins of 'Barbarossa' 143   Hitler Invades Russia 145
North Africa 149   1941: Naval Losses 151   Russia: The Climax 153
The Japanese Tide, 1941 156   Tojo Takes Charge 158
Attack on Pearl Harbor 161   Collapse in Malaya 164

Into Italy 250   Teheran, 1943 252   'The Dam Busters' 254
The War Against Japan 256   Defending Darwin 256
Burma: The Arakan 257   MacArthur's Offensives: Huon Gulf
Landings 258   The Pacific 260   Eastern Front 261

CHAPTER 9
1944: CLOSING IN ... 262
Leap-Frogging to the Philippines 262   Island-Hopping to Japan 264
Italy: Cassino to Rome 267   'OperationOverlord': The Planning 268
D-Day 270   The Battle for Normandy 272   The Bomb Plot and the
German Resistance 274   Flying Bombs 275   Liberation of Paris 277

CHAPTER 7
1942: FIGHTING BACK ... 166
The Fall of Singapore 169   Invasion of Burma 172   Defeat in the East 173
The End in Java 176   A Pause in the Pacific 177   Indian Ocean 179
Loss of the Philippines 180   Battle of the Coral Sea 181
Midway: The Turning Point 184   Collapse in Egypt 187
The Eastern Front 189   Malta 190   The Fall of Tobruk 190
To the Caucasus! 193   The Darkening Scene 194
Alamein: The Defence 196   South-West Pacific: New Guinea 199
Retreat from Kokoda 200   Milne Bay 203   Securing the Solomon
Islands: Guadalcanal 204   Clearing the Coast: Gona-Buna 207
Egypt: Desert Victory, 1942 209   North Africa: From Torch to Tripoli 214
Stalingrad 216   Weapons of War 218
Special Section: Brutal Rule: The Axis Empires 221
'Holocaust': The Final Solution 226   Japan's Empire 229

PART III
THE WAY TO VICTORY: 1943–45 ... 231

CHAPTER 8
1943: TURNING THE TIDE ... 232
The Last Act in Africa: Tunisia 234   Air War: Europe 236
The Battle of the Atlantic: Winning 240   Eastern Front: Kursk 242
Sicily: The 'Soft Underbelly' 243   The Fall of Mussolini 247

Eastern Front: Victory All the Way 278   Hitler's Allies Fall 279
Unrest in Greece 281   War Against Japan 281   Return to the
Philippines 285   The Battle of Leyte Gulf 286   The 'Backyard War' 287
Air War: North-West Europe 288   Grim Winter: France and
Belgium 288   Arnhem 290   The Battle of the Bulge 292

CHAPTER 10
1945: THE BITTER END ... 294
The Russian Avalanche 294   Yalta Conference 296
Into the Rhineland 298   Crossing the Rhine 300
The Battle for Berlin 302   The End in Italy 303
The Death of Hitler 304   Victory in Europe 306
1945: Victory in the Pacific 309   The End in Burma 311
Borneo and the Last Campaigns 312
The Berlin Conference – and the Atom Bomb 313
Japan Surrenders 313

THE AFTERMATH ... 316

APPENDIX: The Loss of Life ... 318
ACKNOWLEDGEMENTS ... 318
INDEX ... 319
MAPS: Europe and the Mediterranean 64   Pacific and South-East
Asia 168   The Battle of Alamein 211   East Indies 311

INTRODUCTION

The world war of 1939–45 was the most devastating conflict in history. It has entered the mythology of the twentieth century, and as such retains a presence in our collective memory that the passing of sixty years has not diminished. It began in the sweltering summer of 1939 with the thunder of cavalry charges across the plains of Poland and ended six years later to the sound of jet aircraft, rocket bombs and an explosion 'brighter than a thousand suns' that vaporised in a split second 60,000 Japanese lives, and marked the birth of the Atomic Age.

If anything, World War II has grown more horrifying as the years unfold. Its epic battles, secrets and tragedies are still being revealed. Nothing in history equals it in sheer murderous savagery or in examples of courage, fortitude and sacrifice. 'The Second World War, for most of its survivors, has remained the most intense experience of their lives, and the source of their most vivid recollections,' wrote an American officer who later found himself prosecuting the guilty at Nuremberg. Hitler and Mussolini were the monstrous figures of their time, and when they died — one by suicide, the other shot by his own people — those who fought against them puzzled as to how two such absurd individuals could have achieved such power and caused so much suffering. 'An evil has fallen upon the Earth,' Pope Pius had said, and the Allied nations gradually saw the war as a crusade, a battle against evil, and raised their own leaders and soldiers to the status of heroes. But the other heroes were the men and women who lived through the heartbreak of loss and the millions of innocent victims who lie in unmarked graves, their lives blameless, their names unrecorded. Even the most cynical can no longer say that they died in vain. When Allied victory was achieved in 1945 it was a total victory: Germany, Italy, Japan and their allies lay in physical and moral ruin. World War II was the last world war, and a new and better world, purged of old hatreds, emerged from its detritus. Europe destroyed itself and soon gone were the European empires, which within three or four years of 1945 had mostly disappeared. New forces — and the modern world — had been born.

The loss of life in the war is still difficult to comprehend. As late as 1960 experts estimated that it was close to 30 million. Within a few years this estimate had risen to 55 million and present-day historians suggest the figure is closer to 60 million. Most of the dead were civilians, including millions of children, the victims of mass murder, starvation and epidemics. At the Yalta conference early in 1945 Premier Stalin reminded Prime Minister Churchill that Russia's death toll was enormous, dwarfing those of her Allies: 'We have already lost four million soldiers on the field of battle,' he said, 'and the war is not yet won — and they are human beings, you know.' Field Marshal Alexander, who was present, was astonished by these losses and later asked the War Office in London to investigate the figures. They verified Stalin's claim. But the Soviet Union's total losses are now known to number more than 20 million military and civilian dead. China, whose war from 1937 to 1945 against the Japanese is almost unknown in the West, suffered the loss of 15 million lives. Germany, which mourned more than a million dead soldiers in the trench warfare of 1914–18, suffered seven million dead in the war of 1939–45.

If anything elevates the history of those years it is the story of how millions of men and women living peaceful, ordinary lives suddenly found themselves fighting for something greater than themselves — to put an end to regimes of cruelty and brutality, whatever the cost. How they did it is the subject of this book.

A. K. Macdougall, 2005

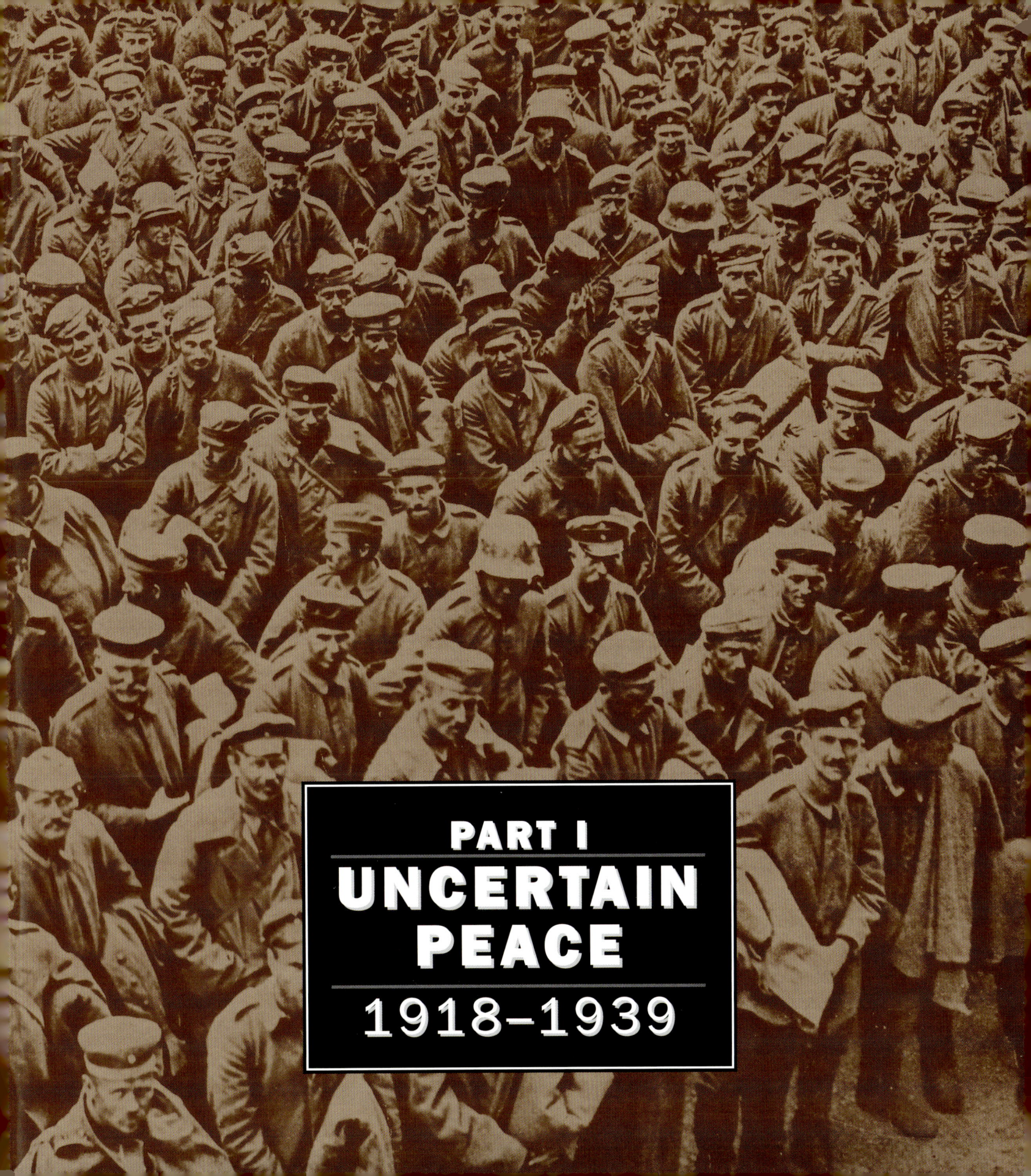

PART I
UNCERTAIN PEACE
1918–1939

CHAPTER 1
DARK VICTORY
1918-19

'There must never be another November 1918 in German history.'
— Adolf Hitler, Chancellor of Germany, 1939

Just before 11 a.m. on the grey, overcast morning of 11 November 1918, gunfire along the front line in France began to slacken. At 10.45 an American artillery officer, Captain Harry Truman, ordered his battery to fire one last salvo. It gave him satisfaction. Twenty-seven years later he would order the last shots fired in a later and more terrible world war. Other gunners fired off a last spiteful salvo of shells and emptied their machine-gun belts before the hour hand reached eleven on their watches.

And then there was silence. The German armies had signed an armistice. The quiet was uncanny. There was little jubilation. Along the entire Western Front from the Belgian plain to the forests of Alsace the opposing armies stood in the muddy terrain, and puzzled over it all. It had been an extraordinary year. Only eight months earlier the Allied armies had faced the prospect of sudden defeat: in early March 1918 Russia's Bolshevik government had signed a peace treaty with Germany that left a third of her territory and population under German control, and eighteen days later Germany, after transporting by rail from the east more than thirty divisions, had launched a series of hammer-blows that nearly reached the English Channel and Paris itself. But from July the Allied armies, strengthened at last by American troops, had launched their own counter-offensives, and there had been no response from their enemy. Germany's armies had exhausted their reserves.

And suddenly the war had ended. Six hours earlier, at 5 a.m., 11 November, German emissaries at Compiègne near Paris had signed the armistice presented to them by Marshal Foch a week before. Its terms were crippling. Field Marshal Haig, Commander-in-Chief of the British Armies in France, had been shown a draft of the terms by Foch and wrote to his wife: 'I am afraid the Allied statesmen mean to exact humiliating terms from Germany, and I think this is a mistake, because it is merely laying up trouble for the future ...' He predicted that many German officers would die rather than accept them. Foch demanded an immediate evacuation by the Germans of the territories they had invaded — not only Belgium but also Alsace-Lorraine (which they had stripped from France in 1871); repatriation of all civilian inhabitants and all prisoners of war; the evacuation of the west bank of the Rhine within thirty-one days; the surrender of the major ships of the German fleet (including ten battleships), the handing over of 5000 field guns and 30,000 machine guns along with 2000 aircraft, 5000 locomotives plus 15,000 wagons and 5000 motor lorries; disclosure of all hidden mines; and the abandonment of the treaties Germany had forced on defeated Russia and Romania. As Germany's military-backed administration disintegrated, the emissaries signed the terms, with misgivings. Within hours the German armies began to trudge back to the Rhine and Allied forces began an orderly advance. The Great War — the World War — was over. After four years of the most savage and destructive war in history and the death of 8 million soldiers, the Allied powers claimed victory over German militarism.

But was it victory? The Germans had signed an armistice — a cease-fire — not a surrender, or so they thought. Their armies on the Western Front were still intact and moving back to Germany with

Inset above: The eagle of Imperial Germany. *Previous page:* The last months of 1918 saw the first mass surrenders of the exhausted German army.
Opposite: Troops of the US 7th Division cheer on news of the signing of the armistice on the Western Front, 11 November 1918.
Opposite right: Proud soldiers of the new republic of Poland formed an honour guard at the signing of the peace treaty with Germany in 1919. Poland's independence lasted just twenty years.

the same grim precision with which they had invaded Belgium and France four years before. In the east, German armies still stood in control of most of Poland, the Ukraine and the Baltic region. In Berlin itself, however, there were wild reports of revolt — rumours of revolution. Only one week earlier, sailors of the High Seas Fleet, alarmed by orders issued on 28 October to raise steam for a last battle with the British fleet, had mutinied, and had taken over the streets of Kiel, where loyal troops had refused to fire on them. Two days before the armistice, workers in Berlin had called a general strike, paralysing what was left of Germany's war effort, and Kaiser Wilhelm had been advised to abdicate, for his army could no longer be relied upon. He had refused, but his abdication was announced from the balcony of the royal palace to crowds of cheering Berliners while in cities from Hamburg and Kiel to Munich and Leipzig government collapsed as mobs of soldiers and workers took over the streets and administration. On 10 November, deserted even by his faithful Field Marshal Hindenburg, Wilhelm had fled to Holland and long exile, and the emissaries already debating armistice terms at Foch's headquarters were ordered by the provisional government in Berlin dominated by socialists to sign any armistice offered. Soon the great German field armies would dissolve, splintering into armed bands of socialists, Bolsheviks and right-wing *Frei Korps*.

Austria-Hungary had asked for an armistice on 3 November, four days after the Turkish Empire had requested one. Bulgaria had collapsed six weeks earlier. In Vienna Emperor Karl's offer of full autonomy to his subject peoples had been a last desperate attempt to keep his empire intact, but Poles, Czechs, Slovaks, Croats, Serbs and Slovenes and even Hungarians now demanded their own states, and his army had simply disbanded itself in the face of a new Italian offensive. In London Winston Churchill, the turbulent 44-year-old Munitions Minister, had described the dramatic events as 'a drizzle of empires, falling through the air'. The Russian Tsar had fallen eighteen months earlier and had already been killed by Bolsheviks. The old autocratic empires that had dominated Europe for centuries had collapsed in a matter of weeks. What would take their place?

FROM ARMISTICE TO PEACE TREATY

On the night of the armistice, to the sound of crowds jubilantly celebrating the end of the war, Prime Minister Lloyd George dined at 10 Downing Street with his Cabinet colleague Winston Churchill, who had been a dynamic First Lord of the Admiralty until the Gallipoli disaster of 1915; and with the Chief of the Imperial General Staff, General Sir Henry Wilson, who noted in his diary: 'LG wants to shoot the Kaiser. Winston does not ...' Churchill recalled that the conversation concerned 'the great qualities of the German people, on the tremendous fight they had made against three-quarters of the world, on the impossibility of rebuilding Europe without their help'.

The Allied powers were under no delusion that Germany had been defeated. Their principal concern was how to punish the enemy and frame a formal treaty that would leave her permanently enfeebled. Lloyd George — 'the man who won the war' — was soon to call a general election, pledging to the electorate to make the Germans pay for the suffering they had caused, to 'squeeze Germany like a lemon until the pips squeak'.

The armistice of 11 November and the collapse of German power took everyone by surprise. In Munich, a German corporal discharged from hospital on 10 November 1918, one day before the armistice, felt despair. A fortnight earlier he had been temporarily blinded at Ypres after a British gas bombardment. His name was Adolf Hitler. 'There followed terrible days and even worse nights,' he later wrote. 'I knew that all was lost. Only fools, liars and criminals could hope for mercy from the enemy . In these nights hatred grew in me, hatred for those responsible for this deed ... Miserable and degenerate criminals. The more I tried to achieve clarity on the monstrous event in this hour, the more the shame of indignation and disgrace burned my brow. What was the pain in my eyes compared to this misery?' He would call Germany's humiliation a 'betrayal', 'a stab in the back' and wrote of that moment: 'My own fate became known to me. I decided to go into politics.' The rest of his life would be an act of revenge against those who had slighted and ridiculed him in his early years, and against the Jews and Socialists — the 'November criminals' — whose willingness to sign the armistice had humbled his adopted homeland.

On 11 November, in Washington, President Woodrow Wilson entered Congress and announced the terms of the armistice, the end of the war. Wilson's peace proposal to the Germans in February 1918, the 'Fourteen Points' which demanded German evacuation of conquered territories and freedom for Europe's minorities, had been eagerly seized on by Germany in the last months of a war as a basis for negotiation, much as a drowning man clutches at straws. Thereafter, Wilson was to give many the impression that he alone had won the war, or at least ended it. His Navy Secretary, Josephus Daniels, and the young Assistant Secretary, Franklin Delano Roosevelt, had walked across to Congress to witness the historic scene. Daniels had appointed the young man, whom he described in his diary as a 'singularly attractive and brave, courageous young Democrat leader'. Roosevelt, like Churchill, had enjoyed his nearly five years helping to run a navy; he

loved the sea, the great grey ships and the 17-gun salutes his position merited. He had returned from a visit to the Western Front two months earlier, carried off a destroyer with a bad case of influenza that had developed into pneumonia. It was a particularly virulent strain of the 'flu and it was devastating the world, but Roosevelt was robust, and soon recovered. Many were relieved, for they saw the handsome New York aristocrat as a future Democrat leader, perhaps a future president.

Millions, including those whose immune systems were enfeebled by the privations of war, were not so lucky, and the influenza pandemic would claim the lives of 40 million people before it disappeared in the middle of 1919 as mysteriously as it had come. And now the world was afflicted by another new virus, Bolshevism. It had been born in violence. Even under its later name, Communism, it was a revolutionary movement that promised much and delivered little. Its leaders in Moscow — Lenin, Trotsky and Stalin — who had fled there from Petrograd as the German armies approached in early 1918, were already preaching world revolution. Revolutionaries in Germany were already calling themselves Bolsheviks and staining the red flag of Socialism with blood.

Left: Troops patrol the streets of Berlin during the revolution at the end of the war, 1918.
Below: Royal Navy officers take the surrender of a German submarine, 1918.
Opposite: Adolf Hitler (right) as a soldier in the German Army on the Western Front. He rose only to the rank of corporal but won the Iron Cross first class for bravery at the front.

The Allied armies began the long march into Germany under grey winter skies. The British entered Cologne and to the south, on 1 December 1918 Major-General Douglas MacArthur, a 38-year-old who had commanded the 42nd Division in France, led his troops into the Rhineland and took as his headquarters a castle at Sinzig overlooking the Rhine, where he lived like a king. He looked the part. 'I have never before met so vivid, so captivating, so magnetic a man,' the reporter William Allen White wrote of him. 'His staff adored him, his men worshipped him.' MacArthur's men were already homesick but their general was impressed by the German people, touched by 'the warm hospitality of the population, their well-ordered way of life, their thrift and geniality'. The Rhineland was quiet, seldom affected by extremism of any kind. Just over twenty years later White would lead the movement in the United States to send aid to Churchill's Britain when it faced defeat by Hitler's Germany and MacArthur would be commanding a million men.

In late December 1918 a former Italian soldier and socialist agitator who had turned to nationalism, and whose life would be linked to Hitler's, Benito Mussolini, visited Berlin and witnessed the scenes of revolution. There, armed bands of soldiers and workers had seized members of the provisional government, and only the loyalty of army units defused the situation. He came down with a dose of influenza, but recovered and returned to Milan seemingly invigorated by the experience of revolution.

Already the leaders of World War II are emerging like figures in an early newsreel, briefly sighted, shadowy, flickering but distinct. When Lloyd George crossed to Paris after his election victory to take part in the conference framing a peace treaty, his attitude to Germany was tempering. He was appalled by the harshness of the terms France was demanding. Germany was to be stripped not only of Alsace-Lorraine but also the Rhineland, and her industrial regions and coalmines in Silesia and Saarland. In a memorandum in March 1919, Lloyd George was to remind his fellow statesmen that a punitive treaty might buy peace for thirty years but would leave Germany thirsting for revenge, concluding: 'it must be a settlement which will contain in itself no provocation for future wars, and which will contain an alternative to Bolshevism'. It must be 'a fair settlement of the European problem'. Among the forces that made solution of a lasting European peace impossible was Bolshevism. Lloyd George and Churchill soon resolved to 'strangle Bolshevism at its birth', but Germany was their immediate problem. Faced by France's intransigence, the British Prime Minister found an equally frustrating peacemaker in President Woodrow Wilson, whom he thought lofty, cold and austere, and clearly under the impression that he was the divine instrument to remake a new world. The cost to America had been light: American forces had been engaged in battle on the Western Front in strength only in the last two months of the war, and their 60,000 killed in battle barely equalled those of Australia, a nation with one-thirtieth of her population. Wilson was to become even more self-righteous when he discovered the numerous 'secret treaties' Britain and France had made during the war to gain allies. Few peace conferences have begun in such a feeling of mutual mistrust.

HITLER IN MUNICH

Adolf Hitler found Munich in late November 1918 a 'people's state' controlled by radical socialists and led by a Jewish social democrat, an ageing writer called Kurt Eisner, who had marched with a crowd of supporters to the parliament and simply occupied it without firing a shot, proclaiming a republic. Hitler left Munich in disgust and returned there in the early months of 1919. From Munich he would emerge within a decade as a national figure on the German scene, a disturber of republics, a spokesman for the embittered.

Hitler had always been eccentric. He was not even German. He had been born in Austria and raised as a Catholic. At school, where he was an insolent, mediocre student, he had worn the red–white–black colours of the German Empire instead of the red and white of Austria, for he had despised the polyglot mixture of Magyars, Slavs and Muslims that comprised the Austro-Hungarian Empire, and he had been punished for his cheek. In Vienna, where he had tried to establish himself as an artist, he had lived a shambling life in boarding houses, rejected by art schools and the talented Jews who gave the city its bustling culture. There the Jews comprised 10 per cent of the population. His hatred for the Jews became pathological. By the outbreak of war in 1914 he had been living in Munich for a year, and he immediately enlisted in a German regiment.

After the German Army and their Free Corps auxiliaries crushed the soviets in Munich in May 1919, Hitler became an agent for the army, reporting on subversive elements. One of the first groups he investigated was called the German Workers' Party, whose anti-Marxist philosophy appealed to him so much that he joined it. He was impressed by the philosophy, articulated in a crude booklet by

Benito Mussolini during his war service in the Italian Bersaglieri. Like Hitler, he proved a brave soldier.

of the Imperial army as an instrument of the Emperor. One historian has described the gathering of the cabal in these incongruous surroundings on the Rhine as 'a meeting which would determine the destiny of Japan'.

In March 1919, in the same month that the Bolshevik leader Lenin convened a gathering of Marxists from twenty countries in Moscow and proclaimed Russia's intention to make Communism a world revolution, and the birth of the 'Communist International' ('Comintern'), Mussolini formed a new radical, ultra-nationalist movement, the Fascists, comprised mainly of former soldiers who were disillusioned with the chaos of postwar Italy and the failure of Italy to obtain the territories promised to her before she entered the war on the side of the Allies in 1915. The term 'fascist' had been widely used in Italy for *fascia* meant group, and the symbol he chose for his party was the *fasces*, the bundle of rods bound round an axe that had symbolised the strength and authority of the Roman state. Fascism's heartland was northern Italy, in the strife-torn industrial city of Milan, but in the November elections only one Fascist member was elected to the Italian parliament, and Mussolini knew despair.

Left: Adolf Hitler at the start of his career as a political agitator, Munich, 1919.
Below: Mussolini (left) leads an early parade by the Fascists.

one Anton Drexler, of combining Socialism — the workers' creed — with nationalism. As Socialism preached the brotherhood of man, and nationalism was militaristic, it was an odd combination. Hitler became member number seven of the future National Socialist Workers' Party (there were to be several name changes but they were soon known as the 'Nazis') and before long he dominated its meetings.

Observing these events from Berlin, Leipzig, Munich and Zurich was the Japanese officer appointed in 1919 as military attaché to Germany and Switzerland, Major Tojo Hideki. Japanese were few in Europe, for Japan, while honouring its 1902 alliance with Britain, had refused to send armies to the Western Front and had limited her involvement to seizing German possessions in China and the Pacific, and providing convoy escorts and a handful of destroyers in the Mediterranean. The reason was simple: Japan's army was ill-equipped for modern war. In October 1921 Tojo, quiet in repose but quick as a sabre in argument, would be one of a group of Japanese military attachés who met at the German resort at Baden-Baden, ostensibly to take the waters but in reality to plan the modernisation

CHAPTER 2
THE RISE OF THE DICTATORS
1919–35

By June 1919, when the Allied powers summoned the German government to sign a peace treaty at the Palace of Versailles outside Paris, Germany was still wracked by insurrection, her streets a battlefield between bands of armed Bolsheviks and equally lawless former army units, her government paralysed, her people starving as a result of the Allied blockade. The harsh terms of the armistice had been transformed into even harsher terms of peace: Germany was to be permanently disarmed — her army was to be reduced to a strength of 100,000 officers and men (barely larger than her police force) and she was forbidden to introduce conscription or produce tanks, fighter aircraft or submarines. German-speaking populations would be part of the new Slavic nations created from the ruins of the Austro-Hungarian and Russian empires — notably Poland and Czechoslovakia. France claimed back Alsace-Lorraine and demanded the entire west bank of the Rhine as her best security against further German aggression. Marshal Foch and Premier Clemenceau had lived through two German invasions and were determined to destroy German power forever. When the peace terms were released the German delegates refused to sign them and the German fleet, interned at anchor at Scapa Flow, was scuttled on 21 June — an act that seemed proof that Germany was still capable of treacherous acts. Germany was stripped of her overseas colonies; they were few but were divided between the victors. Of Germany's Pacific islands and territories, those north of the Equator were granted to Japan, those to the south, to Australia.

The Allies threatened to march on Berlin and Prime Minister Lloyd George refused to lift the blockade unless Germany signed, but in face of German protests the Allies gave way in some points. The Rhineland would remain German, but was to be permanently 'de-militarised' (no German troops were to be stationed there); Saarland was to remain under French control but a plebiscite would be held within twenty years to decide whether its people wished to be part of France or Germany. Wilson of the United States and Lloyd George of Great Britain undertook to come to France's aid if Germany ever invaded the Rhineland. It was an empty promise. The United States Congress rejected the Treaty of Versailles and America returned to isolationism, refusing even to become a member of the new League of Nations that had been Wilson's concept.

Part of Silesia — a coal-mining area where the majority of people were Polish — was to be given to Poland. The peace-makers had decided that Poland, which had long been a landlocked state like Hungary, should have an outlet to the Baltic Sea, and be granted a narrow strip of land to the coast. Much of east Prussia was now separated from Germany proper by a 'Polish Corridor'. Germany also lost the great seaport of Danzig, which would be a Free State governed by the League of Nations.

Founded on President Wilson's idealism, inspired by France's implacable hatred of Germany, the Treaty of Versailles signed on 28 June 1919 was a disastrous attempt to remake the map of Europe. The signing took place in the same Hall of Mirrors that the Prussians had chosen to proclaim the birth of a united Germany in January 1871. No insult was spared Germany.

Inset above: The swastika emblem adopted by the German Nazi party and later incorporated in the national flag.
Opposite: Men of goodwill attempted earnestly to reconcile international disputes in the League of Nations, and failed. Here British Prime Minister Ramsay MacDonald (below right) attends a League meeting at Geneva.
Opposite right: Adolf Hitler in Nazi uniform.

An alarming clause in the Treaty of Versailles demanded that Germany accept guilt for starting the war and, in punishment, pay the cost of the conflict in order to repair the damage. 'Reparations' would be decided later, and payments would begin in 1921. Even Woodrow Wilson confided that if he were German he would hesitate to sign so punitive a treaty. Soon Germany's allies would be forced to sign their own treaties which left them stripped of territory and pride. Austria was reduced to a barely viable rump of a state of three million, and three million of its German-speaking citizens were now living within the borders of the newly created republic of Czechoslovakia; indeed they comprised 24 per cent of the latter's population. The Kingdom of Hungary was now a separate state, but stripped of land, principally Transylvania, which became part of Romania. Hungary was now a kingdom without a king, ruled by an admiral without a navy (Admiral Horthy's monarchist forces had driven out the Bolshevik government in Budapest).

Germans comprised 4 per cent of the populations of post-1919 Poland, Yugoslavia and Romania, and 5 per cent of Hungary's, and formed a sizeable minority in the three new Baltic states of Latvia, Lithuania and Estonia. Settled for centuries in these regions, the 'Volksdeutsche' had preserved their German language and customs, and Hitler was to claim them as 'Germans'.

But it was the creation of a Polish state at Germany's expense — particularly the 'Polish Corridor' — that angered Germany more than any other geographical adjustment to her borders. Soviet Russia, whose armies were defeated outside Warsaw by the Poles in 1920, also suffered loss of territory to Poland. As early as 1922 General von Seeckt, the secretive genius who re-built the German Army, stated: 'The obliteration of Poland must be one of the fundamental drives of German policy ... and is attainable by means of, and with the help of, Russia ...' At the same time General Badoglio, chief of the Italian army staff, stated to his government that the existence of Yugoslavia was intolerable to Italy. Italy had imagined dominating the Adriatic and the Balkans, but the peace treaties had thwarted her ambition. Hitler and Mussolini would in time fulfil the generals' expectations.

Containing the seeds of future dissensions, the treaties of 1919 were doomed from the start, yet the borders they drew, and the artificial states they created, were to survive eighty years and a second world war, with the sole exception of Poland (which in 1945 was shifted west 200 kilometres, as if by some mighty earthquake).

Top left: Allied leaders meet in Paris to frame a peace treaty. From left to right: Marshal Foch of France, Premier Clemenceau, Britain's Prime Minister David Lloyd George and Premier Orlando of Italy.
Left: Leading members of the British Empire delegation at the Paris Peace Conference, 1919. In front row, from left to right, are Lord Balfour, Lloyd George, Australia's Prime Minister Billy Hughes, Lord Birkenhead and Winston Churchill.

Scene outside the Kremlin, Moscow, during the funeral of Vladimir Lenin, founder of Communist rule in Russia, 1924.

'This is not a peace treaty,' Marshal Foch was heard to say. 'It's a truce for twenty years.' It had not even brought an end to war, for fighting continued in eastern Europe for another two years where forces, oblivious to treaties, fought against or alongside Russian Bolshevik armies. Finland and the Baltic states would expel Russian armies from their territory and enjoy a short-lived independence, before, like Poland, losing it two decades later.

Nearly 1.7 million Russian soldiers had died in the Great War, but by the end of 1922 Russia's total mortalities are estimated at close to 16 million — victims of war, civil war, disease and famine. By 1924, when Lenin died, and Stalin assumed power, the Soviet Union was secure.

THE WEIMAR REPUBLIC

Having signed a crippling peace treaty the provisional government of the German Republic, assembling at Weimar, approved its new constitution in July 1919. It was one of the most advanced constitutions in the world and in normal times should have provided the firm basis for a new and democratic Germany. It was 'mechanically well-nigh perfect,' wrote William L. Shirer, the American reporter who would later write *The Rise and Fall of the Third Reich*. 'The idea of cabinet government was borrowed from England and France, of a strong popular [elected] President from the United States, of the referendum from Switzerland.' The president, like the former emperor, had the power to choose the chancellor (prime minister). It gave the vote to all Germans over the age of twenty. It contained a fatal flaw, however. During a time of national crisis the president could rule by decree, suspending parliament. He would rely on the army; and the army had supported the fledging republic on the understanding that the republic would support the army. The army, though limited in size, would remain a state within a state. Its activities were kept hidden from the Allied Control Commission supervising Germany's disarmament, and its Commander-in-Chief, von Seeckt, was soon to initiate defence ties and training facilities with Germany's traditional enemy, the now communist Russia.

The Weimar constitution also provided for proportional voting, but this clause led to the formation of so many small parties and splinter groups that in the 1930 elections no fewer than twenty-eight parties fielded candidates.

In 1920 the League of Nations first met at Geneva in Switzerland to bring peace to the world. In 1921 Britain had given Ireland Dominion self-government, and a measure of independence to Egypt while extending her new empire in the Near East by creating Palestine, Transjordan and Iraq from the ruins of the Turkish Empire. One year later Greek armies were driven from Turkey and the two British leaders who had encouraged the Greek venture were both out of office: late in 1922 Prime Minister Lloyd George lost the confidence of his Conservative coalition partners, and was forced to resign his office. In the elections at year's end Winston Churchill lost his seat in the House of Commons. The old Liberal Party was dead. And it seemed that both leaders had reached the end of their turbulent political careers. Lloyd George's was over; Churchill saved his by joining the Conservatives in 1923 and was again soon a cabinet minister.

Across the Atlantic another charismatic future leader was struck down. In the hot summer of 1921 Franklin Roosevelt, holidaying with his family at Campobello, spent a typically strenuous day: he went sailing as a storm blew up, then went fishing, falling overboard into freezing water. He wore out the energy of his guests, who found an excuse to return to New York. He worked on his model boats, then played tennis and baseball with his children. One day in August he complained of feeling unwell. He woke one morning with a temperature, unable to move his legs. Soon he was paralysed from the waist down. Doctors diagnosed infantile paralysis. His recovery would depend, they said, very much on the attitude of the patient. By October his legs had begun to jackknife and the pain was excruciating. It was clear that Roosevelt would never walk again without the aid of crutches. To the grief of his admirers the young Democrat's political career, which held such promise, was over.

Premier Mussolini greets King Victor Emmanuel in Rome after being appointed to power, 1922.

ITALY: THE FASCIST PATH TO POWER

The treaties that Austria, Hungary and Turkey were forced to sign were as onerous as that forced on Germany, and even one of the victorious Allies was appalled by the clauses of the Treaty of Versailles.

Italy had been promised much but received little for the loss of 600,000 men. Britain and France had helped themselves exclusively to Germany's African colonies and Turkey's Middle East domains, Japan and Australia to Germany's Pacific possessions. There was none for Italy. Italy's principal enemy, Austria, was a shadow of a country, but a new rival had emerged in the Balkans in the new 'Kingdom of Serbs, Croats and Slovenes' — Yugoslavia — which disputed Italy's claims for hegemony in the Adriatic. Italy and Greece had been mollified by promises of Turkish islands in the Aegean and parts of Anatolia, but their troops were to be expelled by Turkish armies led by General Kemal, which defied the Sultan's government in Constantinople and soon expelled it.

Mussolini returned to an Italy wracked by strikes. The end of the war had brought a sudden end to armaments production, and the resulting factory lay-offs and a rapid demobilisation of troops brought unprecedented unemployment. By the irony of history the first fascist, authoritarian state, the model and inspiration of Adolf Hitler's Nazi Reich, would emerge in Italy, the least ruthless but most politically unstable of the European democracies.

In the 1921 elections, as Italy was plagued by industrial unrest and its streets witnessed bloody clashes between Socialists and Bolsheviks and right-wing groups such as the Fascists, Mussolini's Fascist Party won 35 seats in the 535-seat Chamber of Deputies. It was a pathetic result — but for the fact that Italy's other political parties were splintered and seldom able to maintain a coalition for longer than a few months.

By year's end the Fascists, who now wore the black shirts inspired by the dark uniforms of the wartime shock troops, the Arditi, had taken control of most of the cities of northern Italy with the exception of Turin (which remained obstinately socialist), and both mayors and municipalities were terrorised by the Blackshirt squads. Government forces suppressed Communist, anarchist and socialist demonstrations with particular severity, but seldom took action against the right-wing squads. Mussolini and his growing number of adherents had learned the power of brutality, and he was quickly shedding his principles. Once stridently anti-clerical and a sworn enemy of big business, Mussolini now sought support from industrial families and pledged his faith in the Catholic Church, stating 'the only universal idea which exists today in Rome is that which radiates from the Vatican'. Against opposition from young firebrands such as Dino Grandi and Italo Balbo, Mussolini in November 1921 transformed the Fascists from a revolutionary movement into a political party, with headquarters in Milan. In February 1922 Premier Bonomi, beset by socialist demonstrations and fascist violence, resigned and was succeeded as Liberal leader by Luigi Facta, a notoriously weak and indecisive politician. Italians waited for the next step in the drama. Mussolini, by now spoken of as one strong figure who could bring order to Italy, decided to keep Facta in power unless a stronger figure — or the army — was chosen to succeed him. He had been urged to march on Rome but instead in March 1922 he visited Berlin. There he noted growing anti-Semitism and reports of the Nazi movement. Both developments disturbed him.

THE 'MARCH ON ROME'

'With the spread of Fascist power and the retreat of official authority, the King and the army had become the final barrier to a Fascist takeover,' one history states. Once ardently republican, Mussolini astonished his supporters by pledging in a widely reported speech his loyalty to the monarchy. On the pretence of forming a coalition, he began negotiations with other political leaders but when he heard that Facta was attempting to form a 'grand coalition', including in his cabinet heroes such as D'Annunzio and consummate politicians such as Giolitti, Mussolini decided that the time had come to strike. He ordered the Blackshirts to march on Rome on 27 October 1922 but to avoid open conflict with the army. General Pietro Badoglio, a Piedmontese like his King, was reported to have said: 'One burst of rifle-fire from the Carabinieri and Fascism will collapse completely.' But of all the senior generals only General Pugliese, commanding the army in Rome, showed energy in defending the kingdom against the threat posed by the Fascists and demanded that the government declare a state of emergency.

Like many of Mussolini's grand gestures, the march on Rome began impressively and became a fiasco. The army, well equipped with machine guns and artillery, easily blocked railway lines and roads, forcing many Blackshirt groups to stand in the rain waiting for orders that never came. But faced with possible civil war, Premier Facta asked King Victor Emmanuel to declare 'a state of siege' — martial law. Facta brought the decree to the King for signing early on the morning of 28 October. Cautioned by his generals not to use force against a party that had, after all, pledged its loyalty to the monarchy, and alarmed at the prospect of civil war, the King refused to sign it. He decided to make another attempt to form a new government. Facta resigned and his successor Salandra was left with no alternative other than to ask Mussolini to join him in a coalition government. Mussolini refused. He demanded total power, or nothing. On the morning of 29 October the palace telephoned Mussolini and invited him to meet with the King. On the following day the King asked him to attempt to form a government. In the afternoon of 31 October the long-delayed Blackshirts made their victory march through Rome. The Fascist era had begun.

Italians were astonished at the respectable image Mussolini now sought to project: he shed his uniform and wore well-cut suits, a bowler hat and spats. Announcing his determination to restore stability to politics, he decided to rid himself of critics in parliament by eliminating opposition parties. In new elections in 1924 an extraordinary new law gave the party that won the majority of votes an automatic two-thirds of the seats in the Chamber of Deputies. Opposition candidates were attacked, but Mussolini professed that he was unaware of any violence. By 1926 Italy was to all intents and purposes a police state, without a legal opposition. Visitors, however, were impressed by the orderly state of the country, the vast program of state-funded construction, the energy of the new regime. 'No government in history', Mussolini boasted in the Fascist journal in 1923, 'has ever been based exclusively on popular consensus … Fascism has already trampled … over the more or less putrid body of Goddess Liberty.' Slowly Fascism would evolve its hideous philosophy: democracy was ineffective if not decadent; freedom was an abstract; the individual counted for nothing except as a cog in the machinery of the state. Force — brute force if necessary — would overcome all obstacles and enemies.

A group of thugs with half-baked political theories, barely represented in parliament, had achieved total power. It had done this by playing on fears of Bolshevism and civic unrest — after itself creating the unrest — and by dumping most of its philosophy, shamelessly cultivating allies and switching loyalties, and using violence, intimidation of opponents and then pure bluff. Its last act was to legalise its mendacity by a bogus 'endorsement' by the electorate. Soon Mussolini was to launch an economic renewal funded by the state and Italy approached economic bankruptcy. A decade later Hitler would follow almost exactly the same manoeuvres to achieve and consolidate his power in Germany — and within six years also face economic bankruptcy, which he solved by launching war.

Mussolini's Fascists soon took on imperial pretensions, harking back to ancient Rome. This grandiose poster shows Mussolini (top) and Italo Balbo (middle left), one of his principal lieutenants.

THE BIRTH OF THE NAZI PARTY

In Munich Hitler was proving an effective speaker, and the larger the audience the more articulate he became. In February 1920 he convened a meeting at the beer hall known as the Hofbräuhaus in Munich attended by 2000 people. They were attacked by Communists and Socialists but Hitler spoke louder and after half an hour 'the applause began to drown out the screaming and shouting'. He had found his feet and tasted the adulation of the crowd. By year's end the National Socialist German Workers' Party, as the movement was now called, had its own emblem — the ancient symbol of the hooked cross, the swastika, which was to become the most dreaded symbol in Europe, and their banners, rejecting the black–gold–red of the German Republic, adopted the old imperial colours. Hitler explained: 'In red we see the social idea of the movement, in white the nationalist idea, in the swastika the mission of the struggle for the victory of Aryan man.'

Funding began to pour in from the unlikeliest of sources — some from the army. By late 1922 Hitler's activities were so widely reported that the United States embassy in Berlin sent its military attaché to Munich to report on the Nazi Party and its leader. He attended an outdoor rally. 'Never seen such a sight in my life,' the American noted in his diary and, after meeting Hitler, wrote: '… have rarely listened to such a logical and fanatical man'. Of the Nazis themselves he reported: 'Less a political party than a popular movement, it must be considered the Bavarian counterpart to the Italian fascisti … It has recently acquired a political influence quite disproportionate to its actual numerical strength.' General Ludendorff, the arch nationalist, was one supporter.

THE NAZI PATH TO POWER

Hitler denounced the Treaty of Versailles, which he blamed on the Jews and the financiers. On 1 January 1923, when German reparation payments lagged, French and Belgian forces invaded Germany and occupied the Ruhr industrial region. Factories and mines creaked to a halt. Allied troops dispersed protesting German crowds with gunfire. Germany responded by declaring a national strike, and printed banknotes freely, sparking an inflationary madness that almost destroyed her middle class. At the beginning of 1923 it took

Left: Growing power: Adolf Hitler (centre) at a Nazi Party rally in the 1920s.
Above: Hitler with General Ludendorff (left) during their trial in 1924.

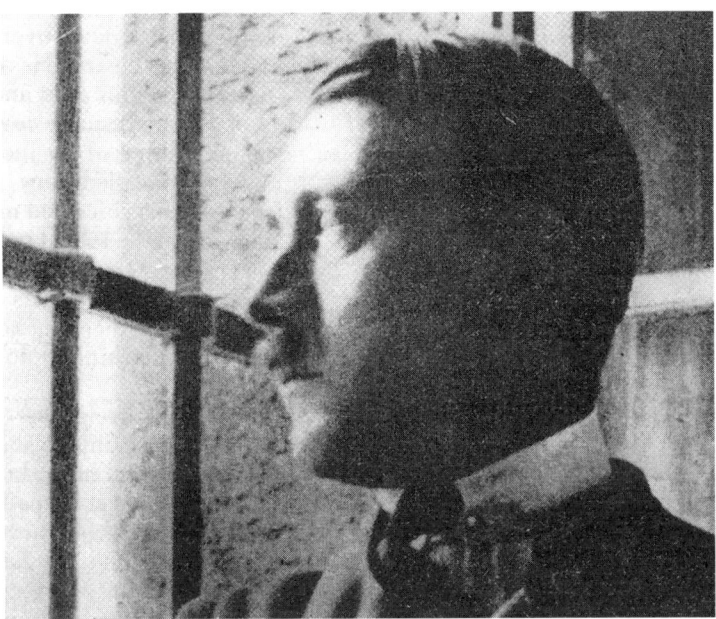

Lonely plotter: Hitler in his cell in Landsberg prison, 1924

75 German marks to buy one American dollar; by year's end it took 4000 billion marks. When Chancellor Stresemann's Cabinet finally agreed to make reparations payments and called off the passive resistance in September 1923, German national feeling was outraged and the President was forced to declare an emergency and govern by decree. In this new trial, the army was again to prove loyal to the republic. In both Saxony and Bavaria the authority of the Berlin government was challenged.

On 8 November 1923 Hitler decided that it was time to act. When Bavaria's newly appointed leader, Von Kahr, was addressing a meeting of several thousand separatists in the beer hall in Munich, Hitler burst in, clutching a revolver, followed by his Nazi Brownshirts, and mounted the podium, where he declared that Bavaria had a new government and that he was the head: 'The national revolution has begun!' General Ludendorff now arrived at the smoke-filled scene and gave his blessing to the new creation. Hitler crowed: ' I want now to fulfil the vow I made to myself five years ago when I was a blind cripple in a military hospital: to know neither rest nor peace until the November criminals had been overthrown, until on the ruins of the wretched Germany of today there should have arisen once more a Germany of power and greatness, of freedom and splendour.' On the following morning, as popular support for the coup faded, Hitler and Ludendorff led a force of 3000 Storm Troopers to the centre of Munich but were confronted there by police and troops, who opened fire. Hitler, unwounded but with bruised pride, was arrested and sentenced in 1924 to a brief period in prison.

The Nazi hierarchy later observed the anniversary of the attempted coup with solemnity but privately Hitler called the failure of the 'Beer Hall putsch' a blessing in disguise. He had made the mistake of attempting to take over an existing government. Next time, he would have his own government already organised, ready for the day when he would be called to power. He had no doubt that the day would come. He had profound faith in his intuition.

Hitler served nine months in Landsberg prison and had adequate time to review his life to date and his achievements — or lack of them. He used the time to write — or rather dictate — his life story, which his secretary Rudolf Hess took down. It was a strange, turgid combination of memoir and half-baked political philosophy riddled with musings on race and destiny and later published as *Mein Kampf* ('My Struggle'). Hitler described France as the 'mortal enemy of the German people' and predicted a last decisive struggle with her. (In fact France had been weakened far more than Germany by the experience of war; her greatness had passed and strength had shrivelled, for her 1.5 million war dead could never be replaced.)

In his confined prison cell Hitler dreamed of spaces — the endless, rolling wheat fields of the Ukraine, the steppes of Poland and Russia. The Germany of the future must have *Lebensraum* — 'living space' — and it must expand to the east. 'Only an adequate large space on this earth assures a nation its freedom of existence … if we speak of earth in Europe today, we can have in mind only Russia and her vassal border states.' The new Reich, Hitler wrote, 'must again set itself on the march along the road of the Teutonic knights of old, to obtain by the sword earth for the German plough and daily bread for the nation.'

Democracy must be eradicated. Only a dictatorship could achieve greatness for Germany. Decisions would be made by one man: 'He alone may possess the authority and the right to command'. 'The state is a racial organism and not an economic organization … ideal virtues alone make possible the formation of a state.' He explained further on: 'All the human culture, all the results of art, science and technology that we see before us today, are almost exclusively the creative product of the Aryan.' The Aryan race 'is the Prometheus of mankind … from whose shining brow the divine spark of genius has sprung at all times … It is he who has laid the foundations of and erected the walls of every great structure in human culture.' Hitler's knowledge of history was extremely patchy, but he was writing at a time when Germany was the home of crackpot theories such as 'geopolitics' and eugenics, which were devised not to explore the riddles of humankind but to justify the often violent course of history. He wrote: 'The existence of a master race presupposes that of an inferior one.' Among the inferiors were the Slavs and the Jews. They would be Hitler's first victims.

Hitler emerged from prison in December 1924, an older but not necessarily wiser man. He found the Nazi Party banned and his own future a dismal one. Europe's time of troubles had ended. It seemed that the Hitlers of the day, the extremists, the street-corner demagogues and rabble rousers, were a thing of the past. The first fascist dictatorship, Italy, was displaying remarkable restraint in both domestic and international affairs, and even Churchill praised Mussolini as a success.

DAYS OF HOPE: THE MID-1920S

In the mid-1920s the world scene brightened further with an economic boom that was to last for much of the decade, ending only in the Wall Street 'Crash' of 1929 and a depression that engulfed the world. In these optimistic years the possibility of another World War was inconceivable. In 1922 also Britain agreed to pay her war debt to the United States at 3.5 per cent interest, an annual sum of 35 million pounds sterling for the next sixty-two years; it proved as feasible in practice as world disarmament, but it strengthened her resolve to recover her own war debts, particularly from Germany, which was patently unable to pay.

Life in Germany returned to normal. The League of Nations in Geneva was regarded as a guarantor of world peace. In 1922 the Washington Naval Treaty, an attempt to defuse Japanese-American rivalry in the Pacific, had limited the size of the world's navies and Britain, France and Italy had also joined as signatories. The great wartime battleship fleets were scrapped. Britain, (including her self-governing Dominions, as they soon became known) and the United States were each limited to navies whose battleships' total tonnage would not exceed 525,000 tonnes; Japan's was limited to 315,000 tonnes; and France and Italy each to 175,000 tonnes. The Washington Treaty was — in the words of the historian A.J.P. Taylor — 'the only effective agreement on limitation of armaments ever made'. Until 1935 Britain did not lay down a single battleship, converting instead several whose keels had been laid to aircraft carriers.

The world was experiencing both economic and political stability. One historian, John Lukacs, has called the years from 1924 to 1929 'the zenith of peace in eastern Europe … There was hope and prosperity in these years.' Germany was flourishing and now receiving American loans to enable her to meet reparations payments — only in retrospect would this be seen as ridiculous. In 1925, when the old monarchist Hindenburg was elected President, Chancellor Stresemann, who was dedicated to reconciliation and peaceful progress, signed with Aristide Briand of France a pact at Locarno that guaranteed their existing frontiers; Britain, Belgium and Italy also signed the pact, undertaking to come to the assistance of any signatory power whose frontiers were invaded. Germany was admitted to the League of Nations. French occupation troops left the Rhineland. Germany was no longer a pariah among nations. For a brief decade Berlin displaced Paris as the cultural centre of Europe and Germany led the world in art, architecture, graphic art, cabaret and cinema, and a free morality that shocked even Parisians.

The Locarno Pact has been described as the high-water mark of hope in the interwar years. The world had seemingly buried the enmities of the past. 'Is this the end?' Winston Churchill wrote in 1927, on the last page of his history of the 1914–18 war. 'Is it merely a chapter in a cruel and senseless story? Will a new generation in their turn be immolated to balance the black accounts of Gaul and Teuton? Will our children bleed and gasp again in devastated lands? Or will there spring from the very fires of conflict that reconciliation of the three giant combatants, which would unite their genius and secure in safety and freedom a share in rebuilding the glory of Europe?'

Churchill himself was out of office by 1929, and was to spend ten years in the political wilderness. The giant figures of the past were disappearing: Marshal Foch, symbol of victorious France, died in 1929. His last words are said to have been: 'If France is in danger, send for Weygand.' His wartime chief of staff, the youthful General Maxime Weygand, assumed Foch's mantle. As if marking his passing and the end of a tradition of spirited attack, France began in that year the building of a line of fortifications along the Franco-German frontier and named it after the War Minister who had championed its construction, André Maginot. The Maginot Line ran from the Swiss frontier to Belgium and consisted of underground forts and massive gun turrets impervious even to direct hits. It was France's 'Great Wall', designed to defend her from any future Teutonic invasion. It was said to be impregnable, and proved to be so. Unfortunately it ended where the Belgian frontier began. What if a future German Army again invaded France through Belgium? Strategists explained that Belgium would be alarmed if the line were continued to the English Channel; engineers explained that the Flanders soil was sandy and not conducive to deep earthworks and concrete emplacements; financiers protested that there were insufficient funds to continue the line anyway. Marshal Pétain, hero of the defence of Verdun in 1916 and an expert on fortresses, declared that the forests of the rugged

A fort of the Maginot Line facing the German frontier.

Ardennes region of south-east Belgium were impenetrable and formed as effective a barrier to a modern army as the Maginot Line. If a future German Army again invaded Belgium, French armies would advance more rapidly than they had in 1914 and fight the decisive battle on the Belgian plain west of the Ardennes. This was the strategy adopted by the French high command until the day in 1940 when German tanks emerged from the forest of the Ardennes and decided France's fate in just five days.

At the Imperial Conference, held in London in 1926, discussion focussed for the first time in two decades principally on trade matters, not defence, and from the meeting of Empire leaders emerged (at Canada's urging) a new definition of their status. Lord Balfour announced that the self-governing Dominions (Canada, Newfoundland, Australia, New Zealand, South Africa and southern Ireland) were 'autonomous communities within the British Empire ... united by common allegiance to the Crown'. The independence of the Dominions in the 'British Commonwealth of Nations' was legalised by the Statute of Westminster (1931) but Australia and New Zealand did not bother to ratify it at all, for their reliance on Great Britain in almost every aspect, from finance to defence, was complete.

INCREASING MILITARISM OF JAPAN

The growing power of Japan seemed to concern only the United States, China and Australia. In 1922 Britain, under pressure from the United States and from Australia, New Zealand and Canada, did not renew its 20-year-old alliance with Japan but instead agreed to the development of a great naval base at Singapore for a British Pacific fleet. 'You had an alliance with us on Sunday, you broke it on Monday, and started a Base on Tuesday,' a Japanese general complained to the British military attaché in Tokyo in 1922.

Work on the base proceeded slowly. As early as 1924 the British Treasury pleaded shortage of funds. Singapore's future fleet would also require a dry dock for the battleships' hull maintenance, another great expense. Singapore Naval Base was destined to be completed only in 1938, when it possessed a newly arrived floating dock but no battleships to put in it.

Japan's intentions proved impossible to predict. Modernised industrially and modelled politically on Western systems since the 1870s, yet built on military conquest, its society remained essentially feudal. Only one citizen in ninety had the vote. Japan had always been a warrior state and the armed forces occupied a special status. Since 1900 the ministers of the army and the navy were senior serving officers with direct access to the Emperor, circumventing Cabinet. Their resignation over matters of policy could bring down a government. This remained so until the defeat of 1945.

In 1925 criticism or ridicule of the Emperor was made a punishable offence. The Emperor at the time was an imbecile but the inscrutable prince who replaced him in 1926, taking the name Hirohito, was more intelligent than his appearance suggested. Nevertheless, the mid-1920s would be remembered in Japan as a liberal period when Western

Police were the only German uniformed personnel permitted in the Rhineland, the German territory on the west bank of the Rhine until Hitler marched his troops in during 1936.

music and dress and foreign education were widely accepted, though freedom of speech was little known. In the 1930s, as Japan, the source of the world's cheapest mass-produced goods (they were a byword for shoddiness) felt the effects of the Depression, liberal influences began to die.

THE GREAT DEPRESSION

On October 1929, the bubble burst and on the New York Stock Exchange shares crashed overnight, wiping billions off the value of the nation's largest companies and most of its smallest, and ending a decade of growth, speculation and overspending. There was to be no quick recovery. The crash of 1929 was the first shock to the world's economic well-being and its repercussions spread rapidly. In 1930 the Western world was facing an economic slump — 'the Depression' — that engulfed all developed countries in the next two years. Production fell, unemployment rose.

HITLER ACHIEVES POWER

In Germany, Hitler had spent seven years building the organisation of the Nazi Party, organising it on a regional basis. Each *Gau* — or region — was controlled by a *Gauleiter* answerable only to him. Hitler had given up ideas of a coup. He would achieve power through parliament, taking advantage of the rivalries and inadequacies of his opponents. To many observers he remained ludicrous and his Chaplin moustache and strange uniforms and gauche manners did not help. An increasing number of people found him spell-binding. In conversation his voice was deep and he was not without a crude wit, and many were transfixed by his extraordinary blue eyes, which deflected their attention from the idiocy of his sayings.

The Depression that hit central Europe in 1930 came like a gift from the gods. Hitler proposed a program to deny power to the Communists, whose supporters were growing in number, to achieve full employment and renew German industry, and he received substantial financial support from industrialists who saw him as the only alternative to Socialism or Bolshevism. In 1928 the Nazi Party won a paltry twelve seats in the Reichstag, but in September 1930, more than six million Germans voted for the Nazis, an eight-fold increase. By 1931, when five million Germans were out of work, Gregor Strasser, one of Hitler's advisers, prophesied: 'All that serves to precipitate a catastrophe ... is good, very good for us and our German revolution.' When Heinrich Brüning, the devout Catholic leader of the Centre Party, was appointed Chancellor, he had to resort to ruling by presidential decree. By October 1931 Hitler was a significant political leader and was received by President Hindenburg, who described him as a 'Bohemian corporal'. Hitler decided to run for President. Early in 1932 the 85-year-old Hindenburg, who was looking forward to spending his retirement on his Prussian estates, was urged to run again for election as President for one reason only: to deny the chance of power to Hitler. Hindenburg won 49.6 per cent of the vote, Hitler 30 per cent; but as the winner needed 50 per cent or more of the vote, a second election was necessary. Hindenburg then won 53 per cent of the vote, and Hitler increased his vote to nearly 37 per cent. One of Hindenburg's first acts was to suppress Hitler's private armies. In the resulting uproar, Chancellor Brüning was forced to resign and the Reichstag was dissolved. In the elections of 31 July — the third time Germany had gone to the polls in five months — the Nazi Party polled 37 per cent of the vote — winning 230 seats in a house of 608 members.

The Nazis were now the largest single political party in Germany but still lacked a clear majority. Rumours spread that a Nazi coup was in the offing. Chancellor von Papen asked Hindenburg to once more dissolve the Reichstag, but was too slow in tabling his motion and the Nazis in the Reichstag, joining with the Communists, passed a vote of no confidence in him. New elections were set for 6 November. To their surprise the Nazis won only 196 seats — a loss of 34 seats. Hindenburg was urged to rule by decree, but the army said it could not maintain order. Murmuring 'I am too old and have been through too much to accept the responsibility for a civil war,' Hindenburg

Above: Adolf Hitler: an early studio portrait of the Führer (Leader) of the Nazi Party.
Right: Hitler at a street rally. The tall figure on the right is his friend 'Putzi' Hanfstaengl, who later displeased him and had to flee to a neutral country

appointed as Chancellor a born intriguer, General von Schleicher, who immediately offered a Cabinet position to Gregor Strasser, one of the leading Nazis. Strasser considered the offer, for by now the Nazi Party was bankrupt and losing votes. Schleicher was unable to form a coalition and asked Hindenburg to again dissolve the Reichstag and let him rule by decree. But Hindenburg had began discussions with Hitler as to the possibility of the Nazis joining a coalition government. Hitler agreed, on condition that he was made Chancellor. Schleicher tendered his resignation on 28 January.

HITLER BECOMES CHANCELLOR

On 30 January 1933, President Hindenburg invited Hitler to be Chancellor of Germany, heading a Cabinet in which Hitler's Nazis held only two other posts, those of Interior Minister (Frick) and Minister of Police in Prussia (Göring). Göring's ministry, however, gave the Nazis control of two-thirds of the police in Germany. Yet it was widely considered that Hitler, in his minority position, was now effectively neutralised, that he would be content with his figurehead role, and that the rabble-rouser was no match for the skilled right-wing politicians with whom he shared government, particularly Hugenberg's Nationalists.

Hitler's seizure of full power was rapid. On the day after his appointment his propaganda chief, Dr Josef Goebbels, confided to his diary: 'In a conference with the Führer, we lay down the line for the fight against the Red terror. For the moment we shall abstain from direct counter-measures. The Bolshevik attempt at world revolution must first burst into flame. At the proper moment we shall strike.'

Less than a month later, on the night of 27 February 1933, the Reichstag building itself burst into flame, and in its fires were destroyed much of what remained of freedom in Germany. It is still not known who was responsible for the act of arson — Goebbels seems to have been astonished by the act but Göring later claimed to have done it. A Dutch simpleton and Communist was later found guilty and executed for the deed. It was probably caused by the Nazis — but Hitler blamed the deed publicly on the Communists and Göring shouted as he watched the flames, 'Every Communist official must be shot, where he is found.' On the next day Hitler asked President Hindenburg to sign a decree for 'the Protection of the People and the State' that suspended all liberties 'as a defensive measure against Communist acts of violence endangering the State' and introducing the death penalty for those responsible. Within a week Nazi storm troopers and the police had arrested Communist leaders, many of whom were tortured and killed or driven into hiding or exile.

In the 3 March 1933 elections the Nazis still failed to achieve a clear-cut majority, obtaining 44 per cent of the vote. But when the Reichstag met on 23 March, Hitler asked deputies to vote on a bill that would grant him total powers to take measures to safeguard the Reich. The Nazis had won 288 seats but still needed a two-thirds majority to change the Weimar constitution. Normally he would

Moment of triumph: Chancellor Hitler greets President Hindenburg (right). In the background is Hermann Göring (in helmet) and Admiral Raeder.

have faced opposition from the two parties that had been his toughest opponents in elections and street fights — the Communists and the Socialists. Fortunately for Hitler, all 82 Communist deputies were in jail or in hiding and the 82 Social Democrats, to their honour, refused to vote for the bill. Hitler needed the 52 votes of the Catholic Centre Party to give him the necessary two-thirds majority, and by bullying them he got them; the 'Enabling Act' was carried. This extraordinary Act gave Hitler total power and he lost no time in taking over every function of rule and in remaking Germany in his own image. Within a week he had dissolved Germany's state parliaments, his first step towards centralising all power in Berlin.

On 1 April 1933 a boycott of all Jewish shops was instituted, the first step in an attempt to eradicate a Jewish presence. Orthodox Jews made up only 1 per cent of Germany's population, yet they were seen as un-German, a threat, not least because of their success in the professions, and in universities and culture. There was hardly an area of German life where the Jews had not made an impression or a contribution.

Wireless programming, newspapers, book publishing, theatre and cinema were placed under the direction and control of Dr Goebbels. All political parties were abolished — except the Nazi Party. In May trade unions were abolished and the works of writers considered decadent were publicly burned in bonfires. Education, previously the responsibility of the states, was centralised and nazified. Youth organisations from the Boy Scouts to Catholic youth groups were banned and soon all German boys were forced to join the 'Hitler Youth', girls the League of German Maidens. Jews were driven from universities. Soon the professors who replaced them were sounding like Nazi street thugs. Professor Wilhelm Mueller of Aachen wrote in his book *Jewry and Science* that even Albert Einstein's theory of relativity, for which he had received the Nobel Prize, 'was directed from beginning to end towards the goal of transforming the living — that is, the non-Jewish — world of living science' and the acclaim which Einstein had enjoyed was rejoicing over 'the approach of Jewish world rule which was to force down German manhood … to the level of a lifeless slave'. The Director of the Institute of Physics in Dresden proclaimed that 'Modern Physics is an instrument of Jewry for the destruction of Nordic science.' Even medicine was to be perverted by Nazi theories of racial superiority and doctors were among the first to join in the program to eliminate those deemed to be racially or mentally inferior.

In March 1933 Göring formed the *Geheime Staatspolizei* (Secret State Police), soon known as the 'Gestapo'. By the end of the year the Nazis had opened fifty 'concentration camps' in which political and other prisoners languished behind barbed wire and were treated with systematic brutality. First crammed with Communists, the camps were soon filled with socialists, pacifists, homosexuals, Jews and Gypsies — all the minorities that aroused Hitler's contempt or hatred. Late in 1933 Germany walked out of the League of Nations after a bogus offer to disarm if other European nations did the same. (In 1934 one of Hitler's most devoted lieutenants, the cold, colourless Heinrich Himmler, who had formed the black-uniformed SS, began to develop the Gestapo's powers as an arm of the SS.)

By 1934 only one body had not yet been overawed by Hitler: the Reichswehr — the army. And only one obstacle to this remained — the uniformed members of the very party that Hitler ruled: the SA Brownshirts who, under Ernst Röhm had grown to a strength of 2.5 million, ten times the size of the army. Rumours spread that the SA was planning a counter-revolution, but most of the rumours were spread by Hitler. President Hindenburg and the army demanded that the Chancellor do something about the SA and Hitler was quick to oblige. On 30 June Himmler's SS arrested and killed out of hand the SA's leadership — this was 'The Night of the Long Knives'. The killings sent a shudder through Europe.

Just over a month later President Hindenburg died. Hitler immediately assumed the dual posts of President and Chancellor, and then abolished the first one, creating a new position for himself as Reich Chancellor and Führer. As Commander-in-Chief he ordered all officers and men of the armed forces to pledge allegiance to him and him alone: 'I swear by God this sacred oath, that I will render unconditional obedience to Adolf Hitler, the Führer of the German Reich and people …' First to swear obedience were the officer corps, who prided themselves on their honour. 'Later and often', writes William L. Shirer, 'by honouring their oath they dishonoured themselves as human beings and trod in the mud the moral code of their corps.' Many generals despised Hitler as Hindenburg had, but few were as contemptuous of the dictator as General von Witzleben, who described Hitler to his officers openly as a 'madman'; ten years later Witzleben would be strangled on Hitler's orders and his agony filmed for the dictator's pleasure.

Within four years German unemployment had fallen from six million to one million, thanks to Hitler's policy of public works and armaments manufacture. In 1934 Nazis in Vienna killed Austria's Chancellor Dollfuss. Mussolini, who regarded Austria as a barrier to German southward expansion, condemned the act and Hitler was forced to disown the deed and assure the world that he was

Chancellor Hitler in formal attire inspects the guard in Berlin, 1933.

committed to peace. But he had already ordered the army — renamed the Wehrmacht — to triple its strength by April 1934. In June of that year he ordered Admiral Raeder to keep secret the construction of submarines and two battle cruisers that were far in excess of the 10,000-tonne limit allowed by the Treaty of Versailles — they were of 26,000 tonnes and history would know them as the *Scharnhorst* and the *Gneisenau*. Göring had vacated his police duties to create an air force. Pilots were already being trained by the civil airline Lufthansa or posing as members of the League for Air Sports and designs were being drawn up for new aircraft. Soon after the Nazis came to power Germany intensified production of synthetic oil and perfected synthetic rubber; both were made from coal.

In November 1933 Winston Churchill spoke in the House of Commons of threatening events in Germany: 'We read all the news [of] the military spirit which is rife throughout [Germany]; we see that a philosophy of blood lust is being inculcated in their youth … We see all these forces on the move, and we must remember that this is the same mighty Germany which fought all the world and almost beat the world … No wonder there is alarm throughout the whole circle of nations which surround Germany.' In November 1934 Churchill informed the Commons that Germany already had an air force and declared that 'the strength of our national defences and especially of our air defences is no longer adequate to secure the peace, safety and freedom of Britain's people'. Prime Minister Baldwin acknowledged that Germany was building military aircraft but stated that 'these were few'.

In the Nuremberg laws of September 1935 all Jews were deprived of citizenship; they were henceforward 'subjects' of the Reich, to be ostracised, hounded or starved. Many among them fled Germany and sought refuge in England, France or the United States. A new dark age had overtaken Germany and Europe.

ROOSEVELT AND THE NEW DEAL

In the same month that Hitler was called to power in Germany, January 1933, Franklin Delano Roosevelt assumed the presidency of the United States. His election win in November 1932 had been a landslide. Few knew that he was crippled and could walk only with the help of leg braces and the strong support of another person. He was confined for most of the day to a wheelchair. But his was a powerful personality, and those who had labelled him a charming lightweight reconsidered their opinion. He had stood as a vice-presidential candidate in 1928, when the Republicans won office under Herbert Hoover. Hoover was everything Roosevelt was not: a cold, humourless man who seemed incapable of coping with the economic blizzard that descended upon the United States in 1929–30.

In a world of despair and darkening horizons Roosevelt's strong voice projected buoyant optimism. 'We have nothing to fear', Roosevelt told Americans in his 1933 inauguration speech, 'but Fear itself.' He saw the nation's economic crisis as the first challenge. To relieve the six million unemployed he, like Hitler, embarked on a government-sponsored and -funded building and construction program. In June the National Recovery Act initiated a federal program of roadways and dams. Business confidence began to recover. Roosevelt gradually put America back on its feet, giving to Americans confidence in themselves and their government. Roosevelt radiated hope and energy.

Above left: Britain's wartime leader Lloyd George (right) twice met Hitler and described him as a 'very great man'. Winston Churchill (left) saw Hitler as a threat to peace in Europe.
Below: Franklin Delano Roosevelt in 1928, four years before his election to the presidency of the United States.

CHAPTER 3
THE MARCH TO WAR
1935–39

The 1930s would be a dark decade of international gangsterism and the year 1935 marked the point when the dictator powers dropped their peaceful mask and revealed their true intentions. Germany's rearmament could no longer be concealed, and in February 1935 Britain and France proposed granting Germany equality of armaments in exchange for Hitler's guarantee of the borders of the eastern European states — an 'eastern Locarno Pact'. The long process of appeasing Hitler had begun.

Hitler announced on 10 March 1935 that Germany had already built an air force, and waited for world reaction. There was none, other than muted protests from the democracies and the League of Nations. One week later (16 March) he announced the introduction of military conscription and his intention to build an army of 500,000 men (that is, about 36 divis-ions). He had broken the first chains in the Treaty of Versailles. Again, there was no reaction other than polite protests.

In a speech from the Reichstag on 21 May 1935 he reassured an anxious Europe that Germany wanted peace: 'the principal effect of every war is to destroy the flower of the nation … Germany needs peace and desires peace! Whoever lights the torch of war in Europe can wish for nothing but chaos.' He offered to reduce armaments, and to limit the German Navy to 35 per cent of the strength of Britain's. Britain eagerly grabbed this offer and it did this without consulting its ally France or the League of Nations disarmament offices. The Anglo-German Naval Treaty limited Germany to a naval strength one-third of Britain's and permitted Germany to build submarines, which had also been forbidden by the Treaty of Versailles. It allowed Hitler to increase naval building — a measure he had not contemplated — while at the same time it limited British construction. Germany laid down two giant battleships, each of 45,000 tonnes — the future *Bismarck* and *Tirpitz* — while Britain, being a signatory of the Washington Treaty with the United States and France, was limited to capital ships of 35,000 tonnes. Creation of a modern fleet for Singapore and the Pacific now seemed remote. 'What a windfall this has been to Japan!' Winston Churchill thundered in the House of Commons. 'The British Fleet, when this programme is completed, will be largely anchored in the North Sea. This means that the whole position in the Far East has been gravely altered …' Germany proceeded to build five battleships, submarines, cruisers and sixty-four destroyers. 'It was thus not a limitation on German rearmament but an encouragement to expand it,' as Shirer writes.

Worse still, Hitler was gathering allies while neutralising his opponents. In 1934 Germany had signed a treaty of friendship with Poland, which had been the cornerstone of France's eastern European alliances. Poland was no longer a democracy; indeed, in 1926 it had been one of the first states to succumb to rule by the military when Marshal Pilsudski and his 'colonels' took power. France's Foreign Minister, Louis Barthou, set out to strengthen France's alliances. He was a republican in the mould of Clemenceau and Poincaré. In October 1934 he welcomed King Alexander of Yugoslavia to Marseilles, but both men were killed there by an assassin in the pay of Italy and Croatian nationalists. Their successors lacked their strength and willpower.

Inset above: **Nationalist China, whose flag is shown, was the earliest victim of international aggression when Japan invaded her in 1937.**
Opposite: **Hitler and Reichsmarschall Göring at their moment of triumph, the bloodless entry into Vienna, 1938.**
Opposite right: **By 1939 Germany's army was the most modern in Europe.**

In February 1934 Paris had been rocked by riots that some observers feared might destroy the Third Republic itself; in Vienna in the same month the right-wing Austrian government was bombarding the workers' suburbs with artillery, effectively crushing the Social Democrats. As the effects of the economic depression spread across Europe, people began to lose faith in their fragile democracies. Fascism grew in appeal and in strength. Parliamentary governments began to fail.

By early 1938 the only nations in eastern Europe with democratic freedoms were Czechoslovakia and Finland. Within little more than a year both were to become victims of the dictators. Western European countries weathered the storm of political upheavals and retained their democratic forms, but fascist and extremist groups emerged in all of them. Even England had its British Union of Fascists, who wore black shirts and demanded authoritarian rule; even Ireland had its blue shirts. The English-speaking nations, with their tradition of two-party democracy and regular elections, came through the years of adversity best of all. In 1935 the Conservatives were returned to power in the British elections; they were to remain in power for ten years.

1935: ITALY MARCHES

In January 1933 Mussolini had greeted the coming to power of the Nazis with delight, saying 'The victory of Hitler is also our victory.' But Italy still projected a peaceful image and Mussolini appeared the soul of reason. He saw the possibility of a future alliance with Germany while voicing his concern about the threat of 'Prussian militarism'. He had deplored the Nazi putsch in Vienna, supported Chancellor Dollfuss and encouraged him to set up a one-party state. He had not been impressed by Hitler when they first met in 1934 and described the portly Göring as 'an ex-inmate of a lunatic asylum'. He was appalled by the bloodshed in June 1934 when Hitler had disposed of his supposed enemies.

Mussolini's obsessions were no longer domestic but imperial. He announced publicly that Italy's ambitions were directed towards Africa and even Asia. He began looking back longingly to the era when Imperial Rome ruled the known world and adopted the pose of a Caesar. His building program adopted that of the emperors. In April 1933 Italians travelling along the new Avenue of the Empire in Rome passed marble maps showing the extent of the Roman empire. Critics called the Duce a 'sawdust Caesar'. Italy's worsening economic position, its reliance on imports and its burgeoning birth rate could perhaps be solved by the acquisition of a larger empire in northern Africa. There, Italy's colonies from Libya to Eritrea were mostly desert, costing much and producing little. Italians formed the majority of the European population of the prosperous colony of Tunisia, but Tunisia was French.

An Italian attempt to conquer the last independent African kingdom, Abyssinia (Ethiopia) in 1896 had failed miserably but in December 1934 Mussolini ordered 'the total conquest of Ethiopia'. He would direct the campaign personally (from Rome) and use an army of 300,000 men. Still fearful of Germany, in April 1935 he welcomed the prime ministers of Britain and France to Stresa and pledged his support to their efforts to contain Germany. He made sure at the meeting that no discussion about Ethiopia was tabled. At the same time he spoke of going to war against Britain and of invading the Sudan if necessary, and initiated discussions with Hitler about an alliance. Mussolini was now playing the double game that would prove his ruin. In May France signed a mutual assistance pact with Soviet Russia and soon announced an extension of military service from eighteen months to twenty-four months. Hitler was to describe these action as provocations.

On 2 October 1935, after protesting about unprovoked aggression by Ethiopian forces, the Italian army invaded Ethiopia, supported by bombers. The advance was timid and made little progress, but the League of Nations condemned Italy as an aggressor, and ordered economic sanctions be imposed on her. The British Mediterranean fleet moved to war stations and the possibility of war grew. In December Britain's Foreign Minister Hoare, and his French counterpart, Pierre Laval, proposed a compromise, suggesting that their countries hand over some of their African territories to Italy, but public indignation forced both men to resign. Only Laval would make a comeback.

The Ethiopian campaign revealed Italy's inadequacies. The Fascist Blackshirt divisions lacked ardour in battle, and were untrained for the exertions of modern warfare, while the army was ill-equipped and poorly led. Italo Balbo, the renowned airman and most popular of Mussolini's younger colleagues, protested that the 'political, diplomatic, financial, and, indeed, even military preparations had been completely inadequate'. Mussolini sent Marshal Badoglio, Italy's best-known military commander, to the scene, ordering him to use whatever measures he thought necessary to achieve victory. Early in 1936 Graziani's army in Eritrea advanced while Badoglio's forces moved forward in the north destroying villages by air bombardment, and dropping poison gas on any enemy groups they encountered. Badoglio entered the capital of Addis Ababa in May. Few Italians had died in the campaign — her 5000 fatalities were mostly native Askaris — but Ethiopia claimed to have lost close to half a million lives. The Ethiopian Emperor, Haile Selassie, went into exile aboard a British warship and made a dignified appearance before the League of Nations, ignoring the catcalls and jeers of Italian diplomats and journalists, and Mussolini proclaimed King Victor Emmanuel 'Emperor of Ethiopia'. Badoglio was made Duke of Addis Ababa.

Mussolini had flouted the authority of the League of Nations and had got away with it. Britain and France, overestimating Italy's strength and influence, continued to court him.

1936: SHIFTING ALLIANCES

In Berlin Hitler had denounced the Franco–Soviet Pact to the French ambassador in 'a long tirade'. The pact was approved by the French parliament in February 1936, and Hitler made his next move soon afterwards. Despite warnings by his generals of possible French counter-measures, he sent German troops into the Rhineland on

7 March 1936, where they were greeted by cheering crowds. Hitler had ordered them to withdraw immediately if French troops confronted them, but none did. General Gamelin, the French Commander-in-Chief, had been asked to draw up plans for this eventuality, but informed his government that the army could make no effective response. France's strength was concentrated in the Maginot Line, and had no mobility though it was still the most powerful army in western Europe. France's Foreign Minister Flandin flew to London to gather support for joint action but met with indifference. Churchill recorded Flandin's words of warning: 'If you do not stop Germany by force today, war is inevitable, even if you make a temporary friendship with Germany.' Prime Minister Baldwin, as wary as British leaders had been in 1914 of being dragged into war by France, stated simply to Flandin: 'England is not in a state to go to war.' This was true, but France *was* prepared. Flandin returned to his country 'with the dismal conclusion that the only hope for France was in an arrangement with an ever aggressive Germany'.

In the House of Commons debate on the Rhineland invasion (26 March) Foreign Minister Anthony Eden called for joint planning by the staffs of Britain, France and Belgium, and Churchill said: 'We cannot look back with much pleasure on our foreign policy in the last five years. They certainly have been disastrous years ... we have seen the most depressing and alarming change in the outlook of mankind that has ever taken place in so short a period. Five years ago all felt safe ...' When the Baldwin government called for a vote of confidence eleven days later Churchill predicted that Germany would construct a defensive line along her new, expanded frontier (the future Siegfried Line) and thundered: 'Herr Hitler has torn up treaties ... the creation of a line of forts ... will enable the German troops to be economised on that line and will enable [their] main forces to swing round through Belgium and Holland.'

France's great system of alliances now began to unravel. Her allies in the 'Little Entente' — Czechoslovakia, Yugoslavia and Romania — began to drift away. Belgium soon withdrew from defence arrangements with France (1937) and declared her neutrality in the event of war, leaving a wide gap to the west of the Maginot Line that was never filled. Soviet Russia was slowly emerging from its self-imposed isolation to counter Germany's growing threat, urging Communists in Europe to collaborate with democratic parties to form 'popular fronts' against the fascists, but France soon had another hostile power on her borders: Spain.

SPANISH CIVIL WAR

In Spain the bloodless removal of the monarchy in 1931 had led to a succession of unstable elected governments that failed to solve the problem of introducing democracy to a society that was still basically a nineteenth-century authoritarian state resting on the twin pillars of the Catholic Church and the army. Both these institutions regarded the Socialist government in Madrid as one dominated by Communists and anarchists and incapable of preserving order. In July 1936 the Spanish army in Morocco under the command of General Francisco

'Obey! Fight!' Two of the mottos of Fascist Italy. Mussolini is seen addressing a rally. Behind him stands Starace, one of his most ruthless lieutenants.

Franco defied the authority of the Madrid government while in Spain itself troops seized Pamplona and other cities in the north and commenced to march on Madrid. In Madrid and Barcelona the risings failed, and they would remain the strongest Republican centres in the military rebellion that quickly became a civil war. It was fought with savagery from its first hours and would take 500,000 lives.

Within five days of beginning the revolt Franco had appealed to Germany and Italy for arms and assistance in his war against the 'Marxists'. Help was readily given. Although exhausted militarily and financially by the Ethiopian war, Italy despatched an expeditionary force of 'volunteers' that eventually numbered 70,000 men; Mussolini thought the war would be over in seven weeks, but it lasted three years. Germany's help was more effective — an air force including modern bombers known as the Condor Legion, which bombed Republican-held villages ruthlessly, destroying Guernica so completely that the name became synonymous with the horrors of modern war. Volunteers from Britain, France, the United States and most European countries enlisted in International Brigades to defend the Spanish Republic and Soviet Russia sent aircraft and pilots to assist them.

The fighting in Spain was a dress rehearsal for the coming world war, and its immediate effect was to draw Germany and Italy closer together. In September 1936 Mussolini made his first state visit to Berlin, where he addressed a crowd said to number a million at the Maiefeld. He returned home astonished by the display of might

Fatal friendship: Hitler and Mussolini photographed during the latter's visit to Berlin in 1936.

and power he had witnessed, and convinced that Italy's future lay with Germany In October 1936 Count Ciano, Italy's Foreign Minister, paid his first visit to Hitler to discuss the formation of an alliance. Ciano, a playboy who had married Mussolini's daughter Edda, was ill-equipped for the role of diplomat, but was a sharp observer of the Nazis, whom he loathed while agreeing that close ties with Germany were essential. Hitler told him that Germany and Italy together could conquer not only Bolshevism but the entire West, and that the British would soon seek some sort of agreement with them. 'In three years Germany will be ready,' Hitler assured him. On 1 November 1936 Mussolini addressed a vast crowd in the Piazza del Duomo in Milan and announced: 'One great country has recently gathered a vast amount of sympathy among the masses of the Italian people: I speak of Germany.' Certain problems between the two nations had been overcome by the signing of agreements. 'This Berlin–Rome line is not a diaphragm but rather an axis around which can revolve all those European states with a will to collaboration and peace.' This was the first public mention of the novel word 'Axis' to describe the strengthening bond between the two dictatorships.

Two months later Göring, Hitler's economic overlord, told Germany's leading industrialists in a secret meeting: 'We live in a time when the final battle is in sight. We are already on the threshold of mobilisation and we are already at war. All that is lacking is the actual shooting.' Early in 1937 Hitler informed the Reichstag: 'The time of so-called surprises is ended.' Europe heard these words with relief and the year would be one without incident or crisis. Yet it was during 1937 that Hitler made his decision to go to war. On 5 November 1937, a date Shirer describes as 'the decisive turning point in the life of the Third Reich' (it was 'Bonfire Day' in English-speaking countries) Hitler summoned his Foreign Minister (Neurath) and his armed forces chiefs (the Minister of War, Blomberg, and Fritsch of the army, Raeder of the navy and Göring, chief of the Luftwaffe) to the Reich Chancellery in Berlin. Here he informed them that 'Germany's problem could be solved only by means of force' and 'Our first objective ... must be to overthrow Czechoslovakia and Austria in order to remove any threat to our flank in any possible operation in the West.' War must come soon — by 1943 it would be too late, for Germany's enemies would be stronger, and his own weapons outmoded. His military men were shocked, but before long all had been removed from their positions. With Blomberg's departure Hitler took over his post as Commander-in-Chief and abolished the War Ministry, replacing it with his own creation — the *Oberkommando der Wehrmacht*, or *OKW* (High Command of the Wehrmacht) and as his Chief of Staff he chose General Wilhelm Keitel, a toady of the Nazis. As successor to Blomberg as C-in-C of the army, Hitler appointed General von Brauchitsch. Joachim von Ribbentrop, who had been an embarrassment as ambassador to London, took the place of the old diplomat von Neurath as Foreign Minister. 'On that day the Nazi revolution, it might be said, was completed.' Hitler now had about him the persons he found most congenial, for none questioned his actions.

1937: JAPAN: DARK CLOUDS, RISING SUN

If the march of events in Germany caused concern, the events in Japan caused puzzlement. The effects of the Depression on Japan's economy were profound. To Europeans and Americans Japan's society was unfathomable and its mentality curious. The most disciplined society in Asia, it was prone to acts of violence that appeared to be officially condoned. Any diminution of Japanese power was seen as a national insult.

As early as 1928 the Japanese secret service had carried out the assassination of the warlord of Manchuria, Chang Tso-lin, to prepare the ground for their eventual takeover of the region. In September 1931 the Japanese army based on the Kwantung peninsula — Japan's sole enclave on the Asian mainland apart from Korea — manufactured an incident that gave them an excuse to invade Manchuria. They blew up part of the railway line and blamed it on the Chinese. Emperor Hirohito instructed them to 'proceed with prudence and caution' and to limit their incursion to seize Mukden and southern railheads. This was accomplished on 18 September 1931 — in one day — at the cost of two Japanese lives and the death of 400 Chinese soldiers. The League of Nations appointed a commission to report on what China described as unprovoked aggression. In January 1932 Colonel Itagaki, political mastermind in the Kwantung army (and one of seven Japanese leaders later hanged in Tokyo by the Allies as a war criminal) ordered his chief troublemaker, Major Tanaka, to create an incident in Shanghai to deflect international attention from Manchuria. A group of monks were set upon there by toughs in the pay of the Japanese Secret Service, and Japan demanded an explanation from China and threatened retaliation. On 28 January 1932 Japanese forces landed in Shanghai and aircraft from aircraft carriers bombed civilian areas, but the Chinese resisted strongly; after nearly six weeks a cease-fire was negotiated. The 70,000 Japanese were withdrawn in late March.

The proclamation of the puppet state of Manchuria — Manchukuo — had occurred on 1 March. In May 1932 young officers assassinated the Japanese Prime Minister, Inukai, seemingly as punishment for his lack of enthusiasm for the Manchurian and Shanghai adventures. In April Lord Lytton arrived to visit Manchuria before compiling his report for the League of Nations. His report, published in September, found that 'without declaration of war, a large area of what was indisputably Chinese territory has been forcibly seized and occupied by the armed forces of Japan'. At Geneva the Japanese delegate Matsuoka explained that Japan wanted no more territory, but in December Japanese forces seized Jehol Province from China. In February 1933, when the League of Nations condemned Japan's invasion of Manchuria by forty-two votes to none, Japan withdrew from the League. The pattern had been set. For Japan there was no going back.

In Japan an old animist religion, Shintoism, was resuscitated, which professed that Japan itself was a creation of the gods and the Emperor the son of Heaven.

As Japan's belligerence grew, China's strength waned. Even after the rise of General Chiang Kai-shek and his Kuomintang in 1925, China remained fragmented, its regions ruled by warlords paying only lip service to the authority of the central government. In 1934 Chiang's forces attempted to eliminate Mao Tse-tung's Communists. Mao then led his followers on one of the epic marches in history to the far north-west of China, where he rebuilt his support and waited.

In the same year, 1934, Japan, having achieved permission to build a navy 70 per cent the strength of the American, started laying down new battleships far in excess of anything built so far. Japan had long smarted under the treaty terms that limited her naval strength to little more than half that of Britain or the United States.

General Yamashita, one of the most capable of Japan's commanders. An antagonist of General Tojo, whose power soon became total, Yamashita was opposed to war with the European powers but led the army that conquered Malaya and Singapore.

'I'm smaller than you,' a Japanese negotiator remarked to an American, 'but why should I have only 60 per cent of the food you have on your plate?' The 'super battleships' *Yamato* and *Musashi* were launched in 1936, by which time any chance of limiting naval building had passed. Weighing in at 73,000 tonnes, these were the largest warships ever built and fired the largest shells ever designed — projectiles 18.1 inches in diameter. Admiral Yamamoto, a rising star in the Imperial Navy, deplored their construction. An enthusiast for aviation, he pointed out that numerous aircraft-carriers could have been built for a fraction of the battleships' cost.

In February 1936 the citizens of Tokyo travelling to work found troops stationed throughout the city. The soldiers, shivering in the snow, seemed puzzled and looked as if the were waiting for orders. Another clique of junior officers had mounted a coup, rousing their soldiers in the 1st Division in the hours before dawn and ordering them to occupy key positions in the city. The ringleaders' motives are still not clear. They were seemingly opposed to shedding Japanese blood in foreign entanglements but quite willing to shed it at home, for they attempted to assassinate the entire Japanese Cabinet and succeeded in killing several ministers in cold blood. Hirohito disapproved of their venture and within days their rebellion was crushed. In their manifesto presented to the Emperor, the rebel officers protested that 'After humble reflection as children of the Land of the Gods, we submit these grievances to the one Eternal God, the Emperor, under whose high command we serve ... increasingly Japan is pursued by foreign troubles, and riding at the mercy of the waves, becomes the butt of foreign ridicule ... Russia, China, England and the United States are within a hair's breadth of ensnaring our Land of the Gods and of destroying our culture ... at this moment when the 1st Division has just heard its Imperial order of dispatch overseas we cannot but look back [with concern] on conditions at home ...' Fourteen of the twenty surviving officers were later executed by firing squad.

Japanese troops treated China's cities as their own backyard. Japanese infantry photographed in Shanghai in the 1930s.

In November 1936 Japan joined Germany in signing 'the Anti-Comintern Pact' to demonstrate their opposition to the Soviet Union. The growing influence of the expansionist army clique could not be halted. In the next elections the Constitutionalists — who were committed in theory at least to parliamentary rule — received a minority of votes. The army was increased from seventeen divisions to twenty-four, while a quarter of the commissioned officers were retired. Hereafter only active serving officers could hold the ministries of War and the Navy. Despite protests from an army faction that favoured a confrontation with Russia and seizure of eastern Siberia, planning proceeded for a full-scale invasion of China, whose government's authority seemed to be collapsing. Manchuria and the Peking area were controlled by Japan, Outer Mongolia by Russia, the northwest by Mao Tse-tung's Communists. Only in central China along the Yangtse Valley was Chiang Kai-shek's authority established, centred on Nanking. In December 1936 Chiang, while visiting the city of Sian (Xi'an), was kidnapped by his own governor and for thirteen days held prisoner. He was released only when he pledged to cease operations against the Communists and stand firm against the true threat, the Japanese. For decades Japan had sought to bring China under her influence by subtle means and sometimes violent reminders of her strength. Now only armed force was left to Tokyo. A generation later Sir William Webb, the Australian judge who sentenced the Japanese leaders to death by hanging, would reflect on the ambivalence of Japanese society: 'Anthropologists, poets, priests and diplomats, each in their own fields, have found, on study, that the Japanese world contains a logic and a beauty of its own,' he wrote, and like others wondered how this beauty was transformed into medieval brutality.

In June 1937 Prince Konoye, an ambivalent leader, was appointed Prime Minister. Five days later the Chief of Staff of the Kwantung army, General Tojo, excused himself from a banquet in Manchukuo, to send a cable to Tokyo stating: 'When viewed against our present state of affairs in China, we deem it most important and desirable, in order to eliminate the threat in our rear, to strike a direct blow against and into the Nanking regime ...'

JAPAN INVADES CHINA, 1937

On the night of 7 July 1937, an incident was contrived near the Marco Polo bridge in Peking, which marked the demarcation line between Japanese and Chinese forces. The Japanese outpost accused the Chinese of abducting one of their men and commenced shelling the Chinese. The Japanese advanced south from Manchuria and in late August 1937 landed more troops at Shanghai, where fighting was furious. In November a Japanese fleet landed 60,000 men 70 kilometres south of Shanghai and advanced towards the city, forcing the Chinese to withdraw to the Yangste delta. By early December 1937 a Japanese army had advanced 300 kilometres up the Yangtse River to Nanking, burning villages and killing civilians as it progressed. Chiang had moved his government to Hangchow on 7 December, leaving an army of 300,000 troops to defend Nanking, which was stormed a week later. There a new aspect of Japanese civilisation was revealed. Japanese troops commanded by General Matsui butchered between 100,000 and 300,000 captured Chinese troops and civilians in the conquered city. Among them were 5000 women who were raped before being killed, and much of the city was put to the torch. Survivors were sheltered by appalled American, British and German envoys and missionaries. The American gunboat USS *Panay*, anchored in a bend of the Yangtse, was attacked and sunk by Japanese aircraft.

The Japanese showed no contrition. The fighting since July had cost more than 100,000 Japanese casualties — figures that indicate the savage cost of the war to both China and Japan that would be fought for the next eight years. To people throughout the world already dismayed by Nazi Germany's brutal treatment of its Jews and by the bloodshed in Spain, it seemed that the world was going mad, that all civilised restraints had gone. 'Before Warsaw, before Buchenwald,' writes the historian of those days, David Bergamini, 'Nanking was the great atrocity. It convinced many Americans, for the first time, that the governments siding with Germany in the Anti-Comintern Pact were genuinely evil.'

In October 1938 the Japanese landed at Canton, near Hong Kong, and the 200,000 Chinese defenders withdrew into the hinterland. China's seaports were now in Japanese hands. Japan now offered peace to China. Usually amenable to compromise, Chiang Kai-shek replied: 'This is a war of the Chinese people … this is a people's war.' In November, as the Japanese armies approached Changsha, the Chinese put the city to the torch and withdrew, burning crops and villages as the Japanese had done, before breaking the Yellow River dykes and flooding the land. Up to one million Chinese peasants died, but the floods barely impeded the enemy's progress.

For the first time aid flowed to China from the United States — namely loans and the nucleus of an air force under a retired US Army Air Corps officer, Colonel Claire Chennault, who would become one of the legendary figures of World War II. A powerful 'China lobby' grew in the United States and China's leaders Chiang and his glamorous American-educated wife were portrayed as the valiant leaders of one of the few nations brave enough to stand up to naked aggression. Among their particular champions was the publisher of *Time* and *Life* magazines, Henry R. Luce, who had been born in China, the son of Methodist missionaries, and who was blind to the corruption that marked Chiang's government. Matsui, who laid waste to Nanking, was hanged by the Allies for the crime eleven years later. Japan's war with China was the first act in the drama of World War II, and it was to consume the bulk of Japan's armies until their defeat in 1945. Chinese military and civilian deaths were so high that statistics were not kept after 1938, but are estimated at 15 million.

Chiang Kai-shek, Sun Yat-sen's successor as leader of China in 1924, led a fragmented and disunited nation against Japan's encroachments from 1931 to 1945.

ARMING FOR A NEW WAR

Left: Modern aircraft: Italian Savoia Marchetti bombers over Spain, 1936.

Right: The shape of the future: the Americans pioneered the design of powerful four-engined bombers. An early photograph of a Boeing B-17 bomber, later famous as the 'Flying Fortress'.

British rearmament had begun in 1935 and it progressed in fits and starts. The navy began a rebuilding program, and the RAF began drawing up plans for modern bombers. Politicians, the press and the public demanded that rearmament be speeded up, but behind the scenes remarkable advances were being made. Over the preceding decade the development of aircraft and the growth of wireless — radio — had been dramatic. Air travel was in its infancy, and the Depression had killed many of the bright aviation initiatives of the 1920s. As early as 1928 two intrepid Australians had flown the Pacific Ocean — an expanse nearly three times the breath of the Atlantic — in a remarkably robust, three-engined aircraft designed by the Dutch genius Anton Fokker. It was of metal construction, with an enclosed cockpit, and had an enormous wingspan, and the crew carried wireless as a navigation aid. By year's end the two Australians had established an airline to connect Australia's capitals, but their venture became a casualty of the Depression. It was not until 1940 that Pan-American Airways opened an air route across the Pacific, from California to New Zealand and Australia. The revolutionary Fokker aircraft became the model for the Junkers transport adopted by the Luftwaffe.

Wireless had played little part in the 1914–18 war. Most ships were equipped with wireless, but the Royal Navy at Jutland still relied on signalling orders by flag, as Nelson had done; this had tragi-comic results when battleships were unable to see clearly the admiral's fluttering pennants through the mist and battle smoke and executed the wrong manoeuvres. Armies on the Western Front relied on telephone lines for communication in the front line: signallers unrolled the cables as they followed the advancing infantry, but their cable lines were often cut by shell-fire, and contact with forward elements was lost.

During the 1920s, with the development of amplifiers, wireless programs including music recitals, interviews, dramas and talks were broadcast widely and by the early 1930s many if not most homes had wireless receivers — radios. In December 1932 King George had made the first live Christmas broadcast from Buckingham Palace via the BBC, and short wave had carried his voice around the world. In World War II radio would be the principal weapon of propaganda and the medium by which Winston Churchill's speeches would damn his enemies and inspire his own people. Television was also being broadcast by the BBC in the late 1930s, and Hitler watched events in the 1936 Berlin Olympics on television, but the images were blurry, the cost of receivers high, and development of TV received little encouragement. The infant medium was regarded as one without a future. The picture tube, however, would be an essential component in radar and the anti-submarine version adopted by the Royal Navy — asdic.

RADAR Britain saw the main threat to its security as the air. Writers and newspapers predicted that Britain's congested cities would be devastated by fleets of enemy bombers and clouds of poison gas. The first steps to counter these threats were unspectacular but effective. By the outbreak of war most of the British population was equipped with gas masks and in wartime it was an offence not to carry one. Batteries of anti-aircraft guns, strong searchlights and barrage balloons were stationed around London and principal cities, and simple air raid shelters constructed.

Measures were taken to try to locate fleets of approaching bombers, and these efforts saw the birth of Radar (the American term for Radio Direction Finding or RDF). It was born when aircraft interfered with wireless. In late 1934 staff at the British Post Office, who were experimenting in sending messages by wireless, noticed that their transmissions were constantly affected by approaching aeroplanes, and asked the government's Radio Research Station at Slough if it could investigate the phenomenon. The Chief Scientist there was a Scot, Robert Watson-Watt. He had already been asked by the Air Ministry to report on the feasibility of 'death rays' — an invention by science fiction writers described as capable of destroying entire cities. In January 1935 Watson-Watt calculated that the generation of electromagnetic waves of sufficient heat to burn and vaporise anything in their path was beyond existing capacities, and concluded by asking the Air Ministry official, 'Well, if the death ray is impossible, how else can we help you?' He was informed about the GPO's problem and asked to carry out experiments in locating aircraft by using radio beams. One month later he set up a transmitter that bounced wireless signals off an RAF Heyford bomber flying at a height of 10,000 feet [3000 metres]. The speed of

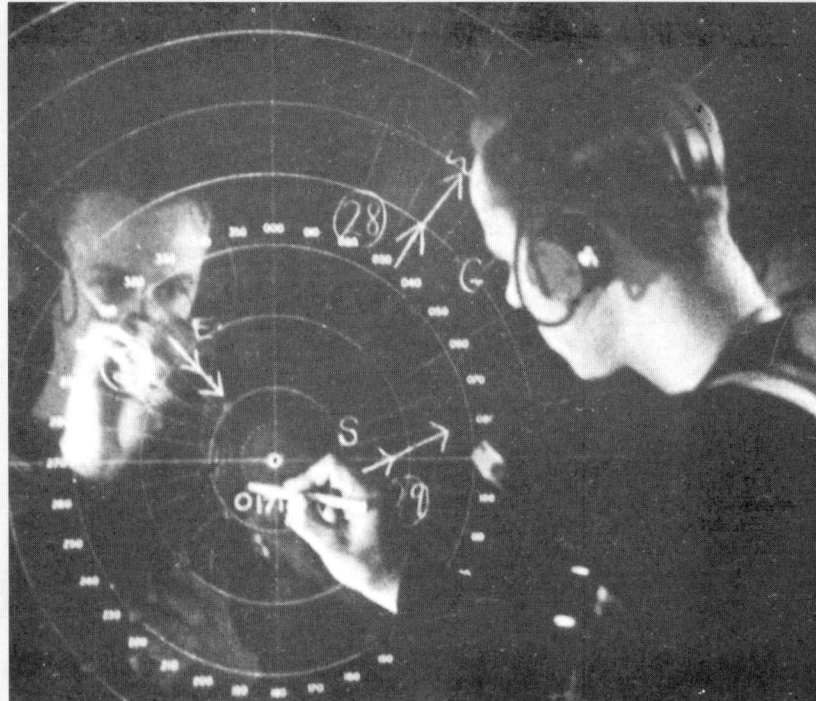

Radar and Asdic were developed by Britain on the eve of war and proved vital, respectively locating approaching enemy aircraft and submerged submarines.

sound was known, and by timing the echoes received on the ground he and his scientists were soon able to calculate the distance, and later the altitude and speed, of approaching aircraft. By 1938 towering wireless masts were rising along the south and south-east coast of England. They became Britain's principal early-warning system. The Germans, who were also developing radar, thought they were ordinary wireless transmitters.

Britain's slow progress in the face of growing German power alarmed Winston Churchill, who urged the creation of a sub-committee of the Committee of Imperial Defence (CID) to plan the air defence of Great Britain. Early in 1935 Churchill and his friend the scientist and Cambridge professor Frederick Lindemann were invited to join an Air Ministry committee. Adolf Hitler's announcement in March 1935 that Germany had formed an air force — the Luftwaffe — and that it was already stronger than the air forces of Britain and France combined, intensified British preparations for an air war. Hitler contributed to British efforts by expelling some — if not most — of Germany's outstanding scientists who happened to be Jews. Britain provided them refuge and Lindemann gave them employment in the laboratories of the University of Cambridge. The young scientific prodigy R.V. Jones, later to head Churchill's wartime Scientific Intelligence department, would remember the arrival there of scientists of the calibre of Erwin Shrödinger and Leo Szilard, Kurti and Mendelssohn.

A German official photograph showing an Enigma encrypting machine (lower left). General Guderian is pictured in his command vehicle during the Battle of France in 1940.

ENIGMA It was a simple-looking machine yet its workings were complex. The 'Enigma' encrypting machine had been invented in 1919 by a Dutchman as a way of encrypting secret business letters for transmission by telegram and during the 1920s was being manufactured in Berlin. All the major powers read each other's mail or secret messages or attempted to. The German Army showed interest in the machine and so did Japan. The US military attaché bought one of the machines, and as it was too big to fit into the embassy's diplomatic pouch, shipped it to the US Signals Corps in Washington, where its workings were examined. Japan used an early Enigma as the basis for its own code machine known as 'Purple', but American code experts had broken its ciphers long before war broke out.

Enigma looked like a combination of a typewriter and a cash register, and incorporated elements of both. It was powered by electricity. It had a keyboard behind which lay a spider web of wires connected to a series of wheels — rotors — and it contained a second keyboard, whose letters lit up. An operator hitting the key B, for example, would see the letter F appear; if the setting of the wheels was changed, striking the letter B would result in an L, and so on. The letters lit up in this way would then be transmitted by wireless in morse code and decoded by the receiver, providing he set the wheels on his machine in exactly the prescribed position. These wheel settings were changed daily.

CRACKING 'ENIGMA'

After Hitler came to power the Enigma was withdrawn from the market. As many as 100,000 machines were supplied to the Wehrmacht during the course of the war. Enigma's workings were so complicated that they were thought to be impregnable. In addition to the original three rotors, two spares were supplied; later a fourth rotor was included in the design. A message's possible permutations are said to have been in the region of 6,000,000,000,000,000. Intercepted wireless messages looked like gobbledegook, but skilled Allied codebreakers invented the forerunner of the computer to process the data. It was a process of elimination. Code-breakers often look for one word — perhaps the address of the sender that appeared on all messages from that source — and the deciphering of that one word can lead them to unravelling the sense of the rest of the message.

Polish Military Intelligence, which conscripted the most brilliant mathematicians from Warsaw University to assist them, was the first to probe Enigma's workings and successfully decode German messages, though it took a week or more to decipher many of them, a delay that rendered the work of little use in time of war. The Poles offered their discoveries to the French. At a meeting in Paris with British and French intelligence officers in January 1939 Polish Intelligence handed over the fruit of their discoveries — and an Enigma machine.

By April 1940 British Intelligence at the code centre at Bletchley Park were deciphering the first German messages, and by war's end were reading every message they had intercepted, passing on to the Prime Minister and his chiefs of staff the information, which was code-named 'Ultra'. The Intelligence passed to commanders in the field was code-named 'Boniface' and was claimed to come from very reliable sources, which many thought implied information from secret agents. The Germans, who congratulated themselves on breaking numerous Allied codes and successfully listening into

Churchill's and Roosevelt's trans-Atlantic conversations, had no idea that their armed forces ciphers had been broken. Ultra could not win battles, but it gave Allied commanders some indication of the enemy's strength or intentions. It was the war's best-kept secret and remained so until 1974 when its existence was revealed.

AIR POWER

BOMBERS Air power would be the decisive weapon in World War II but few realised how completely it would dictate the course of battle and the fate of nations. Bombers were seen as the weapon that could ensure the safety of the British Isles by striking the enemy before he reached the English coast. Fighter aircraft — interceptors — were of lower priority.

By 1936 American aviation development had far outstripped British. The Americans, who were themselves rearming against a possible Japanese threat, also shared the belief that the bomber would be the decisive factor in a future war. As early as 1935 the Americans developed the Boeing B-17 (Flying Fortress), a metal-fuselage bomber, to attack enemy fleets. It was designed to fly long distances with a heavy bomb weight at high altitudes to avoid both anti-aircraft fire and as its nickname implied, it bristled with machine guns to ward off fighters, and was far superior to the under-armed, wood-and-fabric British bombers designed to attack European targets. Late in the same year the first Douglas 'Dakota' flew in California — an all-metal, twin-engined transport aircraft capable of carrying twenty passengers. By 1938 it had been adopted by most of the world's airlines — the US Army Air Corps also ordered it, calling it the C-47; the British called it the DC-3. Slow but safe, a pilot's dream, it became the work-horse of the Allies and more than 10,000 were built; some C-47s were still seeing service in Vietnam in the 1970s.

Above: Hitler with his air force chiefs some time after 1935, when the existence of the Luftwaffe was revealed to the world. *Below:* The late 1930s became an era of extraordinary innovation in the world of aviation. Here a Parnall seaplane is catapulted from its hangar on the deck of the British submarine M-1. The submarine later sank and the new weapon did not go into mass production. But during the coming war Japanese submarines carried aircraft, one of which flew over Sydney in May 1942.

Left: The Douglas DC-3, adopted by the Dutch airline KLM in the 1930s, became famous in the Allied air forces as the Dakota transport.

When Britain began to build up its air defences, designs were called for in 1936 for four-engined 'heavy bombers'; these would not appear until 1941 and Britain would begin the war with two-engined 'medium' bombers such as the Wellington, with a speed of around 250 mph, capable of carrying a bomb load of only 4500 pounds. Some medium and light bombers had evolved from civil aviation's small, fast executive aircraft — the Bristol Blenheim was one of these. It was fortunate that Hitler also overrated the power of his existing bombers and never developed a heavy bomber force.

All the combatants overrated the potential of bombers. They were terrifying weapons against defenceless civilian targets in Spain, China, Poland and France, but it was another matter when they flew at night, had difficulty finding their targets, and faced anti-aircraft fire and attack by swarms of fighters. In 1939 all bombers (apart from the Flying Fortress) were too slow, too frail to carry heavy bomb loads, lacked adequate machine guns to defend themselves, and were bereft of bomb-aiming equipment. The British had power-operated turrets (these were lacking even in the Flying Fortress) but the RAF's early bombers' size — or rather wingspan — was restricted because they had to fit into the hangars already constructed! Thus the two-engined Hampden had a wingspan of only 77 feet, the Whitley one of 84 feet.

The two great heavy bombers of the future — the Halifax and the Lancaster — were originally designed as two-engined aircraft, and the latter — the 'Lanc', 'the war winner' — evolved from the sluggish two-engined Manchester, which was structurally sound but underpowered; when two extra engines were fitted and the wingspan lengthened to 102 feet, a masterpiece was born, a bomber capable of carrying a 22,000-pound bomb load (something beyond the capacities even of a Flying Fortress). The Stirling was equal to the Lancaster in size and wingspan, but responded slowly to the controls, and had few enthusiasts. By late 1943 it was phased out of active operations.

FIGHTERS Fighters were regarded as pursuit aircraft, interceptors, the best defence against swarms of bombers, along with anti-aircraft guns. The Germans also saw aircraft, particularly dive-bombers, as tactical weapons to aid ground troops. The British did, however, possess two of the world's finest fighter aircraft, developed from prototypes that had flown as early as 1934. In 1936 the streamlined Spitfire, the RAF's first all-metal fighter and the first to fly at speeds exceeding 300 mph (500 kph), made its first flight. Powered by a Rolls-Royce Merlin engine that gave it a maximum speed of 362 mph, and armed with four machine guns in each wing, it had been designed originally by Reginald Mitchell for the Supermarine Company to break speed records. It was a classic aircraft — a dream to fly, but in the words of one RAF historian, it remained a dream, for production was slow until 1940.

In 1936 the Air Ministry also ordered 600 of the new Hawker Hurricane fighter, almost the equal of the Spitfire in speed (it had a cruising speed of 318 mph). Their future foe, the German Messerschmitt Bf 109 fighter, which flew as early as 1935, was slightly faster than both the Spitfire and the Hurricane, but the British fighters were more manoeuvrable and easier to turn at high speed, and this was to give then an edge over the 'Me109' in dog-fights. Faster than the Me109E and the two-engined Me110 was the Focke-Wulf 190, which appeared in numbers after 1940. (A total of 20,000 Spitfires and 13,000 Hurricanes were to be produced by war's end; and 35,000 Messerschmitt 109s — and 20,000 Focke-Wulfs.)

Above: One of the early American pursuit (fighter) aircraft that never made it into mass production.

Above right: One of the successful early modern fighters: prototype of the Hawker Hurricane which was ordered in quantities by the Royal Air Force and broke the back of the Luftwaffe in the Battle of Britain in 1940.

Right: A snapshot of Blitzkrieg: German infantry on exercises with tanks.

TANKS AND ARMOURED DIVISIONS

Britain had invented the tank but the Germans invented the 'armoured division' — Panzers — and were to use them with deadly effect. In 1917 British armies had used masses of tanks to break the German front and in 1918 to help shatter it, but tanks were seen as an adjunct to infantry attacks, along with artillery. When the British Army returned to its peacetime strength and resumed its role as an imperial police force, British tank development stagnated; light tanks and armoured cars were found to be more useful. The French — who had used hundreds of Renault light tanks in their summer 1918 offensives — by the late 1930s had developed the heavy tank (32-tonne monsters armed with powerful 75-mm cannon but capable of a speed of only 30 kph). The French saw the tank solely as a defensive weapon. Military theorists — Liddell Hart in England, Guderian in Germany and de Gaulle in France — were predicting the use of masses of tanks in fast-moving 'armoured divisions' of hundreds of tanks, but Germany put the idea into practice. General Heinz Guderian was the visionary. He suggested the creation of a division of more than 300 tanks accompanied by motor-borne infantry to exploit gains, mobile artillery, and anti-tank guns and engineer units to bridge any obstacle. Wireless communication was essential. It was no accident that Guderian had served as a wireless officer in a cavalry division in 1914. Light tanks were ideal for reconnaissance and for parades but his medium tanks must be powerfully armed. If assisted by dive-bombers their impetus would be unstoppable. The German Luftwaffe, which provided the Wehrmacht's anti-aircraft guns, worked in close cooperation with the Panzers. Germany also developed 'Light' or motorised divisions — a mobile semi-armoured formation, consisting of only one battalion of eighty tanks and three regiments of motorised infantry.

British battleships shown here steaming in line ahead were the backbone of the Royal Navy. But the crucial naval battles of World War II in the Mediterranean and the Pacific would be fought by aircraft carriers.

Britain, in a belated effort to catch up with Germany, developed heavier tanks but all lacked firepower: one of their most successful marks, the Matilda, was so heavily armoured that shells bounced off the hull, but was slow, and was used as an infantry tank (I-tank). British engines (some of them taken from London buses) were inferior to German: in desert conditions they seized up more regularly, and in early tank battles wireless communication often broke down completely.

Starting from scratch, the Germans developed tanks that their enemies could only attempt to copy. By war's end, in the last battles in defence of the Reich, German monster tanks — the heavily armoured and powerfully gunned 'Tigers' — could outshoot any Allied tank pitted against them and losses could be replaced in a matter of days. In 1942 the American-made Sherman was a superb tank and became the most widely manufactured tank in the Allied armies but by 1945 it was obsolete, yet was still being sent into battle. It is doubtful if any Allied tankmen went into battle in the last years confident of fighting German armour on equal terms.

By late 1935 Germany had formed three tank divisions. Oddly, the French and German armies still relied mainly on horse-drawn artillery and transport but by the outbreak of war Germany had six tank divisions. Poland and France had none.

THE BRITISH ARMY

Britain's army in 1939 was the only fully motorised army in the world, though little larger than the six divisions that had crossed to France in 1914. Its modernisation had been dramatic. As late as 1938 its troops were still wearing the uniforms of the 1914–18 war; a battle dress was then introduced. (One of the first generals to wear it, because he found it comfortable, was an eccentric major-general named Bernard Montgomery.) In that year a dynamic new War Minister, Leslie Hore-Belisha, appointed as Chief of the Imperial General Staff a young General, Viscount Gort, VC, and promoted a new crop of major-generals. Among them was Harold Alexander who, at the age of forty-five replaced Bernard Freyberg as the youngest major-general in the army. (Freyberg had been retired because of a heart condition: he was later to lead the New Zealand Division though the entire course of World War II.) When the British Expeditionary Force left for France in 1939 it was well equipped, with motor lorries, mobile machine guns (Bren carriers), its artillery armed with 25-pounder field guns drawn by vehicles (the 25-pounder had replaced the 18-pounders of 1914–18).

The Royal Navy on the eve of war was weaker than it had been in 1914, but unlike its enemies (apart from Japan) it possessed aircraft carriers. Britain's assets were to be its manpower — drawn from a worldwide Empire — its industrial capacity, its wealth of scientific intellect (which was soon applied breaking enemy codes and ciphers by mathematical means) and lastly but most importantly, the stability and strength of its democratic institutions. Democracy would prove a hard nut to crack.

1938: THE ANSCHLUSS

'This man — Hitler — is Germany's destiny for good or evil. If he goes over the abyss — which Fritsch believes he will — he will drag us all down with him. There is nothing we can do.'

— Ulrich von Hassel, whose diaries record the dark years before his own execution by the Nazis

The groundwork for Hitler's takeover of Austria had been laid in 1936. In that year the small republic's Chancellor Schuschnigg, who was determined to preserve his country's independence even if it meant accommodating many of Hitler's demands, was forced to lift the ban on the local Nazi Party. But in January 1938 Austrian police uncovered evidence of a planned Nazi revolt and took appropriate action. Two weeks later, on 12 February, Hitler invited the Austrian Chancellor to Berchtesgarten, his mountain retreat overlooking the Alps. On arriving, Schuschnigg remarked on the beauty of the panorama of the Alps but Hitler snapped, 'We did not gather here to speak of the fine view or the weather', and launched into one of his celebrated tirades, stating that Austria's whole history over the centuries had been one of high treason, and ending 'I am telling you that I am going to solve the so-called Austrian problem one way or the other.' He reminded the Austrian of his small country's isolation, and after a tense lunch presented his ultimatum. Local Nazis must be appointed to the government in Vienna. Under threat of immediate invasion by Germany Schuschnigg signed the agreement, but was given four days to carry it out. On his return he announced he would call a plebiscite on the subject of union with Germany, to be held on 13 March. On 11 March, when local Nazis had taken over the streets of Vienna, Hitler demanded that his puppet Artur Seyss-Inquart be appointed Chancellor, and that the new Chancellor request Germany to send in forces to 'prevent bloodshed'. This was done and on 12 March German troops entered Austria; two days later Hitler entered Vienna in triumph, and stood on a balcony of the Hofburg Palace before a crowd of hundreds of thousands of delirious Austrians. While the cheering rose to a crescendo the SS was already arresting Jews and nearly 70,000 opponents of Nazism. Austria had ceased to exist. Its seven million people were now citizens of 'Ostmark' in the new Greater Germany, the 'Third Reich'.

German troops invade Austria, March 1938. Here they enter Salzburg to the cheers of many of its citizens.

1938: CZECHOSLOVAKIA CEASES TO EXIST

Hitler now turned his gaze to Czechoslovakia, the last remaining democracy on his borders. It looked a model nation, yet it was an amalgam of nationalities and they included more than three million Germans who had long inhabited the region bordering Austria — the Sudetenland. Hitler had encouraged their desire to be part of the German Reich, and the Prague government had shown remarkable patience with their agitations and occasional outbreaks of violence. 'It is my unshakeable will that Czechoslovakia will be wiped off the map,' Hitler informed his inner circle on 28 May 1938. The Czechs were everything he hated: they were Slavs and they were democrats. They had built along their mountainous borders with Austria a strong defence system, and their Skoda factories produced some of the finest armaments in Europe.

In an attempt to mediate, British Prime Minister Chamberlain, who had succeeded Stanley Baldwin early in 1937, sent a mission to Prague under Lord Runciman in June 1938 but Hitler had already ordered the invasion of Czechoslovakia to take place by 1 October at the latest. The German generals were alarmed, for the Czech fortresses were strong and Germany was still not ready for war with their victim's ally France; they also felt sure that Britain would this time intervene. They informed London by secret emissaries that they were prepared to arrest Hitler if war came. On 10 September Göring, Hitler's garrulous mouthpiece, said at the Nuremberg party rally that 'This miserable pygmy race [the Czechs] is oppressing a cultured people, and behind it is Moscow and the eternal mask of the Jew devil.' Two days later Hitler demanded 'justice' for the Sudeten Germans, which resulted in an outbreak of fighting by Sudeten Germans. On 13 September Chamberlain asked Hitler if they could meet and discuss the problem. Hitler was astonished by the offer. He had no wish for any mediation. Chamberlain landed at Munich airport on 15 September and met Hitler at the Berghof. There he informed the German dictator that he personally favoured 'the principle of self-determination of the Sudeten areas' but would need to consult his colleagues and confer with the French. On 21 September the British Prime Minister urged the Czechs to accede to Hitler's demands and next day flew to Godesberg to see Hitler again. On 24 September the Czechs mobilised. This threw a spanner in the works. Chamberlain, heartened by Hitler's pledge that this was his last territorial demand in Europe — 'We want no Czechs,' Hitler had shouted — returned to London to win Cabinet approval and confer there with Premier Daladier of France. France had already ordered partial mobilisation. On 28 September Britain mobilised the fleet and ordered it to its war stations. In London air raid precautions were authorised and soldiers were seen digging slit trenches in Hyde Park. Britain's Dominions informed London that war must be averted. President Roosevelt and European leaders appealed to Hitler to show restraint and even Mussolini offered to act as mediator.

On 29 September the leaders of Britain, France and Italy arrived in Munich and there, just after midnight, signed the agreement authorising German troops to enter the Sudetenland on 1 October.

Below: The Munich conference, 1938, in which Czechoslovakia was handed over to Hitler's Germany. From left: Prime Minister Chamberlain of Great Britain, Premier Daladier of France, Hitler, Mussolini and on far right, Italy's foreign minister (and Mussolini's son-in-law) Count Ciano.
Opposite: The end of what was left of Czech independence: German troops enter Prague, March 1939.

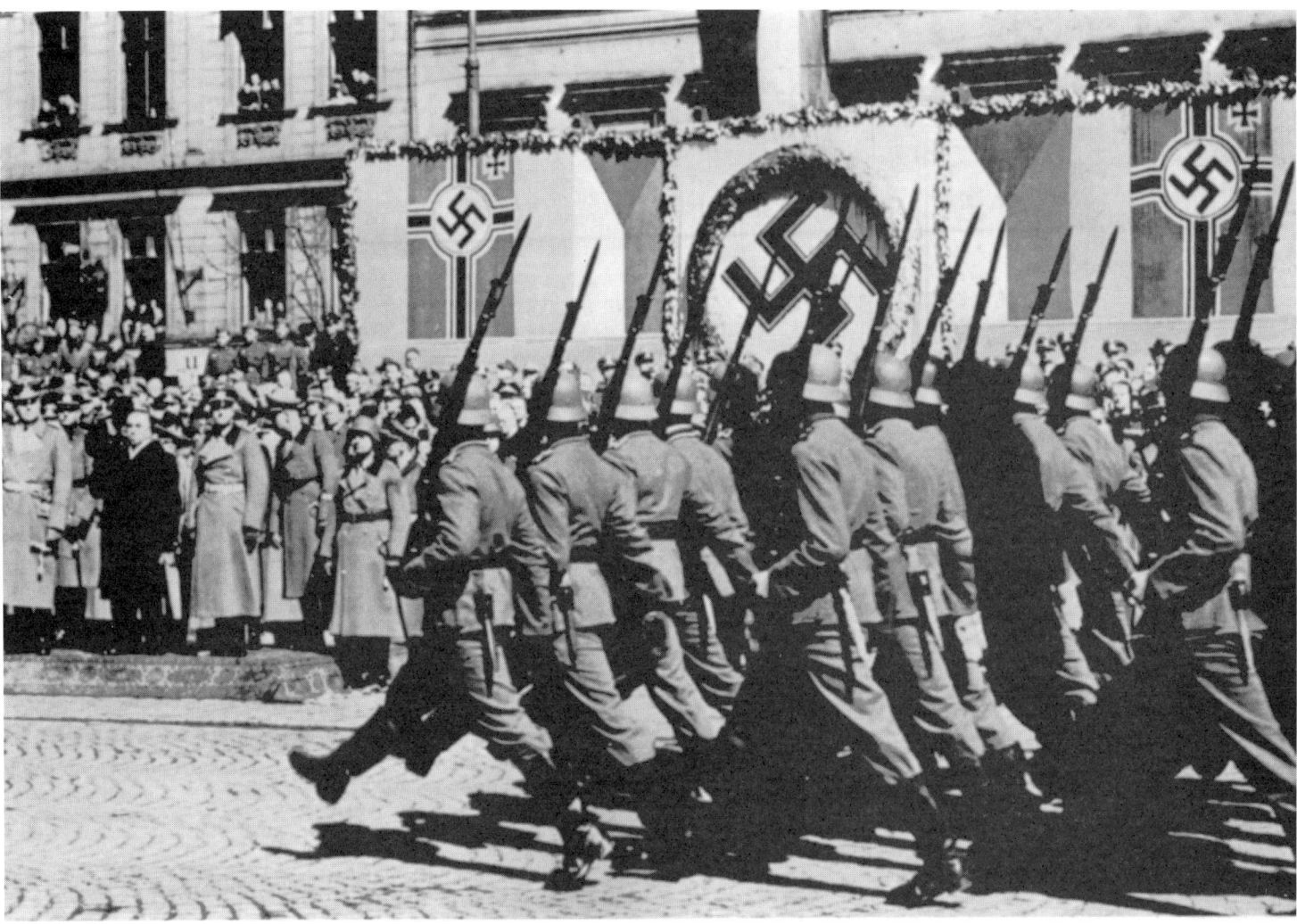

President Beneš, who had not even been asked to attend the conference to witness the dismemberment of his country, handed over government in Prague and flew off to self-imposed exile in London.

Chamberlain flew back to London and announced at the airport to cheering crowds that Europe had achieved at Munich 'peace for our time'. Praised as the man who had averted war, he lived with this delusion for another six months. His cabinet colleague Alfred Duff Cooper resigned in protest; the Foreign Minister Anthony Eden had resigned as early as March 1938 over Chamberlain's meddling in foreign affairs and secretive dealings with Mussolini. Winston Churchill thundered in the House of Commons that 'we have sustained a total and unmitigated defeat', but his voice was drowned out by Chamberlain's supporters. But he persisted: 'All is over. Silent, mournful, abandoned, broken, Czechoslovakia recedes into the darkness … I find it unendurable, the sense of our country falling into the power, into the orbit and influence of Nazi Germany … Do not suppose that this is the end. This is only the beginning of the reckoning. This is only the first sip, the first foretaste of a bitter cup …'.

STALIN AND THE SOVIET UNION

The Soviet Union had emerged form the shadows in 1935, when Stalin's new Foreign Minister, Litvinov, announced a policy of cooperation with the Western democracies. Russian aid enabled the Popular Front government in Madrid to withstand Franco's forces for nearly three years, but little else was done to halt the fascist powers.

Stalin remained an enigma. In 1936 Russia's own purgatory began when Stalin proceeded to eliminate the 'old Bolsheviks', intellectuals and the officer corps of the Red Army, which he sensed was disloyal. By 1938 he had shot all his Marshals except two, fifty-seven of his eighty-five Corps commanders and more than a hundred of his divisional commanders, nearly all of whom were innocent of any treason. The 'Great Purge' had a calamitous effect on the leadership of the army in the coming war. Millions of innocents in addition to dedicated Communist Party members were consigned to labour camps — 'gulags' — from which relatively few would emerge alive. To the outside world, Stalin seemed as inhuman and perhaps as insane as his sworn enemy Hitler.

Grim meeting: summoned to a conference by Hitler, President Hacha of Czecho-Slovakia (as it was now known) is met at the railway station. In the resulting discussions with Hitler Hacha suffered a heart attack just before he signed away what was left of his country to German rule.

1939: THE END OF APPEASEMENT

In January 1939 Hitler addressed the Reichstag in a shrill tone, vowing: 'If the international Jewish financiers ... should again succeed in plunging the nations into a world war the result will be ... the annihilation of the Jewish race throughout Europe.' Appeasing Hitler yet again and any hopes of avoiding another European war came to a sudden end early in 1939. On 14 March Slovakia declared its independence from Czechia and next day German forces rolled into Prague, extinguishing what remained of Czech independence; Chamberlain was devastated. In a speech at Birmingham two days later he threw away his prepared speech and reproached Hitler for breaking his assurances to respect Czech sovereignty. On 29 March Chamberlain announced that the Territorial Army (reserves) would be doubled in strength and two days later went further, informing the House of Commons that 'in the event of any action threatening Polish independence' Britain — and France — would give Poland 'all support in their power'. Hitler was enraged, shouting: 'I'll cook them a stew they'll choke on!' On 3 April he ordered his armed forces to prepare 'Case White', the invasion of Poland, to take place any time from 1 September onwards.

On 21 March Ribbentrop summoned the Polish ambassador and brought up the subject of Danzig and the Polish Corridor. Two days later Hitler, having demanded the cession of the Memel region from Lithuania, arrived in Memel on the battleship *Deutschland* and addressed the Germans of the city, where he was received with rapture.

In late March 1939 General Franco's army entered the silent streets of Madrid. The last defenders of the Republic had fled, mostly over the border to France. Count Ciano wrote on 27 March: 'Madrid has fallen and with the capital, all the other cities of Red Spain. The war is over. It is a new, formidable victory for Fascism, perhaps the greatest one so far.'

ITALY INVADES ALBANIA

In January 1939 Chamberlain and his Foreign Minister Lord Halifax visited Mussolini in Rome in another vain and misguided attempt to wean Italy from closer ties with Germany. The British Prime Minister did not impress the Italian leader, who observed that 'people who carry an umbrella can never found an empire'. Mussolini was now directing his propaganda against France, demanding the return of predominantly Italian regions — Tunis, Corsica, Nice. While harbouring resentment about Hitler's seizure of Czechoslovakia he decided to establish a permanent presence in the Balkans. On 7 April 1939 Italy landed troops in Albania. The small kingdom had been an economic dependency of Italy almost since its birth and, as its army was largely officered and trained by the Italians, it offered no resistance. King Zog and Queen Geraldine fled. The only result of Mussolini's aggression was a British pledge of military support (13 April) to Greece and Turkey.

Two days later President Roosevelt asked the two dictators for assurances that they would not attack any more European nations — and appended a list of 31 countries. Hitler, describing the letter as 'a result of infantile paralysis', made sport of it in the Reichstag as he pledged solemnly not to attack them. He spoke with sarcasm and his speech was broadcast across the world and carried by the major networks in the United States. On 27 April Chamberlain announced the introduction of conscription. Unfortunately, as Churchill lamented, it did not give Britain an army, but it was a step at least, and the Dominions, eager for peace at any price at the time of Munich, pledged support to Britain. Australia, where R.G. Menzies had become prime minister after the death of Joseph Lyons, pledged to Britain that if war came in Europe she would 'make common cause' with the Mother Country.

The pledge of support to Greece by Chamberlain, whom the dictators regarded as a weakling, was taken seriously by Mussolini at least, and 'reinforced his determination to accept the German offer of a formal alliance,' in the words of one of his recent biographers. The alliance was signed with fanfare in Berlin on 22 May. Pledging mutual support in time of war, 'The Pact of Steel' as the dictators termed it, was to be a fatal embrace for both Germany and Italy.

On the following day Hitler explained to his senior officers his decision to invade Poland, whatever the consequences. 'Further successes can no longer be attained without the she shedding of blood. Danzig is not the subject of the dispute at all. It is a question of expanding our living space in the east … There is no question of sparing Poland.' But then he contradicted himself: 'It must not come to a simultaneous showdown with the West — France and England.' He had no wish for a two-front war that had sapped the Kaiser's strength in 1914–18. Then he dwelled on the qualities of the race he most admired: 'The Britisher himself is proud, brave, tough, dogged, and a gifted organiser. He has the love of adventure of the Nordic race and [possesses] geopolitical security and protection by a strong sea power and a courageous air force.'

1939: THE NAZI–SOVIET NON-AGGRESSION PACT

In mid-April 1939 Russia had offered to discuss an alliance with Britain and France to counter German moves, but the Western powers dallied for three weeks before proposing that Stalin come forth with a guarantee of the borders of his neighbours. For the next month discussions between Britain and Russia continued fitfully. Friction was developing in Danzig, where the local Nazis were smuggling in arms. Hitler informed the League of Nations commissioner in Danzig, a Swiss, that 'if the slightest thing was attempted by the Poles, he would fall upon them like lightning'. British diplomats begged the Polish government to reach some sort of understanding with Russia. The Poles rejected such a notion. On 3 August von Ribbentrop spoke in Berlin to the Soviet ambassador of Germany's wish to 'place German–Russian relations on a new and definitive basis'. Stalin and his new Foreign Minister, Molotov, who had replaced the congenial Litvinov, were thinking along the same lines. Ribbentrop received no rebuff.

On 5 August the British and French military mission left for Moscow. They proceeded by passenger liner and when they arrived in Moscow a week later, Stalin did not deign to receive them but delegated his comrade, Marshal Voroshilov. The Soviets were astonished to discover that the British and French officers had no powers to negotiate an alliance, just to discuss one.

In 1943, in the last pages of his diaries, before he was taken out to be shot by his father-in-law's Fascist firing squad, Count Ciano recorded his meeting with Ribbentrop at Salzburg on 11 August, 1939:

'Well, Ribbentrop, what do you want?' Ciano asked by way of conversation. 'The Corridor or Danzig?'

'Not that any more,' Ribbentrop replied. 'We want war!'

In a desperate attempt to restore relations with Italy Prime Minister Chamberlain visited Rome in January 1939. Mussolini did not even bother to attend a formal wreath-laying ceremony. Behind Chamberlain is his foreign minister Lord Halifax who championed the policy of appeasing the dictators. On Halifax's right is his private parliamentary secretary Lord Home who became Britain's Prime Minister in 1963.

The unlikely alliance between Nazi Germany and Communist Russia astonished the world. This caricature by an artist in a neutral country satirises Hitler and Stalin trying to march in step.

Ciano recorded that the German with the 'cold metallic eyes' spoke in 'much the same tone that he would have used about an inconsequential administrative detail ... I felt that the decision was irrevocable, and in a flash I saw the tragedy that threatened humanity.' He warned the German that England and France would be involved and returned to Italy 'disgusted with the Germans'. Ciano advised Mussolini to tell Hitler frankly that Italy could not enter the war under such conditions.

Hitler had moved fast. On 19 August, after the Soviets had agreed to sign a commercial agreement with Germany, Stalin invited Ribbentrop to come to Moscow. On the next day Hitler wrote to Stalin, offering to sign a non-aggression pact. On 23 August Ribbentrop signed the pact at the Kremlin in the presence of a genial Stalin. Hitler was equally jubilant. His arch enemy was now his friend. A clause in the pact related to the fate of Poland, which would be divided between Germany and Russia. The world was stunned by the announcement of the pact. France placed her frontier forces on war alert and the next day commenced mobilisation, calling up 330,000 reservists.

One day earlier Hitler had again addressed his chief lieutenants. Germany must go to war — 'we have nothing to lose; we can only gain' — and outlined Germany's parlous economic state. He did not reveal that paper money had funded his rearmament program and a system of bartering goods had been the only way the Reich had paid for its imports, but he stated: 'Our economic situation is such that we cannot hold out more than a few years. Göring can confirm this.' He informed them that on the morrow Germany would be signing a treaty with Russia, which he stated 'has no interest in maintaining Poland'. He described the British and French as 'little worms' (or 'small fry') — 'I saw them at Munich — and told them that operations against Poland would begin on 26 August.' Hitler exclaimed: 'Close your hearts to pity! Act brutally! Eighty million people must obtain what is their right ... Be steeled against all signs of compassion!'

On the day after the announcement of the pact world leaders pleaded with Hitler to follow the path of peace. President Roosevelt, Pope Pius XII and the monarchs of western Europe suggested that negotiations continue or offered to act as mediators.

German propaganda prepared the way for war, describing fictitious Polish attacks on Germans living in Poland, giving accounts of refugees fleeing and reports that Poland was mobilising. (It wasn't, for fear of provoking a German attack.) Hitler needed a spark to warrant a German entry into Poland and Himmler's SS provided it. Concentration camp prisoners were taken to the frontier, to simulate a Polish attack on the German radio station at Gleiwitz. Their dead bodies, dressed in Polish uniforms, would give the world proof that the Poles had attacked first.

Göring, alarmed by the thought of a premature war, intimated to Western contacts that negotiations would be welcomed but the British ambassador in Berlin reminded Hitler that his nation would stand by her pledge to help defend Poland. Hitler postponed the invasion several days. It would now take place just before dawn, at 4.45 a.m. on 1 September 1939.

PART II
THE EDGE OF DEFEAT
1939–1942

CHAPTER 4
BLITZKRIEG!
1939

GERMANY INVADES POLAND

At dawn on 1 September 1939 the German battleship *Schleswig-Holstein* opened fire on the Polish fortress guarding Danzig, and German armies invaded Poland from the west, the south and the north while the Luftwaffe bombed Polish airfields and communications without cease.

In the morning Hitler drove to the Reichstag, then housed in the Kroll Opera House. Few crowds of Berliners observed his progress and those few who did were subdued. Gone were the cheering crowds who had greeted his every appearance. He said: 'This night, for the first time, Polish regular soldiers fired on our own territory [this was a reference to the sham attack on Gleiwitz]. Since 5.45 am we have been returning fire, and from now on bombs will be met by bombs ... The Polish state has refused the peaceful settlement of relations which I desired, and has appealed to arms ... In order to put an end to this lunacy, I have no other choice than to meet force with force.'

As the world watched Blitzkrieg unfolding and fast-moving German tank columns cut through Poland's two-million-strong army with ease, Hitler awaited with some trepidation the reactions of Britain and France. On the evening of 1 September both nations presented notes to Berlin demanding that German forces withdraw from Poland — these notes struck Ribbentrop as the next thing to an ultimatum.

Last minute attempts took place to postpone the inevitable. Mussolini proposed an armistice and another conference. But his ambassador was told that Britain was not interested in further negotiations. On 2 September Chamberlain informed the Commons that no reply had been received from Berlin. The Labor leader shouted: 'I wonder how long we are prepared to vacillate at a time when Britain and France and all that Britain stands for, and human civilization, are in peril ... we must march with the French.' The French themselves were hesitating to march, pleading for another forty-eight hours in which to complete their mobilisation. The British Cabinet told them that further delay was impossible. At 9 a.m. on 3 September ambassador Henderson handed the German Foreign Ministry an ultimatum that unless German assurances of a cessation of attacks on Poland were received by 11 a.m. 'a state of war will exist between the two countries'. The ministry interpreter hurried to the Reich Chancellery with the document. He found Hitler at his desk and read out its text. There was complete silence. 'What now?' Hitler said, looking at Ribbentrop. Ribbentrop replied that a similar note could be expected from the French.

Göring said, 'If we lose this war, God have mercy on us!' A witness recorded the dismal scene: Goebbels stood 'in a corner by himself, downcast and self-absorbed'. Hitler had no argument with the British Empire; he admired it and for the next year never gave up hope that he could reach accommodation with it. Hitler's hatred was reserved for the 'Jewish–Bolshevik conspiracy' that had thwarted Germany's destiny. He had destroyed the Treaty of Versailles. He had no fear of France. His ambitions lay in eastern Europe, where his new Reich would obtain the 'living space' it needed and grow on the ruins of Bolshevism.

The French ambassador in Berlin left to deliver his note at 10.20 a.m., reiterating that France would fulfil her obligations to Poland, but was not to see Ribbentrop until just after midday: Ribbentrop had been attending a reception for Russian diplomats.

Previous page: **Hitler informs the Reichstag that German forces have entered Poland, 1 September 1939.** *Inset above:* **A German poster holds promise of victory.** *Opposite:* **German photograph showing Polish troops surrendering during the campaign in 1939.** *Opposite right:* **German aircraft over Poland. This photograph shows Messerschmitt-110 aircraft. They proved an effective terror weapon against civilians, but were remarkably slow when faced by fast Allied fighter aircraft.**

The British declaration of war followed at 11 a.m. and was announced by Prime Minister Chamberlain in a BBC broadcast from 10 Downing Street that was carried by short wave around the world. 'This is a sad day for all of us,' he said, 'and to no one is it sadder than to me. Everything I have worked for, everything that I have believed in during my public life, has crashed into ruins ... I trust I may live to see the day when Hitlerism has been destroyed and a liberated Europe has been re-established.' Just after he finished speaking the air raid sirens sounded in London. It was a false alarm, but the sinking at nightfall of the liner *Athenia* by a German submarine, with the loss of 112 lives, brought home the reality of war on its first day. Within three days three more British ships had been sunk, and this set the pattern of loss over the coming years.

The French declaration of war was passed by parliament six hours later, at 5 p.m. (European time), 3 September 1939.

One encouraging note was struck. On 3 September Winston Churchill was recalled to his old post of First Lord of the Admiralty and ships of the Royal Navy received the signal 'Winston is back.' On the same day Anthony Eden was recalled and offered the Dominions portfolio. They had been among the most articulate enemies of appeasement.

Thus the world went again to war.

THE BRITISH EMPIRE GOES TO WAR

Britain could count on the support of the Empire and Commonwealth, but what form this support would take was unknown, for its leading members — the 'self-governing Dominions' — were, since the passing of the Statute of Westminster (1931), independent nations, free to pursue their own foreign policy. Few did, and most did not even bother to ratify the statute, for their economic and strategic reliance on Great Britain was real. They were free to remain neutral in time of war.

The first voices to appear on the wireless pledging support to Great Britain were Australian ones. Within half an hour of Chamberlain's direct short wave broadcast from London, which reached Australia at about 9 p.m. local time, on Sunday 3 September, Prime Minister Menzies broadcast to the nation from Melbourne. In words as articulate as Chamberlain's he stated that Britain and France had declared war on Germany and that 'as a result, Australia is also at war'. He continued: 'Great Britain and France, with the co-operation of the British Dominions have struggled to avoid this tragedy ... but their efforts have failed and we are, therefore, as a great family of nations, involved in a struggle which we must at all costs win ... Honest dealing, the peaceful adjustment of differences, the rights of independent peoples to live their own lives, the honouring of international obligations and promises, all these things are at stake.'

New Zealand's Prime Minister Michael Joseph Savage, who had been born in Australia, told New Zealanders: 'Behind the sure shield of Britain we have enjoyed and cherished freedom and self-government ... Where she goes, we go.' Savage belied his surname: a studious, already ailing man, who came from an Irish-Catholic Labour background, he had no love for the British Empire, but he saw Hitler as evil, and he asked the United States legation in Berlin to deliver New Zealand's declaration of war by hand to the Reich Chancellory.

Australia and New Zealand, with Britain, thus became the first nations on the planet to declare war on Hitler and Nazism. The Viceroy of India declared on the same day (3 September) that India was also at war, without consulting the Council of Princes, but his act was not challenged by prominent nationalist leaders other than Subhas Chandra Bose. The leaders of the growing independence movement, Gandhi and Nehru, had made known their abhorrence of Nazism.

Canada's declaration of war followed on 10 September, one day after Prime Minister Mackenzie King had recalled parliament to debate the action, as he had promised Canadians he would do. Newfoundland, which was still referred to widely as 'England's oldest colony', also declared war.

KING GEORGE OF ENGLAND

PRESIDENT LEBRUN OF FRANC[E]

Ireland — Eire — proclaimed neutrality, but Prime Minister Eamon de Valera, who still regarded Ireland as an occupied — and divided — country (Northern Ireland, where the Protestants were in a majority, had remained part of the United Kingdom in 1921), took no steps to stop southern Irishmen enlisting in the British forces, as tens of thousands were to do.

Ireland (Eire), though a member of the Commonwealth, remained neutral throughout the war. British conscription was never extended to Northern Ireland because the Catholic minority in Ulster would have been affected. Though Churchill was exasperated with Eire and often threatened to invade the South, he never did, and late in 1941 de Valera reiterated, for Allied ears, that Ireland was a 'friendly neutral'. He later allowed Allied aircrew who had landed in the South by mistake to be quietly repatriated over the border while keeping straying German aircrews behind barbed wire, and insisted that the German ambassador in Dublin hand over his wireless transmitter, which was lodged in the safe of a Dublin bank. This was the extent of his assistance to the Allied war effort.

In South Africa two political figures, one-time allies and both former Boer generals, took differing courses. On 4 September Prime Minister Barrie Hertzog attempted to keep South Africa neutral but his motion to this effect was defeated narrowly by the interventionist faction led by Jan Christian Smuts, eighty votes to sixty-seven. Hertzog asked the Governor-General to dissolve parliament but the latter instead appointed Smuts as Prime Minister. 'Smuts took South Africa into the Second World War out of concern for the future of the human race, and in particular for that of Europe,' states one South African historian.

All of these nations had welcomed the Munich agreement which averted war in 1938. They now hoped that the war would be a short one and none made pledges of aid and troops to Britain as they had done in 1914. There were no crowds cheering the news of war, just a quiet sense of resignation and little enthusiasm.

POWERFUL NEUTRALS

The United States declared neutrality, but President Roosevelt said in a national broadcast on the night of 3 September that he did not expect Americans to remain neutral in their hearts. He had recalled his ambassador from Berlin in disgust after the outbreak of Nazi violence against the Jews in November 1938 and was openly pro-Allies but he led a nation that was determined to avoid involvement in another European war. 'Isolationist' sentiment and anti-British feeling were strong, and not just among the Americans of German or Irish origin.

Eight days later (11 September) Roosevelt initiated one of the great correspondences in history by writing to Winston Churchill, whom he had met once before in London in 1918, to tell him 'how glad I am that you are back again in the Admiralty' and inviting him to write to him 'to keep me in touch personally with anything you want me to know about'. With Chamberlain's permission Churchill was to write to Roosevelt regularly, enjoying 'a long and memorable correspondence' and laying the foundations of a partnership that would win the war.

Italy, whose leaders were appalled by the German–Soviet pact and the German invasion of Poland, declared 'non-belligerency', a strange status between peace and war.

THE EMPIRE MARCHES, BUT SLOWLY

The Imperial Conference of 1937 had resulted in public affirmation of 'the unity of the Commonwealth' in the event of any external threat and the following two years had seen a belated but rapid strengthening of the Dominions' defences. But in many ways they were less well prepared militarily than they had been in 1914 and could do little to help Britain during 1940. After mid-1941 their contribution would be dramatic and instrumental in achieving victory.

The declaration of war on Germany by Australia and New Zealand was an emotional response by their people, nearly all of whom came from British (and Irish) stock, and was a show of loyalty, more than a pledge of aid and assistance. Their prime ministers had not bothered to summon parliament before issuing declarations of war through their Governors-General, but Canada and South Africa, with substantial numbers of non-British people in their populations, observed the

German diplomats leave their country's embassy in London for internment and repatriation to their homeland, September 1939. Ironically the figure in the foreground, Dr Theo Kordt, was a prominent anti-Nazi.

parliamentary niceties and took the precaution of debating the issue. South Africa's Boer population was generally hostile to the Allied war effort, Canada's French-speaking population indifferent. Both countries would in time raise great armies of volunteers — Canada's totalled one million, South Africa's 200,000. India would raise the largest all-volunteer army in history, more than two million strong.

1939: THE END OF POLAND

The shells fired by the *Schleswig-Holstein* on the Westerplatte forts at Danzig at 4.45 a.m. on 1 September 1939 were officially the first shots fired in World War II, and they were fired without any declaration of war. A month later the forts were still holding out under a deluge of 12-inch shells but elsewhere Poland's defences had been quickly destroyed.

The German battleship *Schleswig-Holstein* (top), shelling the Polish forts (below) near Danzig, 1 September 1939.

On the eve of war France's Commander-in-Chief, General Maurice Gamelin, who had been Marshal Joffre's chief of staff in World War I, admitted that France could not launch an offensive in the west until seventeen days after war had begun, but stated that Poland could hold out for at least six months, for the Poles were renowned for their impetuous bravery. For fear of provoking Hitler, Poland had delayed ordering mobilisation until the day before the Germans attacked and at least ten divisions were not even mobilised. The Polish front was defended by only seventeen divisions when the Germans invaded, and another twenty-two divisions were marching to their positions or were still in barracks. Against this disorganised defence Germany employed the majority of her western forces and hurled fifty-five divisions (later increased to sixty-three) including five Panzer (tank) and eight motorised (or light armoured) divisions, advancing in two Army Groups — in the north under von Bock, in the south under von Rundstedt.

Poland's disorganised field armies were effectively destroyed in seventeen days. Even the Germans marvelled at their success. Poland was the first demonstration to the world of *Blitzkrieg* — lightning war — in which air forces, particularly dive-bombers, were combined with fast-moving tanks and motorised artillery and infantry. The hot, dry summer had left the roads and fields hard enough to take armoured vehicles; no bad weather delayed their progress.

At dawn on 1 September German army units entered Danzig. Polish workers bravely defending the post office against German troops and local Nazi units were later shot as insurgents because they were not wearing military uniforms. Across the Polish-German frontier German armies moved with precision. The Luftwaffe destroyed Poland's 500 antiquated aircraft, most of which were caught on the ground, within the first two days.

Poland was perfect tank terrain, flat and open along its borders; only the southern frontier had a mountain barrier. To defend her 2000 kilometres of border with under fifty divisions was patently impossible, and Marshal Smigly-Rydz, in pre-war discussions, had resolved to fall back to the rivers, but the rapidity of the German advance destroyed his strategy. By the fifth day of war General von Brauchitsch, who had planned the campaign without reference to or interference from the Führer, was claiming to his officers that Poland was already beaten.

The tanks of General Heinz Guderian's 19 Panzer Corps were charged by Polish lancers from the Pomorze (Pomeranian) Army, but crossed the Vistula on 6 September. The Polish Pomorze and Poznan armies fell back to Warsaw and were set upon by the German 8th Army approaching from Lodz. Here, from 10 to 19 September, along the Bzura River was fought one of the toughest battles of the campaign, but it ended with the surrender of 170,000 Polish troops near Kutno. The Poles were not lacking in valour; what they lacked were effective command and modern weapons. By 14 September the Germans had begun to besiege Warsaw, which was bombed relentlessly, and next day Guderian's tanks had reached Brest-Litovsk to make contact with the Army Group advancing from the south. In the wake of the advancing Wehrmacht came the SS squads, who began a systematic rounding up and killing of Jews.

THE RUSSIANS INVADE

On 17 September Polish armies retreating to the east sighted Russian forces approaching and thought they were coming to their assistance; instead the Russians opened fire. Rather than wait for the end of fighting Stalin had ordered his own invasion of Poland to secure as much of the stricken nation as he could. On the following day the Polish government and a large number of the Polish forces — nearly 100,000 men in all — on the south-eastern frontier crossed into Romania, one of the few nations on its borders not yet under German sway.

Opposite top: **Polish lancers displayed the customary valour of the Polish soldier, but were decimated by German tanks.**
Opposite: **German troops awaiting orders for the final advance into Warsaw.**

Left: 'Stuka': The Junkers-87 dive-bomber was fitted with a siren to increase its terror. Like the Me-110, it proved vulnerable to Allied fighter aircraft after 1940.
Below: Polish troops being herded into captivity under German guard, 1939. Poland was to suffer the death of six million of its soldiers and civilians during the war.

On 28 September, after a 14-day defence, the Polish Army in Warsaw surrendered. 'The wheel always turns,' a Polish general said at the capitulation. The Poles defending the peninsula north of Danzig fought on until 2 October. Hitler, in claiming victory, announced that 700,000 Poles were in German hands (their battle casualties are still unknown), for the loss of 10,000 Germans killed, 3400 missing and 30,000 wounded.

Of Poland's small navy only five submarines escaped, two to Britain and three to Sweden, where they were interned. Few of the Polish soldiers in German hands would survive the war. Another 200,000 fell into Russian hands and the fate of their officers became one of the first war crimes. Nearly 8000 Polish officers, nearly all of them reservists — including lawyers, doctors, engineers, journalists, public servants, the class Stalin termed 'intelligentsia' or 'class enemies' — were murdered by the Soviet Secret Police in a wood near Katyn by a shot in the back of the head; their bodies were buried in shallow graves, which were discovered by the Germans when they overran the region nearly three years later. The Nazis, past masters at mass murder, revealed to the world a Soviet atrocity but Stalin maintained that the officers had died by German hand. Fifty years later the rulers of the Soviet Union would apologise to Poland for the crime.

THE FATE OF POLAND'S JEWS

The fate of Poland was quickly settled. On 21 September Himmler's right-hand man, Reinhard Heydrich, submitted a copy of his plans to 'clean' up Poland (a copy was sent to Army High Command). It proposed that Jews be herded into the cities. A final solution to 'the Jewish problem', he added, would take time to achieve but some of his *Einsatzgruppen* ('task forces'), following the wake of the German Army, had already begun the process. On 3 September an SS unit, entering the frontier town of Wieruszow, had arrested twenty Jews, many of them prominent citizens of the town, and lined them up for execution in the market square. When the daughter of one of them ran up to say goodbye to her 63-year-old father, an SS man shot her; the men were then shot. On the following day, in the city of Czestochowa, 180 Jews were shot. In Bedzin on 8 September, the SS drove 200 Jews into their synagogue, locked the doors and set fire to it. Such appalling scenes were to be repeated countless times during the six years of war.

With the eastern provinces now under Soviet rule and the northern regions rejoined to Germany, what was left of Poland became the landlocked 'General-Government', under the rule in Cracow of a ruthless Nazi named Hans Frank who on his second day in the job spelled out his role: 'The Poles shall be the slaves of the German Reich.' Hitler had told him: 'The men capable of leadership in Poland must be liquidated ... there is no need to send these elements to Reich concentration camps.' They would be killed on the spot. Like Stalin, Hitler believed that the intelligentsia must be disposed of quickly. Jews must be isolated in the cities, where hopefully they would die of starvation. Over a year later Frank addressed his headquarters staff with these words: 'As far as Jews are concerned, I want to tell you quite frankly that they must be done away with in one way or another ... Gentlemen, I must ask you to rid yourself of all feelings of pity. We must annihilate the Jews.' How this was to be done had not yet been decided.

Above: Two Russian tank men (left) with German troops (including the black uniformed Panzer soldier) when their two armies met in conquered Poland, 1939.
Below: Poles who survived the invasion of their country and made their way to Britain and France kept alive the spirit of Polish resistance to Germany. Here General Sikorski, leader of the Free Polish government, introduces the Duke of Kent to Polish military and naval officers early in 1940. Sikorski, a popular leader, was killed in an air crash in 1943.

Hitler, flanked by his generals, reviews the entry of the German army into Warsaw, October 1939. Seen directly below the figure of Hitler is Erwin Rommel, the future Field Marshal and 'Desert Fox'.

In Warsaw the last of the city's Jews, who formed a third of its population, were herded into the slum area known as the Ghetto in October 1940; the 250,000 Jews in Lodz (where they formed 30 per cent of the city's population) were also isolated in a ghetto. The December days of 1939 had taken their toll but in the winter ending 1940, denied adequate food and any fuel for heating or cooking, they began to die like flies from cold, starvation, disease and random killings. By mid-1942, 30,000 Polish Jews had died, a third of them by execution. Worse was to come.

In February 1940 the SS found the ideal location for a major concentration camp near Cracow. It was a town of 12,000 people with an old army barracks and some factories, and stood on the main rail line. By June a camp was completed there to house Polish political prisoners. Soon to be built there was a plant for I. G. Farben's extraction of synthetic oil and rubber, and prisoners would provide the labour. This was the beginning of the Third Reich's first grim concentration camp complex. Its name became the most infamous two syllables in the vocabulary of the twentieth century: Auschwitz. But Auschwitz was not initially the worst of the death camps. It was principally a labour camp. Soon in eastern Poland would rise camps whose only purpose was mass extermination — Belzec, Treblinka, Sobibor, Chelmno, Maidanek.

Reports of the Nazis' hideous treatment of the Jews began to filter out. The world at first refused to believe them, or thought they were exaggerations. Over the next few years more than six million Poles were to die under German rule, half of this number being Jews.

BRITISH COMMONWEALTH

It was in the air that the British Commonwealth's contribution to Britain was most dramatically demonstrated in the first year of war. When war came 450 Australians and 500 New Zealanders alone were serving in the RAF as aircrew. In December 1939 Britain, Canada, Australia and New Zealand signed in Ottawa the Empire Air Training Scheme (EATS) agreement, which envisaged the training of 50,000 aircrew a year to man a vast Imperial air force of 100 squadrons.

This output of aircrew was later amended, as it was seen to be far too optimistic. Australia, in addition to forming twenty-five air training schools, would supply one third of a planned monthly intake of 2800 trainees. It would be eighteen months before the first intake of EATS aircrew would complete training, but by war's end the scheme produced 131,530 aircrew, of whom 72,835 were Canadian. It became Canada's major contribution of air force personnel to the war against Germany, and Canada also provided forty-eight RCAF squadrons which served around the globe. Australia, in addition to contributing EATS aircrew to the squadrons based in the United Kingdom, built up her own air force in the Pacific. By war's end the Dominions of the British Commonwealth would provide 40 per cent of all RAF aircrew, and in 1945 nearly half the pilots in the British air forces.

The Commonwealth also provided an inordinately high number of senior officers in the RAF. New Zealanders had automatically enlisted in the RAF before the creation of the RNZAF in 1937, and many Australian and Canadian officers had transferred to the RAF during the domestic defence cutbacks of the early 1930s. When war came in 1939 the Air Officer Commanding-in-Chief, Middle East (AOC-in-C), Air Marshal William Mitchell ('Ginger Mitch'), was an

Detail from Australian recruiting poster calling for volunteers for the Royal Australian Air Force. Many young men, with knowledge of the savage losses suffered by the infantry, volunteered for air crew, thinking they would have more chance of survival in the air force. But fatalities among air crew in World War II were calamitous.

Australian, as was his deputy, Peter Drummond. The Canadian Raymond Collishaw commanded the active squadrons in Egypt, soon known as Desert Air Force. Mitchell's replacement Arthur Longmore was also Australian-born (though he made no mention of this accident in his memoirs). They were soon joined in Egypt by Arthur Coningham, Australian-born but raised in New Zealand — the flamboyant 'Maori' Coningham, who commanded Desert Air Force and later 1st Tactical Air Force in north-west Europe. The first Australian unit to reach the Middle East, Number 3 Squadron RAAF, would become the top-scoring squadron in Desert Air Force.

Coningham's great friend Keith Park, who commanded 11 Group in the coming Battle of Britain, was also a New Zealander. The Australian Don Bennett would survive being shot down over Norway to form and command the RAF's elite 'Path Finder' force in 1942. Two of the top 'aces' in the fighting in France in 1940 would be 'Cobber' Kain, a New Zealander, and Leslie Clisby, a South Australian, who continued to wear his Australian dark-blue tunic, which was increasingly threadbare, until his own death in action. The historian Macaulay had predicted a century earlier that one day a New Zealander was destined to survey the ruins of London; hundreds were to do so in 1940, wearing the blue-grey of the Royal Air Force.

Pride of the Royal Australian Navy at the outbreak of war were the two heavy cruisers *Australia* and *Canberra*. Here *Canberra* leaves Sydney Harbour for service. She was later sunk in the Solomons (1942).

NAVAL DEFENCES

On the outbreak of war Australia's defences, though long neglected, were possibly the strongest of all the Dominions, at least in naval terms. She was also the only one likely to face direct attack and even invasion if Japan committed herself to expansion into South-East Asia. Canada's navy consisted of six old destroyers; New Zealand had no navy at all and relied on two Royal Navy light cruisers permanently stationed in her waters. British officers commanded them but they were almost totally manned by New Zealanders. On the eve of war, HMS *Achilles* and HMS *Leander* quietly left their familiar waters to take up war stations. (They became the nucleus of the Royal New Zealand Navy on its creation in 1941.)

Australia possessed a small but strong squadron, officered by Australian-born and Australian-trained officers, several of whom had already achieved the high rank of Captain. The RAN possessed two heavy cruisers mounting 8-inch guns, dating from the 1920s, *Australia* and *Canberra* and three modern 6-inch-gun light cruisers purchased from British shipyards in the mid-1930s — *Sydney*, *Hobart* and *Perth*, in addition to old ships — the cruiser *Adelaide*, which was too slow and under-armoured to send into a war zone, and a flotilla of six destroyers of 1917–19 vintage on loan from Britain. They were due for scrapping, but they were still capable of 30 knots, and Britain's fleets and convoys were desperately short of small escort ships. By year's end most of the RAN's ships had sailed for the Northern Hemisphere, leaving Australia's shores barely guarded,

Australia and New Zealand were the first of the self-governing Dominions to respond by sending forces to help Great Britain.
Right: Australian volunteers turn for the photographer before boarding a troop ship for the Middle East early in 1940.

and an intensive naval building program had begun, one that would produce by war's end sixty corvettes (small multi-purpose ships originally designed as minesweepers).

In November 1939 the Australian destroyer flotilla — *Vendetta, Vampire, Voyager* and *Waterhen* — following their flotilla leader *Stuart* (under Commander Hector Waller, RAN), quietly slipped out of Australian waters en route to Singapore. Following a request from the Admiralty they were re-routed to the Mediterranean, where, as the 'Scrap Iron Flotilla', they were to win imperishable fame.

ARMY

The Dominions entered the war with public affirmation of faith in victory but private misgivings. The misuse of Empire manhood and the inept strategy of the British government and high command in the war of 1914–18 (which claimed the lives of as many as 60,000 Canadians, and about the same number of Australians and Indians)

South Africa's Prime Minister, General Smuts, led a divided nation into war. He proved a wise adviser to and supporter of Prime Minister Churchill, who rewarded him with a field marshal's baton, and he became widely popular throughout the Commonwealth

left a dark shadow over memories. Both Canada and Australia called for volunteers for the armed services but postponed promising an expeditionary force to help Britain and it was New Zealand that forced Australia's hand when she announced on 9 September that a force of volunteers would serve overseas. Australia's Prime Minister Menzies announced on 15 September that a 'special force' of 20,000 volunteers would be raised, but did not mention whether it was to serve overseas. The British government had sounded out Australia on its intentions to help with troops and had expected a prompt response. Menzies agreed that the Special Force — soon named the 6th Division, Second Australian Imperial Force (2nd AIF), would be sent overseas but protested to his representative in London when the British government informed him that they were sending shipping to pick up the troops: 'Having regard for the importance of co-ordination with New Zealand and ... to the value of releasing British troops from the Middle East, we are prepared to agree ... However, we do so under protest ... We resent being told that shipping is already on its way for the purpose of collecting our troops on January 2 when we are not consulted ... There has been in this matter a quite perceptible disposition to treat Australia as a colony ...'

The Indian government, whose first responsibility was the defence of India, agreed to send two of its existing infantry divisions to the Middle East (4th and 5th Divisions) where they achieved a famous fighting record, but was reluctant to send more.

The 'Second New Zealand Expeditionary Force' (NZEF) was entrusted to the command of Major-General Bernard Freyberg, VC, a hero of Gallipoli who had been raised in New Zealand but had made his career in the British Army. A giant of a man, he had been retired prematurely and in 1939 had promptly offered his services to New Zealand, where few people had heard of him. Thanks to the influence of his friend Winston Churchill he was appointed. 'Tiny' Freyberg would be one of the great fighting commanders of the war and lead his New Zealanders from Egypt, through the battles of Greece and Crete, Tunisia and Italy to the shadow of the Alps.

Major-General Sir Thomas Blamey, a controversial figure who had been General Monash's chief of staff in the victory days of 1918, was appointed to command the 6th Australian Division, and when a 7th AIF Division was soon formed he was promoted to lieutenant general to command the 1st Australian Corps, and the entire AIF. His brigadiers and colonels were, like him, mostly soldiers who had served in the war of 1914–18 and had maintained their links with the militia in the years afterwards. Australia's forces would be commanded throughout principally by these 'civilian soldiers', much to the irritation of the small band of Regulars who had graduated from the Royal Military College at Duntroon. Commanding 6th Division was Major-General Iven Mackay, a former head master of a Sydney grammar school (and known as 'Mr Chips' to his men); leading the 9th Division (formed in 1941) was Leslie Morshead, a former Sydney shipping company executive. Many members of the five divisions of home-based militia volunteered for the AIF, but the AIF remained distinct from them, proud of its volunteer origins. As in 1914 the first convoy of Australians and New Zealanders that sailed early in 1940 was destined for France, by way of the Middle East. As in 1914, fate decreed that the Anzacs would remain in the Mediterranean theatre for two years, and some — the New Zealanders — until war's end.

Canada's 1st Division arrived in England in mid-1940 and was soon followed by more. Commanded by Lieutenant-General Andrew McNaughton, another civilian-soldier (he was a respected scientist), the Canadian Expeditionary Force was, under the terms of its charter from Ottawa, to fight as a Corps, not to be split up, and this condemned the Canadians, who were restless and eager for action, to sit out the first half of the war as garrison troops in the United Kingdom while the Anzacs and South Africans were in the centre of conflict.

THE 'PHONEY WAR'

Meanwhile, all was quiet on the Western Front. The French Army launched an advance in Saarland on 7 September 1939 that penetrated barely ten kilometres before being halted. It was a gesture, the most that Gamelin could risk to help Poland. Twenty days later Hitler ordered plans made for an immediate offensive in the west, but his generals pleaded for a postponement. Soon winter set in. Ahead lay eight months of inaction and what a bemused American senator labelled a 'phoney war'. The Germans called it the 'Sitzkrieg', and Winston Churchill, adopting a phrase privately used by Chamberlain, called it 'The Twilight War'.

The British Expeditionary Force was again crossing the Channel without loss to take up its position on the left of the French line, as it had in 1914. By mid-October 1939 the BEF, numbering four divisions and 150,000 men, was established near its old battlefields in northern France. Soon the BEF would consist of the 1st, 2nd, 3rd, 4th and 5th Divisions reinforced by five Territorial ones under the command of General Lord Gort, VC, an Irish viscount whom the press called 'Tiger' Gort. One of his Corps commanders, Lieutenant-General Alan Brooke, who crossed to France on 17 September and began the diary on that day that continued to war's end, wrote of Gort: 'I could not help admiring him ... But I had no confidence in his leadership when it came to handling a large force. He seemed incapable of seeing the wood for the trees ...'

In September 1939 the British government had obtained passage of the Defence of the Realm Act — known as 'DORA' — which gave it near-dictatorial powers. Many predicted that the restrictions would never be lifted and that Britain, like the dictatorships, would remain a police state. (It was lifted at war's end.) In the same month identity cards were issued to all citizens, even babies, and it was an offence not to carry the card at all times. Gas masks were issued and children were evacuated from London in case of German aerial attack, but no bombing eventuated.

Phony War in France: the commander-in-chief of the British Expeditionary Force (BEF) in France, General Lord Gort, VC (figure on left in group) shows defence lines to Britain's war minister Leslie Hore-Belisha early in 1940. On the right is Major General Bernard Montgomery of 3rd Division, already wearing battle dress. Behind the war minister's shoulder is Lt-General Alan Brooke, Montgomery's Corps commander and between Brooke and Gort, the slight figure of Lord Munster. Gort dispatched Lord Munster to Churchill to plead for more small boats during the Dunkirk evacuation in May 1940.

Europe and the Mediterranean on the eve of the Nazi conquests, 1938

HITLER'S FIRST PEACE OFFER

On 6 October 1939, the day after Hitler watched his troops roll into Warsaw in a victory parade, he addressed the Reichstag and offered peace to Britain and France. 'I have always expressed to France my desire to bury forever our ancient enmity,' he said. 'I believe even today that there can only be real peace in Europe and throughout the world if Germany and England come to an understanding.' He stated that the Polish question would be solved by Germany and Russia but the other problems — the Jewish problem among them — could be settled by a conference of the leading European nations. In closing, he warned, if his overtures were rejected: 'Then we shall fight … There will never be another November, 1918 in German history.' Chamberlain replied to the offer two days later when he told the House of Commons that 'no reliance' could be placed on German promises.

Rebuffed in his search for an easy peace, Hitler ordered another plan made for an immediate offensive in the west. His constant postponements gave the world the impression that he had decided to pursue negotiations rather than commit further acts of aggression. It was not until December that the first British soldier was killed in action. Along the Rhine American correspondents were astonished to see a truce observed. French gun batteries and Germans on the opposite bank went about their duties in full view of one another without a shot being fired. It was an odd war, one in which the only activity took place in the air, or at sea.

WAR IN THE AIR

When war came the RAF's 'first line' strength was far weaker than that of the Germans: the RAF possessed 608 'first line' fighters and 536 bombers; the Luftwaffe had 1215 fighters and 2130 bombers. The French Air Force helped redress the balance; it soon relied on purchases from American factories to augment its strength.

Britain's air force began the war vigorously. It was restricted to solely military targets, and the most obvious ones were Germany's naval bases and shipping. The nature of the air war was revealed on the first RAF raid of the war, a daylight raid mounted on 4 September against German shipping near Wilhelmshaven. The mission resulted in the loss of seven bombers.

When a force of twenty-four Wellington bombers mounted another raid, again in daylight, in December 1939, only twelve bombers returned. Unknown to the British, the Germans had tracked the aircraft on radar, and their fighter defences were strong, The loss of 50 per cent of a bomber force had never been envisaged. Strategists had predicted that 'the bomber would always get through' to rain death and destruction on an unprepared enemy. The raid forced a complete rethinking of RAF strategy. At this loss rate Britain's 500 or so operational bombers could disappear in a fortnight. As the Air Ministry forbade bombing of the Ruhr industrial region because the factories there were 'private property', flights over Germany were restricted to the dropping of leaflets by night, urging the German people to rise up against their dictator. Aircrew were ordered not to

War correspondents found the war in France for the first eight months a difficult conflict to describe as there was no fighting.

toss the bundles out in case they hurt somebody on the ground; the leaflets must float down. The air war on the Western Front became one of patrols, in which stray enemy aircraft could with luck be brought down. In one skirmish in November 1939 French pilots flying American Curtiss fighters shot down eight Messerschmitts for the loss of one of their own. Deeds like this contributed to a fatal sense of complacency. (The Luftwaffe added more powerful engines to their Messerschmitts — in 1940 the Me 109E would be the fastest fighter in the world, faster even than the Spitfire.)

It was a strange beginning to a war that would later see the destruction of cities under tonnes of high explosive and incendiaries, killing tens of thousands of civilians in one night.

THE WAR AT SEA

At sea the Allies felt confident. The combined British and French navies numbered more than 600 warships, Germany's just over a hundred (and their number included only 50 submarines). German merchant shipping was quickly driven from the seas, and after the sinking of the *Athenia*, German U-boats restricted their targets to enemy warships. They scored early successes, sinking the old carrier HMS *Courageous* and then entering the anchorage at Scapa Flow, whose anti-submarine defences were not complete, to sink the old battleship HMS *Royal Oak* (November 1939).

At the Admiralty Winston Churchill was oppressed by memories. 'No one had ever been over the same terrible course twice with such an interval between,' he wrote 'when great ships are sunk and things go wrong.' He had been dismissed from his post as First Lord of the Admiralty in 1915. *Courageous* had been without her destroyer escort when, 'by a hundred-to-one' chance she had been sighted, slowly turning into the wind to land her aircraft, by an enemy U-boat. 'In twelve months', Churchill surmised, when Germany had hundreds of submarines, 'we must expect the U-boat war to begin', and he contemplated the future with dread. An early enemy 'secret weapon' — the magnetic mine — caused losses, until the Royal Navy countered it by 'degaussing' (demagnetising) ships' hulls.

HUNTING THE *GRAF SPEE*

Another threat to Britain's lifeline was posed by German warships operating on their own. Where were the enemy 'pocket battleships'? These were warships barely 10,000 tonnes in displacement, but carrying 11-inch guns and capable of a speed of 26 knots, giving them a firepower and a speed far in excess of any British cruiser. To track them down required 'hunting packs' of battleships, cruisers and even aircraft carriers. Churchill's mind went back to the anxious months of 1914 when the German Pacific Squadron eluded more than fifty Allied warships and took almost five months to destroy.

The pocket battleship *Graf Spee* had left German waters in the week before the invasion of Poland, and on 30 September sank a British ship off the west African coast. By mid-November, she was sinking ships off Madagascar. When another British ship was sunk on 2 December, the commander of one hunting group, Commodore Henry Harwood, guessed that the *Graf Spee* would then head for the south Atlantic sea lanes, where rich pickings could be found among merchant ships steaming from the River Plate ports to Europe. He was commanding three cruisers: the heavy cruiser *Exeter* and two 6-inch-gun cruisers *Ajax* and *Achilles* (the latter was manned by New Zealanders), when they sighted smoke on the horizon at 6.14 a.m. on the morning of 13 December. It was the *Graf Spee*. Six minutes later the British cruisers opened fire and now began a running battle in which they attacked from three quarters, successfully forcing *Graf Spee* to divide her fire. By 7.40 a.m. *Exeter* had been hit so savagely by the 11-inch shells that she had to drop out of the battle but after 80 minutes of action *Graf Spee*, which had also been damaged, turned away under cover of a smoke screen and made for Montevideo The two light cruisers, both of which were damaged by enemy shells, kept up the pursuit, sticking to the German's tail like terriers. Just after midnight the *Graf Spee* entered Montevideo while the pursuers steamed outside the three-mile limit, waiting for her to emerge. Strong British task forces converged on the scene, and Captain Langsdorff, forced by international law to leave a neutral harbour within three days, informed Hitler: 'Escape into open sea and break-through to home waters hopeless.'

At the outbreak of war Britain implemented the sending of ships in protected convoys, a measure that increased their chances of surviving German submarine attacks.

Captain Hans Langsdorff, of the pocket-battleship *Graf Spee*, with some of his sailors. Langsdorff, who was not a fervent Nazi, took his own life after he was forced to scuttle his ship.

Hitler ordered him to scuttle his damaged ship. On the evening of 17 December the *Graf Spee* blew herself up at the mouth of the River Plate. Her captain shot himself. 'The effects of the action off the Plate gave intense joy to the British people and enhanced our prestige throughout the world,' Churchill wrote. HMS *Achilles* became HMNZS *Achilles* in 1941 on the creation of the Royal New Zealand Navy and she and her sister ship *Leander* survived the war and numerous actions. *Exeter* was to be lost in action against the Japanese in 1942.

German U-boats scored some dramatic early successes but proved ineffective in their war against British convoys in the first year of war. Germany began the war with fifty-six submarines and by September 1940 had the same number — they had only managed to replace the twenty-eight they had lost. And soon the German surface navy was to be almost destroyed in the Norway campaign.

When France fell and provided Germany with sea ports and bases along its entire Atlantic seaboard, the U-boat war took a new and aggressive course.

HITLER'S WINTER OFFENSIVE PLANS

Hitler had predicted that Britain's only effective weapon was blockade — but now he had ample foodstuffs and raw materials flowing to him from the Soviet Union. He had stated that France's only capacity lay in an offensive from the Maginot Line, but their one attack in Saarland had petered out after a few days. He sensed, correctly, that his enemies were fighting a defensive war, hoping that time would bring about his collapse. When his generals complained that the weather was worsening and could make operations difficult, he answered that they were equally difficult for his enemies.

Hitler on 27 October 1939 ordered an offensive in the west to begin on 12 November. He soon postponed the attack, the second of fourteen postponements as the worst winter in decades settled over the Western Front and made any movement impossible. The historian William Shirer believes that events on 8 and 9 November may have influenced Hitler's decision to postpone an offensive: after leaving the anniversary reunion of his cronies at the Munich Hofbräuhaus a bomb went off there, killing or wounding seventy. The German press blamed the attack on the British Secret Service, whose cleverness they exaggerated, and next day the SS kidnapped two British secret agents from the Dutch frontier town of Venlo.

On 23 November Hitler decided: 'I shall attack France and England at the most favourable and earliest moment. Breach of the neutrality of Belgium and Holland is of no importance. No one will question that when we have won.' Again his generals objected to Brauchitsch — von Leeb was horrified to think that Germany 'for the second time in twenty-five years was intending to invade Belgium'. Hitler informed the General Staff that they were defeatist and that he would suppress opposition to his plans with 'brute force'. This was enough to cow his proud Prussians. On 27 December 1939, as the weather worsened and his generals got cold feet, Hitler again postponed the offensive in the west.

At this same time the Allies had agreed to a new plan of operations. If Germany invaded the Low Countries General Gamelin had resolved to advance into Belgium and confront the enemy along the Scheldte. In mid-November he outlined a more complicated plan to establish a line along the Dyle River, which corresponded to a line from Antwerp to Namur. This was the plan adopted, despite many misgivings by his generals — and by the British, who were under his operational command. General Ironside, who had taken Gort's post as Chief of the Imperial General Staff (CIGS) wrote that 'we are strongly of the opinion that the German advance should be met in prepared positions on the French frontier' rather than rush into Belgium. It was adopted, however, by the Allied Supreme War Council on 17 November. Its advantage was that it would deny the Germans Antwerp and enable the Anglo-French forces to link up with the Belgian Army at Louvain. Great reliance was placed in the Belgian Army — seven divisions strong in 1914, it was now twenty-two divisions, an army nearly three times the strength of the Dutch Army. Liège, the great fortress of 1914, was now as strong as the Maginot Line, and a new defence line — the Albert Canal and its fortress of Eben-Emael — had recently been constructed. The Belgians and the Dutch, fearful of provoking Germany, consistently refused to enter staff discussions with the Allies to plan a common defence.

SECRET WEAPONS

ROCKETS

Two months after the war began, in November 1939, the British Naval attaché in neutral Norway was handed a package that had been left overnight on a window ledge of the British embassy in Oslo. It was forwarded to London, where the scientists opened it gingerly, for they thought it might be a bomb. It contained a long letter signed simply, 'A German scientist who wishes you well', and which contained details of Nazi scientific advances. Also included was a mysterious tube which turned out to be a top-secret German proximity fuse for an anti-aircraft shell. The letter informed the British that Germany already had radar, had devised radio-controlled torpedoes and was developing rocket projectiles at a place called Peenemunde on the Baltic coast. Military Intelligence thought the letter was a hoax, and their suspicions were seemingly confirmed a week later when two of their agents, lured to the Dutch border at Venlo to meet bogus 'anti-Hitler German officers' were kidnapped by German Intelligence. But the young scientist R.V. Jones felt sure the letter was authentic, and he remembered the name Peenemunde. It was the research and testing area for the German 'secret weapons' — the V-1 rocket bombs and the V-2 supersonic missiles — which more than four years later fell on London.

ATOM BOMBS

In Germany and Britain spectacular advances had been made in the 1930s in nuclear physics. It was discovered that some metals possessed extraordinary amounts of heat. The New Zealand-born physicist Ernest Rutherford had discovered the three types of uranium radiation and later formulated the theory of atomic disintegration which accounted for the immense heat energy radiated from uranium. He described the atom as a miniature universe in which the mass is concentrated in the nucleus, surrounded by planetary electrons. In 1934 Italy's Enrico Fermi split the nuclei of uranium atoms by bombarding them with neutrons. Another pioneer in nuclear physics, the Hungarian-born Leo Szilard, fled from Germany to England and thence to the United States in 1938. In the same year, Fermi received the Nobel Prize for Physics and left for the United States immediately after the award ceremony in Stockholm. Albert Einstein, who had won the Nobel Prize for Physics in 1921, left Germany in 1933 and was now working at Princeton University.

The expatriate physicists were alarmed by the thought that Nazi Germany might develop a devastating 'atomic bomb'. In August 1939 Szilard and another Hungarian-born scientist, Edward Teller, asked the famous Einstein, whose genius was widely recognised, to write directly to President Roosevelt and inform him that scientists in Berlin had achieved the fission of uranium atoms and that it could be possible to achieve a nuclear 'chain reaction' which could be harnessed into bombs of extraordinary destructive power. The letter was delivered to Roosevelt in October 1939 by their friend, financier and White House adviser Alexander Sachs, who read it out aloud to the President. Roosevelt pondered and said, 'Alex, what you are after is to see that the Nazis don't blow us up.' It was not until 1940, however, that Roosevelt ordered that research on an atomic bomb be intensified. This was the birth of the 'Manhattan Project', which worked for the next five years under conditions of utmost secrecy and growing urgency. In 1942 the world's first nuclear reactor was operating at the University of Chicago, and scientists were working in a hundred establishments including a camp at Los Alamos in the deserts of Nevada, where the weapon could be tested. German progress was slow. Lacking adequate uranium, they intensified production of a substitute, 'heavy water'; but French scientists hid their own valuable stocks, and Norwegian and British commandos destroyed the heavy water shipments from Norsk Hydro in heroic endeavours in the middle of the war. In the end, the race for the atom bomb was a race, the Allies won.

1939: WINTER OF DISCONTENT

British and French strategy in late 1939 resembled the confusion of the worst months of 1917 and 1918. The armies were inactive, as they had been over the winter of 1914–15 and the Allies' best chance of victory was seen as maintaining the deadlock on land while depriving Germany of the raw materials of war by way of a blockade.

Only three weeks after the outbreak of war in September 1939 the future British Foreign Secretary, Anthony Eden, confided to the Australian-born senior official at the Foreign Office in London, Rex Leeper, that Chamberlain's government 'was incapable of waging vigorous war' and predicted 'reverses' before ultimate victory was achieved. When Australia's High Commissioner in London, Stanley Bruce, urged consideration of peace initiatives, Churchill angrily replied that Hitler 'had his hands dripping with the blood of the Poles, and the task was to fight him until he was defeated'. Menzies, who like Bruce was hopeful of a peace settlement, agreed that Churchill was a 'menace'. Many in Chamberlain's Cabinet were reported to favour 'making a peace before war starts'.

But by this stage a new war had broken out. Finland was fighting for its existence and soon Norway and Denmark would absorb the attentions of Hitler.

FINLAND

Having swallowed eastern Poland Stalin was already taking measures to further safeguard his western frontiers. On 24 September 1939 he summoned Esthonia's foreign minister to Moscow and demanded the right to establish Soviet bases there. In October he demanded the same rights from Latvia and Lithuania. Later in the month he presented to the Finns a demand that they evacuate the territory adjacent to Leningrad and cede them bases including Petsamo, Finland's only ice-free port on the Arctic Sea, and Hango, the port on the Gulf of Finland. The Finns were prepared to discuss all the Russian demands except the last. The Soviet reply was the bombing of Helsinki on 30 November and a massed invasion along the length

Right: Bogged in the snow: Russian tanks were quickly immobilised in Finland's harsh winter and Soviet troops isolated and destroyed piecemeal by Finish troops.

of the Finnish frontier. Finland, whose history had been blameless, appealed to the League of Nations.

The Russians had left their attack too late. Winter had set in. In the forested wastes of central Finland, the Finns, small in number but skilled in winter warfare and in moving quickly and silently on skis, allowed slow-moving Russians columns to enter and attacked as night fell, cutting their lines of retreat. The Russian armies floundered. In the south the attackers were confronted with a strong line of forts and emplacements — the Mannerheim Line, named after Finland's national hero, Marshal Mannerheim, who had expelled the Bolsheviks in 1919 and was once more appointed their commander-in-chief. By the end of the year the Russians had made no progress. At last a small and peaceful democracy had stood up to the dictators and held them at bay.

'I sympathised ardently with the Finns and supported all proposals for their aid,' Churchill later wrote. In an extraordinary decision, both Britain and France decided to send assistance to Finland. Seemingly, they had forgotten that their enemy was Germany, not Russia. The French late in 1939 even suggested that Allied aircraft bomb the Russian oilfields at Baku to deny oil shipments to Germany. Messages of sympathy, promises of support and several dozen aircraft reached the Finns, but no Allied ground troops, for Sweden and Norway refused to allow them to cross their territory, though permitting Swedish volunteers to join the Finns. Hitler derived a certain glee from the misfortunes that had befallen his ally Stalin in Finland and also extended some aid to the Finns. Russian mortalities exceeded 50,000 — some say they totalled 100,000, most of whom froze to death. The defeat of the Soviet armies in Finland was confirmation to Hitler that they were now a second-rate force.

As winter prevented all further movement the Russian armies in Finland waited for the coming of spring. In March 1940 they would launch their major offensive. But already Scandinavia was absorbing the strategic attention of Britain and France — and Germany.

PLANS FOR FINLAND AND NORWAY

Churchill's eyes were already riveted on the remote northern Norwegian port of Narvik, from where a rail line led over the frontier to the Swedish iron ore mines. From Narvik iron ore was shipped to Germany, loaded on freighters that clung to Norwegian territorial waters — the Leads — to evade attack. In Churchill's eyes seizure of Narvik would close the iron ore traffic to Germany, cripple her war industries and present the Allies with a base from which they could supply the Finns. Churchill wrote a minute on 15 December 1939 to his Cabinet colleagues: 'It cannot be too strongly emphasised that British control of the Norwegian coastline is a strategic objective of first-class importance.' The Cabinet hesitated to breach Norwegian neutrality. No decision was made. A month later he wrote again: 'Just look at the arguments which have had to be surmounted in the seven weeks we have discussed this Narvik operation … One thing is absolutely sure, namely, that victory will never be found by taking the line of least resistance.'

CHAPTER 5
DEFEAT IN THE WEST
1940

PLANS FOR THE GERMAN OFFENSIVE

On 10 January 1940 Hitler ordered the offensive against France and the Netherlands to begin one week later. Unfortunately, a German aircraft flying to Cologne from Munster became lost in the mist on that very day and was forced to put down in Belgian territory. One of its passengers was carrying plans for the offensive and his attempts to burn the papers were unsuccessful. The Belgian General Staff was alarmed by their contents. King Leopold flew to The Hague to confer with Queen Wilhelmina and the Belgians forwarded copies of the papers to French headquarters — this was the first direct contact from neutral Belgium since 1937. At Hitler's headquarters General Jodl described the event as 'catastrophic'. Hitler was furious, and Keitel later related: 'The Führer was possessed, foaming at the mouth, and pounding the wall' while threatening dire punishment of the General Staff, whom he accused, with good reason, of treachery. The offensive was cancelled. France and the Low Countries had achieved a reprieve.

But it was only a short one. On 12 January 1940 General Erich von Manstein, the chief of staff of General von Rundstedt, sent to Hitler's headquarters a suggestion that the invasion plan be altered, and that the centre of gravity be shifted east to Sedan — otherwise, as an offensive it might degenerate into trench warfare. He suggested that it was 'essential that another army, having crossed the Meuse at Sedan, drives to the south-west'. This army would have to attack from the Ardennes, a rugged, forested corner of Belgium that was considered impassable for tanks. In mid-February Hitler spoke to Manstein, and grasped the significance of the plan. He had always been a risk-taker. On 15 March Guderian, who had also become an enthusiast, affirmed that his Corps' tanks could break through the Belgian frontier posts by the end of the first day, by the fourth day would reach the Meuse and cross it on the fifth. Hitler asked: 'Then what would you do?' Guderian replied: 'Unless I receive orders to the contrary, I intend on the next day to continue my advance westwards. The supreme leadership must decide whether my objective is to be Amiens or Paris. In my opinion the correct course is to drive past Amiens to the English Channel.'

This was the plan adopted for the 'Ardennes breakthrough', which was achieved exactly to the timetable Guderian outlined.

PLANS FOR NORWAY

In January 1940 Hitler had decided to invade Norway and Denmark, but it was not until 20 February that he committed himself to a firm date. Historians wonder if his decision was forced by the boarding of a German ship, the *Altmark*, which was sheltering in Norwegian territorial waters, by the British destroyer *Cossack* four days earlier. It was known that the *Altmark* was carrying British merchant seamen taken off ships sunk by the *Graf Spee* and Churchill ordered Captain Phillip Vian on *Cossack* to free them, even if it meant entering Norwegian waters. British sailors had boarded the *Altmark* at nightfall and as the German crew fled across the ice, freed the captives held below to the shout 'The Navy's here!' It was a blatant flouting of a neutral country, but Churchill recorded that in a dark winter 'it warmed the cockles of the British heart'.

Summoning General von Falkenhorst to Berlin, Hitler explained: 'The occupation of Norway by the British would be a strategic turning

Inset above: **For the British, 1940 was to be the time of trial and triumph.**
Opposite: **Calm before the storm. French troops during the Phony War on the eve of the German attack.**
Opposite right: **Five weeks after invading France German troops were parading past the Arc de Triomphe in Paris. France signed an armistice one week later.**

Finland's national hero, Baron Carl Gustav Mannerheim, who drove the Bolsheviks from Finland in 1919, was recalled to service as Commander-in-Chief in 1939. Despite his aristocratic birth and career as a former Tzarist general, Mannerheim was a convinced democrat who attempted to save Finland from further Soviet threats by fighting on Hitler's side.

THE END IN FINLAND

When the Russian armies resumed their offensive in Finland in early March 1940 their strength was overwhelming. Finland signed an armistice on 12 March that left her independent, but with loss of much territory. Then came the turn of Latvia, Lithuania and Esthonia, which in the same month had to accede to further Soviet demands that robbed them of their rights. In June 1940 Russian troops simply moved into the three Baltic states and Stalin incorporated them into the Soviet Union. Fifty years later they would, like Poland, be the first to break away from a Soviet Union that was already crumbling from within.

A week after Finland signed an armistice, French Premier Daladier, identified too closely with the Finnish debacle, was replaced by Paul Reynaud, a feisty leader who like Churchill had constantly warned in the 1930s of the threat to France posed by Germany. Churchill wrote to Reynaud: 'I rejoice that you are at the helm, and that Mandel is with you.' A week later (28 March) the new French ministry came to London, where Chamberlain announced that a pet project of Churchill's — 'Operation Royal Marine', which involved launching mines along the Rhine — was ready, and outlined Britain's plans for landings in Norway. Finland was already forgotten. Alarmed by possible German retaliation to mining the Rhine, Reynaud suggested an alternative — to lay mines in Norwegian waters to stop iron ore shipments. It was decided to commence this operation on 5 April. The Allies also decided that if Germany invaded Belgium and Holland in the meantime, they would send forces there 'without waiting for a formal invitation'.

On 3 April the British War Cabinet discussed intelligence just received that Germany was amassing a force whose only destination could be Scandinavia; the Swedes had reported that shipping was gathering in north German ports, along with an army rumoured to number 400,000 men. The armada was so large that few could fail to notice it. The invasion force amounted to seven divisions — in numbers, far short of the 400,000 men reported — along with 800 warplanes and more than 200 transport aircraft. Cabinet ordered the Admiralty to begin laying mines in Norwegian territorial waters on 8 April and that a force be readied for landing at Narvik. Late on 7 April British reconnaissance aircraft reported that a German fleet was approaching the Skagerrak. In case it was heading for the North Sea and Norway the British Home Fleet left Scapa Flow on that same night. British cruisers, then embarking troops, left Rosyth for Narvik two hours later.

Thus the early hours of 8 April revealed two invasion fleets steaming for Norway — one British and one German. Before dawn extensive British minefields had been laid outside Narvik.

movement that would lead them into the Baltic … the conquest of Norway …will protect our imports of Swedish iron ore.' In reality an invasion of Norway had been suggested by Admiral Raeder, who had pointed out the advantage to Germany of having air and naval bases along the entire Norwegian coast to threaten British convoys and the British North Sea fleet. In attempting to destroy British sea power, Raeder was to succeed in Norway in destroying most of his own surface navy.

Alfred Rosenberg, Hitler's racial theorist, pointed out that the Scandinavians were Germanic, part of the great Nordic people, perfect citizens of the new Reich. And the Führer was informed that many prominent Norwegians favoured his policies, including Vidkun Quisling, a former officer and War Minister who had founded a fascist party in Norway and was said to have many followers.

BIRTH OF THE ALLIED NORWAY EXPEDITION

On 2 March Premier Daladier of France, without consulting London, agreed to send a force of 50,000 men to aid the Finns, in addition to a hundred bombers. Britain and France together made plans for an expeditionary force of 100,000 men. 'The Finnish campaign was Gallipoli again, and worse … run up in the slapdash spirit which had characterised the expedition to the Dardanelles,' writes the English historian A.J.P. Taylor. British volunteers from infantry regiments began training on skis in the French Alps as the expeditionary force gathered. On 12 March the British Cabinet agreed to landings at Narvik and other ports on the Norway coast. But on the same day the Finns were forced to accept armistice terms from the Russians.

Left: Captain Philip Vian with his officers on the bridge of the destroyer HMS *Cossack*. Vian later distinguished himself in the Mediterranean and rose to the rank of full admiral.

Below: British troops en route to Norway practising lifeboat drill as an escorting destroyer passes.

Above: King Christian X of Denmark was a popular monarch and his conduct during German occupation increased respect for the monarchy. He is shown with his son and successor Crown Prince Frederik.
Below: A French artist's impression of one of the few resounding victories of the Norway campaign. On two occasions British warships steamed into Narvik fiord, sinking the German invasion fleet.

DENMARK INVADED

German forces rolled over the Danish frontier at dawn on 9 April and met little resistance. Troops hidden in German freighters tied up in Copenhagen only a stone's throw from the Amalienborg Palace disembarked and before breakfast were exchanging shots with the Royal Guards, whom King Christian ordered to cease firing. Not a shot was fired by the Royal Danish Navy. The brief war had cost twenty German casualties and the lives of thirteen Danish soldiers.

Under German occupation Denmark received from Hitler special consideration. The Kingdom preserved its monarchy, government, laws and defence forces, and lost only freedom of speech. Churchill called Denmark 'Hitler's Canary'.

NORWAY

Norway was a different proposition and here King Christian's brother, King Haakon, fought and refused to admit defeat. The Norwegian campaign raged for more than two months. In the early hours of 9 April ten German destroyers entered Narvik harbour. They were hailed by two Norwegian guard ships which were immediately sunk, taking with them nearly 300 Norwegian sailors. Narvik's garrison was surrendered without a shot being fired, by their commander, Konrad Sundlo, a follower of the Norwegian fascist Quisling, to the German troops led by a daring Bavarian, General Dietl. 'Thereafter the capture of Narvik was easy,' lamented Churchill, 'It was a strategic victory — forever denied us.'

German mountain troops in Norway, 1940. These soldiers are possibly from an Austrian or Bavarian alpine unit. The ski caps they wear later became general issue to all German soldiers in 1943.

Similarly the Germans landed at and occupied with ease Trondheim, Bergen (where coastal batteries crippled a German light cruiser, which was later sunk by British aircraft), Kristiansand and Arendal (where a British submarine sank the cruiser *Karlsruhe*).

At the same time, a German fleet was moving through the pre-dawn mists of Oslo fjord. In the darkness Norwegian forts opened fire on them, but after dawn German troops were landed and captured the batteries. A Norwegian minesweeper opened fire on the oncoming warships, damaging the cruiser *Emden*, and the forts' torpedoes sank the cruiser *Blücher*. The German invasion flotilla turned back, but German troops pressed on to Oslo, securing the airport, where by afternoon transports were touching down and disgorging more troops. The citizens of Oslo went to work to the sight of German troops entering the city and German bands playing in the city square. The King and his government had already fled and made their way north, from where they were determined to continue resistance.

THE BATTLES FOR NARVIK

Narvik now became the focus of fighting. On the second day of war, at dawn on 10 April, a flotilla of British destroyers — *Hardy*, *Hunter*, *Havock*, *Hotspur* and *Hostile*, steamed into Narvik fjord and took by surprise the German destroyers and the invasion convoy of twenty-three merchant ships. The British ships sank two German destroyers, damaged three others and sank six transport ships. On leaving the scene they encountered the other five German destroyers, which claimed two British warships, but the three surviving destroyers sank another transport on reaching the open sea. Three days later Admiral Whitworth, flying his flag in the battleship *Warspite*, led another bold attack into Narvik fjord and destroyed the remaining eight German destroyers. Dietl's landing force was now stranded and Whitworth signalled the Admiralty: 'I recommend that the town be occupied without delay by the main [Allied] landing force.'

Left: Norway's fascist leader Vidkun Quisling. Appointed by the Germans as Minister-President of Norway in 1942, he proved a callous leader and was shot by the Norwegians as a traitor after the war, in 1945.
Below left: Crown Prince Olav, (left), King Haakon's son and successor, seen with Norwegian officer in 1940.

What now followed was a sad story of wasted opportunities and timorous action. The British force steaming for Narvik under the command of Major-General P. Mackesy landed instead on 15 April at Harstat, a small port on a neighbouring island, 100 kilometres from Narvik. Mackesy had been given conflicting orders. Instructed to avoid heavy casualties at Narvik if faced by strong resistance he was also ordered to 'act boldly'; he chose a middle course. He built up his base and his strength at Harstat — to the frustration of the Royal Navy's commander on the spot, a fiery Irishman, Admiral Lord Cork, while the Germans, given an unexpected reprieve, reinforced Narvik and its coastal defences (discovering 325 Norwegian machine guns in barracks there was a godsend to them).

On 15–16 April British forces also landed at Namsos and Andalsnes to converge on Trondheim. Two separate campaigns were now being fought. The troops, ill-equipped for fighting in the snow, lacked tanks, air support and adequate anti-aircraft guns to combat the incessant German air attacks. The Germans enjoyed air superiority in Norway from the first day and exploited it to the full. So little progress was made that on 26 April the Allied Supreme War Council decided to evacuate forces from the new landings and concentrate all their forces against Narvik — in other words, to give up central Norway. Strong French reinforcements were already on the way to Norway but the decision to evacuate positions led to angry recriminations in the House of Commons, and Chamberlain was held to account for a campaign that was rapidly proving hopeless.

Meanwhile King Haakon threatened to abdicate if his ministers contemplated surrender and determined to hold out in northern Norway to the end. By 7 May the two highly-trained French demi-brigades (one of them from the Foreign Legion) and a Polish demi-brigade were landed and readied to move on Narvik. They would prove to be the outstanding Allied soldiers of the campaign. But three days later the German Blitzkrieg broke over the Low Countries and France and the Norway expedition became a sideshow, a campaign waged with inadequate resources and one in which the Allies had shown little confidence. As France crumbled, the decision was made to evacuate the Allied forces, but this must be done in a way that would not alienate the Norwegians. A new British commander, Lieutenant-General C.J.E. Auchinleck, who had relieved the luckless Mackesy, was on a cruiser in the bombardment force on 28 May when the French and Poles, with some Norwegian troops, fought their way into Narvik and captured it for the cost of 100 casualties. The six thousand remaining Norwegian civilians greeted them with cheers but by late on 31 May most Allied troops at Narvik had been re-embarked. On 7 June the last troops were re-embarked from Harstat, along with the French rearguard from Narvik. The King of

Norway, his son Crown Prince Olav and his ministers sailed aboard a British cruiser for Scotland. Hearing that Allied convoys were at sea the Germans attempted to sink them; the force in which Auchinleck was sailing was subjected to air attack but came through unscathed. The carrier HMS *Furious* was not so lucky. After evacuating the last ten Hurricanes from the RAF's single squadron, which had operated from iced-over airfields (their pilots had bravely made their first touch-down on a carrier's deck) the carrier, escorted by only two destroyers, was sighted by the battle cruisers *Scharnhorst* and *Gneisenau* and sunk, along with both destroyers, for the loss of 1474 men; there were only 45 survivors. Some 25,000 Allied troops had been evacuated to Scotland; they had suffered 5000 casualties, as had the Germans. General Auchinleck was disturbed at the generally poor showing by British troops, most of whom had been badly trained Territorials, and he felt their problems went beyond their inadequate equipment: 'By comparison with the French, or the Germans for that matter, our men for the most part seemed distressingly young, not so much in years as in self-reliance and manliness generally ...' This criticism was suppressed in his official despatch. Many senior British officers in France shared a similar despair at the poor impression made by many French troops, particularly the reservists who were slovenly and ill-disciplined.

Germany had lost three cruisers and ten destroyers; her two battle cruisers were under repair along with three more cruisers. One month later, as Hitler prepared his invasion of England, he would have to attempt to carry it out without a navy.

THE FALL OF CHAMBERLAIN

The conduct of the Norway campaign had eroded what confidence was left in Prime Minister Chamberlain. When he rose in the Commons to speak on 7 May he was greeted with catcalls. One Conservative member, Admiral of the Fleet Sir Roger Keyes, attended the Commons in uniform — his tall figure gleaming with gold was a sight as impressive as *Warspite* steaming into Narvik fjord — and supported the Labour Party's criticisms; another Conservative backbencher, Leo Amery, shouted at Chamberlain the contemptuous words used by Cromwell when he dismissed the Long Parliament: 'You have sat for too long here for any good you have been doing. Depart, I say, and let us have done with you!' On the following day Lloyd George stated that Churchill, as First Lord of the Admiralty, should not be forced to shoulder the responsibility for 'what happened in Norway' — the Navy had been outstanding — and asked the Prime Minister, who had called for sacrifices in the war effort, to 'sacrifice his seals of office'. After the debate Chamberlain admitted to Churchill that he felt he could not go on. On 9 May Chamberlain decided to form a coalition government. In the afternoon Churchill was called to 10 Downing Street, where he found Chamberlain and Lord Halifax, the Foreign Minister; they were soon joined by the Labour leaders, Clement Attlee and Arthur Greenwood, who discussed a coalition but made no firm promise until they had an opportunity to sound out their members.

French alpine troops embarking from Norway to return to France, 1940.

CHURCHILL AT THE HELM

On 10 May the storm broke in western Europe. At 11 a.m. Churchill was again summoned to 10 Downing Street, where Chamberlain and Lord Halifax were waiting. The Prime Minister told him that Labour had rebuffed his overtures and that he was intending to resign. He had only to recommend to the King his successor. 'Usually I talk a great deal,' Churchill recalled, 'but on this occasion I was silent.' There was no doubt that both Chamberlain and the King would prefer Halifax to succeed Chamberlain. To break the long silence Halifax spoke, and disqualified himself. He felt it would be impossible to lead the nation from his position as a peer in the House of Lords. Churchill received a message summoning him to Buckingham Palace at 6 p.m. It was just a two-minute drive from the Admiralty. There the King asked him to form a government. Churchill told the King he intended to form a national government, including Labour and Liberal ministers.

At the age of sixty-five, Churchill had achieved his dream of the prime ministership, but at a time of impending disaster. 'I felt as if I were walking with destiny,' he later wrote, 'and that all my past life had been but a preparation for this hour and for this trial.'

EVE OF BLITZKRIEG

In the spring of 1940 the Allies were committed to a waiting war, ready to counter any German move but unsure where it would fall. The Allied generalissimo, Gamelin, was confident of withstanding any German offensive. The Maginot Line was impregnable. (As indeed it proved to be — some of its forts were still holding out in early July, ten days after the French surrender.) On paper his strength was equal to that of the enemy: Germany possessed 134 divisions, the Allies — if they included eight Dutch and 22 Belgian divisions — counted their strength at 135 divisions (94 French, 10 British and one Polish, formed in France from Poles who had escaped or were living there). Both France and Germany had more than 2500 tanks, and France now had two armoured divisions with another two in process of formation. (The 4th Armoured was soon entrusted to the command of the young prophet of tank warfare, General Charles de Gaulle). In his dank, echoing headquarters in the fortress of Vincennes outside Paris, Gamelin was a shadowy figure, but eternally optimistic. In late March French counterespionage were informed that 'German Intelligence is making urgent inquiries into the state of the major roads along the Sedan–Abbeville axis. Questions included the width of bridges, the appearance of the river banks, the depth of the water courses …' Gamelin paid little heed to reports like this. Defending the line at Sedan, near the Ardennes, was General Corap's 9th Army consisting of seven divisions, all but two of them second-line, many of them reservists, lacking anti-tank guns and adequate artillery. The 2nd Army to its south was little better, though its commander, General Huntziger, was youthful and vigorous. Gamelin made no changes to his dispositions; these armies would be the first to be struck by the Panzers. His best troops were held in the west for an anticipated advance into Belgium. If he had visited more of his armies over the long winter and early spring he would have discerned a lowering in morale among a number of them. The Communists among the soldiers viewed the war as a capitalist one; the right-wing looked upon the dictatorships with admiration; conservatives viewed the Third Republic as corrupted by party politics.

One officer was dedicated to France and the Republic, which he saw as endangered as never before. In early January 1940 Colonel Charles de Gaulle, commanding the tanks in the 5th Army in Alsace, was visited by his old friend Léon Blum, the former Socialist Premier.

An effective partnership: King George VI (left) with Prime Minister Churchill.

Brigadier-General Charles de Gaulle (right) with France's President Lebrun during the latter's visit to the front lines early in 1940.

'The few dozen light tanks attached to my command are no more than trifles,' the soldier said, stating that the lesson of Poland had not been learnt. Two weeks later he sent Blum a plea for the creation of a 'mechanised army': 'Sooner or later the present conflict will be characterised by movement, surprise, incursion and pursuit whose scale and speed will go infinitely beyond the most shattering events of the past. Let us not deceive ourselves! The war that has begun may well be the most widespread, the most complex and the most violent of all those that have devastated the world …' On 3 May Premier Reynaud received an equally eloquent letter from de Gaulle, whom he knew well, which informed him that 'the French military system is conceived, organised, equipped and commanded contrary to the law of modern warfare. There exists no more pressing need than that of radically reforming the system …' De Gaulle offered to serve under him 'in this work'.

On 9 May, just as Britain was preparing to change its government, that of France resigned. Premier Reynaud, dismayed by Gamelin's incompetence, decided to force the general's resignation and take over the post of Minister of War. Confident of being reappointed Premier, he informed President Lebrun and was awaiting his decision, when Hitler made his decision for him: at 9 p.m. on 9 May Hitler had ordered the offensive in the west — Case Yellow — to begin the following morning. Next day the German invasion came and Reynaud withdrew his resignation. He wrote to Gamelin: 'General. The battle has begun. One thing only counts: to win the victory.'

General Maurice Gamelin, the French Commander-in-Chief in 1939 who was removed from his command only after the German armies had broken the French front.

BLITZKRIEG IN THE WEST

DUTCH AND BELGIANS RESIST NAZI DRIVE; ALLIED FORCES MARCH IN TO DO BATTLE; CHAMBERLAIN RESIGNS, CHURCHILL PREMIER

Left: German parachute troops ford a Belgian river under fire, May 1940.

The long-awaited storm broke in the West at dawn on 10 May 1940, when German armies crossed into Belgium, the Netherlands and Luxembourg and the Luftwaffe began heavy bombing of French airfields. German tanks made good progress along the narrow roads of the Ardennes. The Grand Duchess of Luxembourg, her small defenceless country once more witnessing the march of German forces, left her capital in time to reach France and safety.

THE DUTCH COLLAPSE

The Dutch had counted on their flooded regions to hold up an invasion, but Germany used airborne forces to seize key points in the kingdom, and they did this ruthlessly. The Germans quickly seized the Maas (Meuse) bridges on the morning of 10 May before they could be detonated. Airborne troops landed at three airfields at The Hague in an attempt to seize the Queen and her government, but Dutch troops drove them back. Paratroops seized the bridges to

Left: German troops with light artillery fight their way forward in Holland.
Above: Belgian troops welcome British forces as they enter Belgium to try and stop the German flood. Eighteen days later Belgium had been crushed.

Rotterdam, and the single Panzer division allotted to the conquest of the Netherlands reached them late on 12 May. 'The power of resistance of the Dutch army has proved to be stronger than anticipated,' Hitler stated in a directive. 'Political as well as military considerations require that this be broken speedily.' Early on 14 May a German officer with a white flag crossed one of the bridges to Rotterdam and demanded the city's surrender or face bombing. The bombers appeared overhead as he was negotiating and devastated the centre of the city. Rumours spread that up to 30,000 people had been killed. In reality nearly 80,000 were made homeless but fatalities from the bombing totalled 814. When German tanks rolled into Rotterdam, 'Fortress Holland' had been breached. The Dutch Army had lost 2100 killed, 2700 wounded.

Queen Wilhelmina and the royal family escaped to England aboard a British destroyer, but General Winkel-mann signed the Dutch cease-fire, which took effect on the morning of 15 May.

'BLOOD, TOIL, TEARS AND SWEAT'

On 13 May Churchill addressed the Commons for the first time as Prime Minister. He did not spare the members from grim tidings. All the news was bad. 'I have nothing to offer', he told them, 'but blood, toil, tears and sweat.' He made no summary of the war situation, but warned: 'We have before us an ordeal of the most grievous kind.'

BELGIUM INVADED

The suddenness of the German attack paralysed Belgian resistance as much as the shock of war had affected the Dutch. German gliderborne troops landed on the top of the fortress of Eban Emael, which dominated the point where the Meuse River met the Albert Canal and, using explosive charges and flamethrowers took the surrender of its 1200-strong garrison early on 11 May for the loss of 25 casualties.

On the sunny spring morning of 10 May British and French forces entered Belgium to the cheers of the Belgians and sped north. By the following day the army of General Henry Giraud, a spirited French commander, had entered Holland, on the same day that Brigadier-General Charles de Gaulle was ordered to take command of the French 4th Armoured Division. By 15 May, the Allied forces in Belgium had reached their prescribed defence line along the Dyle and had linked up with the Belgian Army, which was retreating to the Antwerp–Louvain line. On that day French 'Light Mechanised' divisions encountered the 4th Panzer Division, and the 3rd British Division, commanded by Major-General Bernard Montgomery, had counter-attacked successfully, denying the enemy easy entry into Louvain.

And then came calamity, one so unexpected that it ranks as one of the catastrophes of European history. The Germans had broken the French front at Sedan where seventy years before a French army had been surrounded by German armies.

SEDAN: THE GERMAN BREAKTHROUGH

By 11 May it was clear that the Germans were active in the Ardennes sector. 'Advancing against the four French light cavalry divisions and two cavalry brigades with their 300 tanks and armoured cars were no less than seven Panzer divisions totalling 2270 armoured vehicles,' records one historian. The French defensive screen retreated across the Meuse next day and blew up the bridges. Late that day, in the north, Rommel's 7th Panzer Division was the first to cross the river using a weir at a point between Namur and Dinant in Belgium and by early next day (13 May) his engineers were bridging the Meuse. It now became a race to plug the gaps, for the river banks of the Meuse were undefended. In the early hours of 13 May German troops paddled across the river at Houx and by noon Rommel had established a bridgehead three kilometres deep. 'At Houx, like the first trickle through a dam, began the penetration that would soon breach the Meuse like a flood,' writes John Williams. For some reason no counterattack was launched against the bridgehead. Further south Guderian's Panzers were emerging from their forest cover and massing on the far side of the river. The French defenders were subjected to aerial bombing until mid-afternoon, and then artillery shelling at a scale they had never imagined possible. It ceased precisely at 4 p.m. when the crossings began. 'Everywhere, the stunned, smoke-blinded French were quickly overwhelmed,' writes Williams. Sedan's defenders saw tanks appearing, and a panic ensued. They were French tanks retreating. On 14 May Guderian's tanks crossed the river and sped on to Sedan and surrounded it.

Thus by 14 May German tanks emerging from the Ardennes had pushed aside the thin forces in their way, pulverised the defenders and broken the front held by the French 9th Army. During that day French counter-attacks failed to dislodge them and air attacks on the bridges failed with heavy loss of aircraft. Reynaud telephoned Churchill in the morning of 14 May to tell him the grim news, and pleaded that Britain send more fighter aircraft.

The German armour entered Sedan and then sped westward, towards the Channel. On the morning of 15 May Churchill was awoken by another telephone call from Reynaud, who told him that the counterattacks had failed, that the road to Paris was open and that 'the battle was lost'. On the following day the Prime Minister flew

Leopold III, King of the Belgians, son of the heroic Albert II, exercised unusual powers in military matters under the Belgian constitution and masterminded his country's unsuccessful defence. A popular monarch at the outbreak of war, he was forced to abdicate in 1950.

Left: Prime Minister Churchill listens grimly as General Georges, one of Gamelin's senior field commanders, explains the parlous condition of France's army.
Below: French troops manning an anti-tank gun. Weapons like this were ineffective against concentrated German bombardment from aircraft, artillery and tanks.

to Paris to confer with the French Cabinet, accompanied by General John Dill and Major-General Hastings Ismay, who would remain at his side for the rest of the war. 'I have never forgotten the complete despair on the faces of Reynaud, Daladier and Gamelin as we entered the room,' Ismay later wrote. Gamelin showed on maps where the German breakthrough had occurred. Churchill asked about the French strategic reserves to plug the gap. 'Aucune' ('There are none'), Gamelin replied. Churchill promised to send ten more squadrons of Hurricanes, knowing that the RAF's fighter strength in Britain was only thirty-nine squadrons (a minimum of sixty squadrons was considered necessary for Britain's own fighter defence).

RETREAT IN BELGIUM

On 17 May the Allied forces in Belgium began their retreat to more secure lines. Major-General Alexander, commanding 1st Division, heard the order to retreat from his neighbouring division; he had received no orders from his Corps commander for two days. He was delighted to hear that he was now under the command of General Brooke of 2 Corps, who wrote: 'It was a great opportunity to see what [Alexander] was made of; and what an admirable commander he was when in a tight place. It was intensely interesting watching him and Monty during those trying days, both of them completely imperturbable and efficiency itself, yet two totally different characters. Monty with his quick brain. Alex ... completely composed and appearing never to have the slightest doubt that all would come right in the end. It was in those critical days that the appreciation I made of those commanders remained rooted in my mind and resulted in the future selection of these two men to work together in the triumphal march from Alamein to Tunis.'

By 19 May the British in the south had evacuated Arras and Gort, the British Commander-in-Chief, reported that the French 1st Army on his right had 'faded away' and that he intended to withdraw to Dunkirk and 'fight it out with his back to the sea'. This alarmed the Cabinet, who ordered Gort to withdraw south towards Amiens–Arras and link up with the French. On the same day General Giraud, retreating from Holland to Le Catelet, was captured by German units.

'BE YE MEN OF VALOUR'

On 19 May Churchill made his first broadcast as Prime Minister. It was memorable, and its closing words were a battle cry: 'This is one of the most awe-inspiring periods in the long history of France and Britain. It is also beyond doubt the most sublime. Side by side, unaided except by their kith and kin in the great Dominions and by the wide Empires which rest beneath their shield — side by side, the British and French peoples have advanced to rescue not only Europe but mankind from the foulest and most soul-destroying tyranny which has ever darkened and stained the pages of history. Behind them — behind us — behind the Armies and Fleets of Britain and France — gather a group of shattered states and bludgeoned races: the Czechs, the Poles, the Norwegians, the Danes, the Belgians — upon all of whom the long night of barbarism will descend, unbroken even by a star of hope, unless we conquer, as conquer we must; as conquer we shall.'

He then drew on the thundering lines from Chapter 3 of Book 1 of Maccabees from the Apocrypha. 'Today is Trinity Sunday,' he said. 'Centuries ago words were written to be a call and a spur to the faithful servants of Truth and Justice: "Arm yourselves, and be ye men of valour, and be in readiness for the conflict; for it is better for us to perish in battle than to look upon the outrage of our nation and our altar. As the Will of God is in Heaven, even so let it be."'

On the night of 20 May German tank columns passed Amiens, cutting off the Allied armies in Belgium, and headed for Boulogne.

WEYGAND AND PÉTAIN ARRIVE

France turned to its ageing heroes of the Great War to inspire the nation. The spry, 73-year-old General Weygand, recalled from Syria, was appointed to Reynaud's Cabinet and the post of Supreme Commander, finally replacing Gamelin. On the same day Marshal Pétain, aged eighty-four, was asked by Reynaud to join his government as Minister of State and Vice-President of the Council (cabinet). The French revered Pétain as the defender of Verdun in 1916, a commander who inspired his soldiers' devotion. Others knew him as anti-republican, fascist in his tendencies, and always a pessimist. On 21 May Weygand flew to Ypres to confer with King Leopold and stressed that the Belgian Army must fall back from the Escaut to the Yser. Next day Weygand saw Reynaud and Churchill at Vincennes, and outlined his plan for a joint British and French attack towards Bapaume and Cambrai with eight divisions; Amiens must be retaken.

The attack never took place. Gort, determined to retreat to Dunkirk and lacking confidence in the French, had attacked near Arras on 21 May with two divisions (5th and 50th) and his newly arrived 1st Tank Brigade. His seventy-four tanks stopped the SS Totenkopf Division and 7th Panzer, before they fell victim to the enemy's remarkable 88-mm guns (anti-aircraft guns that could be also used as field artillery). Four days earlier de Gaulle's division — barely 100 tanks — had delivered a similar sharp blow to the enemy north of the Aisne and he asked permission to drive north to link up with the armies in Belgium. His request was denied.

RETREAT TO DUNKIRK

Churchill returned to London on 21 May in buoyant spirits, impressed by the vitality of Weygand. He was sobered by Eden's record of a telephone call from Gort's aide-de-camp Lord Munster who informed him that 'the position was very grave', that the BEF's lines of communication were cut; he had had to drive two hours to the coast to make the phone call. He added that 'there was no co-ordination between ourselves and the French on our right'. Worse still, the French 'were not prepared to fight, nor did they show any signs of doing so.' On the evening of 23 May Churchill went to Buckingham Palace and informed the King that if the Weygand counter-offensive was not successful the BEF might have to be withdrawn from France. This operation, the King noted in his diary, 'would mean the loss of all guns, tanks, ammunition & all stores in France'.

On 23 May Gort ordered the two divisions in the south at Arras to fall back. Weygand protested this action. On the same night the British evacuated their forces from Boulogne and the Germans reached Calais, whose garrison Churchill ordered to fight to the last bullet. On the morning of 24 May Churchill cabled Reynaud, complaining that that there was no coordination between the British, French and Belgian armies, and that Belgian headquarters had received 'no directive'. That same evening Reynaud cabled Churchill that the BEF had 'carried out a withdrawal of forty kilometres towards the ports, which naturally compelled General Weygand to modify his arrangements'. In fact, Gort had set aside two divisions to assist Weygand's offensive but was receiving disturbing reports that 'the Belgians had no fighting spirit left in them' and that captured plans showed that the Germans were about to launch a tank attack at the point where the British and Belgian armies met — between Ypres and Menin. At 6.30 p.m. Gort made the final decision to retreat to Dunkirk, and use the two divisions earmarked for Weygand to plug the gap at Ypres, which was currently defended by a single brigade. Independently, in London Churchill had come to the same conclusion: the Weygand offensive would not materialise, and the British forces must retreat to the coast. That night General Ironside offered to resign as CIGS. 'Fortunately Ironside is gone and Dill who inspires great confidence is to take his place,' Churchill's Private Secretary, John Colville, wrote in his diary. The race to the sea had begun.

Map showing the territory conquered by German armies in less than seven weeks of fighting in France.

SURRENDER OR FIGHT ON?

The day of 26 May 1940 was to be a crucial one in the history of the war. In the morning Churchill informed the Cabinet that there was 'an odd chance' of evacuating 'a considerable proportion' of the BEF from France. Lord Halifax suggested that as there was now little chance 'of imposing a complete defeat upon Germany', it was now a question of 'safeguarding the independence of our own Empire'. He mentioned that the Italian ambassador had sought an interview to suggest 'fresh proposals for a peace conference'. Churchill replied that peace and security may well be achieved 'under German domination of Europe', but that it was a development 'we could never accept'. At lunchtime he saw Reynaud, who informed him that he could hold out no hope that France had 'sufficient power of resistance'. This was the first indication that France was considering an end to the war. In the afternoon Halifax again brought up the subject of peace negotiations, using the Italians as mediators. Churchill objected, stating that Britain must show Hitler 'that he could not conquer this country'. The cabinet minutes record that there would be no objection to approaches to Mussolini. Halifax endorsed this, stating that if none of Britain's independence was threatened 'we should be foolish if we did not accept them'.

This was the closest Churchill came to considering any form of peace negotiation. At 5 p.m. the Admiralty sent this signal to the Flag Officer at Dover: 'Operation Dynamo is to commence.' The evacuation by the navy of the British Army at Dunkirk had begun.

Gort's BEF began moving towards Dunkirk over roads clogged with refugees and French troops and transport. They were not troubled by tank attacks, and wondered why. On 23 May Hitler had ordered his Panzers to halt. The sandy flat land was not conducive to tank warfare, and he wanted to keep his armour intact for the next blow — the destruction of the French armies. The encircled Allies would be left to the Luftwaffe.

Exhausted Belgian troops rest by the roadside as a British lorry passes, May 1940. In 1914 the Belgian army had fought for two months before retreating into France and continuing the struggle. In 1940, facing a more murderous onslaught, it collapsed in eighteen days.

The British retreat was notable for am amazing manoeuvre by Montgomery's 3rd Division, which his Corps commander and long-time friend Lieutenant-General Brooke asked him to carry out. It involved Montgomery moving his entire division — 14,000 men — to the Yser, on the night of 26 May, across the lines of communication of three other divisions. 'It was a task that may well have shaken the stoutest hearts,' Brooke recalled, 'but for Monty it might just have been a glorious picnic'.

On 27 May Churchill conferred with his advisers to find out just what Britain's resources were in the event of invasion. Military defences were few and Germany might attempt to subjugate Britain by 'air attack alone' but they stated with confidence that the morale of Britain's people would offset Germany's advantage in numbers and matériel. The Prime Minister was also heartened by a telegram from the Australian Prime Minister, Robert Menzies, pledging 'the whole of [Australia's] resources to victory.' An Australian troop convoy was on its way, Canadian troops were already landing in Britain. Churchill noted: 'It will be a splendid episode in the history of the Empire if Australian, New Zealand & Canadian troops defend the Motherland against invasion.' On the previous evening Australia's High Commissioner in London, a former prime minister, Stanley Bruce, had taken a gloomier view, urging to Chamberlain that Britain ask Roosevelt or Mussolini to mediate a peace. Even Chamberlain was shocked when he related the story. At a cabinet meeting on 27 May Halifax again brought up the possibility of an Anglo-French approach to Mussolini to act as a mediator. Churchill and most cabinet members objected to the notion.

LITTLE SHIPS TO THE RESCUE

On 27 May the Admiralty began searching for smaller vessels, and boatyards were scoured for motor launches. 'At the same time', recorded Churchill, 'lifeboats from liners in the London docks, fishing craft, lighters, barges, and pleasure boats — anything that could be of use along the beaches — were called into service. By the night of the 27th a great tide of small vessels began to flow towards the sea, first to our Channel ports, and thence to the beaches of Dunkirk and the beloved Army.'

By 31 May more than 400 small craft, as if carried by some spontaneous emotion, were lifting troops from the beaches of Dunkirk and ferrying them to larger ships. The majority of troops were evacuated by Royal Navy destroyers from the long mole at Dunkirk but the role of the little ships lives in legend. Nearly 900 vessels reached Dunkirk to play their part.

At 10 p.m. that night Churchill hurriedly summoned the Cabinet to tell them that King Leopold of the Belgians had asked for an armistice. The Belgian Army laid down their arms at dawn, 28 May.

DUNKIRK: THE EVACUATION UNDER WAY

The Belgian surrender laid bare the entire western flank of the BEF. Around Dunkirk 200,000 British troops and 160,000 French were encircled and defending a wide perimeter. On the first day the navy had evacuated only 14,000 men. On 28 May Churchill met the other four members of the War Cabinet at the House of Commons. Halifax and Chamberlain again urged encouragement of Italian peace initiatives but Churchill growled that 'nations which went down fighting rose again, but those which surrendered tamely were finished'. At the meeting's end two dozen government members crowded into the room, where Churchill told them of France's plight and the grim position at Dunkirk. He told them that Britain must fight on, whatever the cost. 'I am convinced', he ended, 'that every man of you would rise up and tear me down from my place if I were for one moment to contemplate parley or surrender. If this long Island story of ours is to end at last, let it end only when each one of us lies choking in his own blood upon the ground.' They cheered him, and others rose to pat him on the back. Churchill was deeply affected. There was to be no more talk of negotiations.

On the following morning Churchill heard that 40,000 troops had been evacuated from Dunkirk. About 2000 soldiers were being taken off every hour, but every hour the situation in the bridgehead worsened. On 29 May Major-General Alexander despatched one of his officers, the Prime Minister's nephew Johnny Churchill, to London, to point out the need for smaller boats to help evacuate the troops. Gort had already sent his aide, Lord Munster, to London with the same message, and both young officers arrived next morning at 10 Downing Street at the same time, with the same message.

At 6 p.m. on 30 May Gort called a conference at the headquarters at La Panne, twenty kilometres up the coast from Dunkirk. Already 3 Corps had been taken off and most of 2 Corps. Now only 20,000 British troops remained, and 120,000 French. Brooke, who had been ordered to leave, handed over 2 Corps's command to his best divisional commander, Montgomery. Gort was to return to England; 1 Corps was to form the rearguard. Barker, commanding 1 Corps, was distraught and close to breaking down. Montgomery took Gort aside and begged him to appoint a 'calm and clear brain' to command the last men off. 'Put in Alex,' he said. Barker joined the group of senior generals returning to England, and next day Alexander found that he was commanding 1 Corps and responsible for evacuating the remaining British troops. He was told that 'troops of the French Army should share in such facilities for evacuation'; if worse came to worst, he was authorised to capitulate. Alexander had no thought of capitulating. His troops' discipline was holding. Many had lost their weapons or had thrown them away, but there was no sign of panic. German bombing of the beaches was a regular occurrence, but the sand absorbed most of the blast. The troops cursed their air force for its absence, but RAF Fighter Command was tackling bomber swarms before they appeared and some pilots were flying four sorties a day.

Opposite: 'Alex': Major-General the Hon. Harold Alexander, a son of the 4th Earl of Caledon, was the youngest divisional commander in the British army, and entrusted with commanding the rearguard at Dunkirk. He ended the war as Supreme Allied Commander, Mediterranean, and Britain's youngest field-marshal.

LAST DAYS AT DUNKIRK

Late on 30 May Alexander told the French Commander at Dunkirk, Admiral Abrial, that the troops were not in a fit state to hold on and that he was going to withdraw the British force at midnight because enemy artillery would soon render embarkation impossible. Abrial, angered, replied: 'I must point out that the last British troops will only escape because the French are still fighting.' Both commanders were apparently under a conflicting set of orders. Alexander telephoned Eden in London, and Eden ordered that British and French be evacuated on a '50-50' basis. Alexander agreed to delay the evacuation of his Corps until the night of 1 June. Alexander carried out the evacuation in his calm and unflappable fashion, impeccable in spotless uniform with its Guards cut, and remained another day. He cruised the beaches in a motorboat in the early hours of 3 June to ensure that no British troops were left and then boarded a destroyer for England.

Operation Dynamo came to an end on 4 June, 1940. A total of 338,226 Allied troops had been evacuated from Dunkirk — including 113,000 French. Some called it a miracle. Churchill called it a

Below: **The evacuation of the army from the beaches of Dunkirk, May 1940. From the painting by Charles Cundall in the Imperial War Museum, London.**

Left: General Sir Alan Brooke was another commander who emerged from the campaign in France with his reputation enhanced. He was commanding Home Forces when Churchill chose him as professional head of the British army and his principal military adviser late in 1941. Field Marshal Viscount Alanbrooke's wartime diaries are an important record of their turbulent but successful relationship in planning Allied strategy.

ordered the landing of another one in France. On 2 June Lieutenant-General Alan Brooke, who had reached England from Dunkirk two days before and had slept for thirty-six hours, was summoned to the War Office in Whitehall and told by his old friend the CIGS that he was to return to France to form a new BEF. 'As I look back on the War,' Brooke wrote, 'this was certainly one of my blackest moments ... To be sent back again into that cauldron with a new force to participate in the final stages of French disintegration was indeed a dark prospect.' He was told he would be given the 51st Highland Division, which was still in France, the 52nd Lowland, and the newly arrived 1st Canadian Division. He arrived at Cherbourg and on 14 June saw Weygand, who told him the French Army was disintegrating, and said that it had been decided to hold Brittany as a redoubt. But Brittany had no defence lines. Brooke's force accomplished nothing and was re-embarked as word of France's collapse came through on 17 June.

deliverance. They left behind 75,000 vehicles, 1200 field guns and 11,000 machine guns, or so Hitler boasted. The German Army had taken prisoner 1.2 million Dutch, Belgian, French and British troops. German losses amounted so far to 60,000, of whom 20,000 had been killed.

British matériel losses were enormous, but among the BEF's corps and divisional commanders who returned to England in bedraggled state were the future leaders of the British Army — Brooke, Alexander, Montgomery, Leese and Dempsey among them.

'WE SHALL NEVER SURRENDER'

On 4 June Churchill reminded the Commons that 'wars are not won by evacuations' and that despite the escape of the British Army, Belgium and France had undergone 'a colossal military disaster'. He ended his speech with a stirring challenge to Hitler: 'Even though large tracts of Europe and many old and famous states have fallen or may fall into the grip of the Gestapo and all the odious apparatus of Nazi rule, we shall not flag or fail. We shall go on to the end ... we shall never surrender.'

Having brought out one army from Dunkirk, Churchill now

THE SOMME LINE

The last phase of the Battle of France began on 5 June. It was over in five days. Having retreated to the Somme, the French armies, now reduced to seventy-one depleted divisions, were facing an enemy twice their strength and which included four divisions withdrawn from Poland and Denmark. This was France's agony and the fighting was severe. 'By nightfall', Colonel-General von Bock noted, 'the French were defending themselves stubbornly.' In the east, however, the German 9th Army reached Soissons and in the west Rommel's 7th Panzer Division had broken through, forcing the French 7th Army in the centre to withdraw to align itself with the new receding front. Rommel then swung west to the coast, trapping most of four French divisions and the 51st Highland Division on the cliffs of St Valéry, where on 12 June he took the surrender of nearly 40,000 men.

Right: 'Il Duce' (the Leader). Mussolini attempted to project authority and arrogance in official portraits but was quick to panic when events turned out to Italy's disadvantage.

Below: Mussolini, flanked by Blackshirts, reviews Italian troops, 1940. He attempted to instil in Italy's soldiers the mentality of the German army, but was not successful.

ITALY ENTERS THE WAR

On 10 June 1940 Mussolini declared war on France and Britain. For all his braggadocio he had tried to avert European war in 1938 and 1939, informing Hitler that Italy was unprepared for any conflict. He boasted of Italy's '40 million bayonets' and the number of his divisions, but he had increased the size of his army by halving the strength of his existing divisions and forming new ones. All except the Fascist Blackshirt divisions were under strength and lacking equipment; his light tanks made a flash show on parade but would prove useless toys in the mountains of the Balkans and the deserts of Libya. His generals reminded him that his army was not capable of waging war until 1942 at the earliest. The Italian people detested the Nazis. He left it to his embarrassed son-in-law and Foreign Minister, Count Ciano, to inform the Allies. 'It is a dagger blow at a man who had already fallen,' said the French ambassador. 'The Germans are hard masters. You, too, will learn this.' In his diary Ciano wrote: 'I am sad, very sad … may God help Italy.'

Italian forces made little headway against French defences along the snow-covered mountains on the French frontier, and Mussolini was robbed of a crushing victory.

They had better fortune in north Africa. In July Italian forces invaded British Somaliland, where the small British garrison staged a fighting withdrawal — any form of retreat angered Churchill. In September Marshal Graziani's army in Libya crossed into Egypt, its slow progress through the melting heat shadowed by British aircraft and armoured cars. By December it was comfortably camped inside the frontier but showing little inclination to proceed further. In Cairo General Wavell, the Commander-in-Chief, Middle East, seemed unconcerned, and laid plans to attack it suddenly, cutting its lines of communication. This he was to do in spectacular fashion.

FRANCE: THE LAST ACT

On 12 June Weygand, his armies now reduced to fifty-one divisions, ordered a withdrawal to the Loire. On 14 June German armies entered Paris. During the preceding nine days the French had suffered colossal casualties. France's military losses of nearly 100,000 killed and 200,000 wounded mainly occurred during the June days, when disorganised troops, moving along roads crammed with a million refugees and harried from the air, fought as best they could. Some units gave up the fight, but the losses they inflicted on the Germans (who suffered 150,000 casualties) showed that the battle for France had been a bloody one. British casualties were fairly light at 68,000, but the overwhelming majority of these were prisoners of war, and no official figures exist on the proportion who were killed and wounded.

The air war, an often forgotten aspect of the campaign, was intense: the Luftwaffe lost 1284 aircraft, the British 931 (of which more than 500 were fighters) and the French more than 500.

On 13 June Churchill made his last flight to France for four years. He knew that the French Army had reached the end of its will and ability to fight. Reynaud's government had established itself at Tours where Reynaud informed him that Weygand had recommended that France seek an armistice while there were enough troops to maintain order. He had appealed to Roosevelt for aid. On leaving, Churchill saw the tall, expressionless figure of General de Gaulle at the doorway and greeted him with the words (in French): 'The man of destiny'. De Gaulle, who had been called into the government by Reynaud on 6 June as an Under Secretary of State, said nothing. Churchill was comforted by one thing: he knew that Reynaud was determined to continue the war at Britain's side from her overseas Empire, and with her powerful fleet. Reynaud responded optimistically to Churchill's proposal of a union between France and Britain — 'the Union will concentrate its whole energy against the power of the enemy, no matter where the battle may be. And thus we shall conquer.'

On 16 June Reynaud faced a Cabinet that had already resolved to seek armistice terms. Weygand is said to have exclaimed: 'In three

French soldiers troop into German captivity, 1940. They remained prisoners of the Germans until the end of the war in 1945.

weeks England will have her neck wrung like a chicken.' To form a union with Britain, Pétain added, was like joining 'a corpse'. Reynaud was exhausted and dispirited. In the evening he advised President Lebrun to appoint Marshal Pétain in his place. Barely two dozen French deputies resolved to fight on by establishing a government in north Africa. They included Georges Mandel, Clemenceau's former chef de cabinet and Daladier. (On the signing of the armistice they were treated by the French as traitors.)

On the following day Churchill accepted the inevitable, and made a broadcast: 'What has happened in France makes no difference to our actions and purpose. We have become the sole champions now in arms to defend the world cause. We shall do our best to be worthy of the high honour. We shall defend our Island home, and with the British Empire we shall fight on unconquerable until the curse of Hitler is lifted from the brows of mankind …'

On 18 June, four days after the Germans had entered Paris, the new French government at Bordeaux began negotiations through the Spanish ambassador for an armistice. From London on that day General de Gaulle, who had flown from France the day before with Reynaud's permission, broadcast an appeal over the BBC for the French to keep fighting: 'Is the defeat final? No!' He asked the French to rally to him. 'Whatever happens, the flame of French resistance must not and shall not die.' Few heard his broadcast and even fewer rallied to his cause.

On 22 June the French delegation signed the armistice at Compiègne. They signed the papers in the same railway carriage in which Marshal Foch had dictated terms to the German emissaries in 1918. Hitler was seen in newsreels stamping his feet in delight. By the terms of the armistice Germany occupied northern France including Paris and the entire coastline from Belgium to the Spanish border. The French fleet was to be demilitarised, and Germany disclaimed any claim to it. The 1.5 million French prisoners of war would remain in German custody until the signing of a peace treaty. Several more clauses in the armistice terms reflected shame on the signatories: Anti-Nazi German refugees who were political activists were to be handed over to the Nazis (several were soon beheaded by the Germans as traitors) and any French citizen or soldier bearing arms for another country would suffer summary execution.

The Germans were to seize on this legal framework as the years wore on: in 1940 eight Frenchmen were shot by German firing squads; between September 1941 and March 1942 the figure had risen to 236, in addition to 353 shot as hostages in reprisal for acts of resistance by others. By war's end more than 40,000 French men and women, arrested as hostages, would be executed by the Germans and the Vichy militia.

'Unoccupied France' became the 'French State', ruled from the spa resort of Vichy, and the near-senile Marshal Pétain became 'Head of State'. A somewhat discredited political figure, Pierre Laval, one of the many who had been in the pay of the Italians for much of the 1930s emerged, and his first act was to lobby among the deputies still present to vote out of existence the once proud Third French Republic; this was accomplished on 10 July.

FRANCE DIVIDED

The two-thirds of France administered from Vichy maintained the fiction that it was independent, and still controlling a vast overseas Empire. But France would be an obedient vassal — and in some ways an ally — of Nazi Germany in the coming years, and only a handful of patriots, some of whom shared de Gaulle's almost mystic sense of France's destiny, continued to fight against the occupier. There was no act of organised resistance in France during the first year of German occupation. Resistance would slowly grow, as it did in the rest of western Europe, but it was not until mid-1942 that resistance groups became a force to reckon with.

France's position was unique: it was not only the oldest Continental democracy, birthplace of personal freedoms, but the only nation whose collaborationist government publicly announced their hope for a German victory, thinking that in the New Europe that was emerging France could play a civilising role. One recent French historian of this time of trial admits that of all European nations France, in terms of collaboration with Nazism, 'comes out at the bottom of the scale'.

'The years of occupation indubitably left a painful splinter in the memories of the French people,' continues Philippe Burrin, 'for a cherished image of France was damaged by all the compromising deals struck [by the Vichy government] with one of the worst regimes in Europe … The experience of the Second World War overturned the glorious image of the Great War …'

The world at his feet: Hitler stamps his boots in delight at the moment of the signing by France of the armistice, June 1940.

BRITAIN AT BAY

Britain now faced the threat of invasion. Prime Minister Churchill's energy astonished his colleagues. Civil servants viewed his arrival at Downing Street with alarm, for he was known to keep long hours, often working past midnight. They were not deceived. Yet soon he won their devotion. He often barked but never bit, and showed true remorse when his impatience was manifested. He appointed Clement Attlee, the Labour leader, as Deputy Prime Minister and the formidable former union leader Ernest Bevin as Minister of Labour. He appointed his friend the press baron Lord Beaverbrook as Minister of Aircraft Production — this was the only appointment that King George VI questioned, courteously reminding Churchill that the Canadian was a controversial figure. But Beaverbrook's energy got the aircraft 'out of the factories and into the air'.

In early June 1940 Britain possessed barely one fully equipped division to defend the English coast; the troops returning to France had left all their equipment behind and their morale was low. (The Guards battalions alone had returned with their arms and equipment, and their discipline shamed others.) War Minister Anthony Eden called for volunteers to form the 'Local Defence Volunteers' but Churchill found their title uninspiring, and named them the Home Guard. Comprised of male civilians and some ex-soldiers and led by retired officers, and armed originally with primitive weapons ranging from clubs to pitchforks, the Home Guard grew to a strength of 1.5 million. Churchill ordered plans be drawn up to set the Channel on fire if the enemy launched an invasion fleet. All placename signs in southern England were taken down to confuse any would-be invaders, but the measure served only to confuse travellers.

In June 1940, having already asked their chiefs of staff to present him with plans for an invasion of Europe, Churchill ordered attacks to be mounted on German-occupied Europe by small groups — he immediately thought of the Australians for this task — and volunteers were called for to form 'commandos', to be landed by ship or by parachute behind enemy lines. It was the beginning of 'Combined Operations', and he offered its command to his old friend from Gallipoli days, Admiral of the Fleet Sir Roger Keyes. Commando units began training in the mountains of Scotland. Their early successes were few but their actions did much to raise morale. As early as 22 June Churchill ordered General Ismay to take steps to form 'a corps of at least five thousand parachute troops'. It was the birth of 1st Airborne Division. Churchill instructed Hugh Dalton, his Minister for Economic Warfare, to 'set Europe ablaze'; a 'Special Operations Executive' (SOE) was formed to infiltrate agents into occupied Europe, to create subversion and sabotage behind enemy lines.

INVASION THREAT

When would the Germans invade? Churchill's advisers suggested that the most likely times would be at high tide, near dawn, on nights without a moon. It was not known whether they would drop poison gas. The civilian population of south coast ports should be evacuated. He decide that London would not be declared an Open City, as Paris had been; on the contrary it would be defended block by block. Churchill assured one MP that London 'would devour an invading army, assuming one ever got so far. We hope however to drown the bulk of them in the salt water.' His only consolation was the receipt of Enigma decrypts that Germany possessed only 1250 first-line bombers not 2500, and word that arms and ammunition were arriving from the United States to equip an army that still lacked adequate weapons.

On 14 July Churchill broadcast to the people, stating that 'we await undismayed the impending assault. Perhaps it will come tonight. Perhaps it will come next week. Perhaps it will never come … we shall seek no terms, we shall undertake no parley; we may show mercy — we shall ask for none.' And he urged the people 'to strive without failing in faith or in duty, and the dark curse of Hitler will be lifted from our age'.

When the Germans landed church bells would be rung to warn the populace, and the codeword 'Cromwell' broadcast to alert the forces.

'Winston': Prime Minister Winston Churchill photographed in 1940. Behind him can be seen his devoted wife Clementine, who shared his trials and tribulations through a long marriage.

THE BATTLE OF BRITAIN

On 18 June 1940, the anniversary of Waterloo, Churchill had spoken in the House of Commons of his determination to fight on, whatever the cost. 'What General Weygand has called the Battle of France is over,' he said. 'The Battle of Britain is about to begin. Upon this battle depends the survival of Christian civilisation. Upon it depends our own British way of life and the long continuity of our institutions and our Empire. The whole fury and might of the enemy must very soon be turned on us. Hitler knows that he will have to break us in this island or lose the war. If we can stand up to him, all Europe may be free, and the life of the world may move forward into bright, sunlit uplands; but if we fail, then the whole world, including the United States, and all that we have known and cared for, will sink into the abyss of a new dark age made more sinister, and perhaps more protracted, by the lights of perverted science. Let us therefore brace ourselves to our duty and so bear ourselves that if the British Empire and its Commonwealth lasts for a thousand years men will still say: "This was their finest hour."'

On 22 June France signed the humiliating armistice that left half her country under German occupation. For the next year Britain and her Empire stood alone against Hitler.

Right: The target roundel worn by all military aircraft of the British and Commonwealth air forces. The yellow outer ring was added to the red, white and blue during wartime.
Below: A flight of RAF Hurricane fighter aircraft.

ANOTHER PEACE OFFER

On 19 July 1940 Hitler offered Britain peace in a speech in the Reichstag, stating 'I see no reason why this war need go on …' The offer was rejected out of hand. 'Late in the evening', wrote Count Ciano, when the first cold British reaction to the speech arrived, 'a sense of ill-concealed disappointment spread among the Germans.' Hitler, the Italian recorded, 'would like an understanding with Britain. He knows the war with the British will be hard and bloody …'

In response to a Swedish offer to mediate, Churchill replied that 'His Majesty's Government intended to prosecute the war against Germany by every means in their power until Hitlerism is finally broken and the world relieved from the curse which a wicked man had brought upon it.' These words left little scope for misinterpretation. Hitler had already made plans for an invasion: Operation Sealion.

'Since England, despite her militarily hopeless situation, still shows no sign or willingness to come to terms,' Hitler directed on 16 July, 'I have decided to prepare a landing operation against England, and if necessary to carry it out.' Within six weeks more than 4000 barges, boats and freighters were to be requisitioned to transport the invading armies. All that remained was to secure control of the English Channel by eliminating Britain's air force. 'If, after eight days of intensive air war the Luftwaffe has not achieved considerable destruction of the enemy's air force, harbours and naval forces,' Hitler wrote in a minute to Marshal Göring on 31 July, 'the operation will have to be put off till May 1941.'

'Our fate now depended on victory in the air,' Churchill was to write. Much also depended on decrypts from Enigma and early warning of approaching enemy formations, and here England's radar system proved its worth. The RAF's fate now depended on Fighter Command's forty-nine squadrons equipped with fast, modern Hurricane and Spitfire fighter aircraft, known to history as 'the Heavenly Twins'. Both were capable of speeds exceeding 300 mph (500 kph). So was the German Messerschmitt Bf109 which was, in fact, slightly faster than either of them. The Me 109E could reach 374 mph against the Spitfire's 364 mph and the Hurricane's 327 mph. Hurricanes were the backbone of Fighter Command in the summer of 1940, though Spitfires were to eclipse them in fame. The twin-engined Messserschmitt 110 'fighter destroyer' was slow, and its losses would be high. The British aircraft were more manoeuvrable, quicker in the turn — a vital asset in close fighting — and better armed than the German, and they could stay in the air longer than their enemy, whose fuel would be quickly exhausted in prolonged flights and combat. More important than aircraft were the pilots, who could not be as easily replaced. Dowding's fighter pilots — his 'chicks', as he called them — numbered only 1300. Fighter Command included four Polish squadrons and one Czech. All would soon be in battle.

British factory production was increasing but on 1 July the RAF had only 463 Hurricanes and 286 Spitfires, and of these 728 aircraft only 591 were serviceable and ready for battle. They faced three *Luftflotten* based along the Channel Coast and in Norway numbering 2600 aircraft — including 1131 medium bombers, 316 dive-bombers and 809 single-engined fighters. Daily these figures would fluctuate as aircraft were lost or damaged, others replaced at a rate that makes the final daily computation of strengths and losses still difficult to state with accuracy.

FIRST PHASE

Most historians, however, agree that the Battle of Britain itself began on 10 July with German attacks on England's southern ports and Channel shipping; the first phase lasted until 18 August, its intention being to clear the southern coast and draw the RAF into battle. In July the RAF lost 51 aircraft, the Luftwaffe 127. In August British losses reached 367 and the Luftwaffe's 699 as RAF fighters began decimating German bombers, dive-bombers (both of them slow targets) and Me 109s. The day Göring designated as 'Adler Tag' — Eagle Day — 15 August, was the crucial mid-point of the battle: all twenty-two RAF squadrons in the south were engaged, yet sufficient reserves were on stand-by in the north to savage 100 bombers sent against Tyneside and destroy 30 of them. Total losses for the day were 76 German aircraft, 34 British. No air force, not even the Luftwaffe, could sustain daily losses of this magnitude.

SECOND PHASE

From 16 August onwards the Luftwaffe gave up its attempts to destroy Britain's vital radar masts — a fatal error — and switched its full weight on to the destruction of Fighter Command and its airfields in southern England. The conduct of the battle by Air Marshal Dowding, AOC Fighter Command, and his deputy, the tall New Zealander Keith Park who commanded 11 Group covering south-east England, has been described as ranking among 'the great defensive victories of the war'. In the last ten days of August the RAF lost 126 pilots. Park thereafter ordered a halt to pursuing the enemy over the Channel. Fighters were to concentrate on shooting down the bombers and avoid dog-fighting their fighter escorts. The Australian-born Richard Hillary scored his first kill on 29 August when his flight of eight Spitfires was ambushed ('bounced') by twenty Messerschmitts; he shot down one of them. He was to claim four more before being shot down over the Channel and hauled out, terribly burned about the face. He would survive, his face repaired by the New Zealand surgeon Archie McIndoe, to write the classic of air war, *The Last Enemy*, and become a symbolic figure of his time. Another Australian, Pat Hughes of Tumut, shot down fourteen enemy aircraft and was credited with a share in the destruction of three others before losing his own life: he was the top-scoring Australian pilot of the Battle of Britain.

Opposite: **Air Marshal Sir Hugh Dowding, Commander-in-Chief Fighter Command, masterminded the victory in the Battle of Britain.**
Inset: **Flight-Lt Richard Hillary, one of the 'aces' of the Battle of Britain. Shot down and disfigured by flames, he wrote the wartime classic *The Last Enemy* and returned to flying in 1943 when he was killed in action.**

BOMBS ON BERLIN AND LONDON

Hitler had so far strictly forbidden the bombing of London. But on the night of 24 August a Luftwaffe bomber accidentally dropped bombs over the East End of London. In retaliation Churchill ordered Berlin to be bombed and the following night a force of forty-three RAF bombers mounted the first mission over the German capital (eighty had set out but half of them got lost and failed to find the target. Their epic flight of 1200 miles (2000 km) enraged Hitler and elated the British public. Thus began, by accident, the bombing of British and German cities, a campaign that would devastate the Third Reich.

On 7 September, assured by faulty intelligence that the RAF was down to barely 100 pilots, Göring began the Luftwaffe's 'Blitz' to destroy the British capital. This was another fatal error, for the RAF used the respite from attacks on their airfields to repair the runways and bases and concentrate their strength on destroying the bomber swarms.

British Spitfires. Spitfires were outnumbered by Hurricanes in Fighter Command in 1940 but were even faster and more deadly than 'Hurries'.

THE CLIMAX

The German attacks climaxed on Sunday 15 September when their bombers and fighter escorts were assailed by 300 Hurricanes and Spitfires drawn from Park's 11 Group and Douglas Bader's five-squadron 'Big Wing' from 12 Group. On this day Churchill drove over to Uxbridge, 11 Group's headquarters, from where Air Marshal Park was controlling the movements of his twenty-five squadrons. In his memoirs Churchill wrote of the scene. He observed the central table on which the approaching enemy formations were mapped, as were the dispositions of the fighters being sent up to meet them. A row of light bulbs showed which squadrons were airborne. 'Presently the red bulbs showed that the majority of our squadrons were engaged'; soon all the bulbs were glowing red. Park telephoned Dowding, asking for three squadrons from 12 Group.

'What other reserves have we?' Churchill asked. Park replied: 'There are none.' The British squadrons were now having to return to their airfields to refuel, where they would be easy prey from marauding enemy groups. But then the map showed that the Germans were slowly returning to their own bases. Soon the table was clear. German losses for the day amounted to fifty-six aircraft. The British had lost twenty-six aircraft, but thirteen of their pilots parachuted to the warm green earth of England, to fight another day. The Luftwaffe's losses had become unsupportable. The British regarded lost pilots as more serious than lost aircraft. (British factories were replacing their fighters at a rate of 500 per month, against the enemy's production of 140 a month.)

Left: British magazines sought to keep up the people's morale with pictures like this, but Britain was vastly outnumbered in aircraft and pilots when the Battle of Britain began, and victory hung in the balance.
Opposite: Wartime magazine depicts German aircraft.

INVASION POSTPONED

Two days later, on 17 September, Hitler admitted defeat: A Wehrmacht order deciphered from Enigma informed the British that Hitler was postponing the invasion of England. The bombing of London continued, and so did the loss of German aircraft. The RAF was proving indestructible. Hitler had faced his first defeat. German losses by 31 October (when the Battle of Britain ended) reached 1,733 aircraft. British losses were half that number — 915 aircraft, and their fatalities exceeded 500 pilots.

It was freedom's battle. The RAF's 3000 pilots who flew in the Battle of Britain included men who burned with hatred for the Germans : 147 Poles, eight Czechs, 29 Belgians and 14 Frenchmen. They included volunteers from neutral countries: seven Americans, ten Irishmen. The Commonwealth nations were represented by 94 Canadians (they had their own squadron), 101 New Zealanders, 22 Australians (of whom 14 were killed), 22 South Africans (of whom nine were killed) and a Palestinian. These fatality rates were far in excess of the 17 per cent recorded by Fighter Command as a whole during this period. Forty-seven New Zealanders died in the combat over France and England. 'The Commonwealth provided some of the best and bravest flyers,' wrote Len Deighton in *Fighter*, 'and suffered disproportionate casualties'.

Though 80 per cent of Dowding's young fighter pilots were from the United Kingdom, their 'top ten' aces included a Czech (Emil Frantisek, who preferred to fly with the Poles and destroyed seventeen German aircraft; he enjoyed shooting down stragglers as they made for the Channel), a Pole, two New Zealanders and an Australian, Pat Hughes. Deighton reminds us that of the RAF's top eight aces of the entire war only two were English: 'Johnnie' Johnson and Neville Duke. 'The others were Canadian, Australian, Irish, French and two South Africans.'

One young British pilot, A.V.W. Rosewarne, wrote to his parents shortly before he was killed in 1940: 'Today we are faced with the greatest organized challenge to Christianity and civilization that the world has ever seen, and I count myself lucky and honoured to be the right age and fully trained to throw my full weight into the scale. You must not grieve for me, for if you really believe in religion and all that it entails, that would be hypocrisy. I have no fear of death; only a queer elation …

'The Universe is so vast and ageless that the life of one man can only be justified by the measure of his sacrifice. We are sent into this world to acquire a personality and a character … that can never be taken from us.

'Thus at my early age my earthly mission is already fulfilled. But you will live in peace and freedom and I shall have contributed to that.'

Churchill's words were equally eloquent. In his tribute to the pilots of Fighter Command he said, 'Never in the field of human conflict was so much owed by so many to so few.'

After the Battle of Britain Göring, always popular with the German people and something of a buffoon, never re-established himself in the Führer's favour. He retained the rank of Reichsmarschall and command of the Luftwaffe, but in Hitler's inner circle he was replaced by figures even more brutish and sinister.

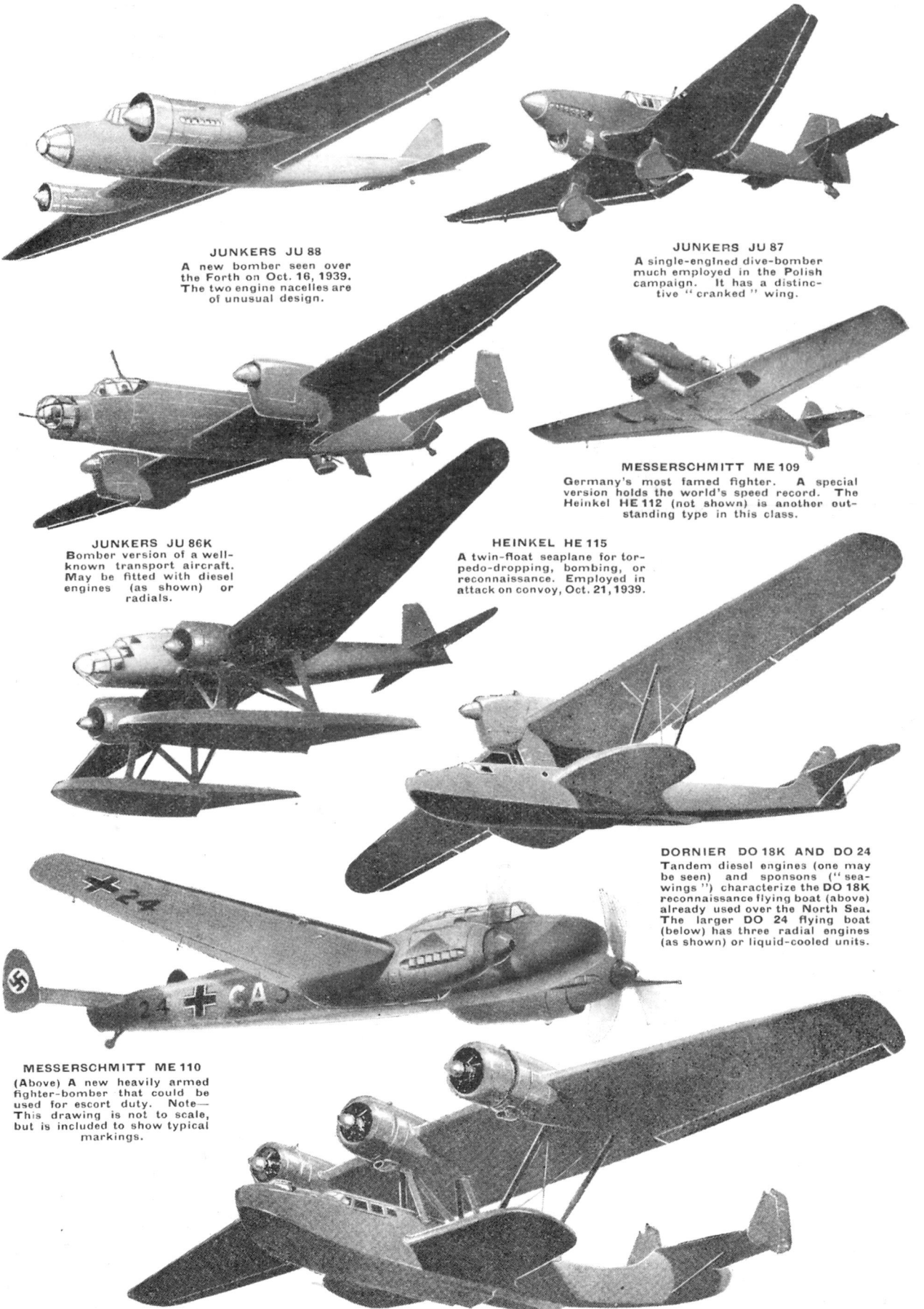

JUNKERS JU 88
A new bomber seen over the Forth on Oct. 16, 1939. The two engine nacelles are of unusual design.

JUNKERS JU 87
A single-engined dive-bomber much employed in the Polish campaign. It has a distinctive "cranked" wing.

MESSERSCHMITT ME 109
Germany's most famed fighter. A special version holds the world's speed record. The Heinkel HE 112 (not shown) is another outstanding type in this class.

JUNKERS JU 86K
Bomber version of a well-known transport aircraft. May be fitted with diesel engines (as shown) or radials.

HEINKEL HE 115
A twin-float seaplane for torpedo-dropping, bombing, or reconnaissance. Employed in attack on convoy, Oct. 21, 1939.

DORNIER DO 18K AND DO 24
Tandem diesel engines (one may be seen) and sponsons ("sea-wings") characterize the DO 18K reconnaissance flying boat (above) already used over the North Sea. The larger DO 24 flying boat (below) has three radial engines (as shown) or liquid-cooled units.

MESSERSCHMITT ME 110
(Above) A new heavily armed fighter-bomber that could be used for escort duty. Note— This drawing is not to scale, but is included to show typical markings.

The new French government. In front row (second from right) Marshal Pétain stands next to General Weygand. In the middle: Pierre Laval whom Pétain was forced by the Germans to appoint as his premier. On the left of Laval is Paul Baudouin, and on the far left, Admiral Darlan.

THE FATE OF THE FRENCH FLEET

After France's fall, one factor occupied Churchill's thoughts to an obsessive degree, and it caused him more concern than the destiny of the French overseas Empire: the fate of the French fleet. He was unaware that Admiral Darlan, who was a known Anglophobe and rose to great influence in the Vichy administration, was just as determined as he that Germany should never have the use of the fleet. Its main vessels lay anchored in Toulon harbour and were fated to be scuttled there in November 1942.

Churchill no longer believed French assurances. If the French fleet were seized by the Germans it would outnumber the British Mediterranean fleet and, if joined by Italy's modern warships, would overwhelm the Royal Navy. On 3 July Churchill ordered the British fleet to offer the French admirals at the naval bases at Oran and the commander of the French squadron at Alexandria a variety of choices: to join the British in the fight against the Axis; to sail their ships with reduced crews for British ports to be interned; or to sail to a port such as Martinique in the West Indies where they would be demilitarised under United States supervision; or to scuttle their ships. If these conditions were not acceptable, the Royal Navy would 'use whatever force may be necessary to prevent your ships from falling into German or Italian hands'. When the French admiral at Mers-el-Kebir base (Oran) rejected these terms Admiral Somerville's fleet opened fire on the French ships, sinking a battleship; two more battleships were beached; one escaped to Toulon, as did the cruisers from Algiers. Close to 1600 French sailors died. Only at Alexandria was bloodshed averted: after long negotiations Admiral Godfroyl agreed to Admiral Cunningham's request to demobilise his ships, which sat out the next two years of war with skeleton crews.

The act shocked the Axis leaders into the realisation that Britain had finished talking or negotiating, and was willing to go to any extremity to avoid defeat; but it poisoned French national sentiment against Britain and almost destroyed General de Gaulle's infant Free French movement from the outset.

DE GAULLE AND FREE FRANCE

A young French public servant and economist, Robert Margolin, was disturbed by the calm acceptance of defeat by his superiors and colleagues. '1940 is a date in the history of France which marks not only a military defeat without precedent but also, for the political elite with but few exceptions, a moral collapse of which I know no other example. As soon as I got to London I joined the Free French.' De Gaulle continued to appeal to the French to continue the battle. In a broadcast on 19 June he appealed for the governors and forces in the French colonies in Africa to disregard the armistice: 'Soldiers of France, wherever you are, rise up!'

To de Gaulle military collapse was one thing, supine acceptance of defeat another. The former governments of Poland, Czechoslovakia, Norway, the Netherlands, Belgium, Luxembourg had formed governments in exile in London; only the monarchs of Denmark and Belgium had remained in their capitals — the first because he had no choice, the second because he hoped to alleviate the suffering of his people. (This proved to be a misguided decision, for Hitler found Leopold obstinate and his speeches long-winded, and soon ignored him completely.) France had no one — except de Gaulle.

'All my life I have thought of France in a certain way,' Charles de Gaulle would write in the famous opening lines of his classic memoirs. 'This is inspired by sentiment as much as by reason. The emotional side of me tends to imagine France, like the princess in the fairy tale or the Madonna in the frescoes, as dedicated to an exalted and exceptional destiny.' If France fell short of his expectations it was attributable to Frenchmen, 'not to the genius of the land … In short, to my mind, France cannot be France without greatness.' He would endeavour to restore France to her greatness.

From his modest headquarters in London's Carlton Gardens de Gaulle set out to reconquer an Empire. His means were pitiful, his supporters few. Barely 1000 of the 100,000 French troops evacuated to England joined his cause; the rest chose repatriation to France. But slowly his followers grew in number. A young army captain, Claude Hettier de Boislambert, would later proudly claim to be the first officer to join de Gaulle; another captain, Pierre Koenig, who had fought in the Foreign Legion in Norway, also joined the Free French. In July a fair-haired, blue-eyed young officer, still wearing bandages from a head wound received in the fighting in France, presented himself to de Gaulle. His name was Captain Philippe de Hauteclocque, the son of a vicomte whose family traced their history back to the Crusades, and who had left his wife and young children at their chateau in Picardy to make his way to England. 'I settled his destination at once,' de Gaule wrote. 'It would be the equator.' In August Hauteclocque, who had taken the name 'Leclerc' to protect his family in France, left by aircraft with Boislambert and René Pleven (a future French premier) for French Equatorial Africa to rally the French possessions there. It was the beginning of one of the great personal epics of the war: Leclerc — de Gaulle's 'young and glorious general' — would later cross the Sahara, liberate Paris and lead his tanks into the ruins of Berchtesgarten, ending there his own crusade to restore France's lost honour. He, like Koenig, would become a posthumous Marshal of France.

In Indochina, General Catroux, a senior general whose admiration for de Gaulle had begun when they shared captivity together in a German castle in 1916, objected to the Vichy government's kow-towing to the Japanese and left for London, where he became de Gaulle's most respected senior colleague. In Somaliland General Legentilhomme also rallied to de Gaulle but was forced to escape to Egypt before the Vichy authorities arrested him. On Cyprus an entire unit of *fusiliers marins* declared for de Gaulle; in Syria Colonel Collet soon led his cavalry over the border to Palestine to join the Allies; all the young men from a fishing village in France sailed for England in a smack to join de Gaulle. From these small beginnings a mighty force would grow.

THE DAKAR FIASCO

Boislambert and Leclerc supplanted the administration of Cameroon and Chad in July–August 1940 with barely a shot fired. Churchill and de Gaulle resolved on another *coup de main* to bring over French West Africa to the Allied cause and gathered an invasion force with strong Royal Navy protection to seize the major West African port of Dakar. It was hoped that the sheer strength of the force would intimidate the French authorities. It included the battleships *Barham* and *Resolution*, the aircraft carrier *Ark Royal*, several cruisers and ten destroyers.

On the morning of 23 September the force, joined by the cruiser HMAS *Australia*, was off Dakar and de Gaulle sent Boislambert and emissaries ashore under a white flag. The Vichy authorities showed where their loyalties lay by immediately arresting them for treason, by rejecting demands for surrender and by opening fire from shore batteries. *Australia*, under heavy fire, sank the destroyer *L'Audacieux*. For the next three days the French and British exchanged fire and *Resolution* was hit by a torpedo. On 25 September the fleet withdrew. It was a humiliating defeat for Churchill and de Gaulle, who viewed Dakar's rejection of his overtures as a personal insult, and the British action further poisoned French feelings for the Allied cause. In Australia Menzies was criticised for permitting Australian participation in action against a nation for which Australians had a long affection.

General de Gaulle with Prime Minister Churchill in a portrait that captures their relationship. This was never free of a slight mutual suspicion, and yet it became one of deep regard.

THE SEA LANES

German use of seaports on the French coast dramatically altered the nature of the war at sea and losses of shipping to German submarines increased to crisis proportions In October 1940 the attacks, in one historian's words, became 'an unremitting massacre' — in that month Admiral Doenitz had only twenty-one submarines at sea but they hunted in packs and sank nearly sixty ships totalling more than 350,000 tons, an average never again reached. British convoys to and from America and Canada were routed around the north coasts of Ireland and Scotland. The British had little with which to combat the growing U-boat threat other than increased destroyer escorts and using flares to light up the scene during night attacks. But in that month the C-in-C Western Approaches (whose headquarters were soon moved from Devon to Liverpool) ordered the creation of 'escort groups' of up to eight warships. Warships and Coastal Command aircraft were soon carrying depth charges, ASV radar and VHF radio telephones and in early 1941 Coastal Command itself was placed under the operational control of the Admiralty. But aircraft could only patrol a distance less than half the expanse of the Atlantic, and the mid-Atlantic 'gap' beyond the range of British and Canadian aircraft remained critical.

Now the Germans introduced a long-range aircraft that hunted like a hawk. The Focke-Wulf Condor, originally designed as a long-distance airliner, had a range of 2000 miles (3200 kilometres) and

Above: A depth charge launched by a Canadian warship explodes.
Left: The U-boat 'ace' Captain Otto Kretschmer (lower right) and his officers and men.

could thus fly 1000 miles (1600 kilometres) into the Atlantic and attack shipping before returning to its bases in Norway or France. The Condors sank fifteen ships in their first month of operations. No British light bomber was fast enough to catch them or well-enough armed to tackle them.

From March 1940 surface raiders disguised as harmless merchantmen began to slip out of German ports, accompanied (from a distance) by supply ships and tankers, also masquerading as neutral ships. The raiders mounted hidden guns and torpedo tubes, and laid minefields, and they roamed as far as the Pacific, even sinking shipping on the Australia–New Zealand run. In August 1940 the raider *Orion* sank the *Turakina*, a freighter armed with a single 4.7-inch gun, in the first naval battle fought in the Tasman Sea. The deadly 7000-tonne raider *Kormoran* (which also carried an aircraft) was to claim Australia's pride, the cruiser *Sydney*, in a battle in which both ships were sunk, in the Indian Ocean in November 1941.

Late in 1940 German pocket battleships felt safe enough to venture into the Atlantic. Another passenger ship converted to an armed merchant cruiser (convoy escort) and well known in Australian waters, the *Jervis Bay*, encountered the pocket battleship *Admiral Scheer* in the Atlantic in October 1940. The AMC, 'like a mother hen interposing herself between her chicks and a marauding fox', gave battle, as the converted liner *Rawalpindi* had done with heroism when faced by the *Scharnhorst* and the *Gneisenau* in November 1939, and suffered the same fate; she was sunk by the *Scheer*'s 11-inch shells but her sacrifice enabled all but five ships in her 37-ship convoy to escape. Her Irish captain was awarded a posthumous Victoria Cross. When the *Scheer*, after nearly six months raiding in the South Atlantic and the Indian Ocean, slipped back into Norwegian waters in late March 1941 she had claimed seventeen ships, and had completed 'the most successful cruise of the entire war by a conventional surface raider'. The foray of the *Scheer* demonstrated the inadequacies of the Royal Navy at a time when its energies were concentrated on keeping open the vital Atlantic lifeline. In eighteen months of war the British had lost 5.5 million tonnes of shipping, two-thirds of this to submarines, and in return had sunk only thirty-six U-boats. It seemed a losing battle. By war's end the Allies would account for more than 700 German submarines, but the tide in the Battle of the Atlantic would not turn in their favour for another thirty months of constant and mounting losses, and many factors other than the courage of their sailors and airmen would be instrumental in winning their long-delayed victory.

Prime Minister Churchill inspects British troops, 1941. On the right is Major General Hastings Ismay. 'Pug' Ismay was Churchill's devoted personal Chief-of-Staff throughout the war, and his genial nature helped defuse many explosive situations between Churchill and the armed forces chiefs.

THE BRITISH EMPIRE AT WAR: THE PACE QUICKENS

The British Commonwealth's complacent attitude to the War was to change when France fell and Britain faced invasion. In Australia volunteers swamped recruiting centres, and there were soon four AIF divisions, all of them destined for long overseas service (6th, 7th, 8th, 9th). Australia also raised an AIF armoured division (which never saw service as a division overseas), and by mid-1941 had an army of twelve divisions — five infantry and two cavalry in the militia and five all-volunteer AIF. By war's end one million Australians were in uniform — an extraordinary effort by a nation of only seven million people. (Canada, with a population of 11 million, also raised armed forces of one million; Britain, with a population of 45 million, was planning on raising only 32 divisions). New Zealand raised two divisions for overseas service — the famous New Zealand Division under General Freyberg in the Mediterranean, later renamed 2nd NZ Division (implying that the 1914–18 division was the 1st), and 3rd NZ Division which saw limited action in the Pacific.

Australia, which had begun the war with 168 aircraft, most of them obsolete, was to end the war with one of the largest Allied air forces (the fourth largest according to some calculations). The Royal Canadian Navy by war's end had grown from six destroyers to a fleet of 471 fighting vessels, one of the largest of the navies, and Canada's air force grew to a strength of 250,000 personnel.

As in the 1914–18 war, Australian troops were the first Dominion forces to enter battle in spectacular — and rowdy — style. Their victories in Libya and in the defence of Tobruk in 1941 captured the world's headlines and crowded out the fine achievements of the two South African divisions, also comprised of volunteers, some of whom had driven the length of Africa to join the army in Kenya and the Sudan, helping to conquer the Italian empire in Ethiopia. In the Mediterranean and North African campaigns of 1941 and well into 1942, 80 per cent of the combat divisions in the theatre were drawn from the Dominions or from India and their major component was Australian (the 6th, 7th and 9th Divisions), with the New Zealand, the 1st and 2nd South African, the 4th and 5th Indian. By mid-1942, 25 per cent of all Middle East squadrons were South African.

The 2nd Canadian Division was fated to suffer 3000 casualties in its first action, the ill-planned attack on Dieppe in August 1942. By that date Canada had formed five divisions, two of them armoured.

It was not until July 1943 that 1st Canadian Division entered battle when it landed in Sicily; from that point on the Canadians were constantly in battle in Italy and formed their own Army in north-western Europe. Up to 100,000 Canadians served in Italy, and there were 6000 fatalities; 250,000 Canadians served in north-western Europe, among whom there were more than 11,000 fatalities. Canada's mortalities in the war totalled 40,000, just exceeding those of the two Anzac nations combined.

The issue of conscription had torn all the Dominions apart politically in 1916–17, and had served only to divide their populations. New Zealand solved the problem of forcing a Conscription Bill through parliament by simply ending voluntary enlistment in May 1940; thereafter all males of military age were liable for active service overseas. South Africa maintained all-volunteer forces which reached five divisions in strength, raised for service only on the African continent, but later sent an all-volunteer armoured division to Italy. Australia, proud that her armies in 1914–18 had all been volunteers, introduced conscription for overseas service in 1943 without domestic or political upheaval (Canada did the same in 1944). The war had transcended political differences and become one of survival.

THE USA

FROM NEUTRAL TO UNOFFICIAL ALLY

In May 1940 Prime Minister Churchill had warned President Roosevelt of the possibility of 'a Nazified Europe established with astonishing swiftness', and asked for increased aid, notably in old destroyers. As France was falling in June 1940 the President, facing increasing anti-war and anti-Allied sentiment in the United States — and with another election at year's end — could only respond to Reynaud's plea for help (June 1940) by saying that his nation was doing all that it could: 'This is so because of our faith in and our support of the ideals for which the Allies are fighting … I am, personally, particularly impressed by your declaration that France will continue to fight on behalf of Democracy, even if it means slow withdrawal, even to north Africa and the Atlantic …' When Mussolini attacked France soon afterwards, Roosevelt described the act publicly as 'a stab in the back'. Hitler responded by calling the President 'that Jew Rosenfelt' (the President had no Jewish blood, his name was Dutch).

When Churchill, as aware as Roosevelt that Britain's cash reserves were exhausted, asked to be given destroyers, the President hit on a solution — a deal. He would trade the old destroyers for 99-year leases on British naval bases in the Western Hemisphere, from Bermuda to Jamaica. 'Congress will raise hell about this,' he predicted, but in September 1940 he went ahead and announced it as an executive decision.

As the world scene darkened, Roosevelt announced that the nation must prepare, while reiterating that no power would draw the United States into war. In 1939 the all-volunteer US Army amounted to barely 300,000 men. It would later grow to a strength of eight million. In September 1940 Congress passed a conscription bill — 'the draft' — which called up 20-year-olds, chosen by ballot, for one year's military training. They called themselves the 'OHIOs' — Over the Hill in October (when they would be allowed to return to civilian life) — but Roosevelt next year extended military service to two years, dashing their hopes.

In November 1940 Roosevelt won re-election — this time by only 27 million votes to the Republican candidate's 22 million — but he saw the victory as endorsement of his foreign policy. He entered his third term already exhausted, and knowing that war was inevitable.

In correspondence with the President, Churchill spelt out Britain's straitened economic position. By November 1940 Britain had sold two-thirds of its assets in the United States; the Americans had been paid squarely for their supplies to Britain: the US Navy had even sent a cruiser to South Africa to pick up gold in payment of British Empire accounts. In November the House of Representatives passed Roosevelt's masterpiece: unlimited military assistance to Britain and her allies without the need for them to pay for it. Roosevelt explained to reporters in his genial way: 'We've done away with the dollar sign!' He called it 'Lend-Lease', explaining to sceptics that the United States was 'lending' equipment to the Allies, who would return it or replace it with goods of similar value when the crisis had passed. He fooled no one. America's industry was booming as never before as war production rose. He could afford to be generous.

In a nationwide broadcast on 13 December 1940 the President made clear his nation's role: America must become 'the great Arsenal of Democracy'. Over the next six months the United States moved closer to full engagement in its undeclared war on Hitler.

THE BLITZ

Following the accidental dropping of German bombs on London Churchill had ordered retaliation. On the night of 25 August 1940 a force of eighty British bombers set out to raid Berlin. Just a week later, on the first anniversary of the outbreak of war Hitler, angered by the British bombing raids, vowed: 'If they attack our cities, we will simply erase theirs!' For the next 57 days up to 200 German bombers each night bombed London. The first 'Blitz', as Londoners called it, lasted without let-up until 3 November. The bombing was indiscriminate. As RAF night fighters proved ineffective in the first three nights the city relied thereafter on its anti-aircraft guns and searchlights probing the night sky to pick out targets. Churchill's government moved to underground headquarters in their 'War Room', the basement of the huge concrete 'Annexe' that still stands near Storey's Gate adjacent to St James Park.

In November Göring shifted the weight of the German bombing to the industrial Midlands. On 14 November Coventry was devastated and 400 people killed in one night. Then Birmingham, Sheffield, Manchester and Leeds were struck. The dockyards and ports of Southampton, Liverpool, Plymouth and Glasgow received regular punishment. The people appeared to be coming through it well: the raids were dreaded, but morale remained high, though many would live with the fear and trauma of those nights all the days of their lives. London under bombardment reminded Churchill of a giant prehistoric animal, wounded, yet refusing to die. Cities — including German ones — would prove difficult to annihilate; even when buildings were destroyed, life continued; citizens emerged from their shelters when the 'all clear' sounded, the rubble was cleared; services were reconnected.

The Germans soon discontinued bombing under a full moon: targets were easy to locate but so were their own bombers, many of which were caught by anti-aircraft guns or the growing force of radar-equipped night fighters. They continued bombing well into the first half of 1941 in total darkness. Göring boasted of his secret weapon. When it was discovered that the Germans were using radio beams to guide bombers to their targets, the British first jammed them and then thought of something cleverer: they sent false beams which led the bomber streams off course. One enemy bomber landed in Devon, with the crew thinking it was in France. Once Dublin was bombed instead of Belfast. It was called 'bending the beams' (though radio beams cannot be bent), and it deflected the worst of the bomb tonnage from British cities.

In May 1941 the Blitz of British cities slackened off. Hitler began moving his Luftflotte to the east, prelude to his attack on Soviet Russia.

'The Blitz': British Air Raid personnel carry a casualty from a ruined house during a respite from the German bombing.

Above: The White Ensign of the Royal Navy, also flown by all navies of the Commonwealth.

WAR AGAINST ITALY

Italy's sudden entry into the war in June 1940 — like that of Turkey's in 1914 — transformed the quiet backwater of the Mediterranean and the Middle East into a theatre of operations, indeed the main theatre of war for British armies for the next two and a half years. For the latter half of 1940 there would be no land battles. The major threat to Britain's hold in the Mediterranean was Italy's large and modern navy and the major actions in 1940 would be fought at sea. Italy's fleet was powerful, possessing six battleships and nineteen cruisers alone, yet it lacked radar and sufficient oil and its tactics were dictated from Rome. It had 50 destroyers and 115 submarines. An equal threat was the Italian air force — the Regia Aeronautica — which had a strength on paper of more than 2000 aircraft, many of them based in Libya and in Ethiopia, which were garrisoned by large armies.

In the air and on land the British forces were barely adequate for defensive, much less offensive, purposes. The Air Officer Commanding-in-Chief (AOC-in-C), Air Marshal Sir Arthur Longmore, initially had 40 fighters and 130 other aircraft to face 400 Italian machines in Libya and 170 in East Africa. General Wavell's army was similarly outnumbered.

The collapse of France under the weight of the German offensives twelve days after Italy entered the war threw the entire weight of maintaining the link to Egypt onto the Royal Navy's under strength Mediterranean fleet. Its commander, Admiral Sir Andrew Cunningham, a Scot, would prove to be Britain's greatest fighting admiral since Nelson.

Cunningham's trump cards were his aircraft carriers, which helped to redress the balance. Against the Italian fleet Cunningham could initially muster only the carrier *Eagle*, four old battleships (only his flagship, *Warspite*, had been modernised), ten cruisers, twenty-five destroyers and a dozen submarines. He saw his assets in his captains and men. An irascible man who seldom gave praise, he paid tribute to them after the war in his memoirs: 'Their enthusiasm and devotion were beyond praise. I had reason to thank the system and tradition that produced such fine seamen ... Our ships might be old, and there was much that we lacked. Nevertheless, we had our personnel, and through that, we were able to forge a weapon that was as bright and as sharp as highly-tempered steel.'

Two ships of the Scrap Iron Flotilla: HMAS *Stuart* (left) and HMAS *Vendetta*.

Early in 1940 the five old Australian destroyers that comprised 'The Scrap Iron Flotilla' were the only destroyers Cunningham had, and he developed a special admiration for them and for their unorthodox leader, the legendary Commander 'Hec' Waller, RAN. 'The officers and men of these Australian destroyers out here are magnificent material and are quite wasted in these old ships,' Cunningham wrote to the Admiralty. 'Tovey has suggested that they might be transferred lock, stock and barrel to five new ships and used at home. They certainly are the most willing and undefeated fellows I have ever had to do with.' Events proved the change impossible. The Australians manned their old crocks through the next year of war.

Egypt, site of the great naval base at Alexandria, had been nominally independent since 1936 but a treaty clause permitted Britain to maintain armed forces there. While proclaiming neutrality, Egypt became the main base in the war against the Axis in the Middle East, and King Farouk and his court took obvious pleasure in any setback suffered by the British.

Britain possessed the two keys to the Mediterranean — Gibraltar in the west and the Suez canal in the east — and Malta, the island fortress in the central Mediterranean that would become the hinge on which victory hung. Malta's air defences at the outbreak of war consisted of three ancient biplanes that were dubbed Faith, Hope and Charity. Its harbour at Valetta proved an ideal base for submarines. Malta was to stand a siege of more than three years.

Cunningham was an aggressive leader. Within an hour of the Italian declaration of war he took the fleet to sea to 'trail his coat' in the Ionian Sea, the first of many vain attempts to entice the enemy ships out to give battle. On 22 June he faced the problem of a French squadron anchored in Alexandria that was now 'out of the war' if not hostile. Using all his powers of tact, Cunningham talked the French Admiral Godfroy into neutralising his ships on 7 July; thereafter they lay at anchor in Alexandria, inactive, until November 1942.

On 27 June 1940 Cunningham sent Vice-Admiral Tovey's 7th Cruiser Squadron, which included the Australian light cruiser HMAS *Sydney*, from Alexandria to rendezvous with an Egypt-bound convoy near Cape Matapan, in south-western Greece, and escort it in. Tovey's force sighted three Italian destroyers at 6.00 p.m. on 28 June and immediately engaged them; *Sydney* sank one of them that was already on fire while the other two made off.

BATTLE OF CALABRIA

On the night of 7 July Cunningham again took the fleet to sea, intending to meet a convoy 150 miles (240 kilometres) east of Malta. At 8 a.m. on 8 July a submarine reported sighting an Italian fleet 200 miles (380 kilometres) east of Malta, and thus 500 miles away. At 3.10 p.m., as the British fleet came under Italian air attack, a carrier aircraft reported the presence of two battleships, six cruisers and seven destroyers 90 miles north of Cunningham's position and the Admiral altered course to intercept them. Just after 3 p.m. on 9 July Cunningham's cruisers, in the van of the fleet, sighted the enemy and, coming under heavy fire from the battleships, hauled around to the north. Eight miles behind was Cunningham, flying his flag in *Warspite*, with the destroyers, and eight miles behind the flagship were the rest of his battleships, straining to catch up. The Italians turned away under cover of a smoke screen and *Warspite* scored a hit on Admiral Riccardi's flagship. At 4 p.m., after suffering another hit, Riccardi broke off the action and Cunningham ordered his destroyers to make a second attack. At 4.45 the Italian destroyers retired, joining the main fleet and leaving one of their number, *Zeffiro*, to lay a smoke screen. The *Zeffiro* became the target of every British gun and was quickly sunk. The fleet returned to Alexandria from the Battle of Calabria on 13 July.

THE CAPE SPADA ACTION

On 17 July 1940 *Sydney* was ordered to support the Royal Navy destroyers *Ilex*, *Hero*, *Hasty* and *Hyperion* on a sweep north of Crete. Unknown to them, two of Italy's fastest light cruisers, *Giovanni Della Bande Nere* and *Bartolomeo Colleoni*, had slipped out of Tripoli bound for Leros in the Aegean.

At 7.20 a.m. on 19 July the destroyers sighted the Italian cruisers off Cape Spada, Crete, and wirelessed their position and made for their lives. As luck would have it *Sydney*'s captain, John Collins, had decided to remain in the area, feeling that he should keep an eye on the destroyers in case they ran into superior forces. The Australian cruiser was only 40 miles (70 kilometres) away. He had no idea whether the enemy cruisers mounted 8-inch guns or 6-inch ones, but he ordered full steam ahead to the destroyers' position. He maintained radio silence. Accompanied by the destroyer HMS *Havock*, *Sydney* tore through the water at 30 knots. 'Meanwhile,' Admiral Cunningham was to write, 'we had intercepted the signals at Alexandria and I was

Opposite: The action off Cape Spada: HMAS *Sydney*, (foreground), chasing the *Bartolomeo Colleoni* with the British destroyers straining to keep up with her. From the painting by Frank Norton in the Australian War Memorial, Canberra.

on tenterhooks … All I knew was that the destroyers were being chased, and that Collins, regardless of the odds, was closing them at full speed. After that, dead silence.'

At 8.20 a.m. HMAS *Sydney*, speeding at an incredible 37 knots, sighted the enemy. At 8.29 a.m., with battle ensigns flying, she fired her first salvo at a range of 19,000 metres and by 8.35 a.m. *Sydney* had scored a hit on *Bande Nere*'s funnel and begun to register repeated hits on *Colleoni*, which by 9.25 a.m. was dead in the water. Captain Collins ordered a destroyer to sink her and chased the *Bande Nere* but the latter was too fast and *Sydney*, having expended almost all her shells, had to give up hope of catching her. She had suffered no casualties. It was a stirring action in a dark moment of the war. The Australian cruiser had emulated the action of her predecessor, the first HMAS *Sydney*, which had sunk the German raider *Emden* in a brisk sea fight at the Cocos Islands in 1914. The war correspondent John Hetherington, after interviewing her captain in Alexandria, described Collins, Australia's future Vice-Admiral, as 'of medium height and build, almost boyish, and with a great sense of humour'.

THE RED SEA

In August 1940 Italian forces advanced into British Somaliland, the tiny desert enclave on the Red Sea, and after a fighting withdrawal the small British garrison was evacuated.

The Red Sea patrol was a floating hell. In high summer the heat was oven-like; men's gums bled, teeth rotted because of lack of calcium; the shores were featureless, the duty monotonous. Italian bombers from East Africa periodically raided Aden and the six enemy destroyers and eight submarines based at Massawa were a constant threat to convoys steaming north to the Suez Canal. Two new Australian sloops joined Red Sea Force late in 1940: HMAS *Parramatta* and HMAS *Yarra*.

TARANTO

The Italian invasion of Greece on 28 October 1940 gave Britain a new ally, Greece, but placed another strain on Britain's Middle East commands. Convoys carrying aid and reinforcements to Greece would face an ever-present threat from the Italian Navy. Cunningham decided that if the Italian fleet would not come out, he would attack

it at its main anchorage at Taranto in southern Italy. He wanted to launch his coup on Trafalgar Day (21 October), but a fire in his carrier *Illustrious* forced a delay. Reconnaissance flights from Malta revealed that barrage balloons had been placed around the anchorage and nets around the battleships. His second carrier, *Eagle*, developed fuel-line difficulties possibly caused by all the Italian near misses. The attack would be launched by a single carrier, *Illustrious*, on the night of 11 November 1940, when the moon was suitable, while a force of cruisers carried out a feint by steaming into the Adriatic and creating mayhem.

Cunningham took his fleet to sea on 6 November — the battleships *Warspite*, *Valiant*, *Malaya* and *Ramillies* and the carrier and destroyers; they came under air attack but *Illustrious* moved off without detection to a position south of Cephalonia, 170 miles (270 kilometres) from Taranto. One of her reconnaissance aircraft reported five battleships in Taranto and a sixth was later reported entering harbour. When night fell *Illustrious* launched her aircraft. Two of them dropped flares over the harbour to illuminate the targets and they were followed by two waves of Swordfish biplanes carrying torpedoes. The battleship *Italia* was sunk by three torpedoes, the *Conti de Cavour* was hit by one torpedo and also sunk, the *Caio Dulio* was hit and sank by the bows. A cruiser and two destroyers were also damaged. '*Illustrious* manoeuvre well executed,' Cunningham signalled with understatement to Rear-Admiral Lyster in *Illustrious*. It was a stunning victory that altered the balance of naval power. First on the scene to inspect the damage in Taranto was the Japanese naval attaché, who forwarded a full report to Tokyo. The daring surprise attack was the model for the Japanese attack on the American fleet at Pearl Harbor over a year later.

In their Adriatic foray on the same night the cruisers *Sydney*, *Orion* and *Ajax* and two destroyers sank a merchantman and left another transport and a destroyer ablaze without loss — Cunningham called it 'a riotous night'. By sheer initiative Cunningham had gained time and temporary naval supremacy in the eastern Mediterranean.

AID TO GREECE

Italy's invasion of Greece in late October 1940 led to a fateful infusion of British aid. It was not enough to turn the stalemate in Albania into victory but it was enough to anger Hitler, who was alarmed at the prospect of British bases on the European mainland.

'On November 16 we saw five British cruisers glide into the harbour at Piraeus, edge over to the quays and disgorge several thousand men,' wrote an American correspondent in Athens, Leland Stowe. 'Those five cruisers made perfect targets for the Italian bombers, but Mussolini's air force was still busy waging war on women and children ... A tremendous throng of Greek civilians cheered the Tommies deliriously as they rode up to Athens singing "Tipperary" at the top of their voices ...' An officer of HMAS *Sydney* wrote: 'Our reception was amazing. Every piece of rising ground and every rooftop was packed with cheering Greeks ...'

1940: GREECE AND THE BALKANS

The war was spreading like a stain over Europe. Romania had clung to the illusion of a French alliance until the fall of France in June 1940 left her isolated and alone. In that month the Soviet Union demanded the return of Romania's northern province of Bessarabia, and also Bukovina. Mussolini had cultivated close relations with Romania, whose volatile people claimed to be Latin, not Slav — and also with Hungary, as counterweights to Germany's hegemony. Unfortunately, Hungary and Romania, both soon to fall into the Nazi orbit, were traditional enemies, and Hungary was threatening to go to war against Romania to recover territory lost to her in 1919.

THE ROMANIAN DILEMMA

As early as July 1940 Hitler had encouraged Romania, which was fearful of further Soviet demands, to invite German units into the country, ostensibly to train her army but in reality to guard the rich oilfields at Ploesti. On 30 August 1940 Hitler orchestrated an 'accord' by which Romania returned all of northern Transylvania to Hungary. It was signed in Vienna. Count Ciano recalled: 'The Hungarians can't control their joy when they see the map. Then we hear a loud thud. It was Manoilescu [the Romanian envoy], who fainted at the table.' More excitement followed. The Romanian people were outraged by the loss of territory and blamed King Carol, who so far had managed to keep the lid on the rising power of the local fascist party, the Iron Guard. On 7 September he was forced to flee his kingdom accompanied by several dozen trunks full of gold and jewels and his mistress Madame Lupescu, for long exile in Portugal. He left his young son Michael behind as King, a pawn in the hands of the clique that now took power. Their leader was General Ion Antonescu, whom Hitler soon came to regard as his most impressive ally. Hitler consoled Antonescu with the promise of rich new provinces in Russia when he attacked the Soviet Union, and here he kept his word. On 20 September Hitler ordered strong forces into Romania, where they soon established themselves, with no complaint from Antonescu. A loyal ally of Britain and France in the war of 1914–18, Romania was soon to be an enemy.

Thus was Hitler presented in one stroke with fuel for his armies and a vital, secure southern flank for his impending invasion of Soviet Russia.

Opposite: **In Berlin Ribbentrop announces the signing of the Tripartite Pact between Germany, Italy and Japan, September 1940.**

1940: THE TRIPARTITE PACT

On 27 September 1940 Germany, Japan and Italy signed the 'three power pact' that made the Axis an international phenomenon, one in which the three powers agreed to create a 'New Order' in the world. Two days later Japanese troops moved into northern Indochina, despite the protests of the Vichy French administration.

The pact was signed with great fanfare in Berlin, where Count Ciano found the atmosphere cool. On the previous night there had been five hours of British bombing. 'Even the Berlin street crowd, a comparatively small one, composed mostly of school children, cheers with regularity but without conviction. Japan is far away. Its help is doubtful ... Another thing that contributes to the depressed spirit of Berlin is the constant recurrence of air raids ...'

Another witness to the event, the American correspondent William Shirer, was taken by surprise by the pact: he had wondered why schoolchildren in the Wilhelmstrasse were waving Japanese flags. He had barely slept because of the week of British bombing, but, having grown to loathe the Nazis and dislike the Germans, he wrote: 'The British should do this every night ... The damage done was not great. But the psychological effect was tremendous.' He had spent the previous evening drinking with 'Lord Haw-Haw', William Joyce, a Briton who broadcast Nazi propaganda on Berlin radio. 'Haw-Haw can drink as straight as any man and, if you can get over your initial revulsion at his being a traitor, you find him an amusing and even intelligent man,' Shirer wrote. (Joyce was Irish-born but a British citizen; his place of birth did not save him from being hanged as a traitor after the war.)

On 20 November Hungary joined the Axis pact, and was followed five days later by Romania and Slovakia. Only Bulgaria, Yugoslavia and Greece remained outside Hitler's orbit. Even the Soviet Union intimated (26 November) that it might join the Axis pact but demanded in exchange too many concessions, including removal of German troops from Finland, and also that Turkey provide a base for the Russians close to the Dardanelles. Not even Hitler could fulfil this demand. 'Stalin is clever and cunning,' Hitler observed. 'He's a cold-blooded blackmailer.'

ITALIAN PLANS FOR GREECE

Mussolini was enraged by his fellow dictator's bloodless seizure of Romania. On 8 October Ciano was ordered to 'take action in Roumania to elicit a request for Italian troops. He is very angry because only German forces are at present in the Roumanian oil regions.' This was beyond even Ciano's powers, but four days later the Duce's anger had still not abated. 'Hitler always presents me with a fait accompli. This time I am going to pay him back in his own coin. He will find out from the papers that I have marched into Greece.'

Above: Hitler and Mussolini during their meeting at the Brenner Pass in 1940.
Below: Hitler greeted by Marshal Pétain at Montoire, 1940. Ribbontrop stands on the right.

Eager for a quick victory, Mussolini on 14 October ordered the invasion of Greece; it was to take place on 26 October. But on 17 October Marshal Badoglio told Ciano that he and the three armed services chiefs were opposed to the Greek venture. 'The present forces are insufficient ... All of Badoglio's talk had a pessimistic tinge,' Ciano recorded. 'He foresees the prolongation of the war and with it the exhaustion of our meagre resources.' The invasion was postponed two days.

Hitler guessed that something was afoot. To plan a Mediterranean strategy he arranged to meet the Spanish dictator Franco on the French-Spanish border on 23 October, and then Marshal Pétain and lastly Mussolini. Franco made so many demands in his high-pitched voice over a meeting lasting nine hours that Hitler for the first time in his life could barely get a word in and confessed afterwards that he'd 'rather have three or four teeth pulled out than go through the experience again.' Franco could see no advantage to Spain in entering the war. She coveted Gibraltar, but knew it was strongly defended; after the fall of France she had seized Tangier, which was not. Pétain, whom Hitler met the following day at Montoire, was more accommodating and put his signature to a bulletin stating: 'The Axis Powers and France have an identical interest in seeing the defeat of England accomplished as soon as possible.'

By now exhausted, Hitler met Mussolini at the railway station in Florence on the morning of 28 October to be greeted on the platform by a beaming Duce and the words: 'Führer, we are on the march! Victorious Italian troops crossed the Greco-Albanian frontier at dawn today.'

ITALY INVADES GREECE

Before dawn that morning the Italian minister in Athens had called on the Greek Premier, General Metaxas, and presented an ultimatum whose acceptance would have made Greece an Italian satrapy. Metaxas, caught in his dressing gown, replied simply: 'No'. The anniversary is still celebrated in Greece as 'No' Day. Italian forces were already advancing over the Greek frontier from Albania, but made little progress. Troops were too few, all were under-equipped, and they were soon faced by the rigours of the Greek winter. World opinion was outraged that Italy had attacked a small nation with barely a quarter of her population, and Greece's brave and successful defence delighted Churchill, who promised to fulfil Britain's 1939 pledge of aid. There was little to send apart from four RAF squadrons of Blenheims and open-cockpit Gladiator fighters which performed prodigies of valour in the bitter cold in the skies over Epirus and Albania in the winter of 1940.

HITLER'S PLANS FOR INVADING RUSSIA ...

Early in December 1940 Hitler approved plans for the invasion of Russia — its codename was 'Operation Barbarossa' — and on 18 December issued his top secret 'Directive 21' explaining that his objective was to conquer Russia 'in a quick campaign' as far as a line running from Archangel to the Volga River.

There would be three major thrusts into the heart of the Soviet Union. Finnish and Romanian armies would assist them. One offensive would advance into the Baltic states and then to Leningrad; the second, south of the Pripet Marshes would drive through White Russia (Belarus) and then swing north, trapping the Russian armies; only then would the drive to Moscow begin. A third thrust would advance through the Ukraine to Kiev. Romanian forces in the far south would advance to Odessa and along the Black Sea coast, prelude to seizing the Donetz basin industrial region.

The invasion was to take place on 15 May 1941. Hitler placed extraordinary reliance on both Romania and its armies. When the ultra-fascist Iron Guard attempted a coup in Bucharest in January 1941, it was repressed by the Romanian army and Hitler congratulated Antonescu on his vigorous action. The fascist leader Horia Sima spent the war in Germany.

... AND GREECE

Fear of 'the English' establishing bases and airfields at Salonika — as the Allies had done in an earlier war — which would leave the Ploesti oil fields open to air attack, and a need to help the Italians in Albania, led Hitler on 23 December 1940 to order plans be made for 'Operation Marita': an invasion of northern Greece, to take place on 26 March 1941, when the snows had melted and the ground had hardened sufficiently to carry his armoured divisions. Only northern Greece was the objective: he had no plans to absorb the entire country and its islands.

DECEMBER 1940

The dramatic year ended with astonishing news. The under-strength British army in Egypt had launched an offensive that by month's end had evicted the Italians from Egypt. At dawn on 9 December 1940 O'Connor's force attacked from their position south of Mersa Matruh and crashed through the Italian lines, while his infantry advanced along the coast road and his light tanks and armoured cars thrust inland. In three days, for the cost of 624 killed, the British captured nearly 40,000 prisoners, and drove the enemy from Egypt.

On 12 December Wavell cabled the CIGS in London, General Sir John Greer Dill, that the 4th Indian was to be withdrawn, 'leaving Western Desert to 7th Armoured Division and 6th Australian Division'. The following day Churchill cabled his 'heart-felt congratulations on your splendid victory.' How that victory was achieved, exploited and then cast away is described in the next chapter.

Greece's unexpected repulse of the Italian armies gave hope to many that the Axis advance into the Balkans could be halted.

CHAPTER 6
THE WIDENING WAR
1941

The deserts of Egypt and Libya stretch from the Nile Delta to the mountains of Tunisia. A great empty amphitheatre, they would be the principal British battlefield for the first two and a half years of war.

The British war correspondent Alex Clifford, who covered the north African war with his colleague and comrade the Australian Alan Moorehead, wrote of its monotony: 'You leave Cairo by the dead-straight, double-tracked motor road which leads to Mena. And there, the great pyramid of Cheops squats ... you quit the green luxuriance of the Nile Valley and swing out abruptly into the desert ... when you reach the coast you turn due west, and immediately you are in the desert proper ... a beige-coloured, slightly undulating landscape ... sometimes the scrub faded away, and there was nothing but hard, bare sand. Sometimes there were great ridges of stone. Always there was dust — dust as fine as snuff or flour which can seep through closed lips and eyelids, through any clothing ... And this desert was empty — uncannily, almost frighteningly empty.'

In summer the temperatures exceeded 50 degrees C in the shade, but there was little shade. In winter before the sun reached its meridian it was cold, and the nights were freezing. From March to May the hot winds — the khamsin — came from the Sahara, blanketing everything with a fine layer of sand. Water was non-existent. Yet occasionally the desert dwellers — the Bedouin — and their camels appeared from the sea of sand to the south, possibly from the few oases there.

'At Mersa Matruh, two hundred miles from Alexandria, we reached a shallow rise and for the first time saw trees. They were poor things — a few dusty tamarisks and a clump of sagging palms — but they were green. And among them were little white houses arranged in broad, straight, intersecting streets, a mosque and two hotels.' Beyond lay the blue Mediterranean. All desert towns looked the same:

straggling buildings on the water's edge. It was an alien landscape.

Italy had a formidable army in her African possessions. Fourteen divisions comprising 250,000 Italian and native troops were in Libya, and another 200,000 in Italian East Africa (Abyssinia, Eritrea and Somalia).

In Egypt the General Officer Commanding-in-Chief Middle East, General Sir Archibald Wavell, had a handful of divisions, none of them at full strength, all of them still undergoing training. As five regular British Army infantry divisions had fought in France, the garrison troops in Egypt and Palestine were formed into the 6th British Division. They were fine, well-trained regulars but they were never to fight as a division and after the arrival of the first Australians — also named the 6th Division — the British formation was renamed 70th Division (it would end its odyssey in Burma). Wavell's tank brigades, barely a hundred cruiser tanks in all, became the 7th (Armoured) Division — the only division that fought in the desert war from the opening shots in 1940 to victory in 1943. It was still known as the 'Desert Rats' when its tanks rumbled into northern Germany under Montgomery in 1945; one of the legendary divisions of the war. Wavell's mounted units of Yeomanry patrolling on horseback in Palestine became 1st Cavalry Division; they too were never to fight as a division, but many of their personnel were later to man tanks in the desert war.

Inset above: the leaping kangaroo, divisional vehicle badge of the 6th Australian Division, the famous fighting formation that fought in Libya, Greece and Crete in 1941.
Opposite: Australian infantry of the 6th Division listening to an address by their Prime Minister Mr R.G. Menzies near Benghazi, February 1941.
Opposite right: Young soldiers of the Waffen-SS, by repute among the toughest troops in the German army.

Thus Wavell's infantry divisions in Egypt and the coming battles in Libya and in east Africa were to be mainly Empire or Dominion troops. When the convoy carrying the first brigades of the 6th Australian Division and the New Zealand Division reached Suez in February 1940, Wavell sent the former into camps in Palestine because he 'did not want them running riot around Cairo' as had occurred in World War I. The 'Diggers' enjoyed their spell in Palestine where the Jewish settlers were friendly, the Arabs less so. Even the trees were familiar: they were eucalypts, which need little water.

In September the AIF moved to Egypt, where the 'Kiwis' were already based. The Australians were exuberant troops, as difficult to handle out of the line as their fathers had been, but tough soldiers. Their officers trained them hard: three-day route marches into the desert were common. Like the New Zealanders, they seldom mixed with British troops but always enjoyed contact with the 'Kiwis' even if drinks resulted in brawls. Yet there was to be little of the contempt that Anzac troops showed towards the British conscripts whom they fought alongside in 1917–18, for the 6th British Division was made up of English, Scottish, Irish and Welsh regulars. All troops entered the war against the Italians full of confidence.

THE HIGH COMMAND

The land, sea and air commanders in Egypt — Wavell, Cunningham and Longmore — assured Prime Minister Churchill of their confidence in holding the Middle East, provided that weapons — particularly aircraft and tanks — and reinforcements reached them. General 'Archie' Wavell was outwardly the image of an orthodox British general. Stocky and stolid, he wore a monocle, but this was to cover the loss of an eye at Ypres a quarter-century before. He was an intellectual with very unorthodox views on generalship. He wrote beautifully but seldom spoke; he had written a biography of his old chief, whom he idolised, Field Marshal Lord Allenby. During the war scare with Italy in 1935 the Egypt command had set up a 'Mobile Force' and begun reconnoitring the coast and desert. The coastal terrain was hard, like gravel, and solid enough to take tanks; the interior was a sea of shifting sand but it was found that trucks could traverse the dunes if tyre pressure was reduced. Wavell set up an unconventional unit from volunteers, equipped with Ford trucks armed with machine guns, called the Long Range Desert Group (LRDG), and Freyberg allowed New Zealanders to join it. LRDG became one of the most successful of the 'private armies' that roamed as far south as Siwa Oasis, the walled city made of sand, and ventured behind enemy lines, raiding airfields before disappearing into the distance.

Wavell had predicted the Italian advance into Egypt, checking its progress as far as Sidi Barrani, and was already planning a counter-offensive. In October 1940 he asked General Maitland Wilson (GOC British Troops Egypt) to examine the chances of an attack against the Italian forces in Egypt: 'The operation I have in mind is a short and swift one. taking every advantage of the element of surprise.' Wavell flew to London where he met Churchill for the first time. The Prime Minister found Wavell taciturn and impervious to demands for an immediate offensive. The two failed to establish a rapport.

Commanding 'Western Desert Force' was a soldier of genius, Lieutenant-General Richard O'Connor, a small bird-like Irishman gifted with an almost uncanny tactical sense. The Dominion forces were still not complete, so his strike force would consist of 7th Armoured Division and 4th Indian Division (like all Indian divisions, one-third of its infantry was British). The extended Italian front was to be pierced by tanks followed by infantry after a brief, sudden bombardment; the attacking forces would then 'fan out', cutting the enemy's communications, fulfilling one of Wavell's dicta: 'Interior lines at night are a general's delight.' He moved his army forward under cover of night until they were in position near Sidi Barrani. Two days later, on 9 December 1940, they attacked the Italian camps and within two days the enemy was in pell-mell retreat from Egypt.

Wavell's next objective was the port and fortress of Bardia, just over the Libyan frontier, and which was known to be strongly fortified. Wavell hoped the Italians would evacuate it. Three days later he informed London that 'the Italians have apparently decided to hold Bardia. It may be necessary to dig this fox.'

Marshal Graziani had suggested concentrating his forces further west at Tobruk but Mussolini ordered Bardia to be held, if only to slow the British advance. The 'impregnable fortress', as Rome Radio described it, was defended by 400 guns and 45,000 troops — more than double the number Wavell's Intelligence had estimated.

Bardia's outer defences were strong: 30 kilometres of blockhouses, minefields and barbed wire, and a major obstacle: a deep anti-tank ditch. There could be no tank attack until the ditch was filled in at certain points; the wire would have to be blown by 'Bangalore torpedoes'; it would be, initially at least, a foot soldiers' battle. The infantry were to be assisted by just eighteen British tanks — sturdy, slow Matildas that were so heavily armoured the Italian anti-tank shells bounced off them..

THE AUSTRALIAN VICTORIES

BARDIA In the early hours of 3 January 1941 the Australian attack on Bardia began. The first companies of the 6th Australian Division's premier battalion (the 2/1st Battalion, City of Sydney's Own — they carried the prefix 2 to distinguish themselves from their famous forerunner, the 1st Battalion of the 1914–18 war) went forward on a three-kilometre front, cheering, shouting and singing, their voices almost drowned in the noise of their own artillery bombardment.

Within half an hour they had seized and bridged the anti-tank ditch and then broke the wire and took the enemy posts before swinging north. Following them were the 2/2nd Battalion and the first tanks, which surged across 'the bridge' at 7.00 a.m. through the breach in the perimeter to sweep south; the 2/3rd advanced in their wake.

The entire 16th Brigade was now inside the enemy perimeter. Nearly two battalions of the 17th Brigade went in after noon. By nightfall the Australians were a kilometre deep into Bardia's defences. On the following day they were clearing the wadis to the south while

Above: A still from a newsreel captures the sight of Australian infantry running into battle during the attack on Bardia.
Left: Lt-General Richard O'Connor (left) with General Wavell the Commander-in-Chief, Middle East

others with their Bren carriers and tanks had reached the coast itself. Bardia fortress had been cut in two; 30,000 prisoners were in Australian hands. Italian gunners were still firing their field-pieces when General Mackay drove into Bardia in his command car, astonished by the sight of masses of Italian prisoners. All resistance at Bardia ceased in the early afternoon of 5 January 1941.

The Australians had lost 130 killed and 326 wounded; they had taken more than 40,000 prisoners, 127 tanks, 400 guns. O'Connor, originally so sceptical and impatient, signalled 'Well done, Australia!' From Blamey came the message 'You have abundantly justified the confidence I have always had in your qualities of leadership. By its success the 6th Australian Division has established the new AIF.' In London, audiences watching newsreels of the battle jumped to their feet, shouting 'Good old Aussies!' and the *Daily Express* described the Australians as 'the cream of the Empire troops and the finest and toughest fighting men in the world'. *Life* magazine, in its pictorial coverage, wrote of the 'big, rowdy Australians who carry horse-play to terrible lengths in war'.

CAPTURING TOBRUK The next objective, the port of Tobruk, was ringed by strong outer defences (nearly 50 kilometres of barbed wire and machine-gun posts) but was less heavily garrisoned. While the 7th Armoured deployed, distracting the enemy on the western perimeter, and the fleet bombarded the town, the Australians attacked before dawn on 21 January, on a six-kilometre front in the south. The sappers again bridged the anti-tank ditch for the tanks (now only twelve in number) and lifted the mines.

The Australians storm Post Eleven, an Italian strongpoint at Bardia, where the fighting was bitter. From the painting by Ivor Hele in the Australian War Memorial, Canberra.

Another brigade attacked just before 8 a.m. on 21 January, pushing north into heavy fire from Italian machine-gunners and tanks dug 'hull down' in the sand to serve as artillery. The Australians fought their way forwards and by dusk the eastern sector of the fortress was in Australian hands. At nightfall the exhausted troops were resting in darkness lit by the glare of exploding Italian stores and ammunition; the scuttled cruiser *San Giorgio* was burning in the harbour.

The end came on 22 January. Enemy positions were found abandoned and the Bren carriers rumbled into the streets of Tobruk without opposition. At Tobruk the 6th Australian Division had taken 25,000 prisoners and 208 guns; they had lost 49 killed and 306 wounded. Within five days the first British ships were entering Tobruk harbour to off-load supplies. The Australians continued their advance.

TO BENGHAZI On 19 January 1941 Hitler and Mussolini met to discuss the African disaster. For Mussolini, it was a summons more than an invitation, and the Führer, apparently disillusioned by his fellow dictator's grasp of strategy, asked him to bring with him his military advisers. For Mussolini, it 'was a protracted torture of embarrassment' but Hitler promised to send military forces to Libya to assist the Italians. In Rome three days later (22 January) Count Ciano spoke to Mussolini with equal bluntness: 'At Sidi Barrani they spoke of surprise. Then you counted upon Bardia, where Bergonzoli was, the heroic Bergonzoli. Bardia yielded after two hours. Then you placed your hopes in Tobruk ... Tobruk has been easily wrested from us. Now you speak with great faith of the escarpment of Derna. I beg to differ from your dangerous illusions. The trouble is grave, mysterious and deep.' Four days later Ciano left for war service and his candid diary was put aside for three months, which saw a further decline in Italy's fortunes and a dramatic change in the direction of the war.

The British advance continued, encountering little resistance. The 7th Armoured reached Mechili and the Australians entered Derna on 29 January to find the town evacuated by the Italians; their 17th Brigade entered Giovanni Berta on 2 February after crossing tortuous terrain but the Italians again had slipped the net. Barce fell three days later and on the following day, 6 February 1941, Australian troops entered an almost-deserted Benghazi in pouring rain after an advance so rapid that even the dynamic O'Connor was amazed.

The 7th Armoured, now charged with the task of cutting off the retreat of the main body of the Italian armies, was low on petrol, its strength depleted by mechanical breakdowns. But breaking all textbook rules, the British tanks struck across the desert and trapped the enemy at Beda Fomm where on 7 February they took the surrender of more than 20,000 Italians along with 1500 vehicles, 20 guns and 100 tanks. O'Connor's tanks reached the border town of El Agheila on 8 February, and there, at the southern end of the Gulf of Sirte, they halted.

'WE SHALL NOT FAIL OR FALTER'

On the same day Lend-Lease was approved by the US House of Representatives, and soon aid and munitions would be pouring into Britain from American factories. President Roosevelt's special representative Harry Hopkins wrote to Churchill: 'As I leave for America tonight I wish you great and good luck — confusion to your enemies — victory for Britain.'

Lieutenant-General O'Connor pleaded for permission to push on the remaining 800 kilometres to Tripoli, 'the glittering prize', and seize all of Libya. British Commonwealth forces had advanced 700 kilometres and captured 130,000 prisoners, shattering eleven divisions and destroying all Italian hopes of a conquest of Egypt. Australian troops had made a spectacular entry into the war, as they had on Gallipoli in 1915, and were destined to play a crucial role in the fighting in north Africa for the next two years.

On 9 February Churchill made his first broadcast for five months. After nine months of almost continual defeat, he was full of hope for the future, and it was one of his most memorable orations. He spoke of the 'mighty tide' of goodwill and aid that was coming from America and of Britain's growing strength, and reminded his listeners: 'In order to win this war Hitler must destroy Great Britain. He may carry havoc into the Balkan states; he may tear great provinces out of Russia, he may march to the Caspian; he may march to the gates of India. All this will avail him nothing. It may spread his curse more widely throughout Europe and Asia, but it will not avert his doom ...' And in words for American listeners he vowed: 'We shall not fail or falter; we shall not weaken or tire. Neither the sudden shock of battle, not the longdrawn trials of vigilance and exertion will wear us down. Give us the tools, and we will finish the job.'

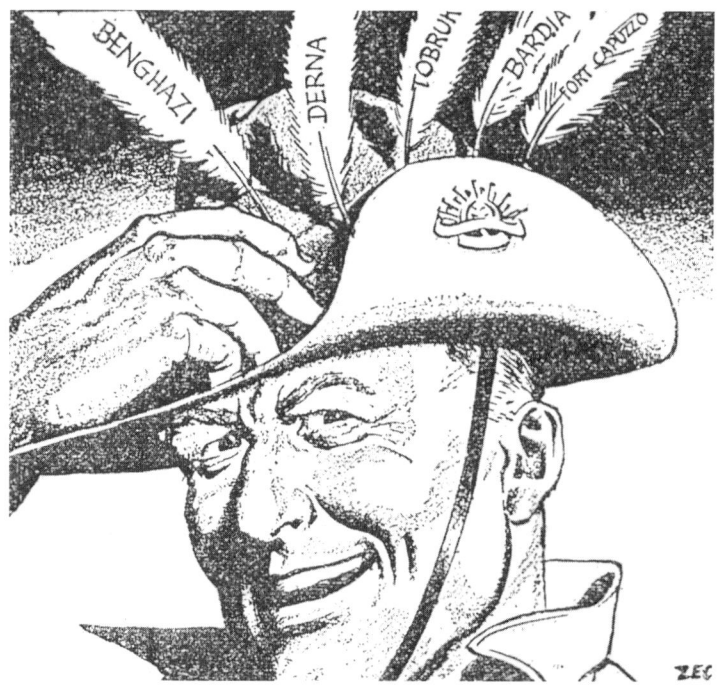

Above right: **The Australian victories in North Africa early in 1941 captured the imagination of the world.**

Below: **By mid-1941, after the German invasion of Russia, Britain had hopes that Germany would collapse under the strain of war. These hopes were not fulfilled.**

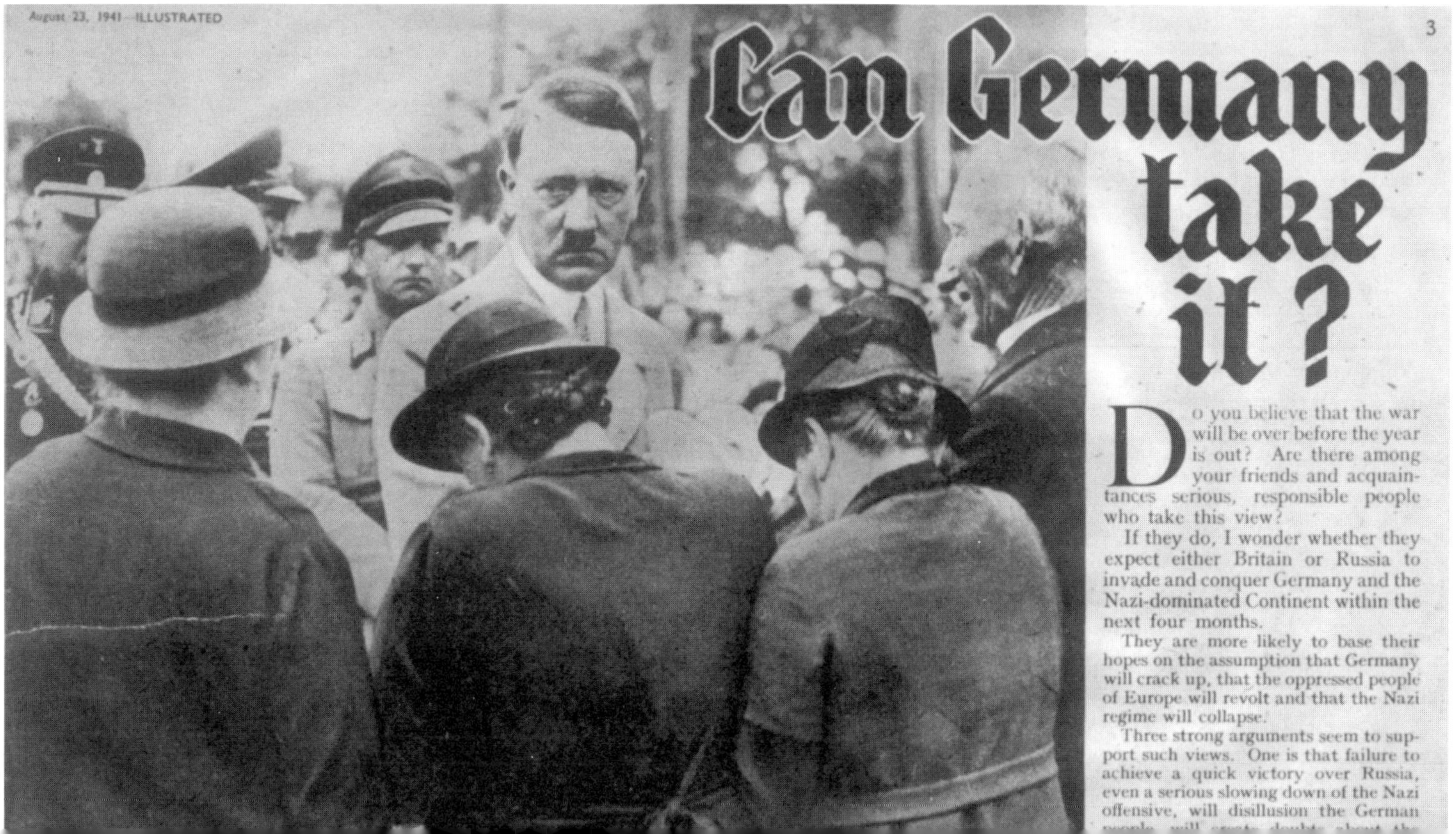
August 23, 1941—ILLUSTRATED 3

Can Germany take it?

Do you believe that the war will be over before the year is out? Are there among your friends and acquaintances serious, responsible people who take this view?

If they do, I wonder whether they expect either Britain or Russia to invade and conquer Germany and the Nazi-dominated Continent within the next four months.

They are more likely to base their hopes on the assumption that Germany will crack up, that the oppressed people of Europe will revolt and that the Nazi regime will collapse.

Three strong arguments seem to support such views. One is that failure to achieve a quick victory over Russia, even a serious slowing down of the Nazi offensive, will disillusion the German

A PAUSE IN AFRICA: AID TO GREECE

On the following day Churchill made the decision to halt the advance in north Africa and send forces instead to Greece. 'It would be wrong to abandon the Greeks, who were putting up a magnificent fight, and were prepared to fight the Germans ...' he explained to Cabinet. This proved to be one of the great strategic miscalculations of the war and his closest advisers voiced their concern. His private secretary, John Colville, noted in his diary: 'Desmond Morton told me there was great opposition to the PM's decision not to press on to Tripoli but to divert our effort to Greece and Turkey. In continuing our African campaign we had the practical certainty of winning all North Africa ... In forming a bridgehead in Greece we ran the risk of another Dunkirk. The CIGS felt so strongly about it that he was almost thinking of resigning.' In those rosy days, as Italy's African empire was collapsing, Churchill saw the chance to build a Balkan alliance against German expansion. On 12 February his Foreign Secretary Anthony Eden and the Chief of the Imperial General Staff (CIGS), General Dill, left for Egypt and Greece to assess the situation. Churchill, who was deeply fond of Eden, cabled Wavell in Cairo to take all precautions 'for safety of our two Envoys, having regard to nasty habits of Wops and Huns'. On that same day, Wavell spoke to the Australian Prime Minister Robert Menzies of a 'Salonika campaign' without mentioning that Australian troops would be involved, and was seen poring over maps of Greece, which had replaced those of north Africa. He explained wryly that he was 'preparing for his spring campaign'. Initially opposed to the Greek venture, Wavell, who had assured Churchill that the desert front was secure, was now an enthusiast for it.

Churchill's two envoys were delayed at Portsmouth and then Gibraltar by appalling weather and their flight did not reach Cairo for a week, during which much was to happen.

ROMMEL: THE DESERT FOX

On the same day that Eden set out for the airport and Menzies heard of the possibility of a Greek expedition, 12 February, General Erwin Rommel flew to Tripoli. He had flown directly from Italy and did not delay in assessing the situation. Just one week earlier he had been summoned to Berlin from his division in France by Hitler and appointed to command the German forces being sent to Libya, and the Italian motorised forces there. He was promised two divisions, to be called the 'Afrika Korps'. The 5th Light Division would reach Tripoli by mid-April, the 15th Panzer by the end of May. They were being sent on the understanding that Rommel would fight a forward defence, not hold a line around Tripoli.

Erwin Rommel was already known to Hitler. He had commanded the Führer's personal escort battalion in the entry into Czechoslovakia in 1938 and was regarded as a fervent Nazi, which he was not. He was apolitical, but extraordinarily ambitious. Born in 1891, he had won Germany's VC — the *Pour le Mérite* — on the Italian front, and had led the 7th Panzer Division in the French campaign, when he was marked out for higher command. He was a master of mobile warfare, ready to take risks, quick to respond to crises, sometimes disturbingly impetuous, and soon his victories and German propaganda would make him the nation's most popular military commander — the 'Desert Fox'. He was also decent and chivalrous, winning the admiration of his enemies.

At the end of the meeting Hitler showed Rommel some of the English-language illustrated weeklies featuring Wavell's victories, and the general found particular interest in 'the masterly co-ordination these showed between armoured land forces, air force and navy'. He lacked naval forces but he would use these same tactics against the British. Flying on to Rome and Catania, Rommel was informed that he would be under the overall command of Marshal Graziani but the luckless Graziani was relieved of his command on 10 February and returned to Italy in disgrace. Rommel soon gave up any idea of taking orders from his successor Gariboldi; he would fight his own war.

Rommel was depressed by the low Italian morale in Tripoli, writing 'most of the Italian officers had already packed their bags and were hoping for a quick return trip to Italy'. On the afternoon of his arrival he took off in a light aircraft and flew over the desert to the east, surveying the terrain and finding little or no evidence of a British advance. Returning to Tripoli that night he ordered Gariboldi to move his 10 Corps — the remnants of the Brescia and Pavia divisions — forward to the Gulf of Sirte, and also the Ariete, even though it was down to sixty obsolete tanks ('they were far too light and had only been used to chase the natives round Abyssinia'). Apart from a small force of Luftwaffe aircraft, this was all Rommel had to build on, and he asked the Luftwaffe to begin bombing raids. He ordered dummy tanks made and mounted them on Volkswagens to mystify British aerial reconnaissance. Two days later the first German troops began disembarking at Tripoli. On 17 February Rommel wrote to his wife: 'My lads are already at the front, which has been moved 350 miles to the east. They [the British] can come now.'

While Rommel was gradually building up his forces, and elements of the 5th Light were pushing forward, the British forces facing them were rapidly being reduced. The 7th Armoured Division had returned to Egypt, for its tanks needed repairs to their treads, and was replaced by the 2nd Armoured Division, but this was a division in name only, for it consisted of a single brigade of 100 tanks (another of its brigades had been detailed for Greece). The 6th Australian Division was embarking for Greece, replaced by the newly arrived 9th Australian Division, based in Tobruk with a brigade of the 7th Australian Division. Correctly surmising that only one brigade of German tanks was in north Africa, Wavell wrote on 2 March: 'I do not think that with this force the enemy will attempt to recover Benghazi.'

When Rommel struck, the attack came like a bolt from the blue.

General Erwin Rommel, Commander of the German Afrika Korps.

TO GREECE

A desperate year in the Mediterranean, 1941 began in the flush of victory. Prime Minister Menzies, on the first leg of a six-month overseas tour, attended a glittering victory banquet in Benghazi attended by General Blamey and his commanders. Mackay and O'Connor had both received knighthoods. In Wavell's own words, 'the minimum possible force' was defending his gains as he began the difficult task of reorganising his forces for fresh commitments, certain that the Axis force would require at least two months before mounting an offensive.

On 18 February 1941 Wavell informed General Blamey in Cairo that a force of 126,000 men — 'Lustre Force' — had been promised to the Greeks, and that it would consist of the 6th and 7th Australian Divisions, the New Zealanders, a British tank brigade and a Polish brigade. It would be commanded Lieutenant-General Henry Maitland Wilson, Wavell's trusted right-hand man. 'Jumbo' Wilson shared Wavell's dislike of Australians, whom they valued as soldiers but thought lacked the fine discipline of the British soldier. In return Blamey thought Wilson unintelligent ('not enough grey matter'). Menzies, who thought Admiral Cunningham was 'the No 1 personality I have so far encountered on this journey', found Wavell inscrutable and described Wilson in his diary as 'tall, fat and cunning'. When Blamey protested that the force merited the appointment of a Dominion commander Wavell replied that only 42,000 of the troops would be Australian or New Zealanders. Assured by Wavell that Menzies had approved the use of Australian troops, Blamey ordered the 6th Division to prepare for embarkation and for the newly arrived 9th Division (whose first brigades had been routed to England for a period) to take over the forward positions on the Libyan front. The New Zealander Freyberg later explained that he had simply been ordered to 'get ready and go'. In all 17,125 Australians and 16,720 New Zealanders would be committed to Greece. They would form the only combat infantry there and more than half the total number of troops sent before Hitler struck.

GREECE EXPOSED TO AXIS ATTACK

Soon events moved so rapidly that all plans — Axis and Allied — were thrown into disarray. On 1 March 1941 Bulgaria joined the Axis Pact, bowing to Hitler's pressure, and permitted the entry of German troops; by nightfall the Wehrmacht was on the Bulgarian-Greek frontier within a day's drive of Salonika. The entire north-east of Greece was now defenceless.

1941: THE BATTLE OF CAPE MATAPAN

British convoys to Greece continued unimpeded, but the Italian fleet remained a threat to them. On the morning of 27 March 1941, Admiral Cunningham recorded in his memoirs, 'one of the flying boats from Malta' reported sighting a force of four Italian warships south-east of Sicily and steaming in the direction of Crete. In fact, British Intelligence had learned from decrypting enemy wireless signals that a major part of the Italian fleet was already at sea. Among the fleet proceeding to the Aegean was the battleship *Vittorio Veneto*, armed with 15-inch guns and capable of a speed of 31 knots (the speed of a destroyer), and she was flying the flag of Admiral Iachino.

Knowing that the departure of the British battle fleet from Alexandria would be noted and reported to the Italians, Cunningham waited until nightfall before boarding *Warspite*, and leading his other battleships — *Barham* and *Valiant* — to sea, accompanied by the aircraft carrier *Formidable*. His light cruisers, including HMAS *Perth*, were already at sea. Twelve hours later, at 7.40 a.m. on 28 March, Cunningham recorded that one of *Formidable*'s aircraft reported 'four Italian cruisers' and some destroyers off Cape Matapan. The Italians soon encountered Cunningham's light cruisers, which were 90 miles (145 kilometres) ahead of him, and engaged them. Cunningham's battleships increased speed to join them, but *Warspite* had been limping at barely 22 knots because of condenser trouble. At about 11 a.m. Pridham-Whippell's cruisers, already under fire from 8-inch shells, came under fire from *Vittorio Veneto*. 'Our cruisers turned away under cover of a smoke screen and ran for it at full speed; but had a very unpleasant time, being closely straddled by 15-inch projectiles,' Cunningham later wrote. 'The situation did not look too good.' Cunning-ham sent *Valiant* ahead to the rescue of the cruisers and then ordered *Formidable* to launch her planes and to seek out the battleship. While the carrier executed manoeuvres to head into the wind and launch them he pressed on, asking also for bombing attacks to be mounted on the fleeing Italians from the squadrons in Greece.

At noon, just before he caught up with his own cruiser force, 'a RAF flying boat' (or so he recorded in his memoirs) reported sighting two Italian Cavour-class battleships and some heavy cruisers, which were retiring to the west (to Cunningham's relief the battleships turned out to be cruisers). 'We settled down to a chase,' Cunningham wrote, 'and it was clear it would be a long one.' Fortunately the easterly wind dropped and *Formidable*, rejoining the fleet, could fly off her aircraft into the westerly wind as she steamed behind in line. *Vittorio Veneto* was already damaged by *Formidable*'s air attacks and limping along at half-speed (15 knots), and was then struck three more times by the Fleet Air Arm. Determined to make contact with the enemy, Cunningham ordered his cruisers to catch up with *Vittorio Veneto* and her cruiser escort, at full speed, and made plans for a night battle.

At about 6.30 p.m. *Warspite*'s own spotter aircraft reported that the Italian battleship and cruisers were only 45 miles away. As darkness fell, Cunningham ordered his destroyers to attack them with torpedoes. But where were the other 'two battleships and cruisers' that had been sighted? Just after 9 p.m. Pridham-Whippell reported that his radar had spotted an unknown ship just 5 miles to port of him; an hour later *Valiant*'s radar reported the same. Just after 10.25 p.m. *Warspite* sighted two enemy heavy cruisers (*Zara* and *Fiume*) and 'a light cruiser' blithely crossing the bows of the battle fleet from starboard to port. Cunningham must have blessed the invention of radar, with which Italian warships were not equipped (nor, oddly, was *Warspite*). The Italians were within point-blank range — 3800 metres — when *Warspite* opened fire; at the same moment a British destroyer turned her searchlight onto the targets and *Valiant* also opened fire, and then *Barham*. 'The plight of the Italian cruisers was indescribable,' Cunningham wrote, 'and in a short time the ships themselves were nothing but glowing torches and on fire from stem to stern.' Minutes later he sighted three Italian destroyers, which had been following the cruisers, and one of them launched torpedoes. Cunningham's destroyers — *Stuart*, *Greyhound*, *Havock* and *Griffin* — now attacked to finish off the enemy cruisers and any sizeable ship they saw. The scene was pandemonium, lit by explosions and darting searchlights, and *Formidable* nearly received a broadside by mistake. The destroyers 'had a wild night and sank at least one other enemy destroyer,' the Admiral wrote.

At 11 p.m. Cunningham withdrew his battle fleet from the scene, but an hour later HMS *Havock* reported sighting another cruiser, the *Pola*, which had been crippled at dusk by one of *Formidable*'s aircraft. Cunningham's striking force of destroyers 60 miles to the west steamed back at full speed, took off the Italian crew and sank her. Fearful of being found in daylight by Axis aircraft, Cunningham called off the chase and set a course for Alexandria. When dawn broke the *Vittorio Veneto* had escaped but Cunningham was relieved to see that none of his eight destroyers had been lost. In the battle called Matapan, the Royal Navy had sunk three Italian heavy cruisers (*Zara*, *Fiume* and *Pola*) and two destroyers at no loss to themselves. One British aircraft had been shot down. The Italian Navy was no longer a threat to the convoys to Greece or to those that might have to evacuate the expeditionary force.

Sketch by a British officer on HMS *Havock* of the Italian cruiser *Pola* under attack in the night battle of Matapan.

Prince Paul, Regent of Yugoslavia, inspecting troops in Belgrade with his ward, the future King Peter.

On 4 March Hitler warned the Yugoslav regent that his kingdom risked destruction if it resisted joining the Axis. General Wilson, disguised in civilian clothes, arrived in Athens to find the Greek government and the Commander-in-Chief, Papagos, depressed and 'defeatist' at the possibility of a German invasion from Bulgaria. Reluctant to withdraw forces from the Bulgarian frontier to a more easily defended line running from Vermion to Mount Olympus — the destination of Lustre Force — the Greeks compromised, detaching three of their divisions to guard the British flank.

On the following day, 5 March, Blamey wrote to Menzies of his grave doubts about the Greek venture. 'The whole of the fighting troops are Australian and New Zealand. It is clear that, broadly speaking, the fighting is the function of the Dominion troops while supply and Lines of Communication is the main function of the British. Past experience has taught me to look with misgiving on a situation where British leaders have control of considerable bodies of first-class Dominion troops while Dominion commanders are excluded from all responsibility in control, planning and policy.' One day earlier Churchill had cabled to Eden: 'I feel very much the fact that we are not using a single British division.' Blamey was also puzzled by the absence of British formations. In February he had been told that Britain intended sending a total of 14 divisions to the Middle East during the course of 1941 — a division a month; but only one British division — the 50th Northumbrian — would reach the desert army before year's end. As in Greece, Dominion divisions would bear the brunt of combat in the Middle East until the end of 1942.

On 7 March the first echelons of Lustre reached Greece — the New Zealanders, all of them jubilant at the thought of action after a year of training and an end to jibes that their fern-leaf emblem was regarded by Hitler as 'an olive branch of peace'. Over the next four weeks they and the 6th Australian Division landed and moved north to take up positions on the Yugoslav frontier, warmed by the sight of Greece in the spring and by the welcome given by the Greeks.

GREEK CONCERNS

Greece was exhausted from four months of war. All feared a German invasion as a result of the landing of a British force. The higher ranks of the Greek Army were riddled with right-wing officers who had great contempt for the Italians but blind admiration for the Nazis. Metaxas had imposed a semi-fascist regime in Greece in 1936, and had called back the exiled King George to give his government legitimacy. His regime was little different from Italy's, except that it was pro-British. Metaxas had died and his successor was more democrat than dictator.

On 22 March 1941 Churchill cabled an impassioned plea to the Yugoslav Premier. 'If Yugoslavia and Turkey stand together with Greece, and with all the aid that the British Empire can give, the German curse will be stayed and final victory will be won.' He encouraged his ambassador in Belgrade to use as much influence as possible to cultivate resistance to Axis demands. Yugoslavia's regent, Prince Paul, the younger brother of the murdered King Alexander, was Anglophile, but known to Churchill as 'Prince Palsy', a socialite and a weakling, sure to choose the line of least resistance. The extent of the activities of the British Secret Service in Yugoslavia is still not known, but they soon bore fruit.

On 25 March the Yugoslav delegates, summoned like errant schoolboys to sign the Axis Pact, arrived in Vienna to sign it. Greece appeared doomed. Anger in Yugoslavia at their action was loud. In Belgrade the German ambassador's car was stoned. But on the following day, 26 March 1941, an extraordinary event occurred — extraordinary to all who did not understand the mercurial, volatile and often violent nature of the Serbs. Serbian officers led by the air force commander, General Simovich, took over in Belgrade. Troops occupied all government buildings and the radio station, which broadcast the news that the government had been replaced and that the boy, Prince Peter, was now King Peter II. The new government assured Hitler that there would be no change in the relations between the two countries.

'I thought it was a joke,' Hitler later confided, when the news of the Belgrade coup was brought to him. In a fury, he ruthlessly ordered the Wehrmacht 'to destroy Yugoslavia as national unit ... with unmerciful harshness.' The attack on both Yugoslavia and Greece was to take place on 6 April. On the night of 2 April German troops entered Hungary, whose Premier, Count Teleki, overcome by shame, shot himself. On the following day German plans to divide Yugoslavia were finalised — Croatia would form a separate state, to be ruled by the arch-terrorist Ante Pavelic. The rest of the hapless kingdom would be shared between Germany, Italy, Bulgaria and Hungary. Even Romania was offered a slice, and her troops were to be the only ones to enter without committing atrocities.

Because of the dislocation to his plans for the attack on Russia, 'Barbarossa' would be postponed from 15 May to 22 June. It was the single most calamitous decision of Hitler's bloodthirsty career. He would later rue the fact that his offensive to take Moscow before the snows fell failed by 'just six weeks' — the six weeks that the Balkans campaign consumed.

Churchill greeted news of the Belgrade revolt with delight but all attempts by Eden and Dill to bring Yugoslavia into a military pact with Greece foundered on Belgrade's well-founded fears of German retaliation. Disaster loomed for the Anzac forces in Greece. Fortunately, evacuation plans had already been worked out.

Wavell had decided that no further troops would be sent to Greece, for the desert front was crumbling under Rommel's offensive. On 4 April Rommel's forces had entered Benghazi and the British forces were retreating to Tobruk and even further east.

Shadow over the Balkans: a German Stuka above the Yugoslav capital of Belgrade just before the city was bombed. Below winds the Danube River.

THE FALL OF YUGOSLAVIA

A German army in Bulgaria under Field Marshal Wilhelm List was about to launch Operation Marita into northern Greece when the Yugoslav coup came. He had command of 15 Panzer Corps, 13 Mountain Corps and 30 Infantry Corps, and was awaiting 50 Corps (three infantry divisions). His fifteen divisions were now to strike west into southern Yugoslavia on the first day, while in Austria, Colonel-General Baron von Weich's ten divisions stood poised. The Wehrmacht was using excessive force to crush a country that had not yet mobilised.

On the morning of 6 April 1941 the Luftwaffe bombed Belgrade without declaration of war or warning, causing enormous civilian loss of life. (The young Austrian-born *Luftflotte* commander, General Loehr, was later executed by the Yugoslavs for this deed and other war crimes.) In the north Weich's troops broke through the frontier defences on the first day and took Zagreb on 11 April; on 13 April one of his columns entered Belgrade; on 15 April he received the surrender of the disintegrating Yugoslav armies at Sarajevo.

List's army took Strumica by nightfall on 6 April. They faced a strong resistance from Greek forts but reached Salonika on 9 April and forced the surrender of the Greek Thrace armies next day. Not wishing to be delayed by masses of prisoners, List ordered the Greeks disarmed and dispersed to their homes. His decision was endorsed by Hitler who admired the Greeks to excess, and released many of their officers under parole, as he had done with the Dutch. Ahead lay tougher fighting against the Anzacs.

Above: **Yugoslav soldiers are rounded up by German troops, April 1941.**
Right: **Field Marshal List who directed the German campaign in the Balkans.**

The Yugoslav government had fled but on 18 April the Yugoslav armed forces surrendered. German fatalities in the brief campaign numbered just 151. Some Yugoslav officers refused to surrender and took to the mountains to fight as partisans — the 'Chetniks' (an old Serb name for armed bands).

Yugoslavia was still alive when it was dismembered. The surgery was rapid and painful. On 25 April, a cold and blustery day, Count Ciano was in Ljubliana. 'The people have a distraught air but are not hostile. I see Pavelic, surrounded by his band of cut-throats …' Slovenia was divided between Germany and Italy, and a functionary told him 'the German treatment of the population is actually worse than cruel. Armed robberies and killings occur every day. Churches and convents are looted and closed.'

THE FALL OF GREECE

On the day war came to the Balkans, Wilson from his headquarters at Katerini told Blamey and Freyberg that the 7th Australian Division and the Poles were being retained in Egypt. Stranded high in the snow-capped mountains north of Thessaly, two Anzac divisions and a brigade of 100 British tanks supported by barely 80 airworthy RAF aircraft faced an avalanche of ten German divisions and an entire *Luftflotte* of 1000 aircraft. On the same night German bombers raiding Piraeus wrecked the port by a lucky hit on the transport *Ian Fraser* which was carrying 200 tonnes of TNT; eleven other ships were also sunk. Greece's main port was now unusable.

On 8 April 1941 the SS 'Adolf Hitler' Regiment was ordered to advance into Greece through the Monastir Gap. This motorised formation, recruited from the cream of Hitler Youth and formed originally as the Führer's black-coated personal bodyguard, would be the first Nazi formation to meet Anzac fire in Macedonia. Snow fell on the Anzac lines on the evening of 9 April and at dawn the next day the freezing troops looked down from their positions on a stream of Greek and Yugoslav refugees moving down the Vevi Valley south of Monastir. Next day the Germans took the Monaster Gap and poured south.

The sudden collapse of Yugoslavia had already made the Vermion–Vevi line untenable. At 2 p.m. Wilson and Mackay ordered a withdrawal south to the Olympus–Aliakmon line; for the 16th Brigade this meant a nightmare 50-kilometre trek over mountains 1000 metres high.

On the morning of 11 April, Australian battalions and British tanks fought off German tanks and infantry before retreating for the loss of sixteen anti-tank guns. Next day, at Ptolemais, the enemy destroyed thirty-two British tanks, and lost only four tanks in the process. The mist had now cleared, leaving the skies open to the Luftwaffe. On 13 April, the fourteen Greek divisions on the west flank of the Anzacs and facing the Italians on the Albanian front began their retreat before they were encircled, but they were too late. By 20 April most were forced to surrender.

ANZAC CORPS REBORN

Blamey was now in de facto command of the ground forces, and on 12 April he designated them 'Anzac Corps', adding the words 'the task ahead though difficult is not nearly so desperate as that which our fathers faced twenty-six years ago'. Feeling that the Greek forces were disintegrating, Wilson ordered a further retreat to the Thermopylae line. This entailed giving up half of Greece. Calamity would result if the Germans struck suddenly and seized Larisa, the road junction through which the retreating forces would have to pass. Brigadier Stan Savige, arriving at Blamey's HQ ahead of his brigade, was ordered to cover Kalabaka. He arrived there to find the town full of officerless Greek troops and their commander, General Tsolakoglou, uncooperative.

In this German propaganda photograph Greek civilians are seen welcoming a German soldier in Salonika. German rule was soon to increase in severity.

By the morning of 16 April ten German divisions were now confronted east of the Pindus by six shattered Greek divisions and two Anzac. In the Pinios Gorge — the fabled Vale of Tempe — 150 emerging German tanks were tackled by Anzac infantry. By nightfall the unequal battle ended, the defenders falling back, some units becoming completely lost in the mountains.

But by 18 April four of the seven Anzac brigades had withdrawn through Larisa. In Athens the Greek Prime Minister, Korysis, committed suicide. Early next day all three forces got clear. By 20 April the main force of Anzac Corps had managed, by blowing bridges and cratering the roads, to place 80 kilometres of broken road between their rearguard and the advancing German columns.

At Brallos Pass, looking down on the plain of Lamia, Australian artillery prepared for a long delaying action. But on 21 April Wavell informed Blamey that the entire force would begin evacuation three days hence. On the same day the few remaining Hurricanes of the RAF fought their last battle over Athens, downing thirty Axis aircraft for the loss of five of their own. In this battle 'Pat' Pattle, the South African 'ace', was killed.

At Thermopylae the New Zealanders stood. Here, exchanging fire with German tanks on 21 April, they fought a three-day rearguard action. On 23 April, the King of the Hellenes left Athens with his government to continue the battle from Crete, and Blamey closed down Anzac Corps HQ before flying off to Egypt with Mackay. Freyberg chose to be the last to leave.

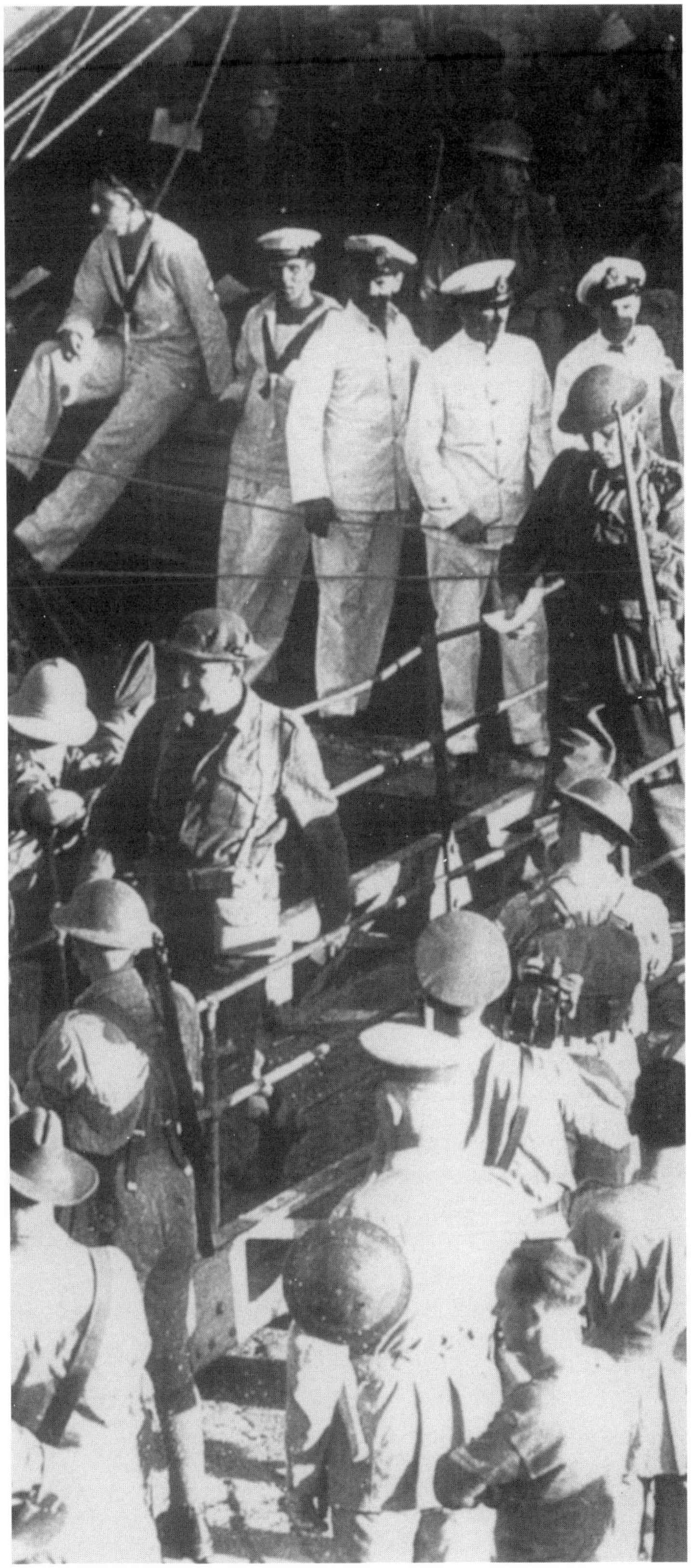

Right: British and Anzac troops evacuated from Greece and Crete land at Alexandria on a British destroyer.
Below: General Sir Thomas Blamey (left) wearing Australian slouch hat photographed in Greece with General Sir Henry Maitland Wilson who was in overall command of the Greek expedition. 'Jumbo' Wilson ended the war a field marshal.

On 24 April the Greek Army capitulated. General Papagos ordered his men to keep the roads clear to enable the Anzac forces to reach their evacuation beaches and the first troops were taken off that night. To the end, the Greeks cheered them. 'They appeared broken hearted that our efforts to help them had brought disaster on our force,' Freyberg wrote.

EVACUATION FROM GREECE

Evacuation under cover of night continued on Anzac Day (25 April); two ships of the Scrap Iron Flotilla with RN vessels took off more than 5500 troops on Anzac Day and *Stuart*, *Voyager* and HMAS *Perth* embarked troops at Nauplion in the Peloponnesus. Although German paratroops seized the Corinth Canal on 26 April, separating the Anzac forces in Attica and the Peloponnesus, the 16th and 17th Australian Brigades were safely evacuated from Kalamata near the south-western tip of Greece. As the first light of dawn broke the last ship pulled out, rather than face certain destruction if caught by Axis aircraft in daylight. On 27 April the Germans entered Athens and hoisted the swastika over the Acropolis. On the next day the last New Zealand brigade was taken off, but lost several hundred troops of the rearguard who fought on until they were overwhelmed.

Of a total of 64,000 British and Dominion troops on the Greek mainland, 12,000 (including Cypriot and Palestinian non-combatant units) fell into German hands. Australia had lost 320 killed, 484 wounded and 2030 taken prisoner. New Zealand's losses were similar. Five hundred men had been killed in the loss of six ships to enemy air attack during the evacuation. But the Anzacs had made a fighting retreat of 500 kilometres with the loss of only one complete infantry battalion. The exhausted divisions, their brigades separated, gradually began to regroup in Egypt and Crete (to where one-third of the force had been carried by the navy).

German losses in the Balkans campaign were just 5000 — 1100 killed, 4000 wounded. They had captured 270,000 Greek troops and nearly 100,000 Yugoslav. Both Churchill and Menzies were held to account in postwar years for the Greek disaster. Churchill held that Britain had a moral obligation to help the Greeks that overrode military considerations. Wavell had simply never envisaged the Yugoslav and Greek field armies collapsing as rapidly as they did.

TOBRUK: THE DEFENCE

On 10 April 1941, six days after capturing Benghazi, and while the forces in Greece were retreating in the face of the German invasion, Rommel's forces attacked Tobruk, and were driven off by brisk fire from the Australians defending its perimeter. The desolate seaport had been isolated by the rapid British retreat and was to remain so for eight long months. Like the eight-month campaign on Gallipoli, it became a vivid chapter in Australian military history. It also became the scene of the first outright defeat inflicted on German forces in the war.

The collapse in Libya in the previous week had been dramatic. Rommel had struck suddenly on 31 March at Mersa Brega, destroying with ease the British armoured brigade patrolling there. Defying Hitler's request for a 'limited offensive' he pushed east rapidly, telling his officers that the Suez Canal itself was within their grasp.

The day of 3 April was one of confusion and it saw practically no ground fighting. Wavell had recalled O'Connor to take over from Lieutenant-General Neame, in whom he had lost confidence, but Rommel then struck towards Mechili and entered Benghazi. Neame, whose misfortunes had not ended, was among the last to leave at the tail of his retreating forces, driving his staff car with O'Connor in the back seat, but lost contact with the other vehicles. Attempting to reach Derna, now with his driver at the wheel, he instead blundered into a German column, which took them prisoner. Two days later, on 6 April, Major-General Gambier-Parry also fell into German hands, along with Australian units, but only after the tough stand by the latter had enabled the 9th Division to withdraw in good order towards Derna and Tobruk.

Flying into Tobruk on 8 April Wavell appointed Major-General Lavarack of 7th Australian Division as GOC of the crumbling Cyrenaica command and ordered him to hold Tobruk for 'at least two months'. He gave the same order at the airfield to Major-General Leslie Morshead, GOC of the much travelled but so far untested 9th Australian Division, which was now in Tobruk. When Lavarack returned to take command of 7th Division on the Egyptian border, Morshead became fortress commander. Small in stature, quiet of manner, unsparing, he was a hard and resolute commander. His troops called him, with affection, 'Ming the Merciless', after the comic-strip character (their Prime Minister Menzies was also lumbered with the nickname, but without affection).

In Tobruk Morshead had 31,000 men of whom 24,000 were combat troops. He had his untried 9th Division of three brigades plus the 18th Brigade of the 7th Division. He also had the British 3rd Armoured Brigade (down to just 45 tanks) and eight regiments of British gunners (field artillery anti-tank and anti-aircraft) who were to win his admiration. 'There'll be no Dunkirk here,' Morshead told his officers. 'There is to be no surrender and no retreat.'

An Australian soldier shelters from the incessant bombing and shelling in Tobruk, 1941

THE SIEGE BEGINS

By 11 April, the day Bardia fell to his troops, Rommel had surrounded Tobruk and called on the garrison to surrender, dropping leaflets with this demand, most of which were put to more practical use. He sent in a major attack by tanks and infantry on Easter Sunday, 13 April, but met a ferocious resistance, losing sixteen out of the thirty-eight tanks engaged. On that day, Corporal J.H. Edmonson (2/17th Battalion) won the AIF's first Victoria Cross of the war. Following his officer with five others in a bayonet charge on an enemy position containing six machine guns, they killed twelve Germans and drove out the rest. Mortally wounded, Edmondson kept fighting until he dropped.

Next day the Afrika Korps attacked again with infantry accompanied by fifty tanks, but the Australians decimated the infantry and the British gunners, firing over open sights, knocked out seventeen tanks. The day ended with Axis losses of 400, most of them taken prisoner; Australian losses were 26. A captured German officer protested: 'I cannot understand you Australians. In Poland, France and Belgium once the tanks got through, the soldiers took it for granted that they were beaten. But you are like demons. The tanks break through and your infantry still keeps fighting.' The Australians seemed to be enjoying the battle.

Wavell cabled Morshead that the defence of Egypt now rested on retaining the fortress: 'I know I can count on you to hold Tobruk to the end.' In a private appraisal, however, he wondered whether the garrison could withstand a siege, writing that 'it depends on whether the port can be kept open'.

On 16 April 1941 an Italian force, battalion-strong, was captured to a man by the 2/48th battalion for the loss of one Australian killed. That evening, stunned by the bloody repulse of his attacks, Rommel, who had cabled Berlin for more troops and admitted his inability to continue his drive eastwards, wrote optimistically to his wife: 'The battle for Tobruk has calmed down a bit, the enemy are embarking, so we can expect to be taking over the fortress ourselves very shortly.'

For the next two weeks Rommel intensified aerial bombardment of Tobruk and the Luftwaffe mounted nearly 700 sorties over the seaport. The defenders dug themselves in for a long stay. Radio Berlin described the defenders as 'Ali Baba Morshead and his Forty Thousand Thieves' (an unkind reference to Australia's origin as a colony of convicts in 1788) who were 'caught like rats' in a trap, so the Australians, who were thick-skinned, called themselves the 'Rats of Tobruk' (the nickname the 9th Division would carry throughout the war).

Morshead had made an impregnable fortress out of the flat, featureless seaport. Half of his thirteen battalions held the outer perimeter, the 'Red Line'. About three kilometres behind them he constructed a second ring of defences, the 'Blue Line'; around Tobruk Harbour itself lay a third defence ring, the 'Green Line', containing his HQ, a reserve brigade and his tanks, carriers and armoured cars. It was defence in depth, with reserves ready to plug any breach. Trenches and caves were dug or extended to provide cover from the almost ceaseless air attacks.

Churchill was delighted by Tobruk's fine defence but, possibly recalling the defence of Ladysmith by a force that outnumbered its Boer besiegers ten to one, reminded the CIGS on 22 April: 'We must not forget that the besieged are four or five times as strong as the besiegers. There is no objection to their making themselves comfortable, but they must be very careful not to let themselves be ringed in by smaller forces … twenty-five thousand men with 100 guns and ample supplies are expected to be able to hold a highly fortified zone against 4500 men at the end of 700 miles of communications, even though those men be Germans ...'

On 30 April the Axis forces attacked again and by next day had taken the high ground and established a salient, but at such cost that Rommel stopped the attacks on 3 May. In three days of fighting the Axis had lost 950 men, the defenders 800. Churchill cabled Morshead: 'The whole Empire is watching your steadfast and spirited defence of this important outpost of Egypt with gratitude and admiration.' In May and again in August the Australians attacked the salient but were unable to recapture it.

On 3 May Churchill told his private secretary, Colville, that Tobruk could be the modern counterpart of the defence of Acre that had dashed Napoleon's plans to conquer Syria: 'It was a speck of sand in the desert which might ruin all Hitler's calculations.'

In early May 1941 Morshead was writing to Blamey to protest the removal of the last Hurricanes, adding: 'If we only had a brigade of Matilda tanks we'd clear the whole show up ... The men are in good fettle. They are a grand lot ... Health is good considering the conditions — a dust storm practically every other day and half a gallon water a day. The (British) artillery are splendid fellows. The brigade commanders are all on their toes, particularly Lloyd and Murray.'

Rommel's extraordinary advance had outdistanced his fuel and ammunition supplies and exhausted his troops. At Tobruk they were harried by night raids from the Australian lines. At Sollum Brigadier William Gott's mobile force struck and then recaptured Fort Capuzzo. British Commandos made a night raid on Bardia, carried there and back by the RAN destroyers. In mid-year came the scorching heat of summer. The caves of Tobruk would become caverns of sweltering heat when the temperature outside reached 50 degrees C. Fresh water was strictly rationed. But still Tobruk held on.

MENZIES IN LONDON

Australia's Prime Minister, Menzies, arrived in London from Egypt in mid-February. He had come expressly to urge reinforcement of defences in Singapore and the sending of modern aircraft to Australia, but found himself observing the unfolding of a series of strategic disasters. He was soon appalled by Churchill's meddling in military affairs and his lack of concern about the Japanese threat. The great friendship between the Commonwealth statesmen was to be a post-war flowering.

To Major-General John Kennedy, the Director of Military Operations at the War Office, Menzies confessed that with one Australian division surrounded at Tobruk and another high and dry in Greece he hardly dared return home, and 'might as well go on a trip to the North Pole'. Kennedy saw the Australian as 'an exceptionally shrewd and able man, with a caustic wit'.

On 14 April Menzies attended a War Cabinet meeting at which Churchill (whom Menzies in his diary termed sarcastically 'the Master Strategist') stated: 'Tobruk must be held as a bridgehead or rally post from which to hit the enemy.' Menzies retorted: 'With what!' and wrote in his diary that night: 'The Cabinet is deplorable ... the Chiefs of Staff are without exception Yes Men ...Winston is a dictator; he cannot be overruled, and his colleagues fear him ...' Menzies decided to stay in London a few more weeks.

He flew home in May via Canada, where he told Mackenzie King that an imperial War Cabinet was necessary to keep Churchill in check and arrived in Sydney after an absence that had lasted six months. He found confidence in his leadership eroded and was forced to resign the prime ministership in August, to be succeeded by his deputy and coalition partner, Arthur Fadden, a blunt farmer who was an uninspiring leader. In October 1941 the two independent MPs who had kept the conservatives in power crossed the floor, and John Curtin and the Labor Party took over government. They were to lead Australia through the tragedies and triumphs of the next four years of war.

Australian Prime Minister Robert Menzies visiting Australian airmen at a base in England during 1941.

THE BATTLE FOR CRETE

On 25 April Hitler ordered plans made for 'Operation Mercury — the capture of Crete. The island would be seized by Göring's airborne forces. Crete must be captured in seven days, not a day more. The invasion of Russia — 'Barbarossa' — must not be delayed further. The task was entrusted to General Kurt Student's crack 11th Air Corps of 22,000 paratroopers and glider-borne infantry, the victors in the invasion of Holland and Belgium — 'The toughest soldiers in the German army,' Hitler boasted, 'tougher even than the Waffen-SS!' They would be carried from the mainland, and supported, by the 1000 aircraft of General Loehr's 4th *Luftflotte*. The battle for Crete was the last act in the Greek drama. It was to be a tragedy, but an epic one.

The island, rich in history and legend — it was the island of Theseus and King Minos had ruled an empire from the city of Knossos — was the last bastion of British defence in the central-eastern Mediterranean. Loss of Crete could bring the Axis to within bombing distance of Alexandria and could threaten Cyprus. Just 250 kilometres long, it possessed a deep-water harbour at Suda Bay, but this was on the north coast, as were its airfields at Heraklion, Maleme and Retimo. Mountains formed the spine of the island; tracks led over them to a rugged south coast where the mountains fell to the sea. 'It seems clear from our information', Churchill cabled Wavell on 28 April after seeing Ultra intelligence, 'that a heavy airborne attack by German troops and bombs will soon be made on Crete. The island must be stubbornly defended.'

On 30 April 1941 Freyberg, who was about to depart for Egypt, was informed that he had been selected to command the island's defences. Within a day he was cabling Wavell that his force 'can and will fight, but without full support from Navy and Air Force cannot hope to repel invasion. I feel that under the terms of my charter it is my duty to inform New Zealand government of the situation in which greater part of my division is now.' He also signalled that there were only six Hurricanes on the island. At the same meeting on Crete, Wilson had received from Wavell the biblical injunction 'I want you to go to Jerusalem and relieve Baghdad!' War had just broken out with Iraq.

Below: German paratroops landing on Crete, 21st May 1941.
Below right: Major-General Bernard Freyberg, GOC of the New Zealand Division, who commanded the British and Commonwealth forces in Crete. The legendary New Zealander, wounded nine times in battle, survived the war to become his country's governor general as General the Lord Freyberg, VC.

On 1 May 1941 Freyberg cabled his government, urging it to exert pressure on the British to send him reinforcements or to review the decision that Crete should be held. But four days later he sent Churchill the heartening message: that he was not at all nervous at the prospect of an airborne invasion, while adding 'combination of seaborne and airborne attack is different'. His troops were in 'great form', but he was anxiously awaiting extra fighter aircraft, equipment and transport. His obsession with repelling a seaborne attack was to result in his neglect of the defences of the vital airfields.

Flying with impunity from mainland Greece, German aircraft began bombing Crete on 13 May, heralding a week of 'softening up'. By 19 May only six British aircraft were left on the island and these were flown to Egypt. Of the six outdated Fleet Air Arm aircraft at Maleme four had been shot down, plus three of the Hurricanes, though the latter had often tackled ten times their number.

Freyberg had on Crete nearly 50,000 troops, but close to 10,000 were poorly armed Greek troops, and half the remainder were non-combat troops (12,000 of the 15,000 garrison at Suda were service corps men or RAF ground crew, untrained to fight as infantry, and known by the latter as the 'odds and sods'). Of the Anzacs — 7700 New Zealanders, 6500 Australians — nearly all were infantry, as were 5000 British. Freyberg had only a dozen tanks and 68 anti-aircraft guns. He stationed at Maleme airfield and along the coast five New Zealand battalions, Australian battalions at Retimo, and most of the British 14th Brigade at Heraklion. Some British officers were afraid to drive past AIF bivouacs, for the Australians had a reputation for shooting at headlights.

The troops rested, enjoying the spring sunshine and wildflowers, and the friendliness of the Cretan people, whose own menfolk — the tough Cretan Division — had been lost in Albania. It was the lull before the storm, only disturbed by regular German bombing of shipping in Suda Bay and the positions around the airfields. The enemy was careful not to bomb the landing strips.

OPERATION MERCURY

Early on the clear morning of 20 May 1941 the troops defending Crete heard the drone of approaching aircraft and looked up to see a sight they would never forget and many would never see again: the sky was filled with hundreds of aircraft from which blossomed like anti-aircraft explosions puffs of white: paratroopers, who floated down amid the gunfire. 'I stood on the hill enthralled by the magnitude of the operation,' Freyberg later wrote, 'looking out to sea I picked out hundreds of planes, tier upon tier coming towards us.'

Ahead lay a day of the most bitter and bloody fighting British and Commonwealth troops had known in nearly two years of war. Hundreds of paratroops were shot as they floated down helpless in their harnesses, and shooting them became a sport. Sixty gliders landed in the Maleme sector, lurching through scrub or crashing into gullies and were raked by tornadoes of small arms fire. Paratroops fell over the ruins of Knossos near Heraklion and were hunted down. Greek civilians armed with ancient weapons joined in the hunt for those who had landed and were trying to organise themselves. By nightfall nearly 4000 Germans had been killed or wounded. At Retimo German aircraft had found no evidence of defences and the paratroopers drifting down on the airfield only 100 metres from the surf were decimated by the Australians. Yet the surviving Germans took the crests of the two rounded hills overlooking the airfield — the 'Charlies' — which would see bitter fighting as the Australians attempted to drive them off.

Even more miraculously, the Germans had taken Hill 107 which dominated Maleme airfield. If an airfield was lost, so was Crete. Just

'Tougher than the Waffen-SS': soldiers of the German airborne forces boarding their Junkers transports before the Crete invasion.

German paratroopers falling on Australian lines on the first day of the Crete invasion, 21 May 1941. From the painting in the Australian War Memorial, Canberra.

before midnight the New Zealanders began falling back from their positions there. They had been subjected to a tornado of bombing all day and were regrouping. Freyberg was concerned, but he was assured that his artillery still dominated the airstrip and that nothing could land there. A counterattack to recover the lost position would be mounted in the morning, but organising the counterattack meant drawing troops from another sector by night, for the roads were not safe to move along by day because of German aircraft. The counterattack at Maleme was not mounted for two more days, and it fell to pieces.

Night fell on northern Crete to the crackle of gunfire and the moans of the wounded. Morning revealed that the defenders were standing firm, including the Greeks, who were barely armed at all. As early as 8 a.m. on 21 May a German aircraft had run the gauntlet of fire at Maleme and touched down. General Kurt Student resolved to hurl every man he could to the airfield. By 4 p.m. the 4th Mountain Division were pouring from transports. He would later admit that if a heavy counterattack had been mounted on Maleme on 20 May his men would have crumbled.

When more German paratroops were dropped behind the New Zealand lines the 28th (Maori) NZ Battalion fixed bayonets and wiped them out; only one-third of the German force survived. On the evening of 22 May Freyberg approved plans to withdraw the NZ Division from the coast to the Galatas area.

CRETE: THE SEABORNE INVASION

Only at sea was an Allied victory achieved. On the night of 21 May Cunningham's fleet sunk a flotilla carrying reinforcements 30 miles off Crete. Not one vessel survived. The next day was one of disaster. Caught in daylight by the Luftwaffe, the battleship *Valiant*, in which Sub-Lieutenant Prince Philip of Greece was serving, was hit by two bombs; his uncle, Captain Lord Louis Mountbatten, commanding the destroyer HMS *Kelly*, lost his ship but survived; the cruisers *Gloucester* and *Fiji* and the destroyer *Kashmir* were also sunk.

THE END APPROACHES While the Australians at Retimo mounted constant counterattacks to remove a tight enemy grip on the roads, the British brigadier at Heraklion made no attempt to break through to them. The lull on 24 May was used by the Luftwaffe to bomb the western seaport of Canea into rubble and by General Ringel to plan a decisive battle next day. On the same day the first British reinforcements reached Suda Bay — forward elements of Colonel Robert Laycock's two Commando battalions; the bulk were landed two days later, when the fate of the island had already been decided.

German troops confer with a Luftwaffe officer during the battle for Crete.

SUDA TO GALATAS: 'STAND — FOR NEW ZEALAND!' The Germans, using flamethrowers, seized Galatas village on 25 May from the exhausted New Zealanders, who straggled out, done in. The Kiwis were not known for losing their nerve but a few shouted 'Back, back ... they're coming through in thousands!' Lieutenant-Colonel Kippenberger, acting as Brigadier, was shocked. Drawing his revolver he shouted: 'Stand! Stand for New Zealand!' The men sat down under the trees and rested. In the background they could hear the guttural shouting of the Germans and spasmodic shooting. Kippenberger decided to mount a counterattack. Dozens of men joined him. Just after 8 p.m., two clattering British tanks headed back into Galatas, with 200 New Zealanders running behind them through the olive groves, shouting battle cries. One young officer, Sandy Thomas (once described as the officer 'most like the young Freyberg'), was to write 'one felt one's blood rising swiftly above fear and uncertainty until only an inexplicable exhilaration, quite beyond description, remained ... Nothing could stop us.' They cleared the village house by house. (Thomas was one of the wounded who was captured, though he was later to escape.) But by 26 May 3000 fresh German troops were being airlifted in daily and the Suda Bay sector was in danger of being surrounded. Pressed by four enemy regiments the New Zealanders holding Galatas were ordered to withdraw to a line east of the Australians.

On the same day as the charge into Galatas a young British officer named Michael Forrester led a crowd of Cretan men, women and children clutching primitive weapons and followed by yapping dogs in a massed charge against a group of paratroopers, all of whom were killed. It was valiant, but the Cretan civilians later paid a terrible price for their bravery. And many were shot out of hand, the Nazi penalty for fighters not wearing uniform. The deeds of the people of Crete added new legends to an island already rich in lore.

The battle of Crete had now lasted a week. Food, water, ammunition — all were in short supply. The heat was intense. The bombing and strafing never ceased. The stench of death, of bodies bloated in the sun, lay heavy on the island. On that day Freyberg signalled Cairo 'Our position is hopeless. Provided a decision is reached at once a certain proportion of the force might be embarked.'

The pressure on the Suda sector was increasing and even Brigadier George Vasey doubted whether his men could hold on. Freyberg ordered the Australians to fall back, entrusting the withdrawal of the 'British Composite Brigade' to General Weston. He neglected to amend its orders; marooned, it fought on in Canea until 28 May.

At the road 1.5 kilometres south of Suda Bay's docks dubbed 42nd Street, the Maori Battalion and two Australian battalions charged with fixed bayonets into the advancing Germans on 27 May amid the olive groves and chased them back nearly two kilometres, killing nearly 300 of them. No one had ever seen crack German troops turn tail and run before. Ten Australians were killed and twenty-eight Maori wounded in this remarkable action.

On 27 May, as the long and agonising retreat over the White Mountains began, General Halder, Hitler's Chief of the General Staff in Berlin, noted in his diary: 'OKW is demanding a holding up of the starting date of Barbarossa.' The next day Hitler, his patience at an end, sent Student in Athens the humiliating cable: 'France fell in eight days. Why is Crete still resisting?' The Germans were still unaware that the retreat had begun.

One group of Australians never received orders to retreat. The two Australian battalions at Retimo under Ian Campbell made repeated attempts to break through Perivolia to Retimo town and fought on till the morning of 30 May, when German tanks suddenly appeared from the direction of Heraklion. For the loss of 120 dead, the Australians had killed 700 Germans and captured 500 others, many of whom lay in the 27 tents full of wounded under the hot sun within Retimo's perimeter. With no escape possible, their commander formally surrendered, but many of them refused to give in and took to the hills, from where a number made their way with the help of Cretan people to Turkey, and resumed the war.

THE RETREAT In the afternoon of 27 May Freyberg received Wavell's permission to retreat over the White Mountains to Sphakia, a small fishing village on the south coast. The long retreat through extreme heat, with the troops subjected to continuous aerial attack, became what Freyberg himself called 'a Via Dolorosa'. Some units kept their order and discipline; others degenerated into a rabble or broke into lines of stragglers. Some lorries drove past exhausted troops refusing to pick them up; men were seen carrying their mates. They stood and fought and retreated through the fields and villages, moving at night when the Luftwaffe was less of a threat.

The fleet began to take the troops off the beaches as Sphakia on the night of 28 May. Of the three cruisers and ten destroyers sent in, one cruiser, HMS *Orion*, and two destroyers were sunk. On the night of 29 May Cunningham sent in eleven ships including HMAS *Stuart* and HMAS *Perth* (the latter was hit by a bomb on the voyage to Egypt) and took off 6000 men. In the dark of 30 May the Australian destroyers Nizam and Napier took off 1500 more and Freyberg received orders to leave. He told Laycock: 'You were the last to come, so you will be the last to leave.' Laycock, who apparently thought himself too important to be taken prisoner, achieved a revision of this order in an interview with General Weston, who also had no desire to remain. Laycock and his 200 men found places for themselves on a departing warship. One of his officers was the novelist Evelyn Waugh; already a cynic, he would depict in his postwar trilogy the battle of Crete as a black comedy. 'Out of all those left behind,' writes Antony Beevor in his account of the battle of Crete, 'the Australians of Lieutenant-Colonel Theo Walker's battalion, the 2/7th, had the right to feel the most bitter. Assured places on the ships, he had marched down to the back having maintained the perimeter on the "top storey" until the last moment.' One of the Australian officers, writing in prison camp, recorded that they arrived to hear the sound of anchor chains being raised as the last ship departed. The marooned troops surrendered next day.

Cunningham sent the navy in one last time, explaining: 'It takes the Navy three years to build a new ship. It will take three hundred years to build a new tradition. The evacuation will continue.' On the night of 31 May his warships brought off another 4000 British and Anzac troops.

Of more than 7000 New Zealanders on Crete, 4000 were casualties, 671 were killed, 2200 captured and nearly 2000 wounded. They had won two more VCs, awarded to Sergeant A.C. Hulme and to Lieutenant Charles Upham. The Australians had suffered 274 killed, 507 wounded and lost 3000 as prisoners of war; three complete battalions had been lost. A total of 12,000 British and Dominion troops had been taken prisoner.

Below: New Zealand infantry – 'Digs' – after their evacuation from Crete.
Below right: Soldiers of the Maori Battalion on board an Australian destroyer on the voyage to Alexandria.

At the Battle of Crete, the Mediterranean fleet was all but destroyed. It had saved the army, but at a terrible cost; 2000 officers and men of the Royal Navy had been lost at sea. Three cruisers and six destroyers were sunk; the battleships *Warspite* and *Barham* and a carrier were badly damaged; eight cruisers including Perth would require weeks of repair work. Of 2000 Royal Marines on Crete half had been lost, many in the rearguard at Sphakia.

Britain's affection for the monarchy was strengthened by the Royal family's conduct during the war. King George and Queen Elizabeth remained in London during most of the bombing.

SINK THE *BISMARCK*!

One drama interrupted the sad saga of defeat. On 21 May reports reached the Admiralty that Germany's giant new battleship *Bismarck* had left the Baltic and was anchored in Bergen fjord, accompanied by the heavy cruiser *Prinz Eugen*. Their objective could only be a foray into the Atlantic sea lanes, where at that moment eleven British convoys were at sea. Few British warships could confront the *Bismarck* with any chance of surviving her massive 15-inch shells. Within a day both ships were north-east of Iceland and on 23 May were sighted by patrolling British cruisers. 'The hunt was on; the quarry was in view; and all our forces moved accordingly,' wrote Churchill. The fast battle cruiser *Hood* and the new battleship *Prince of Wales*, both of them armed with big guns, steamed to intercept *Bismarck* and early on 24 May sighted and engaged the enemy. *Hood* opened fire at 5.52 a.m. at a range of 25,000 yards (approx. 25 kilometres) and *Bismarck* replied, scoring a hit on *Hood* which set a fire alight that reached her magazine. At 6 p.m., after *Bismarck* had fired a fifth salvo, *Hood* suddenly blew up. Of her 1500 men, only three survived.

Prince of Wales, armed with 14-inch guns, continued the battle but was also hit by *Bismarck*'s shells — one of which struck the bridge — and disengaged, but continued to shadow the German ships in company with her two cruisers, while other task forces steamed to join the battle. The Home fleet — among which were the new battleship *King George V* and the carrier *Victorious* — planned to reach the scene by early 25 May.

Bismarck had also been damaged, having been struck below the waterline by two shells that pierced an oil tank. Late on 24 May she turned to engage *Prince of Wales* and soon *Prinz Eugen* left (she made it back to France). At 10 p.m. *Victorious*'s torpedo bombers sighted *Bismarck* and launched an attack, scoring a torpedo hit on her below the bridge. Early next morning the cruisers shadowing *Bismarck* reported that they had lost sight of her. Thinking she was heading for the North Sea the Royal Navy followed, but *Bismarck*, losing oil, was heading for Brest on the French coast. The British units, having been at sea for four days, were also short of fuel. It appeared that *Bismarck* had escaped.

But at 10.30 a.m. on 26 May an RAF Catalina aircraft sighted the *Bismarck*. Just after 7 p.m. a Swordfish from *Ark Royal* launched an attack on the German battleship, scoring two hits, one of which destroyed her steering gear. *Bismarck* was now crippled, steaming in circles. At 8.47 the pursuing British battleships *Rodney* — armed with massive 16-inch guns — and *King George V* caught up with her and opened fire on her within a minute of each other. *Bismarck* was struck and seen to be burning. *Rodney* now closed, firing broadsides from a point-blank distance of 4000 yards. By 10.15 *Bismarck*'s guns were silent, but she refused to sink. Twenty-five minutes later the cruiser *Devonshire* closed to launch torpedoes; it was *Bismarck*'s death blow, and she turned over in the heavy seas and disappeared. Of her 2000 officers and men only 110 could be rescued by British ships.

The Germans had suffered enormous losses. Their 6000 casualties, including 4400 dead, show the intensity of the fighting. The paratroops were never again launched as a division; henceforth they fought as infantry. Some authorities claim the Germans lost 200 aircraft destroyed and another 150 damaged. It had been a bitter and costly battle for both sides. One irrefutable fact remained: the fleet had lost its domination of the eastern Mediterranean.

The loss of Crete saw the sacking of Longmore. 'It's a mess, but Longmore is certainly not to blame,' his successor, a Scot named Arthur Tedder, would write in his diary. Longmore's blunt demands for modern aircraft — Hurricane IIs, Beaufighters, Typhoons and Blenheim Vs — had angered Churchill. Tedder and his deputy, the Australian, Drummond, were to prove more diplomatic; their losses exceeded replacements each month during 1941 and the two new RAAF squadrons in the Middle East — 450 and 451 — were unable to become operational for nearly six months due to a shortage of both aircraft and pilots.

The people of Crete retain a particular love for those who fought beside them in the grim days of May 1941, especially for the Australians and New Zealanders who had come so far to fight and die. On the 60th anniversary of the invasion, a younger generation — paratroops of the Greek Army — would stage a re-creation of the parachute landings. To veterans at the ceremonies on Crete, amid the crowds of holiday-makers watching in amazement as the sky filled with hundred of blossoming chutes and puffs of coloured smoke, the memories it evoked would not be light ones.

1941: ETHIOPIA

Italy's declaration of war left her southern-most African colonies in East Africa stranded. Ethiopia and its south-eastern neighbour Somaliland, and Eritrea on the Red Sea, were now cut off from supply and reinforcement. Mussolini observed their loss from afar with indifference and cursed their garrisons for not fighting more strenuously.

As early as April 1940, when Wavell flew to South Africa to meet Prime Minister Smuts for the first time, he planned to use South African forces against the Italians. In the meantime he would foment rebellion against them. For this task he selected an obsessive young major named Orde Wingate, who had organised Jewish guerrillas during the Arab uprising in Palestine in 1938 and become a fervent Zionist. In early January 1941, after the Australian capture of Bardia, Wavell flew to Khartoum to arrange with General Platt, commanding in the Sudan, to begin his attack on Eritrea, and met there Haile Selassie, who had been evicted from the throne of Ethiopia in 1936. A fortnight later he re-entered his country and raised the flag of rebellion 50 kilometres inside Ethiopia, but few tribesmen rallied to his cause.

Officers and men of a British destroyer of the Mediterranean fleet photographed during 1941.

Platt's forces opened the northern offensive from the Sudan on 11 February, entered Eritrea and soon reached the approaches to its mountainous fortress, Keren, which stood on a plateau a little over 1000 metres above sea level. His forces were now strengthened by 4th Indian Division, which made good progress until the Italians blasted the sides of the Dongolas Gorge, blocking the single, winding mountain road to Keren. Here the toughest fighting of the campaign was to take place. The 5th Indian Division joined in the offensive. 'It is going to be a bloody battle,' General Beresford-Pierse of 4th Indian warned, 'against both enemy and ground. It will be won by the side that holds out longest.' The British would have to clear the road under heavy fire and hails of shells. On 16 March the British and Indians took Fort Dologorodoc; Italian losses were 5000. The 30,000 Italians defending Keren — mainly northern Italian units who fought boldly — launched no fewer than eight counterattacks before the fortress fell after a 53-day siege. British casualties were nearly 4000. But the road to Eritrea was opened and by 8 April Massawa was in British hands.

Wavell now had a surplus of troops in Kenya — 70,000, of whom only 10 per cent were British, but including the South African division that had driven north overland from the Union. Lieutenant-General Alan Cunningham, younger brother of the Admiral, informed Wavell that he would advance in the far south into Somaliland to seize the port of Kismayu. The Italians evacuated it three days later; Mogadishu fell to Nigerian troops on 25 February.

Cunningham's forces, advancing over tortuous terrain, entered Addis Ababa on 6 April (the Emperor arrived a month later, his procession led by a bearded Orde Wingate riding on a white horse). In two months Cunningham had taken 50,000 prisoners for the cost of 150 dead. The last Italian army, barely 5000 strong, defending Amba-Alagi under the command of the Viceroy himself, the Duke of Aosta, surrendered after two days of fighting on 16 May. The last Italian garrison held out until September. In the words of Wavell's admiring official biographer, 'The East African campaign was Britain's first complete victory in the Second World War.'

Two more successes were to brighten the gloom following the loss of Greece and Crete and Libya.

IRAQ

Iraq's politics had always been turbulent, but not violent. In 1930 Britain had relinquished her mandate over the kingdom of Iraq, which she had created in 1921 from the ruins of the Turkish Empire, while maintaining rights to transit forces over the country, and airfields at Lake Habbaniyah, west of Baghdad, and at Basra where an important port and oil refinery stood at the head of the Persian Gulf on the Shatt-al-Arab waterway.

Late in March 1941 an extreme nationalist, Rashid Ali, had become Prime Minister, and began to cultivate links with the Axis powers. On 3 April 1941 Rashid and several army officers known as 'The Golden Square' carried out a coup in Baghdad and forced the Regent and his ward, the boy king Faisal, to flee to safety aboard a British gunboat. It had been a bloodless coup. It was almost a carbon copy of the coup in Belgrade except that a boy king was being removed rather than installed.

Churchill ordered troops be landed at Basra. General Auchinleck, the Commander-in-Chief in India, was quick to respond and an Indian brigade landed there on 18 April. The Iraqi government demanded that they leave. Their demand was ignored. The situation worsened. By late April 7000 refugees had reached the large RAF base at Habbaniyah, which was strongly defended by 2000 troops, many of them local, who had remained loyal to the British. On 2 May a force of 4000 Iraqis had invested the base and begun firing artillery shells on it. More than eighty aircraft were based there — twenty were soon lost to Iraqi shells, but others were fitted with bombs and began retaliating.

Wavell resisted Churchill's pleas to crush the revolt rapidly. 'I have consistently warned you that no assistance could be given to Iraq from Palestine,' Wavell cabled, 'our forces here are stretched to the limit.' Churchill found Wavell's tone offensive and began to regard him as an overstressed and tired man. But a hastily organised 'flying column' of armoured cars aided by units of the Transjordan Arab Legion set out to cross the desert to the scene of fighting — a minor epic that would take them 1000 kilometres to Baghdad itself. On 18 May the column reached Habbaniyah, where the Iraqi besiegers had melted away, and pressed on to Falluja next day, where after brisk fighting that cost twenty-two British lives, it seized a bridge and advanced to Baghdad, entering the city on 30 May. Rashid Ali and his Cabinet had already fled. The Regent and his young charge returned to their palace. Both of them would be killed in a military coup seventeen years later, the first upheaval in Iraq's drift into the hands of extremists led by Saddam Hussein.

INVADING SYRIA

To add to Wavell's mounting problems, Syria was now becoming a base for Axis intrigue. On 6 May, at the outbreak of the Iraq revolt, the Vichy government in France bowed to Axis pressure and granted the Germans and Italians landing facilities in Syria. Within a month 120 Axis aircraft had made use of Syrian airfields, while rendering little or no assistance to the Iraqis. General de Gaulle, with a handful of followers, had rallied Equatorial Africa to the flag of Free France, and had long urged that Vichy control of Syria be challenged. He underestimated the antipathy the Vichy French felt towards his cause, and to Britain's. In the latter part of 1940 de Gaulle and General Catroux had attempted to initiate contact with the French government, but had been rebuffed. Indeed, Vichy's antagonism towards their movement grew as the months passed. In Syria and Lebanon the Governor, General Dentz, commanded an army of 38,000 men, with 90 tanks; he also possessed a force of 100 aircraft. The rugged terrain was also an obstacle to any invading army, as Wavell well knew from his years as a staff officer with Allenby in the Holy Land.

Wavell was reluctant to embark on any fresh adventures, if only because of his lack of forces. The War Office, no doubt with Churchill's urgings, informed him that there was no alternative to action against Syria and ordered him to organise a force for the purpose. General Blamey viewed an advance against Syria as 'largely a gamble'. Wavell had considered three divisions, one of them armoured, as the minimum required to invade Syria; de Gaulle had asked Wavell for four. All that Wavell could provide were two brigades of the Australian 7th Division — the so far 'Silent Seventh' — and an Indian brigade (the 5th). De Gaulle would provide two Free French brigades. The troops would cross the frontier with flags displayed, and were ordered not to open fire unless they were fired upon.

De Gaulle was convinced that the British, initially cool towards a venture into Syria, planned to supplant French influence there. France had granted a form of autonomy to both Syria and Lebanon in 1936, as Britain had done with Egypt, while maintaining the right to base armed forces there. On the eve of invasion de Gaulle announced that both countries would be granted immediate independence. The British demanded that the proclamation be issued in their name also. De Gaulle objected to this; in the end both Britain and France issued separate promises of independence: it was the first of the comic solutions and compromises resorted to by de Gaulle and Churchill in their stormy alliance. De Gaulle was to accuse Churchill's old comrade

Soldiers of Free France photographed in the Middle East on the eve of the invasion of Syria, where French fought against French.

After the conquest of Syria the region became the principal training area for British and Commonwealth forces. Australian divisional cavalry (the black beret denotes their arm) photographed in a Syrian village late in 1941

and adviser to the Free French, Major-General Louis Spears, of sinister manipulations for the rest of the war; once a passionate Francophile, Spears finished the war an embittered Francophobe.

General Maitland Wilson, who remained in Jerusalem during the campaign, ordered the 7th Australian Division's two brigades to advance in two thrusts, one along the coast road to Beirut, the other over a mountain road to Rayak airfield, while the 5th Indian Brigade would move with the Free French forces towards Damascus.

On 8 June 1941 the invasion of Syria began. The Vichy French forces opened fire at first sight of the invading troops. Attempts by British Commandos to seize the bridges over the Litani River failed, and the leading Australian battalion had to ford the river under fire. A pontoon bridge was constructed but the Australians, once across in force, met more fierce French resistance. The second Australian brigade was similarly held up by resistance but seized Merdjayoun on 11 June, by which date the Indians had taken Kuneitra and the Free French were only 15 kilometres south of Damascus.

On the coast the Australians, now supported by naval bombardments, entered Sidon on 15 June, outpacing the inland advance. Jezzine was also taken on 18 June, as the Indian brigades stormed Kiswe. The Vichy French, fighting with an unexpected stubbornness, were now launching counterattacks in strength. Heavy French attacks in Jezzine were repulsed but Kuneitra fell on 16 June, only to be recaptured by British troops the following day. Merdjayoun, the region where the borders of Lebanon, Syria, Transjordan and Iraq met, was a scene of bitter fighting.

The campaign had now bogged down. Reinforcements, the British 16th Brigade and battalions of the 6th Division, had now joined the attackers. The 2/3rd Battalion, after overcoming bitter resistance, took the hills overlooking Damascus, which the French had evacuated. On 21 June, for the second time in twenty-three years Australians troops entered Damascus, the oldest city in the Middle East. An Australian attack on French positions north of Jezzine on 24 June failed, with heavy casualties. Fortunately, during the campaign, Vichy aircraft did not appear in strength, for only two fighter squadrons (80 Squadron RAF and 3 Squadron RAAF) were available to provide air cover.

Palmyra, in central Syria, stoutly defended by the Foreign Legion, fell to British forces sent from Iraq on 3 July, the day that Major-General Slim's leading brigade of 10th Indian Division, also advancing from Iraq, entered Syria. Lavarack now decided to concentrate 7th Division on the coast and press on to Beirut. The major obstacles in their way — the Damour River and the ridge overlooking it — were stormed by the Australians on 30 June, while further inland Beit ed Dine was captured. It was now possible to surround Beirut by an advance through the mountain country.

ARMISTICE IN SYRIA

With Damascus fallen and Beirut now cut off, General Dentz signed an armistice effective on 12 July 1941. The lights went out at the signing and when the electric current was restored General Catroux found that his gold-encrusted kepi had been stolen. He blamed the Australians present.

Lebanon and Syria passed into British and Free French control and became a training area for Allied troops, and yet another burden to defend. A relatively small proportion of the Vichy French troops rallied to de Gaulle's cause; the majority chose repatriation to France. The month-long campaign had cost the Australians alone 1600 casualties, including 416 dead.

Syria was the only complete victory of 1941. In the Western Desert Wavell had launched his counteroffensive, 'Operation Battleaxe', on 15 June, intending to drive back Rommel and relieve Tobruk but it was called off two days later after the loss of 30 cruiser tanks (mostly to enemy action), with 57 Matilda tanks going out of action (mostly due to mechanical failure) and a thousand British casualties. The failure of 'Battleaxe', combined with Churchill's exasperation with Wavell, sealed the C-in-C's fate. On 22 June 1941 Wavell was informed that he was to exchange places with the Commander-in-Chief India, General Sir Claude Auchinleck, a younger man. On the same day Germany invaded Russia.

Wavell had fought campaigns in Egypt and Libya, in Greece and Crete, in Italian East Africa, Iraq, Syria and again in Libya, most of them within the space of just seven months. In another six months he would be asked to shoulder an impossible burden, doomed to failure — to defend the Far East with minimal resources. History would treat him more kindly than Churchill chose to.

IRAN

Less than two months later British forces entered Iran (Persia), where Axis agents were also active, as indeed they were in Afghanistan. The kingdom was even more strategically important than Iraq, for its oil fields were extensive and it formed a land bridge to southern Russia. This operation was left to the new command based in Iraq and even Auchinleck, Wavell's successor, was not distracted by its preparation. To relieve the burdens on GHQ at Cairo, the Middle East region had been divided into area commands — 8th Army was responsible for Egypt; 9th Army for Syria, 10th Army for Iraq. General Quinan of 10th Army would carry out the Iran invasion. Churchill was concerned that the Iranians might seize hostages among Europeans working at the refineries.

On the night of 24 August a motley British flotilla set out to seize the vital Iranian ports at the head of the Persian Gulf. At dawn on 25 August part of the force including HMAS *Kanimbla* (then carrying Indian troops) carried out a 'cutting out' expedition in the Nelson manner: boarding parties seized unsuspecting German merchantmen at Bandur Shapur while the troops secured the port. Meanwhile, part of the flotilla shelled and stormed Abadan's defences where the Iranian admiral and his troops fought bravely before being overwhelmed; the port and refinery were captured almost intact.

Further north HMAS *Yarra* was the first ship to reach Khorramshahr, where she sank the Iranian sloop *Babr* with ten salvoes before steaming up the Karun River, firing on defence positions on the banks and boarding two enemy gunboats. On the same morning, 25 August, British forces crossed into Iran from Iraq while Russian troops entered the country from the north. This campaign was also mercifully short and almost bloodless. Strong pressure was brought upon the Shah to abdicate in favour of his young son, and this he did on 16 September. Anglo-Russian forces entered Tehran the next day. The bulk of British forces were withdrawn once a new Shah was installed and the transport system — particularly the railways — were secured, and Iran became a vital Allied supply artery to the Soviet Union for the remainder of the war. The old Shah died in comfortable retirement in 1944; his son Reza would remain on Iran's throne until 1979. Churchill excused his high-handed action by explaining that Britain and Russia in 1941 were fighting for their lives, and that Iran's independence was restored after the war. Russian forces showed a reluctance to leave, but vacated northern Iran in 1946.

Soldiers of the Indian Army were the unsung heroes of World War II. Muslim, Hindu and Sikh soldiers, all of them volunteers, formed one of the largest Allied armies – two-million strong – and fought from the Middle East and Italy to Burma.

BRITAIN AT WAR

At war's end Churchill would say: 'Our record in this war has been a good one. History will show this.' His wartime coalition with the Labour Party (and a token Liberal presence) proved a success, free of the dissensions and inter-party rivalries of the previous war's coalition, and it introduced measures and restrictions never previously contemplated in British life. Identity cards had been issued to all citizens (even children) as early as 1939 and in January 1940 food rationing was imposed. Households were ordered to reduce coal consumption to two-thirds of their peacetime level. By mid-1941 nearly 50 per cent of the workforce was employed on government work, from factories to the armed services. The Minister of Labour, Ernest Bevin, in 1941 took over the total direction and allocation of workers, and ordered the conscription of women. 'Neither was attempted systematically in any other belligerent country,' writes A.J.P. Taylor. 'Both worked smoothly.' The same historian points out that Britain became a completely socialist state, similar to that Lenin had imposed by force in the Soviet Union. But personal freedoms were not extinguished or challenged; freedom of the press remained, and though Churchill often threatened to close down some newspapers that criticised his war direction, he never carried out his threat. Herbert Morrison, the Home Secretary, closed down only the Communist paper The Daily Worker, which had become an apologist for the Nazi–Soviet alliance.

War production was rapidly increased. By 1942 the British Army had enough rifles to last it ten years but not enough men. The demands of industry and agriculture — and the two competing services — limited the army's growth to two million men. General Brooke, the Commander-in-Chief, Home Forces, was more concerned about the lack of senior commanders. 'It is lamentable,' he wrote in his diary, 'how poor we are in Army and Corps commanders; we ought to remove several, but Heaven knows where we shall find anything very much better ... The flower of our manhood was wiped out some twenty years ago ...'

Shortly afterwards he heard that he was to lose another tank brigade to the Middle East. 'When will the War Office learn not to break up armoured formations which it had taken months to build up?' he asked. A handful of generals received his full confidence — Alexander, Montgomery ('so quick at grasping all the essentials') and rising stars such as Horrocks and McCreery. They were mostly dynamic men, popular with their men, and would all be future Army and Corps commanders.

Until 1942 — a crisis period — British shipyards were replacing the tonnage lost to enemy attack (which averaged, for the first two years of war, two ships a day). Taxes paid for half Britain's war costs, loans the balance. American aid in the form of Lend-Lease (1941) was crucial, but Lend-Lease was a two-edged sword. Britain had to take what America sent her and, having expended her dollar reserves in the USA, she virtually ceased to be an exporting country. In the words of the British economist J.M. Keynes: 'We threw good house-keeping to the winds. But we saved ourselves, and helped to save the world.'

Long before Goebbels in 1943 proclaimed 'Total War' in Germany and began conscripting women and utilising slave labour, Britain was operating under a total war economy.

1941: THE USA, FROM NEUTRALITY TO ALLIANCE

In late January 1941 British and American staff officers first met, to begin joint planning in case the United States entered the war against both Japan and Germany. To these discussions, which lasted until March, representatives from Australia and New Zealand were invited.

A British artillery corporal explains the workings of a heavy gun to female soldiers. Many of London's anti-aircraft batteries consisted of female gunners and their aim was exceptionally good.

'These were fighting words from a neutral nation and a direct challenge to the dictators, an Anglo-American answer to the Tripartite Pact, and it promised a better world than that being forged by Hitler.

To Prime Minister Menzies of Australia, whose efforts to alert Churchill to the danger posed by Japan had been persistent but fruitless, Churchill wrote (15 August) that 'if Japan becomes involved in war with the United States she will also be at war with Britain and the British Commonwealth ... I feel confident that Japan will lie quiet for a while ...'

In September 1941, after American destroyers came under attack from German U-boats, Roosevelt ordered them to shoot back. On 31 October the destroyer USS *Rueben James* was torpedoed by an enemy submarine with the loss of 100 men, including all her officers. American forces were in effect at war long before it was declared. When war came to America in December 1941 the nation reeled in a state of shock, but it was ready for war, with an army under training and a strong navy based in both the Pacific and the Atlantic.

Left: President Roosevelt and Prime Minister Churchill meet for the first time in the war in Newfoundland in August 1941, to form a strong partnership. Between them stands Admiral King, the US Navy Chief of Staff.
Below: General George C. Marshall, the US Army Chief of Staff throughout the entire course of the war. In Washington Roosevelt relied on his wisdom and experience to such an extent that he would not let him take up a field command. After the war Marshall became an equally outstanding Secretary of State under President Truman.

The Lend-Lease Bill was passed by the Senate in March 1941. Soon Roosevelt ordered the United States Navy to escort British convoys to the mid-Atlantic to ease the strain on the British and Canadians. In July 1941 he sent US troops to occupy Iceland, a Danish territory, to take over from the British garrison there.

In August 1941 Roosevelt met Churchill at Placentia Bay in Newfoundland. Both arrived there on warships — the President in the cruiser USS *Augusta*, the Prime Minister on the new battleship *Prince of Wales* — and brought their military and political advisers with them. The meeting's main purpose was to initiate ways of defeating the Axis and to get to know each other. The two leaders hit it off well and drafted and issued the 'Atlantic Charter' — a bill of rights for the peoples of the world, promising self-government for the subject peoples: 'They hope to see established a peace, after the final destruction of the Nazi tyranny, which will afford to all nations the means of dwelling in security within their own boundaries [so that] they may live out their lives in freedom from fear and want.

1941: WAR IN THE AIR

It was time for the British air force to strike back, but its weapons were ineffective. Losses were high and results disappointing. Fighters carried out raids — 'sweeps' — over occupied France; they shot down more than 100 Luftwaffe aircraft but lost more than 500 pilots, many of them to anti-aircraft guns. The medium bombers achieved astonishing results. They often mounted attacks by day, which was gallant but foolish. After a daring low-level attack by fifteen Blenheim bombers on the Bremen docks on 4 July 1941 (in which half the attacking aircraft were lost) their leader, Wing Commander Hugh Edwards, a 27-year-old Australian, was awarded the Victoria Cross. He became the first British Commonwealth airman to win the 'big three' — the VC, DSO and DFC, and survived the war to become Governor of his home state, Western Australia. But these losses could not be sustained.

Lacking four-engined bombers capable of carrying heavy bomb loads, without navigational aids to pinpoint targets, RAF Bomber Command was a blunt sword for the first three years of war, unable to destroy more than 3 per cent of Germany's industry. 'Bomb damage in Germany was negligible before 1942,' states the *RAAF Official History*. By late 1943, by trial and error, it would become the most effective weapon of destruction yet devised.

In June 1941, when the first RAAF bomber squadron in Britain (455 Squadron), formed by EATS-trained aircrew, became operational it had to remain idle for months because of the shortage of medium bombers (as the two-engined bombers were now called). Ordered in July 1941 to bomb enemy industrial targets and 'thereby erode civilian morale' in the vital Ruhr Valley, Bomber Command also lacked fighter protection and powerful aircraft and bombs (the heaviest bomb being used was the 500-pounder). It had only one Hampden — 'the flying suitcase' — to send on its first raid on Germany on 29 August 1941. Most British bomber squadrons could tell a similar story.

Britain's bomber offensive in the six months from August 1940 had claimed just 975 German lives and could be counted a failure. In the costly RAF bomber raids of 1941 loss rates often reached 10 per cent, without inflicting notable damage on the German cities attacked — Frankfurt, Berlin, Hüls, Cologne, Mannheim, Essen, Dusseldorf, all of which would become familiar names to aircrew by war's end. A

A fine shot of a flight of British Wellington bombers above the English countryside. The 'Wimpey' was unable to carry a heavy bomb load but was of strong construction and its reliability made it a favourite of bomber pilots. It was still in use at the end of the war.

On the eve of the invasion of Russia, Hitler explains his plans to his closest confidants: From left, Göring, Field Marshal Keitel and Himmler.

report in August 1941 revealed that only one-third of the bomber force was dropping its loads within even ten kilometres of its targets. It was obvious that more scientific aids and a change in night-time 'stick-bombing' tactics were required. Thus, during 1941, Britain's fighter air-strength would be concentrated on defending her cities, her bombers at striking ineffectively at targets in Germany, and Coastal Command in helping the navy fight the Battle of the Atlantic — the long campaign against the U-boat menace that would reach a climax in 1943.

By mid-November 1940 the Luftwaffe's Blitz on Britain's cities had killed 15,000 civilians. But Germany's aircraft-production industries were already under strain. By mid-1941 they were constructing more than forty different types of aircraft, and output of even vital makes was slowing in comparison with British. By late June 1941, on the eve of the invasion of the Soviet Union, the Luftwaffe's 'first-line' strength (2770 planes) was not much greater than that of a year earlier (2600). There was also a labour shortage and Field Marshal Milch, entrusted by Göring with the expansion of the Luftwaffe, estimated that the armaments labour force would have to be increased from 1.3 million to 3.5 million just to double the annual production of 1200 aircraft to 2400. At that stage the USA alone was producing 1400 aircraft a month. General Ernst Udet, depressed by the insoluble chaos and by Göring's rages, committed suicide late in 1941. General Jeschonnek was to take the same way out in 1943 when Göring berated him for his failure to prevent British mass bombing of German cities.

Hitler cancelled production of heavy bombers. Soon slave labourers would augment the workforce. The only achievement of 1941 was production of a remarkable new fighter, the Focke-Wulf 190. It was faster than the Me 109. Soon four FW 190s would be manufactured for every Me 109.

1941: GERMANY INVADES RUSSIA
THE ORIGINS OF 'BARBAROSSA'

Hitler had decided to invade Russia just after the conquest of France. On 21 July 1940 he had told Brauchitsch to start preparing plans for it. Brauchitsch suggested that the campaign would take eight weeks and require up to 100 German divisions. On 29 July Hitler told his High Command of his intention to invade Russia, explaining (in General Halder's words, committed to his diary): 'Britain's only hope lies in Russia and America. If that hope in Russia is destroyed then it will be destroyed for America too, because elimination of Russia will enormously increase Japan's power in the Far East.' Hitler said, 'The sooner Russia is smashed, the better.' He would strike with two great armies — one directed at the Baltic states and Moscow, one towards Kiev and the Dnieper. His Directive 21 outlining the invasion of Russia — 'Operation Barbarossa' — was issued on 18 December 1940. In February 1941 the Führer, who was known to change his mind, informed his High Command of his

Josef Stalin, ruler of the Soviet Union.

firm and final decision to invade Russia three months hence, on 15 May. He was determined to destroy the 'pestilence' of Bolshevism and create in its place a new German Reich spreading from the plains of Poland and the wheat fields of the Ukraine to the Urals. In early March Hitler held a conference of his service chiefs and outlined the nature of the war he would wage against Russia. General Halder again kept notes of the Führer's speech: 'The war against Russia will be such that it cannot be conducted in a knightly fashion ... This struggle is one of ideologies and racial differences and will have to be conducted with unprecedented, unmerciful and unrelenting harshness. The Commissars [Communist Party officials] are the bearers of ideologies directly opposed to National Socialism. Therefore the Commissars will be liquidated. German soldiers guilty of breaking international

Hitler looks over the maps with his principal army chiefs. On his right stands Field Marshal von Brauchitsch; on his left, General Franz Halder.

law will be excused.' The generals were angry at the thought of condoning murder and protested to Brauchitsch, who did nothing. On 13 May Keitel issued the directive — the infamous 'Commissar order' — stating that 'persons suspected of criminal actions will be brought at once before an officer. This officer will decide whether they are to be shot.' This gave great latitude to the Wehrmacht. On the same day a directive entrusted Himmler's SS with 'special tasks' and Himmler was authorised to act independently of the army. The Nazi racial theorist Rosenberg was given the task, which he regarded as a pleasure, of drawing up a new map of Russia: the Soviet Union would be divided into protectorates and regions for German settlement. Göring, in charge of economic planning for a conquered Russia, and his office specified on 23 May that Russia's food must be sent to Germany even if the Russians starved. 'There is no doubt that as a result many millions of persons will be starved to death if we take out of the country the things necessary for us' — but this was considered inevitable.

THE INVASION DELAYED

As we have seen, Hitler's timetable was thrown out by events in Yugoslavia in late March 1941. In deciding to invade Yugoslavia and all of Greece, he would have to divert forces to accomplish the task and delay Barbarossa a month at least. The invasion of Russia, he ordered, would now take place on 22 June 1941. It was midsummer day and two days before the anniversary of Napoleon's invasion of Russia in 1812. If any of his generals reminded him of this fact, there is no record of it. Russia had been defeated in 1918 by German armies that were less well-equipped than the Wehrmacht. The Red Army was the largest in the world — nearly five million strong. It possessed 34 armoured divisions and the Soviet Air Force had 7300 planes. These figures did not daunt Hitler.

The Führer was confident. He assured his generals: 'We will only have to kick down the door, and the whole rotten structure will come crashing down … When Barbarossa commences, the world will hold its breath …' For 'Operation Barbarossa' Hitler was to hurl against Russia an army of 3.4 million men — 111 divisions, with 40 more in reserve — and no fewer than 2700 aircraft.

In the north Field Marshal von Leeb's Army Group of 29 divisions was to smash through the Baltic states to Leningrad; in the centre Field Marshal von Bock's Army Group of 49 divisions (including nine armoured and six motorised), would advance through White Russia (Belorus) towards Moscow, and Field-Marshal von Rundstedt's Army Group consisted of 43 German divisions and 14 Romanian would advance in the south. Von Rundstedt would be confronted by 77 Soviet divisions plus 14 motorised brigades, and his advance was expected to be slower. In addition, 12 Finnish divisions would move on Leningrad, which was soon subjected to a siege that would last 900 days.

Stalin remained oblivious to the threat. As early as April 1941 Churchill had warned him that intelligence showed a build-up of German forces on Soviet borders. Soviet spies in Switzerland — the famed 'Lucy Ring' — and as far away as Tokyo (where Richard Sorge warned Moscow on 15 June that the attack would begin on 22 June) forwarded warnings but they went unheeded. Stalin's front reported hundreds of violations of air space by German aircraft spying out the land, but Stalin was content with a formal protest. He had never trusted Hitler but decided that nothing yet must be done to provoke a German attack.

On 15 June Churchill wrote to Roosevelt that 'it looks as if a vast German onslaught on Russia is imminent … Should this new war break out we shall of course give all encouragement and any help we can spare to the Russians, following the principle that Hitler is the foe we have to beat.' Roosevelt endorsed this decision and Churchill implemented his promise, pledging aid to Russia on the first day of the invasion. Informed by Hitler of his plans on the day before the invasion began, Mussolini eagerly offered an entire Corps to participate in the war against Bolshevism; Spain's Franco offered a division — the Blue Division. In Occupied Europe, Germany was to call for volunteers to join special Waffen-SS units to crush the Communist empire and found a ready response: soon French, Belgian, Dutch, Norwegian and Danish forces were serving in Russia

The Red Army's secret weapon. Soviet T-34 tanks proved superior to German Panzers

HITLER INVADES RUSSIA, 1941

At dawn on 22 June 1941 Hitler's armies crossed the Soviet borders on a front stretching 2500 kilometres from the Arctic to the shores of the Black Sea. The Russian front collapsed, as Hitler had predicted, like a pack of cards. Nowhere did Russian troops hold their frontier in depth. Even the much vaunted 'Stalin Line' along the old Russo-Polish border had wide gaps in it; its forts gave the only stiff resistance the invaders met in the first weeks.

By the end of the first day one German armoured division in 39 Panzer Corps penetrated 100 kilometres. Stalin closeted himself in the Kremlin in a state of shock, unable to speak or issue orders for a day. German artillery, air attack and the speed with which their forces advanced cut Soviet communications, and entire divisions were rounded up, leaderless. By the end of the second day Russia's air force along the front had been destroyed, mostly at their own airfields. The grey-green columns of German infantry marched on through the heat and dust of summer, exultant and astonished at how many people in the Baltic states, and Russians and Ukrainians, welcomed them as liberators.

Above: German motorised infantry: tracked vehicles crammed with infantry follow the tanks into Russia. *Below:* Fighting their way into a Russian city in July 1941, a German Panzer Mark III (the most widely produced German tank of the war) seen with infantry after setting an enemy vehicle ablaze.

THE FIRST MASS MURDERS

Behind the armies came the SS and its 'task groups' — the Einsatzgruppen. These murder squads were often recruited from ex-convicts and were also empowered to recruit local fascists or thugs to assist them in their grisly duties. As Martin Gilbert, a historian of the Holocaust, states, '… the slaughter in the East began on the first day of the German invasion'. In the frontier village of Virbalis, the SS were assisted by local policemen. The Jews were forced into anti-tank trenches about two kilometres long and machine-gunned. 'Lime was thereupon sprayed upon them and a second row of Jews was made to lie down. They were similarly shot.'

The Germans entered Kaunus (Kovno) in Lithuania on 26 June. There hundreds of Jews were taken outside the town and killed. 'Even before the German killing squads reached a region,' records Gilbert, 'the local population often attacked the Jews who had lived in their midst for centuries. These attacks were not pogroms to beat and wound, to loot and burn, but attacks to kill: to destroy a whole community at one swift blow. In the first five weeks of the German invasion of the Soviet Union more Jews were killed than in the previous eight years of Nazi rule.'

Russian soldiers after their surrender to German troops.

By year's end 200,000 Lithuanian Jews would be killed, mostly in mass shootings; only 36,000 survived. Communist Party members, Commissars and Russian soldiers were also killed, but these were relatively few in number. Wireless reports to Berlin from units boasting of the numbers they had killed were intercepted by the British and Churchill broadcast to the British people on 24 August, describing how 'whole districts are being exterminated … Since the Mongol invasions … there has never been methodical, merciless butchery on such a scale.' The war in Russia would be a war of extermination, for both sides.

THE ADVANCE CONTINUES

In the south von Rundstedt's Army Group took Lvov on 30 June. On 8 July German pincers closed at Minsk around the broken remnants of 32 divisions, and captured nearly 300,000 men and 2500 tanks. In the north the Germans had taken not only Kaunus but the Latvian capital Riga by the end of June, and were entering Estonia.

On 3 July Stalin made his first broadcast to the Russian people since the invasion. He ordered 'scorched earth': nothing must be left for the invader. What could not be carried away must be destroyed. Five days later Hitler's chief of staff wrote that 'of the 164 infantry divisions which the Red Army mobilised, 89 have been completely or partially destroyed … The Russians can no longer offer a continuous front even using the best defensive positions.' He considered that 'all in all, I can already say that we have carried out the task entrusted to us, which was to crush the mass of the Russian army between the Dvina and Dnieper rivers.'

On 2 August three Russian armies were surrounded at Kiev and the survivors of 22 divisions — more than 100,000 men — fell into German hands. On 8 August more than 300,000 Russians were taken prisoner after bitter fighting at Smolensk. And on 5 August Romanian armies numbering 18 divisions (aided by a single German one) had advanced as far as Odessa, which was subjected to a siege that lasted until mid-October, when the great seaport fell. 'The Marseilles of the East' became Romanian and their inefficient rule proved to be relatively relaxed for the civilians in their conquered territory compared to the genocidal hell that was the fate of the rest of Russia.

But the cost of these stunning victories to the German Army was staggering. Many Soviet troops had fought to the death. (Others had taken to the woods and marshes to fight as guerrillas.) In less than two months German casualties had reached a total of 390,000, of whom 100,000 were killed or missing. All the campaigns since 1939 before the invasion of the Soviet Union — Poland, the Low Countries and France, the Balkans and Libya — had cost just 90,000 German dead.

Opposite top: German anti-tank gunners score a direct hit, Russia, summer 1941.
Opposite left: Marshal Semyon Timoshenko, who was one of Stalin's most favoured military commanders but failed to live up to his master's expectations.
Opposite right: General Erich von Manstein, who ranks with Guderian as one of the German army's most brilliant commanders. Like Guderian he never made it to the rank of field marshal.

A CHANGE IN PLANS

Hitler now ordered a change in his master plan. He ordered a halt in the advance towards Moscow. Army Group centre would instead send reinforcements to the Army Groups in the north and south. 'The essential target to be achieved before winter is not the capture of Moscow,' Hitler ordered, 'but the conquest of the Donets coal and industrial region together with the interruption of oil supplies from the Caucasus. In the north, Leningrad must be invested and German forces must link up with the Finns.' Two days later, on 23 August, Guderian, whose tanks were only 300 kilometres from Moscow, saw Hitler and protested at the change, which would send his Corps on a 1000-kilometre detour. He protested in vain.

In the south German forces proceeded rapidly; by the end of August von Rundstedt's forces had reached the Dnieper. Kiev, capital of the Ukraine, and its defenders were soon encircled. 'Kiev must be held at all costs,' Stalin ordered, refusing his generals' pleas to withdraw before the German trap closed. At Kiev in mid-September close to half a million (according to some statistics as many as 666,000) Russians were captured, along with more than 800 tanks and more than 3000 guns.

On 5 September Army Group North's leading Panzers caught their first glimpse of Leningrad, the fabled St Petersburg. Fifteen days later Hitler ordered that the city must 'be wiped off the face of the earth'. Its population must be left to starve. Göring himself told Ciano a few weeks later: 'this year between twenty and thirty million persons will die of hunger in Russia … certain nations must be decimated. Nothing can be done about it.' The Reichsmarschall related that in some camps Russian prisoners had resorted to cannibalism; he joked to others that some had even eaten the guard dogs. The Greeks were already dying of starvation. So too would the Russians.

When Ciano visited Hitler's general headquarters in late October, Ribbentrop sent the Italian warm, sweetened milk to help his cough. The following day they shot game and dined well. While driving the Italian foreign minister to the station next day Ribbentrop exclaimed: 'Hitler's New Order in Europe will ensure peace for a thousand years.' Ciano ventured that a thousand years was a long time, even though Hitler was a genius. Ribbentrop conceded: 'Let's make it a century.'

Below: Young German soldiers stop to fill their water canteens during the invasion of Russia.
Right: German soldiers shelter from enemy fire in a Russian village.

1941: NORTH AFRICA

By late June 1941 the campaign in the Western Desert had been pushed from the headlines by the German war in the Soviet Union. Wavell's failure to break through to Tobruk in mid-June led to another five months of stalemate. The seaport's garrison was reduced to 22,000 to ease the problems of supply by sea that had taken a toll of so many ships. In mid-July General Blamey, who was alarmed by medical reports of the deteriorating physical condition of the Australian garrison, asked the new Commander-in-Chief, Auchinleck, to consider relieving them. They had been in Tobruk for four months. Auchinleck dismissed the idea and Cunningham pointed out to Blamey that bringing them out could see the loss of more ships. But the Australian government supported Blamey and ordered that the 9th Division be replaced by fresh British troops. The evacuation began in August and finished in the last weeks of October, when British troops and a Polish brigade took over the defence, but there was still an Australian unit in Tobruk when the siege was lifted in December.

It had been a defence with few precedents. The Australians had tied up three Italian divisions and three of Rommel's valuable German battalions, and had suffered 3300 casualties, including 800 dead. For the first time in the war resolute infantry had withstood tanks, Stukas and constant air attack. In a way they had broken the myth of the Blitzkrieg.

'CRUSADER' BEGINS

On 18 November 1941 Auchinleck launched the long-planned and long-awaited offensive intended to destroy Rommel's armour and relieve Tobruk: 'Crusader.' A violent thunderstorm on the eve of battle failed to dampen the high morale of the army but slowed its progress.

Now named Eighth Army, the desert force, commanded by General Sir Alan Cunningham, was a formidable grouping of two Corps, 30 Corps (comprised of his tank divisions) and 13 Corps (his infantry, in which the veteran New Zealand Division had pride of place). Of the New Zealanders in the Middle East, the Australian war correspondent Alan Moorehead was to write: 'This wonderful division took a great deal of its fighting morale from its English general, Freyberg, the VC who through two wars had probably been more critically wounded more often than any other living man.' In the coming days Freyberg was to keep his head while other generals were losing theirs — and their careers.

British and Anzac troops at the front line in Tobruk watch a distant tank skirmish. On 7 December tanks from Tobruk linked up with the advancing New Zealanders and a British general signalled: 'Tobruk is as relieved as I am'. On the same day Japan attacked in the Pacific and the desert war took second place to the dramatic Allied collapse in the Far East.

Caught off-balance in the first two days, Rommel reacted swiftly, and the battle 'became a dusty, smoky swirl of confusion, disaster, muddle, heroism and glory. What really happened, incident by incident, engagement by engagement, can never be sorted out,' Auchinleck's biographer John Connell has written. All the British inadequacies in desert fighting were revealed — from confused orders and faulty tactics to ineffective communication between units (principally malfunctioning wirelesses) and tanks undergunned and prey to mechanical breakdowns. By 19 November 4th and 7th Armoured Brigades had reached Sidi Rezegh ridge, only 15 kilometres from Tobruk but Cunningham ordered 13 Corps to the south to advance from near Bardia only on 21 November. By 22 November Rommel's aggressive tank commanders and his deadly anti-tank guns — particularly his 88-mm anti-aircraft guns which could also be used as field artillery — combined with mechanical failures had eliminated nearly half of Auchinleck's 600 tanks, and 30 Corps's advance towards Tobruk was stopped dead.

By the nght of 23 November, with the 5th South African Brigade destroyed and reports that only 75 tanks were left, General Cunningham lost his nerve. Rattled, he suggested to Auchinleck that the battle be broken off. Auchinleck sacked him on 25 November, replacing him with one of his Corps commanders, Lieutenant-General Neil Ritchie, another Scot. On the same day Rommel further shook the British command by launching his armour in a wild 'dash to the wire' of the Egyptian frontier, almost capturing Cunningham at an airfield.

Lacking clear orders from Cunningham, the New Zealanders' commander, Freyberg, had made on 23 November the crucial decision to press on with his division to Tobruk from the toehold he had gained on Sidi Rezegh ridge. Seven days later the New Zealanders were rolled over by German tanks in a desperate battle at Sidi Rezegh but the link-up with the Tobruk garrison was made. It was severed again by Rommel, but Afrika Korps' forced retreat soon afterwards saw the siege of Tobruk finally lifted on 7 December 1941, the very day that the war against Germany and Italy became a world war.

The adversaries: *Left:* Wavell's successor as Commander-in-Chief, Middle East, General Sir Claude Auchinleck. He, in turn, was sacked by Churchill when British victories turned to dust in mid-1942.
Above: General Rommel with his aide Captain Aldinger.

On 24 December 1941 British tanks entered Benghazi for the second time in a year, and by early January 1942 Rommel had retreated another 150 kilometres to El Agheila, back to where he had started from in March 1941.

'Crusader' had seen the Luftwaffe and the Italians outnumber Desert Air Force by 600 aircraft to 540; the Tomahawks and the Hurricanes were outclassed. 'We must stop England thinking that

New Zealand infantry pass a British tank after the link-up had been made to the Tobruk garrison, December 1941.

second-class aircraft will do out here,' Air Marshal Coningham wrote to his chief, Tedder, but no Spitfires would be released to the Middle East until June 1942.

Eighth Army had suffered nearly 18,000 casualties — 5000 of them in the New Zealand Division, who had again proved themselves outstanding soldiers. Rommel had lost 300 tanks and 33,000 men. Afrika Korps had been mauled but not destroyed.

NAVAL LOSSES

The navy kept Tobruk supplied but paid a high cost. The route from Alexandria and Mersa Matruh to Tobruk — 'Bomb Alley' — was subject by day to Axis air attack and threatened at night by minefields and submarines. On the night of 24 June 1941 the Australian sloop *Parramatta*, which had left long service in the Red Sea with relief, fought off an attack by 50 dive-bombers that had sunk HMS *Auckland* and managed, with help from *Vendetta* and *Waterhen*, to pick up many of the troops and crew from the British ship. On 29 June the old *Waterhen*, the beloved 'Chook', was crippled by a dive-bomber; with her back broken she sank the next day off Sollum.

She was the first Australian warship to be lost in the war. Her companion on the day she was hit, HMS *Defender*, was herself sunk eleven days later; *Vendetta* again helped to take off the crew. *Vendetta* was to be the last of the old destroyers to leave the Mediterranean, departing for Singapore in October 1941. On 27 November 1941, as the new desert offensive was ending, *Parramatta* was torpedoed north-east of Tobruk while escorting a transport carrying ammunition to that besieged port. Only 24 of her ship's company of 160 survived; among those lost was her captain.

HMAS *Voyager*, limping into Alexandria on 13 July on one engine, was ordered home eleven days later and *Stuart*, the famous flotilla leader, left on 22 August; her captain 'Hec' Waller, a man Cunningham described with rare emotion in his memoirs as 'one of the finest types of Australian naval officers, greatly loved and admired by everyone', flew home ahead of his ship to take command of a cruiser. The Tobruk shuttle service had already claimed a savage toll of ships, a cost that caused the C-in-Cs in 1942 to decide that Tobruk must be considered expendable if threatened again. Five warships and 21 smaller vessels had been lost. Cunningham was proud of the navy's record: his men had taken out of Tobruk over eight months 34,000 personnel and 7000 prisoners and taken into the fortress 33,000 troops and 72 tanks.

The last months of 1941 were devastating for the British and Commonwealth navies. In November the number of Axis air raids on Malta reached 175 and it seemed clear that they were intended to reduce the island to rubble and destroy its harbour and facilities. On 13 November the aircraft carrier HMS *Ark Royal*, which had just launched fighter reinforcements in the waters west of Malta, was torpedoed by a U-boat, fortunately with little loss of life but great loss of prestige: *Ark Royal*, which the Axis had claimed to have sunk many times, was not only a modern carrier but had been an unconquerable symbol of pride to the Royal Navy. On 25 November Cunningham had taken his battle fleet to patrol between Crete and Libya and was in his bridge cabin on HMS *Queen Elizabeth* when he felt the ship shudder. On reaching the bridge he saw astern the battleship *Barham* stopped dead and listing to port. She had been hit by three German torpedoes. 'The poor ship nearly rolled over on to her beam ends, and we saw the men massing on her upturned side.' Then there was a shattering explosion as her magazine blew up, and she disappeared, taking with her 865 officers and men.

And then, early on 19 December 'something very unpleasant' — as Cunningham described it — occurred in Alexandria harbour. There was an explosion under a tanker, then another under the forward turret of the battleship *Valiant*, and then one under the flagship herself, *Queen Elizabeth*: Cunningham was standing aft by the ensign staff on her when he was hurled nearly two metres into the air by the whip of the ship. Italian frogmen using limpet mines had crippled the last two battleships in the Mediterranean fleet.

On the same day 'Force K', sailing from Malta in an attempt to intercept an Italian convoy off Tripoli, met with disaster. Three cruisers — *Neptune*, *Aurora* and *Penelope* — hit mines and the first of them then hit two more in succession. The destroyer *Kandahar*, moving in to rescue *Neptune*'s men, also hit a mine which blew off her stern. *Neptune* then hit a fourth mine and began to sink. Nothing could be done to help the stricken ship: mines were everywhere, dawn was soon to break and the seas were running high. Only one man survived from among her ship's company of more than 700, which included 150 New Zealanders. Among her dead was Captain Rory O'Connor, RN.

Far away, in the Indian Ocean, Australia suffered a loss that was felt like a blow to her heart. The famed cruiser HMAS *Sydney* was reported 'missing, believed lost'. Returning to Fremantle from escorting a convoy to Singapore, *Sydney* was off the Western Australian coast near Carnarvon when she sighted an approaching merchant ship. It was 4 p.m., 19 November 1941. The two ships drew closer. *Sydney* ordered the vessel by searchlight signal to identify herself. When the unidentified ship replied that she was a Dutch ship, *Sydney* drew even closer, and the two ships were just a kilometre apart when the suspect vessel suddenly hoisted the German war flag and opened fire from hidden guns at point-blank range with such devastating effect that the Australian warship, after scoring one hit on her enemy, was soon on fire, wracked by explosions. She drifted off and was soon just a glow on the horizon before disappearing completely. None of *Sydney*'s 645 officers and men survived. To some it seemed like an omen.

She had encountered the German raider *Kormoran*. The German ship was hit by a shell from *Sydney* that set her afire, endangering the mines in her hold. Her captain ordered his men to abandon ship and they were later picked up drifting in boats.

The Australian light cruiser HMAS *Sydney* which achieved a famous fighting reputation in the Mediterranean battles of 1940, only to be sunk with all hands in a battle to the death with the German raider *Kormoran*.

RUSSIA: THE CLIMAX
ON TO MOSCOW

The advance on Moscow was to start on 15 September but was delayed until 2 October. Barbarossa itself had been delayed five weeks; this last delay of three weeks was to prove fatal to Germany. Winter came early, and a few days before the launching of the offensive, which began well, rain began to fall, and occasional snow. The mud slowed progress; the snow was to stop it dead.

Army Group centre was now 78 divisions strong; with no fewer than 31 Panzer divisions and 19 motorised ones. On 7 October German motorised divisions reached the city of Vyazma, which was soon encircled when an entire Panzergruppe drove north from Smolensk. The 'Vyazma pocket' collapsed, and with it an army of 663,000 Russian soldiers, 120 tanks and more than 5000 guns. It was a greater disaster for Russia than Kiev.

The city to Moscow's south held out against ruthless German assaults but within days the Germans had reached to within 80 kilometres of Moscow; some units pushed on even further and sighted the spires of the Kremlin. Stalin's government evacuated Moscow, and on 10 October General Georgi Zhukov, one of the few Russian commanders who had not lost his head or reputation in the preceding three and a half months, was appointed commander of its defences. On 20 October Moscow declared a state of siege — in effect, martial law. On the same day the intermittent rain over the German front became a downpour, bogging their supply columns, which with every day's advance by the forward troops became harder to sustain.

The bells of Kiev: an exultant German soldier atop the cathedral in the capital of the Ukraine, 1941

In mid-November 1941, when winter set in, a last effort was made against Moscow. Two of the Panzer divisions had only 50 tanks left out of the 300 they had started with in June. The troops, not equipped with winter clothing, froze. In Germany there was an appeal for winter clothing, and soon many of the troops were wearing fur coats and hats donated by women. By the last days of November total German losses since the invasion had mounted to 750,000, a large proportion of which were casualties caused by frostbite. Vehicle parts froze too; engines had to be kept running to avoid seizing up but this exhausted fuel; the artificial rubber in engine parts — buna — turned solid and cracked like wood.

But in the far south, more Russian disasters occurred. On 19 November the Germans took Rostov, and Manstein's armies broke into the Crimea, which was quickly overrun except for the fortress seaport of Sevastopol. 'October and November 1941 were the grimmest months in the whole of the Soviet–German war,' writes Alexander Werth, who served as a correspondent in Russia and later wrote a history of the war there, 'only to be equalled by October 1942, when the fate of Stalingrad hung in the balance.'

Since the invasion in June the Red Army had lost 2.8 million men, mostly as prisoners; yet it was still increasing in strength, even though many of its new divisions were low in numbers. In place of panic and despair, the Russians had recovered their resolution and their infinite capacity to suffer. Within three weeks the temperature had dropped from minus 12 degrees C to minus 35 degrees C (4 December) and the bitter cold was intensified by winds from the Arctic and the east.

Zhukov was to be celebrated as one of the outstanding military commanders of the war, yet he was ruthless, caring little about loss of life. There were signs of panic in Moscow. This was dealt with ruthlessly. Deserters were shot out of hand; other troops were marched to the front under NKVD escort. Half a million Muscovites were conscripted to build a system of trenches and anti-tank ditches that formed a defence line 15 kilometres deep.

From the east also came massive reinforcements to the Russian armies. Soviet Intelligence had learned that Japan had cancelled plans to attack the Soviet Union, and had adopted its second option — a sudden strike in South-East Asia. The great Siberian army was transported west to join in the defence of Moscow. Allied aid also was now reaching Russia. To the beleaguered Russians Churchill had sent 500 Hurricane fighters alone, denuding his defences in Malaya, with tragic results. Anglo-Russian forces had entered Iran in August, and the country was now a principal supply line to Russia.

Above: Like a scene from Napoleon's retreat from Moscow. The horses on which the German army relied for transport suffered terribly.
Below: German troops in December 1941 were still lacking adequate winter clothing.

THE COUNTEROFFENSIVES BEGIN

By the end of the first week of December 1941 the German armies outside Moscow had reached the limit of their exertions. Russian forces there now totalled fifty divisions. On 5–6 December 1941 the Red Army launched its counteroffensives, not just in the region of Moscow, but also along a 1000-kilometre front. Outside Moscow, Zhukov attacked with no fewer than ten armies; to his north Koniev (his great rival for Stalin's favour) attacked with four and in the south Timoshenko pushed with strong forces towards Kursk. Their aim was to crush the flanks of Hitler's Army Group centre and annihilate it. For the first time Panzer divisions were forced to retreat, often leaving their tanks behind. Kalinin fell. 'West of Moscow and in the Tula area,' wrote a British war correspondent, 'miles and miles of roads were littered with abandoned guns, lorries and tanks, deeply embedded in the snow.' By mid-December the Russians had

advanced between 30 and 70 kilometres and had recaptured Kaluga. They found in retaken towns and villages evidence of a Nazi presence: bodies of murdered civilians; corpses hanging from makeshift gallows. In his November speech Stalin had called for the death of every German on Russian soil, and brutality would be repaid with brutality.

Above: At Leningrad the Russians brought supplies and reinforcements into the city using the frozen surfaces of the lakes.
Right: General Georgi Zhukov, the 44-year-old general whom Stalin appointed to take over from the failed Voroshilov on the Leningrad front in September before sending him in October to defend the crucial front at Moscow. From Moscow Zhukov launched the Red Army's first successful counter-offensive in December 1941, saving the city. A year later Zhukov was promoted to the rank of Marshal. He ended the war as the most outstanding of Russian military commanders.

A CHANGE OF COMMAND

'The liquidation of Brauchitsch is the topic of the day,' Ciano wrote in his diary (22 December 1941). 'British and American radios talk of nothing else. The German embassy is staggered by the news.' Hitler never gave Brauchitsch another thought, except to damn him as a fool, calling him 'a man of straw.' To Goebbels three months later Hitler described his deposed C-in-C as 'a vain, cowardly wretch … and a nincompoop'.

Churchill was also dissatisfied with his own chief soldier, General Sir John Dill, whom he thought too pessimistic and tired. On 1 December 1941 General Sir Alan Brooke, Commander-in-Chief, Home Forces, took over his duties as CIGS at the War Office. Churchill had been impressed by Brooke, with whose elder brother he had soldiered in India forty years before. Like his predecessor, and the two generals Churchill had picked out for high promotion, Montgomery and Alexander, Brooke came from Northern Ireland. He was admired throughout the army, was robust, capable of standing up to the Prime Minister and of bearing pressures seemingly without strain. He spoke with the rapidity of a machine-gun. (His frustrations were committed daily to his diary or to letters to his beloved wife, and they would later form one of the most candid portraits of war at the top.) Brooke — the future Field Marshal Viscount Alanbrooke — would be one of the makers of victory.

DARK CHRISTMAS

On 16 December Field Marshal Bock, who was near nervous collapse, asked to be relieved of his command; he was succeeded by von Kluge; and three days later Hitler sacked von Brauchitsch and took over his post. He would now dispense with a commander-in-chief. Hitler had predicted that the German front would run from Archangel to the Black Sea. He was far short of his goals. Leningrad, Moscow, Sebastopol, the oil of the Caucasus still eluded him. The Red Army had recovered.

Hitler had gambled and lost. He realised this on the very day, 7 December 1941, when British forces lifted the siege of Tobruk, and when Japan took the gamble of its own life — a sudden conquest of South-East Asia following a surprise attack on the American Pacific fleet at Hawaii. On that same fateful day the Nazis began the systematic gassing of 40,000 Jews at Chelmno in eastern Poland in an attempt to exterminate the entire race.

The European conflict had become a world war, one unlike any conflict previously fought, and waged by enemies that had abandoned any pretence to humanity. To the Allies it soon became a crusade, one they must win at whatever cost. The alternative was too terrible to contemplate.

THE JAPANESE TIDE, 1941

Japan's imperial ambitions had grown alarmingly after June 1940, when the Vichy French government in Indochina acceded to Japan's demands that they close off supply lines from Hanoi to southern China. One week earlier Emperor Hirohito had discussed the future of French and Dutch possessions in East Asia, which were now isolated. On 12 June Japan signed a non aggression pact with Thailand, which was anxious to claim back provinces on the Indochina border that had been lost to the French. On the next day the Yonai Cabinet in Tokyo was asked to resign to make way for a new Prime Minister, Prince Konoye, who had won the Emperor's approval to introduce one-party government. Early in July Japan initiated another attempt to achieve a cease-fire in China: a representative of Chiang Kai-shek met with senior Japanese officers in Changsha and, while refusing to sign an armistice, agreed to observe an unofficial truce with the Japanese in regions that were free of Chinese Communist forces. 'Though little known and almost entirely undocumented in the West, this unsigned truce was in reality observed rather strictly in the field until Japan's defeat five years later,' writes David Bergamini in his exhaustive study of the Emperor Hirohito's role in this period.

Konoye chose as War Minister General Tojo Hideki — 'the Razor' — and as Foreign Minister Matsuoka Yosuke. Matsuoka assured the American ambassador in Tokyo that Japan loved peace but that the United States must recognise that a 'New Order' was emerging in the world. On 27 July the Japanese Cabinet and the armed forces chiefs of staff met to implement the decision to foster closer ties with Germany and Italy and undertake 'to include the English, French, Dutch and Port-uguese islands of the Orient within the substance of the New Order'. The Imperial Navy protested at this policy, stating that the army had still failed to achieve victory in China, while the army accused the navy of fearing the possibility of war with the United States. The Emperor ordered the two arms to work harmoniously together.

In August 1940 Matsuoka used the phrase 'Greater East Asia Co-Prosperity Sphere' for the first time to describe his nation's economic ambitions. On 22 September 1940 Japan demanded and obtained from the Vichy French the right to base forces in northern Indochina (Tonkin). Four days later the United States ordered an embargo on exports of scrap iron and steel to all nations other than the British Commonwealth and the Americas: it was aimed specifically at Japan. The next day (27 September 1940) Japan joined Germany and Italy in the Tripartite Pact, which was signed in the Reich Chancellory in Berlin. In the pact the three powers announced their intention to establish a 'New Order' in their own regions.

Below: The Emperor Hirohito presides over a meeting of the Japanese cabinet. The role played by Hirohito in Japan's march to war is still a puzzle to historians
Bottom right: The war flag of the armed forces of Japan.

Japan now took on the drab appearance of a fascist state. Early in 1941 Admiral Nomura, who had known Roosevelt when he had served in Washington a generation earlier as naval attaché, was despatched to the United States as Japanese ambassador. In the following month Matsuoka left for Germany and Italy to discuss closer ties with the Axis. In Berlin Hitler promised that if Japan found herself at war with the United States, Germany would also consider herself at war with the Americans. It was one of the few promises Hitler ever kept.

Japan had long nursed a fear of Russia. The German invasion of the Soviet Union in June 1941 encouraged Matsuoka to press for a Japanese invasion of Siberia. He was overruled. On 1 July 1941 Cabinet cancelled plans for a 'Strike North' against Russia and decided instead to occupy all of Indochina as preparation for an offensive in the south to seize the British, American and Dutch possessions there. The oil of the Dutch East Indies and Burma, the tin and rubber of Malaya, the rice of Indochina, were now regarded as essential for Japan's survival.

On the same day, 1 July, President Roosevelt wrote to his Interior Secretary and petroleum administrator, Harold Ickes, to caution him against taking premature measures to cut off Japan's oil supply:

'The Japs are having a real drag-down and knock-out fight among themselves ... trying to decide which way they are going to jump — attack Russia, attack the South Seas (thus throwing in their lot definitely with the Germans) or whether they will sit on the fence ... it is terribly important for the control of the Atlantic for us to help keep peace in the Pacific. We simply have not got enough Navy to go round ...' Roosevelt's intelligence sources were excellent: his navy code-breakers had been reading Japan's diplomatic and naval codes for years.

On the following day (2 July 1941) the Japanese Cabinet met at the Imperial Palace and adopted a position paper stating that 'preparations for war with Great Britain and the United States will be made ...' On the same evening Hirohito was disturbed to hear from General Yamashita, who had just returned from eight months in Germany, that Japan's army was woefully ill-equipped by European standards. It lacked modern arms — from paratroops and medium tanks to heavy bombers; even its radar was primeval by comparison to British and German radar systems. (Japan did not possess an air force — its aircraft belonged to either the army or the navy.) The general recommended that any thought of war be postponed two years until the army could be modernised. Fortunately for Japan, their agents, who moved freely around South-East Asia, reported that European and American defences in the region were threadbare.

On 24 July 1941 the Japanese made their move into southern Indochina, sending a fleet into Cam Ranh Bay and then landing 30,000 troops in Saigon. While tolerating the existence of the French administration, Japan had, by this stroke, secured airfields and harbours within close distance of the Malay Peninsula. American retaliation was swift. Two days later President Roosevelt froze Japanese assets in the United States, closed the Panama Canal to Japanese shipping and swiftly placed an embargo on exports of oil and rubber to Tokyo. The pace towards war was quickening.

On the same day, 26 July, the mastermind of 'Unit 82' charged with planning Japan's southward thrust, a relatively junior officer called Lieutenant-Colonel Tsugi, presented his outline of the coming conquests. The Army Chief of Staff, General Sugiyama, congratulated Tsugi and asked him how long the seizure of southern Asia would take. Tsugi replied that if war was launched on 3 November, Japan could capture Manila by the new year, Singapore by 11 February, Java by 10 March and Rangoon by the Emperor's birthday (10 April). Events caused the war's launching to be delayed until early December, but the timetable was to be kept almost to the day — and Rangoon would be entered by Japanese troops one month earlier than Tsuji had estimated: 8 March.

The militarist group's influence was now almost total. On 15 September Admiral Yamamoto, who viewed war against the United States (where he too had served as a naval attaché) as a disaster for Japan, dutifully produced his plan for an attack on the US Pacific fleet at its anchorage at Pearl Harbor. Present at this meeting were two senior soldiers, Count Terauchi and General Yamashita, who promised their full support to the navy's plans. Yamamoto assured Cabinet that the Imperial Navy would 'run wild' against the European possessions in southern Asia and the Pacific but could never hope to defeat the United States. Once Japan had enlarged its empire some sort of negotiated peace would have to be achieved. Yamamoto knew at first hand of America's almost limitless resources and capacities. Japan (70 million people) produced more than 7 million tons of steel annually but the United States (150 million people) produced 70 million; between 1941 and 1944 Japan was to manufacture 60,000 aircraft, the United States 260,000. By war's end the US Navy would close on Japan with a hundred aircraft carriers ranging from giant fleet carriers to mass-produced 'baby flat-tops' carrying only two dozen aircraft. Nearly two million Japanese would die as a result of the war.

Japan decided that if further negotiations with the United States could not achieve benefits by 15 October, war would result. Roosevelt was adamant that before any relaxation of economic restrictions could be considered Japan must undertake to evacuate China. On 15 October that ambivalent figure Prince Konoye, after warning President Roosevelt through a secret envoy that some gesture must be made to Japan to avoid war, resigned in despair as Prime Minister. He hoped to be succeeded by the Emperor's uncle Prince Higashikuni, but Hirohito had already prevailed upon General Tojo to accept the onerous burden of the prime ministership.

TOJO TAKES CHARGE

On 17 October 1941 an American reporter in Tokyo for the *New York Times*, Otto Tolischus, wrote in his diary: 'The inevitable happened — the Army took over the Government. Hideki Tojo assumed the premiership, and kept the War Ministry. For the first time since the military government of the "taikuns", political, military and police power became concentrated in the hands of one man. And to demonstrate to the Japanese and to the world that it was the Army, and not just another general, who now ran the Government, Tojo had himself promoted to the rank of full general and remained on the active list.' Tolischus reflected that 'nobody had tipped Tojo' and wrote: 'Now the United States knows it is dealing with the Army directly. But military spokesmen stress the danger of rupture unless the negotiations are speeded up.'

Tojo announced that 'actions, not words' would be his motto, and said: 'The national policy calls for a successful settlement of the China Incident and the establishment of the Greater East Asia Co-Prosperity Sphere', while vowing to push diplomacy with the total power of the nation. He ordered an intensification of 'national mobilisation'.

JAPAN'S PLANS FOR WAR

On 3 November 1941 — one of the original dates for launching war — Japan's Supreme War Council considered the forces it had at its disposal, and those of its prospective enemies. The first blow would be the attack on the US Pacific fleet at Pearl Harbor a month hence. Negotiations, however, would continue with the United States and special envoy Kurusu would be despatched to join Nomura in Washington, if only to show Japan's sincerity. Japan would offer to withdraw forces from China, but only after a peace treaty was signed there; forces in northern China would be removed gradually over a period of twenty-five years. The talks were doomed to failure.

ALLIED DEFENCES

Chief of Staff Sugiyama was confident of a quick victory. Allied forces in South-East Asia were being markedly increased — Washington had just despatched more than thirty Flying Fortress bombers to the Philippines — but he informed Cabinet that 'the enemy forces are scattered ... Being able to attack with surprise and with our strength concentrated, we will be able to defeat the enemy units one at a time. Once we land successfully, we are quite sure we will win.'

Allied joint planning to counter a Japanese attack had begun, as mentioned, as early as February 1941, when British (including Australian and New Zealand), American and Dutch officers had met in Singapore. This meeting was the first of a series in which the ABCD powers — American, British, Chinese, Dutch — attempted to develop a common strategy. What they lacked were the means with which to undertake strong defensive measures. All their hopes were placed on 'the Malay barrier' — Dutch-ruled Indonesia, the Malay Peninsula and the great naval base at Singapore, which had been completed in 1938 with the arrival of a graving dock large enough to dry-dock a battleship. But Singapore lacked battleships — or indeed any capital ships.

In 1939 Churchill had stated: 'Singapore is a fortress armed with 15-inch guns and garrisoned by 20,000 men. It could only be taken after a siege by an enemy of at least 50,000 men ... Moreover, such a siege, which should last at least four or five months, would be liable to be interrupted, if at any time Britain chose to send a superior fleet to the scene.' Churchill persisted in describing Singapore as a fortress, but it was simply a naval base, an extensive complex of fuel throughout Malaya, but they lacked anti-aircraft defences and most of them lacked adequate aircraft. Churchill sent 500 Hurricane fighters to Russia in the six months following the German invasion in June 1941, where they accomplished little. They could have turned the tide of battle if they had been sent to Malaya instead. When Japan struck in December 1941, air defences for Malaya–Singapore would number barely 161 aircraft, all of them obsolete.

The Australian government was particularly alarmed by the state of Malaya's threadbare defences. In July 1940 Australia sent there the first of four RAAF squadrons (they were later joined by a single New Zealand squadron). They were equipped with American aircraft — Hudson light bombers and Buffalo fighters. In February 1941 the 8th Australian Division, which was about to leave for the Middle East, was instead diverted to Singapore, where it joined two recently-raised Indian divisions (9th and 11th divisions). All three of these formations were under-strength, consisting of two brigades instead of three. (The 8th Division's third brigade was split up into battalion-sized garrisons for the islands to Australia's north, and was to suffer the same tragic fate as the two brigades in Malaya.) The 8th Division's commander, Major-General Gordon Bennett, a cantankerous but gifted leader known to his men as 'Ginger', began training his troops in jungle fighting, particularly the mounting of ambushes, but the Indian troops remained committed to static defence — manning beach defences, training in constructing road blocks. Few thought the Japanese would attempt to approach Singapore down the length of the rugged, jungle-covered Malay Peninsula. Malaya command possessed no tanks.

Above: General Hideki Tojo: when he took over the prime ministership in October 1941, war became inevitable.

Bottom right: Senior Australian commanders photographed in Singapore on the eve of war: on the right Major-General Gordon Bennett, commander of the 8th Australian Division, talking to Captain John Collins, RAN, the former commander of HMAS *Sydney*, who was attached to British naval headquarters in Singapore.

tanks, workshops, barracks and office buildings on the northern coast of the island. The southern seaward approaches to the island of Singapore and its teeming harbour in the south were defended by formidable batteries of naval guns and minefields strong enough to deter any frontal attack by an enemy fleet, but no fixed defences existed on the north of the island or in Malaya itself. Constructed as the base for a powerful Far Eastern fleet, Singapore possessed in 1939 no more than a handful of destroyers. In that year the British chiefs of staff faced reality and recommended that the air force take over the principal defence of Singapore by establishing a strength of 336 aircraft (22 squadrons), and that two divisions of troops be based there. A subsequent British Commonwealth military conference in Singapore in October 1940 suggested that air defences be increased to 566 modern aircraft. A series of airfields were constructed

But confidence was high that the garrison could repel and defeat any Japanese attack. Churchill regarded Japan as a second-rate power that would shrink from resorting to war. In April 1941, when the British military attaché in Saigon gave a lecture to officers in Singapore he described the Japanese army as a 'first class fighting machine, composed of tough soldiers, efficiently led'. The General Officer Commanding rose to his feet to refute this claim, telling the officer afterwards that 'it was vital not to depress the chaps'. His successor, Lieutenant-General Arthur Percival, refused to authorise the construction of trenches and gun positions in case the preparations alarmed the local populace.

Percival's superior, the new British Commander-in-Chief Far East, a retired RAF air marshal, Sir Robert Brooke-Popham, assured the Australian government that his first-line fighters, the obsolescent Brewster Buffaloes, were 'more than a match' for any Japanese aircraft. Thus, the appearance of the remarkable Mitsubishi 'Zero' was to take the Allies completely by surprise. Originally devised for carrier use, the Zero, lightly constructed, powerfully engined and heavily armed, was capable of up to 360 mph (600 km/h), and was faster than any Allied fighter. Only Hurricanes and Spitfires could have tackled the Zero with confidence. But no Spitfires were released from the United Kingdom's defence for use in any other theatre of war until March 1942. Hurricanes were never to arrive in time or in sufficient numbers. Unlike most Allied fighters, the Zero lacked armour-plating (particularly around the cockpit) and self-sealing fuel tanks, and American fighter pilots, flying slower, heavier aircraft, were later to take advantage of the Zero's weak points — if they managed to get close enough to one.

Prime Minister Menzies' efforts to obtain modern aircraft during his visit to London early in 1941 were fruitless. He had arrived at the height of the Blitz and there were no planes to spare. Churchill agreed, however, to send one Hurricane to Australia for use at flying shows and recruiting drives. It arrived without guns. When the Japanese struck, it was the only modern fighter aircraft on Australian soil.

Australian fears had been mollified by Churchill's affirmation in August 1940 that he thought it 'unlikely' that Japan would invade her and his assurance that 'If, however, Japan set about invading Australia and New Zealand on a large scale, we should then cut our losses in the Mediterranean ... and proceed in good time to you and with a Fleet able to give battle to any Japanese force.'

In September 1941 the British Admiralty recommended that an Eastern fleet be despatched to Singapore over the next four months — one built around the powerful but immensely slow old 'R' battleships — *Revenge, Ramillies, Royal Sovereign, Resolution* — which by January 1942 would be joined by three aircraft carriers. Prime Minister Churchill overruled the Admiralty and ordered two of their most modern and powerful capital ships be sent to the East immediately, hoping they would have a 'deterrent' effect on Japan. The new battleship HMS *Prince of Wales*, flying the flag of Admiral Sir Tom Phillips and the battle-cruiser HMS *Repulse* with an escort of destroyers reached Singapore on 2 December 1941. The aircraft carrier that was to have accompanied them had been damaged and they had proceeded without her. Six days after their arrival Japan declared war. Two days after that, both great ships were sunk by enemy aircraft off the coast of Malaya.

JAPAN'S STRENGTH

Japan had 51 divisions and an army two-million strong. It would use only 11 or 12 divisions in the coming offensives. Four 'Armies' would be allocated to the campaign: the 14th Army to seize the Philippines and Borneo; the 15th Army to take Burma, the 16th Army for Java and the largest, the 25th Army of three divisions, for the conquest of Malaya. They would be supported by 500 modern aircraft and by naval and amphibious forces. In naval strength alone Japan was dominant: she possessed eleven aircraft carriers, whereas the Americans had only three in the Pacific. Each side had eleven battleships (counting the four near-obsolete R-class British ships), 100 destroyers and 100 submarines, but Japan had a strong air fleet, while the Allied aircraft were outdated and few in number. Lacking rapid and substantial reinforcement, the Allied air forces would be quickly eliminated.

Yamamoto's 'Combined Fleet' began gathering in Japanese waters on the night of 14 November prior to the long voyage to Pearl Harbor. Three days earlier the Admiral had written to a friend: 'What a strange position it is in which I find myself. I am having to lead in a decision diametrically opposed to my personal beliefs. And I have no choice but full steam ahead.' Yamamoto's fleet, which included six aircraft carriers under Admiral Nagumo's command, left the Inland Sea on 26 November 1941. It maintained radio silence as it pushed into the mist of the north Pacific Ocean, just beyond the limits of American air reconnaissance. On 2 December, as Tokyo wirelessed to Yamamoto's fleet the signal that meant negotiations had failed and that war would start on 8 December, US Naval Intelligence reported that Japan's carrier fleet had completely disappeared — 'lost'.

Other Japanese fleets were at sea. On 6 December an Australian reconnaissance aircraft based at Kota Bharu in the extreme north of Malaya reported sighting a convoy of 13 warships and 22 transports about 260 miles (over 400 kilometres) from the Malay coast, sailing south from Indo-China. Malaya Command ordered 'First Degree of Readiness'. The pilot lost sight of the convoy in the low monsoonal cloud. An hour before the attack on Pearl Harbor, these ships would land troops on the coast near Kota Bharu, launching the Pacific War.

ATTACK ON PEARL HARBOR

Two days later Admiral Nagumo's carrier fleet had reached waters 230 miles (nearly 400 kilometres) north of Hawaii. At 6 a.m. on Sunday 7 December, they launched 183 aircraft — 51 dive-bombers, 89 torpedo-planes and 43 Zero fighters. Their leader sighted Oahu Island at 7.35 a.m. Twenty minutes later the raiders saw below them the US Pacific fleet anchored in Pearl Harbor — eight battleships, eight cruisers and thirty destroyers, apart from dozens of supply ships — and began their attacks. In five minutes four of the battleships had been hit by torpedoes and were then hit by armour-piercing shells dropped from bombers and by dive-bombers. The battleship *Arizona* was struck by a bomb that blew up her boilers and ignited her magazine: she exploded, broke in two and sank, taking with her 1104 sailors. The battleship *Oklahoma* was hit by three torpedos and capsized, *West Virginia* sank after four hits, *California* was set on fire from her fuel tanks and foundered. *Nevada* got under way but was beached in a sinking condition. Of the battleships only *Maryland*, *Tennessee* and *Pennsylvania* escaped with minor damage. Three cruisers were also damaged in the air attack and 170 aircraft destroyed for the loss of only nine Japanese planes. The second Japanese attack wave, however, met a storm of anti-aircraft fire and lost twenty aircraft. A total of 2403 American servicemen died.

Yamamoto, leading the combined fleet back to Japanese waters, was depressed to hear that no American carriers had been in Pearl Harbor. They had been the principal objective of the attack. He had no idea where they were. In fact Vice-Admiral Bill Halsey was ferrying aircraft to Wake Island in the carrier USS *Enterprise*; USS *Lexington* was on a similar mission to Midway Island. *Saratoga* was undergoing refit in California and a month later was to be struck and damaged by an enemy torpedo. But the other two carriers would later change the course of the Pacific War.

Above: Japanese photograph of 'Battleship Row' in Pearl Harbor under attack, 7 December 1941.
Right: President Roosevelt.

'DAY OF INFAMY'

Due to delays in decrypting Tokyo's long-winded declaration of war, the Japanese ambassador in Washington, to his horror, was not handed it to deliver to the US Secretary of State, Cordell Hull, until after the bombs had fallen on Pearl Harbor. Hull received him with cold contempt. Churchill heard the news reports of the Pearl Harbor attack on a wireless broadcast late on 7 December and immediately telephoned Roosevelt. The President told him that the reports were true: 'We're all in the same boat now.' Churchill went to bed and 'slept the sleep of the saved and thankful'. He knew that Germany, and Japan, were doomed. Next day, having issued with relish a declaration of war on Japan, he made plans to leave for Washington to discuss with his new ally the defeat of their enemies.

To Roosevelt, the sneak attack on Pearl Harbor was proof of Japan's mendacity and treachery. Appearing before Congress he described Sunday 7 December as 'a day of infamy' and asked for an immediate declaration of war on Japan, but not on Germany. Hitler, who heard the news of Pearl Harbor at his headquarters on the Russian front, hurried back to Berlin and on 11 December addressed the Reichstag, describing Roosevelt as 'mad, just as Wilson was' and poured vituperation on him, before declaring that Germany too was at war with the United States. What could well have been an American war against Japan alone was now a world war. America proved to possess the ability to fight two wars at the same time.

CHURCHILL GOES TO WASHINGTON

Prime Minister Churchill left for Washington in the new battleship HMS *Duke of York* on 12 December. His voyage would take eight days, through cold and mountainous seas. He took with him his chiefs of staff, except for General Brooke, who had just taken over as CIGS. By the time he arrived to be greeted by Roosevelt and take steps to forge a 'Grand Alliance' the Allied powers had suffered a series of staggering defeats in South-East Asia and the Pacific.

GUAM AND WAKE ISLAND

On 10 December nine Japanese ships appeared off Guam in the Mariana Islands, and troops aboard them seized the island after three hours of fighting with the American defenders. On 11 December a Japanese convoy attempted to land troops on Wake Island, a tiny coral atoll only 600 miles (1000 kilometres) from the Japanese-held Marshall Islands and used as an overnight stop for the Pan-American flying boats on the new Pacific run. Wake Island's coastal guns sank a destroyer and damaged another, forcing the Japanese to steam away. They returned in strength on 22 December with two carriers and landed 1000 men. With their guns destroyed, the island's garrison of US Marines was forced to surrender.

HONG KONG

The Japanese, 30,000-strong, struck on 8 December and by 13 December had overwhelmed the New Territories on the mainland, forcing a British withdrawal to Hong Kong Island. On 18 December 10,000 Japanese landed on the island, seizing the water reservoirs in the mountains and beginning a bitter five-day attempt by British, Indian and Canadian troops and local volunteers to dislodge them. The Japanese advance was followed by widespread massacres of prisoners, including the murder of sixty patients and the bayoneting of nurses in the hospital outside the defences of Fort Stanley. Major-General Maltby surrendered Hong Kong on Christmas Day 1941.

THE PHILIPPINES

At his headquarters in Manila in the Philippines, General Douglas MacArthur felt confident of repelling any Japanese attack. Just short of his sixty-second birthday but looking twenty years younger, MacArthur had been about to retire as Commander-in-Chief of the Philippine army (of which he had made himself a field marshal), when he had been restored to the US Army active list with the rank of four-star general in July 1941 and been promised large reinforcements. After fifty years of American rule judged even today as benevolent, the Philippines Commonwealth was almost self-governing and due to receive full independence within five years. MacArthur enjoyed a special prestige among Filipinos. He commanded barely 20,000 American troops, a division of well-trained Philippine Scouts and 80,000 hastily trained young Filipinos, who had been called up only two months earlier.

MacArthur had been reinforced by 35 modern Flying Fortress bombers just before war broke. These were the weapons he intended to use to destroy an invasion armada. Having no protective shelters, 18 of them and 53 of his 107 fighters on Luzon were wiped out by Japanese bombing on the first morning of the war; bombers also created ruin at the Cavite naval base. The first Japanese forces landed in the Philippines on 10 December, bringing in tanks, and the main invasion armada carrying 40,000 troops appeared in Lingayen Gulf on 22 December. The Japanese made rapid progress as the defenders withdrew.

Macarthur decided to pull back and attempt to defend the main island, Luzon. At the same time he activated plans to stockpile supplies in the Bataan peninsula, which formed the western coast of Manila Bay; there he would hold out until the promised reinforcements reached him. Informed of a later decision to evacuate Manila and withdraw all forces to Bataan, President Quezon was appalled, threatened to declare the Philippines neutral, and insisted on declaring Manila an 'open city' to save it from being razed by Japanese bombers. MacArthur's inglorious step-by-step withdrawal of his forces to Bataan was carried out with precision, and his two retreating forces blew up more than 180 bridges to slow down the Japanese. MacArthur and the Philippine government left Manila on Christmas Eve 1941, when Admiral Hart's outnumbered naval squadron, the US Asiatic fleet, left for Singapore and Java. The admiral himself closed down his own Manila headquarters and departed for Java in a submarine, leaving behind a small flotilla of subs and a handful of motor torpedo boats to defend the 6000 islands of the Philippines.

1941: THE WIDENING WAR

Above: Japanese prisoners were few in the early months of the Pacific war, and photographs of them even rarer. These Japanese soldiers were captured by American forces in the Philippines in the first months of war.
Right: The Japanese enter Hong Kong December 1941.

On the last day of the year 1941 the first Filipino–American forces began crossing into Bataan and manning the first of its defence lines. They had enough supplies for a month. Here, and on the small rocky island outcrop named Corregidor at the mouth of Manila Bay, MacArthur would make his stand. His appeals to Washington for reinforcements went unheard. In January a recently promoted Brigadier-General named Dwight Eisenhower of the Plans Department advised General Marshall that America's principal strategic concern should be the defence of Australia. A convoy heading for the Philippines was directed to Australian ports.

RETREAT IN MALAYA

Thunderstorms broke over northern Malaya in the early hours of 8 December (7 December US time). Just before 1 a.m. messages reached the RAAF squadron at Kota Bahru airstrip two kilometres from the coast that Japanese forces were landing from ships offshore. Seven of the Australian Hudson light bombers made repeated attacks on Japanese shipping, often at mast height, sinking a transport vessel and a dozen barges and damaging two other ships for the loss of two aircraft. But by late afternoon the 5000-strong invading force had overcome the Indian troops manning the beach defences and the airfield itself was under sniper fire. The remaining Hudsons were ordered south to the airfield at Kuantan.

Seven of the RAAF squadron's Buffalo fighters at Sungei Patani were destroyed on the ground by Japanese air attack; and the remainder were ordered south to Ipoh. This set the pattern for the next month: Japanese destruction of British air strength and seizure of airfields by fast-moving columns of troops, allowing the Japanese to gain mastery of the air in northern Malaya in the first two days of war.

Other Japanese forces were landing further north, over the border on the Thai coast at Singora and Patani, where after a few shots (one of which winged Colonel Tsuji) Thai forces ceased fire and ended their kingdom's brief war against Japan. Japanese forces were soon to enter Bangkok without firing a shot.

LOSS OF FORCE Z

In these days of gloom, one factor gave Churchill hope and confidence: the presence in Singapore of the battleship *Prince of Wales* and the battle cruiser *Repulse*, whose powerful guns could destroy any invasion convoy. Late on the afternoon of 8 December Admiral Tom Phillips took the great ships to sea to search for the invasion convoys off Kota Bahru. Phillips was informed before sailing that his ships — 'Force Z' — could not be provided in the north with air cover. He left under grey and heavy skies, accompanied by four destroyers On the following day he sighted three aircraft. Aware that his presence

Sailors from the sinking battleship *Prince of Wales* abandon ship. Many are trying to reach the deck of an escorting destroyer.

would soon be known to the Japanese — and having found no sign of an enemy fleet — Phillips turned south to return to Singapore.

Just before midday on 10 December Phillips's force was attacked by a wave of enemy aircraft; the two great ships successfully avoided all the torpedos but a bomb hit *Repulse*, causing little damage. Soon afterwards the force was attacked by waves of torpedo-bombers, one of which struck *Prince of Wales*, destroying her steering. *Repulse* was then struck by torpedos and bombs and the two giant ships were sunk. (More than 800 British sailors died, including Phillips and Captain Leach in the flagship, who were last seen standing alone on the bridge.

Churchill was told the news by the First Sea Lord, Admiral Pound. 'In all the war I never received a more direct shock,' he later wrote. Nearly 2000 men were picked up by their destroyer escorts. In two days Japan had destroyed the major capital ships of Britain and the United States in the region. The Imperial Japanese Navy's nine battleships and ten carriers now commanded the Pacific, facing serious threat from only three American carriers, whose whereabouts were unknown.

COLLAPSE IN MALAYA

In Malaya the campaign was fought in monsoonal downpours, which hardly delayed the Japanese. No one had envisaged an attack in northern Malaya at the outset of the southern monsoon which raged from December to March. Nor was the next Japanese move forecast: from Kota Bharu on the east coast the Japanese landing forces proceeded briskly through a brigade of the 9th Indian Division to the west coast; they marched lightly and quickly along the roads, sometimes using bicycles, followed by light tanks. When a roadblock was encountered the infantry moved through the jungle to encircle it.

The first week of fighting decided the campaign. By 10 December the British command had lost a quarter of its aircraft and the remainder were withdrawn from north-east Malaya, for the lack of fighter protection was resulting in ruinous losses in the bomber force. By the night of 12 December — by which date half of Malaya's air strength had been destroyed — the 11th Indian Division at Jitra had been outflanked and then cut in two, with the loss of 3000 men, before it began a chaotic withdrawal. By early on 14 December the depleted division was assembling at its new position at Gurun when it came under heavy attack and began retreating to a new line on the Perak River. The 9th Indian Division, withdrawn to the mid-east coast, was ordered to defend the Kuantan airfields. The most reliable troops, the 8th Australian Division, still remained inactive in Johore, far to the south.

The GOC Malaya, General Percival, in concentrating his forces in the north, but nowhere in strength, was soon to permit a gradual fighting withdrawal down the length of the peninsula, absorbing brigade after brigade (and even single battalions from the Singapore Island garrison) in a vain attempt to plug gaps in the front.

CHURCHILL IN AMERICA

Churchill left his battleship and flew on to Washington airport on 22 December. 'There was the President waiting in his car,' he wrote. 'I clasped his strong hand with comfort and pleasure.' For the next three weeks the Prime Minister made the White House his home, dislocating its routine and keeping Roosevelt amused in the evenings but up well past his bedtime. Churchill later wrote: 'I formed a very strong affection, which grew with our years of comradeship, for this formidable politician ... whose heart seemed to respond to many of the impulses that stirred my own.'

From the first hour they were united in the belief that all Allied resources must be concentrated on the total defeat of Germany. Japan could wait. Churchill was prepared to pay forfeits for his neglect of the defences in South-East Asia. He saw their loss as inevitable. Proud of his American heritage, he addressed Congress on 26 December, to wild applause. 'Here we are together facing a group of mighty foes who seek our ruin; here we are together defending all that to free men is dear.' In the night he suffered a heart attack — a mild one, which his faithful doctor Sir Charles Wilson informed him was angina pectoris. By the following day Churchill felt well enough to plan a trip to Ottawa. There he addressed the Canadian parliament and met with the same warm reception.

There was less cheer in Australia. In Malaya defences were collapsing. By 18 December 1941 the bulk of the two Indian divisions were attempting to hold a line on the banks of the Krian River, but a Japanese column advancing inland threatened their right flank, forcing a further retreat. Penang had been hastily evacuated by the

John Curtin: taking office as prime minister of Australia in October 1941, he led the nation through the anxious days of defeat. His heart weakened by the strains of war, he died in July 1945 one month before victory.

European residents, leaving the Malays and Chinese to their fate. On 23 December an American correspondent in Singapore wrote: 'The situation is going from bad to worse. There is no indication that the Japanese are being stopped at any point.' By 28 December the Indian and British troops had withdrawn to the Ipoh area. But they were again outflanked. Percival authorised a further retreat south to the Slim River. On 30 December martial law was declared in Singapore.

On 25 December Prime Minister Curtin sent to both Churchill and Roosevelt a plea to reinforce Singapore, ordering R.G. Casey, his representative in Washington, to tell the Americans that 'the stage of gentle suggestion has now passed'. Churchill replied that he did not share the view that Singapore would fall. Churchill, delighted by the offensive in the Western Desert that had relieved Tobruk, had already suggested to his chiefs of staff that Hurricane fighters and up to six bomber squadrons be stripped from the Middle East and sent to Malaya, and that the entire British 18th Division (52nd, 53rd, 54th brigades), then en route to Egypt, be diverted to Singapore. Its main body arrived there just in time to be captured.

On 27 December Prime Minister Curtin stated in an historic article in the Australian press: 'We refuse to accept the dictum that the Pacific struggle must be treated as a subordinate segment of the general conflict ... Without any inhibitions of any kind, I make it quite clear that Australia looks to America, free of any pangs as to our traditional links or kinship with the United Kingdom.' This statement, which enunciated the basis of Australian policy from that day onwards, angered both Churchill and Roosevelt,. Churchill thought it revealed Australia's 'mood of panic' and was to write that it 'produced the worst impression both in high American circles and in Canada.'

ANGLO-AMERICAN ENDEAVOURS

Before Churchill left for London in mid-January 1942, Roosevelt endorsed plans to increase his country's war production far in excess of the increase suggested by his advisers. He ordered the construction of combat aircraft during 1942 be increased from a planned 13,000 to 45,000 and the planned 15,000 tanks be increased to 45,000. Instead of 262,000 machine-guns, American factories would aim for 500,000. And in 1943 war production would aim for 100,000 military aircraft and 75,000 tanks. 'I reported all this good news home,' Churchill wrote.

'During the conference the Americans were impressed by the efficiency and close coordination of the British high command,' writes the American historian Ronald Spector. The three British chiefs of staff met daily with either the Prime Minister or his trusted chief liaison officer, Major-General Hastings Ismay, whereas the two American service chiefs, General Marshall of the army, and Admiral King of the navy (there was no separate US air force until 1947) seldom conferred regularly with each other or with President Roosevelt, who often made strategic decisions by himself. It was decided to set up a unified British–American high command in Washington consisting of the British chiefs of staff or their representatives, and the 'US Chiefs of Staff'. It was the birth of the 'Combined Chiefs of Staff', which would decide the strategy with which to defeat the Axis.

One of its first decisions was to set up a unified command in South-East Asia. The Americans had no wish to appoint one of their own officers to preside over the looming disaster. On 12 December Burma had been placed under the command of the C-in-C, India, General Wavell, who recognised Burma's vital position in the war against Japan and had signalled the CIGS: 'Burma is essential base for operations against Japan, it is only route for supplies to China ... At present Burma is far from secure ... defensive plan seems to have been based largely on hope that our air forces would make enemy approach difficult or impossible by bombing. This is contrary to all experience of this war and anyway we have no bombers.' On Christmas Eve Wavell flew to Rangoon, which was then under Japanese air attack and next day he cabled the War Office: '... Reinforcement of Burma by two fighter squadrons is vitally urgent. Mass exodus of civilian population from Rangoon has created many difficulties for us ...' Four days later the patient but weary Wavell became the obvious choice for the post of Supreme Commander and was so informed by Churchill. He would command all American, British, Dutch and Australian forces (known for short as ABDA) in South-East Asia.

On New Year's Eve the writer and member of parliament Harold Nicolson wrote in his diary: 'Big Ben strikes and 1941 is finished. Not a year on which I shall look back with any pleasure ... It has been a sad and horrible year.'

CHAPTER 7
FIGHTING BACK
1942

Both Churchill and Roosevelt wanted to issue a proclamation to the world and a challenge to the Axis powers. Churchill had first used the term 'United Nations' when representatives of the conquered European nations had gathered in London to pledge their alliance six months earlier; Roosevelt urged adoption of the same words to replace the clumsy term 'Allied and Associated Powers'. On 1 January 1942 representatives of twenty-six nations signed the United Nations Declaration in Washington, vowing to cooperate in the war against the Axis and to achieve victory, which they deemed essential 'to defend life, liberty, independence and religious freedom, and to preserve human rights and justice'. Churchill was to explain: 'The Declaration could not by itself win battles but it set forth who we were and what we were fighting for.' Thus was born the future United Nations Organisation.

On 17 January 1942 Wavell flew to his new ABDA headquarters in Java, situated at Lembang, near Bandung, high in the hills 100 kilometres from Jakarta (Batavia). From its birth it was hardly unified. Only one week earlier Admiral Hart, sent out from the Philippines, had set up his naval HQ at Surabaya at the opposite end of the island. With the death of Admiral Phillips and the departure of his successor to Ceylon (the destined base for the Eastern fleet of old R-class battleships), the Royal Australian Navy's young Captain John Collins, the former skipper of HMAS *Sydney*, soon found himself senior British Commonwealth naval officer in Bandung and became 'Commodore, Far East Squadron' in direct command of all British and Australian naval ships in the region. He had already established a warm working relationship with Admiral Conrad Helfrich, commander-in-chief of the Royal Netherlands Navy in Indonesian waters.

'This is the gravest hour of our history,' Prime Minister Curtin told the nation. The Japanese attack found Australia with all her trained troops — the four AIF divisions totalling 120,000 men — overseas. She had only fifteen RAAF squadrons for home defence. A total of 114,000 men were called up for the militia. On 3 January 1942 the British government suggested to the Australian Cabinet that two of the Australian divisions in the Middle East be moved to the Dutch East Indies (Indonesia) from where they could be used to reinforce Malaya. Churchill had impulsively suggested that the third AIF division — the 9th — return to the Southern Hemisphere, but retracted his offer. In little more than a month the majority of the Australian infantry were leaving the Mediterranean theatre of war, never to return.

Churchill was to pay them fine tribute: 'Australia had sent no less than four divisions, comprised of the flower of her military manhood, across the world to aid the Mother Country in this war, in the making of which, and in the want of preparation for which they had no share ... From the days of Bardia, Australian troops and the New Zealand Division had played a foremost part in the Desert war for the defence of Egypt. They had shone in the van of its victories and shared in its many grievous reverses ...'

MALAYA: THE RETREAT CONTINUES

On 5 January 1942 the Japanese began attacks on the Slim River position, the east-centre of the defences, and two days later fifteen of their tanks struck down the road through the 11th Indian Division

Inset: **For Soviet Russia 1942 was to be another test of the strength of its resolve but the year would end in victory at Stalingrad.**
Opposite: **Image of an Anzac. Captain Charles Upham, a sheep farmer from New Zealand's south island, became the only combat soldier to be awarded the Victoria Cross twice for valour. He was captured in mid-1942 and spent the rest of the war in captivity** *Opposite right:* **The enemy: A Luftwaffe pilot, taken from a photograph widely reproduced in German propaganda magazines.**

(whose anti-tank guns destroyed only two of them) and penetrated to a depth of 30 kilometres behind the Indian lines. When the Indian troops retreated, the northern two-thirds of Malaya had been lost.

On 14 January 1942 the Australian 2/30th Battalion mounted an ambush on the Gemas road that became the first hard knock the overconfident Japanese had received. Warned of the approach of nearly 1000 Japanese troops pedalling on bicycles, the Australians hid in the jungle, let them pass over a bridge and then blew up the bridge, directing point-blank fire at them, killing hundreds of them before withdrawing.

The Australians halted Japanese tanks with close fire from their 2-pounder guns the next day and fell back, having inflicted an estimated 1000 casualties on the Japanese for the loss of 81 officers and men. But on 16 January the Japanese broke through Indian troops on the Muar River sector. The Australian 2/29 Battalion found itself almost alone defending the road to Bakri, but its anti-tank gunners coolly knocked out eight Japanese light tanks with their 2-pounders. Of the 4000 men of the Muar force barely 1000 survived.

Yet another defence line was organised but the Japanese advance continued, outflanking and overwhelming British and Indian positions before they could be established. The prospect of a retreat to 'Fortress Singapore' loomed. On the west coast the line was stabilised only on the night of 25 January. On the same day a Japanese fleet was sighted off Endau. In the last major attack mounted by the air force in Malaya, nine Australian Hudsons accompanied twenty-one obsolete RAF Wildebeestes and three Albacores, scoring hits on five ships, but with the staggering loss of eighteen aircraft.

On 27 January 1942 Percival informed Wavell of the critical situation: 'The enemy has cut off and overrun the majority of our forces on the east coast … it looks as if we should not be able to hold Johore for more than another 3 or 4 days.' Wavell agreed to a withdrawal to Singapore island but next day another disaster fell. The Japanese struck 11th Indian Division savagely: from one of its brigades only 200 men escaped.

General Wavell flew into Singapore on 30 January 1942 and there conferred with his commanders, ordering all air force squadrons except one to fly to Sumatra. Afterwards Major-General Bennett drove through the deserted streets of Johore Bharu and past their bombed buildings. He wrote: 'This defeat should never have been. The whole thing is fantastic. There seems to be no justification for it.'

On 31 January 1942 the last British unit, the remnants of the Argyll and Sutherland Highlanders, barely 90 strong, marched across the Causeway to the skirl of the bagpipes, and shortly afterwards the link to the mainland was blown, leaving a 70-metre gap. With it was destroyed the pipeline bringing fresh water to Singapore. The strait was to prove an ineffective moat. At low tide parts of it were only 1.3 metres deep.

Newspapers told of a fighting retreat caused by 'overwhelming numbers of Japanese', but they had conquered Malaya with only 35,000 men. This number had been sufficient to drive an army of 60,000 defenders into a humiliating 1000-kilometre retreat. Japanese casualties were barely 1793 killed and 2772 wounded. Tens of thousands of the defending force were already prisoners. On 31 January the American CBS correspondent who had moved to Jakarta wrote: 'Evacuees are pouring in from Singapore. British officers, officials, civilians, war correspondents. They are moving here en masse. Very cheerful and chipper, you'd think they had just come from a golf game ...'

The conquest of Malaya was the greatest victory in nearly two months of astonishing success. Hong Kong had surrendered. On 11 January the Japanese had landed in northern Borneo; on 15 January, in Burma. On 23 January they landed at Balikpapan in Borneo and that night four old American destroyers scored a notable victory in an attack on the Japanese convoy in which they sank four ships without loss to themselves. On the same day Japanese forces landed at Rabaul, and on Ambon five days later. There seemed no end to their advances.

'The Australians had fought well. They had taken the offensive, infiltrated, ambushed, and dispelled the growing notion that the Japanese were peculiarly, demonically, at home in the jungle,' writes the American authority on Japan at war, David Bergamini. 'In the last ten days the Australians had inflicted heavier losses on Yamashita's men than they had suffered earlier or would suffer later.

THE FALL OF SINGAPORE

Informed of Singapore's lack of defences — 'no measures worth speaking of had been taken by any of the commanders since the war began' — Churchill was to write in his memoirs: 'I saw before me the spectre of the almost naked island and of the wearied, if not exhausted, troops retreating upon it.' In mid-January 1942 he had cabled Wavell: 'I want to make it absolutely clear that I expect every inch of ground to be defended ... and no question of surrender entertained until after protracted fighting among the ruins of Singapore City.'

On 21 January, however, he informed his chiefs of staff: 'We may, by muddling things through and hesitating to take an ugly decision, lose both Singapore and the Burma Road. If Singapore lasts only a few weeks it is not worth losing all our reinforcements and aircraft.'

'After all the assurances we have been given, the evacuation of Singapore would be regarded here as an inexcusable betrayal,' Australia's John Curtin cabled Churchill. 'Singapore is a central fortress in the system of Empire and local defence ... We understand that it was to be made impregnable ... or be capable of holding out for a prolonged period until the arrival of the main fleet.'

Singapore's peacetime population of 700,000 people was now swollen to nearly a million. The island, barely 40 kilometres long and 20 wide, had drawn its main water supplies from Johore but the pipeline was now cut, and the reservoirs were barely adequate to support the extra mouths. Japanese bombing was constant, food stocks were dwindling, but stores, hotels and cinemas remained open, providing an illusion of normality. The Chinese community provided willing helpers to the ARP services and armed militia.

'The battle of Malaya has come to an end,' General Percival announced, on 1 February 1942, 'and the battle of Singapore has started ... Our task is to hold the fortress until help can come.' Convoys continued to make the 500-mile (800 kilometre) voyage from Sunda Strait to Singapore, mostly under cover of night. The docks were in chaos. War material was looted or removed from its crates. Some officers questioned the sense in wasting lives by sending in further convoys. On 5 February a five-ship convoy carrying 2000 AIF reinforcements, most of them on the liner *Empress of Asia*, came under terrific air attack. It was the last convoy into Singapore.

Percival distributed his forces around the island's entire 120-kilometre perimeter. In the words of the British official historian: 'In trying to defend the whole coast when it was obvious the Japanese

One of the most extraordinary photographs of the war shows Australian anti-tank gunners firing their two-pounder at point-blank range into Japanese tanks at a road block near Muar in Malaya.

would concentrate on one carefully selected point, Percival was weak everywhere, no formation had any reserves for immediate counterattack ...' He divided the northern coast into two sectors and selected the 8th Australian Division to defend the 'West' as far as the Causeway. He allotted the bulk of his artillery to the eastern sector. Singapore was now under constant artillery bombardment but the great guns of the fortress could make little response: lack of high explosive shells, and problems of 'location, lack of range, or limited traverse' prevented them being used.

On 8 February 1942 Japanese shelling increased in intensity on the northern coast as sixteen battalions of infantry prepared to cross the strait. The Japanese crossed the strait in an armada of more than 200 boats and landed on Singapore in the early hours of 9 February on the coast defended by the Australian 22nd Brigade. The defenders fought stubbornly. On returning to his HQ, Percival told Bennett and Lieutenant-General Heath of Indian Corps that if the Japanese reached the Bukit Timah road he would fall back and make a tight perimeter around Singapore city.

Meanwhile, 27th Brigade, assuming that the 22nd Brigade had been overcome, withdrew from the Causeway position to a stronger line three kilometres south. At 9 p.m. on 9 February, however, the Japanese Imperial Guards were crossing the straits to fall upon the 27th Brigade. At 4.30 a.m. the sound of fighting was drowned out by the explosion of two million gallons of fuel as the naval base was destroyed by Australian sappers. The flaming petrol poured down the strait, consuming barge-loads of Japanese, and horrifying stories of this reached the Guards commander, General Nishimura. Suddenly squeamish, he called off further attacks across the water. Over Singapore hung a dark and thickening black cloud.

By the morning of 10 February, Bennett felt confident that the dispositions along the Kranji–Jurong line were sufficient to hold the Japanese but there soon occurred a succession of misinterpretations of Percival's orders that saw the entire line abandoned by nightfall. Wavell again flew into Singapore, arriving on 10 February. He criticised Percival for allowing the Japanese to establish themselves and ordered him to counterattack and retake the Kranji–Jurong line early in the afternoon. He was so exasperated with Bennett's remarks that he told him to 'get the hell out' and take his 'bloody Aussies' with him. Wavell issued an order to his troops: 'We must defeat them. The Americans have held out on the Bataan Peninsula against far greater odds ... It will be disgraceful ... if we yield our boasted fortress of Singapore to inferior enemy forces.'

Thus by the evening of 10 February, the battle-weary defenders were holding the line running the length of Woodlands Road against Japanese thrusts from both north and east. The counterattack failed and enemy tanks now appeared. By 10.30 p.m. the Japanese had reached the outskirts of Bukit Timah village. On the morning of 11 February Bennett ordered that the Japanese be driven from its environs; a motley force was scratched together to defend the reservoirs. Seeing 11th Division's left flank completely exposed, Lieutenant-General Heath ordered 3 Indian Corps to withdraw from the north coast, abandoning the naval base, and establish a new continuous line further south.

On 12 February Percival sadly ordered a withdrawal to a 'tight perimeter' around Singapore city, urging Heath to defend the reservoirs north of the city with the 11th and 18th divisions. 'I consider that the end is very near,' Bennett wrote in his diary. The Japanese were now only five kilometres from the docks and were shelling the city with field artillery. On 13 February Percival met his commanders at Fort Canning. From Bennett and Heath, Percival heard that there was no chance of mounting a counterattack.

Friday 13 February 1942 would be remembered in Singapore as 'Black Friday', as eighty small craft left the harbour — and a city burning under a pall of black smoke. Few of them made it past Japanese surface patrols. On 14 February the sixty-five Australian nurses evacuated from the city two days earlier on the *Vyner Brooke* met with tragedy when the ship was bombed and sunk. A group of twenty-two survivors were captured by a Japanese patrol on Banka Island, forced to walk into the surf, and machine-gunned. Only one nursing sister survived.

On 14 February Japanese tanks and infantry reached the pumping station and the reservoirs. Others entered the Alexandra Barracks Hospital, where they captured the patients and next day bayoneted 100 of their prisoners, nearly all of whom were patients and medical staff. Told that the water supply would last forty-eight hours at best, Percival informed Wavell of his intention to seek a cease-fire. At 5.15 p.m. on 15 February General Percival, accompanied by a small

General Yamashita and his staff in Malaya early in 1942.

group of officers carrying a white flag and the Union Jack, met General Yamashita at the Ford factory on the outskirts of Singapore city to negotiate a cease-fire. Yamashita, with Tsuji at his side, shouted a demand for total and unconditional surrender. The capitulation was signed forthwith, to be effective from 8.30 p.m. the same day.

In what Prime Minister Churchill was to call 'the greatest disaster to British arms which our history affords,' the battle of Malaya and Singapore ended. A total of 130,000 men passed into Japanese captivity. Of this number 67,340 were Indian, 38,496 British, 18,490 Australian, 14,382 local volunteers. In the entire campaign the British command had suffered 8000 casualties (killed and wounded). Japan's losses were 9824, of whom 3500 were killed. Australian losses included 1789 killed and 1306 wounded. Before victory over Japan, nearly 8000 Australian prisoners would die in the hands of their captors.

Determined to reveal the story of incompetence that he had witnessed, Major-General Bennett handed over command of 8th Division to his artillery commander and with two of his staff officers got away from Singapore just after midnight, and crossed to Sumatra and then to Java. To the shock and embarrassment of the Australian government he reached Australia by plane.

Of the 67,000 Indian troops captured, well over 40,000 were coerced into renouncing their allegiance to the Crown to join the Japan-sponsored 'Indian National Army' (INA); few of them joined willingly and the INA, woefully under-equipped, later fought without enthusiasm against the British-Indian army in Burma.

The Japanese 'Co-Prosperity Sphere' would witness the death of millions of Asian civilians from starvation or brutality — nearly 50,000 Malays, more than 100,000 Filipinos and nearly two million Indonesians (the last principally in a cruel forced-labour scheme). The 300,000 Allied servicemen and civilians captured by the Japanese (this figure included 130,000 servicemen taken in the campaign for Malaya and Singapore and 100,000 Dutch civilians in the Indies) suffered throughout the war from a shortage of food, adequate shelter and medical treatment.

For the first few months the British and Australian prisoners who were marched into Changi found conditions bearable. The Australian area, Selarang Barracks, substantial, although food, beds and medical attention were inadequate, fresh water non-existent (water was brought into the camp in carts). They were given a daily ration of one pound (half a kilo) of rice but this was later halved, and then reduced even further. The men were 'despondent and listless' but soon had latrines dug to guard against flies and dysentery. POWs originally saw few Japanese; the wire fences they were forced to erect around themselves were patrolled by renegade Sikhs. In mid-June 1942 conditions would change when the Japanese put their prisoners to work as slave labour.

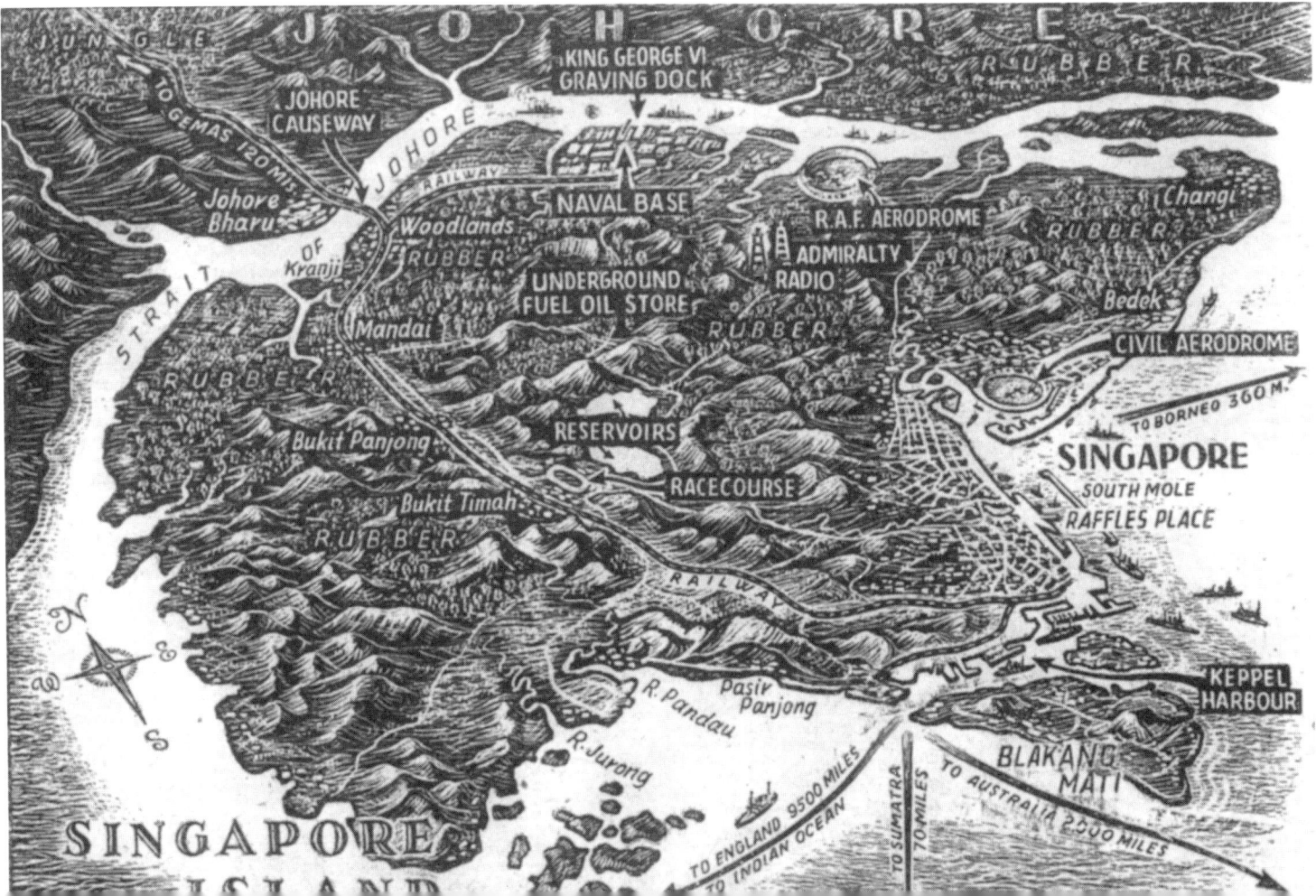

Gurkha troops of the Indian Army defending a riverbank in Burma, 1942.

INVASION OF BURMA

The Japanese had advanced into Burma from Thailand on 16 January 1942, and their forces seized Moulmein after a brisk fight. They pressed on to Rangoon, Burma's port and capital, from where a road led to the mountains of southern China. Burma was defended only by the locally raised 1st Burma Division, which proved unreliable, and the under-strength 17th Indian Division. The defenders fell back to the last main obstacle to the Japanese advance, the Sittang River, but on 20 February met with disaster when the divisional commander approved a brigadier's request to blow up the Sittang Bridge. The explosion was premature for it stranded most of his men on the eastern bank. By next day the division mustered only 3000 men with barely 1500 rifles. Aware that nothing now barred the Japanese advance, Churchill on 21 February 1942 ordered the leading convoy carrying a brigade of the 7th Australian Division, then rounding Ceylon, to make for Rangoon. In Churchill's view the only troops close enough, and capable, of holding Rangoon and southern Burma were the Australians.

Curtin was astonished by Churchill's action and in an angry cable on 23 February protested to him: 'Australia's outer defences are now quickly vanishing and our vulnerability is completely exposed ... With AIF troops we sought to save Malaya and Singapore, falling back on the Netherlands East Indies. All these northern defences are gone or going, now you contemplate using the AIF to save Burma. All this has been done, as in Greece, without adequate air support.' The convoy was immediately ordered back on its original course, towards Colombo. Curtin later agreed to the 7th Division disembarking in Ceylon but the ships carrying them had already progressed to Java or Australia, and two brigades of the 6th Division following in their wake found themselves joining the Ceylon garrison. The Australians were retained there for four months, when they were desperately needed in New Guinea.

Wavell diverted to Rangoon a brigade of British tanks from Egypt and sent three infantry battalions from India. The tanks — petrol-powered American 'Honey' light tanks, driven by the 7th Hussars, were to prove their worth, as were the three brigades of Gurkhas in Burma. From China a Chinese army, little more than three divisions in strength, moved south to cover the approaches to Mandalay, along with a squadron of 'Flying Tigers' — the American Volunteer Group, flying P-40 fighters to assist the dwindling number of Hurricanes in Burma. They were too few and too late.

'But if we could not send an army,' Churchill was to write, 'we could at any rate send a man.' On 19 February Churchill asked Britain's youngest lieutenant-general, the 50-year-old Harold Alexander, who had commanded the rearguard at Dunkirk, to fly to Rangoon and establish order from chaos. 'Never have I taken the responsibility for sending a general on a more forlorn hope,' Churchill wrote. 'Alexander was, as usual, calm and good-humoured ... Nothing ever disturbed or rattled him, and duty was a full satisfaction in itself, especially if it seemed perilous or hard ...' As had happened when Eden was attempting to reach Egypt in the preceding February, appalling winter weather delayed Alexander's departure for a week and he left England on the night of 27 February for the perilous flight to Burma, accompanied only by his aide-de-camp, a 22-year-old Australian officer. The intrepid two survived a forced landing in the Persian Gulf and were not to reach Rangoon until 5 March.

On Friday 13 February another general left for South-East Asia to take command of American forces in China. He took off from Florida in a flying boat for the long flight via the Atlantic and Africa to China. His name was Joseph Stilwell. An old China hand, known to all as 'Vinegar Joe', the 58-year-old combined a forceful character with an innate dislike of his allies, whether they be Chinese or British. He was to meet Alexander several weeks later.

Stilwell, stopping over in Delhi on his way to Chungking, was amused to observe in the huge headquarters of the Indian Army dozens of senior officers who seemed ignorant of what was happening in Burma — 'nobody but the quartermaster knew anything at all.' On 28 February he dined in Calcutta with Wavell, at the gloomy government house. He found Wavell a 'tired depressed man pretty well beaten down' by his constant defeats, and accompanied by an American, Lieutenant-General Brereton, who had lost his air forces but maintained an air of self-importance. He even carried a riding crop. Stilwell, a hard-swearing informal man who often wore old scraps of uniform, murmured to his aide that Brereton probably used it 'to beat off the birds'.

DEFEAT IN THE EAST

Wavell's forces had collapsed in a welter of defeat. In January 1942 the Japanese invaded Borneo while another task force steamed east towards New Britain to secure its great harbour of Rabaul. Defending the port was a single battalion of Australian infantry and a squadron of eight Wirraway aircraft — the Harvard trainers that Australia had manufactured as a fighter plane. The RAAF commander asked for modern aircraft but there were none to send. The Australian government made the hard decision that Rabaul force could be neither reinforced nor evacuated. 'So it was, in mid-January 1942, that with powerful enemy forces poised to strike at Rabaul on the one hand and Ambon on the other, the Australian chiefs of staff faced a military situation for which they had no immediate answer,' writes the RAAF's official historian. 'Without aircraft to strike at the enemy before he struck and to meet his assaults when they came, they were virtually powerless.'

RABAUL AND NEW BRITAIN

On 20 January 1942 nearly 100 Japanese bombers and fighters appeared over Rabaul. The Wirraways were shot down in minutes. Only one survived the action. Next day the squadron leader was ordered by RAAF headquarters in Melbourne to attack the approaching Japanese fleet 'with all available aircraft'. His last remaining Hudson loaded up with bombs and bravely took off to tackle a fleet that included two aircraft carriers, four cruisers and dozens of destroyers and transports. Fortunately for its crew, darkness fell and the raid was aborted. He was ordered to fly out his last planes, leaving the army on its own.

In the meantime the Japanese had landed at Kavieng on New Ireland, which was defended by an Independent Company. Outnumbered, the Australians held on until 30 January when they attempted to escape but were captured at sea. The Japanese landed at Rabaul on 23 January and were met by a furious defence on the beaches before the Australian force moved inland. Their fate was tragic. Of 200 Australians who surrendered, 150 were butchered in cold blood in March. Some eluded the Japanese and were taken off the island in a series of rescue missions mounted over the next four months.

All Europeans except for half a dozen administrators on each island were evacuated from Nauru and Ocean Island. Both islands were later seized by the Japanese.

AMBON

The small island of Ambon was strategically important because of its two airfields. It was defended by 'Gull Force' (2/21st Battalion) and by several hundred Australian gunners in addition to a force of 2600 Dutch Indonesian troops. Gull Force's commander warned army headquarters in Melbourne that his force was inadequate to defend vital points on the island. 'Quite appreciate feelings of lonely garrison,' General Wavell cabled General Sturdee, Australia's Chief of Staff, four days later, 'but am sure Australians will put up stout fight whatever happens.'

On 28 January the remaining RAAF Hudsons were withdrawn to avoid destruction from air raids by the Japanese. Two days later Japanese forces landed. The Dutch Indonesian troops quickly gave up but the Australians defending Laha airfield across the bay fought strongly before surrendering on 2–3 February, when the main body also surrendered. Fifteen Australians had been killed but later 300 officers and men were butchered by the Japanese in a series of mass executions in 'reprisals'. Of the original 1100 men of Gull Force, only 363 were to survive battle and captivity.

Men of the Australian Independent Company in East Timor who retreated into the mountains and fought a guerilla war for a year after the Japanese invasion.

NAVAL ACTIONS

On 2 February 1942, as the fall of Singapore appeared possible, the Allied naval leaders at their headquarters in Java formed an ABDA 'Combined Striking Force', commanded by the Dutch Rear-Admiral Karel Doorman. They did not accept the Australian government's suggestion that the British fleet at Colombo and the US fleet at Pearl Harbor be combined with Java's ships in a single fleet capable of tackling the Japanese Navy.

Doorman commanded little more than a squadron of four cruisers and eight destroyers. It was 'the beginning of three weeks of frustrating, fruitless attempts to check the Japanese flood', states the RAN official history. Doorman led several forays without making contact with the Japanese: when he retired with his force after a small engagement, Admiral Hart wanted to replace him with a more experienced commander but was talked out of it for the sake of Dutch–American relations.

DARWIN ATTACKED

Now came a devastating attack on Darwin by Vice-Admiral Kondo's carrier fleet. At 9.40 a.m. on 19 February ten American Kittyhawks (P-40s), returning from an aborted flight to Java, were landing at Darwin airfield when the first of 188 Japanese bombers appeared. The approaching Japanese had been reported by spotters but RAAF Intelligence at the airfield apparently thought the planes were the Americans returning. Four Kittyhawks were shot down or damaged in minutes, but the Japanese target was the shipping in the harbour — 47 ships. At 10 a.m. 27 bombers in addition to fighters and dive-bombers appeared over the town. The six remaining Kittyhawks were destroyed on the ground and confusion reigned at the airfield. In the raids the American destroyer *Peary* was sunk along with four merchant ships. Bombs rained on the town, killing 35 civilians. At midday another enemy attack was mounted by 40 land-based aircraft from Ambon and Kendari. In these attacks, the Australian home-land's first experience of bombing, Darwin's casualties totalled 556, of whom 238 were killed.

BROOME AND WYNDHAM BOMBED

On 2 March, when a total of 16 Allied flying boats were moored in Broome harbour, Japanese fighters appeared overhead at 9.20 a.m., and destroyed them all. Seventy civilians were killed along with 24 service personnel in the air raid. Japanese air raids also struck Wyndham and even Katherine (300 kilometres inland) while raids on Darwin mounted in intensity. By mid-1942 there would be 16 airfields in the Darwin area and air raids would continue until September 1943: one of the crucial but forgotten battles in Australia's history.

TIMOR

On 20 February Japanese troops began the invasion of both Dutch and Portuguese Timor. After the first days nothing was heard of the Australian defenders in the east — Sparrow Force — and it was assumed that all were captured or killed.

The Japanese landing at Kupang in Dutch Timor met with strong resistance from the Australian 2/40th Battalion, who suffered more than 200 casualties before their retreating column was overtaken by Japanese tanks and they were forced to surrender. The Australian 'Independent Company' in Portuguese Timor, trained to fight as commandos, refused to surrender. After contesting the landing at Dili, they withdrew into the mountains overlooking the port. From there they waged a guerrilla war, raiding Dili itself in April. They were aided by the East Timorese, nearly all of whom, after 400 years of Portuguese rule, were Christians. On 20 April the Australians managed to put together a wireless transmitter out of spare parts and sent their first messages to Darwin.

For the rest of the year they were supplied by air drops and by sea. It was not until January 1943, when Japanese reprisals against the Timorese increased in severity, that the Australians were evacuated. Like the defence of Tobruk, the campaign had taken a heavy toll of ships caught in the Timor Sea in daylight, and among the losses were the veteran destroyer HMAS *Voyager*, which ran aground on a beach and had to be scuttled (September 1942) and the corvette *Armidale*, attacked in daylight by 20 enemy aircraft, and sunk along with nearly 300 refugees and sailors (December 1942). On Timor several hundred Australians had tied up an entire enemy division and inflicted on them 1000 casualties in hit-and-run actions for the loss of 26 of their own men.

JAVA

Java, the main and most populous island in the Dutch East Indies, was defended by inadequate forces: Java's defence rested on five brigades (25,000 men) of Dutch-officered Indonesian troops and 8000 assorted British, with a small number of American gunners originally destined for the Philippines. Included in this number was a brigade of 3000 battle-tested troops of the 7th Australian Division who had reached Sumatra on 14 February before being sent on to Java. There were also 5000 unarmed ground crew of an Allied air force that was soon to shrink to 18 serviceable aircraft.

On that day Doorman took his force to sea to make a sweep to Banka Island and back in search of Japanese ships. On 15 February his force, which included HMAS *Hobart*, came under intense attack, *Hobart* surviving 13 attacks by 107 enemy aircraft without fatalities. One week after the fall of Singapore, on 21 February 1942, Wavell cabled Churchill: 'I am afraid the defence of ABDA area has broken down and the defence of Java cannot now last long … it always hinged on air battle. I have failed you and (the) President here, when a better man might perhaps have succeeded … I see little further usefulness for this HQ.' He added: 'I hate the idea of leaving these stout-hearted Dutchmen.' Next day he was ordered to dissolve his command and return to India, as he had suggested, to his old post there of C-in-C. The defence of Java was now the responsibility of the mixed Dutch, British, American and Australian forces. The troops were under the command of the Briton, Major-General Sitwell, and his air and naval deputies were Air Vice-Marshal Maltby and Commodore Collins.

Dark moment: on the eve of the fall of Java General Wavell (second from left) flies into Batavia [Jakarta] to confer with the American naval commander, Admiral Thomas Hart (left). Behind Wavell is a Dutch liaison officer and on far right General Brereton, the American air force commander in the area.

BATTLE OF THE JAVA SEA

Admiral Helfrich took command of all Allied naval forces. 'This resolute Dutchman', as Churchill called him, formed his ships into two forces, one at Jakarta's port, one at Surabaya. The Japanese invasion of Java was not slow in coming. At 2.30 p.m. on 27 February 1942 Admiral Doorman, alerted at his base at Surabaya by reports from Allied aircraft of two approaching enemy convoys, took his fleet of five cruisers and nine destroyers to sea. His progress was observed by Japanese aircraft. At 4.12 p.m. Doorman sighted the Japanese fleet — Rear-Admiral Takagi's six cruisers and twelve destroyers, escort of the invasion fleet of forty-three transports. In the Battle of the Java Sea, the first surface battle the Imperial Japanese Navy had fought since 1905, HMS *Exeter* was hit in her boiler early in the action and had to return to Surabaya; then two destroyers were sunk by the Japanese, who soon showed their mastery of night fighting. When his destroyers ran out of torpedos Doorman ordered them back to base (one of them, HMS *Jupiter*, struck a Dutch mine and sank); at 10.30 p.m. he encountered two Japanese cruisers and his flagship *De Ruyter* was sunk by torpedos along with the cruiser Java. USS *Houston* and HMAS *Perth* returned to Surabaya.

Commodore Collins, RAN, now commanding the remnants of the naval forces, had already ordered HMAS *Hobart* and the two British cruisers *Dragon* and *Danae* to locate the western Japanese convoy. This force had in fact turned back, and the cruisers passed through Sunda Strait to the relative safety of the southern waters without contacting the Japanese. It was hoped that the last two cruisers, *Perth* and *Houston*, would make a safe run home.

BATTLE OF SUNDA STRAIT

HMAS *Perth* and USS *Houston* left Tanjungpriok on Java's northern coast at 7 p.m. on 28 February to make the dash through Sunda Strait, sailing close to the shore. Just after 11 p.m. they encountered the invasion fleet in Bantam Bay, a vast armada of fifty transports, six cruisers and ten destroyers. They had run straight into the Western Invasion Force.

Perth, already at action stations, immediately chose targets and opened fire, Captain Waller taking her on a five-mile curve through the dark sea, Captain Rooks in *Houston* following in his wake, both ships firing broadsides at the Japanese vessels. It was a wild, forlorn battle, lit by flares, explosions and the flames of burning ships. *Perth*'s forward funnel was hit at 11.27 p.m. and at 12.05 a.m. she was struck by the first of two torpedoes. Stricken, with her ammunition gone, *Perth* was dead in the water. Waller ordered 'Abandon ship' and she went under at 12.25. Waller was last seen standing on the bridge, looking down on the silent turrets.

A Japanese photograph of American soldiers at the moment of surrender in the Philippines, 1942.

Twenty minutes later USS *Houston*, still firing her guns and 'with colours flying', was sunk, taking 600 of her ship's company with her, including her captain. Of *Perth*'s complement of 680 officers and men, 320 were picked up from the water or reached shore to be taken prisoner; only 215 would survive the next three years of captivity. Four Japanese ships were sunk in this famous night action.

THE END IN JAVA

Immediately afterwards Admiral Helfrich, determined to fight to the end in Javanese waters with what ships remained, learned from Palliser that the Admiralty had ordered all British ships to leave the scene 'for India' (Colombo). Helfrich reminded Palliser that he had placed all Dutch warships at the disposal of the British during the battle for Malaya. It was an ugly end to Allied cooperation. The British official history states, disingenuously: 'With nothing left to him but his submarines, even the indomitable Admiral Helfrich realised that continued naval defence of Java was impossible.' Helfrich flew off to Colombo next day. In later years he would tell those close to him that the British and Americans just wanted to cut their losses and go; that the Australian, Collins, was 'one of the few who wanted to fight the Japanese'.

Tragedy followed tragedy. On 1 March the damaged HMS *Exeter* and her accompanying destroyer were sighted and sunk before they could reach Sunda. The four last American destroyers in Javanese waters slipped through the Bali Strait one day earlier and made it safely to Australian waters. It was left to Collins to rescue what he could from the disaster. Sending one last signal ordering all naval ships to leave Javanese waters, he destroyed his code books and set off overland with his small staff to the south coast. Collins reached Tjilitap to find only two Australian corvettes in the harbour and the town full of hundreds of Allied servicemen. He ordered as many people aboard one warship as she could hold and the corvette left for Australian waters that night. Just before noon on 2 March a small flotilla appeared around the point — the sloop HMAS *Yarra*, the Indian corvette *Jumna*, and their small convoy of merchant ships. Soon the four Australian corvettes from Singapore — *Maryborough*, *Ballarat*, *Goulburn* and *Toowoomba* — appeared. Collins ordered *Yarra* to escort its convoy to Fremantle, and arranged for the remaining vessels to depart for home waters at fifteen-minute intervals at dusk.

At 6.30 a.m. on 4 March HMAS *Yarra* (Lieutenant-Commander Robert Rankin) and its slow convoy of three ships were 500 miles (800 kilometres) south of Java when they sighted warships closing on them rapidly. Their pagoda-like fighting tops soon identified three of them as Japanese heavy cruisers — a Japanese strike force that included two destroyers, only eight miles (13 kilometres) behind them and catching up. Five minutes later the first Japanese salvo fell and a shell struck *Yarra* as Rankin ordered the convoy to disperse and the little Australian sloop turned to do battle. At 6.47 a further Japanese salvo carried away her bridge and everyone on it. At 7.00 a.m. her survivors were ordered to abandon ship and took to boats and floats. For three hours the Japanese poured salvo after salvo into *Yarra* from point-blank range but she refused to sink, finally going under at 10.00 a.m. The three ships in the convoy were also sunk. The Japanese made no attempt to rescue any of the survivors before steaming from the scene. Only thirteen of *Yarra*'s men survived after being found clinging to a life raft five days later by the Dutch submarine *K11*. All the other ships ran the gauntlet and reached Fremantle.

On 28 February 1942 the Japanese began landing the first of four divisions on Java at Surabaya, and at points east of Batavia (Jakarta) and near Sunda Strait. The defenders were now without air or naval support. The Japanese made rapid progress inland. Brigadier Blackburn, VC, commanding the Australians, had two alternatives: to take to the mountains and wage a guerrilla war or to surrender. The Dutch commander advised the latter course, telling the Australian that he could expect little support from the inhabitants. The rapidity with which the Dutch East Indies fell and the hostile attitude of the Muslim Indonesians to the Allies was a sad reflection on Dutch rule. The Australians surrendered on 12 March, having suffered only thirty-six fatalities. A thousand Australians were to die in Japanese captivity.

Japanese poster depicting the nation's pride, her pilots.

A PAUSE IN THE PACIFIC

The Japanese armies, everywhere triumphant, were astonished at attaining their objectives in South-East Asia in three months; they had expected a six month campaign and favoured holding the present perimeters. The Imperial Navy, however, advocated an invasion of Hawaii and further incursions into the Indian Ocean. Japan's strategy now evolved from a compromise; it would sever the Australia–America route by taking New Caledonia, Samoa and Fiji after the American carrier force — still its only remaining threat — was destroyed in the battle Admiral Yamamoto planned at Midway.

Meanwhile, on 8 March 1942, the Japanese landed in north-eastern New Guinea at Lae and Salamaua. American Flying Fortresses and RAAF Hudsons raided enemy shipping there two days later. While a convoy carried American troops from Melbourne to New Caledonia, Australian and New Zealand forces, thinly distributed, held the remaining island outposts across the South Pacific.

A NEW SUPREME COMMANDER

On orders from their governments, the chiefs of staff of Australia and New Zealand formulated a proposal on 28 February that 'Anzac Area' (i.e. the geographical limits of both countries) be the base for a counteroffensive against the Japanese and suggested the appointment of a 'Supreme Commander', preferably an American. In March 1942 Roosevelt and Churchill agreed that the Pacific theatre would be the responsibility of the American High Command.

In the Philippines General Douglas MacArthur seemed doomed. In February he had encouraged President Quezon, who had left Manila for the tunnels of Corregidor almost under duress, to appeal to Roosevelt to declare the Philippines neutral. Roosevelt was outraged. MacArthur, who had left his Gibraltar-like island fortress of Corregidor to visit his forces on the Bataan peninsula across the bay only once, was ordered on 23 February to make his way to Mindanao to organise the defences of the southern Philippines, and then proceed to Australia. He told his officers that rather than obey the order he would resign his commission and go to Bataan as an ordinary soldier, but to Washington he replied that his departure could result in a 'sudden collapse' of the defence. Nudged again by Roosevelt and Marshall he finally left on 11 March, speeding through the darkness on a motor torpedo boat with his wife and young son and a dozen officers. After a 35-hour voyage and then a five-hour flight by aircraft, he climbed out of his plane on 17 March at Batchelor airfield near Darwin (which was then being bombed).

Macarthur expected to find immense US forces awaiting his command which he could lead in the liberation of the Philippines. Instead he discovered there were almost no troops at all: the main body of the US 41st Division sailed from San Francisco for Australia the day after the general's arrival, and they were followed eleven days later by the US 32nd Division.

MacArthur reached Melbourne by train on 21 March, delighted by the warmth of the welcome he received there from the Australian government and people. Curtin readily agreed to the suggestion that MacArthur, who had reached hero status in the United and Australia, be appointed Supreme Commander Allied Forces, South-West Pacific Area (SWPA). The Americans made 'South Pacific', which included New Zealand, a separate theatre, the responsibility of the US Navy under the overall command of Admiral Chester Nimitz, C-in-C Pacific Fleet at Hawaii.

By April there were only 33,000 scattered American army and air wing personnel in Australia. There were 43,000 AIF veterans, 63,000 volunteers for the AIF and 280,000 militiamen. General Blamey was appointed Commander-in-Chief of the Australian Army and made MacArthur's deputy in title if not in fact: Commander, Allied Land Forces, but American officers held all other senior positions. On Anzac Day 1942 MacArthur issued his first directive, based on an assessment by Blamey: the Allied land forces were to prevent landings on the 'north-east coast of Australia or on the south-west coast of New Guinea'.

THE FALL OF BURMA

In early March 1942 Rangoon lay under a pall of smoke from demolitions, arson and air raids. Its streets were deserted apart from gangs of looters and fleeing Indian civilians. On 20 February the banks had been closed and the government begun to evacuate Rangoon. Panic had seized the city. Mobs had raided the docks where hundreds of Lend-Lease vehicles were burned. While the Governor dithered about whether to declare martial law, many buildings were set to the torch by looters. An official, soon to leave with his officers for Mandalay, had released convicts, lepers and lunatics from confinement as a humanitarian gesture; the activities of the lunatics gave the doomed city a surreal atmosphere. (These events are not mentioned by Churchill in his war memoirs.) The Japanese were reported to be approaching.

Alexander, arriving in Rangoon on 5 March, mounted a counter-attack on the next day, but on its failure ordered his troops to evacuate Rangoon. His long column, stretching 30 kilometres bumper to bumper, left on 7 March but found the road blocked by the Japanese 30 kilometres north of the city. After a day's fighting and abortive attacks on the road block the Japanese suddenly withdrew to the west, permitting the escape of Alexander's forces. The Japanese troops entered Rangoon (8 March) to find the British had gone. The retreating British column headed north, on what would be a nightmare two-month 1000-kilometre fighting retreat, pursued by two Japanese divisions, the 33rd and 55th, and elements of two others.

On 12 March Stilwell flew into Maymyo, the hill retreat north of Mandalay that was now the seat of government, and met Alexander for the first time. Both generals were under the impression that they

An American wartime view of General Tojo.

General Douglas MacArthur, from an American wartime publication when the general had become Supreme Allied Commander, South-West Pacific. He wears the cap of a Philippine field-marshal; he designed it himself.

were commanding the Chinese forces, which had now grown to a strength of 70,000 men, although they were woefully under-equipped. With Lieutenant-General William Slim (hastily flown to the scene from Iraq) commanding 1st Burma Corps, 'Alex' was to conduct a campaign without an air force — the last RAF Hurricanes were withdrawn on 27 March. Retreating up the Irrawaddy, they received no orders from Delhi so they attempted to hold a line south of the Burma oilfields. But on 1 April the Japanese seized Prome. A fortnight later the British detonated the oilfields at Yenangyaung and fell back after a nightmare battle under choking clouds of smoke.

Central Burma was now gone and on 28 April Alexander ordered Slim to retreat to India. On 30 April the great Ava bridge over the Irrawaddy was detonated; next day the Japanese entered Mandalay without a battle.

Now began the agonising retreat across the Chindwin River to Assam on the mountain border of India, a race against the May monsoon. Alexander's progress was slowed by 150,000 Indian refugees, one-third of whom were to perish of starvation, cholera or dysentery. The monsoon came on 12 May, turning the mountain tracks into mudslides. Alexander watched the last of his troops struggle into India three days later. Joe Stilwell had led his own men out by foot to Imphal. On 25 May Stilwell, recuperating in Delhi, bluntly told newsmen: 'We got a hell of a beating. We got run out of Burma, and it is as humiliating as hell.'

The army had been saved, but it would take three years to retake Burma. The Japanese had conquered it in just three months.

INDIAN OCEAN

On 23 March 1942 the Japanese seized the Andaman Islands 250 miles (400 kilometres) south-east of Rangoon. They then went on a rampage in the Bay of Bengal, while Japanese submarines caused havoc off the southern coasts of India, sinking 100,000 tons of shipping in one week in April. Rear-Admiral Kurita's fleet was a strong one — one aircraft carrier, the *Ryujo*, and six heavy cruisers in addition to destroyers. Vice-Admiral Nagumo's fleet was even more formidable: five aircraft carriers, three battleships, three cruisers and nine destroyers. On the following day, 24 March, Vice-Admiral Sir James Somerville assumed command of the British Eastern fleet at Colombo.

Somerville's fleet was substantial, many of his ships being survivors of the Java tragedy. His five battleships (particularly his 'R'-class) were old and slow but included *Warspite*; he also had three carriers, five cruisers, fifteen destroyers and two submarines. Notified of the approach of a Japanese carrier force, Somerville cleared Colombo and made for waters south of the island. He intended to meet the Japanese fleet at sea but failed to make contact. Short of water and fuel he made for Addu Atoll, 600 miles (960 kilometres) away. He was also soon informed of the overwhelming strength of the Japanese fleet. 'We had narrowly escaped a disastrous fleet action,' Churchill later wrote. On 5 April Nagumo launched his carrier aircraft against the naval base at Colombo, concentrating on its docks and installations. Of the 32 RAF fighters that tackled his bombers, 24 were lost but Japanese aircraft losses were also high. Off the waters of Ceylon (Sri Lanka) Japanese dive-bombers found the heavy cruisers *Dorsetshire* and *Cornwall*, which were leaving Colombo to join Somerville, and sank them both.

On 9 April Japanese carrier aircraft struck Ceylon again, hitting Trincomalee's docks and on the return flight sighted the carrier HMS *Hermes* (whose aircraft had been taken off) and her accompanying destroyer HMAS *Vampire*. The small carrier took direct hits from 40 bombs before capsizing; the veteran Australian destroyer suffered thirteen direct hits and also sank; 300 sailors were lost but nearly 600 British and Australian survivors were later rescued. With this last success, the Japanese carriers steamed out of the Indian Ocean. In their deadly foray in the Bay of Bengal they had sunk 34 ships for the loss of only one ship but had also lost nearly 50 aircraft. Due to this loss of trained pilots the carrier *Ryujo* would play no part in the forthcoming battle of the Coral Sea.

LOSS OF THE PHILIPPINES

Since February 1942 the front on Bataan had been quiet. Japanese forces had been diverted elsewhere. But early in April the Japanese resumed their offensive, against defenders who were now starving. The 'Battling Bastards of Bataan' surrendered to the Japanese on 9 April and 38,000 Americans and Filipinos passed into grim captivity. In Australia MacArthur said: 'The Bataan force went out as it would have wished, fighting to the end its flickering, forlorn hope. No army has done so much with so little, and nothing became it more than its last hour of trial and agony. To the weeping mothers of the dead, I can only say that the sacrifice and halo of Jesus of Nazareth himself has descended upon their sons, and that God will take them unto Himself.'

These were fine words, but Bataan's defenders would have preferred supplies and reinforcements and some cursed their former general as 'Dug-Out Doug'. General Homma, who was by no means an inhumane man, ordered them to be marched north, halfway up the peninsula. He had anticipated 25,000 prisoners but was soon to take three times that number. The Americans and Filipinos were already weakened by malnutrition and disease. Between 7000 and 10,000 of them collapsed and died or were brutally killed on the 'death march' to prison camp.

On 4 May Japanese forces landed on the island fortress of Corregidor and despite desperate fighting on the beaches, they landed tanks, which were reported to be approaching the tunnels where the wounded lay. On 5 May General Jonathan Wainwright cabled President Roosevelt that he was opening parley for a surrender: 'With broken heart and head bowed in sadness but not in shame ... There is a limit in human endurance and that limit has long since been passed ...' To his grief the Japanese demanded the surrender of all American forces in the Philippines. Wainwright, broken in spirit, health and heart, ordered Major-General King, who was commanding the forces in the southern islands, to do as the Japanese demanded.

Having received intercepts of Wainwright's wireless messages to Washington explaining his action, MacArthur cabled General Marshall: 'I believe Wainwright has temporarily become unbalanced ...' The surrender of the few remaining American forces in the southern Philippines followed, though some troops took to the jungle to fight as guerrillas, sustained by the loyalty of the Filipinos. 'Skinny' Wainwright was to share his captivity in Manchuria with General Percival. They were both to stand like gaunt spectres at MacArthur's side when he took the unconditional surrender of Japan in Tokyo Bay three and a half years later.

More than 100,000 Filipinos and 20,000 Americans had fallen prisoner. But the capture of the Philippines and Burma in May 1942 were to be the last complete victories won by the Japanese.

MADAGASCAR

Concerned that the Japanese would seize Diego Suarez, the fine harbour in the Vichy French–held island of Madagascar, a British force landed there in May 1942. The port was seized in two days, but taking the rest of the island was beyond their resources and it lay under Vichy administration until November 1942.

Left: Admiral Isokoru Yamamoto in full dress on the eve of war. The boldest and most charismatic figure in the Imperial Japanese Navy, Yamamoto masterminded the conquest of South East Asia though he warned his masters that war with the United States would inevitably be lost. Discovering that he was visiting Japanese units in the Solomons, the American air force shot down the aircraft in which he was flying in 1943.
Oppsite: A stunning photograph of the British cruiser HMS *Devonshire* drawing alongside a British destroyer in the Indian Ocean. *Devonshire* sank the disguised German raider *Atlantis* in November 1941 and survived the war.

BATTLE OF THE CORAL SEA

'The Coral Sea is one of the world's most beautiful bodies of water,' writes the historian of the US Navy at war, Samuel Eliot Morison. 'Typhoons pass it by; the south-east trades blow fresh across its surface almost the entire year, raising white-caps which build up to long surges that crash on Australia's Great Barrier Reef in a 1500-mile line of white foam. Lying between the Equator and the Tropic of Capricorn, it knows no winter, and the summer is never uncomfortably hot.' These placid waters were soon to be the scene of one of the decisive naval battles of the war, one in which the opposing fleets never sighted each other.

Japan's imperial headquarters were embarking on further conquests. They intended to seize Tulagi in the Solomons and Port Moresby in New Guinea and thus establish control of the Coral Sea, enabling the conquest of New Caledonia and providing bases from which to mount air attacks on Australia. US Naval Intelligence had already cracked their naval code, as early as 20 April Admiral Nimitz, the US Navy C-in-C Pacific, knew that the Japanese intended to mount a seaborne invasion of Port Moresby sometime early in May.

Three Japanese surface forces would be involved. While a small Japanese force seized Tulagi, a convoy commanded by Rear Admiral Kajioka of eleven troop-carrying troopships, escorted by one light carrier, *Shoho*, and four cruisers would steam from Rabaul for Port Moresby. A third fleet under Vice-Admiral Takagi of two Japanese heavy carriers, *Shokaku* and *Zuikaku*, several cruisers and six destroyers, were to destroy any Allied forces in their way. Nimitz despatched to the danger area his carriers *Lexington* and *Yorktown* with cruisers and eleven destroyers under Rear-Admiral Frank Jack Fletcher, who on 4 May bombarded the Japanese landing force at Tulagi in the Solomons before steaming north to try to locate the Japanese carriers.

For the next two days the opposing fleets searched for each other. The Japanese carrier force, by dawn on 7 May, was 200 miles (320 kilometres) to Fletcher's east when their aircraft found and sank an American destroyer and an oiler and reported they had sunk an aircraft carrier and a destroyer. Several hours later, at 8.15 a.m., one of *Yorktown*'s aircraft reported two carriers and four cruisers steaming 175 miles (320 kilometres) north-west of the US carrier force. Fletcher ordered air strikes but his planes discovered only the light carrier *Shoho*, which they sank in ten minutes. Rabaul headquarters ordered the invasion convoy to steam north of the Louisiades, while Fletcher sent after them his cruiser force — 'Anzac Force', now termed Task Force 44. Commanded by Rear-Admiral John Crace, Flag Officer Commanding HM Australian Squadron, who flew his flag in HMAS *Australia*, the fleet included the cruisers HMAS *Hobart*, USS *Chicago* and the destroyer USS *Perkins*. They were attacked at 6 a.m. on 7 May by an entire squadron of twelve Rabaul-based Japanese torpedo aircraft, ten of which were shot down, and minutes later Anzac Force was struck by the first of two attacks by bombers. All attacks were beaten off by superb seamanship and a terrific weight of anti-aircraft fire, as was an unfortunate attack by American B-17 bombers flying from Townsville, who mistook Crace's fleet for the Japanese. A sailor on the bridge of *Australia* remembered Admiral Crace, his face and immaculate white uniform 'drenched with water, blackened by smoke and fumes'; *Hobart* lived up to her nickname 'Flaming Angel' by the amount of gunfire she hurled into the sky.

Below: The heavy cruiser HMAS *Australia*. The '*Aussie*' saw an enormous range of service in World War II from the Arctic Ocean and the coasts of Africa to the Battle of the Coral Sea and the invasion of the Philippines.
Below right: Rear-Admiral John Crace who commanded the Australian naval squadron at the Battle of the Coral Sea. Born in Canberra, he had made his career in the Royal Navy and survived the war to reach promotion to full admiral.

An American painting of the Japanese aircraft carrier *Shoho* in the Battle of the Coral Sea, May 1942. Each side lost only one carrier sunk, but the damage inflicted on two other enemy carriers meant they were unable to play any role in the coming Battle of Midway in June 1942.

Meanwhile Admiral Takagi had sent up his own aircraft to sink Fletcher's carriers. By nightfall on 7 May nine had been shot down and the tragi-comic became commonplace: in the dark six Japanese planes attempted to land on *Yorktown*'s flight deck and nearly a dozen, finally locating their own carriers, 'landed' in the sea by mistake.

On 8 May the two opposing carrier groups grappled with each other and battle was well and truly joined. *Yorktown*'s first attack group of forty-one planes, flying through a heavy squall, did not see *Zuikaku* but sighted *Shokaku* and landed two bombs on her, buckling her flight deck. *Lexington*'s pilots scored another hit on her, and Takagi ordered the lame duck back to the base at Truk. The Japanese hit *Yorktown* with a bomb that penetrated four decks and killed sixty-four men, and they mortally damaged *Lexington* with two bombs and two torpedoes. Wracked by explosions, 'Lady Lex' was listing and burning. For seven hours her men tried to save her but then an internal explosion occurred; her crew were taken off, Captain Sherman being the last to leave, and she was scuttled.

The loss of USS *Lexington*. Her sailors can be seen clambering down the sides of the burning carrier.

The Coral Sea Battle was proclaimed as 'The Battle that Saved Australia' and its anniversary is still commemorated as the first joint victory won by Americans and Australians in World War II. Both sides had lost an aircraft carrier and numerous planes (43 Japanese, 33 American). Tactically it was a draw. Strategically, however, it was an Allied victory. Port Moresby was never again directly threatened by seaborne attack. *Shokaku* took two months to repair and *Zuikaku* a month to replace its aircraft, so neither carrier was able to participate four weeks later in the battle that stopped Japan's seaborne advance in its tracks and changed the fate of the war: Midway.

'THE BATTLE OF SYDNEY'

Sydney, 'the world's most beautiful harbour' in the words of Admiral Morison, the US Navy's official historian, was to be the unlikely scene of a Japanese attack. After the Coral Sea action five I-class Japanese submarines carrying four midget submarines and an aircraft made for the entrance to Sydney. As early as 20 May and again on 30 May the Japanese aircraft flew over Sydney without hindrance on a reconnaissance flight and reported the presence and position of warships. On the night of 31 May three midget submarines were launched. One was caught in the anti-submarine net but two made it past the boom. One of them was sighted and sunk by depth charges but the third launched a torpedo at the cruiser USS *Chicago* but hit instead an RAN boat, the ferry *Kuttabul*, which sank with the loss of nineteen sailors.

A week later, in the early hours of 8 June, a Japanese submarine surfaced off Sydney's eastern beaches near Bondi and fired several shells, which destroyed a block of flats and created pandemonium, but killed nobody. Japanese submarines would remain active off the south-east coast of Australia for another year.

MIDWAY: THE TURNING POINT

The focus of Japanese intentions now moved to two square miles (5 square km) of sand in the north-west Pacific: two American islets known as Midway Island. They lay 1500 miles (2400 kilometres) west of Pearl Harbor, and possessed an airstrip and a wireless station vital to eaves-dropping on hostile messages. To the Japanese they were a stepping stone to Hawaii, but not a vital one. Japan intended to destroy in their waters all the remaining US naval power in the Pacific.

Towards these insignificant specks was steaming under the flag of Admiral Yamamoto the strongest battle fleet ever assembled. It left Japan on 27 May 1942 and it consisted of ten battleships, eight aircraft carriers (carrying a total of 685 planes), 24 cruisers, 70 destroyers, 15 submarines, 18 tankers and 40 other vessels. Soon the armada would split into three. Part of the fleet would be despatched as a decoy and land forces in the Aleutian Islands 1500 miles to the north of Midway, in the hope of enticing the US Pacific fleet from Hawaii. Then Midway would be seized, forcing the Americans to turn and rush the major part of their fleet to its rescue. Then Nagumo's carriers would move west, as if retreating, and Yamamoto would ambush the Americans and destroy them.

Admiral Nimitz had at his disposal forces barely one-third the size of the Japanese. He had three carriers, no battleships, and only eight cruisers, fourteen destroyers and twenty-five submarines. But his code-breakers had warned him that something was afoot; they were not sure of the Japanese objective, Midway, until late May. Nimitz reinforced Midway with every spare aircraft and gun he could find, increased its garrison to 5000 men and ordered them to build trenches in preparation for a massive air bombardment. On 26 May the carriers *Enterprise* and *Hornet* reached Pearl Harbor and were given 48 hours to replenish and rearm; next day *Yorktown* reached Pearl from the Coral Sea action, limping in at 10 knots. It was estimated that repairs to her would take three weeks. Nimitz gave the shipyards three days. Every hour counted. The much travelled *Yorktown*, by now known as 'The Waltzing Matilda of the Pacific' (the American sailors had picked up the Australian slang), flying the flag of Admiral Fletcher, also a veteran of the Coral Sea, left 72 hours later to join her sister carriers in the waters off Midway. The Japanese thought they had sunk her. and were in for a surprise. All three carriers slipped through the Japanese submarine screen without being sighted, but US submarines were already shadowing Yamamoto. All American officers and men knew that they were about to enter the crucial battle of the Pacific War.

On 3 June 1942 the northern Japanese force launched air raids on the Aleutians and began landing troops in the frozen islands. To their south on the morning of 4 June Admiral Nagumo's four carriers, north-west of Midway, launched their first strike on the island. Unknown to him, the three American carriers were stationed north-east of Midway, ready to ambush the ambusher. But the Pacific is a broad ocean and neither knew of each other's exact position. At 6.00 a.m. a Catalina reported two Japanese carriers approaching Midway. Fletcher ordered Rear-Admiral Raymond Spruance, commanding *Enterprise* and *Hornet*,

1942: FIGHTING BACK

to seek them out. Warned by radar of the approach of Japanese aircraft, Midway's defenders had sent their fifteen B-17 bombers in search of the invasion convoy along with thirty-seven torpedo bombers, and then got their obsolete fighters airborne — Buffaloes and Wildcats. In the dog-fights over Midway two Zeros and twenty-two American aircraft were lost. The Japanese bombed the airfield with relative impunity but reported heavy anti-aircraft fire from the defenders. It was decided to mount a second massive strike on Midway.

It was at this moment that the American torpedo-bombers appeared, and hurled themselves against the carriers. They flew to their destruction. Over three hours 44 of the 73 lumbering American aircraft were shot down without making a single hit on the carriers. Having launched 100 aircraft against Midway, Nagumo ordered his remaining 93 aircraft (for the second strike) to be armed with bombs, not torpedoes. It was a decision he would regret. His four carriers were fighting off the abortive American attacks and were attempting

Left: American aircraft over Midway Island.
Below: The master strategist: Admiral Chester Nimitz, Commander-in-Chief, US Fleet, Pacific, who masterminded the battles of the Coral Sea and Midway.

to recover planes from the first strike at Midway and preparing the second strike when, alerted to the presence of an American fleet to his north-east, Nagumo changed his mind and ordered them to be armed with torpedoes instead of bombs. *Enterprise* and *Hornet* had each already launched 50 aircraft, but they would have to fly 150 miles (240 kilometres) and few of them would have sufficient fuel for the return journey. At 9.20 a.m., just as Nagumo was recovering his first wave of Midway raiders, *Hornet*'s torpedo-bombers appeared overhead; all fifteen Devastators were shot down.

Of *Enterprise*'s fourteen dive-bombers ten disappeared into the smoke and never came out of it. Still no hits had been made on the Japanese carriers. Twelve torpedo-bombers from *Yorktown* now appeared; only two survived to limp away damaged. The slow-moving aircraft were sitting ducks, and the few torpedoes they dropped were slow or defective and easily avoided. 'Thus, out of 41 torpedo planes from the three carriers, only six returned, and not a single torpedo reached the enemy ships,' wrote Admiral Morison. 'Yet it was the stark courage and relentless drive of these young pilots of the obsolete torpedo planes that made possible the victory that followed. The radical manoeuvring that they imposed on the Japanese carriers prevented them from launching more planes.'

It seemed that the battle was lost. But at 10.24 a.m., just as Nagumo was launching his next wave, came the 'Miracle of Midway': it came out of the blue in the form of American dive-bombers. For more than three hours they had been searching the ocean for the Japanese fleet, and now they had found it. They were Douglas Dauntless dive-bombers — 17 from *Yorktown*, 32 from *Enterprise*. The carriers below them proved to be a perfect target, their flight decks cluttered with aircraft, bombs, torpedos, fuel lines. They attacked, near vertical in their screaming descent, and in six climactic minutes scored hits on *Kaga*, *Akagi* and *Soryu*, all of which were soon burning and exploding. On *Akagi* Admiral Nagumo's chief of staff recalled that 'the deck was on fire and anti-aircraft and machine-guns were firing automatically, having been set off by the fire aboard ship. Bodies were all over the place ... I had my hands and feet burned ...' Nagumo, who had to descend from the burning bridge on a rope, transferred his flag at 10.47 a.m. to a light cruiser. *Akagi* drifted away and was sunk by a Japanese submarine early next day.

At noon aircraft from the last carrier, *Hiryu*, found the carrier *Yorktown*, which manoeuvred violently at 30 knots to avoid their bombs. But six of the 18 attackers got through her protecting fighters and anti-aircraft fire and hit her severely. Five of Yorktown's six boilers were damaged and her speed dropped to 12 knots; and then she stopped dead. An hour later another attack hit her with two torpedoes and she listed, burning, and appeared about to capsize. Admiral Fletcher transferred his flag to a cruiser. Afloat but abandoned (her crew of more than 2000 men were saved by destroyers), she was finished off by a Japanese submarine next day. But late on 4 June *Enterprise*'s dive-bombers found Nagumo's last carrier, *Hiryu*, and set her on fire with four bombs; she went down next morning. Late on 6 June American aircraft found the damaged cruiser Mikuma and sank her.

By 6 p.m. on 4 June, Yamamoto realised he had gambled and lost. He ordered his remaining fleet to retire to the west while pondering how to break the news of his defeat to the Emperor. Japan had lost 250 aircraft, the Americans 109, but Yamamoto had lost four aircraft carriers — 55 per cent of Japan's carrier force. Only one American carrier had been sunk. 'The abandonment and subsequent loss of the carrier *Yorktown*, so quickly repaired and which so gallantly fought, is the one blot on an otherwise golden scroll of victory,' wrote the US Navy's official historian. The 'Miracle of Midway' — 'The Glorious Fourth of June' — was one of the most unexpected and decisive battles in naval history.

Japanese plans for the seizure of Fiji, New Caledonia, Samoa and the New Hebrides were scrapped. Henceforth she would fight a defensive war.

Admiral Raymond Spruance, US Navy. Modest and reflective, he was arguably the most successful American fighting admiral in the Pacific war.

COLLAPSE IN EGYPT, 1942

In the Middle East and Mediterranean the early months of 1942 again saw all British hopes of total victory dashed to pieces. 'From February to May 1942, the armies rested motionless in the gravel wastes of Gazala. For the troops the long days stretched full of boredom and discomfort. There was nothing to interest the eye but the blank swell of the brown desert; nothing to do but lay mines, dig foxholes and uncoil wire under a sun that grew ever more fierce,' recounts Corelli Barnett in *The Desert Generals*.

'Apart from the heat and shortage of water (less than eight pints per man per day for all purposes including washing) there were the flies, the sweat and dust, desert sores that refused to heal — and the growing and well founded belief amongst British forces that their tanks and artillery were no match for the Germans.' They placed faith in their line of minefields and protected 'boxes' which stretched from Gazala on the coast to the oasis of Bir Hakeim 70 kilometres to the south.

On 21 January 1942, having been chased back to his starting point, Rommel had launched a counterattack, his Panzers catching the British armoured brigades off-balance. British naval power in the Mediterranean was at its lowest ebb and was using what strength it had to keep Malta supplied. The Axis force, their convoys barely

Right: An English illustated weekly depicted the British tank crews in heroic pose but the armour they drove into battle was inferior to that of the Germans, and British tank losses were calamitous.
Below: The new General Grant tanks from American factories were superior to British makes. This photograph shows one of them passing a burning Panzer in the summer fighting of 1942.

Wartime poster showing the fighting men of the United Nations marching to victory. On the left, representatives of the armed forces of the British Empire (note the distinctive headgear of the Australian, New Zealander and South African). On the right of the poster (from top left figure to bottom right): men from Greece, Norway, Belgium, the Netherlands, France, Poland, Czechoslovakia, United States, China, the Soviet Union, Yugoslavia.

hindered, were receiving supplies and reinforcements at the exact moment when 8th Army had stretched itself and its air support to the limit by its advance since November 1941. By the end of 23 January 1st Armoured Division had lost half its 150 tanks and next day lost the rest when 15th Panzer attacked it with a spearhead of 50 tanks which reached Msus airfield. 'It soon became apparent,' the German commander wrote, 'that the British tank crews had no battle experience and they were completely demoralized by the onslaught.' As a result 4th Indian Division, near Derna, was isolated and retreated east.

On 26 January 1942 Churchill, who was returning from Washington to answer for the series of disasters in the Far East, was appalled to hear that Auchinleck was contemplating evacuating Benghazi. Axis forces entered the city two days later and the commander of 13 Corps, Godwin-Austen, was replaced by Brigadier William Gott. On 30 January, with both Benghazi and Derna lost, Auchinleck cabled the Prime Minister: 'I am reluctantly compelled to conclude that to meet German armoured forces with any hope of decisive success, our armoured forces as at present equipped, organized and led must have at least a two to one superiority …'

By February 1942 Auchinleck's army had retreated east 500 kilometres and was now established on a line running south from Gazala and Tobruk to Bir Hacheim. But for the role played by the Desert Air Force in covering the retreat, 8th Army's losses would have been calamitous. With rioting in the streets of Cairo, Britain's position in Egypt was precarious. The disturbances were actively encouraged by King Farouk and a showdown soon resulted. On the night of 4 February British troops and armoured cars surrounded the Abdin Palace in Cairo. After an officer shot open the palace gates the British ambassador, Sir Miles Lampson, presented Farouk with an ultimatum, demanding the appointment of the pro-British Nahas Pasha as head of the government — or Farouk's abdication. Farouk chose the former option but the incident added to the long list of Egyptian grievances against the British.

Other changes took place in the Middle East command, but they failed to satisfy Churchill, who urged Auchinleck to launch an immediate counter-offensive and grew impatient at the delays. On 3 May Auchinleck outlined his difficulties in a long letter to the CIGS, General Brooke, in which he ventured the opinion that strategically it was more important to hold India than the Middle East and that to take on Rommel's strength of 360 tanks he would need at least 700 tanks and therefore could not launch an offensive until 15 June, a month later than he had previously planned. Already angered by Auchinleck's refusal to fly to London for consultations, Churchill was furious and for the first time talked to Brooke of sacking Auchinleck and replacing him with Wavell, or Gort or Alexander.

THE EASTERN FRONT

'Will this winter never end?' Goebbels asked in his diary on 20 March. He wondered if a new ice age was setting in, for the snow still lay heavy on the ground and winter conditions persisted into the first month of spring. Goebbels was depressed. He had learned that Germany's losses on the Eastern Front were already one million, including 200,000 fatalities and 112,000 cases of frostbite. He decided that these figures should be suppressed for the sake of German morale. In April food rationing was introduced in Germany. The wheat fields of Russia were now frozen over. British bombing was increasing in effectiveness. In April much of Lübeck and Rostock lay in ruins. 'The air raid last night on Rostock was even more devastating that those which preceded it ... The situation in the city is in some sections catastrophic,' he wrote on 28 April. Next day Cologne was bombed. 'About a hundred fires were started, some of them of great magnitude,' he lamented. The Propaganda Minister had little good news to impart to the German public.

As the snows slowly began to melt on the Eastern Front both Hitler and Stalin planned new offensives. Against the advice of his General Staff — the Stavka — Stalin made the first move. 'Don't let us sit down in defence with our arms folded, while the Germans attack first,' he told the generals one night in March. 'We must ourselves strike a series of blows to forestall them on a broad front and upset enemy preparations.'

RUSSIA: STALIN'S FAILED OFFENSIVE

Stalin ordered Timoshenko to launch the first thrust against Kharkov. It began on 12 May and by 19 May the Russian armies south-east of the city were in danger of being encircled. In the disaster 240,000 Russians were taken prisoner. In the north the Russian thrust towards Leningrad met a similar fate and nine divisions were encircled, among them their leader, the brilliant 41-year-old General Vlasov, who declared that Stalin was mad and no longer merited his loyalty. He was to raise an army of anti-Communist Russians to fight alongside his new masters the Germans.

In the south a similar crisis developed. In a poorly organised attempt to liberate the Crimea by clearing the Kerch peninsula the Soviet armies found themselves attacked suddenly by Manstein's 11th Army in early May 1942. The Russians collapsed after the destruction of nine divisions, the loss of 175,000 men and 3500 tanks. On the first anniversary of the German invasion, the Soviet Union released statistics showing that her manpower losses had reached the grim total of 4.5 million men. And in June Hitler launched his summer offensive that would carry him to the gates of Asia.

As the snows begin to disappear early in 1942 Hitler plans his next offensive in the East. He is seen with (from left to right) General Jodl, General Guderian in fur collared coat and Field-Marshal Keitel.

MALTA

Early in 1942 Malta's position was critical, its population nearing starvation. Submarines based on Malta continued to 'slaughter' Italian convoys (in Foreign Minister Ciano's words) but the Axis were also sinking most of the ships attempting to reach Malta with supplies and aircraft. Of a convoy of four supply ships sent to the island under heavy naval escort in March 1942 two were sunk by air attack and the others were sunk while unloading in Malta harbour. It was the last convoy to reach Malta for nearly three months. In that month, when the island's air defences were down to six aircraft, Churchill appointed the stalwart general, Lord Gort, VC, as Malta's governor. He chose to live on the same rations as the civilians. In March alone Axis aircraft dropped 2000 tonnes of bombs on Malta, and in April 7000 tonnes. To reinforce the island's air defences Churchill asked Roosevelt if he could spare the large carrier USS *Wasp* to fly in Spitfires for the island's defence.

In May *Wasp* sailed from Gibraltar to a point midway to Malta and launched sixty Spitfires, which arrived to the cheers of the Maltese. *Wasp* then made a second trip, launching more fighters. The Spitfires turned the tide of the air battle. Churchill was grateful and exultant. 'Who said a wasp couldn't sting twice?' he cabled in his note of thanks to the President.

Hitler approved plans for an airborne assault on Malta — Operation Hercules — to be mounted in July. But on 15 June, as his second summer offensive in the Soviet Union got under way, he cancelled it in order to conserve troops and aircraft, and ordered Malta to be reduced by bombing alone. If Malta fell, the Allies' tenuous hold on the Mediterranean was lost.

THE FALL OF TOBRUK

By May 1942 Rommel was re-equipped, rested and ready. On the night of 26 May he attacked 8th Army, his first assault being a feint in the north against the 1st South African Division at Gazala. This was followed by a sweeping advance in the south next day by which he hoped to outflank the British line and then tear north and destroy the British armour before capturing Tobruk. Instead of being concentrated so as to administer a sharp rebuff to the Afrika Korps, Ritchie's two tank divisions were dispersed and the separate brigades were to be destroyed piecemeal. Auchinleck had also taken the precaution of ordering Ritchie not to allow Tobruk to be surrounded nor to surrender. He must fight and maul Rommel's tanks west and south-west of Tobruk. But again Auchinleck's orders were fumbled or disregarded by Ritchie, whose confusion in the first days of the attack was equalled by that of his subordinate commanders, Lieutenant-General Gott commanding 13 Corps in the north and Lieutenant-General Norrie, commanding 30 Corps in the south. Both were astonished by the speed and suddenness of Rommel's advance east of Bir Hakeim. Major-General Messervy's 7th Armoured Division headquarters was overrun early on 27 May and the general escaped capture only by throwing away his red-banded cap and impersonating a private in the melee.

Rommel was also far from happy — he had lost one-third of his tanks, many of them to the powerful M3 General Grant tanks with which 8th Army was equipped (though in insufficient quantities), and within days his forward units were running short of water,

The most widely produced American bombers of the war: B-24 Liberators.

Tough and unflappable soldiers: New Zealand gunners in the Libyan desert, 1942.

ammunition and fuel. His eventual victory was made possible by General Ritchie's indecision between 29 and 31 May. 'The failure of Eighth Army to seize the initiative … was disastrous,' writes one historian. On 1 June Rommel personally led the assault on the marooned 150th Brigade (50th British Division) and overwhelmed it, before ordering the Free French brigade defending Bir Hakeim to be eliminated. On 2 June Auchinleck signalled Ritchie: 'You must strike hard and at once if we are to avoid a stalemate …' On 5 June Ritchie finally began the tank battle for 'the Cauldron', but Rommel was by now rearmed and waiting.

The British preliminary artillery bombardment fell in empty desert, to the delight of the Italians, and 50 out of 70 attacking British tanks were destroyed with ease. 'The heavy British tanks lumbered forward at daylight, providing perfect targets for our anti-tank guns, and ended up in a minefield, where they were simply shot to pieces,' recorded General von Mellenthin. Lacking tank protection and adequate anti-tank weapons, infantry battalions were overrun (Messervy was again almost captured). By the end of the battle called 'Knightbridge', Ritchie's tank strength had been reduced from 300 to 132 and by 7 June his troop losses totalled 10,000, most of them captured. Only in the far south had Rommel been thrown back — by the staunch stand of Koenig's Free French at Bir Hakeim, which was extolled in newspaper headlines throughout the world. Koenig's survivors were finally ordered to break out on 10 June and most of them reached safety.

On 14 June Ritchie ordered the Gazala line evacuated before his divisions in the north were cut off; it was the beginning of another wholesale retreat to the Egyptian frontier and past it, to Mersa Matruh itself. He left Tobruk behind him. Churchill envisaged a strong defence at Tobruk, but Tobruk's commanders, senior among whom was the South African, Major-General Klopper, were unsure whether they were to defend the port or evacuate it. Their orders from General Ritchie were ambiguous and confused.

On 14 June Auchinleck ordered Freyberg's New Zealanders in Syria to move urgently to the desert — 'after', as Churchill wrote, 'a month's needless delay'. Confident that the position in the desert was being stabilised the Prime Minister left for Washington. There, on 21 June, he received the shattering news that Tobruk had fallen and that the Fleet was leaving Alexandria for the safety of the Red Sea. 'This was one of the heaviest blows I can recall during the war,' Churchill later wrote. 'Defeat is one thing. Disgrace is another.'

Tobruk, which the Australians and then the British and Poles had held for eight months, had fallen one day after being encircled. After launching a heavy artillery bombardment and an intense air attack Rommel had attacked Tobruk's perimeter from the south-east, where a thrust was least expected and where the anti-tank ditch had sanded up. A total of 33,000 men, including most of 2nd South African Division, were captured.

Roosevelt's response was immediate: he ordered the 300 Sherman tanks destined for the US 2nd Armoured Division be shipped immediately to 8th Army. Hitler, sensing complete victory, conferred a field marshal's baton on Rommel and ordered the air offensive on Malta to be slackened, a move that Kesselring, commanding the *Luftflotte* bombarding the island, considered 'foolhardy'. All available resources would now be poured into North Africa.

RETREATING TO EL ALAMEIN

On 25 June, the day of stormy debate in the Commons on Churchill's direction of the war, Auchinleck sacked Ritchie and took personal command of 8th Army, ordering a stand to be made on a line running south from Mersa Matruh. On the same day he ordered Major-General Morshead to rush the 9th Division down to reinforce 8th Army. On 26 June 1942 the Australians began moving south, through Syria and Palestine to Egypt, the troops replacing their slouch hats with helmets, their platypus divisional signs on their transport painted over in an effort to keep the move secret. As their trucks roared through Palestine past groups of Jewish settlers the Diggers were heartened by shouts of 'Good luck, Australia!'

On 25 June Rommel told Count Cavallero, the Italian Chief of General Staff: 'I count on being in occupation of Cairo and Alexandria by June 30th.' Three days later Mussolini himself arrived in north Africa, intending to ride into Cairo on a white horse to celebrate the victory. In Cairo itself staff officers began burning top secret files at General Headquarters, preparatory to evacuating the city. Known as 'The Flap' and by some as 'Ash Wednesday', it marked the low point of Britain's fortunes in the war in the Middle East.

More disasters followed. On 26 June 1942 Lieutenant-General Gott ordered his 13 Corps to withdraw from the Matruh area to the east — leaving 10 Corps (50th British Division and 10th Indian Division) behind. In an inquiry a month later General Wilson observed that 'the 13th Corps just disappeared and left 10th Corps up the pole'. Also left up the pole by the collapse of the front, or rather left isolated 40 kilometres in the desert, were the New Zealanders in their positions south of Matruh. The entire division was stranded at Minqar Qaim, with German armour to their east. Freyberg was wounded in the fighting and Brigadier Inglis took command. Forming up their transport at night into a long column, the New Zealanders broke through the German line to rejoin 8th Army in one of the wildest night fights of the desert war. 'Congratulations on your new wound and new glory,' his old friend Churchill cabled to Freyberg. But by now nothing the Kiwis did surprised anyone. And 10 Corps too made a fighting retreat out of the trap. One of its columns had crashed through Rommel's own camp in the night.

By 30 June 1942 the battered 8th Army was holding a new line running south of El Alamein, a forlorn railway station near the coast, barely 100 kilometres — an hour's fast drive — from Alexandria. It was a natural defensive position where the land narrowed to a bottleneck 90 kilometres deep between the Mediterranean coast and the impassable marshes of the Qattara Depression far in the south. It was the 'last ditch' before Cairo.

EASTERN FRONT

Realising that Russia's manpower was virtually inexhaustible and that it was pointless to surround her armies — for new ones arose in their places — Hitler decided early in 1942 to seize the great wheat fields in the south, the oilfields and the industrial region of the Donets basin, particularly the city of Stalingrad on the Volga River.

A German officer on the Russian front, summer 1942.

Oil from the Caucacus, shipped across the Caspian Sea to the Volga River, and the munitions from Stalingrad sustained Russia's armies.

'If I do not get the oil of Maikop and Grozny, then I must end this war,' Hitler told General von Paulus, who would lead 6th Army in the coming offensive. (Paulus, like Vlasov, would later decide that his political master was mad, and after being captured would join the Russians.) Goebbels visited Hitler in his eastern lair in late February, where his leader outlined his new plans. 'The Führer again has a perfectly clear plan for the coming spring and summer campaign. He does not want to overextend the war,' Goebbels noted. 'He is determined under all circumstances to end the campaign at the beginning of October and to go into winter quarters early … perhaps this will mean a hundred years war in the East, but that need not worry us … Our offensive will in all likelihood not begin before the end of May or the beginning of June …'

In Sevastopol and Stalingrad the Russians fought to the death in the rubble of their ruined cities.

1942: TO THE CAUCASUS!

Hitler intended to wait until summer, which would give him time to build up his depleted armies. He asked his allies to increase their forces on the Eastern Front for the final accounting with Bolshevism. Mussolini undertook to send another three divisions if Germany provided then with artillery; Hungary, which had so far contributed little, consented to increase its forces to no fewer than 13 divisions. Romania and even Slovakia would contribute forces.

In April 1942 Mussolini and Ciano met with Hitler and Ribbentrop at Klessheim Castle in Salzburg. Ciano thought Hitler had aged since the winter; his hair was greying. Hitler told Goebbels, who was worried by the state of his health, that he had a horror of snow — a 'physical revulsion'. Ribbentrop, whom Ciano called Hitler's parrot, informed his guests that the war was going well on all fronts — and on the seas. 'When Russia's sources of oil are exhausted she will be brought to her knees. Then the British will bow in order to save what remains of their empire. America is a big bluff …'

Hitler would launch his great new offensive with only half the forces he had hurled against Russia one year earlier: 68 divisions, but they would be aided by 51 divisions from his allies — 27 Rumanian, 13 Hungarian, nine Italian, two Slovak and one Spanish. Only Bulgaria refused to send forces to fight its traditional ally Russia.

THE GERMAN OFFENSIVE BEGINS

On 2 June 1942 the Germans began a massive aerial and artillery bombardment of the last Soviet citadel in the Crimea, Sevastopol, which was defended by 106,000 Russian troops. Marooned by the Axis advance, the Russians had only 38 tanks. Five days later the German–Romanian armies, numbering 203,000 men and 450 tanks, attacked and in three weeks of desperate street fighting occupied the city. Few of the defenders managed to escape. The Germans claimed to have taken 90,000 Russians prisoner, among them 23,000 wounded; the rest were dead. By 3 July the 250-day siege of Sevastopol was over.

In the north on 28 June the Germans launched another offensive in the Kursk–Voronez sector. Only tough fighting saved Voronez — and Moscow — and forced the Germans to swing south towards Stalingrad. 'The Soviet troops, retreating under the pressure of superior enemy forces, nevertheless resisted heroically … But with 1200 planes in this area, the enemy had great superiority in aircraft, as well as in guns and tanks,' explains one Soviet historian. On 28 July Stalin was angered to hear that the Germans had taken Rostov-on-Don (which they had also briefly seized in 1941). They had attacked from the north-east, where no defences existed. Hitler had diverted an entire Panzer corps to capture it, but by so doing he allowed Stalingrad a lifeline. The city now lay open to attack, but would be strongly reinforced over the next four weeks.

Further south the German advance pressed on into the Caucasus mountains. On 11 August the Germans reached the Maikop oilfields, which the retreating Russians had detonated, and were within sight of the Caspian Sea. Alpine troops planted the swastika on the summit of Mount Erebus, from which they could see the foothills of Asia itself.

On 18 August fighting in the area between the Don and the Volga was intense but on 23 August the German 6th Army broke through to the Volga and from a high escarpment looked down upon the tugs and freighters moving slowly on its waters. Beyond, they saw the steppes of Asia. On the next day they began to fight their way into the northern industrial suburbs of Stalingrad, after 600 German aircraft had bombed the city, causing 40,000 deaths. Stalin ordered that the city named after him must resist to the last round. There would be no evacuation, no retreat.

The great industrial city of Stalingrad — the former Tsaritsyn (and now known as Volgograd) — stretched for 50 kilometres along the western bank of the Volga. It would undergo a siege of five months fought with such savagery that no battle in history equals it. Stalingrad would be the nemesis of the German Army.

Germans equipped with light artillery blast their way into Rostov, 1942.

THE DARKENING SCENE

'A THOUSAND BOMBERS'

On the night of 30 May 1942 Bomber Command mounted its heaviest bombing raid of the war, sending nearly 1000 aircraft against Cologne. They dropped nearly 2000 tonnes of bombs and claimed to have caused widespread damage. It was as much a propaganda exercise as a strategic blow, and only one British raid of similar size was to be mounted before 1944 when 1000 aircraft flew against Bremen on the night of 25–26 June.

Professor Lindemann, Churchill's chief scientific adviser, was still predicting that within a year from February 1942 one-third of Germany's population would be rendered homeless by bombing. The bomber was still seen as the instrument of victory. Ahead lay the 'round-the-clock' strategic bombing offensive against Germany.

On 27 June 1942, a convoy (PQ 17) sailing from Iceland to Murmansk in Russia was almost entirely sunk. Admiral Pound at the Admiralty, mistakenly thinking that the giant battleship *Tirpitz* was approaching it, ordered: 'Convoy is to scatter' and withdrew its naval escorts. The merchantmen steamed on unprotected and the ships were picked off one by one. The convoy lost 23 of its 34 ships to German air and submarine attack; 500 of the 600 tanks in the convoy went to the bottom. This disaster, coming soon after the fiasco of February 1942 — the escape of the *Gneisenau* and *Scharnhorst*, which steamed boldly through the English Channel from their French base to the safety of the Baltic — seemed indicative of British ineptitude.

In the Atlantic the U-boat toll on Allied shipping was mounting, worse than in the darkest month of World War I, April 1917, when England faced starvation. In the first four months of 1942 U-boats sank 82 ships in the north Atlantic before shifting their attentions to the south, to the Caribbean and the Gulf of Mexico, where they sank 142 ships in the next few months, for the loss of only 20 submarines. To try to destroy the U-boat bases air attacks were mounted on French bases on the Channel and Biscay coasts while Coastal Command Sunderlands maintained constant patrols, armed with depth charges. By June 1942 at least 60 U-boats were operating in the Atlantic and their toll of shipping was enormous. Between the slow, ponderous Sunderland flying-boats and surfaced U-boats capable of hurling curtains of gunfire at aircraft, some memorable battles would be fought.

Churchill thought of recalling Admiral Somerville's fleet from the Indian Ocean to provide so strong an escort for the Arctic convoys that even the *Tirpitz* would be deterred from venturing out. 'He (Somerville) has been doing nothing for several months and we cannot really keep this fleet idle indefinitely,' he wrote in a minute of 13 July. Again, the Admiralty vetoed the plan. Somerville, Cunningham's great friend (their bawdy signals to each other are part of Royal Navy lore) and a formidable leader, remained in command of the almost inactive Eastern fleet until 1944. A handful of brave

Above: An Allied merchant ship about to sink from a German torpedo.
Below: An Arctic convoy. In foreground a British destroyer HMS *Eskimo* passes an exploding depth charge.

men would achieve what a battle fleet failed to accomplish: midget submarines were to cripple *Tirpitz* and the 'Dam Busters' of the Royal Air Force would later sink her in a Norwegian fjord.

India, meanwhile, was in ferment. In July 1942 the nationalist leaders Gandhi and Nehru had rejected the British government's offer of Dominion status after the war and had called on Britain to 'Quit India'. The security forces had moved quickly and imprisoned both men, but mass demonstrations and some violence broke out and persisted until the end of the year. Some Europeans were murdered. Keeping the peace took most of the strength of the British-Indian army, preventing any opportunity to undertake any offensives in Burma against the Japanese with the few troops they had left.

COMMAND DECISIONS

In mid-1942 Churchill was at wit's end in trying to find a way out of the morass of constant defeat. On 1 July he faced a censure motion in the House of Commons for the loss of Tobruk and his conduct of the war. The motion was defeated next day by 475 votes to 25 but at one stage it seemed that he would be forced to resign. Six days later, when the chiefs of staff vetoed his plan to land in Norway to establish a base to protect the Arctic convoys, he complained to Eden of their negative attitude and suggested: 'We'd better put an advertisement in the papers, asking for ideas.'

Churchill never lacked ideas, but the people of Britain wanted action, not ideas. Powerful public sentiment, manifested in massed rallies in Trafalgar Square, demanded that more assistance be given to Russia, where the Red Army was bearing the brunt of Hitler's war. Public pressure began on Churchill's government to land forces in Europe: 'Second Front — Now!'

Churchill, worried that Stalin, whose armies were again collapsing, would make a separate peace with Hitler, had suggested raids be mounted on the French coast to show the Russians that the Western Allies were active. He called them 'butcher and bolt' raids. This was the genesis of the one-day raid on Dieppe on 19 August 1942 that resulted in 3000 casualties among the 5000 troops involved, nearly all of them Canadian, and one of the largest air battles of the war, resulting in the loss of 150 British aircraft.

Informed by the chiefs of staff that there would be insufficient landing craft for an invasion force in Europe until 1943, Churchill urged that attention be given to a plan long discussed with Washington to land Anglo-American forces in north Africa — Operation Gymnast. In July 1942 General Marshall and Admiral King flew over from Washington to discuss some form of invasion. The Americans suggested seizing the Cherbourg peninsula. The British chiefs of staff were dismayed and criticised the idea so strongly that Marshall gave in and agreed to a north African landing instead: the operation would be named Torch. Churchill was able to signal Roosevelt that the service chiefs had 'reached complete agreement' on the future invasion plan. The President was also delighted and replied: 'I cannot help feeling that the past week represented a turning-point in the whole war and that we are now on our way shoulder to shoulder.' Marshall decided that the youthful, 50-year-old general, Dwight David Eisenhower, would be Supreme Commander of the American forces in the European Theatre of Operations (ETO) to plan the details of the forthcoming invasion. Eisenhower arrived in London soon afterwards accompanied by his deputy, another young general whom Churchill nicknamed 'the American Eagle', the lanky, hawk-nosed and ambitious Mark Wayne Clark.

General Alexander, the hero of Dunkirk and Burma, was designated to command British forces as Eisenhower's deputy in 'Operation Torch'. 'That guy's good,' the modest Eisenhower remarked after his first meeting in London with Alexander. 'He should be Commander-in-Chief instead of me!'

How would the Allied leaders break the news to Stalin that there would be no second front in 1942? Churchill decided to do it personally, and he would fly to Moscow via the Middle East where any sort of victory seemed remote. The ebb and flow of British fortunes in the desert puzzled, angered and embarrassed him. Here, a vast Middle East command of more than 700,000 men — few of whom were combat troops — were facing defeat at the hands of barely a dozen German and Italian divisions.

ALAMEIN: THE DEFENCE

'The enemy is stretched to the limit and thinks we are a broken army,' Auchinleck told 8th Army on 30 June. 'His tactics against the New Zealanders were poor in the extreme. He hopes to take Egypt by bluff. Show him where he gets off.'

In July 1942, in the searing heat of the summer, General Auchinleck and 8th Army fought Rommel to a standstill at Alamein, using defence based on a system of fortified 'boxes' ringed with minefields and barbed wire. On 1 July the 1st South African Division in the north threw back a German attack; on 3 July the New Zealanders 'bounced out' (in one writer's words) and struck the Ariete Division, capturing 44 guns. Rommel's three-pronged assault on the Alamein Box was knocked back. On 3 July Rommel, whose German divisions could barely muster 1300 men, wrote: 'After three days of assaulting the Alamein line I decided that I would call off the offensive for the moment …' But on 4 July Auchinleck launched an offensive by both his Corps. It proved a disappointment and led to the dismissal of General Norrie of 30 Corps. His replacement by Major-General Ramsden came two days later. On 5 July the newly arrived Australians took positions east of Ruweisat Ridge and launched a heavy attack from it two days later.

On 10 July Rommel attacked in the south just as the 26th Australian Brigade attacked in the north, at Tel el Eisa Ridge, taking 1000 astonished and exhausted Italians prisoner. And in what has been described as 'the most important intelligence coup of the entire North African campaign' they also captured the German wireless outpost on Trig 33 and its wealth of documents which revealed that the Germans had penetrated the British Black Code. The code was changed.

On 11 July the 9th Australian Division again attacked, this time against Miteiriya Ridge where they took another 1000 prisoners. On 13, 14 and 15 July the Australians withstood all Axis counterattacks. Of the bitter fighting of 14 July Rommel wrote: 'Fighting continued until long after dark and the Australian infantry showed that they were the same redoubtable opponents we had met in the first siege of Tobruk.' In July the war correspondent Alan Moorehead drove up from Cairo to the Alamein Box manned by his countrymen and was astonished by their appearance and spirit. 'Australians swarmed everywhere and they looked magnificent. None of us had seen such troops before,' he wrote. The Diggers were naked but for shorts, boots and slouch hats. 'Rested — and bored — by their garrison duty, they appeared glad to be back in the Desert.'

But 14 July also saw New Zealanders stranded on Ruweisat, building shelters of rock — 'sangars' — under enemy shelling as they waited in vain for British tanks to turn up. They were overwhelmed and roll call next day revealed that 1400 men were missing; most were soon to endure captivity in the hands of the Germans. Another New Zealand attack one week later again resulted in the Kiwis being overrun when British tanks again left them high and dry on Ruweisat. The troops began to refer to Major-General Freyberg as 'Butch', and held him responsible for the bloodshed. Months later, when Churchill visited the desert army and asked the New Zealanders why they were called Kiwis, one of them replied: 'Because we're nearly extinct, sir!'

On 16 July the Australians launched an attack at Tel el Eisa and on the same day 5th Indian Brigade, with British tanks and anti-tank guns dug in and ready, knocked back an attack by Rommel's armour, claiming twenty-four enemy tanks, six armoured cars and twenty-four self-propelled guns, many of which were destroyed by the remarkable new 6-pounder anti-tank gun. Next day the Australians stormed Makd Khad Ridge. Tel el Eisa was finally secured on 22 July in the last offensive launched by Auchinleck, one that lasted four days (22–26 July). In a separate action the newly arrived 23rd Armoured Brigade, driving the obsolete Valentine tank (which was armed with a 2-pounder), came off badly and in a night attack on 26 July the 2/28th Battalion seized 'Ruin Ridge', but British tank support failed to reach them. Next day the entire battalion was surrounded by German armour and marched into what would be long captivity.

Morshead no longer concealed his contempt for his mediocre Corps commander, Ramsden, who seemed to be 'fighting always in bits and pieces, [resulting in] defeats in detail.' But the Axis army had also suffered grievously. Rommel's reinforcements of high calibre Italian troops had fought well and suffered heavily. One Italian unit, 100-strong, had held an Australian attack on 17 July and emerged with only 16 survivors. July 1942 ended in stalemate, and a bitter one. Brigadier Kippenberger would later write of his New Zealanders' feelings of 'distrust, almost hatred' toward the British tank crews.

CHURCHILL FLIES TO CAIRO

On the last day of July General Auchinleck informed Churchill that he could not mount a new offensive against Rommel before 1 September 1942. Next day, on 1 August, Churchill decided to fly out to Cairo before proceeding to Moscow, to see for himself what was going on. He would take with him only General Brooke — 'Brookie' — and his personal staff. The King, who had long ago overcome his suspicion of Churchill, sent him a letter wishing him God speed and a safe return: 'Your journey will not be too easy physically, and I pray you to take care of yourself …'

Other officers were soon to miss Churchill's bustling presence. Admiral Pound, the First Sea Lord, had said to Major-General John Kennedy at the War Office: 'You cannot help loving that man.' Kennedy himself wrote in his diary: 'Winston certainly inspired confidence. I do admire the unhurried way in which he gets through such a colossal amount of work, and yet never seems otherwise than at leisure. He was particularly genial and good-humoured today. I can quite understand how those around him become devoted to him … he has only one interest in life, and that is to win the war …'

Churchill arrived in Cairo on 3 August. There he was astonished to hear that Auchinleck was suggesting his chief staff officer, Lieutenant-General Corbett, as new commander of 8th Army. After offering the Middle East command to Brooke, who sensibly refused it, Churchill on 6 August sacked Auchinleck and replaced him as Commander-in-Chief Middle East with Alexander, who was ordered to go to Egypt immediately. He flew out next day, accompanied again only by his ADC, and arrived in Cairo on 9 August. The new commander of 8th Army, it was decided, would be the great veteran of two years' fighting, but a tired man: Lieutenant-General William Gott. But on 7 August Gott was killed in an aircraft crash. On Brooke's urging command of 8th Army was given to Bernard Montgomery, who had been selected to replace Alexander as Eisenhower's deputy. He was also ordered to fly out immediately, leaving Eisenhower

Top right: New Zealand infantry building trenches and shelters from rock ('sangars'), Western Desert, summer 1942.

Bottom right: The new commanders. In August 1942 General Alexander (left) was appointed Commander-in-Chief, Middle East and Lt-General Bernard Montgomery took over command of Eighth Army. 'Monty' (right) is pictured on the day of his arrival from England.

perplexed at losing not one but two British Deputy Commanders in three days. Auchinleck, refusing the sop of an empty command, flew to India, facing not only the ruin of his marriage but seemingly the end of his military career. Few men had been so admired by their subordinates and so thoroughly let down by them.

Churchill left Cairo on 10 August for Teheran, the first stop on his journey to Moscow. 'I expect he will be killed in a crash next,' one official noted with concern. Two days later he was flying over the Caspian Sea and the mouth of the Volga. Below him millions of Germans and Russians were fighting in the heat and dust one of the climactic campaigns of the war. On the same night he dined with Stalin in the Kremlin. The first hours were tense and sombre ones. Stalin was angry to hear that no invasion of Europe was planned for 1942. Churchill recapitulated the problems in landing a sizeable army without adequate resources and preparations, and outlined the plan to invade north Africa: 'If we could end the year in possession of north Africa we could threaten the belly of Hitler's Europe.'

This phrase pleased Stalin but the meeting next day was even more painful. Stalin ridiculed the Royal Navy's decision to abandon the PQ 17 convoy and exploded: 'You British are afraid of fighting. You should not think the Germans are supermen. You will have to fight sooner or later. You cannot win a war without fighting.' This was too much for the Prime Minister, who responded by describing with a flow of eloquence how Britain had fought alone for a year and had achieved much. Even the interpreter sat in amazement and put down his pencil, unable to translate it. Stalin broke into a smile and ended up inviting Churchill's party to dinner. There toasts were drunk to the damnation of the Nazis. When Churchill left Moscow on 17 August he knew he had established a rapport of sorts with Stalin. He returned to visit the desert army under its new commanders and then flew back to London confident that affairs were improving markedly.

HITLER AT HIS HEIGHT

In the middle months of 1942 Hitler's power seemed unassailable. The Third Reich was supreme. In the evenings in Berlin he reminisced about his past struggles and rambled about his plans for the future. His 'table talk' was considered so valuable that several of his enraptured secretaries and cronies wrote down every word. In May 1942 he refuted claims by 'foreign journalists' that Germany's alliance with Japan was a 'betrayal of our own racial principles', explaining that 'the present conflict is one of life or death' and the essential is 'to win'. He added that Japan's sudden entry into the conflict came at an opportune time for a Germany enduring 'the surprises of the Russian winter'. His conversations ranged (June 1942) from theology ('It is deplorable that the Bible should ever have been translated into German, and the whole of the Germanic people should have been thus exposed to this Jewish mumbo-jumbo.') to the justice system ('My implacable resolve [is] to have traitors who have been too leniently treated by the courts, handed over to an SS Commando and shot.'). He attributed Rommel's successes in the desert to the superiority of German machinery, particularly the Volkswagen, which he predicted would be 'the car of the future' because of its air-cooled engine. (This was possibly the only one of his predictions that came true.)

In July 1942 Hitler told his cronies that, after Rommel's conquest, control of Egypt would be given to the Italians, who should emulate the British 'who have learned the art of being masters, and of holding the reins so lightly, that the natives do not notice the curb'. Hitler was interested solely in Europe, and obsessed by the notion of connecting Berlin to the East by a system of autobahns, including one direct to the Crimea. He rejoiced that British bombing had failed to destroy his motorways but forced them to be painted black.

'The Russian colossus is being destroyed by its own immobility,' Hitler confided in August 1942. 'The British Empire is dying because of the smallness of its motherland.' Of the German armies in the Crimea he vowed: 'No power on earth will eject us!' And of Russia he said: 'The worst of our winters is now behind us. In a hundred years' time there will be millions of Germans living there.' To Hitler, the possibility of defeat did not exist.

Adolf Hitler in genial mood was at the height of his power and influence in the summer of 1942.

SOUTH-WEST PACIFIC

The first outright land defeat of the Axis powers would occur not in Russia or in the desert but on the jungle-covered island of New Guinea in the south-west Pacific. It would be fought not by millions of men and divisions of tanks but by hundreds of men, and its strategic implications would be profound.

After the American victory at Midway in June 1942 the Joint Chiefs of Staff in Washington ordered offensives to reoccupy New Britain and New Ireland and clear the Japanese from the Solomon Islands and New Guinea. The directives were as implausible as they sound and were far beyond Allied resources. The war against Japan was to be three separate wars — in Burma, in the Pacific Ocean itself, and in the south-west Pacific, where General MacArthur was starved of equipment and reinforcements. His great assets proved to be his tough Australian troops, his new air force commander named George Kenney, and his small but growing surface fleet of American and Australian warships and transports — soon known as 'MacArthur's Navy'.

The nightmare terrain of Papua–New Guinea where Japanese troops met their first outright defeat at the hands of Australian troops.

The offensives — an amphibious invasion of the Solomons at Guadalcanal and Tulagi by the US Navy and Marines and operations by MacArthur's troops in Papua New Guinea — were to begin in August 1942. In September General Wavell ordered an offensive on the western coast of Burma to recapture Akyab Island, once the monsoon had abated in November. In all these operations Japanese troops were to resist with fury. In New Guinea they were to strike first — and meet their first rebuff.

NEW GUINEA

'Burma is hell; but from New Guinea no one returns alive.'

— Japanese saying

In July 1942 the Japanese landed at Buna and Gona on the northern coast of the Papuan peninsula, within striking distance of Port Moresby. Only the narrow but rugged Owen Stanley Range separated them from their goal. Thwarted by the Coral Sea battle in their move to seize Port Moresby by seaborne invasion, the Japanese set about taking it by land, risking the perils of reaching it by way of the trail that led from Kokoda to the foothills above Moresby.

Striking back: in March 1942 American carriers launched bombers at sea to strike a direct blow on Tokyo. The damage inflicted was minimal, but the raid lifted Allied morale and reduced that of the Japanese.

The Japanese were as ignorant of New Guinea's geography as most Allied commanders. The Kokoda Trail, as the Americans described it, was a narrow, winding track, near vertical in parts, covered in mud and barely wide enough in its steepest parts for one man. The Japanese General Horii, conqueror of Rabaul, brought his white horse with him, hoping to ride it over the mountain track into Port Moresby.

Few Australians, apart from missionaries, goldminers and traders, had settled in New Guinea; few Dutch had visited the island's western half which had long been part of their East Indies empire. The terrain was the most rugged in the south-west Pacific region: mist-shrouded mountains and hidden valleys were inhabited by savage tribes. The humidity of the coast was suffocating; in the Highlands, rain fell incessantly. It was a jungle world, alien to anything most Australians and Americans — or Japanese — had ever known.

The rain forests that covered the mountains and valleys were so thick that no sunlight penetrated the vegetation. In 'the worst part' of the Kokoda Trail, battles were fought in darkness; kunai grass grew two metres high on the lowlands; jungle tracks were turned by downpours into mud, often waist-deep; foul gases and mists rose from the swamps to merge into the perpetual cloud. The island was disease-ridden; sores — even scratches — turned into suppurating ulcers; dysentery, blackwater fever, scrub typhus and the malarial mosquito were to take a higher toll of troops than combat casualties. Vegetation and insects took on strange mutations. Snakes, leeches and spiders — all larger than any on mainland Australia — were an extra horror. To the Japanese New Guinea would be where more than 100,000 of their men would die.

MacArthur, who had moved his headquarters from Melbourne to Brisbane, had little knowledge of the state of affairs, the terrain and the climate of New Guinea. He chose not to visit the front until October. Instead he sent two of his staff officers to report on conditions and they returned shaken, telling him they did not see how human beings could live there, much less fight.

THE DEFENCE OF PORT MORESBY For two years Port Moresby had been garrisoned by a token force of Australian militia troops. Militia forces were restricted to defence of 'Australian territory', which since 1919 included eastern New Guinea. They were depressed to find themselves there. The 2000 Australian civilians had been evacuated. Like that other isolated northern garrison at Darwin, Moresby was hit by Japanese bombs in February — the first of the seventy air raids it was to endure over the next six months. Few in the garrison had any illusions about their ability to withstand a heavy attack. There were no fighter aircraft until late March 1942 when a squadron of RAAF Kittyhawks arrived, to the delight of the troops. Before they were transferred to Milne Bay in May the Kitties shot down thirty-five Japanese bombers, losing twenty-two of their own aircraft in the process. By mid-May, when General Blamey ordered a militia brigade to Moresby and another to Milne Bay, the fine harbour on the eastern tip of Papua New Guinea, there were still only two RAAF squadrons based at Moresby.

The average age of the militiamen was eighteen and some of the youngsters had had as little as three months' training; hundreds went AWL in Australian ports when they heard of their destination and one troopship sailed from Townsville nearly empty. The all-volunteer AIF derided the conscript-based militia as 'Chocolate Soldiers' — 'Chokkos'. The 12,000 militiamen were soon to blunt the first Japanese land offensives in New Guinea.

In June 1942 General Morris, the GOC at Port Moresby, ordered his best battalion — the 39th — to garrison the village of Kokoda.

RETREAT FROM KOKODA The Japanese arrived at Buna and Gona on 21 July 1942. The few remaining residents and Anglican nursing sisters there saw strange ships lying offshore and hastily evacuated the settlements and headed inland. Most would be captured and executed by the Japanese.

From the southern coast a trail led inland through high kunai grass to the village of Kokoda. It was 400 metres above sea level, inland from the northern coast, and had a rubber plantation and an airstrip. The village nestled at a 'Gap' in the foothills of jungled mountains. The hike over the Owen Stanley Range by the mountain track from the south was a week's journey. Local bearers would accompany the battalion.

Defending Kokoda and Buna were only 300 Papuan troops and a company of the 39th (militia) Battalion. On 23 July, as more companies were pushing down from Kokoda to join them, the Australians sighted Japanese troops in jungle green, some pushing bicycles, coming down the track to Awala. The Australians opened fire, the Papuans fled and the Japanese, outflanking the Australians, forced them back to Oivi, two hours' march from Kokoda.

The young militiamen, exhausted after fighting for four days without adequate food or sleep, retreated to Deniki, a village on the track just south of Kokoda where on 27 July they were joined by B Company, 39th Battalion. Hearing that Kokoda was still unoccupied, Lt-Col. Owen led his 80 men back to the village, where they dug in. On the night of 28 July they were attacked by a force of 400 Japanese and deluged by mortar fire. The Australians withdrew to the south through 'a ghostly white mist'. A week later the Australians, reinforced by another company, launched the first of several counter-attacks on Kokoda and some managed to reach the perimeter of the small airfield and dig in. On the following day the Japanese attacked but were driven back by heavy fire. At dusk a weird chanting was heard and then a sudden Japanese mortar and infantry attack began. The Australians fell back to Deniki, which was now also under attack from the Japanese. By 14 August the 39th Battalion, having lost half its effective strength and short of ammunition and food, was digging in for a last stand at Isurava.

Meanwhile, the 7th Division AIF had arrived in Papua: in mid-August the 18th Brigade reached Milne Bay and the 21st Brigade disembarked at Port Moresby. The sea port was now alive with activity. Aircraft took off in their dozens from its airfields to raid Rabaul, Lae and Buna. Truckloads of veteran AIF troops were now rolling out to the foothills of the Owen Stanley Range where the road ended. 'Their appearance was inspiring,' wrote one observer. 'These troops were tested and selected by war. There were no weeds among them. They betrayed no enthusiasm. They did not cheer or catcall. They knew what fighting meant ...'

They were soon gasping with exhaustion as they climbed the mountain track. Of the climb past Ioribaiwa the war correspondent George Johnston wrote: 'There are no resting places. Climbing it is the supreme agony of mind and spirit. The troops, with fine irony, have christened it "The Golden Staircase".' Strong men laden with packs fell exhausted after climbing for minutes; the steep steps pegged out of the ridge collected the rain and became a succession of mud-pits; men's uniforms rotted.

A small army of 600 local bearers carried food and ammunition. AIF gunners managed to haul up two of their 25-pounders on ropes but MacArthur still refused to sanction aerial dropping of food and ammunition. 'Air supply must necessarily be considered an emergency rather than a normal means of supply,' he told Blamey.

MacArthur's tactics changed with the arrival of the dynamic commander of his US 5th Army Air Force, 52-year-old Brigadier-General George Kenney. With Irish cheek Kenney told MacArthur that his airmen could transport 26,000 troops to Moresby's new airfields and keep them supplied by air. 'Give me five days,' Kenney told the general, 'and I'll ship the whole damned US Army to New Guinea by air!' Kenney began sending his dozen B-17s on bombing missions to Rabaul and initiated a program of 'biscuit bombing' by tree-hopping RAAF and US aircraft to supply the front-line troops. MacArthur, who had got rid of his two former air commanders, Brereton and Brett, and was not normally a demonstrative man, dubbed Kenney

Young Australian troops, ankle-deep in mud, on the Kokoda Track during the fierce fighting there late in 1942. This image is a still from Damien Parer's award-winning documentary on the New Guinea campaign.

'The Buccaneer'. In the words of MacArthur's biographer, 'By pushing MacArthur's bomber line 1500 miles north of Brisbane, Kenney transformed Moresby from a garrison under siege to the chief Allied base in the Southwest Pacific.'

By 23 August the AIF troops had reached the militiamen at their positions at Isurava and on 26 August the Japanese resumed their offensive. Brigadier Arnold Potts (21st Brigade) now had two AIF battalions — the 2/14th and 2/16th — and two militia units, the exhausted 39th and the under-trained, inexperienced 53rd Battalions. On 27 August the 53rd Battalion was pushed aside by advancing Japanese Minutes later a deluge of mortar and machine-gun fire fell on the 39th, who fought back furiously. 'The pale ghosts', the 'pathetically young warriors' of the 39th, as their new commanding officer, Ralph Honner, called them with pride, launched two counterattacks.

The Australians at Isurava fought off continuous attacks. By mid-day, 29 August the position of the 2/14th was menaced. The furious battle of grenade and bayonet raged all afternoon; by 5 p.m. one company had repulsed the eleventh attack against it. Four hours later Potts gave permission to the 39th and 2/14th to withdraw halfway to Alola. But by now the Japanese had enveloped the 2/14th and the battalion was scattered by a massive attack.

The Australians had taken a heavier toll of the Japanese than they knew. 'Our losses are great,' wrote a Japanese officer. 'The outcome of the battle is very difficult to see.' General Horii had planned to take Port Moresby within seven days and had committed only three battalions to the attack, but he now launched a massive infantry and mortar attack on Alola and the Australians fell back to a position south of the village. Rollcall later revealed that more than 200 of the 2/14th were missing, including their colonel, who later died in captivity.

On 30 August General MacArthur notified the Joint Chiefs in Washington that 'unless moves are made to meet the changing conditions a disastrous outcome is bound to result shortly'. By that date the Japanese had created a second threat to Port Moresby by landing troops at Milne Bay where, as at Kokoda, Australians were fighting a desperate battle in hideous conditions. It had not occurred to MacArthur that the Australians were holding back the Japanese, whose seven-day march across the Owen Stanley had become five weeks of the toughest fighting they had experienced, against an enemy who for the first time refused to retreat without a fight.

TO THE LAST RIDGE On the Kokoda Track Brigadier Potts ordered a fighting withdrawal to Eora Creek. Without shelter under the pouring rain, the troops' feet were pulpy. The bearers had deserted them. By 1 September Potts knew his men could no longer hold on. The 39th Battalion — 'the bloody heroes', as the AIF troops called them — were done in and making their way to the open valley of Myola along with the 'unreliable' 53rd. By 7 September the Australians had abandoned Myola and were preparing to make a stand at Efogi. From there too they had to retreat under pressure.

The young war correspondent Osmar White saw the wounded, emerging from the primitive dressing stations or operating theatres, hobbling on sticks, refusing assistance. 'That which was fine in these men outweighed and made trivial all that was horrible in their plight,' he wrote. 'I cannot explain it except to say that they were at all times cheerful and helped one another. They never gave up the fight. They never admitted defeat. They never asked for help. I felt proud to be of their race and cause, bitterly ashamed to be so nagged by the trivial ills of my own flesh. I wondered if all men when they endured so much that exhausted nerves would no longer give response, were creatures of the spirit, eternal and indestructible as stars.'

General Horii, at his HQ in Efogi village, now had 5000 combat troops and two mortars in addition to his engineers. Just after daybreak on 8 September the Australians on the ridges were attacked and their perimeter was pierced; retreating to Menari they were pursued remorselessly. Almost the entire 2/27th Battalion had been cut off. More than a week later its survivors would struggle through the jungle to the Moresby road after nights of freezing cold, days of terrible heat and torrential rain. A small number of wounded and their carers left behind were later massacred by the Japanese.

Papuan bearers helped the Australians in the Kokoda Campaign, bringing up supplies and carrying out the wounded.

Now reduced to 307 men, the Australians fell back to Ioribaiwa on 11 September. Reinforced by two more AIF battalions of the 25th Brigade, the augmented Australian force came under murderous mortar and machine-gun fire. A single telephone line still snaked its way to Port Moresby. Brigadier Eather telephoned Major-General 'Tubby' Allen at Moresby and asked permission to establish a firm base on Imita Ridge. Allen's reply was brief: 'There won't be any withdrawal from the Imita position, Ken. You'll die there if necessary. You understand that?' When Lieutenant-General Sydney Rowell, commanding at Port Moresby, heard of Eather's decision he said to Allen: 'Our heads will be in the basket over this, Tubby.'

Next day, on 17 September, as the Australians were digging in at Imita, MacArthur telephoned Prime Minister Curtin and told him he had lost confidence in the Australian troops in New Guinea and intended sending American forces there; he also urged that General Blamey fly to Port Moresby and take personal command. Blamey, ordered to Moresby against his wishes, arrived on 23 September. He was conscious that his presence could be viewed by Rowell as 'interference'.

To Rowell the Kokoda Track was the vital sector and he made no secret of what he thought of MacArthur's tactics of outflanking the mountains which had already seen a hapless company of American troops despatched to sweat over the Kapa Kapa track east of Kokoda. Blamey sacked this fine officer five days later. Rowell was replaced by General Herring, the great 'all rounder' among Australian generals, a former jurist, a born diplomat — Robert Menzies thought he possessed the most outstanding personality of any Australian general. Alternating with Mackay, who was often obsessed with detail, Herring was to command field operations over the coming year. These two men, along with Sturdee and Morshead, retained Blamey's complete trust in their positions of high command.

The troops digging in on Imita Ridge awaited attack for ten days but it never came. The Japanese, within sight of the sea and 'wild with joy' on crossing 'the endless waves of mountains upon mountains,' as one wrote, were exhausted and gathering their strength to support a second amphibious attack on Moresby in mid-October. The first, a landing at Milne Bay, had already been repulsed by Australians in the first complete defeat inflicted on the Japanese Army since the war began.

MILNE BAY Milne Bay was a natural harbour on the south-east tip of New Guinea. Picturesque from the air, it was a humid, steaming place whose shores were disease-ridden and covered in mangroves. Its strategic importance was obvious, and the Japanese intended to seize it as a naval and air base and to defend it strongly. Milne Bay's Australian garrison consisted of a militia brigade and the 18th AIF Brigade with artillery. An airstrip had been scratched out as a base for a squadron of Kittyhawks and one of Hudsons.

Late on 25 August a Japanese convoy of five warships and four transports evaded air attack and slipped into Milne Bay. They began disembarking their troops on its northern shore the same night and

American-made Lockheed Hudson light bombers were flown by the Royal Australian Air Force from the first days of war in Malaya to war's end in 1945.

next day these troops attacked, advancing swiftly west towards the airfields. Kittyhawks and Hudsons, flying around the clock, strafed and bombed the Japanese beachhead in the morning. The 61st Battalion — militia — counterattacked later in the day and drove them back. But the Japanese returned at 10 p.m. using a flame-thrower, which the Australians knocked out with grenades, but after a six-hour night fight the militiamen fell back to the Gama River line, just as the AIF's 2/10th Battalion passed through them to tackle the Japanese.

The AIF troops fought tanks with 'sticky bombs' that refused in the humidity to stick. Without anti-tank guns they were forced to fall back on the night of 27 August but the Japanese attack was held short of Turnbull airstrip. By daybreak the Japanese had again melted away. In the two-day lull that followed the Japanese landed another 800 troops.

Just before dawn on 31 August the Japanese, screaming and shouting, attacked the airstrip in waves. They were cut down by steady fire from the Australians. On 3 September the Australians pushed east along the coast and on the following day met strong resistance. The RAAF fighters were now constantly attacking the retreating Japanese and bombing any vessel approaching Milne Bay. By 6 September the Australians had reached the main Japanese base. On the following night three Japanese warships took off the remaining invasion force, leaving 750 dead behind. The Japanese had underestimated both the strength of the garrison and the fighting qualities of the defenders. 'Some of us may forget', wrote Field Marshal Lord Slim who was trying to rid his British-Indian army in Burma of their fear of the Japanese, 'that of all the Allies it was the Australian soldiers who first broke the spell of invincibility of the Japanese Army.'

A Japanese artist's spirited depiction of one of the many night battles fought in the waters of the Solomons in 1942, from which the Japanese came off best.

SECURING THE SOLOMON ISLANDS

GUADALCANAL On 5 July 1942 Admiral King in Washington had received intelligence that the Japanese had landed on Guadalcanal island near the southern tip of the Solomon Islands that were like scattered pebbles off the south-eastern tip of New Guinea, and that they were already constructing an airfield there. He ordered 'Operation Watch-tower' to begin within the month. The operation was controlled by Admiral Nimitz, Commander-in-Chief Pacific, and would involve the US Navy and Marines.

On the morning of 7 August 1942 an armada of almost 100 warships and transports appeared off the coast of Guadalcanal. The fleet was commanded by Admiral Frank Fletcher, the veteran of the battles of the Coral Sea and Midway, flying his flag in the carrier USS *Saratoga*. The convoy was carrying nearly 20,000 US Marines under Major-General Alexander Vandegrift, and was protected by air cover from three carriers. Those on board remembered the place as eerie, forbidding, overshadowed by the jagged cone of a dead volcano on Savo Island. The quiet was uncanny; the waters were still and the soft wind brought with it the stench of swamp and jungle. But the landing began well. The uncompleted airfield was seized without loss when the Japanese construction team fled into the jungle. The tiny island of Tulagi to its north was also taken in one day, after a brief fight.

Before the operation began Fletcher had called together his subordinates and informed them that he was withdrawing the carriers from Guadalcanal after 48 hours because of the threat from Japanese land-based or carrier-based aircraft. Admiral Kelly Turner, commanding the Amphibious Force, argued strongly with him, but unsuccessfully. An officer present recalled: 'I was amazed and disturbed by the way these two admirals talked to each other. I had never heard anything like it.' Fletcher's action has been widely criticised — he was soon afterwards retired from active command — but few Allied officers present were prepared for the shock in store for them at the hands of the Japanese.

On hearing of the landings, Admiral Mikawa at Rabaul had reacted immediately. Gathering a strike force of seven cruisers he steamed boldly down 'The Slot' — the channel between the main islands of the Solomons chain — on a direct course for Guadalcanal. His fleet was sighted by an RAAF Catalina but its warning did not reach the American admiral, who had split his fleet into three to guard the possible entrances to the landing zone.

Around midnight on 8 August 1942 the Japanese cruisers reached the channel between Savo Island and Guadalcanal. The Allied cruisers off Savo steamed at low speed on patrol, their men tired after two days of action. Mikawa passed an American destroyer but did not open fire, and pressed on quietly at 22 knots. At 1.36 a.m. on 9 August

Mikawa sighted two cruisers and destroyers and his fleet opened fire while aircraft dropped flares, silhouetting the Allied ships. Caught steaming at 12 knots, *Canberra* was struck by two torpedoes at 1.38 a.m. and then hit by twenty-four shells in little more than a minute. Her captain was mortally wounded and fires broke out.

Captain Bode of USS *Chicago*, awakened by the sound of firing, chased a lone destroyer into the dark. Mikawa steamed on to locate the northern cruiser force and promptly sank the cruisers *Vincennes*, *Quincy* and *Astoria*. In one hour the Japanese force had sunk three American cruisers and left an Australian cruiser dead in the water. They steamed back to Rabaul without loss. The Australian squadron's commander, Admiral Crutchley, returned in the flagship at dawn to find *Canberra* sinking, beyond saving. She went down at 8 a.m.

The Battle of Savo Island was — in the words of the American Navy's historian of World War II — 'the worst defeat ever inflicted on the US Navy in a fair fight'. Fearful of an air attack, Admiral Turner withdrew his carriers, leaving the Marines on Guadalcanal on their own. (After an inquiry, Captain Bode of USS *Chicago*, shouldering much of the blame for the fiasco, committed suicide.)

Turner unloaded as many stores as he could and then withdrew his ships, leaving the Marines to their own devices. They had only four days' supply of ammunition. Vandegrift got them to work completing the airstrip — which they called Henderson Field. It became the priceless asset on the forlorn island. On 15 August destroyers delivered much-needed supplies; five days later thirty-one fighters and dive-bombers reached Henderson Field.

The Japanese began to pour troops into Guadalcanal under cover of night, sometimes by submarines, sometimes on destroyers, in a desperate attempt to wrest the island from American hands. By the end of August they had landed 6000 troops under Major-General Kawaguchi, who soon launched the first of what would be ten massive assaults on the American lines over the next six months in their attempt to seize the airstrip. The Americans were to repel all of them while fighting six separate naval battles in the foetid waters off Guadalcanal.

In mid-September Turner pushed a convoy of reinforcements through to Guadalcanal, but lost the carrier *Wasp* (hero of the Malta run) in the process, sunk by a submarine. Guadalcanal would be one of the hardest fought land, sea and air campaigns of World War II and would not end until February 1943.

VICTORY AT KOKODA

On 22 September 1942 Tokyo and Rabaul ordered General Horii to withdraw his force to the coast. His officers urged him to make a final thrust over Imita to Port Moresby but he began his retreat, leaving one battalion to cover the withdrawal, ordering it to stand

American troops in the jungles of the Solomons, 1942. Many would remember the experience as the worst of their lives.

firm just past Myola where a treacherous ravine fell down to the torrent of Eora Creek. Four days later the Australians on Imita Ridge began to advance, only to find that the Japanese had disappeared. The Australians entered Ioribaiwa two days later to find the new work of elaborate defences deserted.

By now both MacArthur and the Japanese high command were focusing their attention on the Buna beachhead. While the Australians pushed over the Kokoda Trail, an American battalion was ordered to move over the Jauva track east of Kokoda, and part of the US 32nd Division was flown to Wanigela before moving towards Buna on the coast.

On the Kokoda Trail Australians troops reached Menari by 2 October without sighting any Japanese. At Efogi they found the unmistakable signs of a starved enemy: native gardens had been torn up; there were indications that the Japanese had been reduced to eating grass, roots and even wood from the trees. The troops buried 200 Australian and Japanese bodies then pushed on to just south of Templeton's Crossing, where they struck the Japanese rearguard on 8 October. After pausing to bring up reinforcements they attacked for two days, suffering 183 casualties, to find on 16 October that the Japanese had again slipped away. On the following day Blamey sent Major-General Allen a signal from MacArthur who felt that 'extremely light casualties indicate no serious effort yet made to dislodge enemy'. By 22 October the Australians had reached the strong enemy position at Eora Creek, a fortified 'keep' bristling with mortars and machine-guns and five days later stormed it.

The wholesale retreat of the Japanese had now begun. The 25th Brigade entered Kokoda village on 2 November and raised the Australian flag. After savage fighting along the track, Ilimo was secured; the Japanese deserted Oivi and headed into the jungle in an effort to escape. By 13 October the Australians had reached the Kumusi River, where their engineers bridged the torrent whose waters had already claimed General Horii, washed downstream and drowned in his eagerness to escape. In four days seven battalions passed over the river by rope bridge, punt or flying foxes.

The Owen Stanley Range had been crossed. Ahead lay the 60-kilometre march to the northern coast over foothills that flattened into a plain of high kunai grass; beyond lay the plantations and swamps bordering the coast. In the four-month campaign the Australians lost 625 killed and 1055 wounded in battle. Thousands more had gone down with malaria and other tropical diseases, but most of them would recover. The Japanese losses were estimated to be close to 10,000. The Japanese had realised that there was no easy way to take Port Moresby, the base they needed to threaten any reinforcements reaching the advancing Allies from Australia.

Kokoda was a campaign fought in rain and mud. It had been an infantryman's battle but airmen had played a crucial role in dropping supplies and providing tactical support. By November a total of eighteen squadrons were operating in New Guinea — eleven American and seven Australian. Kokoda has been hailed as an epic of Australian endurance. It had begun in the shambles of retreat and ended in a complete victory won by men untrained in jungle warfare.

In early November 1942 the Australians from Kokoda and Americans pushing towards the Japanese positions at Buna, Gona and Sanananda on the northern coast of Papua were to find nearly 20 kilometres of deep defences along the coast, defended by 9000 Japanese troops. It was to be the scene of the hardest set-piece battles of the New Guinea campaign.

THE LATER BATTLES OF THE SOLOMONS

The Battle of Savo Island had been the first of Guadalcanal's six major naval battles that absorbed much of the strength of the US Navy. Further naval engagements in late August and mid-September saw the US Navy lose four destroyers and the aircraft carrier USS *Wasp*. But the Marines' perimeter around the airfields held, despite bloody and suicidal Japanese attacks. In October Nimitz appointed the aggressive Vice-Admiral Bill Halsey to command US Navy forces in the Solomons. The fleet broke into cheers when they heard the news. Others cheered quietly the small teams of Australians hidden behind enemy lines with wireless transmitters, reporting to Guadalcanal early warning of any movements they observed of Japanese aircraft and shipping. Wearing the uniform of the Royal Australian Navy in the hope of sparing them possible execution if captured by the Japanese (the uniform availed them no protection; all who were captured were tortured and brutally killed), the 'Coast Watchers' were instrumental in the Americans' survival. Halsey paid these brave men fine tribute: 'Guadalcanal saved the South Pacific and the Coast Watchers saved Guadalcanal.'

In October 1942, in a battle off the Santa Cruz Islands — a group of islands east of the Solomons — the Americans lost another carrier, *Hornet*, but downed 100 Japanese planes. In mid-November Admiral Yamamoto made another attempt to reinforce Guadalcanal with troops and destroy the American fleet, but in a three-day battle aircraft from USS *Enterprise* sank a Japanese battleship, and desperate attacks on the airfield at Guadalcanal were repelled by the defenders. The Imperial Navy now wanted to give up Guadalcanal, but Premier Tojo had decided that the Solomons were more crucial than New Guinea. Another series of naval battles began on 30 November off Tassafaronga, where Japanese destroyers again inflicted a defeat on the US Navy, sinking two US cruisers and damaging three others for the loss of one destroyer. The surface engagements ended on the night of 30 January 1943 when USS *Chicago* was sunk off Rennell Island. It was the last naval battle of the Guadalcanal campaign. On the same day, half a world away, the beleaguered German armies at Stalingrad began surrendering, and the British entered their long-sought prize of Tripoli.

A turning point in World War II had been reached. The long years of defeat for the Allies were ending. In early February 1943 the Japanese relinquished Guadalcanal, evacuating their troops under the noses of the Americans and leaving behind 25,000 dead. Each side had lost twenty-four warships. But the way was clear for Allied reconquest of the Solomons.

CLEARING THE COAST: GONA–BUNA

After Guadalcanal, tough fighting remained in efforts to eliminate the Japanese in their coastal defences at Buna, Gona and Sanananda. On 4 November the 25th Brigade coming down from Kokoda ran into heavy Japanese fire just south of Gona. Supplied by air drops, the Australians attacked constantly. The newly arriving 21st Brigade was down to only 1000 riflemen. Malaria and battle casualties took a savage toll of the two veteran brigades.

Soon the militiamen of 30th Brigade arrived. On 8 December the 39th Battalion stormed and seized half the Gona position while the AIF troops attacked from the beach. In Gona, 600 dead Japanese were found. More than 500 Australians had now been killed or wounded in this action. On 18 December Japanese reinforcements hurrying to Gona were halted on the coast, encircled and overcome. Gona was a bitter foretaste of the coming battle of Buna.

On 30 November MacArthur summoned Lieutenant-General Robert Eichelberger to his HQ in Port Moresby. Disturbing reports had reached the Supreme Commander that the American troops (32nd Division) attacking Buna were not fighting well. In an attack on 21 November they had made little progress. At Buna the Japanese had had ample time to construct deep defences from thick logs, and from these half-underground bunkers whose firing slits were hidden by vegetation they could pour a murderous cross-fire on any assault.

MacArthur told Eichelberger to go the front and replace any timid officers he found, saying: 'Bob, take Buna or don't come back alive!' Eichelberger, who thought MacArthur a great actor and

Finally assisted by light tanks and equipped with jungle greens, Australian infantry push forward through the mangrove swamps of Gona–Buna to destroy the last Japanese defenders.

referred to him in letters to his wife as 'Sarah Bernhardt', arrived at Buna to find the position worse than he expected: Some American forward posts were unmanned and command posts were up to six kilometres from the front.

Eichelberger sacked the American divisional commander, organised the division into two assault groups and mounted an attack on 5 December supported by five Australian Bren carriers. The attack failed to penetrate Buna's defences and the carriers were put out of action, but the lift in the men's morale became marked. Eichelberger, in the forefront of the fighting, was among the wounded.

In December 1942 Blamey wrote to Curtin that 'the American troops cannot be classified as attack troops. They are definitely not equal to the Australian militia, and from the moment they met opposition sat down and have hardly gone forward a yard …' At the same time he was considering replacing the malaria-wasted AIF brigades with fresh militia units.

Buna village was attacked on 14 December, but the Japanese had evacuated it and established themselves in a plantation. Light tanks had finally been ferried around the coast on barges to help break the resistance of the Japanese — eight M3 (General Stuart) tanks, nicknamed with good reason 'Honeys' and manned by Australians. Two were lost in an attack on 18 December but sixteen bunkers were taken.

The last attack was mounted at 8 a.m. on New Year's Day 1943. Two Australian battalions supported by two American ones on their flanks attacked with six tanks. While the tanks poured point-blank fire at the bunkers the infantry threw explosive charges through the firing slits. After nearly three days of fighting, only six Japanese soldiers were found alive; the 18th Brigade suffered more than 900 casualties. Buna was taken.

Right: The Australian Army's Commander-in-Chief General Blamey (left) with MacArthur's dynamic commander at Buna Lt-General Robert Eichelberger.
Below: Weary Australian infantrymen with some of the few Japanese prisoners they took at Gona–Buna.

The tracks leading to Sanananda were still blocked by the Japanese, who refused to budge. It was obvious that more troops and tanks would be required. Lieutenant-General Herring decided to contain the Japanese in the west using 7th Division (14th, 18th and 30th brigades) while Buna Force (US 32nd Division) advanced towards Sanananda along the coast. An attack on 12 January saw the loss of three tanks, and the attack petered out. But on the following day General Adachi in Rabaul ordered the starving defenders to break out and make for Lae and Salamaua. The majority were evacuated by small craft and the Australians advancing to Sanananda Point encountered only scattered resistance, which ended on 22 January. A group of 100 Japanese, nearly all sick or wounded, refused demands to surrender and were killed to a man.

The Papuan campaign had taken the lives of 2165 Australians and 671 Americans. More than 3500 Australians and more than 2000 Americans had been wounded. It is estimated that the number of Japanese killed exceeded 13,000. Nearly 1500 Australians had died in the fighting for Gona–Buna–Sanananda, a campaign that could well have been avoided if MacArthur, less eager for a victory, had chosen to bypass the beachhead. In New Guinea malaria and fever had incapacitated 40,000 Australian troops, in addition to the 4000 battle casualties suffered in the three months from November 1942 to January 1943.

Maintaining their Pacific empire was costing the Japanese dearly, for fifteen divisions were now being employed in holding its perimeter. In the deserts of Egypt another hard-fought campaign waged over six months had reached its climax at Alamein.

EGYPT: DESERT VICTORY, 1942

The three months after the fighting in July 1942 had seen a massive strengthening of 8th Army. Under their new commanders Alexander and Montgomery, the British 8th Army's morale was rebuilt. On landing in Cairo on 12 August Montgomery had listened with disbelief to plans to retreat up the Nile and to Palestine, and promptly informed his commander-in-chief, Alexander, that he was assuming immediate command of 8th Army, not waiting another three days. He ordered that there would be no retreat under any circumstances. The army would fight where it stood, and all transport was to be sent to the rear. The effect was electric. Appalled to find that 8th Army was fighting in brigade groups and 'Jock columns', he ordered the divisions to be restored. Divisional flashes were to be worn and divisional pride to be revived. Soon the Highland Division's 'HD' road sign and the jerboa (desert rat) symbol of 7th Armoured would be chasing the New Zealanders' fernleaf road sign across the face of north Africa.

'Monty' was a born showman who believed that the troops should know their general by sight. He visited his divisions to speak to the soldiers, not the officers, and he appeared wearing an Australian Digger's slouch hat covered in badges. Though he later replaced it with a tank corps beret that became his trademark, Montgomery wore the slouch hat with confidence, for he had spent his entire boyhood in Australia, returning to England at the age of twelve, and his nature contained much Australian truculence and capacity for blunt speaking. A non-smoker and a teetotaller, wiry and physically fit, he was unsparing in criticism of those he felt were 'not up to it'. He idolised only one man — General Brooke — but he admired and liked Alexander, who was his junior by four years but his senior in rank, a full General and already knighted.

'Monty': the commander of the Eighth Army in his light tank and wearing the tank-corps beret that became his trademark.

Alexander and Montgomery have been called the 'winning team' — the generals who turned defeat into victory. They were a perfect combination. Monty upset people, Alex calmed them down. Despite his peculiar personality (one British Army psychiatrist described him as slightly mad), Montgomery had a brilliant gift for generalship and his plans were as aggressive as his own nature. He soon brought out from England officers he knew and trusted — new Corps commanders Lieutenant-General Brian Horrocks to lead 13 Corps (44th and 50th British divisions) and Lieutenant-General Sir Oliver Leese to command 30 Corps in the vital northern sector. Similarly Alexander chose as his chief of staff Major-General Richard McCreery, who had been sent out to advise Auchinleck on armoured warfare; he had been totally ignored by Auchinleck, who preferred the advice of the innovative but mercurial Eric Dorman-Smith. Historians have been surprised that Montgomery never considered the two experienced Commonwealth divisional commanders — Freyberg and Morshead — for promotion to Corps command after their two years' experience in the desert.

Reinforcements and weapons were now flowing into the Middle East at a rate that Wavell and Auchinleck would have envied. During August 1942 alone Middle East command was increased by 400 tanks, 500 guns, 7000 vehicles and three fresh British divisions — the 51st Highland (reborn, after the loss of the original 51st in France), the 44th Infantry and the 10th Armoured. When Montgomery ordered that the 44th Division be brought into the front line immediately, GHQ replied that it was impossible and protested to Alexander, whom they tracked down at the British embassy. He told them coldly and bluntly: 'Do it.'

In the same period Rommel requested from Hitler 200 tanks and 16,000 more men — and received none. Ultra warned Montgomery that Rommel would launch another attempt to break the Alamein line. He was ready for it.

PRELUDE TO ALAMEIN

On 30 August 1942 Rommel attacked towards Alam Halfa Ridge, but his tanks were delayed by minefields and then subjected to attack by Desert Air Force, and the assault was stemmed. In the Alam Halfa battles both sides lost 50 tanks and 100 aircraft. They were losses bearable to Montgomery but calamitous to Rommel. Montgomery could now muster ten divisions — three armoured, seven infantry (in addition to detached brigades), totalling 200,000 men. *Panzerarmee* had two armoured and two motorised divisions and the Italians eight divisions; but the twelve Axis divisions were under strength and desperately short of fuel and tanks. Their fighting strength totalled 100,000 men; they possessed 300 Italian and 200 German tanks.

Montgomery now had 1000 tanks, including 300 newly arrived Shermans. In all, the British had a two-to-one superiority. When Churchill, angered by the delay in launching an offensive, demanded action, Montgomery replied to Alexander: 'Alex, if the attack begins in September it will fail. If we wait until October I can guarantee a great victory and the destruction of Rommel's army. Am I still to attack in September?'

Rommel had laid half a million mines in front of his positions along the 50-kilometre front, but 8th Army now had mine detectors, which the Sappers could use to sweep an path for the infantry. The 6-pounder anti-tank gun had replaced the useless 2-pounder.

After a massive preliminary bombardment 8th Army would make a frontal assault on the Axis positions — with one difference. The infantry would have to precede the armour, lift the mines and 'punch holes', corridors in the German and Italian defences, to allow the tanks to pour through them and then cut the enemy's interior lines as Wavell had done against the Italians in 1940–41 The attack was to fall on the night of a full moon; the infantry, attacking in the dark, would have to negotiate terrain to a depth of 7000 metres through 'minefields a mile deep'. Heavy casualties were expected.

On the coast, 30 Corps was an almost entirely Dominion battle formation. Running north to south it consisted of 9th Australian Division, 51st Scottish Division, New Zealand Division, 1st South African and 4th Indian divisions. It was to bear the main brunt of the battle. Lieutenant-General Herbert Lumsden's 10 Corps, consisting of the armoured divisions — the 1st, 8th and 10th — was to be Montgomery's hammer blow; or such was his plan.

German troops used their 88-mm anti-aircraft guns with deadly effect against tanks. The barrels of the British Army's equivalent weapon, the 3.7-inch ack-ack gun, could not be depressed sufficiently for use against tanks.

One of the most famous photographs of the war showing Australian infantry following their officer into the battle smoke.

ALAMEIN: THE OFFENSIVE BEGINS

At 9.40 p.m. on 23 October 1942, 8th Army's 900 guns opened up in the largest, loudest bombardment of the desert war, deluging and destroying the German and Italian forward artillery before lifting the barrage to fall on the second defence line. Watching the bombardment, Major-General Freyberg was heard to murmur 'If ever there was a just cause ...' before leaving his New Zealand gunners to their job. General Montgomery had already gone to bed. There was nothing more the generals could do. The fate of the battle was in the hands of the infantry standing in the lurid moonlight.

At 10 p.m. 8th Army's infantry advanced, company after company following arcs of tracer bullets to keep them on course. After advancing through hails of mortar shells and machine-gun fire, lifting the mines as they went, by dawn 9th Division had fought their way to the second line and were joined by British tanks. South of the Australians the Scots had suffered heavily and the New Zealanders had made the deepest penetration of all, reaching Miteiriya Ridge.

But the 'northern corridor' was still not opened. Montgomery ordered Lumsden to 'drive' his tank commanders or be sacked on the spot. He later confessed that the real crisis of the battle occurred by the third day. The infantry, in their desperate attempts to 'crumble' the enemy, had suffered in some units casualties of 50 per cent. On 26 October the New Zealanders, having lost half their riflemen, were taken out of the line. Even the famed 7th Armoured Division, which had made little progress, was taken out and rested.

THE AUSTRALIAN ORDEAL

'I knew that the final blow must be put in on 30 Corps' front, but at the moment I was not clear exactly where,' Montgomery was to write candidly in his memoirs 'I ordered that operations by 9th Australian Division towards the coast be intensified, my intention then being to stage the final breakout operation on the axis of the coast road ... All now depended on the Australians. They would have to 'crumble' and destroy the expected German and Italian armoured attacks. In Montgomery's own words, 'crumbling' meant 'eating the guts out' of the enemy.

A column of British-made Crusader tanks, which were greatly superior to the tanks used in 1940–41.

Rommel was now moving almost his entire *Panzerarmee* to block a northern corridor. The full weight of Afrika Korps now fell on the Australians. Attacking at dusk to encircle the enemy salient on the coast, the 2/48th Battalion stormed Trig 29 at bayonet point and the 2/24th almost reached Thompson's Post. On 27 October the 9th Division repulsed every counterattack by tanks and infantry. 'Unfortunately, the attack gained ground very slowly. The British [sic] resisted desperately. Rivers of blood were poured out over miserable strips of land,' Rommel wrote of the Australian stand.

At 10 p.m. on 28 October the 9th Division resumed the attack, advancing 1000 metres and withstanding a massive counterattack that raged all next day. 'The battle had lasted five days,' writes a British historian of the strange inactivity of the British corps to the south of this desperate battle, 'and 8th Army had been motionless for three of them.'

On 30 October the 9th Division again attacked, two battalions attempting to cut the coast road while another pushed north to encircle the enemy pocket there. Advancing through curtains of fire the Australians were forced to fall back to a depression called the Saucer. The two battalions involved — 1300-strong at the beginning of the battle — had been reduced to a total of 95 officers and men. They had taken 544 prisoners. The defenders of the Saucer, soon reinforced, withstood three tank attacks next day. On 2 November, the German and Italian counterattacks slackened. Churchill was to write that 'the magnificent forward drive of the Australians, achieved by ceaseless bitter fighting, had swung the entire battle in our favour'.

To their south British artillery fire was heralding the launching of 'Operation Supercharge' — Montgomery's breakthrough.

'SUPERCHARGE': THE BREAKTHROUGH The New Zealand Division was to play the vital role in the breakthrough. Rested, and reinforced by two brigades of the Highland Division and two British tank brigades, Freyberg's men attacked north of Kidney Ridge on 2 November. The 9th Armoured lost 75 of its 100 tanks in this attack.

On the night of 2 November 1942, however, Freyberg summoned his brigadiers and told them that the enemy was 'cracking'. The tanks of 10 Corps were now attacking, British armoured cars were already streaming behind German and Italian strong points shooting up trucks, tearing past crowds of astonished Germans and Italians. Freyberg ordered his commanders to get their transport ready for the breakthrough. They would advance next day. 'The sheer fighting guts of the Australians, New Zealanders and Scots', writes Montgomery's biographer, 'had given the necessary spur to Eighth Army.' Of the Australians' role, their Corps commander General Leese wrote: 'It was a magnificent piece of fighting by a great Division, led by an indomitable character, Leslie Morshead.'

At 4.30 p.m. on 4 November, with a British advance solidly astride the Rahman Track and 20 Italian Corps broken by 7th Armoured Division, Rommel ordered a general retreat. For the Italian divisions in the south, isolated and lacking fuel for their vehicles, defeat was complete.

Brigadier Kippenberger, driving forward in his staff car, saw General Freyberg near the head of the New Zealand column. 'He was sitting on the outside of a tank happy as a cherub … There were very many signs of complete victory.' The Battle of El Alamein was over. At dawn on 5 November Australian patrols found that the Germans and Italians facing them near the coast had all but disappeared.

'RING OUT THE BELLS!' On 6 November 1942 General Alexander cabled the Prime Minister. 'Ring out the bells! … Eighth Army is advancing.' Rommel managed to make a skilful withdrawal when the pursuit was hampered by sudden rains. His next strong stand would be made 2500 kilometres to the west. The Axis armies in Egypt had been broken and 20,000 Italians and 10,000 Germans taken prisoner. Axis killed and wounded numbered 7800 but 8th Army's battle casualties were almost twice as heavy — 13,560. Rommel had lost 1000 guns and nearly 500 tanks. It had been a bitter, hard-fought battle; Montgomery's tank loses also totalled 500 but most of these could be repaired.

In Churchill's words, 'The 9th Australian Division had [struck] what history may well proclaim as the decisive blow in the Battle of Alamein.' In its last battle in the desert 9th Division suffered 3000 casualties including 620 killed; its casualties since July totalled nearly 6000 officers and men. Since June, the New Zealanders had lost more than 6000 men. The 9th Division left the desert to fight a new enemy, the Japanese; the New Zealanders remained in the forefront of the advance across north Africa. Churchill was to say: 'Before Alamein we never had a victory. After Alamein we never had a defeat.'

Under the guard of two British Military Police ('Red Caps'), German prisoners taken at El Alamein await transfer to prison camps, November 1942. The war in the desert between Axis and Allied troops was one fought with some chivalry. No civilians were caught up in its maelstrom and both sides developed a healthy respect for each other.

American forces landing in North Africa, November 1942.

NORTH AFRICA: FROM TORCH TO TRIPOLI

On 8 November 1942, at the other end of the Mediterranean, British and American troops under the supreme command of General Dwight D. Eisenhower, landed in north-west Africa.

The convoy carrying American troops under the command of Lieutenant-General George S. Patton had left Norfolk, Virginia, on 24 October, heading for three beaches near Casablanca on the Atlantic coast of French Morocco. None on board had any idea whether they would be greeted as friends or as enemies, but they were ordered to display the Stars and Stripes on landing as a token of friendship. Patton was a cavalryman who had gravitated easily to training and leading the US Army's first Armoured Corps, which he had put through its paces in the deserts of eastern California known as 'Little Libya'. He had appeared on the cover of *Life* magazine, a form of fame in itself. To instil pride in his new formation he had designed a uniform consisting of a football helmet and a green jerkin; it was not taken up by the War Department but his troops called him Flash Gordon or Old Georgie. Nearly fifty-seven years old, he was one of the oldest US generals (Eisenhower, his chief, was only fifty) and the most colourful, and he used colourful language. He believed in leading from the front.

The British 1st Army, entrusted to the command of General Kenneth Anderson, was steaming from England in two convoys and heading for six beaches on the coast of Algeria. The British were prepared for strong resistance from the Vichy French forces, but their commanders hoped that Byzantine intrigues in the previous weeks would result in a quick cease-fire. Only a week before, Eisenhower's deputy, General Mark Clark, had participated in a cloak-and-dagger mission to Algiers, landing in the dark from a submarine to be met on the beach by pro-Allied French officers and conspire with them to prepare the way for a bloodless Allied landing. Clark informed them that General Henri Giraud would soon be arriving to serve as Governor. This was astonishing news. Giraud had escaped down a rope from his cell in a German castle in April 1942 and made his way to Vichy France, where Marshal Pétain, to his credit, refused to hand him back to the Germans.

Hitler regarded Giraud's escape from German custody as worse than the loss of a dozen divisions. Churchill saw Giraud's importance in other terms — as a future ally and perhaps even leader of Free France in place of the difficult de Gaulle, who made it abundantly clear that he suspected an Anglo-American conspiracy against France. He referred to his allies as the 'Anglo-Saxons'; Roosevelt had no desire even to meet him. Of Giraud, Churchill wrote to Roosevelt: 'This man might play a decisive part in bringing about things of which you have hopes.' Giraud had been smuggled to Gibraltar on the eve of the invasion of north Africa. Widely admired in the French Army, he proved to be an asset of dubious value — rigid, right-wing and inflexible. Eisenhower's political adviser Robert Murphy had also initiated contact with Admiral Darlan, whose deviousness was a byword and with the Commander-in-Chief in Algeria, General Alphonse Juin; but their actions and final loyalties could not be forecast.

The French fought vigorously to contest the landings near Algiers, Oran and Casablanca. Admiral Darlan was in Algiers visiting his dying son when the Allies landed but he was prevailed upon by Murphy and Juin to order the French forces in Algeria to cease fire at 6.45 p.m. Impressed — and intimidated — by General Patton, General Noguès in Morocco ordered all resistance halted on the morning of 11 November. The Allies and the French had each lost 3000 killed and wounded in the three-day battle.

On the same day, 11 November, German forces entered Unoccupied France, ending the fiction of Vichy autonomy. Only one French divisional commander, General de Lattre de Tassigny, ordered his troops to resist the Germans, but he was arrested by his own staff. Sawing through the bars of his cell, de Lattre escaped, contacted the Resistance, and was flown to London in 1943. A flamboyant man, de Lattre was, like Juin, a brilliant soldier and a sincere French patriot with a hatred of the Germans. Long after Giraud had been relegated to obscurity, they became two of de Gaulle's most trusted and dynamic military commanders. Like de Gaulle's earliest lieutenants Leclerc and Koenig, they were to became Marshals of France.

THE FRENCH FLEET SCUTTLED

Under Allied pressure Darlan ordered the French fleet at Toulon to sail to Allied ports, but on 26 November German troops were already entering the docks. For the fleet there was no escape: the Germans had sown the roadsteads with mines and the ships lacked crews. The admiral in Toulon ordered the ships to scuttle themselves. Explosions ripped apart three battleships, eight cruisers, seventeen destroyers, and sixteen submarines in addition to seventy other vessels. In de Gaulle's words it was 'the most pitiful and sterile suicide imaginable' and he himself felt 'submerged into seas of anger and disappointment'. He viewed Churchill's message of regret, coming so soon after the elevation to authority of Giraud, as anther example of Anglo-Saxon hypocrisy.

But the French Army of Africa (strong in manpower but weak in equipment) was now to join the Allied cause. It seemed that victory in north Africa was just a matter of months away.

PLANNING STRATEGY

Churchill and Roosevelt were already planning their next steps. On 15 November, as England's church bells were pealing in celebration of the victories in Africa, Churchill was discussing future strategy at Chequers with his advisers and Eisenhower's Chief of Staff, General Bedell Smith. Roosevelt had suggested invading Sardinia, Sicily, Italy or Greece. On 17 November Churchill wrote to Roosevelt that the Allies should 'strike at the under-belly of the Axis in effective strength', using north African bases. Both leaders thought it important to obtain Turkey as an ally — this was premature, as were thoughts of an early offensive in the Mediterranean. German troops and tanks were now pouring into Tunisia despite muted protests from the French, and on 1 December Rommel launched a strong attack there, proving that the campaign was not yet over.

Two days later Churchill proposed to Roosevelt and Stalin that they all meet: 'We must decide at the earliest moment the best way of attacking Germany in Europe with all possible force in 1943,' he explained. Stalin declined to attend, but asked brusquely when during 1943 an Anglo-America invasion of Europe could be expected. Any invasion of France was now to be delayed. The chiefs of staff recommended pursuing a Mediterranean strategy. On 30 December Churchill made plans to fly to Morocco. He would meet Roosevelt at Casablanca in January 1943.

Allied commanders meet in Algiers after the armistice with the French forces. From right to left, General Henri Giraud, Admiral Sir Andrew Cunningham, General Dwight Eisenhower and, on far left, their former enemy, Admiral Darlan of France. Behind Cunningham stands Ike's naval aide Captain Harry Butcher; behind Giraud is his aide Captain Andre Beaufre (a future general). One week later Darlan, who had aroused much hatred as a member of the French Vichy government, was assassinated by a young Frenchman whose motives are still unclear.

Field-Marshal Karl Gerd von Rundstedt, the German Army's most respected senior commander who was sacked by Hitler for advocating a withdrawal on the Eastern Front, led the German invasion of Vichy France in November 1942: one of his few bloodless conquests. Rundstedt, an aristocrat who showed his disdain for the Nazis, was sacked from his command three times by Hitler.

STALINGRAD

Over all these events a dark cloud lay: the campaign on the Eastern Front and its epicentre, the great battle for Stalingrad. 'From every house, workshop, water-tower, railway embankment, wall, cellar and every pile of ruins, a bitter battle was waged, without equal even in the First World War with its vast expenditure of munitions,' wrote the German General Doerr. As the first German troops were entering the northern suburbs of Stalingrad in late August 1942 Stalin had ordered the defenders: 'Not a step back!' He despatched Nikita Kruschev to the city to supervise its defence, which lay in the capable hands of General Yeremenko.

Stalin's phrase became the slogan and battle cry of the Russians. The fighting was so close that Soviet tanks were driven from Stalingrad's factories straight to the front line, unpainted, and often manned by factory workers. Every pile of rubble became a stronghold. Soon the defenders were clinging to a narrow strip of land on the west bank of the Volga and ferrying reinforcements nightly across the river from the east. Into the steep cliffs of the Volga the defenders had dug tunnels which sheltered the reserves, the wounded, ammunition and supplies, impervious to shellfire. Some of the giant reinforced-concrete factories such as the October Works were almost indestructible by artillery; in their cellars the defenders hid; in others they were entombed. On the east bank Soviet artillery bombarded the German positions, but was soon running short of ammunition.

A new commander of the isolated Soviet 62nd Army, Chuikov, crossed the river to his command post on the east bank on 13 September, the day on which General von Paulus's 6th Army launched their third major offensive against the city with eleven divisions. They were faced by only three Soviet divisions and fragments of others. Chuikov crossed the Volga under hails of shrapnel, and the air he breathed seemed hotter that the flames themselves. 'Anyone without experience of war would think that in the blazing city there is no longer anywhere left to live, that everything has been destroyed and burnt out,' Chuikov wrote. 'But I know that on the other side of the river a battle is being fought, a titanic struggle is taking place.' On 14 September the Germans broke through in the centre and were driving at speed into the city.

The defenders devised new tactics; they would let through the German tanks — whose armour-piercing shells were poor weapons against buildings and concentrations of troops, and then gun down the infantry, allowing their own handful of roaming T-34s armed with armour-piercing shells to deal with enemy tanks. Artillery bombardments of Soviet positions were no longer effective because of the closeness of the fighting. Thus the battle to hold and secure the ground became an infantry battle, man against man, close-fighting of a kind never before experienced. Often Germans and Russians occupied the same building, fighting to drive the others out. Soviet snipers picked off any target that showed itself. When one group of surrounded Russians was called upon to surrender they instead raised the Red Flag and hurled rocks and rubble at the approaching enemy. By the end of a week, the German attacks were faltering. Autumn was approaching and with it the possibility of another early winter as grim as that of the previous year.

In the Caucasus, far to the south, the German advance had stalled. Lacking reinforcements and faced with an enemy reorganising and fighting with a new stubbornness, General von List pushed towards Baku, the great port on the Caspian, but made little progress. Army Group Centre informed Hitler that a Russian counter offensive might be expected on their front, for Zhukov had been rebuilding his armies and the front was eerily quiet. On 24 September Hitler sacked Halder — whose pessimism infuriated him — as Chief of the OKW and replaced him with General Zeitzler.

On 4 October Paulus, who had informed Hitler that 6th Army was short of supplies and meeting with unexpected Soviet resistance, launched another offensive in Stalingrad. 'This was to be the fiercest, and the longest, of the five battles which were fought in the ruined town,' writes Alan Clark in his history of the Russian campaign. The Russians responded with small groups of 'storm troops' armed with grenades, light and heavy machine-guns and anti-tank weapons. 'Get close to the enemy's positions,' Chuikov ordered them, 'making use of craters and ruins; dig your trenches by night, camouflage them by day; make the build-up for the attack stealthily, without any noise ...' An officer of the 24th Panzer Division wrote that 'there is a ceaseless struggle from noon to night. From storey to storey, faces black with sweat, we bombard each other with grenades in the middle of explosions, clouds of dust and smoke, fragments of furniture and human beings ... The street is no longer measured by metres but by corpses ... Stalingrad is no longer a town. By day it is an enormous cloud of burning, blinding smoke; it is a vast furnace lit by the reflection of the flames ...' The battle ended after three weeks of fighting that had bled white the German 6th Army.

The two dictators visit the Eastern Front: Hitler and Mussolini during an inspection tour in Russia late in 1942.

WEAPONS OF WAR

Russian manpower and American war production were the two deciding factors that would give the Allies victory. American factories supplied not only their own armed forces but through Lend-Lease a large proportion of the Allies', including 15 per cent of the Soviet Union's needs. Allied production figures are staggering. Germany was finally crushed by sheer weight of iron. Between 1941 and 1945 Germany produced nearly 55,000 tanks but the United States produced 90,000 and the Soviets 95,000. During this period the Germans manufactured 79,000 aircraft but the United States produced 300,000 and the Soviets 109,000; Germany produced 68,000 mortars but the Soviets turned out 350,000. These figures exclude Britain's own substantial output. The United States also produced 71,000 naval ships (including 100 aircraft carriers) and three million machine-guns. The United States raised armed forces totalling 15 million men and women. The cost was staggering — more than $250 billion, a debt that had to be handed on to succeeding generations to pay. Given the choice between defeat and debt, the Americans chose the latter.

Wartime production led to an economic boom that continued after the end of hostilities, and factories rapidly adapted to peacetime conditions and needs. The war led to American domination of numerous industries, including aircraft production and design.

One aircraft illustrates American ingenuity: the Consolidated Vultee bomber, known as the B-24. It never achieved the recognition achieved by the Boeing B-17 Flying Fortress but it became the most widely manufactured bomber of the war. Nearly 20,000 B-24s — aptly named 'Liberators' — were produced. Each aircraft consisted of one million parts (including rivets); its thin wings gave it remarkable stability but caused manufacturing problems: midgets had to be employed to crawl inside the wings and feed through the cables and wiring.

Shipbuilding boomed. The desperate need for transport vessels resulted in 'Victory' ships — mass-produced prefabricated merchantmen that took just a week to build. The need for aircraft carriers resulted in the 'baby flat-tops' — small prefabricated escort carriers capable of carrying only twenty aircraft and armed with a single 4-inch gun. They were tossed around like tin cans in storms, but a handful of 'baby carriers' turned the tide in the battle of Leyte Gulf in 1944 by delaying the oncoming Japanese battle fleet, and well merited their production.

Ominously, in 1944 alone the Soviets produced 22,000 tanks.

American mass production: 24-tonne Mariner flying boats (patrol bombers) being fitted out in an east-coast factory.

German troops in the ruins of Stalingrad, 1942.

On 11 November Paulus launched another offensive into the miserable ruins of Stalingrad. It fell apart after four days. Prisoners were no longer taken by either side. On 12 November General von Richthofen of the Luftwaffe, flying over the front line north of Stalingrad, was struck by how quiet it was — there was no gun fire from Soviet artillery — and wrote: 'Their [the Russian] reserves have now been concentrated. When, I wonder, will the attack come?'

COUNTER OFFENSIVE

It came on 19 November 1942, with a massive artillery bombardment north of Stalingrad from 2000 Russian guns. The Red Army fell on the front held by Hitler's unwilling allies, the ill-equipped Romanians and Italians, and within three days had broken through their lines in two places. Through the breaches Zhukov launched no fewer than six armies. The Russians advanced so rapidly that on 23 November their tanks reached the bridge at Kalach over which crossed all the supplies for the 6th Army and which provided Paulus's only escape route. The defenders, thinking they were German tanks, failed to detonate the bridge and it was captured intact. 'The first tenuous link in a chain that was to throttle a quarter of a million German soldiers had thus been forged,' writes one historian, 'and the turning point in the Second World War had arrived.' The snows of an early winter were already falling.

On 22 November the two Soviet pincers met. Stalingrad was now cut off and would soon be surrounded. General von Manstein, who was at Vitebsk preparing for an offensive against his own front, was ordered to report to Field Marshal von Kluge and form a new Army Group in the Don bend to 'to bring the enemy attacks to a standstill'. It would take him at least a fortnight to assemble forces strong enough to break the ring tightening around Stalingrad.

Manstein's command was little bigger than a Corps. He suggested to General Zeitzler that the 6th Army attempt to break out to the south-west before it was too late. Zeitzler had already made the same suggestion to Hitler on 21 November. but the Führer had shouted: 'I won't leave the Volga! I won't go back from the Volga!' Two days later Paulus also asked Hitler's approval to evacuate his Army from Stalingrad, in a message sent directly to the Führer, circumventing his Group commander, Weichs. By now 20 German divisions and two Romanian were cut off in Stalingrad. Hitler ordered them to hold their ground, and informed them they would be supplied by

Above: By late 1942 Hitler's interference in strategy was becoming incessant; it proved fatal to Germany.
Below: Soviet troops during the fighting in Stalingrad, winter 1942.

air. This proved a task beyond the resources of a depleted Luftwaffe and flights were hampered by snowstorms, ice and the Russians' seizure of most of Stalingrad's landing grounds. Soon supplies would be parachuted into the last sector held by the starving garrison. In the last weeks the Germans in Stalingrad were living on one slice of bread per day.

On 12 December Manstein launched his offensive to relieve Stalingrad and by 21 December Hoth's 7th Panzer Army, advancing from the south, in a superhuman effort was within 50 kilometres of the city. At night the German 6th Army could see the signal flares of Hoth's columns. Still Hitler refused to authorise any breakout by Paulus — unless 6th Army also held the city. 'I begged Hitler to authorise the breakout,' Zeitzler later wrote. 'I pointed out that this was absolutely our last chance to save the 200,000 men of Paulus' army.'

Fate and Zhukov again intervened. On 17 December the Russians had struck suddenly in the north, against the Italian 8th Army and opened a gaping hole in the front. The breakthrough quickly became a rout. The Italians retreated in disorder, as did the Romanians to their south. Manstein, whose Army Group Don was now itself endangered, ordered Hoth to halt his push to Stalingrad and send one of his three Panzer divisions north to protect Manstein's own flank. On 29 December Zeitzler reminded Hitler that with the collapse of the southern front, the two armies in the Caucasus could be cut off. Within a few hours' drive of the Grozny oilfields but starved of fuel, the armies received permission to withdraw. One week later the Germans at Stalingrad surrendered.

BRUTAL RULE? THE AXIS EMPIRES

EUROPE UNDER THE NAZIS

In the middle months of 1942 Hitler's Reich stood at its height. Germany ruled the lives of 400 million people and in the words of the historian Chester Wilmot Hitler's realms stretched 'from the Mediterranean to the Arctic, from the English Channel to the Black Sea and almost to the Caspian.' A German army stood at the gates of Cairo, and the Axis or its allies held nearly all of northern Africa. Never before had a single nation achieved rule over so much of the earth's surface in so short a time. Its subjects were cowed, its enemies again reeling. Its ally Japan ruled South-East Asia. By the early months of 1943 the 'Thousand Year Reich' was weakening, but its murderous energy was not yet expended.

On the continent of Europe only three nations remained neutral — Spain, Sweden and Switzerland — and all pursued pro-German policies that made a mockery of the term 'neutral'. Sweden supplied the bulk of the Reich's iron ore and nickel, and even permitted German troops to transit their country. Switzerland's balance of payments remained healthy from its exports of war material to Germany; she permitted trains crammed with Germany's Jewish prisoners to cross her territory and her bankers eagerly accepted deposits of money seized from the Reich's Jewish victims, asking no questions. Having given refuge to 28,000 Jews, the Swiss deported 9000 of them in late 1942 by handing them over to French border police, from whose hands they were transferred to German custody for extermination. The International Red Cross in Switzerland did much to alleviate the privations of Allied prisoners of war, but proved remarkably inept in saving the lives of Jews. Germany's director of the Red Cross was a fervent Nazi doctor who had killed prisoners with poisonous injections; he was later hanged as a war criminal. Spain remained openly hostile to the Allies. Only Turkey, at the easternmost tip of Europe, maintained a policy that was defiantly pro-Allied.

In Europe, Himmler's SS had become a state within a state, possessing its own economic structure, its own factories, and even its own combat forces — the Waffen-SS — the 'fighting' SS — to distinguish themselves from the black-coated quasi-police units who ran the death camps. Both wore the skull and crossbones insignia, symbols of death.

RESISTANCE

Long after the war a French heroine of the Resistance, the Vicomtesse de Clarens, wrote: 'Those who worked underground in constant fear — fear of the unspeakable — were prompted by the inner obligation to participate in the struggle, almost powerless, they sensed they could listen and observe. During the war they could but hope that what they did would be of some service, but seldom knew for sure ... It is not easy to depict the loneliness, the chilling fear, the unending waiting, the frustration of not knowing whether the dangerously obtained information would be passed on — or passed on in time — or recognised as vital ...'

There was resistance in the democratic nations of western Europe but initially it was passive. Their peoples treated the Germans with disdain and hostility but there were few acts of sabotage, because there was no organised Resistance and the punishment for killing German soldiers was high: often ten hostages were shot in public for every German killed. For the first years Nazi rule in the west was light. This would change as Germany's position of dominance came under threat and its demands on the local population grew harsher.

Heinrich Himmler (left), the Reichsführer SS and his principal lieutenant Reinhard Heydrich, photographed in Vienna in 1938. They planned and carried out the extermination of Europe's Jews and the Reich's enemies.

Left: Hitler and his mistress Eva Braun at the 'Eagle's Nest' at Obersalzburg in the Bavarian Alps.

Below: Victim of an early attack by the French Resistance, a German officer in Paris is buried with full military honours.

France, which had led the world in many aspects, led Europe in the extent of its collaboration with the New Order. Many of the patriots who had left France to join the Free French returned as agents and set out to create a network of Resistance cells. Special Operations Executive (SOE) sent its first three agents into France in May 1941 to send back information by wireless and organise Resistance units. Another 477 agents would follow over the next three years; of these 106 were killed in action or executed by the Germans.

It was not until the German invasion of the Soviet Union in June 1941 that the Communists throughout Europe began to direct their energies and remarkable organising skills into the war against Germany; they already had the most effective spy network and would soon have a Resistance to match it. And it was not until mid-1942 that the first armed and organised actions against the Germans took place in France.

Less than 5 per cent of western Europe's people collaborated actively with the Nazis, but even fewer joined the early Resistance groups of patriots. Most people, living in a state of fear, hoped only for liberation and an end to the horror. One of the first actions of SOE in London was to establish escape lines for Allied soldiers or airmen; civilians helping in their escape faced summary execution by the Nazis. Their next task was to send information about German strength and movements back to London. Agents parachuting into Hitler's Europe fought the loneliest of wars. On landing in France, they were either met by Resistance personnel or given a list of safe contacts. But who could they trust? SOE's entire Dutch network had been infiltrated and its codes broken by the Germans, and all agents subsequently dropped into the Netherlands were arrested. At the end of 1943 the Germans themselves informed SOE that they had been hoodwinked, sending a message to London that ended: 'Whenever you will come to pay a visit to the continent you may be assured that you will be received with the same care and results as all those you sent us before. So long.' The Nazis sent the forty Dutch agents and seven Britons to die in Mauthausen concentration camp.

The most celebrated of national Resistance movements, the French, was weakened by factions — Communist and Gaullist dominating all others. It gave birth to the 'maquis' only when young men fled to the mountains or the scrubland countryside ('maquis') to evade the Vichy government's forced labour program late in 1942. French agent networks were also infiltrated. In mid-1943, when the Resistance was effectively detonating rail lines and power stations, de Gaulle sent Jean Moulin, a former préfet, back to France to coordinate the eight Resistance groups; he was soon betrayed and tortured hideously by Klaus Barbie, the Gestapo chief at Lyons, France's second city. Blinded and unconscious, Moulin died of his injuries.

Norway stands high in the history of resistance to Nazi rule. It produced the first figure whose name is synonymous with treason — Quisling — but he was ignored until 1942 by the Germans, who appointed one of their own, Josef Terboven, to rule Norway. (He suicided on the day of the German surrender in 1945 and Quisling was shot as a traitor soon afterwards.) Alerted that 'heavy water' was being produced at the Norsk Hydro plant in the mountains of Vemork, Special Operations sent in a team of young Norwegians to destroy it. The four men were dropped in by parachute in October 1942, but London decided that a stronger force was needed. Two gliders carrying British commandos set out to join them, but both crashed. The survivors of the crashes, though wearing British uniforms, were executed by the Nazis as saboteurs. Another six agents were parachuted in to reinforce the stoic original four in mid February 1943; the joint party attacked the plant one week later, delaying production, and in February 1944 they sank the ferry carrying the precious product to Germany. Happily all the Norwegians survived. It was one of the bravest actions of the war.

Denmark occupied a peculiar status. Its government protested its neutrality and the British respected their odd situation. There was no bombing of targets in Denmark until 1943, when the Resistance began to strengthen and the people of Denmark showed growing disgust with Nazi rule. Hitler allowed elections to be held in March 1943 and was outraged when of 149 seats only three went to the local Nazi party. In August the Nazis took over direct control of Denmark's administration, arresting the King. A month later they arrested the entire Danish police force for refusing to follow orders and shipped a great number of policemen to Buchenwald concentration camp.

In 1940 an Australian woman and her French husband made contact with British agents in Marseilles and organised one of the first

Above: Photographs like this showing friendly relations between French civilians and German troops in France were widely reproduced in the Nazi press.
Below: A French patriot faces a German firing squad in occupied France. Executions like these failed to crush the spirit of the Resistance.

Resistance cells. Her name was Nancy Wake. After her husband was arrested and killed by the Germans she was smuggled into England in 1943, where she went through SOE's tough training course for agents. She was parachuted back into France in 1944 to liaise with the maquis and other Resistance groups in their hit-and-run opera- tions against the Germans, who dubbed her 'the White Mouse' and put a price on her head. Decorated for her heroism, Nancy Wake survived the war.

Violet Szabo did not. A young Englishwoman who had also married a Frenchman, she volunteered for SOE after her husband had been killed at Alamein. She was parachuted into France on the night of D-Day (6–7 June 1944) to take command of the maquis in the Limoges area. Four days later she was fated to encounter the SS Das Reich Division, rushing from southern France to the Normandy beachhead. With a machine-gun she held off 400 Germans for two hours before she ran out of ammunition. She refused to talk under interrogation. Transferred to Ravensbrück concentration camp, she was shot there in the back of the head, holding hands with two other British women agents who suffered the same fate, on 26 January 1945.

Before the Allied landings in France enough British arms had been dropped to equip an army of 20,000 men. In liaison with agents from SOE and its American counterpart OSS (Office of Strategic Services) and units of the SAS, the Resistance began open warfare against the Germans, and paid heavily for it. The great battle through the defiles of the Dordogne to delay the Das Reich Division, in which the writer André Malraux was wounded, was an epic of these days. (The Das Reich slaughtered 600 villagers of Oradour-sur-Glâne in reprisal). Another epic was the *maquisards'* doomed defence of the plateau of Vercors, as they waited for Allied reinforcements that never came. The only gliders that landed on the plateau were German; the villages of the Vercors were burned and the occupants slaughtered. Supplied with arms, ammunition and British and American liaison officers, the French Resistance liberated much of France in 1944 before the Allied armies reached them. As many as 30,000 men and women of the Resistance died in battle. On Liberation the French exacted quick justice on collaborators, shooting perhaps 10,000 of them without trial. At war's end more than 110,000 were arrested for collaboration but only 800 were sentenced to death and the sentences of most of these were commuted to prison terms, as the fires of vengeance died.

ARMED INSURRECTION

The first organised, armed resistance to the New Order occurred in Europe's most violent region, Yugoslavia, where Serb army units had sought refuge in the mountains to continue the struggle against the Germans. In June a Communist leader named Josep Broz — code-named 'Tito' — had left Belgrade to form a resistance group known to history as the Partisans. The first notable attacks on Axis forces occurred in Montenegro. On 14 July 1941 Ciano noted in his dairy: 'Disorders in Montenegro. Shooting by armed bands, and assault on the royal villa of Budua.' Next day he wrote that 'things are going badly. The capital isolated and all the roads leading to it are blocked by the rebels. We have sent forces there from Albania.' In August 1941 the first wireless messages were picked up in Britain from Colonel Draja Mihailovic's Serb guerrillas, the Chetniks, requesting assistance. By the end of the year the deeds of the Chetniks were widely hailed

Below: Yugoslav civilians hanged by the Nazis in the first year of occupation. During the course of the war acts of resistance were punished by executions of hostages who were often seized at random and killed violently.
Bottom: Mountains of corpses. Civilians killed by the Nazis await burial.

Above: Draja Mihailovic (centre) with Chetnik leaders in southern Yugoslavia.
Right: Josep Broz, (at left with his chief of staff in 1944) who under the name 'Tito' organised the Communist-led resistance movement in Yugoslavia known as the Partisans.

as the first sign of a resurgent Europe, yet the Resistance there was fragmented, torn by political and even tribal rivalries, particularly in Serbia, the seed-bed of revolt. In September, when the first British SOE officer arrived in Yugoslavia, Tito and Mihailovic met for the first time to coordinate their actions. In October their combined forces launched an attack on 2200 Germans in the town of Kraljevo; in the next week the Germans executed 1700 townspeople in revenge, setting the pattern of conflict for the next three years: attacks followed by hideous and indescribable reprisals. In these atrocities Ante Pavelic's Croat fascist units — the Ustashi — participated bloodily. The Croats, Catholic by faith, had long despised Serbs, Muslims and Jews and wrought vengeance on them in Bosnia-Herzegovina so appalling in its cruelty that the Italians protested and sought to curb them.

Neither Tito nor Mihailovic could agree on who was to lead the Resistance. Tito, despite his Croat birth, believed in the preservation of a strong Yugoslavia; his rival aimed at creating a strong Serbia under the monarchy and viewed Communists as little better than Nazis. He was to collaborate with the Germans and their Serbian puppet government under General Nedic while fighting Axis forces and Communist Partisans. By mid-1943 Britain, knowing that the Partisans were the most effective of resistance forces, cut off aid to the Chetniks. Yugoslavia was to suffer more than a million dead in a war that degenerated often into civil war, a dress rehearsal for the violent collapse of the country in the 1990s.

Greece reflected the same perplexing situation. Communist-led resistance units were the largest and best organised; the monarchists were the first to receive arms and assistance. Their war against the Germans would become a bitter civil war that began in 1944, and flared again from 1947 to 1949.

'HOLOCAUST': 'THE FINAL SOLUTION'

'The death of one person is a tragedy. The death of millions is a statistic.'
— Adolf Eichmann, SS

Among those marked for death were Europe's 11 million Jews, the bulk of whom lived along the Polish–Russian border lands — the 'Pale'. From the outbreak of war in 1939 until the German invasion of Russia in June 1941, a relatively small number of Polish Jews had died in German hands — perhaps 30,000 had succumbed, the bulk of them by starvation or disease. Mass killings of Jews began on the first day of the German invasion of the Soviet Union. In September 1941 the SS shot more than 33,000 Jews of Kiev in a ravine outside the city called Babi Yar. But bullets were thought to be too slow a method and the prolonged carnage upset even the most hardened of SS thugs. The first mass killings by poisonous gas began in December 1941 when more than 40,000 Jews were killed at Chelmno. To the Nazis even this figure was too few. The Jews in western Europe had so far been left unmolested. The first Jew in the Netherlands had died before a German firing squad on 1 March 1941, condemned for a minor offence. The first Jew was shot in France on 10 May 1941 — one year to the day after the invasion of France.

On 20 January 1942 Himmler's right-hand SS man Reinhard Heydrich had convened a meeting at a villa in Berlin on the banks of the Wannsee. Here, attended by members of many government departments including the Foreign Office, Heydrich explained that the war against the Jews had so far involved their expulsion from German territory and their evacuation to the east. These measures were to be considered an expedient only 'in view of the approaching final solution of the Jewish question'. He went through statistics of Europe's Jews — nearly three million in the Ukraine, 2.3 million in Poland (in the General-Government); 742,000 in Hungary, 700,000 in Unoccupied France, 447,000 in White Russia (Belorussia), 400,000 in the Bialystok area. Germany's allies harboured large numbers — 342,000 Jews in Romania; 88,000 in Slovakia, 58,000 in Italy. He stated that 34,000 Jews were dwelling in Lithuania but did not mention that the other 200,000 had already been killed. Heydrich said that all Jews should be brought to the East, separated by sex; those capable of work would be used on construction duties. 'The inevitable final remainder', he said, 'will have to be dealt with appropriately.' The meeting ended with a discussion of the 'various types of solution' to be used, but no record exists of this discussion. The priority was to arrest and move the Jews to the east. The apprehension of the Jews was entrusted to Heydrich's department head Adolf Eichmann, who was soon visiting countries from France to Greece and who was to supervise the deportations. Other functionaries arranged the transportation by rail of the victims. The construction of 'death camps' began in eastern Poland just west of the River Bug, and located on the railway lines. Chelmno was already operating. The three small concentration camps at Belzec, Treblinka and Sobibor were enlarged. Across the railway line from Auschwitz, a new camp was constructed in a birch wood — Birkenau. And soon another extermination camp opened — Majdanek, where 1,380,000 people were to be systematically murdered.

So far the Nazis had built concentration camps, not extermination camps. The concentration camps were themselves pits of horror, where prisoners died from lack of food and medical attention or random execution — at Buchenwald 63,500 prisoners were to die; at Bergen-Belsen 50,000; at Mauthausen outside Vienna, 138,000 died; at Dachau in picturesque Bavaria 70,000 were killed. But these figures pale beside the statistics of the extermination camps, where millions were killed.

On 30 January 1942, Hitler celebrated his ninth anniversary in power by speaking from the Sports Palace in Berlin. He spoke of his confidence in victory and said that 'the war will not end as the Jews imagine it will, namely with the uprooting of the Aryans, but the result of this war will be the complete annihilation of the Jews ... the hour will soon come when the most evil universal enemy of all time will be finished, at least for a thousand years'. These words were recorded by the Allied wireless monitoring service.

Jews arriving on trains were to be separated into the fit and the unfit. Those considered unfit for work including the old, most of the women and all young children, were immediately taken to the main camp where they were asked to take showers; the showers were in reality gas chambers. The asphyxiated bodies were then removed and burned in crematoria. Auschwitz lay on the main rail network from western Europe and was the destination of most of the Jews transported to the east from that region. As such its name has acquired a special kind of horror but fewer Jews died at Auschwitz than in the four major camps in the region that had no function other than the killing of Jews: Belzec, Treblinka, Sobibor, and Chelmno.

Heydrich — 'the Hangman' — did not live to see the fruition of his plans. In May 1942 he was assassinated in Prague by Czech agents parachuted into the country from England. They were tracked down and killed. The consequences of the assassination were grievous. The Nazis razed the entire village of Lidice, shot its menfolk and deported its women and children. Heydrich was succeeded in his SS functions by the Austrian Ernst Kaltenbrunner. Almost seven feet tall, his face disfigured by a duelling scar, he was one of the monsters of the regime.

On 5 July 1942 the Nazis began rounding up the Dutch Jews. On that day the Frank family, Jews who had fled Germany in 1933 for the safety of Holland, went into hiding in Amsterdam. Their youngest daughter, Anne, was thirteen years old. Her diaries describe the next two years the family spent hiding in rooms in a warehouse until their discovery in September 1944. Anne Frank died of typhus in Bergen-Belsen camp seven months later. Her poignant, heart-breaking diary survived and was published two years after the war.

The first trains crammed with 2000 Dutch Jews arrived at Auschwitz on 17 July 1942. Of this number 449 mainly elderly people and children were immediately gassed. The survivors were taken to the Birkenau barracks and their arms were seared with serial numbers. They went to work as slaves for the Reich until they died or were selected for execution. One day earlier 7000 Jews had been arrested in Paris by the Nazis with the assistance of the French police and taken to temporary accommodation at Drancy, a housing estate. Two days later 1000 of them were taken by train to Auschwitz, where they arrived on 22 July. Of their number 375 were immediately gassed, the remainder sent to the barracks for tattooing and work. Of this total only 17 survived the war.

Thus the pattern of genocide was set. For Europe's Jews it meant sudden arrest in their homes, or orders to report to centres nearby for reasons unspecified, with time only to pack a single article of luggage. They were then forced onto trains — usually cattle trucks — for the long journey to the east and to their deaths. In August 1942, 145,000 Jews were gassed at Belzec; in the same month 140,000 Jews were sent from Warsaw to Treblinka and gassed there. 'More than 400,00 Jews were murdered in German-occupied Europe in August 1942,' writes the historian Martin Gilbert. 'Neither their suffering, not their courage, can be adequately conveyed in words.' Reports of the mass killings were already widely known in Allied circles. In September Prime Minister Churchill threatened retribution; he had little else to use. He described this new crime of the Nazis as 'the most bestial, the

Above right: Himmler (left) shams interest in young Russians during a visit to the Eastern Front.
Below: Jewish men, women and children are herded from the Warsaw ghetto by SS and German Army troops before being transported to extermination camps in southern Poland.

most squalid and the most senseless of their offences …' and added: that Europe's hour of liberation would also be the 'hour of retribution'.

On 19 April 1943, 1200 Jews of Warsaw, alerted that the Ghetto was to be totally destroyed, decided to fight to the death. When a force of 2000 SS troops entered the Ghetto the Jews, who possessed only seventeen rifles and several thousand grenades, held them at bay. The Germans were armed with artillery, flame-throwers and gas. When the last Jewish post, at 18 Mila Street, was overcome, SS General

Entire Jewish families, forced to wear the yellow Star of David, went to their deaths together at Nazi hands. The Nazis showed no pity and, later, little contrition.

Stroop proudly claimed that 7000 Jews had been killed in the fighting; the remaining 30,000 were deported to Treblinka. In June 1943, 150 Jews in Treblinka also rose up, turned on their guards and escaped into the forests.

A young doctor arrived in Auschwitz in May 1943. He was a member of the SS named Josef Mengele. He began conducting medical experiments on Jewish patients. In white medical coat and jackboots he would greet each incoming train and separate those passing him into two groups with a move of his whip: who were to die and who were to live a little longer as workers, before they too were killed. He was to be known as the 'Angel of Death'.

When Churchill heard details in July 1944 of the mass killings carried out at Auschwitz he ordered that something be done. The Jewish Agency had suggested the bombing of the Budapest–Auschwitz railway line, and Churchill ordered the air force to do this. The RAF replied that it was 'out of our power'. The US air forces should be approached to attempt to bomb the gas chambers by day. Churchill heard four days later that the deportation of Jews to Auschwitz had been halted as a result of protests by the Pope and other world leaders. The pause was only temporary. On 11 July he wrote to Eden: 'There is no doubt that this is probably the greatest and most horrible crime ever committed in the whole history of the world, and it has been done by scientific machinery by nominally civilised men in the name of a great State and one of the leading races of Europe …' He stated that those responsible, if found guilty of the crime 'should be put to death'.

In late January 1945 a German businessman, Osckar Schindler, who had employed Jews in his factories and was known for his decent treatment of them, heard of a train that was carrying starving Jews; inside one of the wagons were 100 Jews from Birkenau. By subterfuge Schindler had the wagon transferred to a siding and then took the 80 survivors into his care. Over two years he saved 1500 Jews from death. Throughout the sad story of the Holocaust there were others such as Schindler who helped Jews or sheltered them; but they were too few.

At this stage the Jews of Italy, Bulgaria, Hungary — and Scandinavia — remained untouched. Hitler's allies objected to his rabid anti-Semitism. Italy refused to arrest its Jews and the Italian Army provided protection for Jews in the territories they administered; this protection disappeared when Italy changed sides in the war in September 1943. Finland refused to hand over its tiny Jewish population; the Norwegians, Belgians, Dutch and Danes hid many Jews and the Danish resistance smuggled 6000 Danish Jews across the waters to Sweden in 1943. Tsar Boris of Bulgaria refused to hand over his country's Jews, as did the Regent of Hungary. When both were removed from the scene — the first by sudden death, the second by kidnapping by Nazi commandos — the deportation of Jews proceeded without hindrance. The killing of 400,000 Hungarian Jews became the last act in the tragedy.

Allied propaganda seized on the execution by the Japanese of captured servicemen as evidence of their callousness and brutality.

ALLIED PRISONERS OF WAR

Russian prisoners of the Germans were treated with callousness and cruelty. Those who were not worked to death or executed died of starvation and disease. Typhus took the life of Stalin's son, captured in 1941, before the Nazis had time to use him as a bargaining piece. But American, western European and British Commonwealth prisoners of war (POWs) were generally treated by Germany and Italy according to the terms of the Geneva Convention. They received Red Cross supplies and mail; POWs knew that it was their duty to escape but opportunities were few, and they risked being shot in making the attempt. Escapers' best chance was to reach a neutral country — Switzerland, Sweden or Spain — whence they would be repatriated to their homelands. ('Evaders', men who had not been in enemy confinement, were, according to the Geneva Convention, liable to detention in the neutral country they had reached, with little chance of repatriation.)

For the majority of POWs four long years lay ahead of inadequate food, work for Other Ranks (officers were exempt from work, which gave them ample time to fabricate escape plans), and the monotony and frustration of captivity. With the capitulation of Italy in 1943 the camps in northern Italy were quickly taken over by the Germans and few POWs had the chance to escape. Those who did were invariably sheltered by Italian villagers.

Fewer aircrew than soldiers became prisoners but they were among the liveliest of Germany's unexpected guests. Many RAAF men were incarcerated in a camp at Barth on the Baltic, which in early 1945 held more than 10,000 air force officers — 8000 of them American — and a number of NCOs. Another large RAF and Commonwealth 'Stalag Luft' was at Sagan, near Berlin, where in March 1944, seventy-six Allied air force officers tunnelled their way under the barbed wire in the greatest mass escape of POWs of the war. Among those recaptured, fifty were shot by the Gestapo on Hitler's personal order, including four Australians and two New Zealanders. After the German defeat in 1945 officers of the Judge-Advocate General of the RAF hunted down those responsible and several Nazis were hanged for the crime.

To a castle named Colditz the Germans sent inveterate escapers and prominent captives who might prove useful to them. Even from Colditz some officers escaped.

JAPAN'S EMPIRE

Japan's 'Great East Asia Co-Prosperity Sphere' brought no prosperity to its subjects, only brutality. As early as 12 February 1942 — three days before the capture of Singapore — Emperor Hirohito had summoned Premier Tojo to the Imperial Palace and reminded him 'not to miss any opportunity to terminate the war'. Tojo suggested to Hitler that the Axis approach the Allies to arrange a peace, but Hitler was lukewarm to the idea. Later in 1942 Tojo even asked Admiral Kurusu, who had returned from Washington following the exchange of diplomats, to try to 'arrange the end of the war at an early date'. The old man was astonished, replying simply: 'It is easier to start a war than end one.'

Japan was left with no alternative than to increase its efforts and war production to stave off the inevitable. By early 1943 the loss of Japan's shipping to American submarines operating from their major bases at Fremantle in Western Australia and Hawaii was catastrophic. Obsessed with the strategy of fighting a decisive surface battle, the Imperial Navy was notoriously short of submarines and anti-submarine forces and those they had were ill-trained. On land the position was bleak: a Japanese army of nearly one million men had still not defeated China or brought her to the peace table.

Chinese communities were spread throughout South-East Asia and their hatred for the Japanese was deep. Through the grim years ahead the Chinese were the first to help Allied prisoners with food and to form the core of resistance groups. Harsh treatment of Allied prisoners of war was stipulated by General Tojo. In mid-1942 he informed prison camp commandants that 'it is not necessary to be obsessed with mistaken humanitarian notions' and that prisoners must be made to work for the Emperor.

THE BURMA–THAILAND RAILWAY

In May 1942 the first batch of working parties — 3000 Australians — left camp in Singapore for a destination not disclosed to them. It was the Burma–Thailand railway. In June 1942 the Japanese, concerned about the Allied threat to their shipping to Rangoon and the inadequacy of the roads to southern Burma, began construction of an overland railway to run from Thanbyuzayat in the north in Burma (south of Moulmein) to link up with the Thai railway system 421 kilometres away, at Bampong near Bangkok. Work was to start from each end and meet near Nieke, using as labour local people 'contracted' for the work and promised (but never supplied) good food and pay, and prisoners of war, under the supervision of Japanese engineers and guards. It was to be to be completed by November 1943. The 'Railway of Death' was completed close to schedule, but at enormous cost in human lives and misery. Perhaps as many as 100,000 died on its construction, mainly from diseases such as cholera, beri-beri and dysentery. On its completion British air forces in Burma were active enough to destroy much of the railway in low-level bombing.

THE 'GREATER EAST ASIA CO-PROSPERITY SPHERE'

In 1943 Japan's relations with the conquered countries of South-East Asia changed. Tojo adopted a paternalistic policy, and began this by returning control of the foreign settlements in four Chinese ports, including Tientsin, to their puppet government in Nanking. In March 1943 U Ba Maw, the nationalist leader who had escaped to Japan from a British jail in Burma in 1940, was invited to Tokyo and told that Japan was granting Burma independence by year's end. Ba Maw described members of the Japanese government as 'fine examples and true prophets of the exploding Asian age; dynamic, daring, full of the new Asian consciousness' and quickly drew up a constitution. On 1 August 1943 the Japanese military administration handed over administration to the Burmese.

In July Tojo met in Singapore with Subhas Chandra Bose, the Indian nationalist leader who had once rivalled Gandhi and Nehru in popularity in the Congress Party. Bose had been jailed nine times by the British for his activities — the British took care to treat political detainees and prisoners with great correctness, releasing them to home care if they fell ill — but the shame of prison only intensified Bose's hatred for the arrogance of British rule. He had escaped from home detention to Afghanistan and made his way to Berlin where he attempted to raise an army from captured Indian prisoners of war. Few joined him, but Japan thought he might be more effective in South-East Asia, and he arrived there in a German submarine early in 1943. The forces he raised — the Indian National Army (INA) — were later to fight in Burma under Japanese command. Woefully under-equipped, they were to achieve little.

On 14 October the Japanese-appointed government of the Philippines declared independence and on 5 November 1943 Tojo hosted a great meeting of Asian leaders in Tokyo to implement his new policy of 'Pan-Asianism' and to sign a pact of brotherhood and mutual alliance. Representatives of Burma, the Philippines, Thailand, the puppet rulers of China and Manchukuo and the provisional government of India attended. The only leader not invited was Achmed Sukarno, who had agitated against the Dutch rulers of the East Indies (Indonesia) and regarded himself as leader of the future Indonesia. Tojo explained that the East Indies were too important as sources of raw materials to be granted independence and its people were 'not quite ready to handle all that treasure'. As Japan maintained the fiction of French rule in Indochina, no representatives of her people were invited either. (It was not until their defeat in 1945 that the Japanese encouraged Indonesia and Indochina to declare independence.)

Before following MacArthur to Australia, President Mañuel Quezon had entrusted the government of the Philippines to José Laurel, instructing him to pretend collaboration with the Japanese to lessen the severity of their occupation. But at the Tokyo conference even Laurel got carried away by the significance of the occasion and declaimed: 'One billion Orientals, one billion people of Great East Asia — how could they have been dominated, a great portion of them particularly by England and America? ... God in his infinite wisdom will not abandon Japan and will not abandon the peoples of Greater East Asia.' Other speeches carried the same theme. Asia was being reborn. It was probably the high point of Tojo's career. All Asia was on the march at Japan's side, or seemed to be.

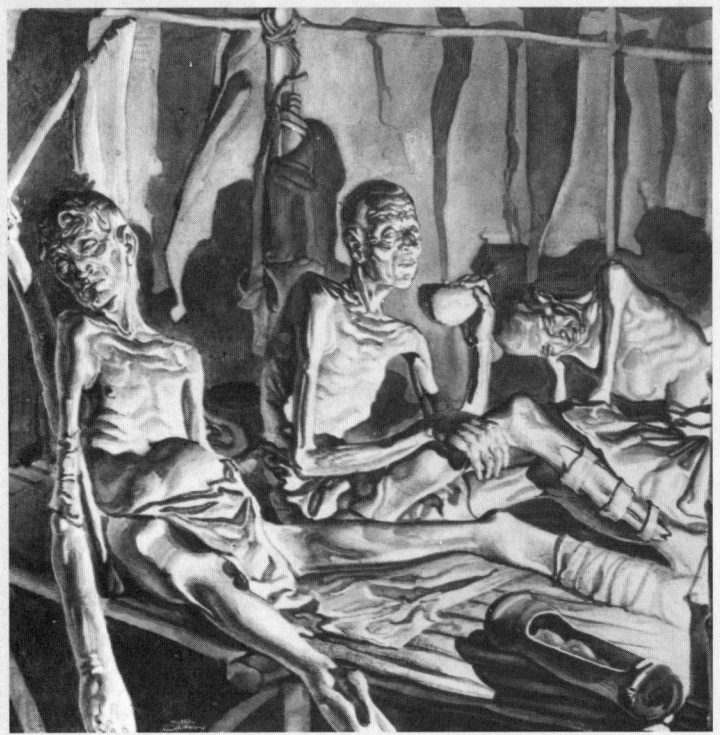

More graphic than any photograph: A painting by an Australian prisoner of war, Murray Griffin, of Australians stricken with illness on the Burma–Thailand railway. From the painting in the Australian War Memorial in Canberra.

PART III
1943–45
THE WAY TO VICTORY

CHAPTER 8
TURNING THE TIDE
1943

On 8 January 1943 three Soviet officers bearing white flags of parley made their way to the German lines in the northern ruins of Stalingrad. They carried an ultimatum for Paulus from General Rokossovski, commanding the Red Army on the Don front. 'The situation of your troops is desperate,' the note ran, 'they are suffering from hunger, sickness and cold ... Your situation is hopeless.' Paulus wirelessed the text of this surrender demand to Hitler and asked for freedom of action to decide his army's fate. His request was denied. On 10 January the Russians launched their last attacks on the German lines. Within a week the Germans were holding only a long pocket of ruins barely 25 kilometres long and 15 kilometres deep. On 24 January the Russians again offered Paulus a chance to surrender. Hitler signalled: 'Surrender is forbidden. Sixth Army will hold their positions to the last man and the last round and by their heroic endurance will make an unforgettable contribution towards the establishment of a defensive front and the salvation of the Western world.'

As the end approached in Stalingrad for the Germans and their allies, Göring broadcast to the German people: 'A thousand years hence Germans will speak of the battle with reverence and awe, and will remember that in spite of everything Germany's ultimate victory was decided there ...' In an equally bizarre action Hitler promoted Paulus to the rank of Field Marshal, explaining that in all German history no holder of that exalted rank had ever surrendered. On the night of 31 January 6th Army's radio operator sent the message; 'The Russians are at the door of the bunker. We are destroying our equipment — ' And then there was silence.

A Russian patrol found Paulus sitting in the gloom of his bunker, too depressed and exhausted to speak. Hitler had expected him to suicide. The great battle of Stalingrad ended in silence.

Of the German army of 285,000 men who had fought at Stalingrad only 91,000 soldiers (among them 24 generals) were still alive to trudge into captivity. Barely 5000 of them survived a typhus outbreak and Soviet ill-treatment to return to Germany twelve years later.

In May 1943, 250,000 Axis troops would be taken prisoner in Tunisia. After three and a half years of constant defeat, the first glimmers of Allied victory were appearing.

When Prime Minister Churchill and President Roosevelt and their chiefs of staff met at Casablanca in mid-January 1943 the whole course of the war had changed dramatically. They could now lay plans for the invasion of Europe itself, once the build-up of American, Canadian and British forces in England made feasible a cross-Channel attack. The invasion of France was slated for May 1944.

Wavell was ordered to launch on offensive from India on the Burma coast in the Arakan (it would be a woeful failure) and in the Pacific the Allies were to plan the seizure of Rabaul and complete the clearing of the Japanese from New Guinea 'in order to retain the initiative and hold Japan.' Admiral King, US Navy Chief of Staff, urged that at least 30 per cent of Allied resources be concentrated in the Pacific for the war against Japan. When MacArthur's plan to

Previous page: Moment of victory: an American and a Russian officer after their armies met up in the middle of Germany, April 1945.
Inset: Badge of the US 5th Army which served throughout the Italian campaign, 1943–45.
Right: Face of defeat: Field-Marshal von Paulus and his officers after the surrender of Stalingrad, January 1943.
Far right: Russian cavalry at full gallop. The Red Army possessed large cavalry forces, but their use in the front line was minimal compared with their propaganda value.

take Rabaul foundered on lack of naval support and landing craft, King won approval for the Commander-in-Chief US Navy Pacific, Admiral Chester Nimitz, to use the major strength of his fleet in seizing the island groups blocking the way to Japan — the Gilberts, Marshalls and Carolines — while Admiral Halsey's ships provided naval support to MacArthur.

At Casablanca it was decided that the bombing campaign against German targets was to be intensified; the growing US Army Air Force in England was to bomb by day, the RAF by night: 'round the clock' strategic bombing which, it was hoped, would break the Germans' will to fight and their industrial capacity. All available resources were to be thrown into the war against the U-boats. Plans were to proceed for a landing in Sicily, to take place once north Africa was secured. On the last day of the conference, having made the two antagonistic symbols of Free France, de Gaulle and Giraud, shake hands in amity before the cameras, Roosevelt announced the Allies' joint resolve to achieve the 'unconditional surrender' of Germany, Japan and Italy, meaning by this not the destruction of their peoples but of the dictators' philosophies, 'based on conquest and subjugation of other peoples'.

LAST ACT IN AFRICA: TUNISIA

But first Tunisia must be cleared of Axis forces. At Casablanca it was decided that General Alexander, who arrived at the conference from the battle front on 15 January, was to take command of both British armies — the 1st and 8th — as Eisenhower's deputy, commanding the operations in Tunisia. Alexander 'made a most favourable impression on the President, who was greatly attracted by him,' wrote his admirer Churchill. 'His easy smiling grace won all hearts. His outspoken confidence was contagious.' Alexander had already established a relationship with Eisenhower based on mutual liking and respect.

On 24 January 1943 the 8th Army entered Tripoli. The next objective was to quickly crush the Axis armies in Tunisia, where the British and American armies advancing from the west were making slow progress in the mud and the mountains. Soon came a rebuff. On 14 February Rommel attacked the American forces at the Kasserine Pass with a strong force of tanks and plunged the US 2 Corps into a chaotic retreat with the loss of 6000 men. 'We have taken a severe licking,' Eisenhower's aide, Captain Harry Butcher, wrote in his diary. Diplomatic by nature, Alexander was privately blunt in his opinion of many of the American troops, whom he described as 'soft, green, and quite untrained. Is it surprising then that they lack the will to fight?' he wrote to Brooke. Visiting British 1st Army headquarters in the north, he was equally critical of General Anderson: 'I am frankly shocked at the whole situation ... Am doubtful if Anderson is big enough for job,' he wrote to Churchill and Brooke; '... hate to disappoint you but final victory in North Africa is not just around the corner'.

Alexander asked Montgomery, advancing in the south, to mount an attack to deflect Axis pressure from the Americans. This he did. 'Well done!' Alexander signalled.

Lieutenant-General George S. Patton, then commanding a Corps in the quiet backwater of Morocco, was ordered to take over 2 Corps on the Kasserine front. He immediately made his presence felt. Tall and impressive, boastful and profane, he was, behind his braggadocio, emotional and sentimental. 'I still get scared under fire, I guess I'll never get used to it,' he confessed in a letter to his wife. Like many Americans such as Joe Stilwell, Patton disliked the British and their air of superiority and doubtful sincerity. 'I think I will have more trouble with the British than with the Boche,' he observed as he left on 6 March for the mountains of Tunisia.

On the same day Rommel attacked Montgomery at Medenine and was shocked to see his attack fail. Montgomery had received warning of the offensive through Ultra decrypts. With 300 tanks in the front, he welcomed an attack and wrote with delight to Brooke that his forces had knocked out more than 50 German tanks and had suffered only 130 casualties. On the same day Rommel left north Africa to take up new duties, entrusting his beloved Afrika Korps and all Axis forces to General von Arnim. Soon von Arnim was to find himself fighting with diminishing resources: Allied air and naval power effectively destroyed any attempt to send him tanks, reinforcements and supplies.

Montgomery in the south was faced with a tough obstacle: the Mareth Line, constructed in the late 1930s by the French to confront any Italian invasion from Libya. It was strongly defended by no fewer than two German infantry divisions, four Italian, and two German Panzer divisions. Montgomery decided to mount a frontal attack as a feint and outflank the line by sending forces on a circuitous 400-kilometre movement around its western flank. For the 'Mareth Left Hook' he chose two of his most resourceful formations, the New Zealanders and General Leclerc's Free French, who had crossed the Sahara to join the British in Tripoli. They would be aided by 8th Armoured Brigade who were faced with the task of pushing tanks through mountainous terrain, and even making their own road. On the night of 20 March Montgomery's guns began their bombardment of the Mareth defences and the outflanking troops moved off on their long march. They were supported by Desert Air Force, whose aircraft effectively eliminated Axis tanks columns in one of the finest examples so far of air force–army cooperation. By 27 March Montgomery could claim victory. He was through the Gabes gap and entered Gabes itself two days later. On 11 April 8th Army linked up with 1st British Army in the north. The two forces hardly recognised each other. Near the end of a 3000-kilometre advance from Egypt, 8th Army's exhausted troops were unshaven, driving vehicles the colour of sand and looked like a bunch of cut-throats. The British 1st Army was spruce in battle dress and green-painted vehicles.

'We were all accustomed to the drab, dull desert scenery. When we passed through the centre of Tunisia and saw fertile valleys, orchards, terraced fields ... we thought we had been transported to Paradise,' an Indian soldier of 8th Army later wrote. 'And then these French people and French children, racing across to our vehicles ... they were very happy.'

A week later Alexander outlined his plans for the final thrust to Tunis: Operation Vulcan. The main attack would be mounted in the north by 1st Army. By 25 April Alexander was able to inform Churchill: 'Enemy continues to resist desperately but this evening there are signs that he is weakening.' Cunningham ordered the fleet to thwart any attempt by the Axis to stage a seaborne evacuation of Tunisia: 'Sink, burn, destroy. Let nothing pass.'

On 6 May Alexander launched his last attack along the Tunis–Medjez road. British tanks entered Tunis and Bizerte next day. On 8 May Alexander cabled Churchill that the Axis forces had 'completely collapsed and disintegrated'. On 12 May von Arnim wirelessed Hitler: 'We have fired our last cartridge. We are closing down forever.' Allied forces took the surrender of 250,000 German and Italian troops. On 13 May Alexander signalled Churchill: 'Sir, it is my duty to inform you that the Tunisian campaign is over. All enemy resistance had ceased. We are masters of the North African shore.'

'And in our ranks the soldiers stripped off their uniforms, washed, and fell asleep in the sun,' wrote Alan Moorehead. 'All Africa was ours.'

VICTORY PARADE

A week later Harold Macmillan, Churchill's political representative stood beside Eisenhower and Alexander to witness the great victory parade in Tunis. The Americans and French had marched past when far off was heard the massed pipers of the Irish regiments and the Scottish Highland Division, leading the British, Indian and New Zealand troops, who marched as if on Horse Guards Parade. Macmillan was near tears at the sight. None of them wore helmets and he could see their proud, suntanned faces. 'All marched magnificently … Some of our generals and colonels are really boys … These men — of this old country — were clearly masters of the world and heirs of the future.' Giraud confessed that in all his life he had never seen such a body of men and to Macmillan afterwards Eisenhower said that 'he had never believed it possible to dream of having such an honour as to command an army like this'.

American troops passing General Eisenhower and his commanders on the reviewing stand, Tunis, May 1943.

AIR WAR, EUROPE

By early 1943 the means were found to achieve victory, in the air as well as in the Atlantic and on the fighting fronts. In February 1942 Air Marshal Arthur Harris, a determined, single-minded leader, was appointed AOC Bomber Command and charged with intensifying the bombing offensive against Germany. The results were shown in May 1942 with the first 'Thousand Bomber Raid' on Bremen and Cologne, a devastating attack that left 250 factories destroyed or damaged. In August 1942 the 8th US Air Force, established on bases in England, began its own offensive against Hitler's Europe, initiating raids by day in B-17s (Flying Fortresses).

As the bomber offensive continued, the scientists began to evolve instruments to improve the precision of night bombing. The Mark XIV bombsight became standard equipment; the radar navigation device, the H2S, which showed 'built-up' areas as a glow on a cathode-ray tube was introduced, along with 'Oboe', a radio-repeater target tracker. German success in jamming 'Gee' and continuing failure of the main bomber force to locate the target saw the formation of a force of 'path finders' in August 1942.

In 1942 Bomber Command lost 1404 aircraft shot down, 2724 damaged, inflicting little damage on Hitler's Europe. This situation would soon change.

THE PATH FINDERS

In 1942 Air Chief Marshal Harris chose as leader of the 'Path Finders' a dynamic, 31-year-old Australian who was already a legend in Bomber Command. The RAAF official history called Donald Bennett 'that brilliant rarity — the almost perfect pilot, navigator and engineer combined' and an 'outstanding leader.' Abrasive, intolerant of failure, Bennett recruited some of the finest pilots in Bomber Command to be first over the target and illuminate it with flares.

The enemy had previously lit fires or released dummy flares to mislead Allied bombers. Now Bennett's 'Pathfinders', aided by their huge Target Indicators, evolved a system of dropping coloured flares to pin-point targets. There were three methods of target-marking: 'Wanganui', when the main force bombed through sky markers; 'Parramatta', when H2S was used; and 'Newhaven', when the bombers simply aimed at the targets indicated on the ground. Losses were high. In their first operation in August 1942, the Pathfinders suffered a 9 per cent loss rate, but the effectiveness of the bomber offensive was to improve dramatically. By 1943 Bennett was using the unarmed, twin-engined, wooden-framed De Havilland 'Mosquito'. He called these fast versatile planes 'the greatest little aircraft ever built'. Mosquitos were later armed with cannon and machine-guns and carried bombs — one of the most adaptable aircraft of the war.

Reichsmarschall Göring was astonished when he inspected a shot-down Mosquito and discovered it was made of wood. After seeing a captured H2S set he described the English as geniuses and told his officers that after the war he intended buying an English radio, because he 'knew that it would work'.

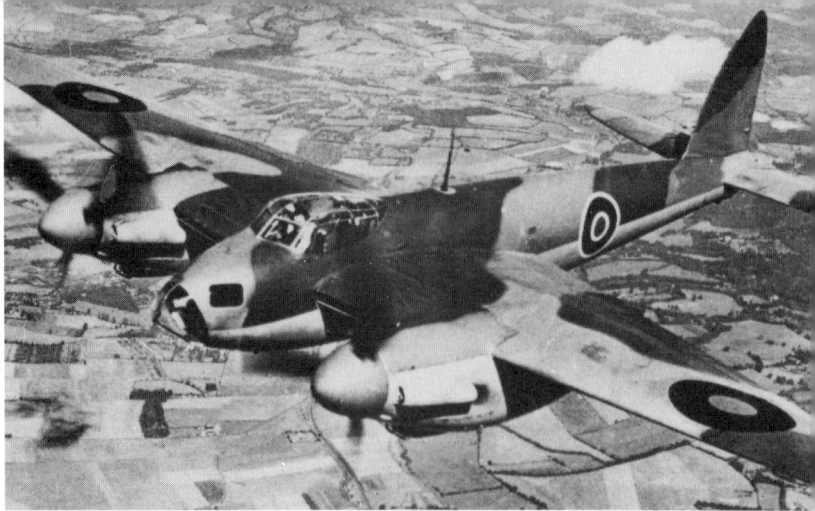

Above top: The astonishing wooden-framed De Havilland Mosquito; light but fast, it could elude enemy fighters.

Above bottom: The jet age begins: first flown in 1943, the British-designed Meteor became, a year later (12 July 1944), the first jet fighter to enter front-line service – only eight days before the Luftwaffe's first jet, the Me 262 appeared.

Opposite: Group-Captain Donald Bennett, the Australian who formed the elite 'Path Finder Force' to lead the bombers to their target.
Above top: Bomber Command, 1943. The strain of war and the mounting losses show on the faces of this Australian crew of a Lancaster bomber.
Above bottom: An Avro Lancaster heavy bomber, 1943. The 'Lancs' were invariably painted black.

BOMBING ROUND THE CLOCK

As a result of decisions reached at the Casablanca conference in January 1943 Allied bombers in England were ordered to concentrate on 'the progressive destruction and dislocation of the German military, industrial and economic system, and the undermining of the morale of the German people to a point where their capacity for armed resistance is fatally weakened'.

'Round-the-clock bombing' began in 1943. In May the US 8th Air Force mounted its first mass daylight raid by 100 Flying Fortresses without fighter protection — they were sitting ducks even at 35,000 feet and even with their armament of eleven machine-guns. In the US 8th Air Force's great attack on the ball-bearing factories at Scheinfurt in Bavaria in October 1943, also mounted without fighter protection, only 30 of the 228 bombers returned unscathed: 62 had been shot down with the loss of 600 aircrew and 138 damaged. After this disaster heavy daylight attacks far into Germany ceased until long-range fighters arrived to fly as escorts. Soon the first of remarkable long-distance P-38 Mustang fighters were escorting the Flying Fortresses, fighting off German fighters on the long approaches to and from the targets.

THE 'LANCASTER' ARRIVES

Bomber Command continued its intensive night bombing and soon had an equally effective weapon. By mid-1943 more than 50 per cent of Bomber Command's front-line strength consisted of a remarkable new heavy bomber, the mighty four-engined Avro Lancaster, which had been phased into service during 1942 to replace the Wellington.

'The Lanc' has been called one of the greatest aircraft ever made, and more than 7000 of them were built. Evolving from the ill-starred two-engined Manchester, it was powered by four Rolls Royce Merlin engines, possessed an airframe strong enough to carry a 22,000 lb (10,000-kilo) bomb load (a feat beyond the capacity even of a Flying Fortress), was capable of flying long distances (4000 kilometres carrying a 3400-kilo load), and could reach a speed of 287 mph at 11,500 feet. In addition, it was astonishingly tough and manoeuvrable; one New Zealander brought his Lancaster back from a mission with its two starboard engines dead.

AIR BATTLE OVER GERMANY

The Battle of the Ruhr began on the night of 5 March 1943 with a raid on Essen by 412 aircraft. The glow from the devastated city could be seen 250 kilometres away. Between March and July 1943 Bomber Command suffered 6000 casualties; 800 of its bombers were shot down and another 2126 were damaged. Dogged by German night-fighters and armed only with .303 callibre machine-guns, they limped home or crash-landed.

'The losses were almost too terrible to contemplate. Fed to the public in small underplayed doses, they seemed insignificant in relation to the retributive effort,' wrote Alastair Revie in his study of the bomber offensive. 'Apart from the wholesale decimation of the flower of Bomber Command's young manhood, these losses were insupportable.' The daily prospect of sudden death was now paramount among the front line crews.' Bomber aircrew suffered higher casualties and won more decorations for gallantry in relation to their number than any other arm of the forces.

Dusseldorf was hammered in May and June 1943. In July and August 75 per cent of the residential area of Hamburg was destroyed and Hanover was plastered. Between April and June 1943 Bomber Command flew a total of 11,000 sorties against the Ruhr. In November 1943 Harris ordered: 'Target Berlin.' He could not have picked a more difficult target. The capital of the Reich lay 600 miles (1000 kilometres) from England and every air mile was pregnant with the danger of night fighters and flak. The five-month offensive almost destroyed Bomber Command. Between November 1943 and March 1944, losses amounted to 1128 bombers and crews.

Two examples provide a picture of the losses suffered. Between March and July 1943, 460 Squadron RAAF flew more than 600 sorties and lost 29 bombers. Starting its history with a dozen bombers this remarkable Australian squadron was to lose 100 in the course of the war. Between January 1943 and February 1944, 75 (NZ) Squadron lost 50 Stirlings; rearmed with Lancasters it lost another 32 aircraft.

Of this period, British fighter pilot John Colville wrote: 'I was distressed by the tense bearing and drawn faces of the bomber crews. At that time, late in November 1943, some 80 per cent were failing to complete unscathed their tour of 30 operations. Of courage they had plenty; but there was nothing but lip-biting gloom registered on those faces.' More than 170,000 young Allied airmen were to die in the air battles in Europe. Of the Commonwealth pilots in his fighter squadron Colville wrote: 'I was attracted by the individualist personalities of the Australians. Many of the Canadians, brave, friendly and resourceful though they were, seemed by contrast to have a rubber-stamped outlook and upbringing ...'

'How much fun was made of the enemy's backwardness!' Göring shouted to his Luftwaffe chiefs in March 1943. 'Make no mistake, gentlemen, the British are going from strength to strength with their much-mocked "four-engined crates" or whatever fine adjectives you dream up for them. He is going to take city after city. It makes no difference to him. He flies with the same navigation to Munich or Berlin, he can fly as far as Warsaw or Vienna ... It makes me furious to see a Mosquito! I turn green and yellow with envy. The British, who can afford aluminium better than we, knock together a beautiful wooden aircraft, and give it a speed which they have now increased again!'

Opposite top inset: Allied air force commanders over-estimated the effectiveness of low-level bombing raids and under-estimated the losses aircrews faced by anti-aircraft fire, enemy fighters, confusion and collisions. This American raid on the Ploesti oil wells in Romania in 1943 resulted in calamitous aircraft losses.
Opposite bottom inset: B-17 Flying Fortress over Europe.
Opposite The 'Mighty Eighth': bomber crews of the US 8th Air Force, based in England, which carried out the major American air offensive in north-west Europe.

THE BATTLE OF THE ATLANTIC: WINNING

In the first three months of 1942 the German submarine peril reached its height. U-boats sank 216 ships, mainly off the Gulf of Mexico and the American east coast; submarine skippers called it a 'duck shoot'. Admiral King in Washington resisted diverting his naval forces to convoy protection and American seamen paid the price for his obtuseness. When convoys and strong escorts were instituted, losses fell. At this time Admiral Doenitz had a strength of 250 U-boats, only 91 of which were operational, the balance being in training. He was to build 1000 — and lose nearly all of them by war's end, but in 1942 he came close to achieving victory.

'During the first six months of 1942 the sinkings of British and Allied vessels were nearly as heavy as for the whole of 1941 and exceeded the whole Allied shipbuilding programme by nearly three million tons,' Churchill wrote in his memoirs, in describing the threat to the Allied lifeline by the U-boats.

But while the strategic bombing of Germany was growing in strength, the battle against the U-boats was slowly being won by the Allied navies and aircraft, with Coastal Command in the forefront, across the Atlantic lifeline. Air cover could protect Allied shipping for only 600 miles (1000 km) at each end of the Atlantic's breadth and by 1942 the U-boats were hunting in packs. Coastal Command was also called on to give protection to the Arctic convoys to Russia that were falling prey to German aircraft, submarines and warships based in northern Norway. In August 1942 sixteen Hampdens of 455 Squadron RAAF flew to Murmansk, two of them crashing in Norway en route,

Above: **Admiral Karl Doenitz, commander of the German U-boat fleet, awards decorations to a returning submarine crew. Doenitz was chosen by Hitler to succeed him as leader in 1945.**
Left: **Shipwrecked survivors of a torpedoed Allied ship.**

to join the force patrolling the Barents Sea. On its return this squadron was to join a New Zealand squadron in the famed 'Anzac Strike Wing'; wreaking havoc on German shipping in the North Sea.

To counter the Atlantic U-boats Britain originally had two measures — strongly escorted convoys and 'hunter' ships equipped with Asdic, which detected the presence of objects underwater. As submarines had to surface at least once every twenty-four hours to recharge their batteries, Coastal Command aircraft, including the Australian Sunderland flying boat squadrons, were fitted in 1942 with 'Leigh Lights' — lamps connected to radar that detected submarines on the surface. In the summer of 1941 the Royal Navy installed a new radar system, Type 271. A further development was HDF, which enabled the hunters to pin-point U-boats' whereabouts from the briefest of radio messages. U-boat codes — their settings were changed every twenty-four hours — were not decoded until 1941 with the capture by a British landing crew of the code-books of the foundering *U-110*. But by 1942 Admiral Doenitz had in turn broken the Royal Navy's codes, enabling him to locate Allied convoys.

The British navy relied on depth charges capable of destroying a submarine if exploding within 8 metres of its hull and 'Hedgehogs' — mortars firing twenty-four depth-charges at once. Coastal Command maintained its long patrols over the choppy waters of the Bay of Biscay where the long-distance B-24 Liberator bomber could now patrol the mid-Atlantic 'gap'.

During 1943 the U-boat packs — sometimes of up to thirty-nine boats — began facing Allied counter-measures so effective that the chances of survival for U-boat crew were one in six. The Schnorkel, which allowed the boats to stay underwater permanently, arrived too late to tip the scales. And the Allies were hunting them with their own wolf packs of destroyers and frigates whose Asdic operators waited for the tell-tale 'ping' in their headphones that revealed a submerged submarine.

In May 1943 a total of forty-three German submarines were sunk and in six days in late July sixteen U-boats were sunk by air and naval attack, nine of them in the Bay of Biscay; of these, three were sunk in one day in an action called 'the most successful battle in the whole campaign'. It all began on 31 July 1943 when a British-manned Liberator radioed a sighting of three surfaced U-boats, two them large tanker 'milch cows'. The call quickly homed in a Catalina, two Halifaxes, an American Liberator and a Sunderland of 461 Squadron RAAF piloted by a 22-year-old Australian. The U-boats zig-zagged and poured a torrent of gunfire at their assailants but one submarine was damaged; two aircraft were hit before the Australian pilot made his run, flying so low that he nearly grazed the U-boat's conning tower, and dropping seven depth charges, which sank the sub in an exploding tower of foam. By a weird coincidence aircraft U-461 had sunk submarine *U-461*; one of the Halifaxes then sank a second sub.

By mid-1943 the mighty battle was almost won. Allied convoys could bring with relative impunity the millions of American troops and the armaments and supplies needed for the invasion and liberation of Europe. This battle of fluctuating intensity had cost the lives of 30,000 Allied seamen and 28,000 German U-boat crews. A total of 2282 ships and more than 700 U-boats were sunk. Surface raiders remained a threat, especially to the Arctic convoys. At the end of March 1943 Churchill informed Stalin that British Intelligence (from Norwegian agents) had reported that the *Tirpitz, Scharnhorst, Lutzow* and nine other warships were in Narvik fjord, posing so serious a threat to shipping that the latest convoy had been cancelled.

SCHARNHORST AND *TIRPITZ*

In December 1943 Enigma decrypts revealed that the *Scharnhorst* was on the prowl off Norway. The Home Fleet under Admiral Sir Bruce Fraser steamed to intercept her and caught up with her in the waters off northern Norway. On 27 December 1943, in the 'Battle of North Cape' — a night battle lit by star shells — *Scharnhorst* was devastated by the powerful guns of the battleship *Duke of York* and was finished off with torpedos.

Now only *Tirpitz* remained a deadly threat. Crippled during 1943 by midget submarine attacks, in 1944 the 'unsinkable' super-battleship moored in her Norwegian fjord was attacked by the Dam Busters (617 Squadron RAF), who dropped armour-piercing bombs on her from a height of 14,000 feet. *Tirpitz* turned turtle and sank, entombing 1000 sailors. There was now nothing left of Hitler's surface fleet.

Heavy seas: A British K-Class destroyer in the Atlantic.

Russian troops follow their tanks into battle. Russia's losses were massive but could always be replaced.

EASTERN FRONT: KURSK

In mid-February 1943, only a fortnight after Stalingrad had fallen, the Germans evacuated Kharkov. In just three months the Russians had pushed back the German front nearly 300 kilometres. But their advance was now ebbing. Hitler flew to the front, and ordered Kharkov retaken. He had appointed Guderian Inspector General of armoured forces, which during 1942 had undergone an extensive overhaul. Most Panzer divisions now had as few as 100 tanks — less than one-quarter of their strength a year earlier. Guderian pleaded with Hitler to restore the Panzer divisions to full strength — if necessary by withdrawing self-propelled guns from infantry divisions — rather than create new, under-strength ones, but he was rebuffed.

Hitler placed much faith in the new breed of 'super tanks' now emerging from German factories — the Tigers and Panthers, which carried guns comparable to the deadly 76-mm guns of the Russian T34 tanks — and self-propelled guns (heavy artillery mounted on the chassis of tanks). During 1943 Germany would produce 6000 tanks but Russia would produce 11,000. No amount of ingenuity could reverse the imbalance, and Guderian soon had to contend with the crazy ideas of the sports car designer Dr Ferdinand Porsche to construct a tank weighing 180 tonnes — three times the size of the Tiger. Porsche also received the Führer's assent to produce a 'giant Tiger' armed with a 100-mm cannon and which he named after himself — the 'Ferdinand'. Only 90 were built.

The Tiger tanks, 60 tonnes in weight, with tracks so broad that they could travel over the roughest ground, were to make their first appearance in battle in the counter offensive near Kharkov, which began on 21 February 1943. Their appearance marked, in one historian's words, 'the end of the Russian tank's role as the undisputed queen of the battlefield', and also made the tank most widely used by the Allied armies — the Sherman — almost obsolete.

The Russians evacuated Kharkov in mid-March, after losing 30,000 men (very few of whom were prisoners) and more than 600 tanks. The German line was now re-established to where it had been in the previous summer. Manstein now laid plans to remove the Soviet salient at Kursk, but the attack was postponed. Hitler apparently hoped the line established would remain permanent. His intimates noticed that he no longer sketched out wild strategic dreams. He had run out of ideas. They noticed that he had aged, and his hands often shook.

Guderian's rival Kluge championed the plan to pinch out the Kursk salient by massive use of armour, spearheaded by the Tiger tanks. Hitler hesitated to give a decision, and even Manstein suggested that any date after April would be hazardous. Guderian was left almost alone in opposition to the offensive. Speer, the new director of armaments, explained that production difficulties were delaying the delivery of the Tigers, but more than 300 of them would be ready by the end of May. With every delay, Russian defences were strengthening.

The Kursk offensive, codenamed 'Citadel', was launched on 4 July 1943 when 2000 German tanks rolled forward north and south of the salient. Their attacking spearheads — Tigers forming the tips — found well-entrenched Russian defences bristling with artillery and anti-tank guns and the Germans suffered heavy losses. Russian tank strength stood at 3600 and behind the forward defence lines Zhukov had gathered his entire reserves — three armies — ready to plug any gaps. None were made. By the end of the first day the Soviet defences had been barely dented and Stalin received the heart-warming signal 'The Tigers are burning'. By 12 July most of the Tigers were destroyed and the Germans were down to 600 tanks, nearly all of which were knocked out in one last savage day of fighting. The German offensive had been repulsed.

Kursk was the last German offensive on the Eastern Front. From that day onwards Germany would be fighting a delaying action against Soviet strength, and most of Hitler's entourage knew the war was lost.

A Red Army mortar battery.

1943: SICILY — THE 'SOFT UNDERBELLY'

On 9 July 1943 an Italian Military Intelligence summary stated: 'An Anglo-Saxon offensive in the Mediterranean is imminent. The enemy attack with massive quantities of equipment and men will be directed most likely against our islands, especially Sardinia, in the Aegean, on the French coast, the Spanish peninsula … and on the coast of northern Europe.' An invasion of Greece was unlikely, it stated, because of strong German reinforcements recently sent there. Early on the next day Allied forces landed in Sicily, where they were least expected. After four years of war, it was the first breach in Hitler's Fortress Europe.

PLANNING 'OPERATION HUSKY'

Allied Intelligence and deception planning had been brilliant, successfully duping the Axis powers into thinking the Allies were intending to invade Sardinia or Greece. In London the 'Double-Cross' Committee devised a macabre plan to deflect German attention from Sicily. On 30 April 1943 the body of a Royal Marine officer was dropped from a British submarine off the Spanish coast at Huelva, and carried ashore by the waves. When the Spanish opened the briefcase they found papers relating to the coming Allied landings in Sardinia and Greece, photographed them and promptly forwarded the copies to German Intelligence. On 12 May Hitler, who was delighted by the discovery of Allied plans, ordered defences in the Balkans to be strengthened, concluding his directive: 'Measures regarding Sardinia and the Peloponnese take precedence over everything else.' When the Allies bombarded the tiny island of Pantellaria south of Sicily in June and took its immediate surrender, Axis Intelligence suspected it was a diversion. Field Marshal Rommel was ordered to take command of German armies in Greece to prepare for the coming invasion.

The whole thing was a hoax. The dead staff officer, Major Martin, was 'the man who never was'. His body was that of a nameless man who had died of pneumonia in a London hospital. The 'top secret' papers in his briefcase were forged by the British.

But planning for the Sicily invasion — 'Operation Husky' — had been stormy and protracted. The first plans, calling for multiple landings along the Sicily coast, had been drawn up by Alexander's staff in the closing weeks of the Tunis campaign (April 1943). Montgomery described them as a 'dog's breakfast' and a 'hopeless mess' and informed Alexander that he intended to draw up his own invasion plan that would land 8th Army in the south-east of the island, near Syracuse. This plan was ultimately accepted. It relegated Patton's US 7th Army to a subsidiary role: they would land on the south coast near Gela. Patton, who had hoped to make a spectacular landing in the north-west and seize Palermo, was incensed at the secondary role assigned to American forces. Allied strategy viewed the seizure of airfields in the south of the island as essential, for northern Sicily was beyond the range of the air forces in Malta and Tunisia.

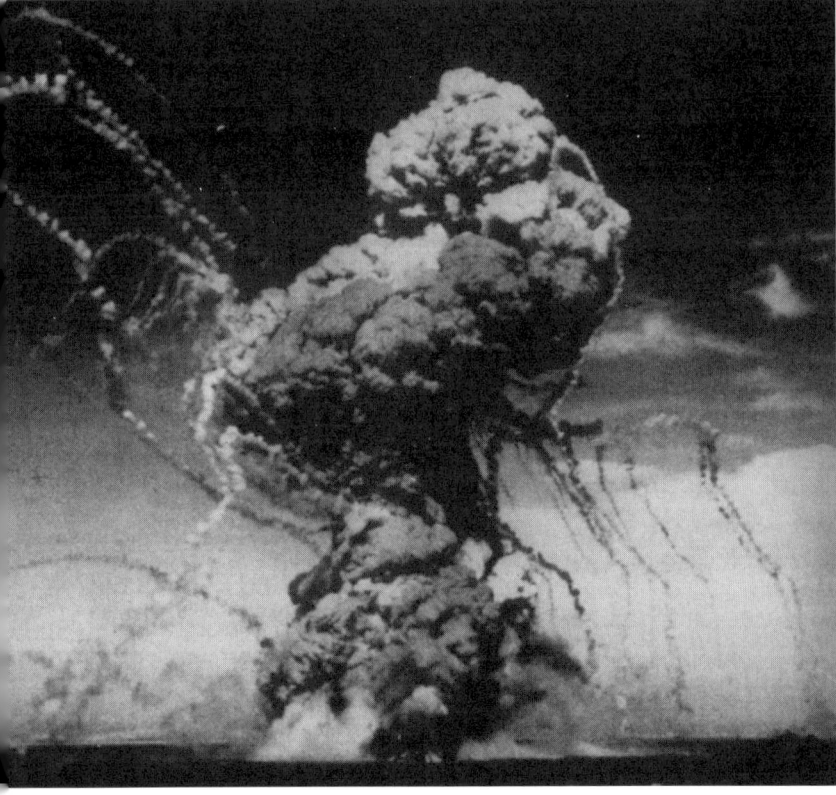

It was the first Allied invasion to make use of the extraordinary amphibious vehicles — DUKWs, known as 'Ducks', for they could waddle onto land — and paratroops. Confidence at Allied HQ on the eve of the invasion was high. It was believed that seven Italian divisions were garrisoning the island, but strong resistance was envisaged only from the two German divisions, identified as the 15th Panzer Grenadier and the Hermann Göring. Three days before D-Day Patton, visiting the crammed harbours, was astonished by the size of the invasion fleets, and typically issued a rousing Order of the Day to his troops: 'When we land we will meet German and Italian soldiers whom it is our honour and privilege to attack and destroy … the glory of American arms, the honour of our country, the future of the whole world rests in your individual hands. See that you are worthy of this great trust. God is with us. We shall win.'

On Malta, the Allied commanders gathered. In the afternoon of 9 July Eisenhower was with Cunningham as weather reports came in of a mounting storm with 40-knot winds. The great invasion armada was already at sea and was the largest assembled to date by the Allies — 3000 ships and landing craft, including 1200 warships, carrying American troops from Algerian and Moroccan ports and Montgomery's British forces from Tunis — a total of seven divisions numbering in all 160,000 men, with 600 tanks. American war correspondent John Gunther was particularly impressed by Alexander's serene bearing: 'He listens well and thinks carefully before he talks … When you mention Montgomery to people, they may curse or grin,' Gunther related. 'Every time I asked anybody about Alexander, I got a reaction of pleasure, genuine warmth, and admiration.' Eisenhower and Alexander went out in the evening of 9 July to a high point above Valetta harbour to watch the Allied airborne forces leave. More than sixty planes and gliders could be seen, picked out by searchlights. 'It was blowing hard and the roar of the aircraft towing the gliders was partly carried away.' As night progressed, the winds dropped, the storms abated and Eisenhower said a silent prayer for his men.

THE LANDINGS

The Allied airborne landings began disastrously. Dozens of gliders were fired on mistakenly by Allied gunners, the strong winds carried many off target and some crashed into the sea, while others made it to Sicily but were landed on a front of 100 kilometres in the southeast of the island.

But the amphibious landings went smoothly: by late afternoon Gela was in Allied hands and the Italian coastal defence unit at Augusta blew up its guns without firing a single shell. Montgomery's 8th Army, including the 1st Canadian Division (in action for the first time in the war) advanced north against minimal opposition while Axis counterattacks were hitting the Americans savagely at Gela,

Left top: Canadian infantry (1st Division) on a troop ship en route to the Sicily landings.
Left: An American ammunition ship takes a direct hit and explodes off the Italian coast.

where for three days the position was critical. Allied warships joined in the barrage of shelling to break the Axis attacks and on 12 July General Guzzoni, commanding all Axis forces in Sicily, began withdrawing to the north-east of the island. There the Germans would put up the toughest fighting of the campaign. On 13 July Mussolini, who described the situation as 'serious and delicate but not desperate', met with General Kesselring, who undertook to send two more German divisions to Sicily, though all realised that these were insufficient to defend the island. The Allies were landing four more divisions.

On the following day General Ambrosio submitted a frank memorandum to the Duce. 'It is useless to search for the causes of this state of affairs. They are the result of three years of war, begun with scanty means, and during which [our] few resources have been burned up in Africa, in Russia and in the Balkans …' He suggested that Italy would require strong German reinforcements to hold the enemy at bay.

Meanwhile the Allies made good progress in Sicily. When Montgomery, attempting to outflank stiffening resistance and take Catania on the mid-east coast, advanced his forces into the American sector, using Route 124, Patton was incensed. The action confirmed his suspicion that the British were stealing his thunder and on 17 July he flew back to Alexander's HQ in north Africa to present his case. Alexander gave him permission to fight his own battle. 'Once loosed, Patton drove his 7th Army as a man possessed,' writes one British historian. 'He took Palermo in a short five-day campaign and then received Alexander's permission to turn eastwards to come up on Montgomery's northern flank for a combined assault on the Etna line and an advance on Messina along the north coast. The American Army had proved itself both in its own eyes and to the world at large. Alexander was never again to make the mistake of underestimating the Americans.'

The chivalrous knight and the Napoleonic marshal: General Sir Harold Alexander (left) with his American subordinate commanding US 7th Army, Lt.-General George S. Patton on the eve of the Sicily invasion. On right is Admiral Kent Hewitt, US Navy.

'Most of the way it was as pleasant a campaign as one is likely to find in war,' wrote a young paratroop commander in 82nd Airborne, Brigadier-General Max Taylor, whose men fought as infantry in the advance and found little resistance from the Italians they faced. His division lost 200 killed in Sicily but took 20,000 Italian prisoners. Patton's divisions — in particular the 2nd Armoured and the 3rd Infantry — moved as if he had lit a fire beneath them. The footsloggers of the 3rd marched 160 kilometres in 72 hours, as the tanks tore past them in clouds of dust and choking heat. Palermo fell to American troops on 21 July, when they entered to the cheers of the Sicilians, and two days later Patton entered the city, taking up residence in the Royal Palace and receiving the cardinal of Palermo like a Renaissance king. On the next day he boasted to war correspondents that his army had captured 40,000 Italians and that future students of war 'will study the campaign as a classic example of the use of tanks'.

In early August both Allied armies began their attack on the Etna line. In Sicily Alexander was faced by a duplicate of the Tunisia campaign: American forces in the west, British in the south advancing against a German-Italian army retreating to the north-east sector where hopefully he would take their surrender. Hitler, realising that Italian assistance was illusory, ordered his forces to evacuate Sicily but they carried out a masterly fighting retreat, gradually shrinking their perimeter around Messina, launching heavy counterattacks, detonating roads and bridges sufficiently to slow down the Allied impetus. Montgomery took Catania on 4 August but German reinforcements were fed into Sicily until 11 August when their evacuation began. Alexander had asked Cunningham and Tedder to do their utmost to destroy the evacuating forces, but nothing was done. 'It was not until 14 August that anyone on the Allied side realised what was happening.' Late on 16 August Patton's forces reached the outskirts of Messina, much of which was in ruins, to more cheers from the populace. On 17 August, when the German commander left Sicily, all his forces had been evacuated across the Straits of Messina, complete with their equipment, tanks and guns, without hindrance from Allied air or naval forces. On the same day Patton drove into Messina to stage a triumphal parade but found a small group of British tanks there already.

It was the height of Patton's fame, but within a month he was in disgrace. On 3 August he had visited a hospital full of his wounded, an experience that always affected him deeply, and was outraged to find there a soldier who was apparently unwounded, but whose nerves had gone. Patton slapped his face and a week later, on looking into another hospital, he shouted at and slapped another GI who confessed his nerves had gone. 'I won't have these brave boys seeing such a bastard babied,' Patton shouted at the hospital commander. Arriving at Bradley's HQ at 2 Corps Patton boasted of his action and Bradley was horrified. Reports of the incidents quickly reached Eisenhower, who was as incensed as Bradley that a senior general had acted brutally towards an enlisted man. He valued Patton more than any of his generals but ordered him to apologise personally to both the soldiers — and in public to all the men in his command. A month later Patton heard that his subordinate Omar Bradley, whom he thought cautious and timid, had been appointed to command American ground forces in the projected invasion of northern Europe. He thought his own career was over.

The battle for Sicily was less than a complete victory, but its political repercussions were enormous and Patton's was not the only reputation it affected. It led directly to the fall of Mussolini and of Fascism.

Scottish infantry (51st Highland Division) in Sicily, 1943.

THE FALL OF MUSSOLINI

In late July 1943 the city of Rome lay under sweltering summer heat. On 19 July the Allies had mounted their first heavy air raid on Rome, a city the Romans felt was inviolate as the seat of the Holy See. Many Romans left the capital. By early afternoon the streets of Rome were almost deserted as its remaining citizens sought some relief from the heat. But in the royal palace, army headquarters and the homes of Fascist leaders Rome was alive with rumours, plans and plots. It was said that Mussolini, depressed about the collapse of Italian resistance in Sicily, was contemplating resigning, for reports of Sicilians welcoming American and British troops as liberators could no longer be kept from the people. Other rumours ran that the King was planning to appoint the ageing Orlando, Italy's Prime Minister in 1919, or Marshal Badoglio — or even Graziani — in the Duce's place. At night Mussolini read the transcripts of telephone intercepts from his Secret Service but apparently placed little credence in the gossip of his government members or of the leaders whom he had removed from positions of power.

Among the leading plotters was Dino Grandi, who had written from Bologna to both Mussolini and King Victor Emmanuel that the Fascist Grand Council should be convened to discuss a complete reform of the way Italy was conducting the war: Mussolini must give up his one-man rule. Count Galeazzo Ciano also saw the removal of the dictator and breaking the alliance with Germany as Italy's only hope of salvation. On 21 July the King's equerry, the Duke of Acquarone, informed Senise that His Majesty was intending to carry out a coup, replacing Mussolini with Marshal Badoglio.

Even the plotters were astonished on 22 July 1943 when Mussolini announced that the Fascist Grand Council would be convened at the Palazzo Venezia at 5 p.m. on 24 July. It had not met since December 1939. They had just two days in which to decide their course of action. On the morning of 24 July General Castellano visited the Chief of the Carabinieri, and outlined plans to arrest Mussolini and leading Fascists. One of Ciano's protégés, a dynamic young general, Carboni, commanding the Motorised Corps, was ordered to bring his units near to Rome; Field Marshal Kesselring at his headquarters at Frascati was assured that it was a measure to defend the city against Allied invasion.

As Mussolini left his villa his wife pleaded with him not to go. She had premonitions that their son-in-law Ciano was plotting against him. He brushed aside her warnings. He would allow his critics to ask their questions and he would answer them, and he expected a long session. He arrived to find his bodyguard absent. The Duce's private secretary had informed their commander, Galbiati, that they would not be needed. 'The square in front of the palace was almost deserted on the hot summer afternoon except for a few plain clothes detectives,' one historian writes. As the meeting began Mussolini, dressed in his black Militia uniform, took his place on the raised dais covered with red brocade from where he had dictated Italy's destiny, with his two oldest colleagues, Marshal de Bono and De Vecchi, on his right, party secretary Scorza on his left. His council sat below him. They were more nervous than their Duce.

This Italian propaganda poster sought to rally the people around King Victor Emmanuel and Mussolini. By 1943, neither figure aroused respect among Italians.

Ciano had come armed with a hand grenade and had given a second one to De Vecchi. Grandi, who had been to confession, would table his demands for change during the meeting.

Mussolini began a long speech reviewing the errors of the past, listing the ways Germany had helped Italy, and denied that he had usurped others' authority. 'No war is popular when it starts. It becomes popular if it ends in victory,' he assured his listeners, and confessed: 'And at this moment I am the most despised and hated man in Italy, but the time has come to tighten the reins.' His talk rambled for nearly two hours, before he called for others to speak. Bottai warned that the Anglo-Americans were intent on occupying Rome — 'the home of Fascism' — and told Mussolini: 'Your speech destroyed our last illusions. The war has gone badly because you, isolated from us, haven't been capable of commanding nor of having yourself obeyed by the Chiefs of the Armed Forces.' Grandi then rose. He demanded that the King be asked to assume effective command of the armed forces, and launched into a bitter condemnation of Mussolini's rule which, he said, had 'lasted too long and with its degeneration has changed the face of its leader, has destroyed and killed Fascism'. Grandi spoke for an hour, declaring: 'The responsibility for this disaster lies not with Fascism, but with the dictatorship.' Bottai and then Ciano spoke, the latter claiming that Germany had betrayed Italy. Only Farinacci, most ardent of Fascists, spoke for a strengthening of ties with Germany. By midnight all were exhausted by the atmosphere, heat and nervous tension. During a brief respite Grandi handed Mussolini his resolution, which carried the signatures of nineteen of those present. Buffarini implored the

Duce: 'Arrest them all. It is a plot.' But Mussolini returned to the chamber and called for a vote. At 2.40 a.m. on 25 July Grandi's motion was approved by nineteen votes to seven.

Mussolini returned to his villa having informed Scorza that he would see the King next day and ask that Marshal Graziani be appointed one of his 'military ministers', in the hope that a restructuring of the government would strengthen Italy's will to win. While he slept fitfully, the plotters informed the King of Grandi's move, and planned to arrest the dictator next day after he left his audience with the monarch.

Mussolini arrived at the King's villa at 5 p.m. on Sunday 25 July. His escort, three carloads of plainclothes police, parked outside the gates. Mussolini began describing the meeting when the King suddenly broke in: General Puntoni, in the next room, heard the murmur of voices and the King's words: 'Things are not going well. Italy is in pieces, soldiers don't want to fight and the vote — the Grand Council vote — was dreadful … I must ask you to leave your post so that I can be free to entrust the government to others.'

Mussolini was dumbfounded. When the King added 'I think the man for the present situation is Marshal Badoglio', Mussolini slumped into a chair, murmuring 'Then it's all over.' The King sought to console him: 'I'm sorry, but the solution couldn't have been otherwise.' The meeting had taken twenty minutes.

The King saw Mussolini to the door and shook hands with him. As Mussolini descended the front steps of the palace a captain of Carabinieri saluted him and said: 'Duce, I have been ordered by the King to protect your person. Please follow me.' Mussolini protested weakly and was escorted to a waiting ambulance in which, guarded by six policemen, he was sped through the streets of Rome to the prison at Trastevere. He was soon transferred to the Carabinieri barracks and then to an island where he had sentenced his political foes, and where, like many of them, he proceeded to write his memoirs, justifying his actions and damning his enemies. Later still he was moved to a ski resort in the Apennines, where he lived on a diet of grapes and milk, played cards, and gossiped with his guards.

By 5.30 p.m. the key members of Mussolini's government had also been arrested and were under detention, and Badoglio was arriving at the King's villa to be appointed Prime Minister. He spoke on the wireless later that night, informing Italians that he had been appointed Mussolini's successor. One of his first acts was to declare the dissolution of the Fascist Party. By nightfall crowds were massing in the streets of every city and town in Italy, celebrating the fall of Fascism. It had collapsed without a shot. Other crowds went in search of Fascists, who quickly shed their party badges; a mob stormed the Fascist headquarters in Rome, which was undefended, and burned its contents, a sad loss to historians. Some Germans, thinking the war was over, joined in the celebrations. Going to bed that night the anti-Fascist philosopher and writer Benedetto Croce, who had compiled the *Italian Encyclopaedia* (one of the few worthwhile initiatives of Mussolini) wrote: 'The sensation I feel is that of a liberation from a sickness which burdened the mind.'

Romans awoke next day to a carnival atmosphere. Flags hung from balconies. Anti-Fascists climbed up the facade of buildings and smashed the Fascist emblems. In the north, Communists came out of hiding and liberated prisoners.

In his broadcast to Italians Badoglio had told them that 'the war continues', but when Hitler heard the news of Mussolini's fall he exploded in fury, describing the Italians as traitors, and shouting: 'What's-his-name said straight away that the war would be continued but that doesn't mean a thing. We can play the same game.' He ordered that German troops take over Italy, occupy Rome, liberate the Duce — and even invade the Vatican, where he suspected plots were hatched and his enemies given refuge: 'We'll take right over — the whole diplomatic corps … that riff-raff. We'll get the whole bunch of swine out of there. Later we can say we're sorry.' He was talked out of these measures. Goebbels, more soberly, wrote: 'It's simply shocking to think that a revolutionary movement which had been in power for 21 years could be liquidated just like that.'

AFTER THE FALL

There is an air of farce about the fall of Mussolini and the 'Forty-Five Days' that followed. In Rome Badoglio was faced with the problem of constructing a government free of Fascists but acceptable to Hitler. Of his sixteen ministers, ten had served in Mussolini's government and three had been senators under Fascism. Badoglio totally ignored them, proclaiming martial law and a dusk-to-dawn curfew, and declaring that any act of public disturbance would be regarded as treason. Italians had tasted complete freedom for just one day. Anti-fascists were freed and allowed to return home but thousands of Communists were still held behind bars. Ciano was one who wisely decided to leave Rome, and German forces began entering Italy in such numbers that the Italian high command protested.

Badoglio initiated contact with the Allies. In the first week of August 1943 one emissary, an Italian marquess, saw the British ambassador to Portugal, who reported to Churchill that the Italian prophesied Communist uprisings in Italy, which would give the Germans an excuse to intervene, that he 'never from start to finish made any mention of peace terms' and that his whole story was 'no more than a plea that we should save Italy from the Germans as well as from herself and do it as completely as possible.' Badoglio sent another emissary to make contact with the British consul in Tangier who, after secret meetings that could have been scripted for a Hollywood spy film, reminded the emissary that the Allies demanded Italy's unconditional surrender. A young general named Castellano, who spoke English perfectly, offered to contact the Allies in Lisbon; when he left Italy by train on Friday 13 August the Germans already knew the purpose of his mission.

In Italy the charade of Axis cooperation continued. When General Zeitzler heard that the Italian high command was concentrating a division at the Brenner Pass — Germany's gateway to Italy — and was withdrawing its 4th Army from southern France and divisions from the Balkans, Hitler ordered his staff to confront the Italians.

A suspected Fascist is arrested by Italians in the days immediately after Mussolini's fall.

Pietro Badoglio, Marshal of Italy, Duke of Addis Adaba who supplanted Mussolini in power in 1943.

On 15 August General Roatta met Jodl at Bologna. Jodl asked the Italian Chief of Staff bluntly if the troops being moved to northern Italy were to be used against the Allies or the Germans, Roatta indignantly replied that such a question was an insult to Italy's honour.

Churchill cabled General Alexander that discussions were proceeding with General Castellano about Italy's surrender and urged him to make the most of the situation. Churchill and Roosevelt, meeting in Quebec, decided to continue negotiations and retain in the Mediterranean enough landing craft (particularly the large tank-carrying LSTs) to effect a landing on the Italian mainland. Eisenhower made plans to land forces at Salerno, near Naples, on 9 September. Two key Allied officers, Eisenhower's Chief of Staff Bedell Smith and Allied Forces HQ's Head of Intelligence, Brigadier Strong, left for Lisbon by air in ill-fitting civilian clothes under assumed names. By nightfall on 18 August they were meeting with Castellano in Lisbon. The Italian was taken aback when they informed him that they required Italy's surrender — Italy wanted to switch sides without surrendering. They asked him to consult with Badoglio and presented him with a wireless transmitter with which to contact them. Heavily burdened, the small Italian general promised to send them a decision in code.

On 19 August Churchill and Roosevelt, meeting for another conference in Quebec, agreed that 'unremitting pressure' was to be maintained against the Germans in Italy but that Operation Overlord — code-name of the Allied invasion of France — should be 'the principal ground and air effort against the Axis in Europe'. On the same day Churchill signalled Alexander: 'Our greatest danger is that the Germans should enter Rome and set up a Quisling-Fascist government. Scarcely less unpleasant would be the whole of Italy sliding into anarchy.' On the same day Montgomery complained that he had been ordered to invade Europe with the 8th Army but had been given no objective! Alexander, who had been distracted in planning a landing at Salerno — Operation Avalanche — replied: 'Your task is to secure a bridgehead on the toe of Italy' and 'engage enemy forces there to give assistance to Avalanche.' On the last day of August General Castellano arrived at Alexander's advance headquarters near Syracuse, where he related that the Germans had already poured nineteen divisions into Italy, and that he still had no authority to sign Italy's surrender. He returned two days later, informing Allied Forces HQ that Marshal Badoglio welcomed an Allied airborne landing at Rome, but wanted to postpone Italy's armistice. Alexander was furious. He demanded that the Italians sign the papers immediately. This was done at 4.30 p.m. on 2 September 1943, but it was agreed that it would not be immediately announced.

INTO ITALY

On 3 September 1943 the British 8th Army crossed the Strait of Messina in the sunshine and landed without opposition at points on the toe of Italy. It was the fourth anniversary of the outbreak of war. The troops were received with cheers by the Italians. An even larger Allied invasion armada carrying two American divisions and one British division of General Mark Clark's 5th US Army began leaving for the beaches of Salerno. The Allies were still concerned about a last-minute betrayal by the Italians. So was Hitler.

On 7 September Eisenhower sent two officers, including Brigadier-General Max Taylor, to plan the landings in Rome with Badoglio. The Americans travelled by torpedo boat under cover of night to the mouth of the Tiber where they were met by Italian officers. In Rome General Carboni told them that the Germans had moved two more divisions near the capital; the airfields were under their control and if an armistice were announced they would seize the city in hours. The paratroop landing was cancelled and the planes recalled just after they had taken off. Badoglio refused to make a broadcast announcing Italy's surrender, so Eisenhower threatened to broadcast the news himself. The troops en route to Salerno heard his voice late on 8 September, only hours before they reached the beaches, and they expected to walk ashore unopposed. Aboard ships they began cheering: the first Axis power was down. One joked they he expected to be greeted by the mayor of Salerno and 'a bottle of vino'.

In Berlin Foreign Minister Ribbentrop telephoned his embassy in Rome to inform them that Italy had surrendered. The embassy officials were astonished, but radio bulletins were already carrying the news. Badoglio broadcast 75 minutes after Eisenhower had done so. Less than an hour later German forces began entering Rome, brushing aside baffled Italian troops on the outskirts of the city and meeting with resistance only as their intentions became clear.

Badoglio, the King and the government left Rome for the safety of Brindisi just before dawn next day. Badoglio had failed to issue any cogent orders to the Italian armed forces. Some units fought strongly against the German, others, awaiting orders from Rome, were rounded up by bluff or intimidation. It was the common people of Italy — men, women and even children — who were the first to seize arms and fight the Germans with fervour.

Two strong characters: General Mark Clark commanding US 5th Army in Italy and (right) Air-Marshal Arthur Coningham, the Australian-born commander of Desert Air Force, in the early stages of the Italian campaign.

American Sherman tanks in Italy. The Allied advance was slow and unspectacular.

SALERNO

The Allied troops landing at Salerno early on 9 September encountered little opposition. Instead of pushing inland rapidly the American General Dawley built up a secure beachhead and began stockpiling supplies. Three days later five German divisions pouring towards Salerno launched their first devastating counterattacks on the Allied lines and almost broke through. Alexander reacted quickly and called for Allied naval shelling of the areas of German concentration while diverting eighteen tank-carrying transport ships to Salerno. Visiting the beachhead on 15 September he found Dawley 'a broken reed' and urged his replacement. By 16 September, when the attacks were repulsed, Salerno beachhead had 200 tanks ashore and 170,000 men; on the next day their troops made contact with 8th Army.

On 1 October the Allies entered Naples, whose people had fought the Germans in the streets for a week. There they found the harbour blocked with sunken ships but they had achieved Stage One of the campaign — taking Naples and the vital Foggia airfields in the south-east that enabled the air forces to cover their operations and even bomb northern Italy. On the same day Hitler authorised Kesselring, the German C-in-C in Italy, to withdraw to a 'winter line' in the mountains south of Rome. It was formed of defensive positions 20 kilometres deep stretching across the Italian peninsula, and its western strongpoint was the lofty mountain peak of Cassino.

The fury of Italian autumn rains now struck the Allied armies. On 5 October their forward elements reached the Volturno River, where the Germans contested the crossing. The river was soon in full flood. Clark's troops crossed the Volturno on 15 October and a fortnight later reached the outposts of the Germans' winter line. In the last week of October Alexander informed Eisenhower: 'Today the situation is that eleven Allied divisions are fighting a frontal battle in country favouring the defence against an immediate strength of nine German divisions, which can be reinforced at any moment …' The Italian campaign, so lightly entered into, would be a gruelling one, with always one more river to cross, one more valley to secure, one more mountain to seize, against a resourceful enemy fighting every metre of the way.

By 8 November Montgomery had pushed his troops as far north as the Sangro River. Normally 30 metres wide, the Sangro was now a raging torrent 100 metres wide; his attack eleven days later, mounted in impossible weather, was thrown back. Another attempt to cross the Sangro on 28 November led to ten hard days of fighting. Even the New Zealand Division, pre-eminent among 8th Army's combat formations, reported that its troops were exhausted, suffering battle fatigue.

When Eisenhower and Montgomery left Italy in the last days of December 1943 to take up their posts in England in preparation for the Allied invasion of northern France, the Italian campaign was already a sideshow, one whose only real value was the absorption of more than a dozen of Hitler's best divisions. In Italy the year ended as it did in Russia — in rain and mud, wind and snow. A fresh campaign would have to wait until the spring of 1944.

THE ITALIAN ORDEAL

Churchill had hoped to spare the Italian people from 'the hot rake of war' being dragged up their peninsula. Alexander had placed much reliance on adding the Italian Army to his forces, but the Germans had dealt ruthlessly with their former Axis partner. When the Allies appealed on radio on 10 September for the Italian Army to rise up against the Germans, the army no longer existed.

Italy's sixty divisions totalled an army of 1.7 million men. Of this number 700,000 were outside Italy, mainly in the Balkans. Two entire divisions in Yugoslavia joined the Partisans; in Italy other units — particularly the elite *Alpini* — joined the Resistance. The 11th Italian Army in Greece surrendered to the Germans on the understanding that they would be repatriated to Italy; instead they were among the 450,000 Italian soldiers transported to Germany to work as slave labourers. More than 40,000 Italian soldiers were killed by the Germans — among them the entire garrison of Cephalonia, off the coast of Greece, where 8400 poorly armed Italians fought off German attacks for a week until they ran out of ammunition. The Germans shot them all and burned their corpses, casting a dark cloud of acrid smoke over the island for days. Greeks there still use the phrase 'The Italians are burning' to describe a dark and threatening sky.

In September Mussolini reappeared in Italian political life. Rescued from his comfortable confinement, he was greeted by Hitler as a long-lost friend. The Duce was one of the few people for whom Hitler had a strong and lasting affection and he later regretted that he had had to impose a 'brutal friendship' on the Italian. In Milan the deposed dictator, a grey shadow of his former self, set up the 'Italian Social Republic' with German support and attempted to create a new army. He was joined by the most cold-blooded of his Fascist adherents who carried out random atrocities against Italian resisters. The work of the Fascist Militia accomplished nothing except the growth of the Resistance, which fought back with equal savagery.

TEHERAN, 1943

On 28 November the 'Big Three' met at Teheran. It was Roosevelt's first meeting with Stalin and he sought to charm him. At dinner the President told Stalin that God was on their side; Stalin retorted that as everyone believed the devil was a Communist, God was probably a 'good Conservative'. The leaders felt confident enough to discuss the fate of Europe once Germany was crushed, and Churchill asked Stalin to promise to respect the independence of the Polish nation. It was a promise Stalin would not keep. Stalin was informed that the invasion of Europe would take place in

Mussolini after his release from captivity by German commandos in September 1943.

THE 'BIG THREE' MEET

In September Stalin had suggested to Churchill and Roosevelt that they meet soon to plan a combined strategy against the Axis. Churchill replied enthusiastically, and suggested the Iranian capital of Teheran as a convenient place. To throw the Germans off the scent, he and Roosevelt would meet at Cairo before flying on to Teheran. Churchill reached Cairo on 22 November and there met Roosevelt.

Opposite: The big three at the Teheran Conference: Stalin, Roosevelt and Churchill. Behind them stand, from left to right, their principal military advisers, Britain's General Sir John Dill and General George C. Marshall (the two men became the firmest of friends and colleagues); Marshal Voroshilov; General 'Hap' Arnold; General Sir Alan Brooke (with hands folded) and Air Chief Marshal Sir Charles Portal; Admiral Sir Andrew Cunningham, and Admiral Leahy, US Navy.

May 1944, but was given no other details. He asked his allies to keep this promise, for the Red Army was tired, saying bluntly that unless a second front was opened 'it would be very difficult for the Russians to carry on'. Despite this warning, it was by all reports a genial meeting of powerful allies.

By 4 December the two Western leaders had returned to Cairo for the second part of their own conference to plan further strategies. Churchill flew on to Tunis and there he complained of tiredness. He slept all day on 11 December. This was unusual for him. At night he told his doctor that he had a sore throat and 'a splitting headache'. His condition deteriorated. Mrs Churchill was summoned to be with him. By 15 December Harold Macmillan was writing: 'PM is definitely worse and has got pneumonia, and they fear pleurisy ... His pulse is very irregular.' Treated with the revolutionary new antibiotic drugs, one of the lasting triumphs of the war, by 19 December Churchill was recovering. 'Papa much better today. Has consented not to smoke, and to drink only weak whisky and soda,' Clementine Churchill reported to her daughter Sarah. Five days later the Prime Minister was holding conferences with his military chiefs. He spent several days convalescing in Marrakesh before returning to England to plan Hitler's own early demise.

THE DAM BUSTERS

On the night of 16 May 1943 the specially formed 617 Squadron RAF, which included a large number of Australian and New Zealand aircrew, carried out the most audacious bombing mission of the war — the breaching, by 'bouncing bombs' of the Moehne and Eder dams in the Ruhr valley. Wing Commander Guy Gibson, DSO, DFC, a 25-year-old RAF veteran of 173 missions, was awarded the Victoria Cross for his qualities of leadership and gallantry on the operation; of the 133 aircrew who flew in the raid, 56 failed to return.

The 'Suicide Squadron' was made up of the most daring pilots in Bomber Command. Two of the most legendary were Australians, 'Mick' Martin and David Shannon. 'The backbone of the squadron were Martin, Munro (a New Zealander), McCarthy (an American) and Shannon,' wrote Air Marshal Sir Ralph Cochrane, 'and of these the greatest was Martin ... As an operational pilot I consider him greater than Gibson and indeed the greatest that the Air Force has produced.' Leonard Cheshire, VC, who commanded 617 after Gibson's passing, wrote: 'I learned all I knew of this low flying from Mick.' Martin survived the war.

An attack on the Dortmund–Ems canal in September 1943 saw 617 Squadron lose fifteen of its twenty-one aircraft. Under the command of the Welshman Willie Tait the squadron was to score a bulls-eye: the sinking of the *Tirpitz*.

Above: A German photograph of the super battleship *Tirpitz* in her Norwegian fiord. In 1944 she became the most prominent victim of the Dam Busters.
Below: The crew of an Australian Lancaster of the Dam Buster squadron. From left to right: Flight Lt J.F. Leggo DFC and Bar, Flight Lt H.B. Martin DSO DFC, Flight Sergeant T.D. Simpson DFM, Flight Lt R.C. Hay DFC and Bar, Pilot Officer B.T. Foxlee DFM. 'Mick' Martin survived the war to become an air marshal in the post-war RAF and win the Air Force Cross.

As the Chinese leader Chiang Kai-shek was also present the leaders devoted the first day to the Far East and undertook to stimulate offensives in Burma. As for Europe, all the Allied armies could hope to achieve was to reach the Pisa–Rimini line, two-thirds of the way up the Italian peninsula. Apart from more military assistance to the Yugoslav and Greek partisans, who had captured Churchill's romantic imagination, there was little more that could be done in the Mediterranean. An attempt to capture the Italian islands in the Aegean — the Dodecanese — had ended in failure and the loss of 5000 British troops because Eisenhower had refused to divert forces — particularly air forces — to what he considered a British sideshow. American suspicion grew that the British had ambitions in the Balkans.

His Majesty King George VI, paid a personal visit to the cruiser HMAS *Shropshire* at Scapa Flow before she departed for action in the Pacific. Captain Collins (centre) and Commander Harries salute to the shrill of bosun's whistles as the monarch returns to shore

THE WAR AGAINST JAPAN

In Tokyo Emperor Hirohito, depressed by news of the defeats at Buna and the southern Solomons, advised his War Minister: 'Give enough thought to your plans so that Lae and Salamaua don't become another Guadalcanal.' Japan's move to reinforce Lae by sea was predictable; it would probably take place under cover of heavy weather. On 1 March 1943 a patrolling B-24 caught a glimpse of a large Japanese convoy through a lucky break in the clouds. The convoy consisted of eight transports, carrying a total of 7,000 troops, escorted by eight destroyers.

Over two days (2–3 March) the convoy was attacked by every bomber Brigadier-General Kenney could muster, including Australian Beaufighters which strafed the ships at mast height. The eight transports and four of the destroyers were sunk for the loss of five American and one Australian aircraft. Up to 3000 Japanese were killed in the victory that MacArthur termed 'the most decisive aerial engagement' so far in the south-west Pacific.

BATTLE FOR WAU

The scene of land operations now shifted to the Huon Gulf and its hinterland, where a small force of Australians — 'Kanga Force' — had been waging a guerrilla war. By January 1943 the Japanese began to reinforce Lae and Salamaua, the coastal settlements on the Huon Gulf. General Blamey finally obtained MacArthur's permission to fly an AIF brigade into Wau airfield — the 17th Brigade, his last veteran brigade.

Wau, set in a narrow grassy valley nearly 1300 metres above sea level, was to be the scene of a desperate battle. By 19 January 1943 the commandos were deployed around the airfield. Two days later Japanese patrols were seen approaching from the north-east along the Black Cat Track (named after a nearby gold mine) leading from Mubo. Early the next day Japanese fire began to fall on the airfield. The first heavy attack on the airfield came on 30 January just as transport aircraft bringing Australian reinforcements arrived, landing through fire from the Japanese.

On 1 February the Wau force began counterattacking vigorously in a ground battle that lasted for days. Two transports had been lost but four Japanese bombers and twenty-five fighters were shot down in the battle. If the Japanese force — 3000 strong — had reached Wau one day earlier the airstrip could have fallen, but by 6 February they had been pushed back to their base at Mubo. They had lost 200 killed.

DEFENDING DARWIN

In May 1943 the Japanese began hitting back in strength. Darwin was now defended by three squadrons of Spitfires — the Spitfire Wing (54 Squadron RAF and 452 and 457 Squadrons RAAF) commanded by

Left: Australian troops on the near-vertical slopes of Green Sniper's Pimple during the battle for Shaggy Ridge, New Guinea, 1943.
Left inset: Like a pitcher in a baseball game, an American hurls a grenade during the Solimons fighting, 1943.

Spitfires of the Royal Australian Air Force that defended Darwin during the long air battle, 1942–43. The red roundel was painted out in the Pacific war to avoid Allied aircraft being mistaken for Japanese.

Australia's leading 'ace' of the war, Wing-Commander Clive Caldwell. He would become a national hero, but few of his young pilots were experienced in combat, and the air battle would be ferocious.

On the morning of 2 May 1943 a force of forty-five Japanese bombers and fighters struck Darwin airfield and were attacked by thirty-three Spitfires, eight of which were lost in the dogfight or in forced landings, though only two Australian pilots were killed. Ten Japanese aircraft (six 'definites' and four 'probables') were destroyed. This set a pattern of combat that lasted until 6 September when the Japanese ceased their raids.

In South-West Pacific Area General Kenney's air forces, though still lacking an adequate number of heavy bombers, totalled 680 RAAF and 770 American aircraft. Air superiority — the key to, if not the instrument of, victory — was gradually being achieved. By April 1943 Kenney was able to begin an air offensive aimed at breaking the 'Bismarck barrier'.

BURMA: THE ARAKAN

The first British counteroffensive in Burma had ended in a fiasco. In December 1942, as the monsoon ended, British-Indian forces set out to recapture Akyab island off the Arakan coast. It would serve as a base for army and air forces to mount an offensive into central Burma. But if Akyab were to be secured, the Japanese would have to be driven out of the promontory that hung like a sword above it, and whose eastern border was the Mayu River. It was appalling country, malaria-infested, and the promontory was mountainous with few roads. Through the Mayu Range, however, ran an east–west tunnel, long disused, that the Japanese had fortified: the battle to dislodge them would take two campaigns over eighteen months.

By early 1943 no fewer than nine British-Indian brigades were in the Arakan, facing constant counterattacks by only two Japanese brigades. The campaign was directed from Calcutta by General Irwin of Eastern Army, who did not visit the scene but instead sent Lieutenant-General Slim of 15 Corps, the hero of the Burma retreat, to report on the situation. Slim was embarrassed by his role but wrote a harshly critical report which inferred that Irwin was unaware of the difficulties his untrained troops were facing. As attacks intensified, most of the British brigades were surrounded or their communications cut. Only the coming of the May monsoon prevented further Japanese advances and averted a British disaster. Days before the rains came Slim was handed a signal from Irwin ordering him to return to Calcutta for a further posting. Minutes later he received a second signal from Irwin: 'Cancel my first message. I have been relieved of my command and you are filling my place. Congratulations.'

Bill Slim, the new commander of Eastern Army — soon to be named 14th Army — would be the architect of victory in Burma, but the battlefront was regarded as a backwater, and victory would take two more years of hard fighting. In May 1943 came two turning points: General Slim was appointed to the command of 14th Army and Orde Wingate's first 'Chindit' column set out on a 2500-kilometre march behind Japanese lines and back, supplied by air and returning after losing one-third of its men but proving that unorthodox tactics worked. In August 1943 Churchill appointed the young, dynamic, publicity-conscious Lord Louis Mountbatten, who had been rescued from his sunken destroyer in the waters off Crete in 1941 to command Combined Operations, as Supreme Commander, South-East Asia Command (SEAC), with orders to get results.

MACARTHUR'S OFFENSIVES

The Joint Chiefs in Washington authorised MacArthur to concentrate on reconquering the Solomons as far as southern Bougainville, New Guinea as far as Madang, and western New Britain. No reinforcements could be sent to him. In broadcasts to the Australian people Curtin spoke bitterly of Australia being condemned to 'a holding war' that could last 'another three years'.

In March 1943 Admiral King ordained that the Central Pacific force under Admiral Spruance would be the US Fifth Fleet, to serve under Admiral Nimitz in the conquest of the Gilbert Islands. Halsey's South Pacific force and Admiral Kelly Turner's 3rd Amphibious Force would be renamed US Third Fleet; and South-West Pacific force with Admiral Dan Barbey's 7th Amphibious Force — 'MacArthur's Navy' — would become Admiral Carpenter's US Seventh Fleet. Each fleet would include several 'task forces'.

Halsey flew to Brisbane in March 1943 to confer with General MacArthur. They hit it off well together and perfected plans for 'Operation Cartwheel' — a two-pronged advance towards Rabaul, involving thirteen separate and sometimes overlapping amphibious operations that would include landings in the Huon Gulf and, it was hoped, would end with Halsey's seizure of Bougainville and MacArthur's landing at Madang on New Guinea's north-east coast.

Japanese raids did little to affect the timetable of MacArthur's next offensive, timed to begin on 30 June 1943. Admiral Halsey's Third Fleet (and the smaller 'Seventh Fleet', which consisted of little more than HMAS *Australia*, HMAS *Hobart* and USS *Phoenix*) was placed under MacArthur's tactical command. The plan involved landings on Woodlark Island and New Georgia; General Krueger's US 6th Army was to push on to Bougainville and western New Britain. It would be an amphibious campaign using landing craft protected by the guns of the fleet. The Australians in New Guinea were to take Lae, Salamaua, the Huon Peninsula and Madang. In May 1943 RAAF Bostons and Beaufighters began continuous raids on Lae and Madang, a prelude to the coming land offensive.

In May an Australian patrol made the first reconnaissance of Nassau Bay, the coastal area selected for the amphibious landing. The Japanese, suspicious of the Australian probes, began to bring in reinforcements and on 20 June launched an attack by 200 aircraft and 1500 troops against the Australian position on Lababia Ridge; the attack was repulsed. The Americans landed in mountainous seas at Nassau Bay on 30 June 1943 but made little progress inland. MacArthur's forces landing on New Georgia met bitter opposition.

TO SALAMAUA

As a prelude to the two-pronged Allied drive on Salamaua, the Australians fought bitterly to secure Bobdubi Ridge and its key position of 'Old Vickers', while Japanese reinforcements pushed down from Salamaua to extend their mountain defence line as far as Mount Tambu. 'This is our 71st day on Bobdubi, and there is no relief yet,' wrote a Japanese sergeant. 'Every day there are bombings. Can the people at home imagine the suffering ...' Five days later, on 28 July 1943, Old Vickers was stormed by the 58/59th Battalion in a charge up the knife-edged ridge, the Australians hurling grenades and firing from the hip.

By 14 August the Americans at Nassau Bay and Australian attacks forced the Japanese to give up Mount Tambu. Plans were now laid to seize Lae by simultaneous land, sea and airborne invasion. In New Guinea General Blamey commanded the largest number of Australian divisions ever seen in a single theatre of war — the 7th and 9th AIF, and the 3rd, 5th and 11th Militia.

LAE

On the morning of 4 September 1943, the day after Allied forces had crossed from Sicily to land in southern Italy, an armada of 152 warships and transports landed the 9th Australian Division east of Lae. Inland, the 7th Division crossed the Markham River and American paratroopers floated down on Nadzab in the first airborne operation of the Pacific War. By 6 September the first plane-loads of 7th Division infantry were landing at Nadzab airstrip. On 11 September General Milford's 5th Division entered Salamaua as the bulk of its 5000-strong Japanese garrison retreated to Lae. Four days later the first men of the 7th Division entered Lae. The battle for Lae cost the Japanese 1500 dead. But 8000 of their soldiers eluded the traps set for them and struggled over the mountains to Sio, under enormous hardships, to live and fight another day.

HUON GULF LANDINGS

Now planning an invasion of New Britain by the US 6th Army, MacArthur delegated the clearing of the Huon Peninsula to the Australians. The 9th Division, 'the Rats of Tobruk', were to land at Finschhafen to secure its valuable harbour, while the 7th Division held the Markham and upper Ramu valleys. There were 5000 Japanese in the region. The battle for Finschhafen and its mountain hinterland at Sattelberg would be a bitter, two-month campaign.

On 22 September 1943 the 9th Division's 20th Brigade stormed ashore 10 kilometres north of Finschhafen, established a beachhead and pushed south. The Japanese at Sattelberg — the 1000-metre-high ridge 10 kilometres inland — began mounting strong attacks on the extended Australian front. By 18 October the beachhead had been cut in two. With reinforcements of Matilda tanks, the Australians fought their way up the mountain road to Sattelberg and took it on 25 November.

Evacuating Wareo on 8 December 1943, the Japanese straggled over the mountain tracks to Madang and Wewak. The 9th Division entered Sio on 15 January, having suffered 1000 casualties. Japanese casualties were at least 8000. The Japanese high command regarded Finschhafen as one of the crucial battles of the war. It had not occurred to them that their hold on it could be wrested away. For the remaining Japanese now marooned in New Guinea little but death lay ahead. Meanwhile the 7th Division had pushed through the Markham Valley to the Ramu River. By early October 1943 Dumpu was securely in their hands.

TO MADANG

While the Australians wearily hauled themselves across the Finisterres, MacArthur replaced his cautious 'island hopping' with a bold new strategy, bypassing isolated Japanese garrisons by skilful use of his overwhelming air power and amphibious fleet. This dramatic strategy saved countless American lives and was described after the war by Tojo as one of the three factors that sealed Japan's doom (the others being the depredations of the American carrier groups and submarine forces). MacArthur's immediate objectives were Bougainville, New Britain and the Treasuries. Landings on all were made by the end of December 1943.

The end of 1943 also marked a pause in Australian army actions in New Guinea. The nation was exhausted by four years of war and the drain on manpower was immense. On 23 December 1943 Blamey announced the end of the Australian Army's active role in New Guinea, in accordance with MacArthur's directive that American forces were to take over active operations. The three weary AIF divisions would return to Australia while the 3rd, 5th and 11th Militia (AMF) divisions took over garrison duties in the New Guinea area.

One obstinate Japanese position in the Finisterres still blocked the road to Madang: Shaggy Ridge, a seven-kilometre-long razorback that had resisted all attacks on it since October. After bitter fighting all resistance on the 'Saddle' dominating Shaggy Ridge ended on 26 January 1944, and the Japanese withdrew. On the eve of Anzac Day 1944 the Australians struggling over the Finisterre Mountains entered Madang. The Huon Peninsula was 'cleared'.

In the seven months from September 1943 to April 1944 the Australians had killed 35,000 Japanese for the loss of 4000 casualties. They had shattered the 100,000-strong 18th Japanese Army. 'In sixteen months of war', the Australian Official History relates, 'the Japanese had passed from the exhilarating heights of victory to the grim verge of defeat.'

Australian infantry pause during the long march over the Finisterre Ranges to Madang in Papua-New Guinea late in 1943.

THE PACIFIC

Any reconquest of the Pacific by the US Navy would involve sending fleets and invasion forces carrying Marines ever westward, seizing the Japanese-held island groups that blocked progress — the Gilberts, the Marshalls, the Carolines and the Marianas, in that order. Many of these were known to be strongly defended, with bases for aircraft and warships. Some were little more than coral atolls in the sparkling blue ocean, but all were potentially deadly.

The Japanese had captured the Gilbert Islands in September 1942; the Marshalls to their north had been a German possession obtained by Japan as a mandate in 1919 and heavily fortified. When the US fleet steamed for the Gilberts group it was a formidable armada. It included two new fleet carriers named after the two already lost in battle, *Lexington* and *Yorktown*, three light carriers, twenty destroyers and the new battleship *Alabama*. In August the 5th Amphibious Corps had been created — mostly Marines. To assist their landing they would use amphibious vehicles named 'alligators' that had been originally devised for use in the Florida swamps. In October 1943 the invasion fleet had gathered its 100 warships and transports in harbours scattered from Hawaii to Fiji and appeared off the two coral atolls in the north of the Gilberts chain named Makin and Tarawa.

The invasion force landed there on 21 November and seized Makin in four days for the cost of 200 casualties — and a carrier sunk by a Japanese submarine with the loss of 642 sailors. The Japanese Combined Fleet stayed snug in their great anchorage of Truk, but attempted to destroy the American fleet with aircraft in a spectacular night attack that achieved no sinkings.

Tarawa was proving more difficult than Makin. It was defended by more than 4000 Japanese, and they survived the massive naval bombardment. By the end of the first day (20 November), one-third of the 5000 US Marines who had landed were casualties; the tide had receded and they were stranded. When the tide rose reinforcements poured in but resistance was not crushed until the end of four days of intense fighting. Only 17 Japanese were found alive. They had inflicted 3000 casualties on the Americans, including 1000 killed. This was a heavy toll. But lessons were learned. The taking of Kwajalein atoll in the Marshalls in February 1944 would be accomplished with lighter losses. Of the 41,000 Marines and army troops landed, 372 died in the week of fighting; and nearly 8000 Japanese were killed. The Pacific War would be a war of attrition, as the Japanese refused to surrender, choosing death instead.

By late in 1943 the American amphibious forces in the Pacific were equipped with an extraordinary range of vehicles, including 'Alligators' (left) and 'Water Buffaloes' (centre).

Before the coming of winter in 1943, the Red Army had driven the Germans from most of the Russian homeland: Russian soldiers after their entry into Smolensk.

EASTERN FRONT

On 7 November 1943 Stalin broadcast to the Soviet people. It was the 26th anniversary of the 1917 Revolution and he described the year just ending as 'the year of the great turning-point'. One month after the July victory at Kursk Russian armies had taken Orel and Belgorod, the two cities north and south of Kursk from where the Germans had launched their last great attempt to destroy Russia's armies. Of Orel's pre-war population of more than 110,000, only 30,000 people were left. In September the Red Army took Kharkov.

The small groups of Partisans who had fought lonely wars in the past two years were now armies in themselves. During 1943 Partisan strength in Belorussia alone had grown from 65,000 to 360,000; by the end of the year there were 220,000 armed Partisans in the Ukraine. At the time of Kursk the Partisans had made 6000 attacks on rail lines in one night, and Soviet historians have estimated that they killed in Belorus and the Ukraine nearly a million Germans over the years 1941–44. The peasants suffered hideous reprisals at Nazi hands — the burnings of villages, mass execution of their inhabitants and deportation to Germany of the young and fit. (More than three million Ukrainians were deported to the Reich.) Often the Red Army entered a town to find it already occupied by the Partisans.

Stalin had finally harnessed the will of his people to fight. Each victory was announced over Moscow radio with thunder rolls of drums and ended with the vow: 'Death to the Germans.' In September the Russians recaptured Smolensk and in November 1943 Vatutin's armies liberated Kiev. Two-thirds of the territory conquered by Germany had been liberated. Possibility of a German victory had vanished.

'Taking together the blows struck at the Germans and their allies in north Africa and southern Italy, the intensive bombing of Germany ... and the regular supplies of armaments and raw materials that we are receiving from our Allies, we must say that all this has greatly helped us in our summer campaign,' Stalin said. 'The fighting in southern Europe is not the Second Front, but, all the same, it is something like the Second Front ...' Germany in 1944, he predicted, would face 'catastrophe'. The year 1944 would be one of even more astonishing victories that would carry Russians armies to the borders of Germany itself. The offensives began even before winter's snows melted: In January 1944 Soviet armies broke through to Leningrad, lifting the 900-day siege.

CHAPTER 10
CLOSING IN
1944

While the armies in Italy and the Eastern Front were deadlocked in the winter, waiting for the snows to recede, the Pacific in the year 1944 was to see the most dramatic Allied advances of the entire war and with them the fruition of Admiral Nimitz and MacArthur's strategy. Even in Burma, the stagnant front, Japan's armies were to meet resounding defeat. In a good omen for the great bounds the Americans were to take in the central Pacific and the south-west Pacific, 1944 was a leap year.

LEAP-FROGGING TO THE PHILIPPINES

MacArthur, having secured Arawe in mid-December 1943, and landed at Cape Gloucester over Christmas, seized Saido in January 1944. He then took a gamble, one of the greatest of his life. Instructed by the Joint Chiefs in Washington to seize Rabaul, Japan's strongest base in the south-west Pacific, he decided to by-pass it, to let it 'wither on the vine'. One of his biographers has likened the shape of the Bismarck Sea to that of a wine cask. In its north the Admiralty Islands formed its cork. MacArthur would go straight for the cork — seizing Manus Island in the small Admiralty group would provide him with a fine anchorage and ground for air bases. He would then boldly launch himself westwards, ever westwards, along the northern coast of New Guinea — to the Philippines. He would let the Japanese in Malaya and the East Indies also wither on the vine. His daring campaigns of 1943 had raised his reputation; those of 1944 would make him one of the great commanders of history.

On 29 February 1944 MacArthur landed troops in the Admiralty Islands. They went ashore on tiny, but strongly-defended Los Negros. MacArthur visited the beaches, which were still under sniper fire, to be present in case a hasty evacuation was necessary. In the drizzling rain he strode, pipe in mouth, to the front and tested the airstrip surface with his stick to see if the coral was hard enough to take bombers. It was. The gamble succeeded and by 9 March RAAF Kittyhawks were landing on the island; during operations Australian warships again lent gunfire support and carried out patrol work.

Emirau Island was seized in March. Awaiting an invasion that never came and lacking aircraft of sufficient range — and adequate fuel — with which to strike the Allies, the Japanese defenders of Rabaul were left in the backwash of the Allied advance. Eighteen months later Australian forces in New Britain were to take the surrender in Rabaul of 90,000 half-starved Japanese, including nineteen generals and twelve admirals.

NORTHERN NEW GUINEA

In April 1944 MacArthur bypassed the 200,000 Japanese at Wewak and landed at Aitape and Humboldt Bay on the coast of Dutch New Guinea, his landings covered for the first time by aircraft from US Navy carriers lent to him for the occasion. In May 1944 MacArthur's Americans seized Wakde and Biak, with RAAF Kittyhawks from Hollandia providing air cover. At Biak the fleet bombarded the shore to soften resistance; the 1000 Japanese defenders fought on until August. Noemfoor Island was invaded in July. In all these operations MacArthur's fleet included the Australian squadron of cruisers and destroyers — Task Force 74. The Japanese launched a desperate attack on Aitape on 10 July but the US 32nd and 43rd divisions supported by the three RAAF squadrons and the guns of Task Force 74, held all attacks and killed 5000 Japanese.

Inset: The Imperial war flag of Japan.
Right: American troops during the seizure of a Japanese-held island in the Pacific.
Far right: An Australian 'Digger' in New Guinea, 1944 carrying a Bren machine-gun.

EASTERN FRONT

By May 1944 the Russians had advanced deep into Poland and across the borders of East Prussia and had driven the Germans from the Crimea. In January they broke through to Leningrad, where they found only 600,000 inhabitants left of the city's population of three million. Leningrad's buildings were in ruins, its palaces deliberately shelled by the enemy. The German armies retreated to Esthonia. In February marshals Konev and Vatutin launched their armies on the Dnieper, encircling the Germans in the Korsun salient. The Red Army pushed over the Dnieper, the Bug and the Pruth rivers, through the Ukraine and reached Jassy in Romania.

The Crimea remained, defended by 200,000 German and Romanian troops. Hitler ordered them to fight to the last round. On 11 April the Russians, with an army of nearly 470,000, attacked and swamped the German defences. One week later only Sevastopol remained in German hands. Hitler ordered a garrison of 50,000 men to defend it and permitted the evacuation of the remainder, but few escaped before the city fell on 5 May. The Russians had defended Sevastopol for 250 days; in 1944 it fell in just four days. Alexander Werth visited it soon after its recapture and wrote: 'From a distance Sevastopol, with its long and narrow bay beyond, looked like a live city, but it also was dead. Even in the suburbs, at the far end of the valley of Inkerman, there was hardly a house left standing. The railway station was a mountain of rubble and twisted metal ... Sevastopol itself, bright and lively before the war, was now melancholy beyond belief. The harbour was littered with the wrecks of ships the Russians had sunk during the last days of the German occupation ...' He recorded that the Crimean Tartars had closely collaborated with the Germans and formed a police force during the occupation. Stalin was to exact a terrible revenge against the 500,000 Crimean Tartars, the Cossacks who had joined Hitler and the Chechens of the Caucasus who had welcomed the Germans as liberators. Even before war's end he deported them en masse to Siberia, where many died.

In June 1944 the Russians would launch the first of their great summer offensives.

ISLAND-HOPPING TO JAPAN

THE MARIANAS

In February Nimitz's forces had taken Kwajalein in the Marshall Islands. Nimitz now proposed a bold leap 1200 miles (1920 kilometres) beyond the Carolines to the Marianas, for these islands could provide bases for the new long-range B-29 'Super Fortresses' to bomb Japan. Nimitz's plan was ridiculed by MacArthur, who feared a diversion of forces from his theatre, and even by Admiral Tom Kincaid. Fortunately Nimitz had a strong ally and supporter in Admiral King in Washington, who reminded MacArthur that switching resources to the south-west Pacific had not been approved at Casablanca. General Marshall supported King and Nimitz, but suggested a compromise. The central Pacific offensives against the Marianas would proceed in June — and MacArthur was to seize Mindanao in the southern Philippines five months later.

The Japanese high command viewed an American seizure of the Marianas as impossible, and had done little to strengthen the defences of their bases on the main island of Saipan. It was only a month before the American blow fell that Tokyo appointed Admiral Nagumo there to command a 'Central Pacific Fleet' that was not yet in existence. Japan sent the 43rd Division to the island in two convoys; one got through but the second was almost destroyed by American air attack. Saipan's defenders numbered 31,000, but they had few fixed or strong defences, for all building materials sent to them had been sunk. Steaming towards Saipan under the command of Admiral Spruance was one of the largest fleets ever assembled — 535 ships, including 101 warships and 15 carriers. They carried an invasion force of 127,000 men, two-thirds of them US Marines. Japan concentrated her fleet at Biak — it included the giant battleships *Yamato* and *Musashi*.

The American naval and air bombardment of the south-western coast of Saipan began early on 15 June 1944. The amphibious forces headed to the beaches at 7 a.m. and the landings went well. Admiral Ozawa, commanding the Combined Fleet, had only half the number of carriers as Spruance but counted on more than 900 aircraft — his own 473 planes on carriers and 500 in the Marianas. He was unaware that most of the latter were already being destroyed.

On 18 June Japanese search planes reported the presence of the main American strike force — Vice-Admiral Marc Mitscher's Task Force 58 and its seven large carriers, eight smaller ones, seven battleships, twenty-one cruisers and sixty-nine destroyers. Mitscher's role was to cover the landings, not destroy the Japanese carriers. Ozawa launched his first air strike next day and met with a shock: his pilots were assailed by a new American fighter that outclassed them, the 'Hellcat', modelled on a captured Zero but far superior in

Invading the Admiralty Islands: General MacArthur with Admiral Tom Kincaid (left) on the bridge of the latter's flagship.

speed and armament. American bombers got through the Japanese anti-aircraft fire and protecting fighter screen — and sank two carriers, a battleship and a cruiser. An American submarine had already sent a torpedo into the carrier *Skokaku*. In the words of the historian John Toland: 'In a few hours Ozawa had lost 346 planes … Japanese naval air power had been crippled, and permanently.'

The exultant American carrier pilots called the day's air battle a 'turkey shoot'. History knows it as the Battle of the Philippine Sea. But many never lived to celebrate the victory. Attempting to reach their carriers before their fuel ran out, scores ditched in the sea. Mitscher broke all the rules of naval warfare: he ordered all carriers to turn on their lights, illuminate their flight decks. Returning pilots saw their carriers lit up like Christmas trees, shining with the lights of victory. American combat losses were fifty planes; another eighty pilots ditched in the sea and those near their own ships were quickly rescued.

Fighting against fanatical resistance, the three American divisions linked up their beachheads on 30 June. Watching his defeat from a cave, Admiral Nagumo committed suicide, with the help of a bullet from a junior officer. The last of the defenders sought death rather than surrender. Many Chamoros jumped to their deaths from the cliffs. One night thousands of starving and weaponless Japanese made primitive spears and charged along the beach, striking two unsuspecting battalions of the US 27th Division, butchering and wounding more than 600 Americans before being killed to a man. On Saipan 22,000 civilians were killed or chose death rather than captivity, along with the entire 30,000-strong Japanese garrison. American fatalities totalled 14,000, a horrifying figure that MacArthur denounced as butchery.

On 21 July Spruance began the conquest of the remaining islands in the Marianas group, landing Marines and army troops on Guam. Five days later the force was attacked by other suicide charges by the Japanese, who came on in thousands into point-blank artillery fire. By 10 August the island was secured and most of its defenders dead.

Above: 'Six down!' An American fighter pilot on his return to his aircraft carrier during the battle of the Marianas.
Below: Carriers and battleships formed the backbone of the US Navy task forces in the Pacific. A 10,000 tonne *Independence*-class carrier (built on the hull of a cruiser) is followed by a 27,000 tonne *Essex*-class carrier and a line of battleships.

On 25 July 15,000 Americans landed on neighbouring Tinian and within eight days took the island. Just a fortnight afterwards Tojo resigned. For the first time Japanese territory was in enemy hands. Japan's last great land offensive, into northern Burma, had also failed. On 18 July Tojo was succeeded as premier by a representative of the Imperial Navy, Admiral Yonai who made no secret of his wish to end a war that Japan had already lost.

ITALY

January 1944 found the Allied armies in Italy stalled in the mud facing Kesselring's winter line. Now named the Gustav line, it stretched across the peninsula, taking advantage of the Apennine mountain ranges and the other natural obstacles — the Rapido River in the west, and on the Adriatic coast the River Sangro. The Allies were tantalisingly close to Rome, but mountains blocked their way, and looking down on their efforts was the towering height of Monte Cassino, whose summit was crowned by the great Benedictine monastery, one of the treasures of medieval religious and architectural history. Only two roads led to Rome, one (Route 7) along the coast; the other (Route 6) was inland and ran north-west to Rome through the Liri valley. It ran across the Rapido River and through the town of Cassino, which lay directly beneath the great abbey. Ruined castles crowned the summit of other peaks such as Monte Camino, but nothing matched the magnificence of the Abbey of Monte Cassino. It had been built in the sixth century by Saint Benedict, destroyed three times and rebuilt again in the fourteenth century.

British infantry in the front line of the Anzio beachhead early in 1944. The fighting at Anzio was some of the toughest and closest of the war.

It would be hard to find a more classic setting for a battle, nor one so forbidding. 'In spring and early summer much of the mountainside is thickly wooded with olive, wild oak, fir and the ubiquitous acacia ... In spring and summer the trees do something to soften the base of the monastery, so that from certain angles it may seem to be reclining on a sumptuous green cushion rather than crouching on a hard mountain top,' wrote Fred Majdalany, who fought there, in his classic book on the coming battle. 'But in winter, when the slopes are bare, and the gales and the black thunderclaps sweep incessantly across from the wild hinterland of the Abruzzi, the Abbey of Monte Cassino hardens into a gaunt symbol of defiance, a great fortress in the sky.'

Field Marshal Alexander, whom even Churchill would accuse of butting his head to no avail against Cassino, had already decided to outflank the obstacle by landing up the coast at Anzio, just south of Rome. Thus the first attempt to seize Cassino was a secondary effort that might draw German reserves from the Anzio landing. Two days before Anzio General Mark Clark launched his 5th US Army across the Rapido in an attempt to bypass Monte Cassino in the south: The attack by the 36th (Texas) Division, mounted in pouring rain and a thick fog under heavy German artillery fire, with units encountering minefields before reaching the river bank, was a confused affair. Some units reached the bank; others were decimated by heavy fire from across the river. After two days and the loss of 1800 men — the fighting tip of a Division — the attack was called off. It left bitter memories among Texans. Further north the US 34th Division made a successful crossing and secured Monte Cairo, and the French Corps in February had penetrated north of the Cassino position; these positions were important bridgeheads but remained a nightmare to hold and supply.

ANZIO

Similar disappointment occurred at Anzio. On 20 January 1944 two divisions landed at Anzio and encountered little opposition. General Lucas pushed his troops more than 10 kilometres and then halted, to build up supplies and establish a strong bridgehead. What followed was a repetition of Salerno. By the time Lucas launched his thrust towards Rome he confronted six German divisions and his congested bridgehead was soon under constant artillery fire. There the Allies remained — maintaining their perimeter in some of the most murderous close-fighting of the war, until May. Churchill complained that he had hoped to land a tiger cat behind the German lines, but all he got was 'a beached whale'. Alexander, visiting the beachhead, raised men's spirits, but General Lucas did not. He was replaced by a fighting general, Lucian Truscott.

SECOND BATTLE OF CASSINO

In March 1944 Alexander ordered a second attempt to force the Cassino line. He would use some of his best troops, 'two of the greatest fighting divisions of the war' — the New Zealand Division, and another veteran division, the 4th Indian, along with the British

78th Division, which had fought well in the mountains of Tunisia. The divisional commanders — Freyberg, promoted to lieutenant-general, was now commanding all three divisions under the title of 'New Zealand Corps' — suspected that the Germans were using the monastery as an observation post, or may even have incorporated it into their defence line, and asked Alexander to have it bombed. There were no Germans in the Abbey. General von Senger, commanding 14 Panzer Corps, and a devout Catholic, had gone to the monastery to attend mass on Christmas Day, 1943, but he and his men had been meticulous in respecting the sanctity of the Benedictines.

The bombing of the monastery began early on 15 February, and the building was almost totally devastated; even its vast walls collapsed in parts. The Germans found its ruins excellent for defence when 4th Indian Division and the New Zealanders began their attacks from the north and south, hoping to converge on Cassino town, which also lay in ruins. After three days the battle had achieved little. Freyberg called a halt on 18 February and prepared to mount a second attempt. He called for the bombing of Cassino town; the attack would be launched by a New Zealanders and an Indian brigade, supported by the New Zealand Armoured Brigade. (Such was their prowess that the NZ Division was one of the few to include a brigade of tanks.) The rest of the divisions would follow. His reserve, the 78th Division, would exploit any breakthrough. Downpours delayed the launching of the attack. It began on 15 March with the bombing of Cassino. The attackers seized two peaks — Castle Hill and Hangman's Hill just below the summit of the monastery — and were about to launch an attack on the summit when, on 19 March, the Germans counter-attacked in strength. Allied tanks were delayed and then ambushed. With casualties approaching 5000 Freyberg called off his second battle.

Alexander decided to wait until the coming of summer weather. In two months, the ground would have hardened. He would launch his fourth attempt to get past Cassino in May. His offensive would be timed to coincide with a breakout from Anzio.

ITALY: CASSINO TO ROME

On 11 May Alexander launched his offensive in Italy. 'The Allied armed forces are now assembling for the final battles on seas, on land, and in the air to crush the enemy once and for all,' ran his Order of the Day. 'To us in Italy has been given the honour to strike the first blow.' This time it was successful. Cassino fell, and the road to Rome was opened. His battle plan was bold. He would have to

The Benedictine monastery on the summit of Monte Cassino, devastated by Allied bombing. The great edifice was rebuilt after the war.

blast his way through the Gustav line into the Liri valley, south of Cassino, which led to Rome, and then launch his second punch from Anzio, where seven divisions were now firmly established. He called upon the French Corps and their tough Moroccan mountain units to advance through the southern mountains while the Canadian Corps and 30 British Corps pushed up the Liri valley. Rome was a fine prize, but he intended to entrap the German army facing him. 'Our objective', he signalled Churchill, 'is the destruction of the enemy south of Rome.' The Holy City would fall as a consequence. Mark Clark's 5th Army was ordered to strike from Anzio and seize Valmontone on the main road to Rome (Route 6) to prevent the escape of the German 10th Army.

The Poles stormed the ruins of the monastery on Monte Cassino on 18 May; the French astonished even Alexander by the rapidity of their advance. Clark had other plans: determined to be the first into Rome, he switched the axis of his attack north, to Rome itself, sending a single division from Anzio to secure the road, a force insufficient to prevent the Germans from escaping to a position north of Rome but adequate to prevent the 8th Army's columns from advancing further. Rome had been declared an 'open city' (undefended) and on 4 June Clark fulfilled his dream of being the first Allied general into the city, accompanied, as always, by official photographers.

Churchill announced the fall of Rome in the Commons on the following day. One day later Allied armies landed on the coast of Normandy. D-Day had arrived and the long-delayed campaign to liberate Europe had begun.

Accompanied by an American priest, General Mark Clark takes in the sights of Rome, June 1944. Next to him sits his chief of staff, General Al Gruenther.

'OPERATION OVERLORD': THE PLANNING

At dawn on 6 June 1944 hundreds of landing craft were making their way through choppy seas towards the beaches of Normandy. They carried American, British and Canadian infantry and tanks in the greatest seaborne operation of the war. Offshore hundreds of Allied warships were unleashing a bombardment of the shore beach defences and the hinterland. In the hours before dawn, 13,000 American and British paratroops and glider-borne troops had been dropped ahead of them and were already fighting to secure bridges and crossroads. 'Operation Overlord' had begun.

The Normandy landings were the fruit of two years of planning. As early as March 1942 General Marshall had presented a plan codenamed 'Roundup' for an invasion of Europe drawn up by his keenest officer, General Eisenhower. It envisaged an invasion on 1 April 1943 and the landing of 50 divisions on the northern coast of France between Le Havre and Boulogne, from a fleet of 7000 landing craft (few of which had even been built). The Americans also presented a second plan, for a landing later in 1942 to be launched only if Russia seemed in danger of collapse, involving five divisions, codenamed 'Sledgehammer'. The latter was soon discarded — or rather modified. Brooke predicted that so small a force would be annihilated; it became 'Gymnast', the landings in North Africa. At the Casablanca conference of January 1943 thoughts had become clarified and a special planning section was created. General Frederick Morgan was appointed Chief of Staff, Supreme Allied Commander (he called himself COSSAC) to plan a full-bodied invasion of France for May 1944.

But who would command the great undertaking? Churchill had hoped to offer the command to Brooke, but the mass of forces would be American and it was clear the commander would have to be one of their own. Brooke was heartbroken at being passed over. The obvious choice was George Marshall, but Roosevelt shuddered at the thought of losing his wise counsel in Washington. Admiral King, a sailor with few good things to say about the army, regarded Marshall as 'the one indispensable man' in Washington. Nevertheless Eisenhower was under the impression he would be taking up Marshall's position as Chief of Staff. It was not until Christmas 1943 that Roosevelt appointed him to command the invasion. Eisenhower hoped that Alexander would be appointed his British deputy in command of the field armies, but the choice fell on Alexander's difficult subordinate, Montgomery.

Within three days of taking up his new command, Montgomery, having read the original invasion plan, voiced his concerns. Morgan and his staff had produced a plan so complete and well thought out that its basic suggestions were not changed, and his chiefs marvelled at the work that went into it. Five thousands vessels had been earmarked for the invasion, including 1000 warships and 3000 landing craft. The historian John Keegan writes: 'The cross-Channel shipment of the assault and follow-up, their escorting, beaching and docking and the ship-to-shore bombardment which would cover the landings were irreproachable in conception', as were plans for the air bombardment, the interdiction by the air forces of road communications, and the elaborate deception plan to mislead the Germans into preparing for an invasion in the Pas de Calais. Until the Allies seized Cherbourg they would be without a harbour, so artificial harbours were constructed — giant floating concrete caissons code-named 'Mulberries' — that could be sunk off the beaches to provide breakwaters. To provide fuel for the armies, pipelines would be laid under the Channel — 'PLUTO' (pipe line under the ocean). An experimental division was formed — the 79th British, under the command of an innovative general, Percy Hobart (Montgomery's brother-in-law); it would provide the amphibious tanks that could 'swim' ashore alongside the infantry divisions. In concept and imagination the planning for Overlord was brilliant.

Montgomery changed the plans. He regarded as insufficient the landing of only three divisions on a narrow stretch of the Normandy coast, with another 12 divisions landing in the next two weeks, He predicted another Salerno — a crowded beachhead that could be pushed into the sea. He wrote to Churchill that that it would lead to 'appalling congestion on the beaches.' He demanded that a minimum of five divisions be landed on the first day, at multiple points along a broad front and stated: 'The initial landings must be made on the widest possible front — 80 kilometres, not 40. It should be preceded by airborne landings.' His plan was adopted and the logistics modified. The Allies would land five divisions on five beaches — two American, two British and a Canadian; these beachheads would be built up to Corps strength from the 30 divisions earmarked for the campaign. The first day, Montgomery felt, would be the crucial one.

Other commanders thought the choice of Normandy ridiculous and suggested landing the invasion force directly on the coast near Calais — the Pas de Calais. This appeared the logical place. The Germans thought so too and there, within sight of the English coast, constructed their heaviest defences. One important element of Morgan's plan was retained. Normandy would be the objective. It would involve a far longer voyage for the invasion fleets from English ports — and how this could be done without the enemy observing them was a concern. It was left to Allied counterintelligence to hoodwink the Germans. This was done brilliantly. Intensive bombing and sabotage of railways and roads on the Calais–Paris axis was mounted. German agents in England — all of whom had been caught and 'turned' — forwarded false information to Germany about the thirty Allied divisions in south-east England ready to fall upon Calais.

This great army did not exist. General Patton was appointed to command the phantom army. Always the actor, he played his part to perfection, inspecting skeleton forces to wide publicity. While thousands of dummy tanks and vehicles were constructed in East Anglia, bogus intelligence was broadcast describing a build-up of Allied forces there. Operation Fortitude misled the Germans by false intelligence and wireless messages that another Allied army would land in Norway, forcing the Germans to increase their forces there. (At war's end, when Hitler's bunker was protected by several dozen teenage members of Hitler Youth, 300,000 Germans were still based in Norway). In February 1944 southern England, where the invasion forces were gathering, began to be sealed off. All travel from England ceased. In May troops were confined to their barracks and camps. A blanket of secrecy settled over the island.

The invading Allies would be facing a German army in France of fifty-five divisions, thirty of which were of top quality. They were backed by a Panzer Group of eleven tank divisions, of which half formed Panzer Group West under the command of the C-in-C, Field

Before the Normandy invasion the senior Allied commanders meet. Eisenhower is flanked by Montgomery and Ike's Deputy, Britain's Air Marshal Tedder. Behind (left to right) are General Omar Bradley, Admiral Ramsay, Air Marshal Leigh-Mallory and Lt-General Bedell Smith.

Marshal von Rundstedt, who had resolved to commit them to battle in a massive counteroffensive only when he deemed it necessary. Rommel, his equal in rank but junior in years, had been appointed to the command of Army Group B in northern France in February 1944. He sought control of the Panzers, but was unsuccessful. Rommel wanted the tanks to be close to the coast, ready to crush any invasion on the first day. 'For the Allies as well as the Germans', he said, 'this would be the longest day.' His old adversary Montgomery predicted that Rommel would 'do his level best to Dunkirk us — by preventing our tanks from landing by using his own tanks well forward.' Montgomery was aware that the seemingly peaceful countryside of Normandy possessed obstacles to an army: it was bocage country whose fields were bordered by thick hedgerows and sunken roads, providing defenders with natural defensive positions from which they would literally have to be dug out.

In his final address to his officers on 15 May Montgomery spoke without his usual bombast. 'We must blast our way on shore and get a good lodgement before the enemy can bring up sufficient reserves to turn us out,' he said. 'Armoured columns must penetrate deep inland, and quickly, on D-Day.' His soldiers, he said, must go into battle 'seeing red', consumed with hatred for their enemy. 'Nothing must stop them — nothing.' In this he failed: his British troops still did not hate the 'Jerries', as they called them, with the passion Montgomery demanded. The invasion would begin on Monday 5 June, when tides would be right and a half-moon shining, ideal for an airborne invasion. All now depended on the weather. The spring weather was perfect. The skies were clear, the seas smooth.

At 4.15 a.m. on 4 June, two hours before the invasion army was due to sail, Eisenhower met his staff and was informed that the weather was deteriorating. He postponed the operation. The Admiralty issued a gale warning to all shipping in the Irish Sea. Convoys, buffeted by strong winds, returned to harbour and high waves crashed in fury on the beaches of Normandy. But the weather experts predicted that the storm would soon clear. The tides and the half moon would not appear for another fortnight. In the evening Eisenhower asked his commanders for their views and then made his decision: 'OK. We'll go.' The invasion would begin on 6 June 1944.

D-DAY, 1944

From the harbours of southern England, from Falmouth and Torbay to Southampton and Harwich, the ships slipped out to sea and by mid-afternoon on 5 June had gathered at a point south of the Isle of Wight. Overhead swarms of fighters flew on constant patrol. No German aircraft or raiding torpedo-boats (E-boats) intruded to report the fleet's presence. In the evening aerial bombardment began of the French coastal defences and communications. Late in the afternoon of 5 June Eisenhower drove down to the airfield where units of the US airborne forces — the 82nd and 101st divisions — were blackening their faces and checking their kits preparing to board their aircraft. He talked to them in his natural way: 'Where are you from, soldier?' and grinned if he found a fellow Kansan. At 10 p.m. the paratroops encumbered with their chutes and their 100-pound kits began boarding. At Harwell airfield, 200 British troops wearing the red berets of the airborne forces began boarding their gliders: they would be the pathfinders for the 6th Airborne, who would be dropped by parachute to seize the left flank of the bridgehead and hold the bridge over the Orne and the canal between Caen and the sea until the seaborne troops and 250 gliders carrying the main force reached them later in the day.

By midnight hundreds of Dakota transports, each carrying 18 American paratroopers, were flying almost wingtip-to-wingtip towards the coast of France. The sound alone was awe-inspiring. Of the 820 aircraft only 20 were lost to enemy fire or through collisions. Over the western extremity of the bridgehead they began jumping from their aircraft: these 13,000 airborne soldiers would be the first to land on the soil of France. They too would be reinforced by glider-borne troops. As dawn approached they could hear the sound of the mighty Allied bombardment of the coast.

THE LANDINGS 'A rising, surging sea carried the invasion fleet uneasily into the night. To the men whose destiny lay beyond the black horizon the voyage seemed lonely and interminable,' wrote the BBC war correspondent Chester Wilmot who landed with the British glider-borne troops. At 6.30 a.m. on 6 June American infantry (9th and 90th US divisions) splashed ashore on the far western extremity of the Normandy beaches, at the beach code-named 'Utah'. Two miles offshore, the amphibious tanks had been launched, and a dozen of them landed in the first wave: 'From (the dunes) came not the expected torrent of fire but fitful and erratic spurts, for the defenders were numbed by the bombardment which still rang in their ears.' By 9 a.m. the infantry and tanks on Utah had broken through the defences and were pushing inland.

But to their left, on Omaha beach, there was slaughter. Here the sand ended in a sea wall and the 7-kilometre beach was covered by German machine-guns, which took a deadly toll of the American infantry of 2nd US Division. The water was so rough that some tanks were not landed; others sank like stones and only two reached the beach. Hundreds of men fell in the shallows, the survivors sheltering behind beach obstacles or at the base of the sea wall. Their reinforcements, 29th Division and 1st Division, met with similar solid resistance and took heavy casualties. 'Two kinds of people are staying on this beach — the dead and those who are going to die,' shouted Colonel G.A. Taylor. 'Now let's get the hell out of here.' The Americans blasted the barbed wire with Bangalore torpedoes and fought their way inland but Omaha cost 2000 Americans killed and wounded.

To the east, the British and Canadians were landing. At Gold beach the 50th British Division, veterans of the desert war, splashed out of their landing craft at 7.30 a.m. to see the amphibious tanks already ashore, firing at the defences. Among them were three tanks equipped with whirling 'flails' to explode landmines, but these tanks were soon knocked out or bogged. The English troops — Hampshires, Dorsets, Green Howards — pushed inland and attacked pillboxes with grenades. By late afternoon their beachhead was secured.

On the far left, the 3rd Canadian Division landed on 'Juno' beach and found most of the defences unscathed by the bombardment. By mid-morning, with the aid of tanks, the Canadians had pushed three kilometres inland and by dark were 12 kilometres inland — one of the finest deeds of a day on which heroism was commonplace.

The 3rd British Division — Montgomery's old command at Dunkirk, inactive in England for four years — landed at 'Sword' beach with twenty-one of their twenty-five amphibious tanks. Inland they encountered German tanks of 21 Panzer Division and the advance stalled. The beaches became congested. On their flank the Commandos had cleared the western edge of Oistreham, and in early afternoon the beleaguered British airborne troops holding the Orne bridge heard the skirl of pipes: Lord Lovat was nonchalantly leading 4th Commando to their assistance. It was another eight hours (9.30 p.m.)

General Eisenhower visits the American paratroops before they boarded aircraft for the invasion.

before 3rd Division infantry reached them. But by the evening of 6 June the Allied armies were ashore, for the cost of 11,000 casualties, of whom 2500 were fatalities. This loss was considered light in view of the magnitude of the operation. The Allied air forces had flown 12,000 sorties without the loss of a single aircraft to the Germans. 'By D-Day', writes Wilmot, 'the Luftwaffe was a spent force.' Montgomery had hoped to seize Caen on the first day. It was a vain hope. For a month Caen was to be the pivot of the German counterattacks.

Hitler still thought the Normandy landings were a feint, and that the main Allies would soon land their major forces at the Pas de Calais. The 15th German Army remained north of the Seine to meet its attack. It was not until 4 p.m. that he permitted the use of his armoured Reserve and Rundstedt signalled 7th Army of 'the desire of OKW that the enemy in the bridgehead to be annihilated by the evening of 6th June since there is a danger of fresh landings by sea and air'. Only two of the Reserve's five Panzer divisions were in Normandy: the 17th SS was 200 miles (320 km) away; 1st SS was in Belgium; 2nd SS was 600 miles (1000 km) away near Toulouse, and its movement north was fated to be delayed by attacks by the French Resistance.

The two Panzer divisions available were to counterattack immediately from Caen. Kurt Meyer of 12th SS was jubilant, describing the British as 'little fish' whom he would soon throw back in the water. Meyer's teenage warriors of the Hitler Youth were soon to strike the

British infantry landing under fire on the beaches of Normandy, dawn, 6 June, 1944.

Left: Field-Marshal Rommel and his chief of staff General Speidel, 1944.
Below: Canadian and British troops with German prisoners on the first day of the Normandy invasion.

THE BATTLE FOR NORMANDY

Now began the hardest part of the campaign: to break out of the bridgehead before stalemate was reached. Rommel and Hitler still believed that another assault was soon to fall on the Pas de Calais; 15th Army remained at full strength and not until late July were divisions sent to help contain the Allied offensives. They came too late. In the west the Americans took the surrender of Cherbourg (26 June), only to find the great port blocked by demolitions. It was not useable till late in August. Supplies had to be brought in to the beaches, using the artificial harbours, but on 19 June a great storm had blown up in the Channel, driving the pontoons onshore, wrecking the harbour in the American sector. But nearly half a million Allied troops were ashore. German Panzer attacks were stopped dead.

Canadians with savagery. By the end of 7 June (when the Allies entered Bayeux, which was liberated without a shot), Allied fighter-bombers had almost destroyed Bayerlein's Panzer Lehr division. Thereafter his formation moved under cover of night. By the end of the second day General Miles Dempsey's British–Canadian troops had linked up and firmly established a bridgehead 30 kilometres wide and up to 15 kilometres deep. By dawn on 8 June their bridgehead had joined the Americans and the Allied bridgehead now ran 50 kilometres along the Atlantic coastline. On 10 June the area was safe enough to allow Prime Minister Churchill and the Allied Chiefs of Staff to visit Normandy and observe their armies' progress. By this stage 14 Allied divisions were ashore and the bridgehead was now 70 miles (110 km) wide, and deepening every day.

On 1 July Keitel telephoned Rundstedt and asked 'What shall we do?' The old Field Marshal replied: 'Make peace, you idiots. What else can you do?' On 8 July the British entered the ruins of Caen and ten days later Montgomery launched an attack by Three Corps — 'Operation Goodwood'. While General Bradley's 1st US Army prepared to launch 'Cobra', Goodwood ground to a standstill but Montgomery's 2nd British Army and 1st Canadian Army were now attracting the weight of German armour in Normandy. When Cobra began on 26 July after the vital crossroads town of Saint-Lô had been wrested from the Germans, it developed rapidly. By 31 July

the American tanks had reached as far south as Avranches. On the following day General George Patton's 3rd US Army became operational. Patton's great moment had come: he unleashed his tanks from Avranches, they overran Brittany (the German-held ports were ignored, except Brest which surrendered after a heavy attack in mid-September). Hitler's generals recommended an evacuation of forces from France but he ordered a counterattack at Mortain by seven divisions on 7 August; the attack was stopped by a single American division, thereafter known as 'The Rock of Mortain', and the offensive

Above: Montgomery's forces enter a village in Normandy. On the right are two Sherman tanks observed by British troops and French civilians.
Below: American troops in a newly-liberated village in Normandy are welcomed by French civilians.

dissipated under Allied counterattacks. Patton's tanks entered Le Mans (9 August) and sped on through towns where they were welcomed by cheering French men, women and children before swinging north towards Argentan.

THE BOMB PLOT: 20 JULY 1944

Just after midday on 20 July 1944 there was an explosion in the conference room at Hitler's East Prussian headquarters — the 'Wolf's Lair'. Hitler staggered into the daylight, his tunic torn, his eyebrows singed, his eardrums burst. Twelve hours later (at 1 a.m. next day) he made a broadcast to the German people, announcing in a raucous voice: 'My German comrades! If I speak to you today it is first in order that you should hear my voice and should know that I am unhurt and well ... A very small clique of ambitious, irresponsible and, at the same time, senseless and stupid officers had concocted a plot to eliminate me ... The circle of these usurpers is very small and has nothing in common with the spirit of the German Wehrmacht ... It is a gang of criminal elements which will be destroyed without mercy ...' When he heard that several field marshals had been implicated in the assassination attempt he told his chief prosecutor: 'I want them to be hanged, strung up like butchered cattle.'

His lackeys had already begun executing the plotters. The junior officer who had inspired the attempt on the dictator's life and almost carried it through had already been shot in the courtyard of the War Ministry in Berlin. He was a young nobleman, Count von Stauffenberg, who would be remembered as the Lochinvar of the German Resistance. This was not the first attempt by Germans to kill Hitler but it would be the last. In its aftermath what remained of German opposition to Hitler was killed off brutally or confined to concentration camps awaiting the executioner's bullet. They failed to save Germany from its final descent into hell but — in the words of the German historian Joachim Fest — their failure 'does not detract from their memory or from the example that they set'. The Germans who resisted Hitler were among the bravest of all, for no power helped them, the Allies mocked their efforts and postwar Germany for two generations depicted them as traitors.

They were of all ages and came from all walks of life, from the clergy and the nobility to the army and university students. Hitler had been correct in describing the General Staff as a nest of traitors. On a number of occasions senior generals plotted to remove him from power but were thwarted at the last moment by their failure of nerve or a change of circumstances. Hitler, like many dictators after him, kept his movements secret, changed his timetables. In his own grotesque way he seemed to have a charmed life.

THE GERMAN RESISTANCE

Late in 1942 the Gestapo had swooped and arrested a group of prominent Berliners whose activities had been monitored by informers. Among the eighty men and women arrested were the nucleus of a Communist cell that formed the heart of the Soviet 'Red Orchestra' spy ring. They included a Luftwaffe officer, Harro Shulze-Boysen and his wife; and Arvid von Harnack and his American-born wife Mildred. All were executed; Mildred Harnack

Field-Marshal von Witzleben in front of the People's Court where he was sentenced to death for treason.

was beheaded on the personal order of Hitler on 16 February 1943.

Two days later two young university students in Munich, Hans Scholl and his sister Sophie, were arrested after they were seen distributing leaflets denouncing the Nazis and their war. They called themselves the White Rose movement. With their professor and a young friend, Christopher Probst, they were found guilty of treason and beheaded. Before her execution Sophie Scholl said: 'What does my death matter if by our actions thousands are awakened and stirred to action? In the same year, 1943, Hitler discovered that his own counterintelligence Service, the Abwehr, was not only riddled with anti-Nazis but led by them: the SS arrested its head, Admiral Canaris and his right hand man, Colonel Hans Oster and many of their officers. The SS and Gestapo took over the Abwehr's duties. Among other prominent figures arrested were the theologian Dietrich Bonhoeffer who regarded Hitler as the embodiment of evil, the anti-Christ, and Count Helmuth von Moltke, whose Kreisau circle had long discussed ways of ridding Germany of its murderous regime but abhorred violence. (Canaris, Oster, Bonhoeffer and Moltke languished in concentration camps until the last weeks of the war, when they were killed by the Nazis.)

It seemed that the spirit of resistance was broken. The arrival of Stauffenberg changed all that. He had lost an eye and an arm in the fighting in Tunisia, yet he would be described as a rare being, a 'complete man': honourable, inspiring, decisive, loyal in friendship and brave. Younger officers gravitated to him. Posted to the War Ministry and often in close proximity to the Führer, Stauffenberg evolved with his comrades an elaborate plot to kill Hitler and replace him with a government free of Nazis that could negotiate an end to the war. Concurrent with Hitler's assassination, units of the Reserve

Army would arrest Nazi leaders under the ruse that they were carrying out an exercise to ensure their safety — 'Operation Valkyrie'. Senior military commanders were sounded out but few, including Rommel, committed themselves to the plot. Most said they would await the outcome; this was enough to see their lives brutally ended by Hitler.

Von Stauffenberg flew into Rastenburg at 10 a.m. on 20 July. He was carrying in his briefcase a bomb with a timing mechanism. He used captured British explosives, which were better than their German equivalent. Before entering the Führer's conference he armed the fuse. It was a sweltering day and the atmosphere in the hut was stifling. He placed the briefcase under the table near Hitler and excused himself. Shortly afterwards, at 12.40 p.m., there was an ear-splitting explosion. Stauffenberg immediately drove unhindered to the airfield and flew back to Berlin, positive that Hitler was dead. From the War Ministry Stauffenberg's comrades sent messages by teleprinter to the army in Paris, Prague and Vienna to arrest the local SS leaders. This was done by army officers with some enthusiasm. At 4.30 p.m. Stauffenberg arrived at the War Ministry. There he discovered that Hitler was not dead and that messages from Rastenburg were already reaching Berlin.

Hitler was injured but alive. Goebbels was being arrested by the army when the officer commanding the Berlin guard battalion, Major Remer, spoke to Hitler himself on the telephone. Hitler ordered him to suppress the rising immediately. One of the principal plotters, General Fromm, tried to save his own skin by condemning Stauffenberg and his officers to death. Their senior plotter, General Beck, who had resigned from the army ten year earlier because of his loathing for the Nazis, was given the opportunity to shoot himself. The younger officers were shot in the glow of head lights in the courtyard of the War Ministry and Fromm sent the message by teleprinter to Rastenburg: 'Attempted putsch by disloyal generals violently suppressed. All leaders shot.' He too was later shot on Hitler's orders.

The trials of eight of the plotters began on 7 August. Many had already been subjected to torture and were treated with indignity by the judge, a rabid individual named Roland Freisler. The following day all were condemned to death, among them General von Witzleben, General Hoepner and Count Peter Yorck von Wartenburg. They were strangled on piano wire hung from steel hooks and Hitler ordered their death throes filmed for his enjoyment. On the same day another group of officers were tried, found guilty and sentenced to suffer the same fate. For months, as the Gestapo mounted a manhunt throughout the Reich, other anti-Hitler figures were tracked down and put on trial. Even their relatives were arrested. Field Marshal Rommel had already been forced to commit suicide because of his contacts with the plotters. Field-Marshal von Kluge also killed himself. General von Stülpnagel, military commander in Paris, shot himself but succeeded only in blinding himself. He too was hanged.

The victims of Hitler's wrath had attempted to save Germany from further suffering. Up to July 1944 nearly 2.8 million Germans had died. By the end of the war another 4.5 million Germans would lose their lives.

FLYING BOMBS AND ROCKETS

Hitler had often spoken to his intimates of his 'secret weapons' that would bring Britain to her knees and give him victory. On the night of 12 June 1944 Hitler unleashed the first of them on London — a pilotless 'flying bomb'. By the end of the month 724 of them had struck the city. Fighter aircraft and AA-guns tried to bring 'the doodle-bugs' down before they reached the city, and in July–August Bomber Command flew 10,000 sorties against the launching sites. On 6 July Churchill informed the Commons that about 2750 flying bombs had been launched against London and had killed 2752 people — 'exactly one person per bomb' — while 10,000 Londoners had been wounded. (Another 2000 airmen were to die in the bombing of the rocket sites that destroyed most of Hitler's terror weapons.) By the end of the first week of September Allied armies had overrun the launching sites. Of more than 8000 V1s launched against London, only about 2400 got to their target, and they had killed 6000 people and injured another 18,000. More than 1000 V1s had crashed after launching; others turned and plunged harmlessly away from their target; fighter aircraft, anti-aircraft defences and the balloon barrage had taken care of others. Churchill was proud of the victory, and of the spirit of the Londoners.

The V1 flying-bomb menace had no sooner been overcome than V2 rockets were launched. These 13-tonne monsters were supersonic and Londoners heard the whine of their approach after they had exploded. Bomber Command again had to divert its main efforts from the bombing of Germany to help neutralise the missile sites, a task completed in December. Many of the missile sites were based in The Hague, and many were fired on Antwerp (which became the target of 8700 V1s and 1600 rockets), Liège and Brussels, causing huge damage. 'The people of Belgium', wrote Churchill, 'bore this senseless bombardment in a spirit equal to our own.' By this stage 1300 V2s had been launched against London, of which number 500 hit the city, causing another 10,000 casualties (one in four of whom was killed).

Top: The V1 'Flying Bomb', also known as the 'Doodle Bug'.
Right: The German rockets were dubbed the 'V2's.

Montgomery's tough fighting had made this advance possible. In the words of his official biographer, the Americans' 'stunning successes in France in 1944 were predicated on the selfless role of British and Canadian troops in Monty's great design'. By 17 August, the day when Patton's tanks reached Orleans, the Canadians had reached Falaise, and the retreating Germans were soon caught there in a trap. Attacked on three sides and subjected to ceaseless air attack, eight German divisions were annihilated in the Falaise Pocket in five days; and the tattered remnants of Hitler's armies in France retreated across the Seine. The Germans had lost 400,000 men (half of them were prisoners of war) and 1300 tanks.

Allied killed, wounded and missing in the 80 days of fighting, principally in the killing ground of Normandy, totalled 210,000; to this figure should be added the lives of 20,000 Allied airmen who died in bombers and fighters over this period.

Above: **American foot-sloggers (infantry) make their way through a French town near Avranches in Normandy.**
Below: **The German defenders of Normandy provided the Allied armies with tough resistance. This soldier's collar and breast plate denotes him as a member of a Luftwaffe security unit.**

SOUTHERN FRANCE

On 15 August the Allies landed in southern France in Operation Dragoon. Churchill had pleaded for its cancellation, saddened to see so many divisions employed for the operation that could have been more effectively used in Italy. But he was on the scene to see General Alexander Patch's US 7th Army go ashore on the Riviera coast. Appropriately, the bulk of the force was French — seven divisions under General de Lattre (his command would soon be renamed French 1st Army) and three American. Inland the French Resistance rose up to delay German reinforcements reaching the landing zones. By the end of August Marseilles had fallen to the French and Americans and the Allies had advanced as far north as Grenoble. Lyons fell on 3 September; one week later Patch's troops linked up with Patton's forward units.

LIBERATION OF PARIS

Paris had already been liberated by another French force. Eisenhower had planned to bypass Paris, but de Gaulle pressed him to reconsider this decision. On 19 August the police of Paris, hearing of the approach of the Allies, refused to follow German orders and began firing on the Germans. They were quickly joined by the men and women of the Resistance and street fighting began. A short truce was called and Gaullist patriots made their way out of Paris to warn de Gaulle that the Communist units were likely to take over the city if it were not destroyed first by the Germans: the Allies must come, and come soon. Late on 22 August Eisenhower gave orders for General Leclerc's 2nd Armoured Division — the spirited veterans of the Sahara — and the US 4th Division to race for Paris.

General Leclerc acknowledges the cheers of the Parisians (and gives the Victory sign) on the day his tanks liberated Paris.

Hitler ordered the German commander in Paris, General von Choltitz, to destroy the city but his 20,000 men, though possessing nearly 100 tanks, were powerless to contain the insurrection. Intermediaries — including the Swedish consul-general — pleaded with Choltitz to spare Paris, the 'City of Light'. On the evening of 24 August the first French tank entered the centre of Paris and by nightfall the bells of Paris were ringing. Next day, as Hitler was demanding angrily of Choltitz: 'Is Paris burning?' Leclerc's entire division was tearing through villages packed with cheering crowds and had entered the city. By day's end French tanks were fighting in the heart of Paris and the hunting down of the last Germans began.

De Gaulle entered Paris on the following day, walking down the Champs Élysées through an ocean of people delirious with joy, to lay a wreath beneath the Arc de Triomphe. It was one of the emotional moments of the war. Two days before Paris fell, Romania had signed an armistice with the invading Red Army, whose summer offensive had brought them deep into eastern Europe and the northern Balkans. The two western and eastern props of Hitler's Fortress Europe had been knocked away. In September 1944 American troops crossed the German border near Aachen. It seemed possible that the European war could be over by Christmas, as Eisenhower had hoped.

ITALY

Churchill regarded the diversion of his forces from Italy to southern France as a grave strategic error, but his pleadings to Roosevelt and Eisenhower that the Riviera landings be cancelled fell on deaf ears. The President, already concerned about Soviet intentions in eastern Europe, was alarmed by Alexander's plans to break the German armies in Italy, enter the Po valley and then proceed via the Ljublana Gap into Slovenia and the plain of Hungary.

Weakened by the transfer of seven divisions to southern France — including Juin's fine French Corps — Alexander, with only twenty divisions, launched his summer offensive on 26 August against twenty-two enemy divisions defending the strongly fortified Gothic line, which stretched across the peninsula. Churchill flew out to Italy to witness the opening battle and watched with Alexander from a hillside north of Florence as the 5th Army moved forward. He could see little but artillery explosions but enjoyed being under enemy shellfire.

The Americans took Futa Pass but were stopped short of their objective, Bologna, by Kesselring's savage counterattacks. In the east, on the Adriatic coast 8th Army, strengthened by the Polish Corps, took Rimini after four weeks of fighting on 21 September and entered the Po Valley and the plains of the Romagna. Then the autumn rains fell, and the water-logged plain became impassable. 'All that is remembered about the Gothic line battles is the heavy losses suffered by both Armies for so little reward,' writes one of Alexander's biographers. As the weather deteriorated, the Allied armies in Italy were condemned to another winter of stalemate. The final thrust to the Alps would have to wait until the coming of spring in 1945.

Russian tank men welcomed by villagers after the Red Army's entry into eastern Poland; this is possibly a posed propaganda photograph.

1944: EASTERN FRONT VICTORY ALL THE WAY

Four days after the Allied landing in Normandy the Russians began their summer offensive. On 10 June Marshal Govorov launched the Red Army against the Finnish defences, broke through them and two weeks later reached Viipuri. Finland initiated armistice talks. On 23 June the clearing of Belorussia began. Field Marshal von Busch pleaded with Hitler to allow him to retreat before the blow fell; the Führer's reply was to sack him and replace him with Field Marshal Model. The Red Army launched 166 divisions on four fronts into Belorussia and by mid-July had taken Vitebsk, Bobruisk and Minsk. At Minsk an army of 100,000 Germans were surrounded; 40,000 were killed and the rest taken prisoner, to be marched through the streets of Moscow to a captivity that few survived. They were all that remained of nearly thirty German divisions.

Much of Belorussia was now a desert. The Germans had ploughed the crops under and destroyed more than a million homes. Close to 400,000 people had been deported to Germany. Yet large Partisan forces had survived in the marshes along the Dnieper, and at one stage they had controlled up to 60 per cent of Belorussia.

INTO POLAND

The Russian advance continued. On 13 July the Red Army took Vilno (Lithuania) and the armies of Marshal Rokossovski entered Poland, his place of birth, taking Lublin on 23 July. On the outskirts of Lublin they discovered an enormous camp ringed with barbed wire and seemingly deserted. It was Majdanek, the extermination camp where between 1.3 million and 1.5 million Jews had been murdered. The British war correspondent Alexander Werth went to Lublin several days later and wrote: 'Despite some bomb damage here and there, the city had preserved some of its old-time charm.' The churches were crowded and the streets full of Russian and Polish troops; the shops were empty but food was available in the markets. People told terrible stories of German rule and of massed hangings in Lublin's squares.

Nothing prepared Werth for Majdanek. It lay only three kilometres from Lublin, within sight of the city's steeples. 'It looked singularly harmless from outide,' he wrote. 'The place was large; like a whole town of barracks painted a pleasant soft green.' The grass was a dull, greenish-grey colour. At one end of the camp there were enormous mounds of ashes: they were human remains, sprinkled with bones. In a field nearby cabbages grew to enormous size; they had been fertilised with human ashes. At the other end of the camp squatted concrete buildings: the gas chambers; and nearby the crematoria, where the bodies were burnt. It was a factory of death, producing nothing but corpses. On one day 20,000 Jews had been gassed at Majdanek; the crematoria could not burn all the corpses, so most of them were buried in mass graves. When Werth related its history the BBC refused to believe his story or to use it. The *New York Times* commented that reports of the Nazi atrocity 'sound inconceivable', while adding that a 'regime capable of such crimes deserves annihilation'.

On the last day of July the Russians reached the Gulf of Riga, cutting off an entire German Army Group in Latvia, where thirty divisions were soon stranded. On the same day the Russians reached the Vistula River opposite Warsaw, entering the suburbs of Praga, and Moscow radio called upon the Poles of Warsaw to rise up against the Germans.

WARSAW UPRISING

Late on 1 August the Polish Resistance in Warsaw emerged from their four years of waiting and began firing on the Germans, confident that the Red Army would soon be entering the city. What now followed was one of the needless tragedies of the war but also one of the most heroic. The Poles, who acknowledged the government in exile in London as their leaders, and had accumulated arms and hidden them until now, tore up concrete pavements and built barricades, hurling petrol bombs against German tanks. They seized ammunition and weapons from dead Germans and waited for liberation. Stalin let the Poles fight and die. One week before the Warsaw uprising he had established a Polish Communist government at Lublin. In response to the Home Army's pleas for assistance, Churchill informed Stalin that he was dropping supplies and ammunition to them by air. On the following day, 5 August 1944, Stalin replied coldly that the 'Home Army of the Poles consists of a few detachments …' On 15 September the Red Army finally secured Praga and was soon to establish a narrow bridgehead across the river in the face of heavy German counterattacks, but Warsaw's agony continued. On 1 October General Bor-Komarowski capitulated to the Germans on the understanding that he and his men would be treated as soldiers, not insurgents. The Germans removed him to captivity in Germany — to Colditz. On 11 October Hitler ordered Warsaw razed to the ground. By the time the demolitions ended 90 per cent of the old city of Warsaw was rubble. Polish historians maintain that of the city's population of one million, up to 300,000 Poles died; the British historian of Europe's resistance, M.R.D. Foot, gives a figure of 100,000 Polish dead. Churchill wrote in his memoirs that 15,000 members of the Resistance were killed and 200,000 citizens were 'stricken'.

HITLER'S ALLIES FALL
ROMANIA

On 20 August, 1944 the Russian armies on the Ukraine front — totalling 90 divisions — struck deep into Romania, encircling sixteen German divisions and what remained of the Romanian Army. The majority of the Romanian troops laid down their arms. The road to Bucharest was open. On 23 August King Michael asked Marshal Antonescu to come to the royal villa outside Bucharest to discuss the gravity of the situation. There the young monarch ordered the dictator to arrange an immediate armistice with the Russians. Antonescu, stupefied, refused. Michael pushed a buzzer beneath his desk and a handful of his own Royal Guards burst into the room and arrested Antonescu. The King then announced in a broadcast that a cease-fire was taking place and that General Sanatescu was forming a new government.

German reaction to this was savage: as Romanian troops in Bucharest began hunting down Germans, the Luftwaffe launched a savage bombing attack on the city. The German minister suicided as Russian forces entered Bucharest — and the nearby oilfields of Ploesti — on 30 August. The Soviet forces were greeted by cheering crowds, and brought with them Romanian Communists who were soon appointed to prominent positions in the provisional government. The Romanian Army was now an ally of the Red Army, and

Above: King Michael of Romania (left) at the front with the nation's dictator General Antonescu whom the King arrested in August 1944 as Russian armies approached
Below: Bulgarians welcome the arrival of the Red Army. Sixty years after these pictures were taken, when the Communist regimes had fallen, King Michael and King Simeon returned to their countries where they were received with warmth.

was to prove a potent force in its new role, suffering heavier battle casualties in the next nine months of war than it had since Romania's unwise entry into the conflict in 1941. From Bucharest the Soviet armies advanced due west, towards Belgrade. Bulgaria now lay prone to attack, and Hitler's armies in the Balkans faced being marooned.

In September a Romanian armistice delegation flew to Moscow to formalise their country's new status as an ally. 'No sooner had the Rumanians gone than the Finns were ready to be received,' wrote Werth of these dramatic collapses. 'The Rumanian armistice was signed on the 12th; and the Finns on the 19th; and then came the Bulgarians.'

BULGARIA

Oddly, the Soviet Union was not at war with Bulgaria. Tsar Boris had sought to maintain friendly relations with Moscow while retaining a certain independence from Hitler. Like Mannerheim of Finland, he had refused to deport his country's Jews, a decision endorsed by their people; no Bulgarian troops fought on the Eastern Front. Boris had died mysteriously after returning from a conference with Hitler on 28 August 1943; since that day a Regency had ruled in the name of his six-year-old son Simeon. On 5 September the Soviet Union declared war on Bulgaria and three days later Soviet armies entered the country. No resistance was offered. Two days later the Bulgarian government declared war on Germany. As in Romania, a purge of anti Communist elements began; among those soon shot as traitors were the three unfortunate Regents, among them the boy king's uncle, Prince Kyril.

Poland, Romania and Bulgaria were now in the Soviet sphere of influence and destined for forty-five years of grey Communist rule. They were soon to be joined by Hungary.

HUNGARY

Like Bulgaria's rulers, Hungary's Regent, Admiral Horthy, had sought to maintain a form of independence from Hitler. Hungary's Jews remained unmolested, and in the nation a certain freedom of speech and the rump of a parliament survived well into 1944. When Hitler accused Horthy of protecting the Jews, the baffled Regent replied: 'What do you want me to do with them? Kill them?' Hitler nodded. Horthy was appalled. As Soviet armies approached Hungary's borders Horthy initiated contacts with the Allies. General Alexander was astonished one day to see a number of Hungarian generals who had flown to Italy to open armistice negotiations. Churchill rejected their overtures: they must deal directly with the Soviets.

By 10 October 1944 General Malinowski's Soviet armies had crashed through the Hungarian and German defence lines and reached to within 70 kilometres of Budapest. Weary of Hungary's passivity, Hitler decided to end the fiction of Hungarian independence and install a local fascist government headed by the leader of the 'Arrow Cross' movement, a deranged anti-Semite, Ferenc Salasi. On 15 October Admiral Horthy broadcast that Hungary was declaring an armistice with the Soviet Union; by nightfall SS units led by Otto Skorzeny had kidnapped Horthy from the palace above the Danube and fought Hungarian army units to a standstill in the city. Salasi was proclaimed premier and — in the words of the historian John A. Lucacs — 'a nightmare reign of horror began'. Salasi provided full facilities to Adolf Eichmann's SS in rounding up Hungary's Jews for deportation and vowed to defend Budapest to the death. A young official at the Swedish legation, Raoul Wallenberg (one of the prominent banking family) saved thousands of Jews by providing refuge for them (he took over buildings in Budapest and declared them part of the Swedish legation). After the Russians entered the city he disappeared. He was to die in captivity in the Soviet Union in 1947.

GREECE AND YUGOSLAVIA

Hitler reluctantly ordered his Army Group South East to evacuate Greece, and southern and eastern Yugoslavia; in the west of the fragmented country they fought for the next six months a bitter campaign against Tito's Partisans. On 15 October a British convoy of nearly 100 ships steamed unmolested to the port of Piraeus and landed troops to garrison Athens. The Germans had gone. On 20 October Tolbukhin's Soviet armies and Tito's Partisans entered Belgrade. Tito would soon prove to be no puppet in Moscow's hands. Only two weeks earlier the Albanian Partisans had entered Tirana.

CHURCHILL IN MOSCOW

Churchill was concerned by the widening rift with Stalin. Deeply saddened by the Soviets' attitude to Poland and their abandonment of the Warsaw patriots, he nevertheless defended Russia's record in the House of Commons, reminding members that 'we must never forget the … measureless services which Russia has rendered to the common cause, through long years of suffering, by tearing the life out of the German military monster'. Russia, he stated, 'had borne the brunt of the struggle on land'. (Indeed, it has been estimated by a British historian that 90 per cent of German military and civilian fatalities occurred on the Eastern Front.)

Churchill resolved to go to Moscow to discuss the chance of the Soviets entering the war against Japan and, more importantly the future of eastern Europe. He would beard the Great Bear (as he often called Stalin) in his den. He flew with his staff from London on 7 October by way of Italy, where he saw Alexander and Wilson. Alexander complained that the 'Italian front was being allowed to wither away' and had been 'wrecked by bad strategy'. Stripped of his best divisions and with no chance of reinforcements (all were being directed to France), he had no hope of breaking the German line before winter set in.

In Moscow both leaders agreed that the two Polish governments — one in London, the other in Lublin — must come to an agreement. Churchill then said: 'Let us settle about our affairs in the Balkans' and suggested that they agree on how much influence the Soviets and Britain should have in the nations now at the mercy of the Red Army. Churchill took a piece of paper and wrote down a list of them, suggesting that in Romania, Russia should have 90 per cent predominance, in Greece 10 per cent, in Yugoslavia, 50 per cent, in Hungary,

50 per cent, in Bulgaria 90 per cent. Stalin readily assented. He had no intention of honouring the agreement. Freedom of choice in all the other nations, pro-western in sentiment and democratic in their political groupings, was soon to be extinguished — except in Greece.

UNREST IN GREECE

British troops and officials who had landed bloodlessly in Greece found themselves in a difficult situation, one that soon erupted into violence. The strongest Resistance forces — the Communist movement (ELAS) and its armed units (EAM) — were undeclared enemies of the right-wing force (EDES) and refused to tolerate the notion of a restoration of the monarchy, regarding King George's ministers as semi-fascist. Churchill's choice as prime minister, the moderate Socialist George Papandreou had announced his willingness to form a coalition government with the Communists, but the latter protested that Papandreou and the British were fostering anti-Communist groups. The militia organised by the Germans, for example, was maintained as a police force. On 3 December there took place a mass demonstration in Athens and firing broke out (it is still unknown whether the shots were fired by British troops, Greek police or Communists) and several demonstrators were killed. The armed Communists struck back, attacking police stations and government buildings. The first part of the Greek Civil War had begun and British troops were caught in the crossfire.

On 7 December Harold Macmillan at his headquarters in Caserta wrote in his diary: 'The Greek news is very bad, and so is the Italian. Greece has a revolution, and Italy is without a government. And in both cases we have drifted apart from our American Ally and a great part of British public opinion is disturbed and hostile.' Four days later he flew to Athens with Alexander to evaluate the situation. They reached the British embassy in the capital to find it under sniper fire and discovered that the small British garrison held barely 5 per cent of the city; some units were cut off and surrounded. Alexander signalled Churchill to suggest that a neutral figure, the widely admired Archbishop Damaskinos, be appointed Regent, and that the insurgents be ordered to withdraw from Athens or face the consequences. Churchill concurred in this. On 12 December Alexander — promoted field marshal on that day to succeed Jumbo Wilson as C-in-C Mediterranean — flew back to Italy to organise the sending of reinforcements to Athens. Churchill decided to fly to Athens to try and sort out the mess, and arrived to everyone's surprise on Christmas Day. In the evening he called a conference attended by the ELAS and EDES leaders, who arrived heavily armed. Electricity had been cut off, so the meeting was lit by hurricane lamps; Churchill was flanked by Damaskinos, Eden, Alexander and Macmillan. They began negotiations to the sounds of a full-scale war — the sound of explosions and rifle-fire; rocket-firing Beaufighters were already blasting EAM positions.

Less than two weeks later the Communists accepted truce terms; in mid-January they began leaving Athens for their refuges in the north. The truce remained in force, though fragile, for another three years.

WAR AGAINST JAPAN

BURMA: JAPAN'S LAST OFFENSIVES

During 1943 the Allies built up their strength on the frontier with Burma, and they built roads. For the Allied nations the Burma front was a forgotten war; there were no dramatic victories to claim, no swift advances. Allied commanders saw the stagnant front as the sole connection with China, for the Indian railways ended at Dimapur high in the mountains of Assam, and from Dimapur roads were being laid to Ledo in the north, connecting it to China. From Dimapur also a road had been constructed south to the plateau of Kohima, which by late 1943 was the main British base on the Burma front, filled with supply dumps, hospitals and all-weather airfields.

Burma was impossible country, yet in 1944 it would see the first and most complete victory inflicted on the Japanese. Burma is bordered to the west, north and east by mountain ranges — on the

General William Slim commander of the 14th Army in Burma. Possibly the outstanding British military commander of the war, Slim led his 'Forgotten Army' (three-quarters of whom were Indian soldiers) to victory over the Japanese in Burma in 1944–45.

frontier with India in the west by the mountains of Assam, in the north and east by the rugged ranges of China. In Burma the rivers run from the north to the south and provide no natural obstacle to armies invading from the north or south. The Central Burma plain is flat and dry, perfect tank fighting country, but Slim's tanks and heavy artillery would have to be brought over the mountains, a task considered impossible. To darken the gloom of any general contemplating a Burma campaign, the monsoon arrived in May and lasted till early November, turning the entire country into a quagmire, pestilential with mosquitos and exotic tropical diseases; the rivers became raging torrents.

Late in 1943 General Slim's 14th Army HQ received intelligence that the Japanese forces in Burma were being doubled in size: no fewer than seven divisions were in the country or arriving there. Japan had resolved on a major offensive, nothing less than an invasion of India through the mountains of Assam. If successful it would effectively sever the Allied lifeline to China along the Ledo road and perhaps even force China to sign an armistice (a prospect that long worried the Western Allies). As 1944 dawned, a major victory became for Japan a necessity, for her Pacific empire was shrinking, natural resources were in short supply, war weariness was pronounced. The risk of waging a major offensive in notoriously rugged terrain was balanced by political benefits, too: Japan would use two divisions of Indian National Army troops, and was confident that the Indian masses would rise up against British control once a victory was achieved.

The Japanese attack in Assam would be the major punch in the two-fisted assault, for in the south they would launch a simultaneous offensive against the British-Indian positions in the Arakan and hopefully clear the way for a coastal advance to Chittagong and thence to Calcutta. The Japanese had nothing but contempt for the British-Indian Army in Burma. Yet in the preceding year both the morale and the equipment of the 14th Army had increased. It had been a long battle to transform a defeated army into one confident of turning back an enemy offensive, and much of the transformation was due to General Slim, and to the newly arrived Supreme Commander South-East Asia Command, the youthful Admiral Mountbatten.

Slim knew that his men would need a preponderance in numbers and equipment to outfight the Japanese, and he determined to provide them with these. In addition, he now had ample and growing RAF and American air forces for ground support and supply. Both Churchill and Wavell had supported Brigadier Orde Wingate in creating the 'Chindits' to make forays into Japanese-held territory. Slim knew that the Japanese could only be defeated by conventional methods — by drawing them into battle on a field of his choosing and subjecting them to concentrated attack by air, tanks, artillery and infantry before cutting off their lines of communications and lines of retreat. In many ways this brilliant soldier was a most conventional general. Indeed by early 1944 Slim saw the coming Japanese offensive as his first real chance to destroy the Japanese army in Burma — reconquering terrain was the last of his priorities.

The 'Burma Road'. Constructed by Chinese labourers as a supply route from Burma to China, the road was one of the civil engineering wonders of the war.

HA-GO! THE ARAKAN OFFENSIVES Slim was to confess that he was initially astonished by the vigour and range of the Japanese offensives. The Japanese 15th Army would use three divisions in addition to INA units in Assam against Imphal–Kohima. On 3 February 1944 one Japanese division — 55th Division — attacked in the Arakan, which was now defended by five divisions (among them 5th and 7th Indian and 81st West African). Despite their numerical inferiority the Japanese cut the roads and broke into the 7th Indian Division HQ, sending its redoubtable commander Frank Messervy to join the retreat — yet again — without his cap. It was Messervy who inspired and directed the desperate defence of the Administrative Box from 6 to 24 February, when the Japanese, faced by mounting counter-attacks, called off the offensive, having lost heavily. By mid-March the Japanese had been driven out of their strong defences in the Tunnels system beneath the Mayu range, and they were then exterminated completely. Only 8000 Japanese had dislocated an army of 180,000 British-Indian troops — but for the first time Slim's troops had stood their ground and fought back. He saw it as a victory. 'For the first time a British force had met, held and decisively defeated a major Japanese attack and followed this up by driving the Japanese out of the strongest possible natural positions,' he later wrote. The Japanese defeat in the Arakan in 1944 was decisive. One of Slim's officers, the 28-year-old Brigadier Mike Calvert, wrote: ' It was the first time a Japanese attack on the continent of Asia had been held by the western powers. The Australians had found out how to do this in New Guinea eighteen months before, but they were a cohesive entity who could trust each other.'

CHINA The last Japanese were being killed in the Arakan when another Japanese force launched an offensive in the north, in Assam — and another in China (the 'U-Go' offensive), in an attempt to seize the airfields at which Chennault's bombers were based. The China-based US 14th Air Force was in General Chennault's view the instrument with which to defeat the Japanese. Stilwell, exasperated with Chiang Kai-shek's ineptitude and Chennault's obsession, signalled General Marshall in mid-May that China 'will squeeze out of us everything it can get to make us pay for the privilege of getting at Japan through China … I contend that ultimately the Jap army must be fought on the mainland of Asia … Is my mission changed?' Marshall informed him that priority would be given to air offensives against the enemy. Soon the first of the super-bombers would arrive at Chinese airfields: the B-29 'Super Fortresses'. Even Chennault, a prophet of air power, was doubtful of their effectiveness. He was happy with his B-17s and B-25s (Mitchell Bombers).

Fuel for the new bombers would have to be flown from India across the Himalayas to four new airfields being constructed in Chengtu. The B-29s were enormous. They were 100 feet long, with a wingspan of 144 feet. They could fly at 350 mph and carry a bombload of 4 tonnes for 3500 miles (about 6000 km). On 5 June the first hundred B-29s in India raided Bangkok; only half of them found the target but the raid was judged a success. Ten days later 92 of them flew from India to Chengtu to refuel and then proceed on their first raid on Japan. Some got lost on the way over the Himalayas, others suffered mechanical failure, others landed at the wrong strips. Sixty-nine of the bombers that took off made it to Kyushu, where they managed to drop a single bomb on the Wawata steel works. The raid accomplished its secondary purpose: the Japanese were alarmed and their morale fell.

After the war a US strategic bombing survey concluded that the idea of basing B-29s in China had been 'unsound'. The 800 tonnes of bombs they dropped 'were of insufficient weight and accuracy to produce significant results'. By October 1944, B-29s were flying from their new Pacific bases on Saipan. After teething problems, they were soon to bomb Japan's cities with devastating effectiveness.

In China the Japanese armies pushed forward, taking Changsha (that much fought-over city) late in June 1944. After a rebuff, they returned to the attack and took Hengyang, 160 kilometres further on. When the Japanese offensives into eastern China and the US airfields were progressing Stilwell was leading his Chinese divisions into northern Burma and Chiang was to blame him for denuding China of valuable forces. It was to be Vinegar Joe's last campaign.

'U-GO! IMPHAL–KOHIMA, MARCH–JULY 1944

Three Japanese divisions launched the heaviest offensive of all — the *U-Go*. If they could defeat the British armies in Assam on the Indian frontier and capture their supply dumps at Kohima, the road to Calcutta and even Delhi lay open to them. Knowing that an attack was coming, Slim had three options: to pre-empt it by advancing across the Chindwin River; to hold a line along the Chindwin; or to consolidate his forces in an easily defended position, namely the Imphal plateau. 'I therefore decided to adopt the third — to concentrate 4 Corps on the Imphal plain, and fight a major battle there to destroy the 15th Japanese Army. I was tired of fighting the Japanese when they had a good line of communications behind them and I had an execrable one. This time I would reverse the order.'

The village of Imphal stands on a lofty plain measuring 30 miles by 20 miles. By early 1944 it was covered by ammunition and food dumps, camps, hospitals. It also possessed one of only two all-weather airfields in the region — air supply and the flying in of reinforcements was essential once the fighting began.

Slim knew the Japanese must attack and break through before the coming of the monsoon rains in mid-May and anticipated an attack in mid-March. He accordingly ordered his forward troops, the 17th Indian Division, to begin withdrawing to Imphal just before that date. But the Japanese, true to form, attacked nine days earlier, on 6 March, near Tiddim, and nearly encircled the 17th Division. By 6 April the Japanese had struck far to the north, towards Dimapur, the rail head (which had a ration strength of 45,000 labourers but no garrison whatever). They had also encircled Kohima, which was defended by a force of only 3000 troops, and had cut its road south

Lt-General Joseph Stilwell (left) in Burma with the 'Supremo' – Admiral Lord Louis Mountbatten – the British Supreme Allied Commander, South-East Asia Command (SEAC). Stillwell had no vanity, Mountbatten had enough for both men.

to Imphal. Slim began to fly in troops from India's Reserve and from the Arakan. 'It was a race between the Japanese and the arrival of our reinforcements,' Slim later wrote.

The defence of the town of Kohima would be the first epic of the great battle. Reinforcements and tanks reached Kohima on 18 April, and Slim decided to defeat the Japanese here rather than divert his forces to Imphal, which he knew had enough supplies and troops to hold out till mid-June. Against Kohima and Imphal the Japanese expended their strength in suicide attacks. 'Now is the time to capture Imphal,' ran an Order of the Day from the major-general commanding 33rd Japanese Division. 'The coming battle is the turning point. It will decide the future of the Greater East Asia War.' He told his men bluntly that few of them would survive; few did. Allied air forces had command of the skies and were strafing and bombing road convoys, and forcing supply craft to hug the river banks and move under cover of night. British and Indian units, supplied by air drops, were now infiltrating behind enemy lines, ambushing reinforcements and cutting communications.

In mid-May came the monsoonal rains, which washed away any Japanese hope of victory. On 22 June Slim's forces reopened the road to Imphal. The Japanese were melting away. On 1 July units of 14th Army reached Ukhrul and a week later destroyed the garrison there. Three weeks later Slim, driving by jeep along the muddy road littered with abandoned enemy tanks, vehicles, guns and corpses, entered the ruins of the village to visit 23rd Division. 'Whole sections of the road had vanished in landslides; the troops, soaked and filthy, were staggering forward across steep slopes through mud ... halfway up to their knees, but everyone was cheerful,' he wrote. 'The litter of the Japanese rout was everywhere; their corpses shapeless lumps in the mud.' On entering Tamu he found 500 dead Japanese, and hundreds of dying ones. There was evidence of a complete breakdown of the Japanese administration. By the end of July the British forces had reached 110 kilometres south of Imphal, and the advance continued. Remaining Japanese strong points were subjected to bombing from the air, and assaults by tanks and artillery, and whole infantry columns outflanked the defenders and took them from the rear: these were Japanese tactics now turned to good advantage.

By late July the 15th Japanese Army had lost 50,000 dead and perhaps 25,000 wounded. Slim's forces had suffered 15,000 battle casualties. They had outfought the Japanese.

MYITKINA FALLS And to make the Allied victory complete, on 3 August Myitkina — 'Mitcheena' as the troops called it — had fallen after a siege of over two months to Stilwell's American, Chinese and Chindit forces advancing on it through impossible country from the north-west. It was a bitter campaign, worsened by the disputes between the commanders on the spot. Frank Merrill's American unit, the 'Marauders', was broken by its exertions and losses (Merrill died of a heart attack in the last days of fighting) and some of his men, weakened by dysentery and dressed in rags, threatened to shoot Stilwell next time he visited the firing line. But the capture of Myitkina and its airfields was an important strategic victory, forever robbing the Japanese of any chance of holding northern Burma. Chiang Kai-shek complained to Roosevelt: '... we have taken Myitkina but we have lost almost all east China, and in this General Stilwell cannot be absolved of grave responsibility'.

1944: TO THE CHINDWIN Slim still felt that the easiest way to achieve victory in Burma and reopen land links to China would be an amphibious landing at Rangoon; but no landing craft were available in 1944 (all were being used in the Mediterranean and the Pacific). He would have to bring his army over the mountains. Once across the mountains, he would fight the decisive battle on the parched and dry central plain of Burma, where he could use tanks and long-range artillery to best advantage — open fighting. He calculated that, given his problems of supply and transport, he could maintain close to five divisions on the Burma Plain, plus two tank brigades (numbering only 200 tanks in all). He would be confronting five reorganising enemy divisions, so his forces were equally matched. But he had air superiority, and air supply and tactical support were to be instrumental in his eventual triumph.

Slim lost an ally when Stilwell was recalled from China in October 1944. 'He was replaced by three generals who divided between them his half-dozen jobs,' Slim later wrote ruefully. Despite his Anglophobia, Stilwell had trusted 'old Slim' as he called him, but his constant criticisms of Chiang Kai-shek's ineptitude and corruption had finally resulted in a showdown. Slim also lost his loyal superior General Giffard — 'Uncle George' to the troops — who was replaced in November by General Sir Oliver Leese, one of Montgomery's star commanders.

Slim's veteran 17th Indian Division — survivor of the humiliating retreat of 1942 — was among the first to discard its mule teams and become fully mechanised; lorries carried the infantry, and jeeps towed his guns. The jeeps' axles had been shortened so that they could be driven onto Dakota transport aircraft and airlifted to the battlefield.

To provide his tanks, Slim would use the veteran 4 Corps, which would have to make its way over 500 km of dirt road from Assam, from Tamu to Pakokku. They made a new road as they went, surfacing it with bitumen-coated hessian, widening it to allow 3-tonne trucks, 50-tonne tanks and transporters to navigate the hairpin bends; Slim watched with wonder as his army moved south through impenetrable clouds of dust — a relief from the rivers of monsoonal mud — and was amused to see the tanks patiently towing their multi-wheel transporters. He ordered his engineers to organise river transport, to use the Chindwin as a supply route protected by armed motor-boats.

On 3 December 1944 the British and Indians crossed the Chindwin River in strength when 33 Corps pushed a brigade across. The Japanese began withdrawing to the Irrawaddy, a wider and more difficult obstacle to 14th Army. With the end of the monsoon in December 1944 Slim's forces began bridging the Chindwin River, often using elephants to carry the logs for bridges and boats. The advance into Burma for the decisive battle had begun.

RETURN TO THE PHILIPPINES

The American advances continued. On 15 September 1944 MacArthur's forces landed on Morotai, just south of the Philippines, and Nimitz's amphibious forces landed in the Palau islands (which lay halfway between the Carolines and the Philippines) and 1st Marine Division went ashore on Peleliu.

PELELIU Peleliu 'turned into one of the toughest, bloodiest operations of the war', writes one American historian. On Peleliu the temperature reached 115 degrees F (46 degrees C), but underground, where the Japanese had dug tunnels and cave systems in the coral, the temperature was even higher. The battle lasted a fortnight and cost the Americans 6000 casualties — for an asset of doubtful value.

The aggressive American island campaign had now destroyed or isolated thirteen Japanese divisions and what remained of Japanese air power now faced two American air forces — the 5th and the 13th — totalling 4000 US, Australian and New Zealand aircraft. Soon MacArthur would fulfil his pledge to the Filipinos: 'I will return.' He had won approval to strike at the heart of the Philippines, at Leyte.

In July 1944 MacArthur had met Roosevelt and Nimitz on Hawaii to attempt to modify the joint chiefs' plan to seize Formosa (Taiwan) and secure the south China coast for the final push to Japan. In his forays Admiral Halsey had discovered that the southern Philippines were lightly defended, particularly Mindanao in the south and Leyte further north, and supported MacArthur in choosing a landing in the centre, on Leyte Island. The Pacific fleet would support the invasion. MacArthur was thus able to bring forward his planned invasion date (20 December) two months — to October.

Early in October Halsey broke the back of Japanese air strength in the region, taking his carrier fleet as far north as Okinawa and as far west as Formosa; he bombarded airfields with impunity while his pilots destroyed close to 500 Japanese aircraft on the ground or in the air, where the remarkable US Navy Hellcat fighter again proved its worth.

Australian troops gradually took over garrison duties from American forces in the South-West Pacific but the Royal Australian Navy's ships would serve in the invasion fleet. They were led for the first time in their history by an Australian officer, Commodore John

US Marines during the battle to clear Peleliu, one of the hardest battles of the Pacific war.

Collins (veteran of the Mediterranean and Singapore), who flew his flag in the heavy cruiser *Australia*, accompanied by HMAS *Shropshire*, the two Tribal-class destroyers *Arunta* and *Warramunga* and the three liners converted to LSIs, *Westralia*, *Manoora* and *Kanimbla*.

BATTLE OF LEYTE GULF Japan would hurl against the fleet at Leyte her remaining carriers and battleships — and its last secret weapon: the kamikaze suicide pilots, who saw in self-immolation their country's salvation. On 20 October 1944 the 'greatest naval force ever assembled' — 738 ships including seventeen fleet carriers and six battleships — gathered off the coast of Leyte under the protection of the guns of Halsey's 3rd Fleet and Kincaid's 7th Fleet. The island was only lightly defended. A force of 20,000 GIs splashed ashore, soon followed by MacArthur himself. The Japanese Naval high command put in motion a massive attempt to destroy the invasion fleet at Leyte Gulf. No fewer than four Japanese battle fleets were steaming to Leyte, their destination unsuspected. Two were coming from Japan, two from Singapore.

Next day, 21 October 1944 — Trafalgar Day — dawned bright and clear but numbers of Japanese aircraft soon appeared over the invasion armada. At about 6 a.m. a Japanese dive-bomber was seen hurtling towards *Australia*. It crashed into the flagship's foremast, exploding on impact, raining in pieces onto the bridge below, causing 100 casualties. The captain was killed and the commodore grievously wounded.

Admiral Kurita now steamed north from Singapore towards the San Bernardino Strait, accompanied by another fleet under Admiral Nishimura which detached and headed for Surigao Strait. They would be joined by a fleet of six carriers under Admiral Ozawa steaming south from Japan. Halsey, guarding the strait and confident that no threat existed to the invasion armada, was alerted to Ozawa's approach and headed north at full speed to destroy his fleet. Ozawa now decided that he should play the role of decoy to attract Halsey's carrier fleet. Another Japanese fleet approached west of Luzon to join Nishimura's force and both headed for Surigao Strait.

Top: A rare photograph of four American fleet carriers in the Pacific.
Above: Admiral William Halsey, one of the most popular and most aggressive American admirals in the Pacific.

Early on 24 October Kurita's fleet of four battleships (including the leviathans *Yamato* and *Musashi*), six heavy cruisers and masses of destroyers steamed unchecked through the San Bernadino Strait and struck south towards the now defenceless transports at Leyte Gulf. The only obstacle in their path was a force of six small American 'escort carriers' (thin-skinned mass-produced flat-tops mounting single 5-inch guns) and their destroyer escorts, which together fought a valiant delaying action. The carriers retreated, launching their aircraft, zig-zagging to avoid the deadly 15-inch shells. One carrier and most of the destroyers were sunk but Kurita was delayed, and now realised that he could not strike and escape before dawn broke. Reluctantly, he ordered his fleet to return the way they had come.

In Pearl Harbor Nimitz was following wireless reports of the actions, and wondered why Halsey's Task Force 34 had disappeared. Halsey's forces were wreaking havoc among Ozawa's fleet and were sinking four enemy carriers. When Nimitz signalled to Halsey: 'Where is Repeat where is Task Force 34? The world wonders.' Halsey was furious at this insult — the last three words had been added by the telegraphist to confuse Japanese decoders, but Halsey was not to know this.

On the night of 25 October Nishimura's southern strike force, detached from Kurita's battle fleet, joined up with Shima's fleet and both steamed into Surigao Strait to catch the Leyte transports from the south. They headed straight into the guns of Rear-Admiral Oldendorf's waiting fleet, which included *Shropshire* and *Arunta*. In the last 'battle line' naval engagement in history, Oldendorf 'crossed the T', his broadsides shattering the Japanese force of two battleships, a cruiser and destroyers; the retreating Japanese were pursued through the night and the following day.

Japanese losses in the complex series of actions known as 'The Battle of Leyte Gulf' included four carriers and three battleships, one of them being the 'unsinkable' giant battleship *Musashi* (64,000 tonnes), which finally went under with 2000 of its men, but only after taking 19 torpedo hits and as many bombs; six enemy cruisers were also sunk. The Imperial Japanese Navy had now ceased to exist.

The Japanese garrisons of the Philippines were marooned. Seven weeks later MacArthur landed forces on Mindoro, south of the main island of Luzon, and at month's end announced that the Leyte campaign was over 'except for some minor mopping-up operations'. MacArthur's 250,000 Americans suffered more than 15,000 casualties but of the 70,000 Japanese who had defended Leyte island only 5000 would see their homeland again. In January 1945 MacArthur would invade Luzon.

THE 'BACKYARD WAR'

For Australian forces the last eighteen months of the war against Japan were an anti-climax. Among the RAAF — and the RNZAF — in the Pacific few personnel had any illusions that they had been relegated to a backwater, fighting a war that passed them by. In 1944 the RAAF in the Pacific amounted to a total of 163,000 men and women; 1st Tactical Air Force based in Noemfoor and Morotai continued to raid targets in the Celebes and Dutch New Guinea in support of Australian land forces carrying out the onerous and unspectacular task of destroying the pockets of Japanese still left. In October and November 1944, as Australians began to move in to clear the Japanese from New Guinea and the northern Solomons, the strength of the Japanese garrisons facing them was unknown. In fact nearly 100,000 Japanese remained on New Britain, 40,000 on Bougainville, 13,000 on New Ireland and 30,000 near Wewak.

Blamey had originally intended to replace American divisions by single Australian brigades, but MacArthur insisted on stronger forces. Accordingly, from his army strength of 430,000 men Blamey selected 12 brigades — the equivalent of four divisions — for the onerous

In theatrical fashion MacArthur wades ashore at Leyte Gulf, fulfilling his promise to the Filipinos: 'I shall return'. On his left is his chief-of-staff, General Sutherland.

task of 'cleaning up'. The loss of lives in the 'backyard war' caused Cabinet early in 1945 to question Blamey's tactics; he answered the criticism by stating that the Americans, content to sit behind their fortified perimeters, had certainly not neutralised the Japanese, and he had ordered that operations be mounted with care to minimise casualties. To fight aggressively was simply part of the Australian soldier's temperament.

The 3rd Australian Division arrived on Bougainville late in 1944. By March 1945 the Australians had forced the Japanese almost to the Buka Passage in the north and were nearly halfway to the Japanese base in the south at Buin. By V-J Day only a sector around Buin itself remained untaken. In the liberation of Bougainville 2000 Australians were killed and wounded; 18,000 Japanese died and only 23,000 remained to surrender in August 1945.

When the 5th Australian Division arrived on New Britain in November 1944, the Japanese had withdrawn to the Gazelle Peninsula to defend their base at Rabaul, but their force was still sizeable, consisting of elements of five divisions (close to 100,000 men), though most of them were starving. The Australians limited operations to seizing the Waitavola–Tol region, which was reached after hard fighting in March 1945, all operations being assisted by air strikes from RAAF and RNZAF aircraft and by Papuan infantry adept in hunting down stragglers.

The 6th Australian Division, AIF, arrived on the northern coast of New Guinea in November 1944 to take over from three American divisions — the 31st, 32nd and 43rd. The Australians also faced an enemy force far more numerous than themselves — the remnants of three Japanese divisions at Wewak and in the mountainous hinterland. It would be a hard campaign.

NORTH-WEST EUROPE
THE STRATEGIC BOMBING OF GERMANY

The Allied bombing campaign over Germany continued into the first quarter of 1944. Bomber Command's losses from flak were now reduced from 10 per cent to 4 per cent with the help of 'Window', strips of metallic foil released to confuse enemy radar. A massive raid on German rocket development sites at Peenemunde on the Baltic in August 1943 had succeeded in delaying the launching of Hitler's 'secret weapon'; construction of the flying-bombs and rockets continued in the underground factories in the Harz Mountains.

Heavy attacks on Berlin, Leipzig, Frankfurt and Stuttgart were maintained. A night raid on Nuremberg on 30 March 1944 was Bomber Command's greatest single disaster — 95 aircraft were lost out of the total bombing force of 795. Although 763 bombers were lost in the first three months of 1944 the effect of Bomber Command's long offensive was beginning to show. The Luftwaffe was now losing aircraft faster than factories could replace them; tragically, German civilian deaths were increasingly high. July and August 1944 were triumphal months for pilots attacking what remained of German shipping. An Australian Beaufighter of 455 Squadron returned from a successful low-level attack on German vessels with part of a ship's mast embedded in its nose after flying through the heaviest flak the squadron had ever encountered.

Commanding 1st Tactical Air Force in the campaign in north-west Europe was the Australian-born New Zealander, Arthur Coningham, whose command was to grow to 1800 aircraft and 100,000 men drawn from seven nations.

From May to December 1944 American and RAF bombers effectively reduced German production of synthetic aviation fuel to 11 per cent of its planned output, a crucial factor in the air war. Mass bombing of Germany had resumed in July 1944 with an attack on Kiel, followed by raids on Stettin, Stuttgart and Bremerhaven. By August 1944 the last U-boats were driven from the Bay of Biscay into Norwegian waters; by October 1944 German shipping in the North Sea had all but disappeared.

Above: 'Ike': Supreme Allied Commander in north-west Europe and a future American president, General Dwight David Eisenhower.
Left (in panel): Rocket-firing Beaufighters destroying enemy shipping off the coast of Norway, 1944.

GRIM WINTER: FRANCE AND BELGIUM

By September 1944, fifth anniversary of the outbreak of war, the advancing Allied armies in western Europe were confident of ending the war by Christmas. The shattered German armies had retreated from France; Montgomery's forces had entered Belgium and had advanced 200 kilometres in two days (the fastest recorded advance in military history) when tanks of the Guards Armoured Division drove into Brussels on 4 September to the cheers of the Bruxellois; the British reached Antwerp the next day. Montgomery would regret that he had failed to clear the German garrisons from the Sheldte estuary: they were to make impossible the use of the great port until the Germans were winkled out in late November. But elsewhere it looked as if the German armies had collapsed completely.

BROAD FRONT OR SINGLE THRUST?

On 1 September Eisenhower had resumed command of all Allied forces in the west, as had been agreed. Montgomery was mollified by promotion to field marshal, but regarded the future with a certain anxiety. Eisenhower was committed to a 'broad front' advance against the German frontier; Montgomery as early as 4 September advocated a solid thrust into Germany's industrial heartland, the Ruhr. He was overruled.

Eisenhower's American armies now outnumbered the British. In addition to Montgomery's 21 Army Group (2nd British Army and 1st Canadian), he controlled Bradley's 12th US Army Group (Hodges' 1st US Army, Patton's 3rd US Army, soon joined by Simpson's 9th US Army). All were making astonishing progress. 1st US Army took Liège on 8 September and entered Luxembourg city on 10 September. Further south, the Americans crossed the German border near Aachen on 1 September. Patton took Verdun and by 16 September was approaching Metz, which was strongly defended. German garrisons still held many of the Atlantic and Channel ports but were cut off from aid and rescue. Nearly all of France had been liberated.

Right: Cantankerous general: General George S. Patton who led the US 3rd Army at a gallop across France, only to be stopped dead on the Franco-German frontier by lack of fuel and Eisenhower's caution. He regarded Eisenhower as excessively pro-British and essentially timid but liked him as a man.

Below: American infantry on their preferred mode of transport – riding a tank through the outer defences (the 'Dragon's Teeth') of the Siegfried Line on the German frontier September 1944.

ARNHEM

Deeply concerned by Eisenhower's refusal to order a full-hearted single thrust into the Ruhr and northern Germany, Montgomery was heartened by his interest in securing a Dutch bridgehead over the lower Rhine. On its journey to Rotterdam, the Rhine passed through the industrial city of Arnhem, which lay barely 100 kilometres north of Montgomery's front on the Dutch–Belgian border. If he could seize Arnhem, Montgomery could outflank the Siegfried Line and then advance sharply east towards the Ruhr. The Allied high command took the gamble. Eisenhower provided the entire Allied airborne army for the operation — the four battle-tested divisions of Normandy fame — 1st and 6th British Airborne divisions, the 82, 101st US Airborne, in addition to a Polish airborne brigade. Montgomery's plans were bold. He would drop the British at Arnhem and then advance by road to link up with them, using Lieutenant-General Brian Horrocks' 30 Corps, while American airborne troops captured the bridges over which they would cross on the way to Arnhem — those at Eindhoven and Nijmegen. This was a tall order, and Lieutenant-General 'Boy' Browning, the dashing commander of the British airborne forces (he was married to the novelist Daphne du Maurier, which added to his glamour), ventured the opinion that Montgomery might be going 'one bridge too far'. Montgomery would brook no further delay, for the Germans were known to be strengthening their defences at Arnhem.

Above: Before being overwhelmed, British airborne troops man a mortar in a ditch near Arnhem.

Left: Lt-General Frederick 'Boy' Browning, commander of the British airborne divisions. From his headquarters at Nijmegen he witnessed the destruction of his corps.

Intelligence reached Allied HQ that an entire Panzer division was resting and regrouping in the forests outside Arnhem, but the report did not receive due attention. On 17 September a great Allied air armada began dropping the paratroopers. The British landed on the north bank and rapidly set out for the city of Arnhem. They had little transport, and few of their radios had survived the drop. A small party reached the northern approaches to the bridge and held it against mounting counterattacks.

The 82nd Airborne captured Eindhoven on 18 September, and 30 Corps advanced full of confidence. The 101st dropped near Nijmegen and after two days of fighting captured the bridge after crossing the river in rubber boats under heavy fire. Now 30 Corps tanks moving north on the exposed road came under deadly fire from German anti-tank guns; many were hit, blocking progress. But by 25 September all attempts to reach the paratroopers on Arnhem bridge and the group to their west had failed and Montgomery ordered the survivors to try to withdraw. Total Allied battle casualties were 17,000. As many as 10,000 Dutch civilians also fell casualty. Arnhem remained in German hands until the great Allied crossing of the Rhine in March 1945.

TO THE SIEGFRIED LINE

To add to the disappointment of Arnhem, the winter came early on the Western front. The November rains turned the front into a quagmire; Allied air support was limited by adverse weather. There would be no end of the war in 1944. Casualties were mounting. The British Army was dismantling anti-aircraft and Royal Marine units to provide infantry reinforcements. Supply was a mounting problem. Patton's advance had stalled in September when his tanks ran out of petrol. An increasingly large 'tail' of the front-line armies soaked up most of the supplies before they reached the front. Of the 11 million men in the US Army (three million of them in the 60 divisions in Europe under Eisenhower) only 20 per cent comprised combat divisions — infantry, armoured and airborne, and of these two million only 700,000 were at 'the sharp end' as front-line infantry and tank crews who took most of the casualties.

These figures confirm that American and British forces were the best supplied of all fighting nations and they tell us two things: the support and service 'tail' of a division controlled the body ('the tail wagged the dog'), consuming the bulk of the manpower just to keep the fighting troops transported, fed and supplied; battle losses in the forward units could not be made up without drawing personnel from other vital services. Both the US and Britain could run out of soldiers and reinforcements if losses were excessive. This point was reached before the end of 1944, forcing the high command to adopt a cautious strategy that possibly prolonged the war.

Metz fell to Patton's army on 1 November, but its outer forts were still resisting. De Lattre's First French Army was working wonders. On 11 November Churchill visited Paris, where he was acclaimed with cheers. And two days later he and de Gaulle visited de Lattre's armies at his HQ near Besançon. Brooke was concerned as de Lattre outlined his coming offensive along a huge front. 'Another case of Eisenhower's complete inability to run the land battle as well as acting as Supreme Commander,' Brooke wrote in his diary. 'Furthermore it is another example of the American doctrine of attacking along the line. The American Army just north of de Lattre is attacking in impossible country in the Vosges; all he will do there is lose men.' As dusk fell Brooke and Churchill watched the French march past. After the young soldiers — boys of the maquis hastily put into uniform — came the weird sound of African pipes and a battalion of the Foreign Legion appeared, moving at their famous slow and steady march. 'Through the falling snow-flakes came a sight I shall never forget. The grandest assembly of real fighting men that I have ever seen, marching with their heads up as if they owned the world, lean, hard-looking men, carrying their arms admirably and marching with perfect precision. They disappeared into the darkness', leaving Brooke (who had been born in France) with a memory he long preserved of the reborn French Army. Under de Lattre's dynamic leadership the French took Belfort on 22 November and Leclerc's tanks entered Strasbourg next day; Leclerc had fulfilled the pledge he had sworn in the Libyan desert never to tire until the tricolour flew again over Strasbourg.

Prime Minister Churchill and General de Gaulle (by now head of state of the provisional French government) visit the armies of General de Lattre de Tassigny (right in photograph) at his headquarters near Alsace, November 1944. General Juin can be glimpsed over de Gaulle's right shoulder and General Brooke in the extreme left of the photograph.

American tanks and infantry move forward through the mud.

There was little else to cheer about, except Roosevelt's re-election as President in November; no man had ever before been elected for four terms. He and Churchill made plans to meet again with Stalin, if only they could agree on where to meet. Roosevelt suggested Malta, Gibraltar, Rome and even Jerusalem. Stalin offered Yalta in the Crimea. On 3 December Churchill wrote to his old friend and confidant Smuts (whom he had made a field marshal in token of his support): 'In spite of Metz and Strasbourg and other successes, we have of course sustained a strategic reverse on the Western Front. Before this offensive was launched we placed on record our view that it was a mistake to attack against the whole front … There is at least one full-scale battle to fight before we get to the Rhine in the north …' Against the extended Allied front a far greater reverse was in store, a blow that would almost sunder the Allied lines.

THE BATTLE OF THE BULGE

Hitler was still capable of springing surprises. To the alarm of his generals he was withdrawing armoured divisions from the Eastern Front, to destroy the Allies on his western doorstep. It was the eve of what the Allies called the 'Rundstedt Offensive' — though Rundstedt, the Commander-in-Chief West, thought it mad and disclaimed any responsibility for it. History also knows it as the Battle of the Bulge.

Hitler had collected a massive army of 10 Panzer divisions and 14 infantry divisions, including the 6th Panzer Army, whose existence was known by Allied Intelligence but thought to be Hitler's strategic reserve. It would spearhead the coming offensive. Hitler hoped the attack would reach Antwerp, severing the British–Canadian armies in the north from the Americans in the south, and leave them both at his mercy.

Montgomery was worried about the thin American line to his south on the Ardennes front and suggested that Patton's 3rd Army be moved north to guard it. Eisenhower, driving through the region on the way to a conference at Maastricht, was also worried: he saw practically no American troops, armour or dumps on his drive. The 75 miles (about 120 km) of front was held by only four American divisions. Bradley's army were still battering their way south of Aachen through the Hurtgen Forest, a bloody advance that penetrated only 12 kilometres into the Siegfried Line and caused 30,000 casualties in its five months' progress, prompting many to question Bradley's competence and reputation as 'the soldiers' general'.

Eisenhower returned to his rear HQ at Versailles outside Paris confident that the weather — the worst in fifty years — would deter any German attack. He played bridge with his officers, pleased to hear that he had been nominated by the President for his fifth star — the first 'General of the Armies' since John J. Pershing in 1918. Eisehower's devoted naval aide, Harry Butcher, noted in his diary (16 December): ' The man who always cautioned his family not to expect him to be promoted has risen from lieutenant colonel to five-star general in three years, three months, and sixteen days — six promotions, one about every six months. He had been a major for sixteen years.' The diary is almost blank for the next six days for the Ardennes avalanche fell just as he was writing these lines.

On 16 December 1944 a total of 14 German infantry divisions supported by the strongest armoured force ever gathered in the west moved forwards against five American divisions on a 100-mile (160 km) front in the Ardennes region. The Tiger tanks made good progress along the narrow roads; their first objective was to seize the road junctions — and perhaps even American fuel supplies. The 6th Panzer Army struck near Monschau after an artillery bombardment from 2000 guns. To its south 5th Panzer Army advanced towards Namur, destination Brussels, while 7th Army pushed its infantry forwards to cover the southern flank. Hearing of the attack, Bradley reacted slowly, thinking it was just a feint, 'a spoiling attack'. Eisenhower, soon confined to his Versailles HQ by reports that German commandos (led by Otto Skorzeny) were dressed as Americans and intending to kill him, ordered Patton to release two armoured divisions to strengthen the Ardennes.

The Americans were resisting strongly, particularly at St Vith, where 7th US Armoured fought back. 'St Vith became a rock of defence on which the tide of assault broke and divided, flowing west in two channels,' writes Chester Wilmot in *The Struggle for Europe*. One SS battle group was kept from the petrol dumps by a wall of flame: US engineers had set up road blocks of fuel drums and set them alight. Early on 18 December Manteuffel's 5th Panzer Army moved quickly on Bastogne, the key town and road junction, which was rapidly reinforced; next day the Germans met the first fire from the 101st Airborne, which had been rushed from Reims 160 kilometres away. The Airborne were to hold Bastogne to the end, their commander, Major General Anthony MacAuliffe rejecting surrender demands with a one-word reply that even the Germans could not understand: 'Nuts.'

Late on 19 December Eisenhower made the unpalatable decision to call on Montgomery, giving him command of all forces north of the breakthrough — including Bradley's 9th Army. Four British divisions immediately moved south to defend the Meuse. Another German hammer-blow fell on 21 December against 1st Army; St Vith fell and by late on 23 December Manteuffell's tanks were only seven kilometres from Dinant. The Bulge was expanding. But Montgomery was certain that the best tactics were to wait until the Bulge grew to its greatest extent, when the Germans had extended their lines — and then to fall on their flanks. On 26 December Patton's tanks raised the siege of Bastogne. Next day the Germans were reeling back from Dinant 'and the spearhead of Manteuffel's 5th Panzer Army lay broken in the snow'.

Hitler determined to continue attacks on the Allied front. Another assault was launched by eight German divisions on 1 January 1945 south of the Saar; two days later another attack was launched against Bastogne. This was 'the fiercest of the Ardennes campaign' but was called off on 5 January when Montgomery's advance threatened the northern flank. On 8 January Hitler admitted defeat by permitting the bulk of his forces to retreat to a firmer defence line. The Germans had lost 90,000 men and the Americans 77,000 (a quarter of whom were prisoners). Each side had lost more than 700 tanks.

The bitter winter of December 1944 witnessed the launching of the last great German offensive in the west. American tanks, shown here, pass wrecked German armour.

CHAPTER 10
THE BITTER END
1945

Snows from the worst winter in fifty years lay over northern Europe in January 1945. The great rivers were iced over. In the Netherlands people ate tulip bulbs to stave off hunger but 15,000 starved to death. The skies were overcast. There could be little air activity or movement over roads and no major offensive by the western armies until the snows disappeared in February and March.

But in the east Russian armies were moving forwards. In response to Churchill's plea to Stalin to prevent if possible German reinforcements to the west, Stalin ordered the great offensive in the east to begin eight days earlier than planned. Hitler dismissed as lunacy General Guderian's warning that the Russians had built up enormous strength and that German reinforcements should be concentrated on the Vistula and not frittered away to defend Vienna and Budapest. The Red Army was now 500 divisions strong (though not all of these were complete) and it would break on the German armies like a flood, and upon eastern Europe like an avalanche. Germany's 164 divisions would be shattered and nearly eight million German civilians whose ancestors had settled in the east up to 900 years earlier would soon be making their sad way west to escape the Red Army. Close to two million Germans would perish in their attempts to escape. The Red Army showed no mercy to those it captured. It was the beginning of the greatest migration of peoples since the Mongol invasions of the thirteenth century.

THE RUSSIAN AVALANCHE

On 12 January the Russians opened up a thundering artillery bombardment of the German lines on the Vistula opposite Warsaw and launched an attack from their narrow bridgehead on the west bank. It was the first of the offensives that would carry them to Berlin. They entered the ruins of Warsaw a week later. On 13 January the Red Army attacked in south-east Poland and advanced within three days almost to Cracow. On 20 January the Red Army entered East Prussia and Silesia and was poised to enter Budapest. The roads were clogged with fleeing German civilians.

On 18 January, as Russian armies approached, the Nazis evacuated the Auschwitz–Birkenau camps where 60,000 prisoners were still alive. After shooting most of the sick, and destroying many of the buildings in a vain attempt to hide the atrocities that had been committed there, the guards herded the rest on foot to the west. Those who fell exhausted were shot by the roadside. The Russians entered Birkenau on 27 January. Horrifying photographs of the few survivors were the first images of the death camps to reach the west; in the next four months there would be many more.

By mid-February the Russians were approaching Breslau (Wroclaw) whose Gauleiter, Hanke, ordered it defended to the last round. It held out until March, when he escaped by light plane. Budapest fell. Posen (Poznan) fell on 23 February. In the north the armies of Rokossovski reached the Baltic coast on 4 March. On 30 March Danzig fell, and the Red Army's Polish division had the satisfaction of accepting the German surrender.

On 8 April Marshal Tolbukhin's troops entered Vienna, where Austrian patriots were already defying Nazi orders and guiding in Russian tanks. On 9 April the Russians took Königsberg after a four-day battle. Five days later Hitler issued an order to his armies in the east: 'The Bolshevik–Jewish enemy stands before the

Inset: **Use of combined air, land and sea forces was a feature of Allied operations in World War II: badge of the US Army Amphibious Units, 1945.**
Opposite: **German prisoners taken by the Americans in the muddy fighting in March 1945. Allied soldiers were astonished at the number of teenage soldiers who surrendered.**
Opposite right: **An Australian Matilda tank rolls forward during the mopping up on Bougainville, 1945.**

Above: Red Army troops reach the Lithuanian coast at Memel.
Below: Russian troops pass the citadel in Koenigsberg, the capital of East Prussia.

gates. If everyone does his duty, the Asian attack will collapse. Berlin will stay German, Vienna will be German again, and Europe will never become Russian.' The Red Army had now established a bridgehead on the west bank of the Oder. It was only 70 kilometres from Hitler's capital. On 16 April the Russians advanced for the last battle — the taking of Berlin.

YALTA CONFERENCE

En route to meet Stalin at Yalta, Churchill flew first to Malta, where he met Roosevelt for preliminary discussions. Churchill was shocked at the great change that had overcome the President. He was grey and pallid, aged; even his eyes reflected none of his renowned vivacity. Churchill knew that much more than a victorious conclusion of the war depended on a successful meeting of the Big Three. 'The only hope for the world is the agreement of the Great Powers,' he had written to Eden. 'If they quarrel, our children are undone.' The two leaders flew on to Yalta where next day the round-table discussions began with Stalin. Stalin explained that he had begun his offensive in the winter to help the Allies. Now what could they do for him? He asked that air bombardment of German communications be increased, particularly in the Berlin–Dresden–Leipzig area, from where he estimated at least forty German divisions were being sent east. Stalin exaggerated; the Germans had sent only four divisions, but the result of this request was the Allied bombing of Dresden just a fortnight later.

As to the future of conquered Germany, Roosevelt suggested that the foreign ministers draw up a plan for its division into zones of occupation; Churchill maintained that one of the zones should be French. He had rejected de Gaulle's demand to be invited to the Yalta conference, murmuring that Canada by her sacrifice had more right to attend than France, but at the same time he wanted France to be recognised as a Great Power. (He was wrong: Canada's war dead of 40,000 was bad enough; France was to mourn 400,000 dead.) Churchill objected to the idea of exacting reparations, pointing out that the procedure had proven unworkable. The subject of Poland occupied more time than any other at Yalta. Stalin demanded that Poland's frontier with the Soviet Union be shifted west at the expense of Germany to the old 'Curzon line'. Initially hostile to the idea of a new 'world government' — the United Nations — Stalin was now receptive, but pointed out that the self-governing nations of the British Empire alone would provide half a dozen representatives, and the Soviet Union only one. He asked for two extra seats, for Belorussia and the Ukraine. It was agreed that a conference of the United Nations would convene in the United States in April. In almost an afterthought Stalin demanded that all Soviet prisoners of war and slave workers liberated by the western armies be returned to the Soviet Union. This demand, to which the Western leaders readily agreed, was to have a tragic outcome. The freed Soviet citizens and soldiers ended up in Soviet camps — the Gulags — which within three years would contain nearly six million souls.

When the three leaders had signed a high-minded declaration promising the nations of Europe the right to 'democratic institutions of their own choice', the conference concluded. Churchill just wanted to get home. Stalin had promised free elections in Poland but few trusted him. Two months later a dozen Polish leaders were invited to Moscow and on their arrival were thrown into Lubianka prison. In Poland itself the Soviets were arresting anti-Communists and threatening to take over government in Romania and Bulgaria. Churchill was oppressed by the thought that the great army of Poles who had fought with British forces in the Middle East, Italy and north-western Europe would find their home enslaved by another ideology. (No Poles were forcibly returned to their homeland.) He was also disturbed by reports of the Red Army's violent progress through East Prussia, where the civilian population was fleeing. There were stories of widespread rape and murder.

Yalta, February 1945: Stalin's interpreter leans forward to translate a remark by President Roosevelt. Behind the big three stand Fleet Admiral King and Admiral Leahy.

THE DESTRUCTION OF DRESDEN

On the night of 13 February 1945, while the Allied leaders were meeting at Yalta to decide the fate of postwar Europe, Bomber Command bombed Dresden, the beautiful capital of Saxony that had so far been spared bombing. On the next two nights American bombers dropped incendiaries. It was one of the most controversial actions of the bombing war and claimed the lives of an estimated 35,000 German civilians and European refugees in the fire-storm, though some historians place the figure higher. (It is clear, however, that the figure of 135,000 killed quoted by English historian David Irving is incorrect, if not a deliberate falsification.)

In one daylight operation over Germany by a force of 143 Mosquitoes, 20 were shot down and 40 damaged: German flak defences were still strong. On 11 and 12 March Australian and New Zealand pilots of Bomber Command participated in the two 'thousand bomber' raids on Essen and Dortmund, which met negligible opposition. The Mosquito Wing, in which Canadian, Australian and New Zealand aircrew served, mounted an amazing low-level attack on Gestapo headquarters in Copenhagen and was now bombing Berlin, though in a February raid 21 of a force of 143 failed to return.

INTO THE RHINELAND

On 8 February 1945 Montgomery launched an offensive into the Rhineland to reach the west bank of the Rhine: 'Operation Veritable'. It began in rain and mud and conditions worsened two days later when the Germans opened the Roer dams, flooding the terrain. The Canadians attacking south-east from the Nijmegen bridgehead made good progress. After hard fighting the British took the Reichswald forest and 5000 prisoners for 1000 casualties. Horrocks of 30 Corps called it 'the grimmest battle in which I took part during the war'. The weather was so bad that 'Grenade', the second, southern thrust to 'pinch out' the Rhineland west of the river by Simpson's 9th US Army towards Düsseldorf, was postponed until 23 February. But when it began it went like clockwork and the Americans took more than two dozen bridges across the Roer. The German forces west of the Rhine were collapsing and surrendering in hordes. Some estimate their losses at 200,000 men. Bradley's ADC noted on 1 March: 'General Bradley estimates that our troops will be on the Rhine this evening ... The general effect of this sledge hammer drive to the Rhine has been reflected in the crumbling resistance up and down the Rhineland.' Bradley's two armies scored remarkable successes.

They struck towards Cologne, which they entered on 6 March.

On 7 March an advance unit of the US 9th Armoured Division reached the lofty heights above the Rhine at Remagen and saw through the mist a bridge filled with traffic. They raced down to it and engineers cut the demolition wires while an infantry platoon raced across it to the far bank.

Above: Field-Marshal Walther Model, image of a Prussian general, ranks as one of the outstanding German commanders of the war. Hitler refused to allow him to withdraw his forces from the west bank of the Rhine, where they were encircled by the Allies. After again being encircled in the Ruhr pocket, Model escaped but shot himself (21 April 1945).
Left: American troops in an M3 half-track.

Eisenhower was delighted and General Hodges, normally a cautious man, responded like Patton, driving his tanks across it before the Germans managed to destroy it by air attack and mines.

Through February and March 1945 three Allied air forces ranged far ahead of the armies, destroying German communications — rail lines, road convoys, canals and barges. 2nd Tactical Air Force had ensured the 'complete air superiority' that Montgomery deemed essential. On 20 March Montgomery sent a message to his troops: 'Events are moving rapidly. The complete and decisive defeat of the Germans is certain … 21 Army Group will now cross the Rhine. The enemy thinks he is safe behind this great river obstacle … And having crossed the Rhine, we will crack about in the plains of northern Germany. Over the Rhine then, let us go. May the "Lord Mighty in battle" give us victory in this, our latest undertaking …' Montgomery told Eisenhower that after surrounding the German armies in the Ruhr, the correct strategy was to go straight for the Elbe — and Berlin.

Left: Cologne after Allied bombing. Allied aircraft destroyed the Rhine bridge but spared the cathedral.
Below: British and Canadian infantry ride forward on a tank during the bitter fighting on the west bank of the Rhine.

In Berlin Armaments Minister Speer told Hitler on 18 March that 'in four to eight weeks the final collapse of the Germany economy must be expected with certainty … After that collapse the war cannot be continued indefinitely' — and that Germany must cease demolitions to retain a basis for existence and reconstruction. Hitler replied: 'If the war is lost, the nation will also perish. Their fate is inevitable … Besides, those who remain after the battle are only the inferior ones, for the good ones have been killed.' He ordered that all industrial plant must be destroyed, all bridges, gasworks, railways. Germany must be turned into a desert. Speer was to spend the next month talking Gauleiters out of following this insane order, and contemplated killing Hitler with poison gas capsules dropped into the air shafts of his underground bunker.

CROSSING THE RHINE

The first troops to cross the Rhine in boats were Patton's 3rd US Army, who landed on the east bank on the night of 22 March south of Mainz. From Oppenheim Patton would make his dash for Frankfurt. On the night of 23 March Montgomery's British troops crossed. Next day his artillery bombardment left little standing of the towns on the far bank. Wesel was now a pile of rubble. 'Pop goes the Wesel,' a British officer remarked, with no compassion. In the far south of the Allied line the French 1st Army crossed the Upper Rhine on 30 March and advanced into the Black Forest.

Crossing the Rhine: American infantry crouch down to avoid German fire as their landing craft approaches the east bank.

On 24 March Churchill stood with Montgomery on the banks of the Rhine to see the airborne troops drop onto the east bank. Sadly 6th Airborne suffered 30 per cent casualties but German resistance was soon broken. Advancing Allied troops were astonished at how rapidly the Wehrmacht was giving up the fight; while small, fanatic SS units and Hitler Youth fought to the end.

STOPPING SHORT OF BERLIN

On 27 March Montgomery signalled Eisenhower: 'My intention is to drive hard for the Elbe using 9th Army and 2nd Army.' The right of the US 9th Army would be directed at Magdeburg and the left of the 2nd Army on Hamburg; he added, cheekily, 'thence via the autobahn to Berlin, I hope'. To Eisenhower, who had outlined the necessity to clear up the Ruhr before anything else, this was outright disobedience. Eisenhower signalled back that as soon as the British had made contact with 9th US Army and the Ruhr was surrounded, 9th US Army would revert to Bradley's command. Worse news followed. Bradley would mop up the Ruhr and then advance to Dresden to link up with the Russians — west of Berlin.

Montgomery's role was to protect Bradley's northern flank. On 28 March Eisenhower, without informing his chief, General Marshall, cabled this decision to Stalin (via the US Military Mission in Moscow). Berlin — and Prague and Vienna — would be left to the Russians. To Montgomery this was Eisenhower's last and greatest act of interference and nothing less than a strategic disaster. Brooke in London was similarly astonished, noting: 'To start with he (Eisenhower) has no business to address Stalin direct. His communications should be through the Combined Chiefs of Staff.' Churchill also protested to Eisenhower: 'If the enemy's resistance should weaken why should we not cross the Elbe and advance as far eastward as possible? ... This has an important political bearing as the Russian armies in the South seem certain to enter Vienna and Austria ...'

It is clear that two cautious men, Eisenhower and Bradley, decided to change the axis of advance. ('Whenever these two get together, they get timid,' Patton had written in his diary.) They were also alarmed by the threat posed to the Allied armies by the so-called 'Hitler Redoubt' in southern Germany that would have to be eliminated. The redoubt proved to be a figment of Nazi imagination. It did not exist. Allied troops entering Bavaria found only undefended towns and villages. By contrast, Soviet control of Berlin and eastern Europe was to be a reality for the next forty-four years.

While seven Allied armies, including the French, were moving into southern Germany to storm a non-existent southern redoubt, Montgomery's two armies were expected to clear the north German coast and seal the border with Denmark before the Russians arrived there first. The going was easy over the north German plain and they passed through towns and villages in which white sheets of surrender hung from windows. Resistance stiffened as the British neared Bremen.

Allied soldiers hardened by years of war were sickened by their discoveries in German concentration camps. Here American troops are seen after entering Ohrdruf concentration camp in Thuringia, where 31 prisoners were murdered by departing guards.

ROOSEVELT DIES

On 12 April President Roosevelt was relaxing at Warm Springs, Virginia, having his portrait painted, when he suddenly let out a cry of pain, clasped his head and slumped forward. He had suffered a fatal stroke. To his widow Eleanor, Churchill wrote: 'I have lost a dear and cherished friendship which was forged in the fire of war. I trust you may find consolation in the magnitude of his work and the glory of his name.' To Harry Hopkins (himself soon to die) he wrote: 'I feel with you that we have lost one of our greatest friends and one of the most valiant champions of the cause for which we fight.'

The world grieved and soldiers were seen sobbing, as it they had lost a father. Franklin Roosevelt had been president for as long as many of them could remember — more than twelve years. The Nazis in Berlin heard the news of Roosevelt's death with delight. Goebbels greeted Hitler: 'Mein Führer, I congratulate you. Roosevelt is dead. It is written in the stars that the second half of April will be the turning point for us. This is Friday, April thirteenth. It is the turning point!'

On 12 April American troops came across a concentration camp, Buchenwald, and were horrified at what they found. Bodies lay everywhere. Next day British troops encountered a camp called Belsen, and were sickened by what they discovered. Survivors in the camp were almost skeletons. Piles of corpses were stacked like firewood. They found execution chambers and torture rooms. The stench of death and decomposition permeated everything.

ENTERING BERLIN

On 13 April the Russians secured Vienna. On 15 April the Canadians wheeled west to seize the northern Netherlands and the North Sea base of Wilhelmshaven. Next day the Americans entered Nuremberg.

THE BATTLE FOR BERLIN

On that day (16 April) the Russians broke the German defence line on the Oder River and advanced the last 10 kilometres to Berlin. Hitler's capital once boasted a population of 4.3 million. One-third of them had left. Berlin, a Socialist and Communist stronghold, had never given the Nazis a majority in national elections. One-third of its buildings had already been destroyed by Allied bombing and in the coming battle close to 100,000 Berliners were destined to die (6000 of them committed suicide). What was left of the city was soon to be a battlefield.

The Russians advanced before dawn in the glare of 200 searchlights and the sound of thousands of rockets. They faced the last large German armies. It would be a battle involving a total of 3.5 million men, 8000 tanks, 50,000 guns and mortars, and 9000 aircraft — nearly all of them Soviet. Seizing Berlin would cost 300,000 Russian casualties including 100,000 dead, but the Russians would take 500,000 prisoners.

On 20 April Hitler spent a miserable birthday in his underground headquarters in Berlin. He was fifty-six but looked twenty years older. He had hoped to spend the day at Obersalzburg, overlooking the Alps, and many of his intimates had gone to Bavaria, but the Americans were approaching Munich. Guests at the bleak celebration included Göring, Himmler, Ribbentrop and the ever faithful Goebbels. At nightfall all but Goebbels left Berlin for safer surroundings. Doenitz, Keitel and Jodl were also present. Hitler, by now drugged by sedatives, was living in an unreal world: two days later he ordered a counter-attack on the Russians by a Corps that had already disintegrated and burst into an insane fury when it failed to materialise. On 23 April the Russians closed the ring around Berlin and were fighting their way into the city, block by block.

On 25 April 1945 the Americans linked up with the Russians at Torgau, cutting Germany in two, leaving the German armies in Hungary, Austria, Czechoslovakia and Yugoslavia to the oncoming Russians.

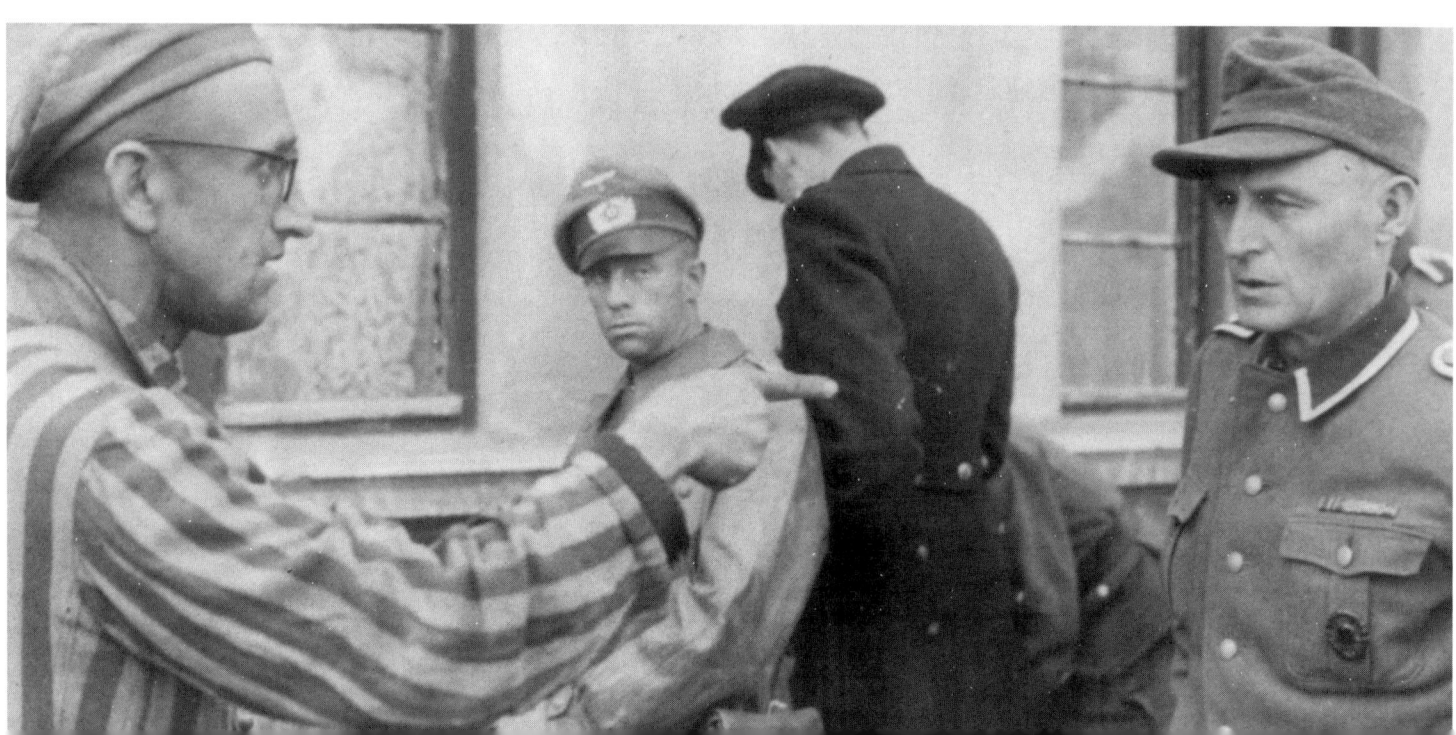

An American army photograph of a liberated prisoner face to face with a guard who had ill-treated him, Germany, April 1945.

Above: The British Commonwealth's warhorse Lt-General Freyberg VC after the New Zealanders entered Trieste in May 1945. He is seen with the commander of the Yugoslav Partisan corps which attempted soon after to take over the city.
Right below: The bodies of Benito Mussolini and his mistress Clara Petacci hanging from a girder in Milan after their execution; most Italians were horrified that his mistress had also been shot.

THE END IN ITALY

Meanwhile the war was ending in Italy. In April also Alexander launched his armies on their last, victorious offensive. His armies had once more been reduced. The Canadians had been withdrawn to north-western Europe, and his forces totalled twenty divisions drawn from a total of twenty-six nationalities — British, American, New Zealand, South African, Polish, Brazilian among them. He was still opposed by twenty-three German divisions, and he had had to fight hard to obtain permission to fight one last campaign. It began with his speciality — the surprise, two-handed punch. The first was delivered by 8th Army on the Adriatic coast with an amphibious crossing of Lake Commachio. The New Zealanders, always in the forefront, stormed the banks of the Senio River and then the Santerno. Five days later the US 5th Army advanced on Bologna, which fell to them on 21 April. Allied tanks now raced for the Po River before the German armies could cross it and establish another defensive line. The German armies, harried from the air and on the flanks by Italian Partisans, collapsed.

Some units reached the banks of the Adige and suffered the same fate; those who could not swim across surrendered. Italian partisans blocked the Alpine passes to prevent any escape. The New Zealand Division sped past Venice for Trieste and entered the city only hours before Tito's Yugoslav Partisans attempted to seize it. During those dramatic weeks the German armies in Italy had already opened negotiations for surrender. Their emissaries had met Allied officers in Switzerland and feared only that Hitler would order them shot as traitors. On 29 April German officers, dressed in civilian clothes, arrived at Alexander's headquarters at Caserta near Naples and signed the unconditional surrender of all German armies in Italy. The capitulation would be announced on 2 May 1945 and take effect immediately.

By this time Mussolini himself was dead and his corpse hanging from a girder in a square in Milan. On 16 April he had transferred the seat of his ramshackle government to Milan. There, in the birthplace of Fascism he decided to make a last stand. A week later railway workers in northern Italy went on strike, paralysing communications. In towns and cities the National Liberation Committee was taking over as the Germans retreated. Fearful of being captured by the Partisans, Mussolini abruptly left Milan in a ten-vehicle motorcade with a German escort for Lake Como, releasing his last supporters from their oath to Fascism.

'But the irrational violence of Fascism could not end reasonably,' writes F.W. Deakin in his history, *The Brutal Friendship*. The roads were now controlled by the Partisans and there could be no escape to Switzerland. One former minister, Buffarint, tried, but was turned back by Italian frontier guards; he later took poison, recovered and was shot. Early on 27 April Mussolini joined the end of a retreating German column. The column was halted and then allowed to proceed by Partisans, but they recognised Mussolini hiding in the back of a German truck and ordered him to get out. They were not sure what to do with him; with Italian humanity they had no thought of executing

him. When news of his capture came to Milan, however, a Communist Partisan squad was sent out with simple orders: 'Kill Mussolini.' On 28 April they took custody of him and his mistress Clara Petacci. On the road beside the lake they ordered their captives to get out, and then shot them both. The squad drove on to Dongo where fifteen other Fascist functionaries were being held, among them Pavolini, Zerbino, Bombacci. They were lined up in the square overlooking Lake Como and shot. Their bodies, along with those of Mussolini and his mistress and of fifteen Fascist militia shot on the same day, were taken to Milan where the crowd vented their fury on the corpses.

THE DEATH OF HITLER

On 28 April Hitler heard from a radio broadcast that Himmler — his 'true Heinrich' — was negotiating the surrender of the German armies in the north through a Swedish Red Cross intermediary, Count Folke Bernadotte. Hitler burst into a rage and then 'sank into a stupor and for a time the entire bunker was silent'. He then heard that the Russians were in the centre of Berlin and nearing Potsdamerplatz, just one block away. Everyone was deserting him, except his mistress Eva Braun. In the early hours of 29 April Hitler and Eva Braun were married. It was destined to be a very short marriage, one without a honeymoon. Hitler then dictated his last will and testament, one without contrition: 'It is untrue that I or anybody else in Germany wanted war in 1939 ... the ruling clique in England wanted war, partly for commercial reasons, partly because it was influenced by propaganda put out by international Jewry ... The seed has been sown that will grow one day ... to the glorious rebirth of the National Socialist movement of a truly united nation.' Copies of this were neatly typed and despatched by messengers dodging the shells and bullets. The Führer suggested that his secretaries leave, advising them to make for the English lines, assuring them that the British 'will still act like gentlemen'. They joined the tens of thousands of troops and civilians attempting to escape west before the Russians arrived.

By afternoon on 29 April Hitler heard that Mussolini had been executed. In the early hours of 30 April he and his wife retired to their quarters. Officers waiting outside the door heard a shot. They found the two bodies on a sofa. Eva Braun had taken poison. Hitler had shot himself in the mouth and had possibly also bitten a poison capsule. There was no time for an autopsy. Their bodies were soaked in petrol and burned in a ditch in the Chancellery garden.

Goebbels informed Admiral Doenitz that he (Doenitz) had been appointed Hitler's successor. Late on 1 May Goebbels and his wife Magda ordered that their sleeping children be killed by injections and then asked an SS officer to shoot them both. Their bodies, too, were burned. The last inhabitants of the Führer Bunker then attempted to escape through the Russian lines. One escapee, General Mohnke, next day reached the Friedrichstrasse railway station and from his elevated view beheld an inferno. 'I now had a panoramic view of the Berlin night time battlefields. It looked like a painting, something apocalyptic by Hieronymous Bosch. Even to a hardened soldier, it was most unreal, phantasmagoric ... flares, shell-bursts, the burning buildings, all these reflected on a low-lying, blackish-yellow cloud of sulphur-like smoke. I could see nothing resembling a clear battle line. But I spotted the launching sites of the Katyushkas [rockets] and I calculated they were only about a mile away in the direction of the Tiergarten ... The Spree was now black, now red, very eerie ...'

Russian troops burst into the great Charité hospital when surgeon Dr Ferdinand Sauerbruch was carrying out an operation. The troops were drunk. 'A wild chase of the nurses and even of the female patients began', and order was restored only by the arrival of Russian officers with drawn revolvers. Other German civilians were not lucky enough to be saved from rape or murder. Such acts became commonplace and increased when the service troops arrived in the wake of the combat soldiers, who were mostly too tired and had seen too much death to carry out atrocities. Russian troops had fought their way up the staircases of the old Reichstag on the day Hitler killed himself (30 April was also the day the Americans entered Munich) and the Red Flag was already flying over the ruins. On 2 May loudspeakers were blaring the announcement that Berlin's last commander, General Weidling, had signed the city's surrender.

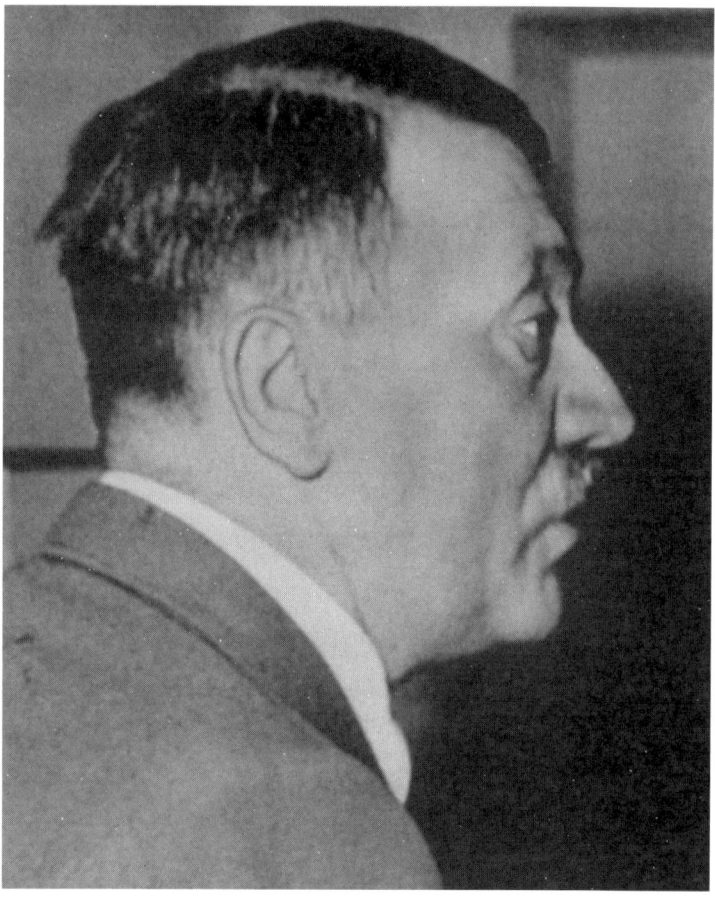

Adolf Hitler in his last year of life, prematurely aged and a nervous wreck kept functioning by drugs.

Above: British troops forced Germans to bury dead prisoners at Belsen concentration camp.
Left: The victims. Two survivors of a concentration camp photographed after liberation.
Below: Some of the first German troops who surrendered in Berlin.

VICTORY IN EUROPE

On 1 May the Russians had reached Rostock and the British entered Lübeck. Two days later General Dempsey's headquarters notified Montgomery that they had been approached by a delegation of four German officers who apparently wanted to arrange a surrender. At his tactical HQ on Luneberg Heath near Hamburg, Montgomery ordered his staff to spruce up and that the Union Jack be raised. He waited for the Germans outside his caravan. On arriving they stood at attention and saluted. Montgomery strolled across to them, looked them over, casually raised his hand to his beret and then demanded in his rasping voice: 'Who are you? What do you want?' He was enjoying the moment. The senior German general replied that he had been sent by Field Marshal Busch to offer the surrender of the German armies retreating from the Russians between Berlin and the Baltic. Montgomery replied that they must surrender to the Red Army.

He then made his own proposal: he would accept the surrender of all German forces facing his own armies, including those in Holland and Denmark. He then lectured them on their ways: 'Your women and children get no sympathy from me — you should have thought of all this six years ago.' A witness recalled that Montgomery 'continued to tongue-lash them, explaining in great detail some of the concentration camps he had seen'. He told them to report back the next day. In the meantime he had a surrender document typed up. To his son's guardian Montgomery wrote that night: 'I really do think the German war is drawing to a close. We took one million prisoners in April, and the total since D-day is over three million.'

Near the Brandenburg Gate a Russian officer announces to his troops the surrender of the German defenders of Berlin, 2 May 1945.

Led by Admiral Friedeburg, the German officers returned next day and at 5 p.m. on 4 May 1945 signed the surrender, accepting Montgomery's terms. The ceremony took place in a tent. It would take effect at 8 a.m. next day, giving the Germans time to wireless the orders to their units. On 5 May Doenitz's government sent Friedeburg to locate Eisenhower to discuss the surrender of all German armed forces. Eisenhower realised they were playing to time to permit as many of their troops as possible to cross to American and British lines before they were overtaken by the Russians. He demanded that they sign an immediate surrender. Jodl flew to Reims, where he was received coldly, and there signed the unconditional surrender on 7 May; to take effect at midnight next day. As the surrender would have to be ratified by the Soviet Union, a third signing took place on 8 May in Berlin, presided over by Marshal Zhukov.

The war in Europe was over. Prime Minister Churchill announced in a broadcast on the evening of 7 May that the next day (8 May 1945) would be a holiday — Victory in Europe Day. On 8 May the 400,000 Germans in Norway surrendered — to the Norwegian resistance army of 45,000 disciplined men who had waited four years for this day. Churchill told the people of Britain in his victory broadcast: 'We must not forget that beyond all lurks Japan, harassed and failing but still a nation of a hundred millions, for whose warriors death has no terrors … Forward, unflinching, unswerving, indomitable, till the whole task is done and the whole world is safe and clean.'

Above: In a tent at his headquarters on Luneburg Heath Field-Marshal Montgomery takes the surrender of German forces facing his 21st Army Group in north west Germany. On his right sits Admiral Freideburg.
Below: The third and final signing of the unconditional surrender took place in Berlin on 8 May 1945 when Field-Marshal Keitel (centre) signed the documents in the presence of Marshal Zhukov. Admiral Freideburg, Doenitz's representative (right) again attended a surrender ceremony and shortly afterwards committed suicide.

Above: Marshal Göring in American hands after his capture. He gave a press conference before being stripped of his fine uniform and confined to a cell.
Below: Red Army soldiers celebrate the end of the war in Berlin.

VICTORY — AND AFTER

When the first rumours of Germany's defeat reached the Allied nations on 7 May people poured into the streets and began to celebrate the coming of peace. Their rejoicing was premature. Stalin demanded that the West postpone announcing the victory until the Germans surrendered to the Red Army in Berlin on 8 May, but Churchill and Truman had not been able to hold back the news. In Prague — one of the few cities spared bombing — German SS units were still fighting the Czech Resistance when the Russians entered the city on 9 May. On that day the last German garrisons stranded in the backwash of war surrendered, from the Aegean islands to Dunkirk. And then peace reigned throughout Europe, disturbed only by the sound of celebrations described as 'the greatest explosion of natural joy yet known to mankind'.

Across the face of Europe millions of people were making their own way home. They numbered nearly 12 million. For half of them there was no home to go to — among them the Germans who had fled from the approaching Red Army, and the Poles who had no wish to return to a Soviet-ruled country. In Allied camps eight million German personnel were in prisons camps. Even before American, British, French and Soviet armies began moving into their zones of occupation, the Western allies were demobilising their forces. Millions returned to their loved ones. As the Allied prisoners-of-war were found and flown back to England — among them 100,000 Americans — the hunt began for the Nazi leaders. Most of Hitler's henchmen were arrested without a fight. Goering gave himself up to the Americans in Bavaria; Doenitz and his rump government were arrested; Ribbentrop was found in a shabby hotel in Hamburg writing his memoirs. On 23 May Himmler was sighted by British officers gathering wood near the Danish frontier; in detention he bit a poison capsule, choosing a quicker death than the fate he had meted out to his millions of victims.

1945: VICTORY IN THE PACIFIC

FROM THE PHILIPPINES TO OKINAWA

In the first week of January 1945 MacArthur's invasion convoy had reached Lingayen Gulf to begin the recapture of Luzon. The ships were struck by kamikaze aircraft whose pilots seemed to single out the old three-stacker HMAS *Australia* for special punishment, which so damaged her that she had to leave the Task Force.

On 9 January General Krueger's 6th US Army landed on the beaches of Lingayen Gulf against little opposition. The campaign was similar to that waged by the Japanese three years earlier. The main American force even landed at the same place as the Japanese had, and progressed rapidly inland. Yamashita, too, evacuated Manila, but a naval landing force arrived there and fought to the end, turning the city into a charnel house and an inferno.

Bataan fell to the Americans and then Corregidor, whose garrison of 5000 fought for eleven days; only 20 survived. MacArthur visited the rock soon afterwards, and ordered: 'Hoist the colours and let no enemy ever haul them down.' Across the bay in Manila, thousands of Filipinos were butchered by the Japanese or caught in the crossfire. The last defenders of Manila were overcome on 4 March and Yamashita was later hanged for a war crime — the Rape of Manila — ot which he was not culpable. It was MacArthur's last campaign of the war. Only five days later the British and Indian forces in Burma entered Mandalay, opening the road to Rangoon.

Above: **American poster published just after the end of the war in Europe.**
Below: **After the landing by American Marines on Okinawa troops bring stores ashore from landing craft.**

IWO JIMA The island of Iwo Jima lay midway between the American air bases in the Marianas and Japan. From Iwo Jima — just over 600 miles (1000 km) from Tokyo, long-range Mustang fighters could escort the Super Fortresses on their raids. The island possessed three airfields and was defended by 20,000 Japanese. Its seizure was entrusted to the 4th and 5th Divisions, US Marine Corps, with the 3rd Division in reserve. and its bombardment by Spruance's battle fleet commenced on 15 February. The Marines started landing after the heaviest bombardment of shore defences in the entire war, but still the Japanese survived it. Marines climbing from the LSTs and amphibious vehicles were pinned down on the beaches. By dusk 30,000 American were ashore, clinging to the beaches and under artillery bombardment; soon rockets fell on them. 'The first night on Iwo Jima can only be described as a nightmare in hell,' the correspondent Robert Sherrod wrote. The Americans raised the Stars and Stripes over Mount Suribachi but half the island was still in Japanese hands. The last resistance was not overcome until 26 March, by which time the last survivors mounted a suicide charge and were cut down. Of the 20,000-strong garrison only 216 had been taken prisoner; 17,000 were dead and the rest hiding in caves where most would die. Iwo Jima was a bloody battle that cost 5000 American lives. President Truman was horrified by the toll.

OKINAWA In March 1945 the Americans began the invasion of Okinawa. Among the ships bombarding the island were the British Pacific fleet, under Admiral Sir Bruce Fraser, and the Australian Squadron. Japan had few weapons left except the blind courage of her warriors. The last super-battleship, *Yamato*, was sent from Japan to wreak havoc in the waters off Okinawa. She only had enough fuel for a one-way voyage and she was sighted on 7 April and sunk. In the first week on Okinawa, few Japanese were found and Admiral Turner wirelessed Nimitz (8 April): 'I may be crazy but it looks like the Japs have quit the war, at least in this section.'

Next day the American troops met with spirited resistance. Okinawa, the last American campaign of the war, would be one of the hardest-fought, lasting three months. The island was defended with suicidal courage and tactics. Nearly 2000 Kamikas aircraft attacked the Allied ships, damaging 34 destroyers in addition to 200 other vessels. Nearly 200,000 Americans were ashore by mid-June when the Japanese resistance began to collapse. The last defenders were hunted from caves; if surrender demands failed they were blasted with hand grenades and entombed by artillery fire. The Japanese commander and five of his staff had chosen death; they were found with their throats cut.

Left: **Wounded American Marine being taken to First Aid during the fighting on Iwo Jima.**
Above: **Over Okinawa the Japanese launched 'Baka' rocket aircraft from larger planes; the single pilot was expected to crash it into American warships.**

A week earlier General Ushijima committed harakiri, murmuring 'the native Okinawans must resent me'. More than 110,000 Japanese died, and so did 75,000 Okinawans. The capture of the island cost nearly 13,000 American dead or missing. To the north lay Japan. In July the Emperor of Japan ordered that the war 'be terminated as soon as possible'. If the Allies insisted on unconditional surrender, however, Japan would fight to the bitter end.

THE END IN BURMA

THE ROAD TO MANDALAY Early in 1945 the British 14th Army had reached the Irrawaddy River and stood poised to cross it and destroy the last Japanese army in Burma. The Irrawaddy is broad and fast-flowing, and presented a major obstacle to an army now mechanised and equipped with tanks. General Slim ordered his engineers to built their own boats, including barges, using if necessary elephants to carry the timber to the river's edge. Slim ordered multiple crossings to confuse the Japanese, hoping that the decisive crossing south of Mandalay by his most powerful Corps, 4 Corps, would go unnoticed by them.

On 9 January, 19th Division pushed its first battalion over the Irrawaddy and established a strong bridgehead. The Japanese, determined to hold Slim on the Irrawaddy, launched savage attacks against the bridgehead for three weeks, and suffered heavily. The 20th Division crossed near Monywa on 22 January, and the entire division was across the river near Myinmu by the night of 13 February, about 50 kilometres from Mandalay. They had established a strong bridgehead 10 kilometres long and three kilometres deep.

All depended on 4 Corps, which Slim planned would strike the decisive blow against the Japanese on the plain at Meiktila south of Mandalay. He saw his men emerging from the jungle hills, 'their jungle green uniforms and their faces were red from the dust, and the jungle itself was red, too, every leaf thick with dust …' Forward elements of 4 Corps crossed the Irrawaddy on 14 February near Pagan, where the mist shrouded 120 temples along the river — 'a place of great beauty', Slim recalled. Meiktila, after hard fighting, fell to 17th Indian Division on 3 March. But this was just the beginning of the battle of Meiktila. Over the next two weeks the Japanese attempted to regain the area and at one stage reached the airfield, where Allied reinforcements and supply aircraft touched down under fire.

By the second week of March 1945 the British-Indian forces had crossed the Irrawaddy in five places, and Allied air forces were blanket bombing Japanese defences and communications. The Japanese were slow to react, as if exhausted and punch-drunk. On 20 March, after stiff fighting, the dusty sprawling city of Mandalay fell to Allied forces and the Union Jack was hoisted at Fort Dufferin on the heights above it. Allied casualties in the Meiktila–Mandalay fighting were 10,000, and losses were much higher for the Japanese.

THE RACE FOR RANGOON With barely six weeks until the monsoon broke, Slim ordered Lieutenant-General Frank Messervy, now commanding 4 Corps, to dash for Rangoon. Plans were laid for an amphibious landing at Rangoon — the seaborne landing for which Slim had pleaded for two years. The more cautious Monty Stopford was to push 33 Corps down the Irrawaddy. Even for the impetuous Messervy this was a tall order. To advance 500 kilometres with tanks he would have to leap-frog his divisions, relying on air supply by using captured airfields. On 21 April Messervy's troops took Magwe; on the following day General Kimura ordered his forces to evacuate Rangoon by 28 April and attempt to escape to the east via Pegu. But Messervy took Pegu, and the Japanese withdrawal from Burma became a shambles, with their exhausted columns overtaken by British tanks, and travel by road impossible.

On 1 May an Allied aircraft flying over Rangoon reported a complete absence of Japanese, and sighted a message painted on the roof of Rangoon jail: 'Japs gone: Exdigitate'. (It was the work of an Australian air force prisoner of war, using service slang for 'Hurry Up.') On the same day Gurkha paratroops landed near Rangoon. On 3 May British landing craft dropped forces at Rangoon docks, and the troops entered the city to cheers from the populace. Slim pressed on to seize Moulmein. Burma had been retaken.

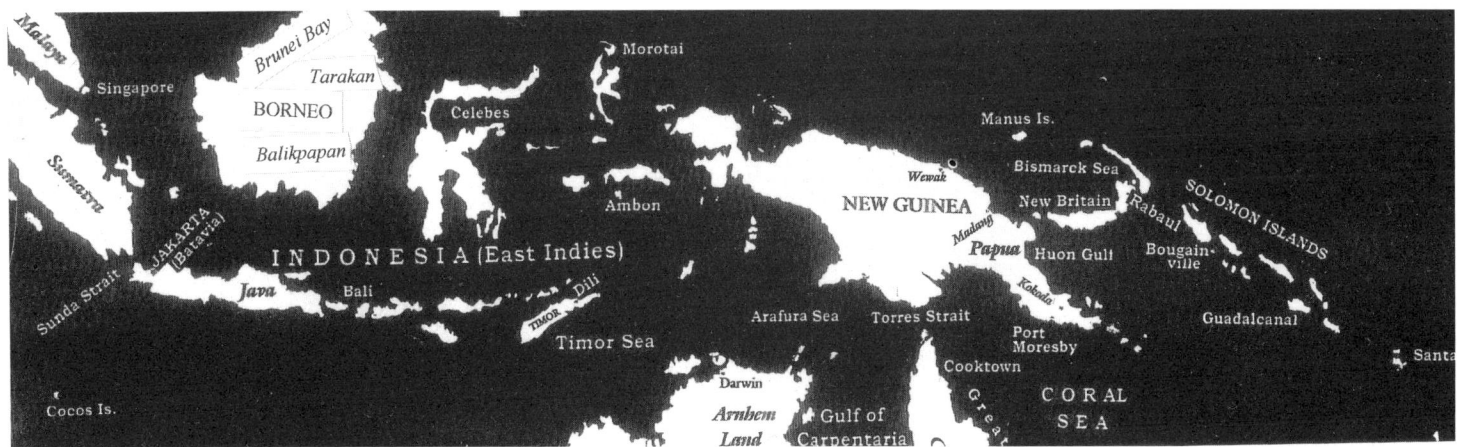

Plans had been made for an offensive early in 1945 by an envisaged 'British-Commonwealth Pacific army' to advance on the Japanese homeland. New Zealand considered recalling her division from Italy to participate in the last assault. These plans were to be rendered null by Japan's rapid collapse after the dropping of the atomic bombs.

BORNEO AND THE LAST CAMPAIGNS

While Europe was celebrating the end of the war, Australian troops were at sea, heading for the last amphibious invasion of the war and fighting their last campaign. They were men of the most famed and travelled of Australian divisions, the 9th, the defenders of Tobruk and the victors of Alamein, and they were heading for Tarakan on the coast of Borneo. The 1945 invasion of Borneo had been agreed upon at the Quebec conference of 1944 as a means of securing the oil of the Indies and bases for the British Pacific fleet. But by early 1945 even the British Chiefs of Staff regarded a Borneo base as too far from Japan to be effective and General Marshall advised MacArthur that the operations would have little immediate effect on prosecuting the war. When Blamey suggested their cancellation MacArthur loftily replied that this would affect his strategy.

After three weeks of bombardment of the shore, the invasion fleet landed the 9th Division at Tarakan on the morning of 1 May 1945, and the troops got two kilometres inland on the first day before clearing the Japanese posts next day with flame-throwers. Tarakan required a month of bombardment by artillery and tanks before the Japanese were overcome. Tarakan claimed 225 Australian and 1500 Japanese lives.

By December 1944, the Australians in New Guinea had pushed into the rugged Torricelli Ranges and along the coast to Wewak, their progress aided by landing craft. The 19th Brigade took Maprik on Anzac Day 1945 and the 16th Brigade entered Wewak in May to find the Japanese had evacuated it. Harried by naval shelling, air strikes and Australian patrols, the Japanese retreated into the mountains, but only 13,500 of the original 40,000-strong Wewak garrison were alive to surrender on the Capitulation, and a further 1000 died soon afterwards.

By war's end New Guinea had claimed a total of 100,000 Japanese lives (some authorities claim the total was nearer 150,000); another 70,000 had died in the Solomons. On 1 June the 9th Division began landing from LSTs and LCIs at Brunei Bay and encountered little opposition other than that on Labuan Island, which was overcome by infantry, flame-throwers and tanks. The 24th Brigade entered Beaufort on 26 June but hard fighting followed when the Japanese counterattacked. More than 1200 Japanese died around Brunei Bay and 114 Australians were killed.

Australian infantry clamber from an American landing craft on Labuan Island, Borneo 1945.

Australian engineers of 2/13 Field Company who went ashore ahead of the infantry to neutralise enemy explosives on the beaches of Tarakan, Borneo 1945.

But more horrifying was the discovery of six emaciated Australians in a village: they were the only survivors of the Sandakan death marches in which more than 2000 Australian and British prisoners of war had died or been murdered by their guards. The indigenous head-hunters were turned loose on the Japanese — even on those 6000 who surrendered, few of whom survived their own death march. Whereas most Diggers regarded the Japanese who surrendered in their thousands with a mixture of distaste, puzzlement and pity, and seldom exacted revenge for the horrors they and their mates had suffered, the 'Beaufort Episode' proved an exception.

On 1 July 1945, five days after engineers had gone in first to blow gaps in the underwater obstacles, the 18th and 21st brigades were carried to the shore at Balikpapan in landing craft under dark clouds of smoke from the burning oil tanks. The Australians made good progress ashore, seizing both airfields without tank support before pushing the Japanese into the hills. Japanese fatalities totalled 1800, while 229 Australians were killed in this, their last battle of the war. Japan assembled a home army of two million to resist the invasions MacArthur planned for late 1945 and 1946.

THE BERLIN CONFERENCE — AND THE ATOMIC BOMB

At the conference held at the palace of Potsdam in July 1945 near conquered Berlin the leaders of the Soviet Union, the United States and Great Britain met to decide the future course of the war against Japan, and to plan for the future. It was to be the last time the 'Big Three' met as Allies. Churchill, who arrived on 15 July, was greatly taken next day with the new president, Harry Truman, who seemed vigorous and decisive. Truman's manner was not deceiving; he was both. In the afternoon Churchill visited Berlin and looked over the ruined Reichs Chancellery above Hitler's bunker. A small group of Berliners, possibly happy to be alive, broke into a cheer when they saw him. 'My hate had died with the surrender,' he later wrote, 'and I was much moved.' Churchill was tired. He had been campaigning prior to general elections he had called for late July. His wartime coalition had dissolved into party politics — he accused Labour of wanting to institute a socialist Gestapo — and now his Grand Alliance was falling apart.

In nearly ten days of meetings much was accomplished. Churchill left the conference on 25 July, the day when the election took place. By the evening it was clear that Labour had won a landslide, with nearly 400 seats against the Conservatives' 213. On 26 July he saw the King and relinquished his seals of office, recommending that the Labour leader, Clement Attlee, be appointed prime minister. Two days later, to Stalin's surprise, Attlee arrived in Potsdam to represent Great Britain.

On 18 July President Truman had told Churchill that the atomic bomb on which American, British and European émigré scientists had been working had been successfully tested in the deserts of New Mexico. It had an explosive power equal to 20,000 tonnes of TNT. Truman had no hesitation about using the atomic bomb to end the war. At Potsdam on 26 July 1945 Truman presented Japan with an ultimatum demanding her immediate surrender, with terrible consequences if it rejected the demand. Japan made no reply.

JAPAN SURRENDERS

On 4 August American aircraft had dropped leaflets over Hiroshima warning that the city would be destroyed unless Japan surrendered. At 8.15 a.m. on 6 August 1945 an American Super Fortress flying from Tinian piloted by Colonel Paul Tibbetts dropped an atomic bomb on Hiroshima. It floated down gently on parachutes and exploded about 200 metres above the ground The airmen saw a purple flash and then a mass of flames (heat so extreme that granite melted within a kilometre of the centre of the blast). In the concussion wave that followed all buildings within three kilometres were destroyed. A huge mushroom cloud rose from the target. 'My God', shouted the co-pilot, 'what have we done!' No fewer than 64,000 Japanese had been incinerated in a split second.

On the following day Foreign Minister Togo stated that Japan should accept the Potsdam Declaration and surrender. Army Chief Anami objected strongly, saying 'Furthermore, we don't even know if

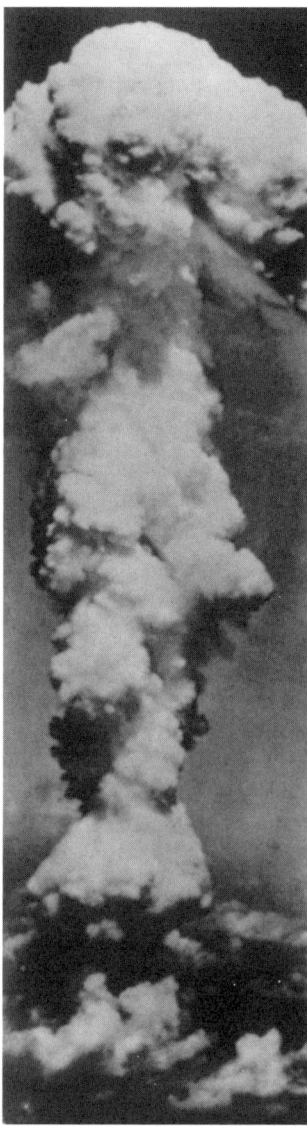

the bomb was atomic.' On 8 August the Japanese ambassador in Moscow approached Foreign Minister Molotov with a personal plea that he initiate peace negotiations with the United States. Instead Molotov handed him the Soviet Union's declaration of war. Russian armies poured into Manchuria, well equipped with tanks and crushed any resistance on their swift progress. Japanese casualties were enormous.

On 9 August an American aircraft dropped a second atomic (plutonium) bomb on Nagasaki and 40,000 Japanese died. In the evening Emperor Hirohito told his Cabinet: 'Ending the war is the only way to restore world peace and to relieve the nation from the terrible distress with which it is burdened.' The Japanese government wirelessed its acceptance of the Potsdam Declaration, providing that the Emperor remained on the throne. The Americans were preparing two more atomic bombs but early on 14 August dropped leaflets instead, informing the Japanese people that their government had offered to surrender. This came as startling news to the civilian population. Just before midnight on 14 August the Emperor signed the document accepting the Allied terms, and ordered his armed forces 'to cease active operations and to surrender arms'. He then recorded the news for his subjects. The recording was put in a safe and broadcast early the next day, 15 August, despite desperate attempts by fanatical officers to find and smash it. Among the Allied nations 15 August was the day that would be celebrated as 'Victory over Japan Day' — V-J Day. The Pacific War had ended as suddenly as it had begun.

When his captains asked what they should do if Japanese suicide aircraft appeared, Admiral Halsey ordered: 'Shoot them down in a friendly fashion.' But the Japanese all over the Pacific accepted their Emperor's command, and the crushing humiliation of defeat. On 28 August an armada of nearly fifty Dakota transports touched down on Japanese soil. Two days later MacArthur arrived at the airfield and clambered from his plane. He was greeted by Eichelberger, and said 'Bob, from Melbourne to Tokyo is a long way, but this seems to be the end of the road.'

In prison camps all over South-East Asia Japanese commandants announced that the war had ended, and retired to their quarters to contemplate the future. In one last act of historic significance the Japanese encouraged their puppet regimes in French Indochina and nationalist leaders in Indonesia to proclaim independence. In Hanoi, the Communist guerrilla leader Ho Chi Minh proclaimed the independence of his Vietnam, and in Java Achmed Sukarno proclaimed an end to Dutch rule of Indonesia and the birth of a republic. British-Indian units landing in Singapore were welcomed by crowds of well-wishers, but other units landing in Saigon and in Indonesia found hostile bands of armed nationalists ready to contest the return respectively of the French and the Dutch troops. Fighting soon broke out and Japanese troops were used to help the British restore order.

On 2 September 1945 representatives of the Japanese government stood on the deck of USS *Missouri* in Tokyo Bay and signed the formal instruments of surrender in the presence of General MacArthur and

Left: The atomic explosion.
Below: The Japanese delegates arrive to sign the unconditional surrender. Foreign Minister Shigemitsu is on the left, army chief Umezu next to him.
Opposite top: General MacArthur reads the preamble before asking the Japanese to sign the surrender documents. Behind him stand representatives of the Allied powers at war with Japan from left to right; China, Great Britain (Admiral Fraser), Soviet Union, Australia (General Blamey), Canada, France (General Leclerc), the Netherlands (Admiral Helfrich), and New Zealand.
Opposite bottom: British Commonwealth and American prisoners of war greet news of the end of the war and the arrival of Allied troops.

officers of all Allied forces, including General Blamey and Commodore Collins of Australia, Admiral Helfrich of the Netherlands and General Leclerc of France. (On the same day, Ho Chi Minh proclaimed in Saigon the independence of Vietnam.) By MacArthur's side stood General Percival, liberated from prison camp. MacArthur then spoke for the broadcast microphones in the language that came easily to him: 'Today the guns are silent. A great tragedy has ended. A great victory has been won … The entire world is quietly at peace.'

MacArthur said that it was his 'earnest hope and indeed the hope of all mankind' that 'a better world shall emerge', one founded on 'faith and understanding — a world dedicated to the dignity of man and the fulfillment of his most cherished ideals — for freedom, tolerance and justice.' Even the Japanese present, aware of the hatred felt towards their nation, were deeply affected by his unexpected words and their call for reconciliation. World War II was over.

Four days later Australian forces took the surrender of the Japanese on New Britain and on 9 September General Blamey took the surrender of the Japanese at Morotai, coldly and without words of warmth. On 12 September Mountbatten, with General Slim at his side, accepted the surrender in Singapore of the Japanese in South-East Asia. Mountbatten, who had hoped to take the surrender personally of the Emperor Hirohito, wrote of his concern about the future to MacArthur: 'I cannot help feeling that unless we are really tough with the Japanese leaders they will be able to build themselves up eventually for another war.' MacArthur thought otherwise: to humiliate the Japanese and their emperor would destroy his attempt to build in the Japanese a new self-respect and a new society. But even Lee Kwan Yew, a student in Singapore (and its future president), who had survived the horrors of Japanese rule and cheered the return of the British, called the day of surrender 'one of the greatest moments in the history of south-east Asia'.

First to be repatriated were the Allied prisoners-of-war, who were found in camps throughout south-east Asia. Thereafter, repatriation of both victors and vanquished was rapid. By early 1946 the Australian forces in the south-west Pacific, once 344,000 strong, had returned home, barely 400 remaining in New Guinea. For millions it was time to pick up the threads of a life disturbed by war.

THE AFTERMATH

'The Germany in which we found ourselves travelling at the end of April presented a scene that was almost beyond human comprehension,' the war correspondent Alan Moorehead wrote. 'Her capital lost and almost razed ... Around us fifty great cities lay in ruins, or at least in partial ruins. Many of them had no electric light or power or gas or running water, and no coherent system of government. Like ants in an ant-heap the people scurried over the ruins, diving furtively into cellars and doorways in search of loot ... Life was sordid, aimless, leading nowhere ...' The Germans called 1945 'Year Zero': the end, the year of nothingness. Few saw it as a new beginning.

The trial of eighteen Nazi leaders began in Nuremburg in the American zone of occupation before judges from the United States, the Soviet Union, Britain and France. The Nazis' crimes or their compliance with them, were so monstrous that new charges were proposed: that of planning and waging aggressive war and of committing 'crimes against humanity'. The trial began on 1 November 1945 and ended on 31 August 1946, when the judges retired to consider their verdicts. On 30 September they passed death sentences on Goering, von Ribbentrop, Keitel, Jodl, Kaltenbrunner, Rosenberg, Frank, Frick, Streicher, Sauckel, and Seyss-Inquart. Goering took poison on the eve of execution but the ten others were led to the gallows on 16 October. Their bodies were cremated and their ashes thrown into a river. Speer, Doenitz, Raeder, von Schirach, and Hess were among those sentenced to prison terms (the last named for reasons of insanity). Hundreds of criminals escaped, some adopting new identities — Mengele and Eichmann fled to South America and the latter was tracked down fifteen years later and hanged in Jerusalem, in the Jewish state of Israel. Sixty years later the hunt continues for those who had escaped the net.

In Tokyo, General Tojo, who had ineptly attempted to shoot himself at the war's end, faced trial and in 1948 he and six other Japanese wartime leaders were hanged for war crimes. As in Europe, civil courts and military tribunals for years placed on trial other individuals charged with murder; of 2400 Japanese found guilty, 809 were executed.

After the explosion of joy to celebrate the end of the war, the Allied peoples felt a sense of loss, not only for their own dead and maimed. Hitler and Mussolini were gone, but so also were the men who had led the Allied nations through the great ordeal: Roosevelt and Curtin of Australia dying from the strain of war; Churchill swept from office; de Gaulle soon to resign as France's premier in disgust with French party politics. Only Stalin remained, to cast a malign influence over the future. Soviet armies remained in eastern Europe, three-million strong, and any democratic opposition to Communist rule was eliminated in eastern Germany, Poland, Hungary, Romania, Bulgaria and Albania. Even Czechoslovakia succumbed in 1948 and only Yugoslavia under Marshal Tito refused to accept Moscow's direction.

The winter of 1946–47 in Europe was remembered as the most severe in memory. People went without fuel for warmth, or adequate food. A Communist takeover of government in Italy and France was predicted. Growing tensions and the chill in relations between the Soviet Union and the West became an undeclared war — the Cold War — that was destined to last almost half a century. The world lived under the shadow of the atomic bomb; fears of nuclear extinction grew after the Soviet Union developed its first A-bomb in 1949. Victory was complete, but at what a cost.

. . . . .

Yet from these anxious times and this state of ruin a new Europe was emerging and the modern world was being born. To the growing Soviet challenge came response. In March 1947 the United States announced that it would defend any nation threatened by Communism and in June announced the 'Marshall Plan' by which it would offer economic assistance to the nations of Europe to help them rebuild their shattered societies. European recovery was rapid. The rubble was cleared, industry rebuilt. The Germans proved eager to create a new and democratic society, as did the Japanese under the benign rule of General MacArthur. The victors demanded no crippling reparations, nor carried out any punishment of the conquered peoples, whom they felt had suffered enough. This was the true victory of World War II. The Allied occupation of Germany and Japan was one of the undeniable triumphs of the era. Within ten years of the war's end both West Germany and Japan were thriving economies.

In the four years after 1945 the old European empires in southeast Asia disappeared. India and Pakistan achieved independence in 1947, Burma and Ceylon in 1948, and Indonesia in 1949. China passed under Communist control in 1949 but even the French extended self-government to most of Indochina in 1946, retaining only Vietnam (this too was lost in 1954). This process of change accelerated.

The occupation of western Germany ended in 1949. In that year the nations of Western Europe formed a mutual-defence alliance under US guidance — the North Atlantic Treaty Organisation: NATO. Like the United Nations Organisation (UNO), founded in 1945, it still exists. The wartime leaders re-emerged, as if the people needed them. Churchill was re-elected in 1951, energetic as ever. Dwight Eisenhower was elected United States president in 1952; de Gaulle was recalled to power in 1958. Churchill, failing in health, retired in 1955. His last words to his cabinet ministers were: 'Man is *spirit*. Never fall out with the Americans'. He was succeeded by Eden, who almost destroyed the Anglo–American alliance in 1956 by seizing the Suez Canal from Egypt by force; and then by Macmillan, who rebuilt the alliance. They had been two of Churchill's close wartime colleagues. Montgomery, now a field-marshal and a viscount and irascible as ever, retired in 1958. When Churchill died in London in 1965, at the age of ninety, he was buried like a king.

As Stalin strengthened his hold over eastern Europe the Australian correspondent Chester Wilmot set out to write a history of the conflict, *The Struggle for Europe* (1952) to explain 'how and why the Western Allies, while gaining military victory, suffered political defeat; how and why in the process of smashing Nazi Germany and liberating Western Europe, they allowed the Soviet Union to gain control of Eastern Europe …' Stalin, descending into paranoia, died in 1953 and his successors soon revealed the extent of his crimes and murders. In numbers alone they dwarfed Hitler's: as many as 20 million Soviet citizens died from execution or in concentration camps — the 'Gulags' — in the last twenty-five years of his rule. World War II did not bring an end to war. Genocidal murder continued, far from Europe — in Asia and Africa, provoked by the last ideology, Communism, and often intensified by racial, tribal and religious hatreds. The 'thaw' in relations between the Soviet Union and the West fluctuated until the 1980s, when the Soviet Union, bankrupted and failing, began to liberalise its society. It made no moves to repress popular risings in eastern Europe in 1989 and itself fell apart in 1990, when Germany was at last reunited.

Europe progressed to peaceful union. One super-power remains, the United States. For all the world's woes, at present more people live in freedom, free of repression, than at any time in human history. This, at least, is reason for hope.

· · · · ·

The Allies had crushed Germany with sheer weight of armament and by a strategy that, for all its errors, proved masterly. Other invisible factors gave the Allies victory and made the defeat of the Axis inevitable. The greatest — the thread that runs through this narrative — was the sheer courage and determination of the men and women who fought. Among the Allied nations observers found no trace of the defeatism and despair so pronounced in the last years of the 1914–18 War. History has now consigned to its subconscious the hideous crimes of the Nazis — they surface as a recurrent nightmare — but the spirit of their victims and foes still shines 'bright and indestructible as stars': the young Jews fighting with rocks against artillery in the ruins of the Warsaw Ghetto; the fatalism of the bomber crews flying steadily on through the darkness and flak above the Ruhr while aircraft on each side of them burst into flames, exploding and plummeting to earth; the captured men and women of the Resistance tortured but unyielding and dying unbroken and defiant; the drawn faces of the infantry, captured on newsreel, as their landing craft bucketed towards the beaches of Tarawa, Normandy, Okinawa, Tarakan …

In 1942 a British soldier wrote anonymously a poem called 'A Soldier: His Prayer', and many committed its lines to heart:

I knew what we were fighting for — peace for the kids, our brothers freed,
A kinder world, a cleaner breed.

Its closing lines could be an epitaph for all those who died:

Help me, O God, when death is near,
  To mock the haggard face of fear —
That when I fall — if fall I must —
  My soul may triumph in the dust.

APPENDIX

THE LOSS OF LIFE

Europe (dead/missing)	Military	Civilian	Jews
American	170,000		
British (UK)	265,000	60,000	
French	250,000	270,000	90,000
Belgian	10,000	50,000	40,000
Dutch	10,000	100,000	90,000
Luxembourg	—	—	3,000
Denmark	—	—	1,500
Norwegian	10,000	—	1,500
German	3,250,000	3,640,000	170,000
Italian	330,000	70,000	15,000
Austrian	230,000	40,000	40,000
Czech	20,000	70,000	260,000
Hungarian	120,000	80,000	200,000
Yugoslav	300,000	1,300,000	55,000
Greek	88,000	325,000	60,000
Bulgarian	10,000	—	7,000
Rumanian	200,000	40,000	425,000
Polish	120,000	2,500,000	2,800,000
Finnish	90,000	—	
Soviet (inc. Baltic States)	13,600,000	6,000,000	1,720,000
Lithuanian	—	170,000	
Latvian	—	120,000	
Estonian	—	140,000	
Totals:	**19,070,000**	**14,730,000**	**5,978,000**

Asia	Military	Civilians
Chinese (estimated)	3,500,000	10,000,000
Japanese	1,700,000	360,000
Totals	**5,330,000**	**15,690,000**

- Under Japanese rule an estimated 120,000 Filipinos died, along with 50,000 Malayans and up to 1 million Indonesians.
- The figures for European fatalities are based on those given in Hans Dollinger's *The Fall of Nazi Germany and Imperial Japan* (1966) and the *Encyclopedia Britannica*

British Commonwealth fatalities

Australian	30,000
Canadian	40,000
Indian	25,000
New Zealand	10,000
South African	7,000
Colonies	7,000

PICTORIAL ACKNOWLEDGEMENTS

Photographs on pages listed below have been supplied by or reproduced with kind permission of the following archives:

Australian War Memorial, Canberra, Australia: Front cover, back cover; 9 (right); 11 (lower); 16 (lower); 59; 61 (left); 107; 113 (right); 115 (both); 116; 125 (right); 126; 128; 130; 131; 133 (both); 135; 138; 142; 149; 150 (left); 152; 159 (lower); 169; 173; 182 (both); 187 (lower); 188; 199; 201; 202; 203; 207; 208 (both); 211; 213; 230; 236 (lower right); 237 (both); 241; 254 (lower); 256 (top); 257; 259; 263 (both); 269; 287; 295 (right); 312; 313

Imperial War Museum, London: 2-3; 7; 37; 57 (lower); 63; 66; 73 (both); 76 (lower); 78; 83 (top); 85; 87; 93; 95 (top); 96; 99; 101; 104-105 (both); 169; 137; 139; 140; 181; 195 (lower); 197 (lower); 209; 212; 245; 246; 253; 255; 266; 271; 281; 290 (top); 291; 305 (top); 307 (top)

National Archives of Australia, Canberra: 61 (right)

New Zealand Archives (and Alexander Turnbull War History Collection, Wellington): 125 (left); 151; 167 (left); 191; 197 (top); 303 (top)

US National Archives and Records Administration (NARA), Washington, DC (including archives of US Army Signal Corps, US Marine Corps, US Navy, US Coast Guard, US Air Force and captured Enemy Records): 9 (left); 141 (lower); 161 (both); 177; 179; 184; 185 (both); 190; 200; 205; 214; 215; 218; 222 (top); 227 (lower); 229; 231; 235; 238; 239 (both); 244 (lower); 249 (top); 250; 251; 256 (lower); 260; 264-265 (all); 267; 268; 270; 273 (lower); 276 (top); 277; 282; 283; 285; 286 (both); 288 (top); 289 (both); 292; 293; 295 (left); 297; 298 (lower); 299 (top); 300 (both); 301; 302; 307 (lower);308 (top); 309 (both); 310 (left); 314-315 (all)

Soviet official: 17, 155 (both), 193, 220 (lower), 233 (both), 242, 261, 278, 296, 306, 308 (bottom left)

Page 38, Bundesarchiv; page 58, *Time-Life*; page 100 (top), page 272 (lower), Canadian Archives; page 189, Ullstein

The balance of the images come from the author's scrapbooks and collection of historic photographs, journals and ephemera gathered over forty years in writing and publishing. If the source or ownership of any illustration has not been correctly acknowledged, the author and publishers apologise and undertake the correct the omission.

INDEX

Abyssinia, (see Ethiopia)
Admiralty Islands, 262
Alamein battles, 192, 196, 209–213
Albania, 46
Alexander, General H.R. (F-M Earl Alexander of Tunis), 42, 86–88, 172, 197, 234, 244–251, 266, 277, 303
Aircraft development, 36–41, 65, 97, 236–239
Air war (Allied), 142–143, 194, 236–239, 288
Ambon, 173
American forces (see also United States), 8, 11, 39, 102, 141, 160–315
Anzio, 266
Ardennes offensives, 82, 293
Arnhem battle, 290
Atlantic, Battle of the, 246–247
Atom bombs, 68, 313
Auchinleck, General (later F-M Sir) Claude, 76, 139, 149–150
Auschwitz–Birkenau camps, 58, 226–227, 294
Australia (and Australian forces), 52, 59–62, 115–117, 126, 149159, 169–178, 182, 192, 196, 209–213, 230, 236, 255–259, 287, 312–315
Austria, 10, 11, 43, 294
'Axis', birth of, 32, 109

Badoglio, Marshal Pietro, 16, 248
'Barbarossa' (invasion of Russia), 143–156
Battle of Britain (1940), 93–96
Belgium, 67, 82–86, 288
Belsen camp, 301
Berlin, battle of (1945), 304
Bismarck, 134
Blamey, General Sir Thomas, 62, 115, 124,149, 178, 208, 259, 315
'Blitz', The, 103
Bolsheviks (Communists), 10–11
'Bomb Plot (1944), 274
Borneo campaign , 312
Britain, 10, 14, 17, 23, 28, 36–42, 50, 140
British Commonwealth (and Empire), 23, 52–53, 59–62, 101–102
Brooke, General Sir Alan (later F-M Viscount Alanbrooke), 63, 156, 197
Bulgaria, 67, 82–86
Burma, 72, 178, 257, 281, 311
Burma–Thailand railway, 240

Canada (and Canadians), 52, 59, 62, 88, 162, 244–245, 250, 270, 276, 299, 303
Cassino battle, 266
Caucasus, Germans reach, 192
Chamberlain, Neville, 44–48
Chiang Kai-shek, 33–35, 156, 252, 284
China, 33–35
'Chindits', 257
Churchill (Sir) Winston, 10, 17, 27–28, 45, 97, 141, 162, 197, 250–255, 266, 275, 278, 291, 297, 307, 313, 314
Clark, General Mark W., 196, 214, 250, 266–268
Collins, Captain (later Vice-Admiral Sir) John, 106, 175, 255, 286
Coral Sea battle, 181–183
Crete battle, 129–133
'Crusader' battle, (1941), 149
Cunningham, Admiral Sir Andrew (Admiral of the Fleet Viscount Cunningham), 105–111, 114–134
Curtin, John, 172
Czechoslovakia, 16, 44–45, 302

D-Day, 270
'Dam Busters' squadron, 254
Danzig, 16, 47, 50
Darlan, Admiral, 98, 214–215
Darwin, battle of, 174, 254
De Gaulle, General Charles, 78–79, 98, 137
Dieppe raid, 195
Denmark, 74
Depression, the, 23
Dresden bombing, 298
Dunkirk evacuation, 84–88

Eichmann, Adolf, 226
Eisenhower, General Dwight David, 96, 214, 268, 289
Enigma decrypting machine, 38
Ethiopia, 30, 135

Fascism (see also Italy), growth of, 13, 18–19
Finland, 69, 72
France, 8, 14, 22, 30, 50, 63, 68, 80–91, 98–99, 222–224
Freyberg VC, General Bernard (later General Lord Freyberg), 129–133
Gamelin, General Maurice, 54, 78
Goebbels, Dr Josef, 25, 189, 302
Göring, Hermann, 32, 50, 94–95,129, 148,236, 308
Gort VC, General Lord, 63
Graf Spee, 66
Greece, 110, 118, 124, 281
Guadalcanal, 261

Himmler, Heinrich, 26, 56, 226–228, 308
Hiroshima, 313
Hitler, Adolf, 10, 12, 20, 24–32, 43 et al
Heydrich, Reinhard, 56, 226
'Holocaust', The (Jewish), 226–228
Hong Kong, 162
Huon Gulf campaign, 258
Hungary, 10, 16, 109, 228, 280

Imphal–Kohima battles, 283
India (and Indian forces), 52, 62, 139, 195, 281–284
Iran, 139
Iraq, 136
Irrawaddy River, 311
Ireland, 53
Italian campaign, 250, 266, 303
Italy, 12, 18–19, 30–31, 46–47, 89
Iwo Jima, 310

Japan, 22–23, 28, 33, 156–186, 229–230, 254–260, 262–265, 281–287, 309–315
Java, defence of, 174–176
Jews, Nazi persecution of, 26, 58, 146, 221–228

Kharkov, 261
Kiev, 147, 261
Kokoda campaign, 199–206
Kormoran, 152
Kursk offensive, 242

Laval, Pierre, 30, 91
Leclerc, General Philippe, 99, 234, 277
Leningrad, 148
Leyte Gulf, Battle of, 286
Libya, 112–119

Lithuania, 146, 296
MacArthur, General Douglas, 11, 162, 177, 199, 207, 256–259, 262, 285–286, 309, 314–315
Maginot Line, 23–24
Majdanek death camp, 226, 278
Malaya, 158, 163–169
Malta, 190
Manila, Rape of, 309
'Maquis' (French Resistance), 224
Mariana Islands, 264
Marshall, General George C., 141, 165, 199, 268
Menzies, Prime Minister Robert, 52, 121, 128
Midway, battle of, 184–186
Minsk, 278
Montgomery, General Bernard (later F-M Viscount Montgomery of Alamein), 163, 197, 209–213, 234, 243–251, 269–276, 288–307
Morshead, Lt-General Sir Leslie, 126, 210
Moscow, Battle of, 153–155
Munich conference, 44
Mussolini, Benito, 12, 18–19, 247–303

Nagasaki, 314
Narvik battles, 75
Nazis, 12, 20–32, 43 et al
Netherlands, 80–81, 158, 222
New Guinea campaigns, 199–203, 205–208, 256–259, 287
New Zealand (and New Zealanders), 52, 124–134, 149–150, 196, 268, 251, 266, 303
Normandy campaign (1944), 268–276
Norway, 69–77, 223

Odessa, 146
Okinawa, 310

Paris, 90, 276
Path Finders, The, 236
Patton, General George S., 214, 234, 244
Pearl Harbor attack, 161
Peleliu invasion, 285
Petain, Marshal Philippe, 84–91
Philippines, 162, 180, 286
Ploesti raid, 238
Poland, 16, 28, 48–50, 54–58, 278
Potsdam conference, 213

Quisling, Vidkun, 76

Radar, 37
Rhine crossings (1945), 300
Rhineland, 31, 298
Ribbentrop, Joachim von, 32, 47, 109, 316
Romania, 108, 279
Rommel, F-M Erwin, 118–119, 149–150, 188–192, 209–215, 234, 269, 275
Roosevelt, President Franklin D., 10, 17, 27, 141, 161–162 et al, 302

Saipan invasion, 264
Schindler, Oskar, 228
Sedan breakthrough, 182
Sevastopol, defence of, 193
Sicily invasion, 244
Singapore, 23, 159, 169–171
Slim, General William (F-M Viscount), 257
Smolensk, 153
South Africa, Union of, 52
Soviet Union, 17, 45–48, 52, 143–148
Spanish Civil War, 31
Stalin, Josef, 11, 45, 144–148, 189, 198
Stalingrad, battle of, 192–194, 216–220, 232
Stilwell, Lt-General Joseph, 172, 179, 284
Sydney, HMAS, 107, 152

Syria, 137–138

Tanks, development of, 41
Tarawa, 260
Teheran conference, 252
Tirpitz, 241
Tito, Marshal, 225
Tobruk, defence of, 126, 149, 191
Tojo, General Hideki, 13, 158, 230, 264, 316
Treblinka death camp, 58, 227
Truman, President Harry S., 8, 313
Tunisia, 234

U-boats, 100, 194, 240
Ukraine, 145, 261
United States of America, 102, 141
Ustashi (Croatia), 225

Versailles, Treaty of, (1919) 14
V-E Day, 307
V-J Day, 314
V1 and V2 missiles, 275

Wake Island, 162
Warsaw, 56, 278, 294
Wavell, General Sir A., (F-M Earl Wavell), 114–139, 165–175
Weygand, General Maxime, 22, 84
Wilson, President Woodrow, 12
Wireless, 36–37

Yalta conference, 296
Yamashita, General, 33, 158, 171, 309
Yamato, 34, 310
Yugoslavia, 18, 121–123, 224

Zhukov, Marshal Georgi, 153–155, 219, 243, 307